MySQL

MICHAEL KOFLER
Translated by DAVID KRAMER

Apress™

MySQL
Copyright © 2001 by Michael Kofler

ISBN (pbk): 1-893115- 57-7

Printed and bound in the United States of America 12345678910

Trademarked names may appear in this book. Rather than use a trademark symbol with every occurrence of a trademarked name, we use the names only in an editorial fashion and to the benefit of the trademark owner, with no intention of infringement of the trademark.

Editorial Directors: Dan Appleman, Gary Cornell, Jason Gilmore, Karen Watterson

Translator, Copyeditor, and Compositor: David Kramer

Managing Editor: Grace Wong

Proofreader: Laura Cheu

Cover Designer: Karl Miyajima

Distributed to the book trade in the United States by Springer-Verlag New York, Inc.,175 Fifth Avenue, New York, NY, 10010 and outside the United States by Springer-Verlag GmbH & Co. KG, Tiergartenstr. 17, 69112 Heidelberg, Germany

In the United States, phone 1-800-SPRINGER;
orders@springer-ny.com;
http://www.springer-ny.com
Outside the United States, contact orders@springer.de;
http://www.springer.de; fax +49 6221 345229

For information on translations, please contact Apress directly at 901 Grayson Street, Suite 204, Berkeley, CA, 94710

Phone: 510-549-5937; Fax: 510-549-5939; info@apress.com; http://www.apress.com

Contents

Preface

MYSQL IS ON THE VERGE of repeating in the database market the success achieved by Linux in the operating system sector. The recipe is simplicity itself: Take a database system that cannot yet offer the completeness of functionality of a commercial database system but that is reliable and offers fast operation without making excessive demands on hardware. Then provide this database system an open source license (general public license, or GPL) and permit free use of it (if it follows certain rules). Since the code is available to everyone thanks to the GPL, programmers throughout the world can improve on and extend MySQL.

In the past few years MySQL has found wide application, above all as a database system for dynamic web sites, and as a free database system it just about represents a de facto standard. In combination with PHP or Perl, MySQL is providing the database system for more and more web sites. (A favorite combination is Linux + Apache + MySQL + Perl or PHP. Such systems are called "LAMP systems" for short.)

However, MySQL is available not only to Linux. Almost every operating system is supported (variants of Unix, BSD, and Linux; Windows, MacOS; and others). Likewise, the use of MySQL is not limited to web applications. For example, the ODBC interface also provides MySQL access to all Windows programmers.

What Does This Book Offer?

This book is an applications- and example-oriented introduction to MySQL. It begins with an extensive introduction (Part I) on installation under Windows and Linux. We also consider the installation of typical components that are used in combination with MySQL (Apache, PHP, Perl, and MyODBC). Building on this, our first example will show the basic use of MySQL.

Part II, "Fundamentals," provides a large amount of background material on the use of the most important administration tools, the database language SQL, the proper design of databases, and the access system of MySQL.

In Part III, "Programming," we emphasize the languages PHP, Perl, and Visual Basic (in combination with MyODBC). Almost all the examples presented can be tried out *live* on my web site.

Part IV goes into the administration of MySQL (backups, use of log files, etc.) and deals with several advanced topics (e.g., BDB, InnoDB, and Gemini tables and transactions; full-text indexes; replication; compiling MySQL).

We end the main text with a reference section (Part V) that provides an overview of the SQL commands of MySQL, the commands and options of the administrative tools, and the functions of Perl and PHP application programming interfaces (APIs).

Finally, three appendices give information on MySQL error numbers, the web site for this book, and suggestions for further reading.

In combination with the example databases and programs on my web site this book should provide a good foundation for the development of your own database applications. In this I wish you much fun and success.

Michael Kofler, May 2001
<mysql@kofler.cc>
http://www.kofler.cc/mysql

Translator's Note

I have been helped enormously in the process of translation by Michael Kofler, the author of this fine book, with whom I have maintained a flurry of e-correspondence between Lancaster, Pennsylvania, USA, and Graz, Austria, throughout the translation of this book. With friendly encouragement, Michael promptly answered all of my numerous queries.

The staff at Apress have been very helpful and friendly as well. I particularly would like to thank Jason Gilmore, who read the entire translation and made numerous suggestions and corrections; Grace Wong and Hollie Fischer, who have taken care of numerous technical details and managed the production process; and Gary Cornell, who enmeshed me in this translation project, my third for Apress.

Arthur Ogawa provided LATEX support, and I thank him as well.

Finally, Laura Cheu checked the typeset files for correct formatting and made many helpful suggestions.

At this point the author, or in this case the translator, having thanked those who assisted him, generally goes on to state that nonetheless, despite all those helping hands, eyes, and hearts, any errors that remain are entirely his own responsibility (while secretly blaming the copyeditor for all those missed typos and the compositor for various formatting snafus and fubars). In this case, however, the translator, having taken on himself the tasks of copyediting and typesetting, is truly left with no one to blame but himself.

The Nitty Gritty

Example Programs, Source Code

To the extent that we are dealing with web applications, all of the applications in this book can be tried out directly on my website (http://www.kofler.cc). There you will also find the source code for all the examples.

In the longer program listings in this book you will find at the beginning of the example a comment line that specifies the file name appearing in the example files on the web site, for example,

```
<!-- php-programming/simpleinput.php -->
```

To save space, sometimes only the most interesting passages in the program code are printed.

Versions

The functions of MySQL and the numerous programs placed in its environment change with every new version—which sometimes appear weekly. The following overview indicates which versions I have worked with.

- **MySQL:** Version 3.23.37.

- **MyODBC:** Version 2.50.36.

- **PHP:** Version 4. The PHP scripts presented in this book were tested exclusively with PHP4. In general, *.php was used as file identifier. If your web server is so configured that *.php3 or *.php4 is required as file identifier, then you will have to alter the names of the PHP files. Otherwise, you will have to modify all links within the HTML and PHP code (this affects primarily <a href=... > and <form action=... >).

- **phpMyAdmin:** Version 2.1.

- **Perl:** Versions 5.0 and 5.6.

- **Apache:** Version 1.3.12.

- **Linux/Windows:** MySQL and the other programs used were tested for this book under Linux and Windows. For Linux the distributions Red Hat 6.2, 7.0, and 7.1 and SuSE 7.0 and 7.1 were employed, and for Windows we used

Windows 2000 Professional (without Service Packs) as well as Windows NT 4 Server (SP 5).

- **Visual Basic, VBA, ADO:** Visual Basic programs were developed and tested with VB6 and VBA6 and ADO versions 2.1 and 2.5.

Notation

- *Commands and functions in SQL, PHP, etc., generally appear in italic (e.g., SELECT). (Note, however, that when the background text is italic, as in the gray "Remark," "Tip," "Caution," and "Pointer" boxes and some section headings, such commands and functions will appear in a* roman *font; e.g.,* SELECT.)

- MENU COMMANDS USE CAPS AND SMALL CAPS (e.g., FILE|OPEN).

- Keyboard shortcuts use this monospace font (e.g., Shift+Delete).

- File and directory names also use the monospace font (e.g., /usr/local or C:\Windows).

- Programs and programming commands are in the monospace font as well (e.g., mysql or cmd.exe).

SQL commands are generally written in UPPERCASE letters. This is not a syntactic necessity, but merely an often observed convention. MySQL does not distinguish between uppercase and lowercase in interpreting SQL commands.

In specifying Windows directories we will often not write out the absolute path, since it depends in any case on the particular installation. We observe the following conventions:

- \Windows\ means the Windows directory (e.g., C:\Windows or D:\WinNT4).

- Programs\ means the directory under Windows for program installation (e.g., C:\Programs or D:\Program Files).

- Mysql\ means the MySQL installation directory (e.g., C:\Mysql or D:\Program Files\Mysql or /usr/local/mysql).

Commands

Many commands will be presented in this book. We will be moving back and forth between the Unix/Linux and Windows conventions. The following two commands are equivalent:

```
root# mysqladmin -u root -h localhost password xxx

> mysqladmin -u root -h localhost password xxx
```

In each case we have given the system prompt (root# for Unix/Linux and > for Windows). You type in only what follows the prompt (here in `boldface type`). Under Unix/Linux it is possible to divide long inputs over several lines. The lines are separated by means of the backslash symbol \. We shall often use this convention in this book. The following command is thus equivalent to the two above:

```
root#   mysqladmin -u root -h localhost \
        password xxx
```

In each case *xxx* is to be replaced by the relevant text (in this example by your password). We have indicated that *xxx* is dummy text by the use of a slant font.

Abbreviations

I have attempted in this book to make as little use of abbreviations as possible. However, there are several abbreviations that will be used repeatedly without being introduced anew in each chapter:

ADO	Active Data Objects (Microsoft database library)
BLOB	Binary Large Object (binary data block)
ISP	Internet Service Provider
ODBC	Open Database Connectivity (interface for database access, particularly popular under Windows)
PHP	PHP Hypertext Preprocessor (a scripting programming language for HTML pages)
RPM	Red Hat Packet Manager (a format for Linux software packages)
SQL	Structured Query Language (database programming language)
URL	Uniform Resource Locator (Internet address of the form `http://www.company.com/page.html`)
VB	Visual Basic (programming language)
VBA	Visual Basic for Applications (programming language within the Microsoft Office package)

Part I

Introduction

#### CHAPTER 1

What Is MySQL?

THIS CHAPTER BEGINS WITH AN overview of the most important concepts from the world of databases and then delves into the possibilities and limitations of MySQL. What is MySQL? What can it do (and what is it unable to do)?

In addition to describing the central functions of MySQL we shall also discuss fully the issue of licensing MySQL. When is one permitted to use MySQL without payment, and when is a license required?

Chapter Overview

What Is a Database?

Before we can answer the central question of this chapter, namely, *What is MySQL?* you, dear reader, and I must find a common language. Therefore, this section presents a beginning database glossary, without going into great detail. (If you have already had significant dealings with relational databases, you can skip the next couple of pages in good conscience.)

There is scarcely to be found a term that is less precise than *database*. A database can be a list of addresses residing in a spreadsheet program (such as Excel), or it can be the administration files of a telecommunications firm in which several million calls are registered daily, their charges accurately calculated, monthly bills computed, and warning letters sent to those who are in arrears. A simple database can be a stand-alone operation (residing locally on a computer for a single user), while others may be used simultaneously by thousands of users, with the data parceled out among several computers and dozens of hard drives. The size of a database can range from a few of kilobytes into the terabytes.[1]

In ordinary usage the word "database" is used to refer to the actual data, the resulting database files, the database system (such as MySQL or Oracle), or a database client (such as a PHP script or a program written in C++). Thus there arises a great potential for confusion as soon as two people begin to converse on the subject of databases.

Relations, Database Systems, Servers, and Clients

A *database* is an ordered collection of data, which is normally stored in one or more associated files. The data are structured as *tables*, where cross references among tables are possible. The existence of such *relations* among the tables leads to the database being called a *relational database*.

Let us clarify matters with an example. A database might consist of a table with data on a firm's customers (name, address, etc.), a table with data on the products the firm offers, and finally, a table containing the firm's orders. Through the table of orders it is possible to access the data in the other two tables (for example, via customer and product numbers).

MySQL, Oracle, the Microsoft SQL server, and IBM DB2 are examples of *relational database systems*. Such a system includes the programs for managing relational databases. Among the tasks of a relational database system are not only the secure storage of data, but also such jobs as the processing of commands for

---

[1] It all started with the megabyte, which is about one million bytes. A terabyte is 1024 gigabytes, which in turn is approximately one thousand megabytes. The prefix "mega-" comes from the Greek for "great," or "large," while "giga-" is derived from the Greek word for "giant." In turn, "tera-" is from the Greek word for "monster." It would appear that numbers once regarded as large, gigantic, or even monstrously huge have become part of our everyday vocabulary.

querying, analyzing, and sorting existing data and for storing new data. All of this should be able to take place not only on a single computer, but over a network as well. Instead of a *database system* we shall often speak of a *database server*.

Where there are servers, there are clients. Every program that is connected to the database system is called a *database client*. Database clients have the job of simplifying the use of the database for the end user. No user of a database system in his or her right mind would wish to communicate directly with the database server. That is much too abstract and inconvenient. (Let programmers worry about such direct communication!) Instead, the user has a right to expect convenient tables, list boxes, and so on to enable the location of data or to input new data.

Database clients can assume a variety of forms, and indeed, they are often not recognized by the user as database programs at all. Some examples of this type of client are HTML pages for the display and input of messages in an on-line discussion group, a traditional program with several windows for managing addresses and appointments, and a Perl script for executing administrative tasks. There is thus wide scope for database programming.

Relational Versus Object-Oriented Database Systems

Relational databases have dominated the database world for decades, and they are particularly well suited for business data, which usually lend themselves to structuring in the form of tables. Except for the following two paragraphs, this entire book discusses only relational databases (though we shall not always stress this point).

Another kind of database is the *object-oriented database*. Such databases can store free-standing objects (without having to arrange them in tables). Although in recent years there has been a trend in the direction of object-oriented programming languages (such as Object-Store, O2, Versant, Objectivity), object-oriented databases have found only a small market niche.

Note that relational databases can be accessed by means of object-oriented programming languages. However, that does not turn a relational database into an object-oriented one. Object-oriented database systems enable the direct access to objects defined in the programming language in question and the storage of such objects in the database without conversion (persistency). It is precisely this that is not possible with relational database systems, in which everything must be structured in tables.

Tables, Records, Fields, Queries, SQL, Index, Keys

We have already mentioned tables, which are the structures in which the actual data are located. Every line in such a table is called a *data record*, or simply *record*, where the structure of each record is determined by the definition of the table. For example, in a table of addresses every record might contain *fields* for family name, given name, street, and so on. For every field there are precise conditions on the type of information that can be stored (such as a number in a particular format, or a character string with a predetermined maximum number of characters). The collection of all of one type of field taken over all the rows of a table can be thought of as a *column* of the table, and we will sometimes be a bit loose in distinguishing fields from columns.

The description of a database consisting of several tables with all of its fields, relations, and indexes (see below) is called a *database model*. This model defines the construction of the data structures and at the same time provides the format in which the actual data are to be stored.

Tables usually contain their data in no particular order (more precisely, the order is usually that in which the data have been entered or modified). However, for efficient use of the data it is necessary that from these unordered data a list can be created that is ordered according to one or more criteria. It is frequently useful for such a list to contain only a selection of the data in the table. For example, one could obtain a list of all of one's customers, ordered by ZIP code, who have ordered a rubber ducky within the past twelve months.

To create such a list one formulates *queries*. The result of the query is again a table, one, however, that exists in active memory (RAM) and not on the hard drive.

To formulate a query one uses SQL instructions, which are commands for selecting and extracting data. The abbreviation SQL stands for *Structured Query Language*, which has become a standard in the formulation of database queries. Needless to say, every producer of a database system offers certain extensions to this standard, which dilutes the goal of compatibility among various database systems.

When tables get large, the speed at which a query can be answered depends significantly on whether there is a suitable *index* giving the order of the data fields. An index is an auxiliary table that contains only information about the order of the records. An index is also called a *key*.

An index speeds up access to data, but it has disadvantages as well. First, every index increases the amount of storage on the hard drive necessary for the database file, and second, the index must be updated each time the data are altered, and this costs time. (Thus an index saves time in the reading of data, but it costs time in entering and altering data. It thus depends on the use to which the data are to be put whether an index is on the whole a net plus or minus in the quest for efficiency.)

A special case of an index is a *primary index*, or *primary key*, which is distinguished in that the primary index must ensure a *unique* reference to a record. Often, for this purpose one simply uses a running index number (ID number). Primary indexes play a significant role in relational databases, and they can speed up access to data considerably.

MySQL

MySQL is a relational database system. If you can believe many diehard MySQL fans, MySQL is faster, more reliable, and cheaper—or, simply put, better—than any other database system (including commercial systems such as Oracle and DB2). Many MySQL opponents challenge this viewpoint, going even so far as to assert that MySQL is not even a relational database system. We can safely say that there is a large bandwidth of opinion.

- The fact is that there is an ever increasing number of MySQL users, and the overwhelming majority of them are quite satisfied with MySQL. Thus for these users we may say that MySQL is *good enough.*

- It is also the fact, however, that MySQL lacks many features that are taken for granted with other database systems. If you require such features, then MySQL is (at least for the present) not the database system for you. MySQL is not a panacea.

In the next couple of sections we shall examine some of the possibilities and limitations of MySQL.

> **REMARK** *In this book we are considering MySQL. Do not confuse MySQL with mSQL. To be sure, MySQL and mSQL have similar programming interfaces (APIs), which merely facilitates the confusion between the two. However, the underlying database systems are completely different. More information on mSQL can be found at* http://www.hughes.com.au/

Features of MySQL

- **Relational Database System:** Like almost all other database systems on the market, MySQL is a relational database system.

- **Client/Server Architecture:** MySQL is a client/server system. There is a database server (MySQL) and arbitrarily many clients (application programs), which communicate with the server; that is, they query data, save changes, etc. The clients can run on the same computer as the server or on another computer (communication via a local network or the Internet).

  Almost all of the familiar large database systems (Oracle, Microsoft SQL Server, etc.) are client/server systems. These are in contrast to the *file-server systems*, which include Microsoft Access, dBase, and FoxPro. The decisive drawback to file-server systems is that when run over a network they become extremely inefficient as the number of users grows.

- **SQL:** MySQL supports as its database language—as its name suggests—SQL (Structured Query Language). SQL is a standardized language for querying and updating data and for the administration of a database.

  There are several SQL dialects (about as many as there are database systems). MySQL adheres to the ANSI-SQL/92 standard, although with some significant restrictions and many extensions.

  This topic will be dealt with more extensively below. Beyond the ANSI-SQL/92 standard, MySQL supports, among other things, several additional data types, full-text indexes, and replication.

- **Programming Languages:** There is a host of APIs (application programming interfaces) and libraries for the development of MySQL applications. For client programming you can use, among others, the languages C, C++, Java, Perl, PHP, Python, and Tcl.

- **ODBC:** There is an ODBC interface for MySQL. With it MySQL can be addressed by all the usual programming languages running under Microsoft Windows (Delphi, Visual Basic, etc.). MyODBC is currently at version 2.5, level 0. The ODBC interface can also be installed under Unix, though that is seldom necessary.

- **Platform Independence:** It is not only client applications that can run under various operating systems. MySQL itself (that is, the server) can also be run under a variety of operating systems. The most significant are Apple Macintosh OS X, IBM OS/2, Linux, Microsoft Windows, as well as countless flavors of Unix (such as AIX, BSDI, DEC Unix, FreeBSD, HP-UX, Open-BSD, Net BSD, SGI Iris, Sun Solaris, SunOS 4, SCO Unix).

- **Speed:** MySQL is considered a fast database system. This assessment has been supported by countless benchmark tests (though such tests, regardless of who has carried them out, should be regarded with a certain degree of skepticism). In part, MySQL's speed advantage is the result of the absence of certain features.

Limitations

This section is aimed at the reader who already has some knowledge of relational databases. We shall use some terms from the world of databases without defining them precisely. (On the topic of transactions alone one could fill dozens of pages!)

However, our explanations should be understandable to the database novice as well. If you are interested in more detail on such background material, then I must refer you to the vast literature (see the Bibliography at the end of the book).

Many of the shortcomings listed in this section can be found on the to-do list of the team of MySQL developers, or have already been implemented. But even if one or another feature is already available by the time this book appears, this does not mean that you can use it in your applications without further thought. The development of database systems, whether by a commercial firm or in the open-source arena, is a very complicated endeavor. So wait until features have been thoroughly tested and have had a chance to mature.

> **POINTER**   *The documentation for MySQL is not at all silent on the subject of shortcomings or missing features. There is a quite readable chapter in the MySQL documentation on the topic "How standards-compatible is MySQL?" There you will find extensive information on the points at which MySQL fails to comply with current standards. Often, a reason for the shortcoming is provided, and sometimes as well some pointers on how to get around the difficulty.*

ANSI-SQL/92 Limitations

ANSI SQL/92 is a standardized definition of the database query language SQL. Many commercial database systems are largely compatible with this standard and also offer many extensions.

MySQL is also conspicuous for its countless extensions, but unfortunately, the compatibility is not so extensive as is the case for other database systems. The points described in greater detail in what follows (transactions, sub*SELECT*s, views, triggers, stored procedures, foreign keys) are examples of the lack of ANSI-SQL/92 compatibility.

These limitations usually make it impossible (or merely very difficult) to adapt existing databases and the associated SQL code from other database systems into MySQL. Conversely, it is almost as difficult to transfer a MySQL solution to another database system if you have not scrupulously employed only the ANSI-SQL/92-conforming features of MySQL. (The temptation to use the useful proprietary features proves in most cases to be too great.)

- **SubSELECTs:** MySQL is not capable of executing a query of the form

```
SELECT * FROM table1 WHERE x IN (SELECT y FROM table2)
```

  This limitation can be circumvented in many cases by setting up a temporary table, which, however, is neither elegant nor particularly efficient. In other cases the limitation must be attacked with additional code in an external programming language.

  There are similar limitations for *DELETE*.

- **Foreign Keys:** MySQL is conversant with *foreign keys*, which help to link two tables. Usually, however, the keyword *foreign keys* also describes the ability of a database to ensure the referential integrity of the linked tables, and at present MySQL is incapable of this.

  Let us suppose that we have two tables, one for book titles and a second for the authors of these books. If you delete an author from the author table, the database system should test whether any book titles by this author remain in the database. If that is the case, then either these titles should be deleted as well or the entire operation should be aborted.

  MySQL is not concerned with such relations. If you delete the author, the remaining book records refer to a no-longer-existing author. (A similar situation obtains on the Internet, where a link all too frequently points to a nonexistent site). Not only is this situation unaesthetic, it often causes serious problems in programming and debugging.

  Therefore, in MySQL database applications the programmer must ensure that the integrity of the data (that is, the relationships among the various tables) is maintained when commands for changing and deleting data are executed.

- **Views:** Simply put, with *views* we are dealing with an SQL query that is considered an independent database object and that permits a particular view into the database. MySQL currently does not support views (though we may expect this feature to be implemented shortly).

  Of course, with MySQL you can always execute those SQL commands that are defined as views in other databases. However, it is impossible to store these queries as objects in the database.

  Views assist in the administration of the database, since it is thereby relatively simple to control access to individual *parts* of the database. Views also help in avoiding redundancy in application development.

- **Stored Procedure:** When we speak of *stored procedures* we are referring to SQL code that is stored within a database system. Stored procedures (SPs for short) are usually employed to simplify certain steps in a procedure, such as inserting or deleting a record. For client programmers this has the advantage that these actions need not operate directly on the tables, but can rely on SPs. As with views, SPs also help in the administration of large database projects. Stored procedures can also increase efficiency in certain cases.

- **Triggers:** A *trigger* is an SQL command that is automatically executed by the server during certain database operations. If a database is incapable on its own of ensuring referential integrity, then it is usually triggers that are brought into play to assist in this. For example, a trigger can be executed every time a record is to be deleted, which would test whether this operation is permissible and prohibit the action if need be.

- **Transactions:** A *transaction* in the context of a database system refers to the execution of several database operations as a *block*, that is, as if it were a single command. The database system ensures that either all of the operations are properly executed or else none of them. This holds even if during the transaction a power interruption occurs, the computer crashes, or some other catastrophe intervenes. Thus, for example, it cannot happen that $100,000 is withdrawn from your bank account without then being deposited into mine if an error intervenes, no matter of what kind.

Transactions also give programmers the option of effectively aborting any number of already executed SQL commands. In many situations this simplifies programming considerably.

There is a range of opinion as to the importance of transactions. The MySQL development team has long held the belief that transactions are not necessary in many applications and that MySQL runs sufficiently securely and stably without them. Furthermore, avoiding transactions yields considerable savings in speed. And finally, every programmer has the option of writing code that ensures that a series of SQL commands terminates successfully or, if not, can be properly withdrawn. (This argument, however, sounds almost as if, say, one were to suggest to C++ programmers that they deal with memory management of objects themselves.)

Be that as it may, MySQL has supported transactions since May 2000 in the form of BDB tables. and also since April 2001 in the form of InnoDB tables. A third type of what can be considered a transaction, Gemini, should arrive shortly. However, the MySQL documentation admits that these new table types have not yet been tested and checked to the same extent as other MySQL features. A further problem is that these new table types are not yet available for all operating systems that support MySQL. In other words, MySQL supports transactions, but this feature will take a while to mature and become stable. See Chapter 12 for more on transactions.

The lack of sub*SELECT*s, views, SPs, and triggers does not greatly restrict the possibilities open to client programmers. It does, however, lead to a situation in which the program logic is transferred from the server level to the client level. The result is more complex or expensive client programming than would otherwise be the case, leading to redundancies in code and problems with maintenance and alteration of code.

Further Limitations

The following limitations actually have nothing to do with ANSI-SQL/92 but nonetheless play a significant role in practice.

- When MySQL is used with standard tables (table type MyISAM), *locking*—that is, the temporary blocking of access to or alteration of database information—is in operation only for entire tables (*table locking*). With other database systems, on the other hand, it is possible to protect only certain records using locking (*row locking*). This is much more efficient when several users are accessing the database at the same time. In many database applications the difference in speed obtained from better locking is so great that MySQL is ruled out as a database system.

  You can circumvent the *table-locking* problem in MySQL by implementing BDB tables. Transactions in BDB tables are executed without *table locking* and are therefore executed more efficiently than they would be with *LOCK*-protected operations in normal MySQL tables.

- MySQL is not able to execute *hot backups*, which are backups during operation without blocking the tables with locks.

- The MySQL server supports a variety of character sets and the associated sort orders, but at present can have only a single *sort order* active at a time. If the sort order must be changed, MySQL has to be restarted. All table indexes must then be reset.

  Especially for those using MySQL with Internet service providers it would make sense if the desired sort order could be set individually for each table or for each client.

- MySQL is currently unable to deal with Unicode or other mutibyte character strings. (Of course, it is possible to treat such data as binary objects, but there are no functions for dealing with character strings, in particular no usable sorting or comparison algorithms.)

- A *development environment* (front end, GUI) for administrative tasks—from database development to backup—has become a given with many commercial database systems. With MySQL there is not merely a development environment, there is a whole dozen of them. To be sure, tools such as phpMyAdmin are already fairly mature and represent a significant alleviation of administrative work, but there is presently no tool that covers the complete spectrum of all administrative tasks in a suitable and user-friendly manner.

MySQL 4.0/4.1

As this book was being finished, MySQL version 4.0 had just been announced but was not yet available, while version 4.1 is most likely still a gleam in the development team's eye.

MySQL 4.0

Despite its shiny new version number, MySQL 4.0 is not set to offer many new functions, but instead, to serve as the basis for future extensions. The following list provides a brief preview of the most important changes to look for.

- The new table types—either already available or soon to be—InnoDB and Gemini should be completely mature by version 4.0. Then MySQL will boast three transaction-capable table types, namely BDB, InnoDB, and Gemini. Additional features of InnoDB and Gemini are support of row-level locking and automatic reconstruction of tables after a crash. Additional details on these new table types can be found at `www.innobase.fi` and `www.nusphere.com`.

- It should be possible to execute hot backups while the system is running (without blocking the entire database).

- The format of files for describing table properties (`*.frm`) is set to change.

- The MySQL server `mysqld` should be available not only as a program, but also as a library, so that MySQL can be better used in *embedded products.*

POINTER *Information on the current status of MySQL development can be found at* `http://www.mysql.com/development/`

MySQL 4.1

Version 4.1 had not even been announced as this book was being written. But according to the MySQL mailing list, this version will contain, among other things, the long-awaited sub*SELECT* commands.

MySQL Licensing

One of the most interesting features of MySQL is the license. MySQL is an open source project. That is, the complete source code of MySQL is freely available. Since June 2000 (that is, since version 3.23.19) the *GNU Public License* (GPL) is valid also for MySQL. It is thus ensured that MySQL will continue to be freely available in the sense of the open source idea. (For commercial applications of MySQL there is a second, commercial, license available in addition to GPL. More on this later.)

Rights and Duties with Respect to the GPL

Open source is often incorrectly interpreted to mean "without cost." It is indeed true that GPL software can be used without payment of fees, provided that one adheres to certain conditions. However, the open source idea goes much further:

- Since the source code is freely available, when there are problems you are not at the mercy of a software vendor.

- When problems arise you can attempt to repair the problem yourself or to implement features that are lacking. Furthermore, you can appeal to the developers' group for help.

- You can be certain that the program code has been read by many developers and does not contain any unsavory surprises (such as so-called back doors such as the database system Interbase had for many years, whereby access to every Interbase database was possible via a hard-coded password).

- You are permitted to alter GPL products, and indeed sell the resulting new programs.

At the end of this list of GPL merits there are a few demerits (for commercial applications). If you wish to use a GPL program as the basis for a commercial product, you must again make your own source code freely available, in the sense of GPL, with the changes made. This is seldom something that developers of commercial products wish to do.

In general, it holds that every program that is derived from GPL software exists under the terms of GPL. Since this feature would often too severely restrict the implementation of GPL programs, there is an additional form of GPL license: In addition to the ordinary GPL, whose rules we have just gone over, there is the LGPL (Library GPL). The LGPL allows for the free use of LGPL software in commercial applications without the commercial code having to be made available in the sense of GPL. (In the case of MySQL, MySQL servers and the administration tools adhere to the terms of GPL, while the MySQL client libraries adhere to LGPL.)

> **POINTER**   *Further information on the open source idea, including the full text of the GPL together with aids to interpretation, can be found at the following addresses:*
>
> ```
> http://www.gnu.org/copyleft/gpl.html
> http://www.opensource.org/osd.html
> ```

MySQL Licensing in Practice

MySQL adheres not only to GPL, but also to a second, commercial, license. According to the application, you can choose between the open source license and a commercial license.

Use of MySQL in the Sense of the Open Source License

The following list collects the different situations in which one may freely use MySQL in the sense of GPL.

- MySQL can always be used internally without cost. It is only when the resulting solution is to be sold to other customers that the question of licensing comes into play.

- MySQL can be used freely within a web site. (The code of PHP or Perl scripts need not be made freely available in the sense of GPL, since you, as a PHP or Perl developer, communicate with MySQL via the MySQL client library, which is subordinate to LGPKL.)

- Likewise, an Internet service provider may make MySQL available to its customers without having to pay MySQL license fees. (Since MySQL is running exclusively on the ISP computer, this application is considered internal.)

- Finally, MySQL can be used free of charge for all projects that themselves run under the GPL or comparable free license. (If you have developed a new free e-mail client for Linux, say, and wish to store e-mails in a MySQL database, you may do so without further ado.)

Use of MySQL with a Commercial License

In the sense of GPL the following uses are prohibited:

- You may not change or extend MySQL (that is, the database server) itself or sell the new version or product thus created without simultaneously making the source code of your changes freely available. You are thus prohibited from developing a new database system based on MySQL if you are not prepared to make your extensions freely available to the MySQL community in the sense of GPL.

- It is forbidden to develop a commercial product, such as a bookkeeping program, for example (without making the code available in the open source sense), that relies exclusively on MySQL as the only possible database.

  The boundaries here are somewhat fluid. Thus according to the MySQL documentation itself it is permissible for a commercial program to provide an option for recording MySQL tables instead of logging files. However, if your program can be used only if MySQL is also available, thus creating a direct dependency on MySQL, then a commercial license is required.

If the limitations of the GPL are not acceptable to you as a commercial developer, then you have the right to apply for a commercial MySQL license. This can prove worthwhile because MySQL remains available to you even if you are unable or unwilling to make your code available in the sense of GPL.

Commercial MySQL licensing fees are calculated based on the number of servers (where a server is a computer, regardless of the number of CPUs). There is no limitation on the number of clients that may access the server. The cost is quite reasonable in comparison to commercial database systems (currently $200 for a license, with a significant reduction starting at ten licenses).

> **REMARK** *If you use MySQL in combination with BDB, InnoDB, or Gemini tables (and not with the default table type MyISAM), the commercial license fee is increased by about thirty percent for each additional table type. The reason for this is the three table types have been developed and are maintained rather independently of MySQL.*

> **POINTER** *Further information on licensing MySQL can be found in the MySQL documentation, in the chapter "MySQL Licensing and Support."*

Support Contracts

You may make a support contract with the MySQL company if you desire commercial support in the development of a MySQL application. You thereby simultaneously support the further development of MySQL.

> **POINTER** *Details on commercial MySQL licenses and paid support can be found at the following address:*
>
> http://www.mysql.com/support/
>
> *Links to various companies that offer commercial MySQL support can be found at the following address:*
>
> http://www.mysql.com/information/partners.html

Alternatives to MySQL

Of course, there are many alternatives to MySQL, particularly if you are prepared to pay (lots of) money for licenses and perhaps also for the requisite hardware. Among these are IBM DB2, Informix, Microsoft SQL Server, and Oracle.

If you are looking for a database in the open source realm, then PostgreSQL is currently perhaps the most interesting alternative. (However, be warned: The discussion between advocates of MySQL and those of PostgreSQL usually resembles more a war of religions than what might be termed measured intellectual discourse.)

Furthermore, there are several formerly commercial database systems that have recently been converted to open source. The two best known of these are Interbase (from Inprise/Borland) and SAP DB.

POINTER   *Much further information on PostgreSQL can be found, needless to say, on the Internet. The following web sites are a good starting point:*

```
http://www.at.postgresql.org/
http://www.postgres.com
http://openacs.org/
```

POINTER   *Comparisons between various database systems (including MySQL and PostgresSQL can be found at the following sites, among others:*

```
http://www.postgresql.org/mhonarc/pgsql-general/1999-11/msg00227.html
http://www.phpbuilder.com/columns/tim20001112.php3
http://www.devshed.com/BrainDump/MySQL_Benchmarks/
http://openacs.org/philosophy/why-not-mysql.html
```

POINTER   *Three home pages on Interbase and open source projects derived therefrom and a page on SAP DB are the following:*

```
http://www.interbase2000.org
http://www.ibphoenix.com
http://firebird.sourceforge.net
http://www.sapdb.org
```

Summary

MySQL is a very capable relational client/server database system. It is sufficiently secure and stable for many applications, and it offers an excellent cost/benefit ratio (not only because MySQL is free itself, but also because it makes comparatively modest demands on hardware). MySQL has thus developed into a quasi standard in the realm of small-to-mid-sized Internet databases (such as for discussion groups or similar applications).

Above all, in the Linux world MySQL is used increasingly by applications as the background database engine, whether it be managing logging data more efficiently than previously or managing e-mail, MP3 files, addresses, or comparable data. MySQL is poised to play a similar role to that of the Jet Engine in the Microsoft operating system (where in many respects MySQL offers s meaningfully better technical basis). Thanks to the ODBC interface, MySQL is now being used in the Windows world for such tasks.

Apart from technical data, MySQL has the advantage over other open source database systems in that presently it is by far the most popular database system. It follows that MySQL has been more thoroughly tested and documented than other database systems and that it is relatively easy to find developers with MySQL experience.

However, MySQL cannot (yet) compete in every respect with the big boys of the commercial database system world. If you must manage highly critical data (to give two examples: on-line banking and management of medical data) or if you have special requirements (such as data warehousing), then MySQL if most likely not going to be your first choice.

CHAPTER 2

The Test Environment

IN THIS CHAPTER WE DISCUSS first of all how to set up the test environment for MySQL on a local computer. Since MySQL usually doesn't run all by itself, but in combination with other programs, this chapter also discusses Apache, PHP, Perl, MyODBC, and phpMyAdmin. We consider installation under Windows and under Linux.

If MySQL has been made available by your Internet Service Provider (ISP) and you are not inclined to install MySQL on your own computer as well, the last section of this chapter gives a brief overview on how under this scenario you can quickly begin your first experiments.

This chapter is geared specifically to MySQL neophytes. If you already have access to a functioning MySQL system, you may feel free to skip this chapter.

Chapter Overview

POINTER   *A detailed description of how you can compile MySQL yourself under Linux can be found in Chapter 12. (The description is valid also for other Linux/Unix systems.)*

Windows or Unix/Linux?

The question of under which operating system to run MySQL can easily lead to fisticuffs, so strongly are opinions held. But we shall remain civil in this section, and perhaps for the entire book. The fact is that MySQL, as well as Apache, PHP, Perl, and most of the other programs that are usually run in conjunction with MySQL, were developed originally under Unix/Linux and were only later ported to Windows.

MySQL in Practice

In practice, that is, on a publicly available server on the Internet, the above-mentioned programs are run predominately under Unix/Linux. (There is scarcely an Internet Service Provider to be found that offers MySQL under Windows.) For this reason alone—the greater deployment in the world at large—the programs running under Unix/Linux have been better and more extensively tested. Possible errors or security holes in the Unix/Linux version of MySQL are thus more likely to be discovered and repaired quickly.

A further argument for deployment under Unix/Linux is that the programs function more efficiently as a rule. This has less to do with the view that Windows is generally slower than Unix/Linux (I have no desire to discuss this issue here), but with the fact that the process and thread models of these operating systems are quite different from each other. Programs such as Apache and MySQL are first and foremost optimized for the programming model of Unix/Linux, not for that of Windows, and this by itself often gives a significant speed advantage to Unix/Linux.

Therefore, the development communities of the programs mentioned above are unanimously in favor of having their programs run under Unix/Linux, and not under Windows. You would do well to take this opinion to heart.

> **REMARK** *When we speak of Windows, we generally mean Windows NT/2000. In principle, MySQL runs under Windows 9x/ME, but there it is impossible to provide reasonable security of the system against unauthorized access.*

Development Environment

Things look somewhat different if you are currently only developing a database application. During the development you will use a test environment that is usually accessible only to you or your team. Thus you have no reason to expect problems in security or in efficiency due to large numbers of accesses to the system. Since there is good compatibility between the Windows and Unix/Linux versions, there is little to be said against, for example, developing a discussion group for a web site first under Windows and then porting the completed solution to the Linux server of your ISP.

If you have at least two computers in your test environment, you can, of course, install MySQL, Apache, etc., on one computer under Linux, and carry out the actual development work (database design, creation of script files, etc., on the second computer under Windows (say, because your favorite editor runs under Windows).

To this extent the entire discussion of Windows versus Unix/Linux doesn't amount to much, and for development you should use the operating system that you find more to your liking.

> **REMARK** *Of course, there are also arguments against Windows even for the development of MySQL solutions. One argument is that by developing the entire project under Unix/Linux you gain considerable experience that will be valuable later during the process of bringing the project on line on a Unix/Linux server (specifically in reference to issues of access rights and security).*

REMARK *Another argument deals with the deployment of system functions that under Unix/Linux usually are available in a form different from that offered under Windows. For example, under Unix/Linux one can simply send an e-mail by program code (such as in a PHP or Perl script). Under Windows there are no standard interfaces for such tasks.*

A final argument is this: If you possess a typical Linux distribution (for example SuSE, Red Hat) on CD-ROM, you also possess all the programs of the MySQL test environment. After the various packages have been installed, everything usually runs correctly at first go, without any further configuration nightmares. On the other hand, if you work with Windows, you must first obtain the individual programs from the Internet, install them, and then configure them in what often is painstaking, frustrating labor.

MySQL (Server Installation)

MySQL is available over the Internet without cost, both as source code and in compiled form for most operating systems. Check out `http://www.mysql.com/downloads`

This section describes the installation of the binary version of MySQL under Windows and under Linux. If you wish to compile MySQL yourself (which makes sense only in exceptional circumstances), you will find relevant information in Chapter 12.

REMARK *When one speaks of MySQL one is usually referring to the database server. A MySQL installation thus usually means the installation of the server, where usually all the client tools are installed at the same time, so that the server can be administered. This is the subject of this section.*

If MySQL is already installed on another computer and you wish only to access that installation, then you need only the client tools. The next section discusses such a separate installation.

Version Numbers

The web sites listed above offer many versions of MySQL. Which should you choose?

Currently (as of May 2001), the use of version 3.23.*n* is recommended. Version 3.23.*n* is considered officially *stable* starting with version 3.23.31. This means that any problems that appear in later versions will be corrected, but no fundamentally new functions will be built into this version.

At the same time, the development of the next version, version 4.0, has already begun. As these lines were being written, there was still no publicly available version of MySQL 4.0 for downloading, but that situation may have changed by the time you are holding this book in your hands.

> **REMARK** *New versions of software are given the attribute* alpha, *followed, as progress continues, by* beta, gamma, *and finally,* stable. *For production use you should not employ a new version until the MySQL development team bestows the attribute* stable.

> **TIP** *If you are developing a web application that is to be installed by an external Internet service provider, you should find out what version is being used. Many ISPs are reluctant (with good reason) to install the most recent version.*
>
> *If your ISP is using an older version of MySQL (many ISPs are still using version 3.22.n), then it is often a good idea to use the older version for your own development. In this way you avoid the situation in which you have used certain functions that will be unavailable on the system of your ISP.*

Installation Under Windows

MySQL for Windows is available as a WinZip archive. To install it, copy the contents of the archive to a temporary directory and there launch `setup.exe`. (With newer versions of WinZip you can simply launch `setup.exe`. WinZip extracts the necessary files on its own into a directory and then deletes the archive when the installation is complete.)

The setup program itself offers no surprises. You may specify the installation location and select the components to be installed. If you stick with the default settings, then the database system, the documentation, and a default setting for access rights (the privileges database *mysql*) are installed into the directory `C:\mysql`. The space requirement is about 20 megabytes. Optionally, you can also install files for benchmark tests as well as libraries and include files (if you wish to develop MySQL clients with C/C++).

> **WARNING** *The setup program takes no notice of any existing MySQL installations. If you wish to update an installation, you should first secure the existing databases, then deinstall the old version of MySQL, and then install the new version. This process is described more fully below.*

Windows NT, Windows 2000, etc.

> **REMARK** *In this book it is generally assumed in descriptions of Windows NT/2000 that the installation of programs is executed by the* administrator *(or by a user with equivalent privileges) and that programs such as WinMySQLadmin are also executed by such a user.*
>
> *An installation without* administrator *privileges is usually impossible. Even with the use of programs without* administrator *privileges there can arise problems with access privileges, related to the manner in which access rights to files and processes are managed under Windows NT/2000. (A description of the access system of Windows NT/2000 is beyond the scope of this book.)*

Under Windows NT/2000, etc., MySQL can be run as a free-standing program or as a *service.* The latter variant fits the process model of Windows NT/2000 better and therefore is to be preferred. For this reason the MySQL server is automatically installed as a service if the installation takes place under Windows NT, Windows 2000, or a later version. This service will subsequently be launched automatically at startup. But for now it does not yet run!

Configuring and launching MySQL manually

If MySQL was installed in a directory other than C:\mysql, then before the first launch of MySQL the configuration file C:\my.cnf or Windows\my.ini must be generated. There the installation directory of MySQL must be specified in the following form (replace Q:/Program Files/mysql by the actual installation directory):

```
[mysqld]
basedir=Q:/Program Files/mysql
```

To launch the MySQL server (it is not necessary to restart the computer) execute SETTINGS|CONTROL PANEL|ADMINISTRATIVE TOOLS|SERVICES, select the service *mysql* with a double click, and click on the button Start (see Figure 2-1).

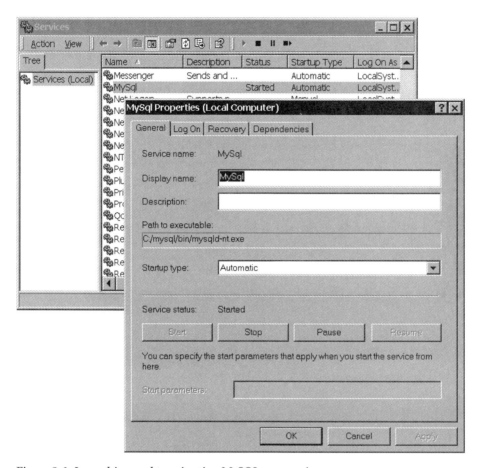

Figure 2-1. Launching and terminating MySQL as a service

Launching MySQL with WinMySQLadmin

With WinMySQLadmin things go somewhat more smoothly. Instead of generating C:\my.cnf or Windows\my.ini yourself, launch the administration program mysql\bin\winmysqladmin.exe installed with MySQL (the simplest method is from within Windows Explorer with a double click).

This program begins by asking for a user name and password. This information is used to create a new administration login for MySQL, which will then be used by WinMySQLadmin. The name and password are stored in plain text in the file Windows\my.ini. Therefore, do not use a password that is used anywhere else in your system.

The program then shrinks into a stoplight icon within the task bar. To launch MySQL execute, with the right mouse button, the commands WINNT|INSTALL SERVICE and WINNT|START SERVICE. The stoplight should change from red to green.

If there are problems at launch, then launch the user interface of Win-MySQLadmin with the right mouse button using SHOW ME. The dialog form START CHECK provides information about possible causes of the launch failure. In the dialog MY.INI SETUP you can examine the file Windows\My.ini, make changes, and then save via SAVE.

In order for WinMySQLadmin to be executed each time the computer is booted up, click, in the dialog MY.INI SETUP, the button CREATE SHORTCUT ON START MENU. This will add the program to the Windows startup directory.

The next time the computer is started the program will automatically be executed and immediately shrunk to an icon within the task bar. With the right mouse button you can operate the most important functions and open the dialog shown in Figure 2-2.

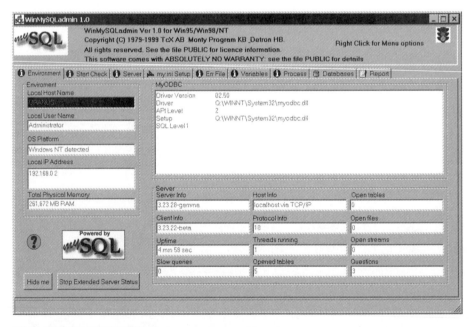

Figure 2-2. WinMySQLadmin

Windows 9x/ME

Installation under Windows 9x/ME is almost identical to that under Windows NT/2000. The only significant difference is that here MySQL cannot be used as a service. (Windows 9x/ME knows nothing about services.)

The result is that the MySQL server is not launched automatically at startup. But that is now the responsibility of WinMySQLAdmin: This program registers itself at the first (manual) launch in the Windows startup directory, and in the future launches the MySQL server at every computer startup.

Installation Under Linux

MySQL is included in most Linux distributions. The installation is here confined to installing the MySQL program package with the distribution's package manager. This is described below in detail for Red Hat and SuSE Linux.

Red Hat: Installation of the Included Version

MySQL 3.23.36 is included with Red Hat 7.1. (Future versions of Red Hat will presumably contain more current versions.) MySQL is divided into four packages, whose RPM files are located on CD 2:

- `mysql-version.rpm` contains the client programs, including the *shared libraries*, which are used by many programs to access MySQL. The client programs (`mysql, mysqladmin`, etc.) aid in the administration of MySQL.

- `mysql-server-version.rpm` contains the actual MySQL server.

- `mysql-devel-version.rpm` contains the libraries and include files for program development in C.

Usually, only the first two of these packages need to be installed. The installation can take place with either `rpm` or `gnorpm`.

```
root# rpm -i /mnt/cdrom/RedHat/RPMS/mysql-3-23-36-1.i386.rpm
root# rpm -i /mnt/cdrom/RedHat/RPMS/mysql-server-3-23-36-1.i386.rpm
```

REMARK *On the Red Hat CD number 2 there is also a MySQL package:* `mysqlclient-version.rpm`. *This package contains an older version of the* `libmysqlclient` *library. This package is needed only if you have installed older programs (e.g., PHP or Perl modules) that require these libraries.*

To determine whether MySQL is already installed on your computer (and if so, in which version), execute the following commands:

```
root# rpm -qa | grep mysql
mysql-3.23.36-1
mysql-server-3.23.36-1
```

To try out your newly installed MySQL server, execute the following command:

```
root# /etc/rc.d/init.d/mysqld start
```

If you want the MySQL server always to start automatically, you must add mysqld to the appropriate init-V run levels. The simplest way of proceeding is to make this setting with chkconfig:

```
root# chkconfig --level 235 mysqld on
```

As database directory, /var/lib/mysql is used.

SuSE: Installation of the Included Version

With SuSE 7.1 you get version 3.23.30 of MySQL. (Future versions of SuSE will contain more recent versions of MySQL.) MySQL is divided into five packages (YaST category *ap*, i.e., *applications*), of which, as a rule, the first three are installed with YaST:

- mysql contains the actual MySQL server.
- mysql-client contains the client programs (mysql, mysqladmin, etc.) for administration of MySQL.
- mysql-shared contains the *shared libraries*, which are used by many programs to access MySQL.
- mysql-bench contains benchmark tests for MySQL.
- mysql-devel contains libraries and include files for program development in C.

MySQL can be launched manually after installation with the following command:

```
root# /etc/init.d/mysql start
```

To have MySQL launch automatically at startup you must change the variable *START_MYSQL* in /etc/rc.config:

```
# change in /etc/rc.config
START_MYSQL="yes"
```

As database directory, /var/lib/mysql is used.

> **REMARK**   *If you use SuSE 7.1 together with Kernel 2.4, you will receive an error message at MySQL startup. Nonetheless, MySQL will launch. To avoid the error message you can get the most current version of MySQL for the SuSE distribution from the SuSE FTP server:*
>
> ```
> ftp://ftp.suse.com/pub/suse/i386/update/7.1/ap2/
> ftp://ftp.suse.com/pub/suse/i386/update/7.1/ap3/
> ```

Red Hat and SuSE: Installation of a Newer Version

Experienced Linux users can, of course, install the most recent version of MySQL from www.mysql.com instead of the included packages. Please note, however, that you may have to deal with some incompatibilities (see the next topic).

Before installation you must back up databases that have already been used (see the section on backups in Chapter 11), quit the MySQL server, and delete the already installed version of MySQL:

- **Red Hat:**

  ```
  root# /etc/rc.d/init.d/mysqld stop
  root# rpm -e mysql-server
  root# rpm -e --nodeps mysql
  ```

- **SuSE:**

  ```
  root# /etc/init.d/mysql stop
  root# rpm -e mysql-client
  root# rpm -e --nodeps mysl-shared
  root# rpm -e mysql
  ```

> **REMARK** *The option --nodeps for deinstallation can be necessary if another package is installed on the computer that requires a particular MySQL package (usually Perl or PHP modules for MySQL).*

Current MySQL packages can be found on the web site www.mysql.com/downloads under the heading *Standard binary RPMs*. There, too, MySQL is divided into five packages:

- Server package

- Package with benchmark tests

- Client package (administration tools)

- Developer package (include files and libraries for program development)

- Shared libraries package (libraries for execution of external programs that access MySQL)

As a rule, you need the server, client, and shared libraries packages. For installation use rpm -i.

In the process of installation the MySQL server is automatically launched. Moreover, entries in the system init-V are carried out, so that MySQL will be launched automatically at startup. To launch or terminate the MySQL server manually, execute the following command:

```
root# /etc/rc.d/init.d/mysql start / stop
```

Incompatibilities After Installation of the Packages from www.mysql.com

> **WARNING** *Sad to tell, every Linux distributor has an individualized notion of how software packages should be managed, in what directories files should be installed, and how programs should be executed at startup. Therefore, only experienced Linux users should install packages that are not specifically intended for your distribution. In other words, if you are not a Linux expert, for a MySQL update you should use only packages that have been created by Red Hat or SuSE particularly for your distribution. You will find such packages in the update or download region of the relevant web site. Unfortunately, it often takes weeks or even months before the latest version of MySQL becomes available.*

Red Hat: The init-V script now has the name mysql (instead of mysqld).
However, since the links for the run levels 2–5 are correctly entered, the newly
installed MySQL version will be automatically executed at startup.

SuSE: The init-V script is installed in the wrong directory. Move it to
/etc/init.d:

```
root# mv /etc/init.d/init.d/mysql     /etc/init.d
```

The new init-V script ignores the variable *START_MYSQL* from
/etc/rc.config. Furthermore, the directories /etc/init.d/rc?.d/ are missing
links to the init script. If you wish MySQL to be started automatically, you
must create the necessary links in the init-V directories /etc/init.d/rc?.d:

```
root# ln -s /etc/init.d/mysql /etc/init.d/rc2.d/S99mysql
root# ln -s /etc/init.d/mysql /etc/init.d/rc3.d/S99mysql
root# ln -s /etc/init.d/mysql /etc/init.d/rc5.d/S99mysql
root# ln -s /etc/init.d/mysql /etc/init.d/rc2.d/K10mysql
root# ln -s /etc/init.d/mysql /etc/init.d/rc3.d/K10mysql
root# ln -s /etc/init.d/mysql /etc/init.d/rc5.d/K10mysql
```

Both Distributions: A further difference affects the internal management
of the package dependencies. During the installation of other packages
(for example, php-mysql) the distributions no longer know that MySQL
has already been installed. With Red Hat you can force the installation of
packages despite the unresolved dependencies with the rpm option --nodeps,
but there is no longer any guarantee that all programs will then work together
correctly. With SuSE you can specify in YaST that the package dependencies
are to be ignored.

Finally, problems are also to expected in distribution updates. In an update
to a new version of the Linux distribution, MySQL is probably left untouched
and will not be updated automatically.

As database directory /var/lib/mysql is used.

As socket file /var/lib/mysql/mysql.sock is now used (instead of
/tmp/mysql.sock). The socket file enables efficient local communication
between a MySQL client and the server without having to use TCP/IP.

If individual programs are no longer able to establish a connection to MySQL
(for example, PHP), then the easiest solution is to establish a link:

```
root# ln -s /var/lib/mysql/mysql.sock    /tmp
```

Another possibility is to use the socket option in /etc/my.cnf to inform all
programs where this file is located.

33

Testing the Installation

To test whether the MySQL server runs and whether you can use it, launch the program mysql. Under Linux you simply execute mysql in a shell window. Under Windows launch mysql/bin/mysql.exe with a double click in Explorer. In this program you execute the command status. Under Unix/Linux the result should look like what is pictured in Figure 2-3.

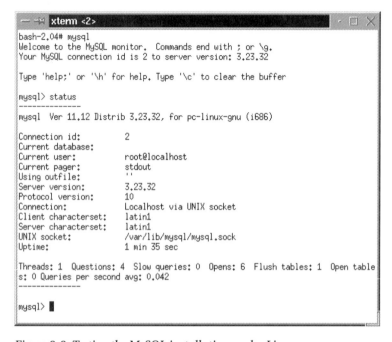

Figure 2-3. Testing the MySQL installation under Linux

If that doesn't work, check whether the MySQL server is running at all. Under Linux you would execute ps -a:

```
root# ps -a | grep mysqld
  1288 pts/1 00:00:00 mysqld
  1290 pts/1 00:00:00 mysqld
  1291 pts/1 00:00:00 mysqld
```

Under Windows NT/2000, take a look at the task manager. There should be a process running called mysqld.exe.

If the MySQL server is not running, you will probably have to start it manually. Under Linux you would use the init-V script mysql[d] start. Under Windows use instead the program WinMySQLadmin.

> **REMARK** *The name* mysqld *is short for the MySQL daemon. This is simply another name for the MySQL server.*
>
> *Under Unix/Linux it is usual to call auxiliary programs running in the background "daemons." (In Windows NT/2000 such programs are called "services.")*

Security

After a default installation MySQL is insecure. Anyone can enter without a password as *root* and has unlimited privileges. (Under Windows the default installation is even more insecure, if that is possible.)

As long as you are not storing any critical data in MySQL, you can continue to use the database system completely unsecured (just be aware of the security risks, however). If you value security, then you will find in Chapter 7 an extensive description of the MySQL access system, including a step-by-step introduction to beginning to secure your system.

Updating MySQL

You will find the most recent versions of MySQL in various formats at www.mysql.com.

> **CAUTION** *In general, it is recommended that you back up all MySQL databases before undertaking a MySQL update.*
>
> *If you update MySQL within a main version, that is, a small version change such as 3.23.30 to 3.23.35, then as a rule you can use your database files without change. In this case the backup is merely a security measure.*
>
> *In the case of a large version change, say from 3.22.n to 3.34.m or from 3.23.n to 4.0.n, then you must make a complete backup and then bring up the database afresh.*

> **POINTER** *Information on making a backup and on migrating between databases of incompatible versions of MySQL, as well as general information on* mysqldump, *can be found in Chapter 11. This section assumes that a small version change is carried out and that therefore the database files can be used without alteration.*

Updating Under Windows

Before you install a new version, you should deinstall the old one. Databases that you have created yourself are not harmed. (Your personal database files in the directory Mysql\data are not touched.)

> **CAUTION** *The database* mysql, *which contains all of the access privilege information, will be deleted. Therefore, create a backup copy of this database before deinstallation (that is, copy the directory* mysql/data/mysql *to another location).*

The configuration files C:\my.cnf and windows\my.ini will normally not be touched during deinstallation. Nevertheless, it is a good idea to make backup copies of these files.

If you wish to use the existing configuration and database files without difficulties, you should install the new version of MySQL in the same directory as it was before.

Before you launch MySQL, you must redeploy the backup copy of the *mysql* database. To do this, copy the secured directory mysql again into the MySQL data directory (mysql/data).

Updating Under Linux

- Execute a backup. (As with Windows, your own database files should remain intact. The database *mysql* might be overwritten by the new version.)

- Terminate MySQL with the relevant init-V script:

    Red Hat: root# **/etc/rc.d/init.d/mysql[d] stop**

    SuSE: root# **/etc/init.d/mysql stop**

- Deinstall the MySQL packages with `rpm -e` or another package management tool (Red Hat: `gnurpm`, SuSE: `yast`).

- Install the updated MySQL packages.

- Restore the *mysql* database. (If the MySQL server was automatically launched after installation, you must first terminate it.)

- Launch the MySQL server.

MySQL-Max

The MySQL standard distribution for $3.23.n$ currently contains drivers for only the table types ISAM and MyISAM. If you want to try out the new table types BDB, InnoDB, and Gemini, you must either wait for MySQL 4.0 or else compile MySQL yourself, or else install MySQL-Max. This is a MySQL server that contains the new table drivers.

Please note that MySQL-Max is currently in beta status (as are also the drivers for BDB, InnoDB, and Gemini) and is not yet available for all operating systems. MySQL-Max is thus currently suited to those MySQL users who would like to test these new table drivers without making too great demands on them. Only when MySQL-Max has attained *stable* status from the MySQL team will this MySQL variant probably become the default installation for most operating systems. It is only at that point that one could recommend the deployment of MySQL-Max in a production system.

Installation Under Linux

If you wish to install MySQL-Max under Linux, you must first install the usual MySQL packages. MySQL-Max contains as its only file `mysqld-max`, which is installed in the directory `/usr/sbin`.

In order to have `mysqld-max` start up instead of the usual version `mysqld`, a suitably adapted init-V start script is necessary. This has been automatically installed since MySQL 3.23.37. If you have a current version of MySQL, then `mysqld-max` will be used automatically after installation.

As a first test after installation you should find out which table types are actually available:

```
user$ mysql -u root -p
Password: xxx
mysql> SHOW VARIABLES LIKE 'have%';
Variable_name Value
```

```
have_bdb       YES
have_gemini    NO
have_innodb    DISABLED
have_isam      YES
have_raid      NO
have_ssl       NO
```

If as in the above example you discover that *DISABLED* is displayed for individual table drivers, then the problem is most likely due to an incorrect or incomplete configuration. Information is usually provided by the MySQL logging file, which under Unix/Linux generally has the name /var/lib/mysql/*hostname*.err (where *hostname* is to be replaced by the name of the computer). Detailed information on the InnoDB start configuration and the use of such tables can be found in Chapter 12.

MySQL (Client Installation)

All of the client programs are automatically installed with the MySQL installation described above. Often, however, the server runs on a different computer, and you require only the client tools to access the external server. In this case a space-saving client installation is sufficient.

With a client installation only various administration programs (mysql, mysqladmin, mysqldump, etc.) as well as the related libraries and character set files are installed. Then you can use these programs to create new databases on the external MySQL server, read existing data, execute SQL commands, and so on.

> **REMARK** *In some situations you can dispense entirely with the installation of client tools on the local computer, namely, when an administration tool is installed on the MySQL computer that runs locally (for example, phpMyAdmin) and can be used over the Internet. If the MySQL server runs on the computer of an ISP, then that is the usual situation; see the last section of this chapter.*

Windows

The zip archive `Winclients-version.zip` with all the files for a client installation can be found at the following address:

`http://www.mysql.com/downloads/os-win32.html`

To carry out the installation, extract the contents of the zip file into the directory of your choice. If the MySQL server uses a special character set (you will see this in the connection process in the error message *Can't initialize character set*), you must then copy the directory `mysql\share\charsets` into the root directory of drive `C:`. The path to the character set files must be as follows: `c:\mysql\share\charsets`

> **REMARK**   *As this was written in February 2001, the client installation files were already nine months old. The files for the client installation are apparently updated less frequently than the files for the server installation.*
>
> *The reason for this is that change is much slower in the client tools than in the server itself. Nonetheless, there have been continual small improvements and corrections in the client programs (such as* `mysql.exe` *and* `mysqladmin.exe`).
>
> *Therefore, check before performing a client installation whether the version is sufficiently current. You may have to do a complete server installation to obtain the current client tools*

Unix/Linux

The most current Linux distributions provide packages for client installation. Simply install the package `mysql-version.rpm` (not `mysql-server-version.rpm`). You can also get such RPMs for the client installation at the download site `www.mysql.com` (*Client programs for i386 systems*), and, in contrast to the comparable Windows package, always in the latest version.

Apache

This section describes a basic installation of Apache and some elementary configuration steps.

Installation

> **POINTER** *Detailed information on the countless configuration possibilities as well as security of the installation can be found in books on Apache and at the Apache documentation site:*
>
> http://www.apache.org/docs/

Installation Under Windows

Apache is available at www.apache.org (and at a number of mirror sites) as an installation program for Windows. Install the file setup.exe on your computer and execute the program.

Under Windows NT/2000 it is a good idea to set up Apache as a service. To do this, execute START|PROGRAMS|APACHE|INSTALL APACHE AS SERVICE. There you can also set the behavior of the program at startup (usually AUTOMATIC, assuming that you want Apache to be launched automatically).

Installation Under Linux

Apache is normally automatically installed under Linux. If that is not the case in your situation, you will have to install the relevant package (usually apache-*version*.rpm).

Configuration and Start

Configuration File

Almost all Apache settings are managed via the configuration file httpd.conf. There you must change, before launching Apache for the first time, the setting

ServerName. You should provide the network name of your computer, for example, the following:

```
# change in httpd.conf
ServerName uranus.sol # Here give the name of your computer
```

Where `httpd.conf` is located depends, of course, on the operating system:

> **Windows:** `Programs\Apache Group\Apache\conf`
>
> **Red Hat Linux:** `/etc/httpd/conf/httpd.conf`
>
> **SuSE Linux:** `/etc/httpd/httpd.conf`

Launching Apache

To launch the program after setting `httpd.conf`, the following commands are necessary:

> **Windows 9x/ME:** START|PROGRAMS|APACHE|START APACHE.
>
> **Windows NT/2000:** In SETTINGS|CONTROL PANEL|ADMINISTRATIVE TOOLS| SERVICES select the service *Apache* and click on START in the service dialog.
>
> **Red Hat Linux:** root# `/etc/rc.d/httpd start`
>
> **SuSE Linux:** root# `/etc/init.d/apache start`

In the case of Red Hat Linux, Apache is automatically installed in such a way that it is launched at startup. For SuSE this is also true in principle, although you must change a variable in `/etc/rc.config`:

```
# change in /etc/rc.config for SuSE
START_HTTPD="yes"
```

Testing the Apache Installation

To test the Apache installation, launch a web browser on the local computer and input the address `http://localhost`. What should appear is the default Apache site with a short infotext that informs you that the Apache installation was successful.

> **REMARK** *The name* localhost *is valid both under Windows and under Unix/Linux as the network name for the local computer. The address* http://localhost *therefore corresponds to* http://your.computer.name *(or whatever you have named your computer).*

Restarting Apache After Changing httpd.conf

After a change in httpd.conf you must restart Apache so that the new configuration becomes effective. Depending on the operating system the restart is carried out in one way or another.

Windows 9x/ME: First, execute START|PROGRAMS|APACHE|STOP APACHE; then START APACHE.

Windows NT/2000: In SETTINGS|CONTROL PANEL|ADMINISTRATIVE TOOLS| SERVICES select the service Apache and click first on STOP in the service dialog, and then on START.

Red Hat Linux: root# /etc/rc.d/httpd restart

SuSE Linux: root# /etc/init.d/apache restart

Creating an Alias (Virtual Directory)

In the default installation Apache enables access to all files and subdirectories of a root directory. The path to this directory varies according to the operating system (in fact, according to the setting of DocumentRoot in httpd.conf). The following list shows the usual default settings:

Windows: Programs\Apache Group\Apache\htdocs

Red Hat Linux: /var/www/html

SuSE Linux: /usr/local/httpd/htdocs

With an alias it is possible to associate a virtual directory on the server with an arbitrary directory on the hard drive on the server. For example, via Apache, with the path http://computer.name/virtual you can access the actual directory e:\data\real or /usr/share/help. An alias is also helpful in simplifying access over the web server to directories located at various places on the hard drive. To do this you should insert an Alias line in httpd.conf according to the following template:

```
# in httpd.conf
Alias /virtual e:\data\real
```

For the change in `httpd.conf` to become effective, Apache must be restarted (see above).

Access Protection for Individual Directories (.htaccess)

It can happen that not all of the directories managed by Apache should be universally accessible. For example, if you install phpMyAdmin for administration of MySQL at an Internet service provider, these administrative tasks should be available to you alone, and not to every web surfer who happens by.

Password File

The simplest method of protecting individual directories is offered by the file `.htaccess`, which is placed in the directory in question. However, it is first necessary to set up a password file. This file can, in principle, be located just about anywhere, though for reasons of security it is recommended to select a directory that is not accessible from without (that is, outside of the directories reachable by Apache).

The password file is generated with the Apache auxiliary program `htpasswd`. Choose the option `-c` (*create*), and specify the name of the password file and a user name. The program will ask you for the desired password, and then it generates the password file, in which the user name appears in plain text, the password in encrypted form.

```
> htpasswd -c site.pwd myname
New password: *********
Re-type new password: *********
Adding password for user myname
```

To add an additional combination of user name and password to a preexisting password file, execute `htpasswd` again, this time without the option `-c`:

```
> htpasswd site.pwd name2
New password: *********
Re-type new password: *********
Adding password for user name2
```

The resulting password file will look something like this:

```
myname:$apr1$gp1 .. ..$qljDszVJOSCS.oBoPJItS/
name2:$apr1$A22 .. ..$OVO1Nc1FcXgNsruT9c6Iq1
```

> **REMARK** *If you wish to execute* htpasswd.exe *under Windows, you have to open a DOS window and specify the complete path name inside quotation marks (usually* "Programs\Apache Group\Apache\bin\htpasswd.exe")*.*
>
> *If you want to create or enlarge the password file in a directory of an Internet service provider, then use* telnet *access to the computer of the ISP (in order to execute* htpasswd *there). Many ISPs make available other configuration aids.*

.htaccess *File*

An .htaccess file protects the entire contents of a directory (including all subdirectories). The file normally consists of the following four lines. Here *AuthUserFile* specifies the complete file name of the password file:

```
AuthType Basic
AuthUserFile /www/username/htdocs/_private/site.pwd
AuthName "myrealm"
Require valid-user
```

AuthName denotes the *realm* within which access is valid. The point is that you do not have to execute a login every time want to access various directories protected by .htaccess. Once you have logged into a particular *AuthName*, this login remains valid for all further directories with this *AuthName* indicator.

For .htaccess this means that you specify the same *AuthName* character string for directories with a common login. Conversely, for varying directories you may specify varying domain names, in which case a new login is required for each directory.

Require valid-user means that every valid combination of user name and password is allowed. Alternatively, you can specify here that a login is permitted only for particular users:

```
Require User myname name2 name3
```

Access to a Protected Directory

As soon as you attempt to read a file from a protected directory with a browser, the web browser presents a login dialog (see Figure 2-4).

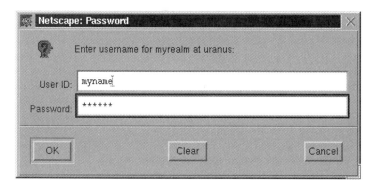

Figure 2-4. Access to a web directory protected by cw.htaccess

> **POINTER** *Further details on user authentication and* .htaccess *configuration can be found at the web address* http://www.apacheweek.com/features/userauth

PHP

PHP stands for *PHP Hypertext Preprocessor* (which is to say that we are dealing with a recursive abbreviation, so beloved in the Unix community). PHP enables the insertion of script code into HTML files. It works like this: Every time a surfer requests a file with the identifier *.php, the web server (Apache, for example) transmits this file to the PHP interpreter. This, in turn, evaluates the PHP code and constructs the resulting HTML document, which is then returned to the web server. The web server then directs the file to the surfer. PHP thus offers a simple way of generating dynamic web pages. No assumptions need be made about the client.

PHP4 has been available since about the middle of the year 2000. However, some Internet service providers still have the older and once very popular PHP3 installed. The two versions are largely compatible, but PHP4 offers a host of additional commands. Before you begin development of your web pages, be sure to find out which PHP version is supported by your ISP.

The examples in this book were developed with PHP4. If you are using PHP3 you will have to make some small changes here and there.

The CGI Version Versus the Apache Module

There are two basic ways that Apache can run the PHP interpreter: as a free-standing program and as a module.

- In the first variant the PHP interpreter is executed as a *CGI program*. The program must be restarted for the translation of each *.php file, which is relatively inefficient. The advantage of the CGI variant is that the installation and configuration are simpler.

- In the second variant the PHP interpreter is run as an Apache module. The module is a sort of extension to the Apache program. It is loaded once and then remains in memory. The advantage of the module variant is that execution is considerably more efficient. Furthermore, some additional functions are available under PHP (for example, HTTP authentication functions).

Under Unix/Linux the PHP module is usually used in the form of a *Dynamic Shared Object* (DSO). This enables the subsequent addition or exchange of Apache modules without Apache itself having to be recompiled.

PHP4 Installation as a CGI Program Under Windows

At the web site http://www.php.net/ you will find the most recent version of PHP4 in two variants: as a WinZip archive and as an installation program. Since the installation program is dependent on the Internet information server, while in this book Apache is used as the web server, you should choose the WinZip variant. Installation is easy. Simply copy all the files in the archive into your favorite directory (for example, C:\php4).

> **REMARK** *At* http://www.php.net *a precompiled PHP for Windows is available only in the CGI version. PHP can be installed under Windows as an Apache module as well. For this you will have either to compile PHP yourself or hunt for a precompiled version on the Internet (for your version of Apache!). The configuration of Apache also looks somewhat different from that described in this chapter. Further information can be found at* http://www.geocities.com/ro_marius/mod_php4.html
>
> *Please note that you can use many PHP libraries only in the CGI version of PHP, since these libraries are not thread-secure. (This means that problems can arise when two subprocesses use the same functions.)*

Registering the PHP Interpreter with Apache

But wait! We are not yet quite done. The next step is to tell Apache where the PHP interpreter is to be found. For this `httpd.conf` must be edited. The following lines provide the required settings so that Apache transmits files with the identifiers *.php, *.php3, and *.php4 to the PHP interpreter.

Please note the unusual syntax of `ScriptAlias` and `Action`. With `ScriptAlias` we have /php4/ defined as an abbreviation for the installation directory of the PHP4 files. This abbreviation is then used again in `Action`, where therefore /php4/php.exe means that `php.exe` is located in the directory that was defined in `ScriptAlias` (and not directly in the directory /php4).

```
# in httpd.conf
ScriptAlias /php4/ "C:/php4/"
AddType application/x-httpde-php4 .php4 .php3 .php
Action application/x-httpde-php4 "/php4/php.exe"
```

For the settings to take effect, Apache must be restarted in the service dialog (SETTINGS|CONTROL PANEL|ADMINISTRATIVE TOOLS|SERVICES).

> **REMARK** *In your test system you can easily configure Apache in such a way that it deals satisfactorily with *.php, *.php3, and *.php4 files. However, on the system of your ISP this is probably not the case. That is, your ISP generally prescribes a particular data type (often *.php3, even if PHP4 is installed). To avoid problems later in the installation of your PHP files on the ISP computer you should use the same file identifier in your test environment as that used by the ISP.*
>
> *In this book we generally use the identifier *.php. If your web server is so configured that the file identifier *.php3 or *.php4 is prescribed, you must make the relevant change to the names of your PHP files. Furthermore, you must adapt all links within the HTML or PHP code (this affects, in particular, <a href= . . . > and <form action= . . . >).*

> **TIP** *Apache is generally installed under Windows NT/2000 as a service, which is started by the user* system. *This has two drawbacks. First, there is a security risk, because* system *(and thus Apache and concomitantly the PHP or Perl script launched by Apache) has unrestricted access to the computer. Second, it is impossible to terminate the PHP interpreter if an infinite loop or similar problem occurs due to a programming error. (Even the Windows* administrator *may not terminate a system process with the task manager. There are, of course, other tools that can do this. But they are generally unavailable.)*
>
> *When it is only a matter of greater convenience in PHP development, then it suffices to assign Apache to the user* Administrator. *The assignment of the Apache service to a user is accomplished in the dialog sheet* LOG-ON *of the service dialog* SETTINGS|CONTROL PANEL|ADMINISTRATIVE TOOLS|SERVICES. *Apache is then executed as a process of the user* Administrator, *and* Administrator *is then allowed to end Apache processes as well as derived processes (PHP interpreter, etc.) at any time.*
>
> *From the point of view of security, however, this configuration is nothing short of catastrophic. It would be better to define a new Windows user (for example, with the name* apache*) and assign it to the Apache service. The user* apache *has only limited privileges (at least read access to all HTML documents, write access to the apache configuration files, and network access).*

PHP4 Installation as Apache Module Under Linux

Red Hat: To use PHP (in combination with MySQL) under Red Hat Linux you should install, with rpm, the package gd (available on CD 1) as well as php, php-mysql, and mod_php (all on CD 2). Finally, restart Apache:

```
root# /etc/rc.d/httpd restart
```

For the connection to PHP to be successful (more precisely, for PHP, which is executed by Apache in the account *apache*, to be able to access the file /var/lib/mysql/mysql.sock), you must still edit the access privileges to the directory /var/lib/mysql:

```
root# chmod a+x /var/lib/mysql
```

REMARK   *If you have installed a newer version (from* www.mysql.com*) of MySQL than that delivered with Red Hat 7, the package system does not recognize that MySQL is already installed and it refuses to perform the installation of* php-mysql. *You can circumvent this obstacle by forcing installation with* rpm -i --nodeps.

   A second difficulty is that php-mysql *expects the library* libmysqlclient.so.9, *while newer versions of MySQL use a more recent version of this library. (With PHP this results in error messages that the functions* mysql_xy *are unknown.) A remedy in this case is a simple link:*

```
root# ln -s /usr/lib/libmysqlclient.so /usr/lib/libmysqlclient.so.9
```

SuSE: To put PHP to work under SuSE you need only install the package mod_php4 and then restart Apache. That's all there is to it!

```
root# /etc/init.d/apache restart
```

If you do not use the version of MySQL provided with SuSE, but rather have obtained MySQL directly from www.mysql.com, then you may need to provide a link to mysql.sock (the connection between PHP and a local MySQL server is accomplished by means of this socket file):

```
root# ln -s /var/lib/mysql/mysql.sock /tmp
```

Testing the PHP Installation

Create a test file phptest.php according to the following template, and save the file in a location where Apache can access it (that is, in the htdocs directory or in an alias directory):

```
<html><head><title>PHP Test</title></head>
<body>
<?php phpinfo(); ?>
</body></html>
```

Now load this page with a web browser. Be sure that the page is not read directly from the file system but via Apache. (For example, you must use http://localhost/phptest.php as the address, not D:\htdocs\phptest.php.) The result should look something like Figure 2-5.

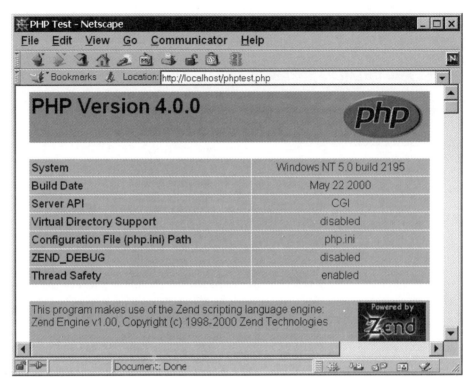

Figure 2-5. PHP 4 runs!

TIP *If it does not function properly and instead of the table shown in Figure 2-5 you get only an empty page or a couple of lines of weird PHP code, the most probable cause of the trouble is that you are looking at the page directly and not via Apache. Please be sure that the path in the web browser contains* http://localhost *and not the direct file name, such as* C:\path\phptest.php*). Other possible causes of the error are Apache configuration problems. Have you restarted Apache after the change in the configuration file?*

Testing PHP in Combination with MySQL

The following program (see Figure 2-6) provides a list of all MySQL databases. (Immediately after installation there are only two databases: *test* is empty, while *mysql* is responsible for the MySQL internal management of access privileges.) The variables *mysqluser* and *mysqlpasswd* can remain empty as long as MySQL access is not secured by a password.

```php
<?php // mysql-test.php ?>
<html><head>
<title>Test PHP and MySQL</title>
</head><body>
<?php
  $mysqluser="";           // user name
  $mysqlpasswd="";         // password
  $mysqlhost="localhost";          // computer name
  $connID = mysql_pconnect($mysqlhost, $mysqluser, $mysqlpasswd);
  $result=mysql_list_dbs();
  echo "<p>Databases at the local MySQL server<p>\n";
  while($row = mysql_fetch_row($result)) {
    echo "<br><i>$row[0]</i>\n";}
?>
</body></html>
```

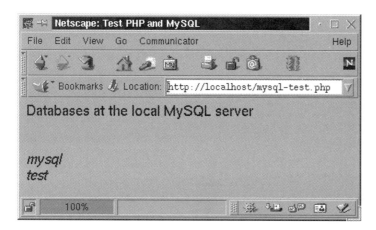

Figure 2-6. PHP can access MySQL

PHP Configuration

Various configuration details of the PHP interpreter are controlled by the file php.ini. This file under Unix/Linux is located in /etc, while under Windows it is in the PHP installation directory.

phpMyAdmin

The best current tool for convenient administration of MySQL is probably phpMyAdmin (Figure 2-7). A condition for the use of phpMyAdmin is, however, the installation of PHP version 3 or higher. (Note that phpMyAdmin consists merely of several *.php or *.php3 files. Thus phpMyAdmin is not only a valuable tool, but at the same time an excellent example of MySQL programming with PHP.)

POINTER   *This section describes only the local installation of phpMyAdmin. Further information on other installation variants (such as for administration of MySQL by an Internet service provider) as well as an extensive description of the application possibilities of phpMyAdmin can be found in Chapter 4.*

Installation

phpMyAdmin consists of a number of *.php or *.php3 files. These files are installed in a directory on the web server. (You may either use a subdirectory of htdocs or set up an alias directory; see above in the section on Apache.)

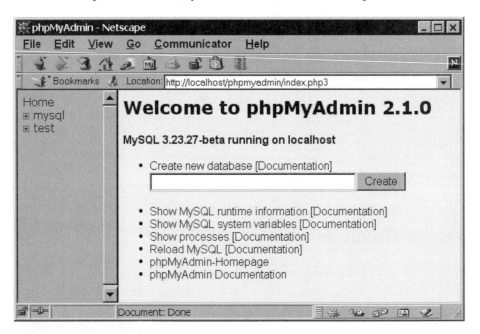

Figure 2-7. phpMyAdmin

Under Windows, phpMyAdmin is provided as a *.zip archive, which can be easily extracted with WinZip. Under Unix/Linux, on the other hand, it is usually a *.tar.gz archive. To extract it use the tar command according to the following template (modify the archive name and target directory according to your individual situation):

```
root# tar xzf phpMyAdmin_2.1.0php.tar.gz -C /usr/local/httpd/htdocs/
```

As long as MySQL is installed in the default configuration (and thus does not require a password for database access), phpMyAdmin should work without any problems. You can test this easily by loading index.php3 or index.php in your browser via Apache.

Specifying a MySQL User Name and Password

If MySQL is already password protected (which is recommended for security reasons; see also Chapter 7), then phpMyAdmin will not be able to establish a connection to MySQL. Instead of the start page an error message will be displayed.

A remedy for this situation is provided by configuring the file config.inc.php. There two or three lines must be changed to inform phpMyAdmin what user name and password are to be used in establishing a connection to MySQL (and also what host name, in the case that MySQL is not installed on the same computer as Apache, i.e., *localhost*):

```
# Change in config.inc.php
$cfgServers[1]['host'] = 'computer.name'; // computer name or localhost
 ...
$cfgServers[1]['user'] = 'username';
$cfgServers[1]['password'] = 'xxx';
```

Protecting Access to phpMyAdmin with a Password

If you are installing phpMyAdmin for administration of MySQL not only in your test environment but also with an ISP, then you are, of course, dealing with a security problem of great magnitude. Not only you, but every surfer as well, can use phpMyAdmin to manipulate your databases (or even delete them if said surfer locates the directory in which you have installed phpMyAdmin). You can prevent such a tragedy by password protecting access to the phpMyAdmin directory with a .htaccess file. (We are no longer dealing with a MySQL password, but one for Apache. The use of .htaccess was described above in the section in this chapter on Apache.)

> **CAUTION** *A second security problem is represented by the file* config.inc.php, *which contains, in plain text, your MySQL host name and associated password. If the PHP configuration of Apache is correct, then these data are evaluated by the server, and the client never sees the original file. Often, however, the computer of the ISP is installed in such a way that the web files can also be loaded via FTP, and then, as they say, you are in deep trouble. Therefore, make sure that it is not possible to read* config.inc.php *by anonymous FTP.*

Perl

Perl is perhaps the best-loved scripting language running under Unix. It is used by system administrators and web programmers (for CGI scripts), among others. However, Perl is of interest to you even if you have no intention of programming in Perl. Namely, there is a host of scripts for various MySQL administrative tasks. (Some are provided with MySQL, while many others can be found on the Internet.) In order for these scripts to be usable, Perl must be installed on your computer.

Installation

Perl Installation Under Windows

Downloadable files for Perl can be found under www.perl.com and www.activestate.com. The currently most popular distribution of Perl (containing a collection of all necessary files together with the installation program) is ActivePerl, which is available as an MSI file free of charge. With Windows ME or Windows 2000 you begin installation simply by double clicking on the MSI file. With older versions of Windows you must first install the Windows installer (a download link can be found at www.activestate.com).

Perl Installation Under Linux

Perl is automatically installed with almost all Linux distributions, since countless administration tools require Perl. You can determine whether Perl is installed and, if so, what version, with the following command:

```
root# rpm -qa | grep perl
perl-5.6.0-9
```

If Perl happens not to have been installed, then you can install the Perl package with rpm or gnorpm (Red Hat) or with YaST (SuSE).

Testing the Perl Installation

Under Windows, create a text file with the name test.pl and the following contents:

```
#!/usr/bin/perl -w
print "Hello world!\n";
print "Please hit Return to end the program!";
$wait_for_return = <STDIN>;
```

Windows: Under Windows it should be possible to launch the file at once with a double click. The program prints "Hello world!" in a DOS window, waits for Return, and then terminates.

If a double click fails to bring about program execution, then open a DOS window and try the following command:

```
Q:\> perl Q:\directory_with_my_perl_files\test.pl
```

Linux: Under Unix/Linux you must first label test.pl as an executable file:

```
user$ chmod u+x test.pl
```

Now the program can be executed:

```
user$ ./test.pl
Hello World!
Please hit Return to end the program!<Return>
```

If this doesn't work, then perhaps the Perl interpreter has not been installed in the directory /usr/bin but in some other directory. Determine what directory this is and make the necessary change in the file test.pl.

> **REMARK**   *Under Unix/Linux it is not usual practice to give Perl files names of the form* *.pl *(even though it does no harm). Nonetheless, in this book we shall use this identifier to make it easier to exchange files between Windows and Unix/Linux.*

MySQL Support for Perl

The installation of Perl is not the end of the matter. Perl is not capable of communicating with MySQL all by itself. Perl must be extended with two auxiliary modules:

- **DBI:** *DBI* stands for *database interface*. With *DBI* modules we are dealing with a general interface for database programming.

- **DBD-Mysql:** *DBD* stands for *database driver*. This module contains the MySQL-specific extension to *DBI*.

Installation of DBI and DBD-Mysql Under Windows

If you use the above-mentioned ActivePerl distribution, then the installation of the two modules is quite simple, since with this distribution the auxiliary program ppm (Perl package manager) is included. The program can be launched in a DOS window. It assumes a running Internet connection. The use of ppm is seen in the following lines:

```
Q:\> ppm
PPM interactive shell (2.1.1) - type 'help' for available commands.
PPM> search DBI
Packages available from http://www.ActiveState.com/PPMPackages/5.6:
DBI [1.14] Database independent interface for Perl
PPM> install DBI
Retrieving package 'DBI' ...
Installing J:\Perl\site\lib\auto\DBI\dbd_xsh.h
Installing J:\Perl\site\lib\auto\DBI\DBI.bs
  ...
PPM> install DBD-Mysql
Retrieving package 'DBD-Mysql' ...
Installing J:\Perl\site\lib\auto\DBD\mysql\mysql.bs
  ...
```

Installation of DBI *and* DBD-Mysql *Under Linux*

Red Hat: With Red Hat 7, alas, only the *DBI* module is included (package `perl-DBI` on the PowerTools CD). Use `rpm` to install this package.

The *DBD::mysql* module can be found in the *contributed* section of the Red Hat FTP server. Your best bet is to look on the Red Hat download site for *perl DBD*. Here is the most recent address of the file:

```
ftp://ftp.redhat.com/pub/contrib/libc6/i386/perl-DBD-msql-mysql-1.2214-1.i386.rpm
```

Download the package to your computer and install it with `rpm`. Unfortunately, the package is installed in the Perl 5.005 directory tree, whereas Red Hat 7 uses version 5.6.0 of Perl. The following command (written on two lines for lack of space) copies the files from Perl 5 into the Perl 5.6 directory tree. The option `-i` ensures that no files are accidentally overwritten:

```
root# cp -iR /usr/lib/perl5/site\_perl/5.005/i386-linux/* \
   > /usr/lib/perl5/site\_perl/5.6.0/i386-linux
```

> **REMARK**   *Perhaps there will exist a current Red-Hat-compatible version of the package* `perl-DBD-msql-mysql` *by the time you are reading this book. In that case, of course, the* `cp` *command will not be necessary.*

SuSE: With SuSE all necessary packages are included. Install, with YaST, `perl_dbi` (category *perl*) and `mysqperl` (category *pay*). You can check whether the packages are already installed with the command `rpm -qa | grep perl`.

Testing DBI *and* DBD-Mysql

The following Perl script shows all databases available to the MySQL server. Immediately after installation these are only *mysql* and *test*. The example will work only if the given user name and password permit access to this table. Change this information as need be. (The words in question are in slant script. If MySQL is still not password protected, then both character strings can be left empty. Information for setting MySQL access privileges can be found in Chapter 7.)

```perl
#!/usr/bin/perl -w
# Test file mysql-test.pl
use DBI();
# establish connection to database
$dbh = DBI->connect(
"DBI:mysql:database=mysql;host=localhost",
"user", "password", 'RaiseError' => 1);
# execute query
$sth = $dbh->prepare("SHOW DATABASES");
$sth->execute();
# show results
while(ary = $sth->fetchrow_array()) {
print join("\t", ary), "\n";
}
$sth->finish();
```

The result of the script will look something like this:

```
localhost  root      Y      Y      . . .
linux.localroot       Y      Y      . . .
linux.local           N      N      . . .
localhost             N      N      . . .
   . . .
```

Apache Configuration for Perl and CGI

If you wish to use Perl via CGI for programming dynamic HTML pages, then Apache will have to be configured accordingly. Usually, Perl CGI scripts are stored in the directory apache/cgi-bin. In order for Apache actually to process the page http://www.mycompany.com/cgi-bin/hello-cgi.pl, the following setting within httpd.conf is necessary:

```
# in httpd.conf
ScriptAlias /cgi-bin/ "C:/Program Files/Apache Group/Apache/cgi-bin/"
<Directory "C:/Program Files/Apache Group/Apache/cgi-bin">
  AllowOverride None
  Options None
</Directory>
```

Those parts in slant script must, of course, be replaced by the directories that are actually used on your computer.

CGI on a Unix/Linux Computer

Note that the files in the cgi-bin directory are executable and that Apache (which usually is executed under the account *apache* or *nobody*) is also allowed to read these files. Use chmod to set the appropriate access privileges.

> **TIP** *Even if you move the CGI files via FTP into the* cgi-bin *directory of your ISP, you must set the access privileges. The FTP protocol provides for this possibility, and most FTP programs are capable of doing so. (With the program WS_FTP, which runs under Windows, you can click on the files with the right mouse button and execute the command* chmod.*)*

CGI on Windows Computers

When Apache and Perl are installed on a Windows computer, the execution of Perl scripts usually does not work properly (error message *Internal Server Error*).

The reason is that Apache evaluates the first line of the Perl script (generally *#!/usr/bin/perl*) in order to search for the Perl interpreter. Under Unix/Linux this works, but under Windows the Perl interpreter is usually somewhere else entirely (for example, in the directory C:\Program Files\Perl\Bin\Perl.exe). The simplest solution is to add the following *ScriptInterpreterSource* lines in httpd.conf within the *<Directory>* tag:

```
# in httpd.conf
<Directory "C:/Program Files/Apache Group/Apache/cgi-bin">
  ...
  ScriptInterpreterSource registry
</Directory>
```

With this you achieve that the location of the Perl interpreter is determined by Apache with the help of the file identifier (which must be *.pl) and the Window registry.

Testing CGI Scripts

To test whether CGI files are executed, create the file cgi-test.pl in the cgi-bin directory:

```perl
#!/usr/bin/perl -w
# Test file cgi-test.pl
use CGI qw(:standard);
use CGI::Carp qw(fatalsToBrowser);
print header(),
  start_html("Hello CGI"),
  p("Hello CGI"),
  end_html();
```

If you are working under Unix/Linux, then you must set the access privileges with chmod g+rx or chmod a+rx in such a way that Apache is able to access the files. Then open the following page with a web browser (see Figure 2-8). Instead of www.myserver.com you must specify the network address of your computer or localhost.

http://www.myserver.com/cgi-bin/cgi-test.pl

Figure 2-8. CGI test page

Executing Perl Scripts with mod-perl

In the above configuration Apache starts the Perl interpreter anew for each script. Needless to say (though we are saying it, aren't we?), this is not very efficient. It is much better to maintain the Perl interpreter in memory. This is accomplished with the Apache module *mod-perl*.

> **POINTER** *The details of installation and configuration of Apache with* mod-perl *would take us too far afield from the subject matter of this book. Further information can be found in good books on Apache or in cyberspace, for example at the page* http://perl.apache.org/guide

MyODBC

ODBC (Open Database Connectivity) is a popular mechanism, particularly under Windows, for uniform access to a wide variety of database systems. The only requirement is an ODBC driver for the database system, which creates the interface between the ODBC system and the database.

> **REMARK** *ODBC is also sometimes used under Unix, and there is also MyODBC for Unix. However, in this book only the Windows application of ODBC/MyODBC is discussed.*

The ODBC driver for MySQL is MyODBC; MyODBC supports the functions for level 0 (and for some functions in levels 1 and 2 in ODBC version 2.5). For installation you should obtain MyODBC from the MySQL web server. It has most recently appeared at the following address:

http://www.mysql.com/downloads/api-myodbc.html

There are three Windows versions:

- MyODBC for Windows 9x/ME with setup program

- MyODBC for Windows NT/2000 with setup program

- myodbc.dll (regular version) and myodbcd.dll (debug version)

On initial installation use the setup program that corresponds to your operating system. If later you wish to update the installation, it suffices to replace the DLL myodbc.dll in the Windows system directory (e.g., C:\Windows\System32). There is no provision for a deinstallation of MyODBC.

> **REMARK** *MyODBC does not assume a MySQL client installation on the computer. If you use ODBC on a computer exclusively for access to a MySQL server that is running somewhere else, then it is sufficient to have MyODBC installed by itself.*
>
> *In MyODBC only the default character sets of the client tools are included. (This includes* latin1, big5, czech, euc_kr, gb2312, gbk, sjis, tis620, ujis.) *If the server uses another character set (option* default-character-set), *then the result is the error message "Can't initialize character set n."*
>
> *The solution is simple. The directory* c:\mysql\share\charsets *must be installed on the ODBC computer. All of the MySQL font files must be copied to that location. (You will find these files on the computer on which the MySQL server is running. If that is a Windows computer, then the path is typically* Program Files\mysql\share\charsets, *while under Unix/Linux is will be something like* /usr/local/mysql/share/mysql).

Setup Program

For the first installation obtain the appropriate setup version of MyODBC for your operating system, unpack the archive into a temporary directory, and execute setup.exe. In the dialog INSTALL DRIVERS a list of all available ODBC drivers will be displayed. There you must select the entry MySQL with your mouse. Then continue the installation with OK

> **CAUTION** *Do not register your approval too early by simply clicking on* OK *without first selecting MySQL. Otherwise, various ODBC libraries will be installed, but not the MyOCBC DLLs.*

The setup program copies the necessary files into the Windows system directory. Presto! Done! If things fail to go correctly, you may want to turn to the ADVANCE settings (see Figure 2-9). With VERSION you can determine which MyODBC version is currently installed.

> **REMARK** *The MySQL documentation announces that the MyODBC installation under Windows sometimes breaks down to the accompaniment of mysterious error messages (for example, that the file* Windows\System\Mfc30.dll *cannot be copied). It is recommended as a solution to this problem to start up Windows in* safe mode. *To activate this mode it is necessary at Windows startup to hold down the* F8 *key. This should lead to a successful installation. I must say that I have installed MyODBC successfully on a variety of computers without having to take these measures.*

There then appears the dialog DATA SOURCES. There you can create DSNs (Data Source Names). These are references to MySQL databases. Once the DSNs have been set up, you can address the associated databases from all ODBC programs under the name of the DSN. DSNs will be treated in detail in Chapter 10.

> **TIP** *You do not have to carry out the DSN definition at once but can wait until you actually want to access a database via ODBC. You can access the dialog DATA SOURCES at any time via the Windows system tools (ODBC or ADMINISTRATIVE TOOLS|DATA SOURCES).*

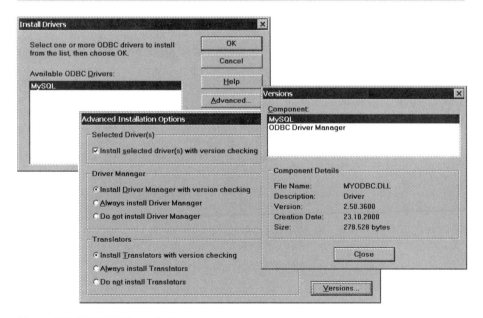

Figure 2-9. MyODBC installation

Code Editors

To complete the testing environment you will need an editor for developing your MySQL programs. If you are developing web applications and are using, say, PHP or Perl, in principle you can use any editor you like, under Windows even notepad.exe. It is more convenient to work with an editor that understands HTML/PHP/Perl, etc., that displays your code in different colors, assists with the insertion of frequently used code blocks, and so on.

The choice of editor is, of course, primarily a matter of taste. But if you are looking for a good editor, the following suggestions might be of some use.

> **TIP** *The following links can be found at my home page:* www.kofler.cc/mysql

Emacs/XEmacs

The editors Emacs and XEmacs are considered by many Unix/Linux fans to be the measure of all things. Their use is complicated and takes a bit of getting used to, but in exchange these editors are probably unsurpassed for their adaptability to your individual requirements, and they are more stable than most other editors. (X)Emacs is obtainable without charge for Unix/Linux and is also obtainable for Windows. (As the names suggest, these two editors have a common ancestor. They are relatively compatible one with the other and differ only a little in their use. Those who prefer clear menus and toolbars will probably refer XEmacs for its ease of use.)

```
http://www.gnu.org/software/emacs/emacs.html
http://www.xemacs.org/
```

Both Emacs and XEmacs work without problems with HTML files as well as with files of most programming languages (Perl, C, etc.). They can highlight different code elements in color, etc. However, the situation is less good at present with PHP support. There is no PHP mode included with the current versions of Emacs and XEmacs. The simplest solution is to select C++ mode. (This, however, does not work properly with HTML code, as one would expect.) So that Emacs/XEmacs will view a PHP file as a C++ file, add the following text to the first line:

```
<?php // -*- C++ -*- --
```

On the Internet one can find certain PHP extensions for Emacs. However, their installation requires a fundamental knowledge of the internal workings of Emacs. Furthermore, there seems not to be any mode that will work properly with both HTML and PHP (and most PHP files contain both of these).

```
http://www.cs.huji.ac.il/~baryudin/php3_mode.html
http://www.challenge.dk/~madsdyd/linux/
```

Special PHP Editors

At the following two addresses you can find a number of links to PHP and HTML editors (for both Windows and Linux):

```
http://www.itworks.demon.co.uk/phpeditors.htm
http://www.phparchiv.de/pages/PHP_Editoren/
```

I have had relatively good experiences under Linux with Bluefish, under Windows with the HTML Kit, and with PHPEd. All three programs are obtainable free of charge.

```
http://bluefish.openoffice.nl/
http://www.chami.com/html-kit/
http://soysal.awak.com/PHPEd/
```

Using MySQL with an ISP

This book generally assumes that you have installed MySQL on your own computer. It is only in this way that you have the possibility of trying out MySQL in all of its many facets. Furthermore, it is helpful to develop MySQL solutions first on a test system and to port them to a web site only after sufficient testing.

However, in principle it is also possible to do without one's own MySQL installation entirely. In this case you develop a dynamic web site based exclusively on the MySQL access that your Internet service provider makes available. Here we shall briefly describe the necessary course of action.

MySQL Administration at an ISP with phpMyAdmin

As a rule, ISPs permit only local MySQL access for reasons of security. You can thus register with MySQL only if you are working locally on a computer of the ISP. But generally that is precisely what you are not allowed to do (it could also be that you have `telnet` access, but that is also seldom allowed due to security considerations).

To the extent that your ISP supports PHP, MySQL administration is still possible. The favored program for this purpose is the PHP script collection php-MyAdmin that we have already mentioned. These scripts fulfill the condition that they can be executed on the ISP computer, while on the other hand, phpMyAdmin can be conveniently used over the Internet (that is, for administration you simply use a browser that runs locally on your computer).

We have already described the installation of phpMyAdmin on a local system. To carry out the installation on an external ISP computer, first unpack the phpMyAdmin archive on your local computer. Then set the access information in `config.inc.php` (ISP host name, user name, password). You should have obtained this information from your ISP. Details on `config.inc.php` can be found in Chapter 4.

Finally, use an FTP client (under Windows, for example, WS_FTP) to move all the phpMyAdmin files from your computer into a WWW directory (such as `phpmyadmin` at your ISP.

If all has gone well, then you can now launch phpMyAdmin with a browser with the address `www.mysite.com/phpmyadmin/index.php` or `-/index.php3`. With phpMyAdmin you can now create and delete your own database tables, add data, etc. You may also in some circumstances be able to use phpMyAdmin for the purpose of creating new databases. That depends on the MySQL administration privileges granted you by your ISP. (Further information on using phpMyAdmin can be found in Chapter 4.)

> **CAUTION** *Everyone who guesses the address of* `phpmyadmin/index.php` *can administer your database just as you can. It is thus absolutely essential that access to the directory* `phpmyadmin` *be secured via a* `.htaccess` *file. The method for doing this is described in the section on Apache in this chapter.*

> **REMARK** *Functionality similar to that of phpMyAdmin is offered by mysql-tool, which is a collection of Perl scripts that must be installed in a* `cgi-bin` *directory. It is especially recommended to use mysqltool when your ISP does not support PHP. See* `http://www.dajoba.com/projects/mysqltool/`

Database Upload

> **POINTER** *If you develop MySQL solutions first locally and then port them to the computer of your ISP, it is necessary to create there a copy of your test database. Thus you must copy the locally created database (perhaps together with all its data) to the MySQL server of the ISP. This modus operandi is often called "database upload." Hints on how to carry out this upload can be found in the last section of Chapter 11.*

#### CHAPTER 3

Introductory Example (An Opinion Poll)

THE BEST WAY OF BECOMING familiar with a new database or development system is to work through a full-fledged example. Thus in this chapter our goal is to create a web site for the purpose of conducting an opinion poll.

To a certain extent this is a trivial example, and its results certainly could be accomplished without the use of MySQL. However, it brings into focus the interplay between MySQL and a script programming language (for this example we have used PHP). Moreover, our example casts light on the entire process of database design from first beginnings right up to the completed application.

Chapter Overview

Overview

Our opinion poll consists of two pages. The file vote.html contains a simple questionnaire with a single question: What is your favorite programming language for developing MySQL applications? The question is followed by a selection of choices for a response (see Figure 3-1). After one of the options is selected and OK is clicked, the result page results.php is displayed (see Figure 3-2).

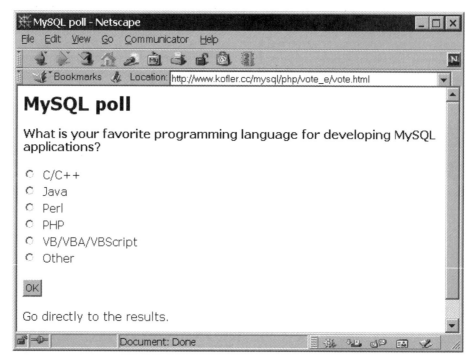

Figure 3-1. The questionnaire

Assumptions

You can try out this example right now. Just wend your way to my web site (www.kofler.cc). However, from a pedagogical point of view it would be better for you to attempt to recreate this example for yourself. For this you will need a test environment consisting of Apache/MySQL/PHP that permits you the following:

- creation of a new MySQL database (that is, you need sufficient privileges to be able to execute *CREATE DATABASE*)

- moving files into a directory on the web server

- executing PHP script files

Information on setting up such a test environment on a local computer can be found in the previous chapter.

A complete understanding of our example requires some basic knowledge of databases. If you have never had much, if anything, to do with databases and as a consequence run into difficulties in understanding what is going on, please do not despair. Chapter 5 provides a complete introduction to relational database systems, while Chapter 6 explains in great detail how to use the database query language SQL.

In this example the programming language PHP will be used. The code is rather straightforward; that is, you should have no difficulty in understanding it even you don't know a word of PHP. However, you should know in general how embedded script languages function in HTML. (The Active Server pages developed by Microsoft are based on the same idea.)

Database Development

To save the results of our questionnaire with MySQL you must first set up a database and then place a table in that database. (Every MySQL database consists of tables. A particular feature of this example is that only a single table is required.

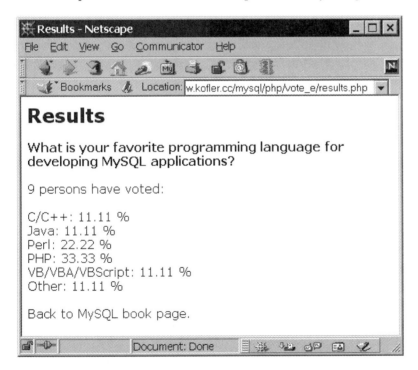

Figure 3-2. Results of the survey

As a rule, that is, when the requirements of the project are more complex, several linked tables will be used.)

Executing `mysql`

Both operations—generating a database and creating a new table—require that you communicate with MySQL. Under Unix/Linux you execute the command `mysql`. Under Windows you search in Explorer for the program `mysql.exe` and launch it with a double click. (The program should reside in the `bin` directory of the MySQL installation directory, that is, in `C:\Programs\MySQL\bin`.)

REMARK   *If* `mysql` *immediately terminates, possibly with an error message such as* Access denied for user xy, *then either access to MySQL is completely denied to user* xy, *or it is protected by a password. In either case you must invoke* `mysql` *with the options* -u name *and* -p:

```
> mysql -u username -p
Enter password: xxx
```

Furthermore, `mysql` *has dozens of other options. The most important of these are described in Chapter 4, while all of them are collected in Chapter 14. Background information on the MySQL security system (access protection, passwords, privileges) can be found in Chapter 7.*

REMARK   *The distinction between MySQL and* `mysql` *is somewhat confusing. MySQL denotes the database server, which normally is launched automatically at system startup. The server runs continuously in the background. (This chapter assumes that the server is up and running.) The program name of the server is, depending on the operating system,* `mysqld` *(Unix/Linux) or* `mysqld.exe` *or* `mysqld-nt.exe` *(Windows).*

In contrast to these we have the auxiliary programs `mysql` *and* `mysql.exe`*. These programs come into play when administration or maintenance are to be carried out interactively. The program* `mysql` *has the task of transmitting interactive commands to the server and displaying the results of these commands on the monitor. The official name of* `mysql` *is MySQL Monitor, but the functionality and mode of action are more reminiscent of a command line interpreter.*

> **POINTER** *Some alternatives to* mysql, *such as the more convenient HTML interface phpMyAdmin, will be introduced in Chapter 4.*

In mysql you can now input commands that will be transmitted to the database server (see Figure 3-3). To test whether a connection can even be made, execute the command *STATUS*. The result should be the display of various pieces of status information about the database (such as the version number).

```
mysql> STATUS;
mysql Ver 11.12 Distrib 3.23.32, for Win95/Win98 (i32)
  Connection id:          3
  Current database:
  Current user:           ODBC@localhost
  Server version:         3.23.32-debug
  Protocol version:       10
  Connection:             localhost via TCP/IP
  Client characterset:    latin1
  Server characterset:    latin1
  TCP port:               3306
  Uptime:                 1 min 5 sec

Threads: 2 Questions: 8 Slow queries: 0 Opens: 7
Flush tables: 1 Open tables: 2 Queries per second avg: 0.123
Memory in use: 8332K Max memory used: 8348K
```

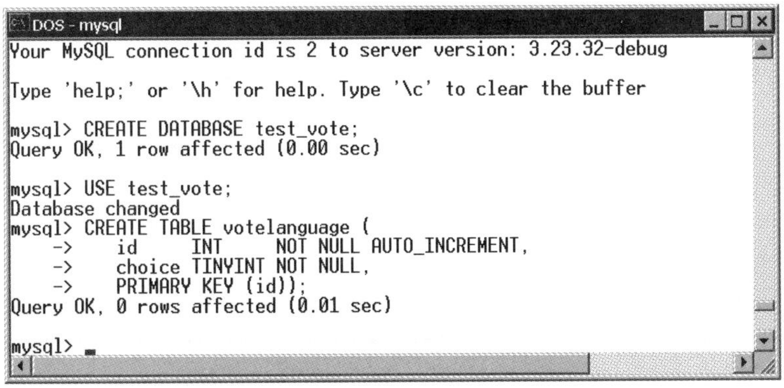

Figure 3-3. The MySQL monitor

> **POINTER** *If problems arise in starting up* mysql *or in executing* status, *the most probable cause is that the database server hasn't even been started or that access has been denied to you. More information on installation can be found in Chapter 2, while information on access and security can be found in Chapter 7.*

Setting Up the Database

To set up the new database *test_vote*, in mysql execute the command *CREATE DATABASE*. Note that that you must end the command with a semicolon. In the following two lines your input appears in boldface.

```
mysql> CREATE DATABASE test_vote;
Query OK, 1 row affected (0.01 sec)
```

The reply delivered by mysql may look a bit weird. The output 1 row affected indicates that in the list of all databases, which internally, of course, is in the form of a MySQL table, one row was changed. What is important here is only that the *CREATE DATABASE* command was executed correctly.

> **REMARK** *The database name* test_vote *was not chosen quite arbitrarily. In the default setting of MySQL access privileges, every user is permitted to create databases on a local computer that begin with the word "test." In particular, when you yourself are not the MySQL administrator (but rely on the help of a system administrator), a name of the form* test_xy *can save any number of e-mails or telephone calls.*
>
> *The drawback of the name* test_xy *is that every user of the local computer can edit, or even delete, the database. This is no problem for this introductory example, but in the case of a real-life application you probably will want to give your database a bit more security. Necessary information on this can be found in Chapter 7.*

Creating Tables

The database *test_vote* has been created, but it is not yet possible to store any information. For this you need tables. To create a new table within the database *test_vote* use the command *CREATE TABLE*.

Before you execute this command, however, you must specify the database into which the table is to be placed. The requisite command for this is *USE*. It determines the default database to which further commands are to be applied. (MySQL is managing other databases besides the newly created database *test_vote*.)

```
mysql> USE test_vote;
Database changed
mysql> CREATE TABLE votelanguage (
    -> id INT NOT NULL AUTO_INCREMENT,
    -> choice TINYINT NOT NULL,
    -> PRIMARY KEY (id));
Query OK, 0 rows affected (0.01 sec)
```

The *CREATE TABLE* command may seem a bit strange at first. But just go ahead and input the boldface commands listed above line for line. (You can terminate each command with Return. The semicolon indicates to mysql that the end of a command has been reached.)

> **TIP** *If you should make a typing error during the input of a command, MySQL will usually inform you of this fact with an error message. You must now repeat the entire command. Using the cursor keys ↑ and ↓ you can recall and correct previously input lines.*
>
> *If MySQL has accepted* CREATE TABLE *in spite of a typographical error (because the command, though semantically not what you had in mind, is nonetheless syntactically correct), you can delete the incorrectly defined table with* DROP TABLE votelanguage;. *That accomplished, you can repeat the command* CREATE TABLE.

Now let us explain what is actually going on. With *CREATE TABLE* you have brought into being a table with two columns, *id* and *choice*. Once the table is filled with data (namely, the results of the survey), the content of the table can be displayed something like this:

```
id   choice
1    4
2    5
3    4
4    3
5    3
...
```

The interpretation of these data is that the first person to respond to the survey chose the programming language PHP, while the second chose VB, and the third selected PHP. The next respondents chose, in order, Perl, Other, Perl, and C. The column *id* thus contains a running identification number that identifies the lines (the data set). The column *choice* contains, in coded form, the selection made by the survey participant, where the numbers 1 through 6 correspond to the programming languages C, Java, Perl, PHP, VB, and Other.

> **TIP** *Like any other specialized subject, the database world has its own argot. Database vocabulary includes the term* data record *for each line of the table above. Instead of* columns *(here* id *and* choice*) one often speaks of* fields.

In order to generate a table with the two columns *id* and *choice* the following command would suffice:

```
CREATE TABLE votelanguage (id INT, choice TINYINT);
```

The result is that the column *id* is declared with the data type *INT*, and *choice* is declared to be of data type *TINYINT*. That means that in theory, 2^{31} individuals (2,147,483,648, that is) could participate in our survey before the range for *id* were exhausted. (If *id* were declared as type *UNSIGNED INT*, then the number of potential participants would be doubled.) In *choice*, on the other hand, there are 2^{16} different values available. (The data types *INT* and *TINYINT* are discussed in Chapter 5 together with the other MySQL data types.)

By this point you may be wondering why I have plagued you with such a complicated command as *CREATE TABLE* when there is a much easier way to achieve the same result. The difference between the complicated and simple variants is the difference between good and bad database creation. (And you wouldn't want me to be leading you astray on our very first example, would you?)

The attribute *AUTO_INCREMENT* for the column *id* has the effect that with each new record the appropriate value for *id* is automatically inserted. Thus when the results of the survey are saved, only *choice* has to be specified, since the database takes care of *id* on its own. This attribute ensures a consistent numbering of the data records, which is important for efficient management of the table.

The attribute *NOT NULL* ensures that actual values must be placed in both columns. It is not permitted to store the data record *NULL* or (in the case of *choice*) not to insert any value at all. Thus this attribute prevents invalid data records from being stored. (Go ahead and try to force MySQL to accept such a data record. It will refuse and present you with an error message.)

PRIMARY KEY (id) has the effect that the column *id* is used to identify the data records. That is the reason that the column was provided for in the first place, but MySQL is not so clever as to be able to read your mind, and it requires that it be informed precisely as to what your wishes are. (In this case *id* is called a *primary key*.) The definition of a primary key has a decisive influence on the speed with which data records can be accessed. That holds especially for linked tables—but let us not get ahead of ourselves. We shall stick for the moment with simple tables, always define a single primary key (and do so, if possible, for an *INT* field with the attributes *NOT NULL* and *AUTO_INCREMENT*).

Why Make It Complicated, When It Could Be So Much Easier?

Perhaps it has occurred to you that we have presented a rather complex solution to an easy problem. It could done in a much simpler fashion. All we need to do is to control six counters, such as in a table of the following form:

id	counter
1	2
2	0
3	7
4	9
5	2
6	1

Such a display would mean that two participants expressed a preference for the C language, none for Java, seven for Perl, nine for PHP, and so on. Each time a preference is registered the corresponding counter is incremented by 1. The database would consist altogether of six lines; one wouldn't have to worry about performance; memory requirements would be essentially zero—nothing but advantages! And all of this is aside from the fact that the six counters could be effortlessly stored in a small text file. In short, MySQL is totally unnecessary for this survey.

All right, then, you are correct! However, such an attitude is helpful only as long as we are dealing with a simple example. What happens when you would like to offer each participant the opportunity to make a comment? What if you allow the participants to fill out the questionnaire only after a login (to rule out the possibility of multiple voting)? What if you wish to record the time and IP address for each participant (again to secure against attempts at manipulating the survey)?

In all these cases you would have to store the responses in a table like the one that we have presented. (The table would have merely to be enlarged by a column or two. The structure of the program can remain essentially the same.) So, if the conception of this example seems a bit overly complicated at first glance, the reason is that we are keeping open the possibility, even in this first example, of a later extension.

The Questionnaire

As we have mentioned already in the introduction, our entire project consists of two web sites. The first page (vote.html) contains the questionnaire. This is pure HTML code (without PHP). The second page (results.php) carries out two tasks: evaluating the questionnaire and displaying the results.

The HTML code of the questionnaire is given here, so that the code for evaluation in the next section will be understandable. Most important are the attributes *name* and *value* of the elements of the questionnaire. All of the radio buttons have the name *vote*, while *value* contains values between 1 and 6. The OK button has the name *submitbutton*, and as *value* the character string *"OK"* is used.

```
<!DOCTYPE HTML PUBLIC "-//W3C//DTD HTML 4.0//EN">
<!-- php/vote/vote.html -->
<html><head>
  <title>MySQL-poll</title>
</head>
<body>
<h2>MySQL- poll </h2>
<p><b> What is your favorite
programming language for developing MySQL applications?</b>

<form method="POST" action="results.php">
  <input type="radio" name="vote" value="1">C/C++
  <br><input type="radio" name="vote" value="2">Java
  <br><input type="radio" name="vote" value="3">Perl
  <br><input type="radio" name="vote" value="4">PHP
  <br><input type="radio" name="vote" value="5"> VB/VBA/VBScript
  <br><input type="radio" name="vote" value="6"> Other
```

```
  <p><input type="submit" name="submitbutton" value="OK">
</form>
<p>Go directly to the <a href="./results.php">results</a>.
<p>Back to the
<a href="../mysqlbook.html">MySQL book page</a>.
</body>
</html>
```

Questionnaire Evaluation and Displaying Results

One can call results.php either directly (for example, via a link) or using the data in the questionnaire. In one case what is shown is only the current state of the questionnaire. In the other case, the data are also evaluated and stored in the database.

Establishing a Link to the Database (mysql_connectinfo.inc.php)

The opening lines of results.php consist of HTML code. Then comes the first task within the PHP code, which is to create a link to MySQL. For this purpose the PHP function *mysql_pconnect* is used, to which three pieces of information are passed:

- user name

- password

- computer name (host name)

If you have installed MySQL yourself on the local computer and have not yet secured it with a password, then you may simply pass empty character strings as parameters. The specification of the computer name is necessary only if the web server (that is, Apache) is running on a different computer from the one that is running MySQL.

It is fundamentally not a good idea to write the user name and password in plain text in a PHP file. Of course, the visitors to your web site will never see the source text of this file (because the PHP code is first evaluated, and the resulting HTML document contains only the PHP output), but configuration errors can occur. The two most common errors are (1) a change in the Apache configuration (for example after an update) that results in PHP files not being executed and thus being displayed in their original form; (2) an incorrect or slipshod configuration of the FTP server, which allows users to read PHP files on your web site directly (i.e., bypassing Apache and PHP).

To avoid making it too easy for strangers to get at your password (while at the same time not having to write this information in every PHP script, which would cause a great deal of work in the event of a change in the MySQL password), the MySQL login information is usually stored in its own file. This file is stored in a directory of the web server that normally is inaccessible (protected by .htaccess). Make certain that it is impossible to get at this file via anonymous FTP.

In the following example this password file has the name mysql_connectinfo.inc.php. It is stored in the directory _private. (If you have not yet secured your MySQL server, you can simply give an empty password.)

```php
<?php
  // <website-root-dir>/_private/mysql_connectinfo.inc.php
  // link data
  $mysqluser="user"; // user name for MySQL access
  $mysqlpasswd="xxx"; // password
  $mysqlhost="localhost"; // name of the computer on which MySQL is running
  $mysqldbname="test_vote"; // name of the database
?>
```

The first PHP instruction in results.php is an *include* command, by means of which mysql_connectinfo.inc.php is loaded. Depending on the location in the directory hierarchy where results.php and mysql_connectinfo.inc.php are located, you will have to edit the path name in *include*.

The function mysql_pconnect returns an identification number that is stored in the variable *link*. In the present example, *link* is used only to identify possible problems in creating the link. In this case an error message is displayed and the PHP code ended abruptly with *exit*. Otherwise, the active database is selected with *mysql_select_db*. (MySQL usually manages several databases, and the effect of *mysql_select_db* is that the following commands automatically refer to *test_vote*.)

Evaluating the Data and Storing Them in the Database

The next task in results.php consists in evaluating the data in the questionnaire and storing them in the database. If results.php was called via the questionnaire of vote.html, then the variable *submitbutton* contains the character string *"OK"*. (Compare the *name* and *value* attributes in vote.html.)

For the sake of security a validation test is carried out for the variable *vote*. (For example, a participant may have forgotten to select one of the choices.) If *vote* contains a valid value, then this value is stored in the database. The SQL command to accomplish this will look something like the following:

```
INSERT INTO votelanguage (choice) VALUES (3)
```

What *INSERT INTO* accomplishes is to insert a new data record (a new row) into the table *votelanguage*. The expression *(choice)* specifies all of the fields of the data record for which values should be passed by means of the command *VALUES (. . .)*. Since MySQL takes responsibility on its own for the field *id* (attribute *AUTO_INCREMENT*; see above), in this example *choice* is the only field affected. Of course, instead of "3" the value of the variable *vote* will be placed, depending on which of the programming languages was selected in the questionnaire. The SQL command thus constructed is then passed along to MySQL with the PHP function *mysql_query*.

> **POINTER**   *If you have never had dealings with SQL and thus are unfamiliar with the syntax of SQL commands, fear not. In Chapter 6 you will find an extensive introduction to SQL. The two commands used in this chapter, namely* INSERT *and* SELECT, *are presumably more or less self-explanatory.*

Displaying the Survey Results

Regardless of whether the questionnaire has just been evaluated, the previous results of the survey must be able to be displayed. (If a new vote has been cast, it will be taken into account.)

First a check must be made as to whether the *votelanguage* table contains any data at all. (When the questionnaire is first placed on the Internet, no votes have yet been cast.) The required SQL query looks like this:

```
SELECT COUNT(choice) FROM votelanguage
```

The SQL command is again executed with *mysql_query*. What is new this time is that a link to the result of the query is stored in the variable *result*. The result of a *SELECT* command is, in general, a table. However, in the above example this table consists of merely a single row and a single column. (Furthermore, *result* contains only an ID number, which is used as a parameter in various other *mysql_xxx* functions. It is the task of PHP to take care of the actual management of the result.)

To evaluate the result, the function *mysql_result($result, 0, 0)* is used, by which the element in the table from the first row and first column is read. (With MySQL functions counting begins with 0.)

Provided that the *votelanguage* table is not empty, a loop is executed to report the percentage of votes cast for each programming language. The requisite SQL queries look similar to the one above, only now the number of data records that contain a particular value of *choice* (for example, 3) is counted.

```
SELECT COUNT(choice) FROM votelanguage WHERE choice = 3
```

For evaluation *mysql_result* is used. Then a bit of calculation is necessary to round the percentages to two decimal places.

Program Code (`results.php`)

```php
<!DOCTYPE HTML PUBLIC "-//W3C//DTD HTML 4.0//EN">
<!-- php/vote/results.php-->
<html><head>
<title>Survey Result</title>
</head><body>
<h2> Survey Result </h2>
<?php
  include("../../_private/mysql_connectinfo.inc.php");
// Create Link to Database
  $link =
    @mysql_pconnect($mysqlhost, $mysqluser, $mysqlpasswd);
  if ($link == FALSE) {
    echo "<p><b>Unfortunately, no link to the database
          can be made. Therefore, the results
          cannot be displayed at present. Please try
          again later.
          </body></html>\n";
    exit();
  }
  mysql_select_db($mysqldbname);

  // if questionnaire data are available:
  // evaluate + store
  if($submitbutton=="OK") {
    if($vote>=1 && $vote<=6) {
      mysql_query(
        "INSERT INTO votelanguage (choice) VALUES ($vote)");
    }
    else {
      echo "<p>Not a valid selection. Please vote
              again. Back to
              <a href=\"./vote.html\">questionnaire</a>.
              </body></html>\n";
      exit();
    }
  }
```

```
  // display results
  echo "<P><B> What is your favorite programming language
          for developing MySQL applications?</B>\n";

  // Number of votes cast
  $result =
    mysql_query("SELECT COUNT(choice) FROM votelanguage");
  $choice_count = mysql_result($result, 0, 0);

  // Percentages for the individual voting categories
  if($choice_count == 0) {
    echo "<p>No one has voted yet.\n";
  }
else {
    echo "<p>$choice_count individuals have thus far taken part
            in this survey:<br>\n";
    $choicetext = array("", "C/C++", "Java", "Perl", "PHP",
                        "VB/VBA/VBScript", "Other");
    for($i=1; $i<=6; $i++) {
      $result = mysql_query(
         "SELECT COUNT(choice) FROM votelanguage " .
         "WHERE choice = $i");
      $choice[$i] = mysql_result($result, 0, 0);
      $percent = round($choice[$i]/$choice_count*10000)/100;
      print("<br>$choicetext[$i]: $percent %\n");
    }
  }
?>
<p>Back to
<a href="../mysqlexamples.html">MySQL-examplepage</a>.
</body>
</html>
```

The Resulting HTML Code

If you are relatively inexperienced with PHP, you might find it helpful to have a look at the resulting HTML code (that is, what the user finally sees in the browser, as depicted in Figure 3-2) as an aid to understanding the program presented above.

```
<!DOCTYPE HTML PUBLIC "-//W3C//DTD HTML 4.0//EN">
<!-- results.php -->
<html><head><title>Umfrageergebnis</title></head><body>
<h2>Umfrageergebnis</h2>
```

```
<P><B>What is your favorite programming language
      for developing MySQL applications?</B>
<p>6 individuals have thus far taken part in this survey:<br>
<br>C/C++: 0 %
<br>Java: 0 %
<br>Perl: 16,67 %
<br>PHP: 50 %
<br>VB/VBA/VBScript: 33,33 %
<br>Andere: 0 %
<p>back to
<a href="../mysqlexample.html">MySQL-examplepage</a>.
</body></html>
```

Ideas for Improvements

Layout

It may have occurred to you that I have not paid much attention to the appearance of things in this example. Naturally, the results of the survey could be presented in a nicely formatted table or perhaps in a colorful bar graph. However, that has nothing to do with the subject of this book, namely, MySQL. Introductions to the attractive presentation of HTML documents, to the PHP programming of various graphics libraries, and the like can be found in quantity in a number of books on HTML and PHP (and, of course, on the Internet).

Questionnaire and Results on a Single Page

It is certainly possible to execute all the elements of our survey—questionnaire, evaluation, and presentation of results—with a single PHP script. However, as a rule it is a good idea for the participants not to see the previous results before casting a vote.

Options

You could make the survey more interesting or more informative by offering additional opportunities for input. In our example there could be a text field for the input of other programming languages or perhaps a text field for optional comments or for information about the professional background of the participants. However, you must consider that the more you ask, the more superfluous data you will collect. (If someone does not want to answer a required question, you may get a deliberately false response.)

Multiple Selection

In principle, you could construct the questionnaire in such a way that a participant could select more than one programming language. In the HTML form you would use check boxes instead of radio buttons. However, the necessary changes in the design of the database are somewhat more complicated. The table *votes* must now be able to store in each data record an arbitrary collection of programming languages. It would be easy, though inefficient, to reserve a separate column in the table for each programming language and then store the value 1 or 0 depending on whether or not the language was voted for. If you do not want the *votes* table to take up any more space in memory than necessary, then you could store a multiple selection as a combination of bits. For this purpose MySQL offers the data type (*SET*). But this option would make the program code for the storage and evaluation of the survey results considerably more complicated.

Protection Against Manipulation

In most Internet surveys the goal is not to obtain information but to promote interest, and thereby obtain a large number of accesses to one's web page. In such cases there is not much point in protecting the survey against misuse. However, if you wish to provide such protection, you have a number of possibilities:

- You could place a "cookie" containing a random number on the participant's computer and store this same value in the database. In this way an attempt to cast additional votes could be easily caught. (The disadvantage is that many Internet users are opposed to cookies and delete all cookies at startup or else prohibit their placement altogether.)

- You could require a login with e-mail address and password. Only those who have registered may vote. You store information in the database on who has already voted. (The disadvantage is that Internet users tend to have little patience for logins. Not many Internet users would give their e-mail address simply for the privilege of filling out your questionnaire.)

It is true in general that you cannot completely prevent such manipulation of a survey. That is, every system of security can be gotten around by someone who puts enough effort into the attempt.

POINTER *There are many complete PHP solutions for questionnaires available, both with and without MySQL support. Before you set about reinventing the wheel, you might want to take a squint at some of the PHP sites on the Internet, for example the following:*

```
http://www.hotscripts.com/PHP/
```

Part II

Fundamentals

#### CHAPTER 4

User Interfaces

THE END USER SHOULD NEVER see MySQL as a program. Instead, a convenient program or several web sites should be used to provide access to the database or assist in the input of new data.

Developers and database administrators, on the other hand, must frequently communicate directly with MySQL, for example, when new databases are created, existing databases enlarged, individual data records added, or queries tested. For such administrative tasks there are several tools that differ in regard to their range of functionality and degree of user-friendliness.

This chapter introduces the most important user interfaces for MySQL. The command program mysql, the HTML interface phpMyAdmin, the Windows program WinMySQLadmin, and the Linux program KSql.

Chapter Overview

Overview

The only *official* user interface for MySQL is currently the like-named program mysql (mysql.exe under Windows). With this program you can carry out almost all administrative tasks, but the Spartan user interface, in the style of a command line interpreter, will not bring you much joy.

The lack of a graphical user interface for MySQL has inspired many programmers. The result is a dozen or so different programs, of which none, alas, can claim to represent a perfect solution. This chapter presents some of these popular programs, without any claim to completeness:

- As already mentioned, mysql offers the least amount of convenience. Nonetheless, this tool cannot be done without. It has the advantage that it is a fixed component of every MySQL installation, is available under all operating systems, makes little demand on hardware, and can be run via telnet.

- WinMySQLadmin is provided with the Windows version of MySQL. The program is of use most of all in the setup and configuration of the MySQL server under Windows. Moreover, the structure of databases can be viewed (but currently not changed).

- phpMyAdmin consists of a collection of PHP scripts. It is used via a web browser, and therefore phpMyAdmin is perfectly suited for the administration of a MySQL server on a remote computer. phpMyAdmin is perhaps the best user interface currently available for MySQL, and it is obtainable without cost (GPL licensing).

- KSql is a Linux program. It is useful in basic administrative tasks.

Brief Description of Some Other Programs

- MySQLmanager, like WinMySQLadmin, is included in the MySQL Windows package and is automatically installed. After registration of the server the program shows a hierarchical tree with all databases, tables, and their fields. At present, that is the limit of the program's functionality, and so one can hardly speak of this as an administrative tool.

- MySQLGui is the first GUI tool presented on the MySQL home page and is, in fact, a product of the MySQL development team. Nonetheless, it gives the impression of nothing more than a colorful prototype. You can execute SQL commands and display the results in a table window, and not much more. Moreover, there in no Windows version, only those for Linux and Unix derivatives.

- MysqlTool is a collection of Perl CGI scripts that cover all the principal administrative tasks (generate and edit databases and tables, view and edit data, execute queries, set MySQL access privileges, manage MySQL processes, etc.). MysqlTool is to some extent Perl's answer to phpMyAdmin. Unfortunately, it is rather complex, and furthermore, it requires root access to the Unix or Linux computer on which the scripts are installed.

- Urban Research SQL Utility (urSQL for short) is a Windows program that gives access to databases of MySQL, Access, Microsoft SQL Server, Oracle, PostgreSQL, etc. The program assumes that MyODBC is installed. This program enables the creation and editing of databases and tables, the viewing and editing of their content, the development of SQL queries, etc. There is rather a large assortment of functions, though the user interface is rather primitive. While urSQL is shareware, it can be tested free of charge.

- Zeos Database Explorer (ZDE) is also a Windows program, with which you can view tables belonging to the database systems MySQL, PostreSQL, Microsoft SQL-Server, and Interbase. The program is most impressive for its astounding speed. If you wish to create MySQL database content under Windows, then this program will certainly be useful. However, it is not really a full-fledged administrative tool, since neither alteration of the database structure nor other administrative tasks are possible.

> **TIP** *Download links to the programs mentioned here (and some others) can be found at my home page:* http://www.kofler.cc/mysql

mysql (Monitor)

In the previous chapter you became acquainted with mysql as a simple command interpreter, with which you can execute SQL commands and view the resulting tables in text mode. This section gives some further tips for using mysql with MySQL.

> **POINTER** mysql *can also be used for a variety of administrative tasks in batch mode, such as for saving tables in ASCII or HTML files or restoring previously backed-up databases. These possibilities for using* mysql *are presented in Chapter 11. There is described how frequently used* mysql *options can be stored in configuration files.*

> **POINTER**   *For more complex management tasks (backups, ASCII import and export, repairing table files, etc.) there are additional command tools provided with MySQL, such as* mysqladmin *and* myisamchk *(see also Chapter 11).*
>
> *A reference to all the options and functions of the command-oriented administration tools can be found in Chapter 14.*

Executing mysql *and Other MySQL Commands*

Unix/Linux: On Unix/Linux systems you simply specify mysql (or the name of another MySQL command) in a shell and press Return. The programs are normally installed in the directory /usr/bin, so that it is unnecessary to provide the name of the directory.

Windows: mysql and most other MySQL commands are generally stored in the directory Programs\mysql\bin. Furthermore, Programs\mysql\scripts generally contains (depending on the version) several Perl script files. Both directories are normally not a part of the *PATH* system variable, which contains all directories with executable programs. Therefore, there are the following possibilities for launching the programs:

- The simplest and most convenient approach is a double click in Windows Explorer. A disadvantage of this procedure is that no options can be passed to the program, yet in most cases it is necessary at the very least to provide the user name and password.
- Via START|RUN you can launch the program in a small dialog window. There you can also provide options. (You can most easily copy the command name together with all directories with Explorer's *Drag&Drop* in the start window.) This method is acceptable in isolated instances, but if the command is to be used frequently, this is much too inconvenient.
- You can open a command window (START|PROGRAMS|ACCESSORIES| COMMAND PROMPT) and there give the name of the program and the complete path. Again, you can save some typing and use Explorer with *Drag&Drop* to copy the name into the window. Alternatively, you can first use CD to move into the directory Programs\mysql\bin.

- In the long run it will prove most convenient to extend the system variable *PATH* to the MySQL tools. To do this execute START|SETTINGS|SYSTEM, click in the dialog sheet ADVANCED, select the system variable *PATH* with a double click, and enlarge the list of directories to include the MySQL `bin` directory and the MySQL `script` directory. Directories must be separated by semicolons. (Figure 4-1 shows the setting of the system variables in Windows 2000.)

From now on, in every command window (regardless of the current directory or drive) input of the MySQL command name is sufficient to execute it.

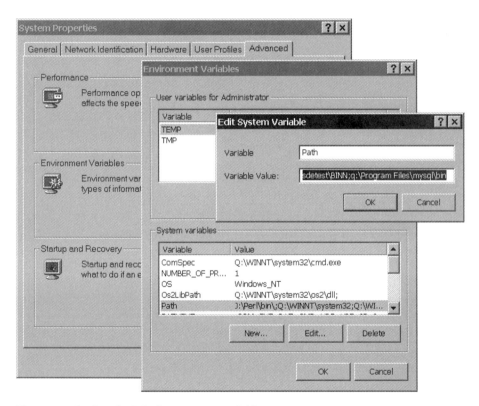

Figure 4-1. Setting the Windows system variables

Using MySQL Interactively

mysql is launched as usual with the options -u and -p. (Of course, one can do without the options if the login name is the same as the MySQL user name or if access to MySQL has not been password protected and so a password is not required.)

Now SQL commands can be input. The commands can extend over several lines and must be terminated with a semicolon (see Figure 4-2).

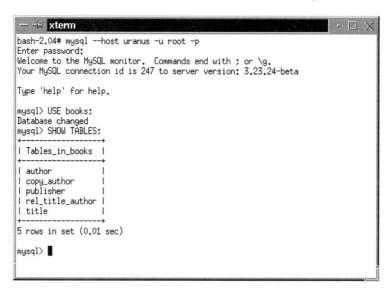

Figure 4-2. Using the MySQL monitor under Linux in an xterm *window*

```
> mysql -u root -p
Enter password: xxx
Welcome to the MySQL monitor. Commands end with ; or \g.
Your MySQL connection id is 248 to server version: 3.23.24-beta
Type 'help;' or '\h' for help. Type '\c' to clear the buffer
mysql> USE books;
Database changed
mysql>  textbfSELECT * FROM title;
```

titleID	title	publisherID	year
1	Linux, 5th ed.	1	2000
2	Definitive Guide to Excel VBA	2	2000
3	Client/Server Survival Guide	1	1997
4	Web Application Development with PHP 4.0	3	2000
6	test	1	2000
7	MySQL	1	2001
9	MySQL & mSQL	4	1999

```
7 rows in set (0.01 sec)
```

CAUTION *You can do a great deal of damage with* mysql. *For example,* DELETE FROM tablename *deletes all data records from the table* tablename *without so much as a "by your leave." And what is more, there is no way of undoing the damage. If you would like to avoid such fatal errors, you should use* mysql *with the option* --i-am-a-dummy. *Then* mysql *permits the commands* UPDATE *and* DELETE *only if they are protected with the key word* WHERE *or* LIMIT. *There are some additional security limitations.*

In addition to the SQL commands you can use some additional commands offered by mysql (for example, *source filename*). These commands do not need to be terminated with a semicolon. As with SQL commands, these are case-insensitive. Each of the commands exists in a two-letter short form, such as \h for *help*. In the short form the commands can also be given at the end of a line; the only place they must be written out in full is at the beginning of a new line. Table 4-1 gives only the most important commands. A list of all the commands can be found in Chapter 14.

Table 4-1. mysql *commands in interactive mode*

\c	clear breaks off input of a command
\h	help displays the list of commands
\q	exit or quit terminates mysql; under Unix/Linux this can also be done with Ctrl + D
\s	status displays status information of the MySQL server
\T [*f*]	tee [*filename*] logs all input and output in the specified file
\t	notee ends tee; the logging can be resumed at any time with tee or \T; note that the file name must be given again
\u *db*	use *database* makes the specified database the default
\#	rehash creates an internal list of all mysql commands, the most important SQL key words, and all names of tables and columns of the current database; then it suffices to input only the initial letters; with Tab the initial letters are expanded into the complete key word; this functions only under Unix/Linux
\. *fn*	source *filename* executes the SQL commands contained in the specified file; the commands must be separated by semicolons

Simplifying Input

Terminating Input: It often occurs, particularly with multiline commands, that you note an error in a line above the one that you are typing and as a result wish to terminate the entire input (so that you can start all over again). To accomplish this, regardless of the cursor position, simply input \c and press Return. Note, however, that (\c does not have this effect within a character string enclosed in single or double quotation marks.

History Function: mysql remembers the last commands that were input (even after program termination!). These commands can be recalled with the cursor keys ↑ and ↓.

Rehash Command: If you execute the mysql command rehash (abbreviation #), then mysql displays a list of the most important SQL key words as well as the table and column names of the current database. All entries in this list can be completed with Tab. That is, you need only type the first few letters and then hit Tab. If there are several possibilities for completion, these are displayed by mysql as a list, and you can then continue your input.

Tips for Using mysql Under Unix/Linux

Scroll Region: Under Unix/Linux, mysql is usually executed in a shell window. Every such program (xterm, kvt, nxterm, gnome-terminal, etc.) offers the possibility of setting the number of lines that are kept in temporary storage. If you provide a large enough value, then you can use a scroll bar to examine previously input commands and copy them with the mouse to the clipboard.

Keyboard Shortcuts: Under most operating systems mysql relies on the readline library. Therefore, the usual suspects in the lineup of Unix/Linux keyboard shortcuts are available for editing input (for example, Ctrl + K for deleting a line from the cursor location to the end, Ctrl + Y for restoring the most recently deleted text). Most of the keyboard shortcuts correspond to those under the editor Emacs.

Private Configuration File: Frequently used options (such as user name and password) can be stored under Unix/Linux in a user-specific configuration file with the name ~/.my.cnf. Options related to all client tools are placed in the group [client], while those relating specifically to mysql go into the group [mysql]. The following lines provide an example. (Further details on creating configuration files can be found in Chapter 14.)

```
# Options for all MySQL tools
[client]
user=username
password=xxx
# Options for mysql
[mysql]
database=mydatabase
```

Since the file contains a password in plain text, it should be protected from prying
eyes:

```
user$ chmod 600 ~/.my.cnf
```

Tips for Using `mysql` *Under Windows*

`mysql` is executed in a command window (where the command interpreter
`cmd.exe`, familiar from the DOS era, is running, for which reason the window
is often called the "DOS window"). Many of the particulars of this program are
configurable. You can access the configuration dialog by clicking on the title bar
with the right mouse button (see Figure 4-3).

- **Color:** In the command window are usually displayed white characters on
  a black background. That is not particularly easy on the eyes. If your eyes
  would prefer a white background and black characters, then consult the
  COLORS dialog sheet to change the setting.

- **Window Size:** There is not much room in an 80×25 character display for
  representing the results of *SELECT*. The dialog sheet LAYOUT comes to your
  aid here, allowing you to change the window size.

- **Scroll Region:** A larger window does nothing to increase the number of
  lines displayed. This setting can be changed by enlarging the SCREEN
  BUFFER SIZE in the dialog sheet LAYOUT. This sets the virtual window size.
  In the window a segment of the virtual window is visible, and you can use
  the scroll bar to see previous commands and results.

- **Clipboard:** The command window offers the not-well-known possibility
  of copying and pasting text to and from the clipboard. To copy, select a
  rectangular region with the mouse and simply hit Return. To paste, click
  anywhere in the window with the right mouse button. For these shortcuts
  to function you must have activated the option QUICKEDIT MODE in the
  OPTIONS dialog sheet.

When you close the configuration dialog you are asked whether the settings should hold only for the current window or whether they should be saved, with the result that the shortcut (link) to cmd.exe will be changed. Choosing the second variant will ensure that in the future the command window will have the properties described here.

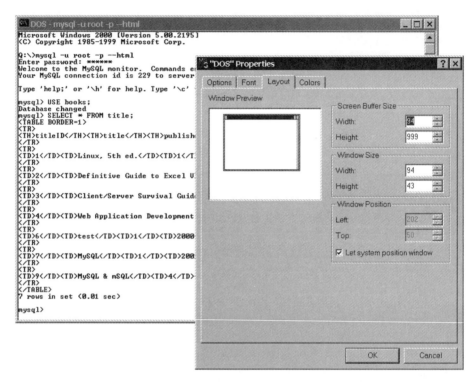

Figure 4-3. Configuration of the MySQL monitor under Windows

CAUTION *In MySQL databases it is standard to use a Windows-compatible character set. In the command window, however, what is used is an older (DOS-compatible) character set. For this reason various special characters (such as ääöüß) are incorrectly displayed in the DOS window. What is worse, the DOS character set is also used in data records that are stored using an INSERT or UPDATE command in the DOS window. If you then look at those data records with another program (for example, with phpMyAdmin), the special characters are seen to be incorrect.*

> **CAUTION** *(continued) The solution is not to input data records containing such special characters in the DOS window with* mysql. *Make such inputs either with another program (phpMyAdmin) or with* mysql *under another operating system (Unix/Linux). If this is impossible, write the input command with a text editor (such as Notepad) and paste it into the DOS window via the clipboard.*

Cygnus Version of mysql Under Windows

In addition to the garden-variety mysql.exe there is also under Windows a second version of the MySQL monitor, namely mysqlc.exe. Internally, mysqlc.exe and mysql.exe differ in that the former was compiled with the Cygnus GNU C compiler (instead of with Visual C++), and therefore the readline library used in the Linux/Unix world was used.

Before you can launch mysqlc.exe for the first time, you must copy the file mysql\lib\cygwinb.dll into the Windows system directory (generally Windows\System32).

Additionally, mysqlc.exe offers more and, to some extent, different keyboard shortcuts from those provided by mysql.exe for editing individual lines. Thus mysqlc.exe is designed for those users who usually work under Unix/Linux and feel lonely in Windows without the familiar suite of keyboard shortcuts.

> **REMARK** *Alas, the* readline *library under Windows NT/2000 does not function particularly well. Although a number of* Ctrl *and* Alt *shortcuts can be used, important shortcuts like* Delete, Home, End *do not work. (Instead, you can use* Ctrl + D, Ctrl + A, Ctrl + E.) *Moreover, special characters like äåöüßé cannot be input. Further information on using the* readline *library under Windows is obtainable at the following addresses:*
>
> ```
> http://www.is.lg.ua/~paul/devel/readline/
> http://www.gwdg.de/~mrickma/ming/
> ```

Terminating mysql

You can terminate mysql with *exit* or *quit* or \q or Ctrl + D (only under Unix/Linux). Under Windows you can also simply close the DOS window.

WinMySQLadmin (Windows)

WinMySQLadmin is a user interface to MySQL that currently is available only under Windows. This program is provided with the Windows version of MySQL and is automatically installed. After the first launch (which is done manually), the program registers itself in START|PROGRAMS|STARTUP and in future will be launched automatically at startup. WinMySQLadmin, for its part, automatically launches the MySQL server if it is not already running.

The program is usually visible as a small icon in the Windows task bar. It uses a stoplight to indicate the state of the MySQL server (see Figure 4-4). A green lamp indicates that the server is running, while red indicates that it is not.

Figure 4-4. WinMySQLadmin as an icon

Displaying WinMySQLadmin

After it has been launched WinMySQLadmin shrinks to a stoplight icon in the task bar. If you click on this icon with the right mouse button, you can display WinMySQLadmin with SHOWME. The button HIDE ME in the dialog sheet Environment shrinks the window again into an icon. In this dialog sheet you can also summon the on-line help for WinMySQLadmin, which, unfortunately, is not much help at all.

Starting and Stopping the MySQL Server as a Service Under Windows NT/2000

When WinMySQLadmin is executed under Windows NT/2000, it automatically registers the MySQL server as an operating system service and then launches this service. Thereafter, you can use WinMySQLadmin to stop the service and to start it again. You can also unregister the service with WinMySQLadmin, but at the next startup the service will be automatically registered again.

MySQL Configuration

At first launch, WinMySQLadmin creates the file Windows\my.ini if such a file does not yet exist. This file can be viewed and edited in the dialog sheet MY.INI SETUP.

Sad to tell, the entire user interface in the dialog sheet (see Figure 4-5) is rather complicated and confusing. The following description explains the effect of the individual dialog elements and how they are related to one another:

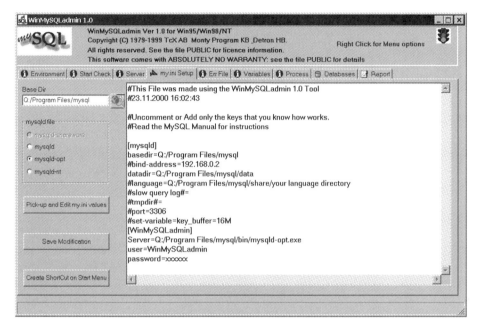

Figure 4-5. Setting `my.ini` *in WinMySQLadmin*

- **BASE DIR:** In this text field the MySQL installation directory can be set (for example, `C:\mysql` or `Program\mysql`). You can then find in this directory the directories `data`, with the MySQL databases, and `bin`, with the MySQL programs and commands. A change in this directory is generally not necessary.

  The directory `set` here is used to determine the file names for the MySQL server (`bin\mysqld.exe` is simply added to the directory). For some reason that is not entirely clear, the option `basedir` in `my.ini` is not changed.

- **MYSQLD FILE:** With these options one can set which of the two or three (Windows NT/2000) MySQL server variants should be launched:

  `mysqld.exe` is the standard server, including debug information. `mysqldopt.exe` is especially optimized for Intel Pentium (and compatible) processors and is the best choice on most systems. `mysqldnt.exe` is provided particularly for Windows NT/2000. This variant is the only one that can be used as an NT service (the other two variants can be used exclusively as stand-alone programs).

- **PICK UP AND EDIT MY.INI:** With this button `Windows\my.ini` is read anew and displayed in the dialog. Any changes made in WinMySQLadmin will be lost.

- **SAVE MODIFICATIONS:** With this button first the settings BASE DIR and MYSQLD FILE are evaluated and saved in the option `Server` of the group `[WinMySQLadmin]`. Then `Windows\my.ini` is saved.

- **CREATE SHORT CUT:** With this button the entry PROGRAMS| STARTUP|WINMYSQLADMIN is generated in the Windows start menu (if it does not yet exist). This has the effect that from now on Win-MySQLadmin will be launched automatically at system startup. This is particularly practical under Windows 9x/ME, under which MySQL cannot be automatically started as a service. This task is taken over by WinMySQLadmin.

> **CAUTION**   *For specifying path names in the configuration file the forward slash (/) must be used, not the backslash (\\), as is usual under Windows.*

> **REMARK**   *Please note that there can be two additional configuration files:* `C:\my.cnf` *and* `DATADIR\my.cnf`*. If there are several configuration files existing simultaneously, they are read in the following order:*
>
> `C:\my.cnf` → `Windows\my.ini` → `DATADIR\my.cnf` (only mysqld).
>
> *Settings in the last file to be read have priority. Using configuration files is discussed in detail in Chapter 14.*

Displaying Status Information

WinMySQLadmin provides much information in the dialog sheets ENVIRONMENT, SERVER, VARIABLES, and PROCESS about the state of the MySQL server: status information, the contents of the status and system variables, and a list of all running MySQL processes.

The dialog sheet ERRFILE displays the (most recent) lines of the file `mysql.err`. In this file are logged various warnings and error messages. The file is usually located in the directory `mysql\data\`. However, the button REFRESH does not always work. If you really and truly want to see the latest state of this file, you will have to open it in an editor.

Displaying the Database Structure

The DATABASE dialog sheet (see Figure 4-6) provides a quick overview of the databases managed by MySQL, with their tables and columns. Unfortunately, at present the database structure cannot be edited (create a new table, edit tables, etc.), nor can the contents of tables be examined.

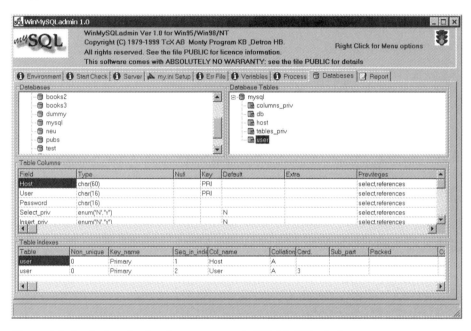

Figure 4-6. Analyzing the database structure in WinMySQLadmin

WinMySQLadmin as a Security Risk

> **CAUTION** *The first time it is launched, WinMySQLadmin asks for a user name and password. If you provide this information, the program registers a user in the MySQL access database. This user has unrestricted access (like* root*). This user is, to be sure, password protected, but this password is placed by WinMySQLadmin in the file* Windows\my.ini *in plain text. Anyone who has access to your computer and knows a bit about MySQL can thereby obtain unrestricted access to MySQL.*
>
> *In the "first aid" portion of the chapter on security (Chapter 7) you will find a concrete introduction on how you can restrict the rights of WinMySQLadmin to some extent in order to reduce the security risk. (At present such security holes cannot be completely closed, because WinMySQLadmin would thereby become unusable; see below.)*

When WinMySQLadmin Doesn't Function

WinMySQLadmin must register like any other client with the MySQL server. For this the program uses the user name and password combination stored in Windows\my.ini:

```
[WinMySQLadmin]
user=username
password=xxx
   ...
```

If these two lines are missing in my.ini, for example because they were deleted for security reasons (the password, after all, is sitting there in plain text), the program is registered with the MySQL server without a password as *odbc@localhost*. This functions, of course, only if the access privileges allow registration without a password. Which operations in WinMySQLadmin are now accessible depend now on the security configuration. If *odbc@localhost* has no privileges other than login, then the following operations are possible in WinMySQLadmin:

- Start and stop the MySQL server

- Display status information (dialog sheets ENVIRONMENT, SERVER, ERR FILE, and VARIABLES)

- Display a list of the user's processes (dialog sheet PROCESS; the processes of other users are not visible)

- Display a list of all databases (dialog sheet `Databases`; however, neither the structure nor the contents of the databases can be examined)

- Generate an error report

> **REMARK** *If you wish to start or stop the MySQL server with WinMySQLadmin under Windows NT/2000, you must log in under windows as* Administrator *or as a user with* Administrator *privileges.*

phpMyAdmin (HTML)

phpMyAdmin consists of a number of PHP scripts that enable nearly all of the administration of MySQL. Thanks to the HTML interface the administration can be carried out with almost any web browser, independent of operating system, locally as well as over a network.

Like other MySQL user interfaces, phpMyAdmin also displays various shortcomings. But all in all, phpMyAdmin is by far the most mature and reliable MySQL administrative tool available when these lines were being written (February 2001).

A particular feature of phpMyAdmin is that in combination with certain browsers (for example, Internet Explorer under Windows) it correctly shows Unicode character strings stored in BLOBs. (However, it is not possible with phpMyAdmin to edit Unicode character strings in BLOBs. In general, MySQL is currently incapable of correctly processing Unicode character strings. As a solution to this problem such character strings are often stored in BLOBs.

Overview of the User Interface

The user interface of phpMyAdmin consists principally of three HTML pages (based on various PHP scripts). If you work with phpMyAdmin you will, of course, stumble on many pages, but the three discussed here (and we shall continually refer to them in this section) represent the starting point for all navigation with phpMyAdmin.

- **Start Page** (Figure 4-7): The initial page `index.php3` enables the selection of desired MySQL servers, the creation of a new database, and the execution of various administrative tasks related to the server.

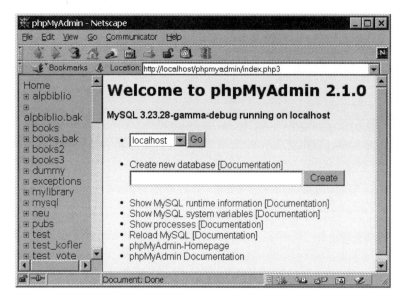

Figure 4-7. Start page of phpMyAdmin shown in Netscape 4.7

- **Database View** (Figure 4-8): The database view provides an overview of all tables of the database and shows a collection of various functions for processing the entire database (generate and delete tables, execute SQL commands, export the database, etc.).

- **Table View** (Figure 4-9): In table view you see all the columns of the database with their properties. Here you can insert columns, edit or delete, and execute various administrative functions for individual tables (rename tables, copy, export, import ASCII files, etc.).

In the left column of phpMyAdmin is displayed a hierarchical list of all databases and tables. You are only a mouse click away from shifting quickly to database or table view.

POINTER

*You can obtain some rather compact on-line help via the start page of phpMyAdmin (*index.php3*) by following the link* PHPMYADMIN DOCU-MENTATION. *Additional and more current information on phpMyAdmin can be found at the following Internet location:*

```
http://phpwizard.net/projects/phpMyAdmin/
```

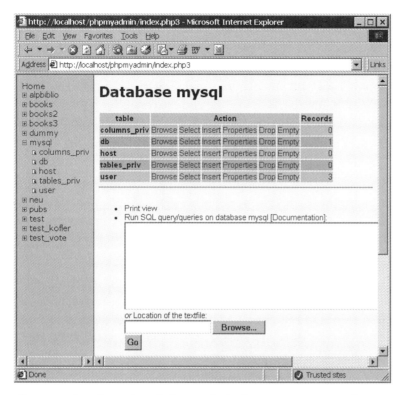

Figure 4-8. Database view of phpMyAdmin shown in Internet Explorer

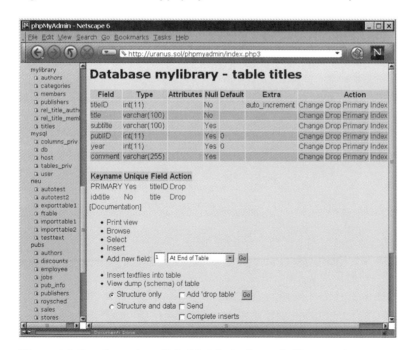

Figure 4-9. Database view of phpMyAdmin shown in Netscape 6

Installation and Configuration

There are several possibilities for installing and using phpMyAdmin:

- In the simplest case both phpMyAdmin and MySQL run on the same local computer (that is, Apache, PHP, MySQL, and the scripts for phpMyAdmin are all locally installed). This installation variant has already been described in Chapter 2.

- It is not much more complicated to install phpMyAdmin locally and thereby maintain a MySQL server that is running on another computer (for example, on that of an Internet service provider). The only problem is that MySQL must be configured on the external computer in such a way that external administration is permitted. ISPs in particular usually permit only local access to the server (that is, by *localhost*).

- For the administration of a MySQL server located at an ISP it is worthwhile to install phpMyAdmin there as well. As a rule, only the script files of phpMyAdmin need to be transported into the file tree of the web server (usually in the htdocs directory). All other conditions (Apache, PHP) are automatically fulfilled by most ISPs. Even access to MySQL is no problem, since phpMyAdmin is now, from the point of view of MySQL, being executed locally.

> **CAUTION** *It happens frequently that phpMyAdmin is installed in such a way that it is accessible to all users over a local network or even over the Internet who know or can guess the network address of the start page. (This is particularly true in the third case mentioned above.) To avoid giving complete MySQL access to just anyone, the access and phpMyAdmin script files must be password protected. Usually, a* .htaccess *file is used. Introductory information on dealing with such files can be found in Chapter 2. Further information can be found in any half-decent book on Apache.*

Configuration of MySQL Access

The complete configuration of phpMyAdmin is accomplished in the file config.inc.php. In the simplest case it suffices to set the three array variables *host, user,* and *password.*

```
# configuration file config.inc.php
$cfgServers[1]['adv_auth'] = false;
$cfgServers[1]['host'] = 'computer.name'; // or localhost
$cfgServers[1]['user'] = 'username';
$cfgServers[1]['password'] = 'xxx';
```

If the MySQL server is running on the same computer as the web server that is executing the phpMyAdmin script files with PHP, then you give *localhost* as the computer name. Optionally, with $cfgServers[1]['port'] the TCP/IP port over which the link is established can be specified. That is necessary only if the default port 3306 is not the one to be used.

> **CAUTION**   *The file* config.inc.php *contains the user name and password in plain text. That is always a security risk. Make sure that unauthorized access to this file, such as via anonymous FTP, is not possible.*

> **CAUTION**   *The extent of the possibilities for administration with phpMyAdmin depends, of course, on the MySQL access rights possessed by the MySQL user whose name phpMyAdmin has used at login (that is,* $cfgServers[1] ['user']= ... *). Therefore, phpMyAdmin is not responsible for access protection, but rather the MySQL access system with the privilege database* mysql, *which is described fully in Chapter 7.*
>
> *Conversely, we see that if only some of the options for phpMyAdmin described below work for you, then it is not that phpMyAdmin is flawed, but that you have insufficient access rights to MySQL. In particular, if you use phpMyAdmin to manage a database located at an ISP, you will generally have access only to your own database. (Otherwise, your ISP would be guilty of a serious breach of administrative etiquette.)*

Secure Authentication

In order for phpMyAdmin to be usable without restrictions, a password (in plain text) must be given in the file config.inc.php for traditional authentication as described above, and this password must allow unrestricted access to MySQL (that is, a MySQL *root* password). Regardless of how good the system as a whole is secured, such passwords in plain text are a thorn in the side of any security-conscious administrator.

Therefore, phpMyAdmin recognizes another authentication system, *advanced authentication*, which is more secure. This system is somewhat more difficult to understand. The following description assumes that you understand the MySQL security system (see Chapter 7).

Authentication is a two-step process:

1. In the first step a link to the MySQL server is established, where only the tables *user* and *db* of the *mysql* database are read in order to determine a list of databases that can be accessed via phpMyAdmin. (The user name/password pair placed in config.inc.php in plain text must now be provided read access to only these two tables. An attacker discovering these data will not be able to do much with them.)

   For secure authentication to be employed, in config.inc.php the array variable *adv_auth* must be set to *true*. Furthermore, the name and password for access to the tables *mysql.user* and *mysql.db* must be specified in the array variables *stduser* and *stdpass* (and not as previously in the variables *user* and *password*).

   ```
   # config.inc.php, secure Authentication
   $cfgServers[1]['adv_auth'] = true;
   $cfgServers[1]['host'] = 'host.name';
   $cfgServers[1]['stduser'] = 'phpadmin'; // only for access to
   $cfgServers[1]['stdpass'] = 'xxx'; // mysql.user and mysql.db
   ```

   On the MySQL server side, the user *phpadmin* must be registered with minimal access privileges. This is accomplished by the following two commands:

   ```
   GRANT SELECT ON mysql.db TO phpadmin@host.name IDENTIFIED BY 'xxx'
   GRANT SELECT ON mysql.user TO phpadmin@host.name
   ```

2. In the second stage of the authentication process the login name and password provided by Apache are used to create the final link to MySQL. For MySQL administrative work the login name and password that were used in the HTTP login to the phpMyAdmin pages are used here.

> **REMARK** *The authentication procedure described here works only if PHP is executed as an Apache module. If, on the other hand, the CGI version of PHP is used, which is the usual situation under Windows, then the attempt at authentication leads merely to an error message. In the web browser* internal error *is displayed, and in the Apache error file,* malformed header from script. *In this case you must use the traditional phpMyAdmin authentication.*

Servicing Several MySQL Servers with phpMyAdmin

Host, user, and password entries for multiple MySQL servers are possible in config.inc.php. If you make such entries, then on the start page of MySQL there appears a listbox with the names of the computers whose MySQL servers can be managed. Selecting one of these names establishes a link to that server.

The variable cfgServerDefault determines with which computer php-MyAdmin establishes a link at startup. If the variable is set to 0, then at startup phpMyAdmin initially sets no link, but merely presents a listbox with the selection of servers.

```
# configuration file config.inc.php
$cfgServers[1]['adv_auth'] = false;
$cfgServers[1]['host'] = 'computer1.name'; // MySQL Server 1
$cfgServers[1]['user'] = 'username1';
$cfgServers[1]['password'] = 'xxx1';
$cfgServers[2]['adv_auth'] = false;
$cfgServers[2]['host'] = 'computer2.name'; // MySQL Server 2
$cfgServers[2]['user'] = 'username2';
$cfgServers[2]['password'] = 'xxx2';
 ...
$cfgServerDefault = 1; // Default Server
```

If you do not wish to have simply the computer name (array variable *host*) displayed in the list box, then you can use $cfgServers[*n*]['verbose']='*name*' to display a different character string.

Additional Configuration Possibilities

In addition to the MySQL access data in config.inc.php you can also set various options. The following list describes only the most important of these, together with their associated variables:

- `$cfgConfirm` = true/false: This variable specifies whether a confirmation query should be displayed before data are deleted (default: true).

- `$cfgMaxRows` = 30: Specifies how many data records should be displayed per page as the result of a query.

- `$cfgMaxInputsize` = "300px": Specifies how wide (in display pixels) input fields for tables should be (for example, the column VALUE in Figure 4-10). The width is valid also for the input field for SQL commands, which is usually too narrow. If you would like to increase this width, you can edit the file db_details.php. The lines in question look originally like this:

```
<textarea name="sql_query" cols="40" rows="8" style="width:<?php
echo $cfgMaxInputsize;?>"></textarea><br>
```

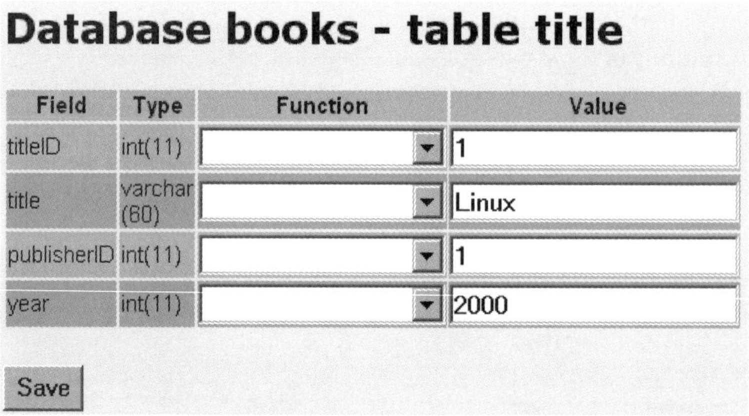

Database books - table title

Field	Type	Function	Value
titleID	int(11)	▼	1
title	varchar (60)	▼	Linux
publisherID	int(11)	▼	1
year	int(11)	▼	2000

Save

Figure 4-10. Adding a data record

With this new variant you can achieve that the SQL input field is twice as wide as it was originally:

```
<textarea name="sql_query" cols="40" rows="8" style="width:600px">
</textarea><br>
```

- `$cfgShowBlob`=true/false: Specifies whether the contents of fields of type *xxxTEXT* and *xxxBLOB* are to be displayed (default: true). If the variable is set to false, then instead of long texts and BLOBs, only the text *[BLOB]* is displayed.

Creating and Editing Databases

If your desires run in the direction of creating a new database, phpMyAdmin can save you the necessity of having to deal with many complex *CREATE TABLE* commands.

> **POINTER** *The following examples are based on the database* books, *which will be presented in the next chapter as an example of normalizing a database. The following chapter contains a great deal of background information and examples on the subject of database design.*

Creating a Database

The creation of a new database begins in the main menu, in which you provide the name of the new database. This database then becomes the active database. (If you wish to insert a table into a preexisting database, then click on that database in the list of databases.)

Creating a Table

In the dialog for table *xy* you will find, among other things, CREATE NEW TABLE ON DATABASE XY. There you give the desired name of the table and the number of columns (when in doubt, just give a number that is too large. You can always leave the extra columns empty). GO leads to the next form (see Figure 4-11), in which you can conveniently set the name and properties of the columns.

Database books - table title

Field	Type	Length/Set	Attributes	Null	Default	Extra	Primary	Index	Unique
titleID	INT			not null		auto_increment	☑	☐	☐
title	VARCHAR	60		not null			☐	☐	☐
publisherID	INT			not null			☐	☐	☐
year	INT			not null			☐	☐	☐

Table comments:

[Save]

Figure 4-11. Design of the table title *in phpMyAdmin*

The use of phpMyAdmin requires a bit of knowledge about the possible and necessary settings for the various data types. For example, you will get slapped with an error message if you attempt to declare a *VARCHAR* column without providing a length, or a *TEXT* column with a length (neither variant is provided for in MySQL). You may then, of course, correct your error.

Under certain conditions phpMyAdmin does not adhere exactly to your specifications, but varies them a bit. Thus in the design of the table that appears in Figure 4-11 it adds the default value of 0 for the columns *publisherID* and *year*. Such high-handedness on the part of phpMyAdmin usually does not cause any trouble.

Changing the Table Design

In the phpMyAdmin table view you can equip each column with an index by a simple click of the mouse. It is just as simple to change the column attributes, such as the maximal length of character strings (link CHANGE). You can delete existing columns (DROP) and insert new columns at any position (ADD NEW FIELD).

> **TIP** *While the creation of new tables works just fine, there are sometimes problems in making changes to a preexisting table. Under certain conditions phpMySQL generates flawed SQL commands whose execution is refused by MySQL. Once you have had some practice with* ALTER TABLE, *you can discover the error in many cases. Then just copy the command into the SQL command input field, correct it, and execute it. (We will discuss below how to execute SQL commands in phpMyAdmin.)*

Inserting, Displaying, and Editing Table Data

Inserting Data into a Table

With INSERT (see Figure 4-12) you can insert individual data records into a table. This is a convenient way of proceeding for a few test records. However, only one data record can be edited (not several simultaneously), so this procedure is rather cumbersome for larger data sets.

- **Functions:** It is often the case in the input of a data record that an SQL function is to be inserted, such as *PASSWORD('xxx')* to store *xxx* in encrypted form. For this phpMyAdmin offers several frequently used functions in the column FUNCTION, including *ASCII, CURTIME, NOW.* Figure 4-13 demonstrates the use of such functions.

- **NULL:** If *NULL* is to be stored in a field, then you must input the four characters *NULL* in the VALUE column. If you simply leave the column empty, then in the case of strings an empty character string is stored, and in the case of numbers the value zero.

> **TIP** *It is relatively tedious to input several data records with phpMyAdmin. In many cases it is more efficient to input the records into a text file and then import them with* INSERT TEXTFILE INTO TABLE.

Displaying Table Contents

With both database view (see Figure 4-8) and table view (see Figure 4-12) the link BROWSE leads to a display of the contents of the table. For this the command *SELECT * FROM table LIMIT 0, 30* is executed. You may then use PREVIOUS and SHOW to move backward and forward through the table. BEGIN displays the first

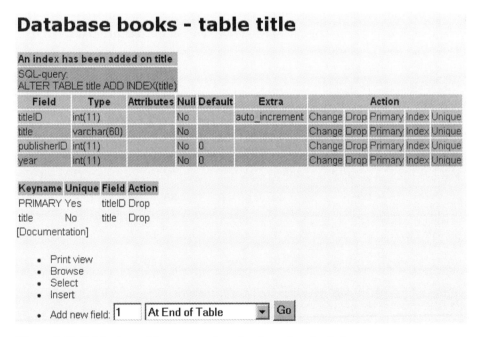

Database books - table title

An index has been added on title

SQL-query:
ALTER TABLE title ADD INDEX(title)

Field	Type	Attributes	Null	Default	Extra	Action			
titleID	int(11)		No		auto_increment	Change	Drop	Primary Index	Unique
title	varchar(60)		No			Change	Drop	Primary Index	Unique
publisherID	int(11)		No	0		Change	Drop	Primary Index	Unique
year	int(11)		No	0		Change	Drop	Primary Index	Unique

Keyname	Unique	Field	Action
PRIMARY	Yes	titleID	Drop
title	No	title	Drop

[Documentation]

- Print view
- Browse
- Select
- Insert
- Add new field: `1` `At End of Table ▾` `Go`

Figure 4-12. Table view with many options for changing the design

Password	char (16)	`PASSWORD ▾`	`xxx`

Figure 4-13. Adding a password

record, while END displays the last. If you specify numerical values in the two input fields after the SHOW button, you can display n data records beginning with the mth. (If you wish to sort the table contents in some way, you must formulate and execute an SQL query yourself; see the following section.)

The value *NULL* is not, unfortunately, identified as such, but is merely displayed in the form of an empty field. *NULL* can therefore not be distinguished in phpMyAdmin from an empty character string.

Binary data (BLOBs) are displayed, depending on the configuration, as ASCII character strings or by the character string *[BLOB]*.

> **TIP** *If you would like to sort a table according to a different criterion, simply click in the relevant column.*

Editing Data

If you click on the link EDIT shown in Figure 4-14, you will land on a new page, in which the data record can be edited. This page looks as depicted in Figure 4-10, where in the column VALUE the previous contents of the record are displayed, where they can be easily edited.

Showing records 10 - 14 (23 total)

SQL-query:
SELECT * FROM authors LIMIT 10, 5

| Begin << | Previous < | | > Show | 5 | rows starting from | 15 | | >> End |

au_id	au_lname	au_fname	phone	address	city	state	zip	contract		
527-72-3246	Greene	Morningstar	615 297-2723	22 Graybar House Rd.	Nashville	TN	37215	0	Edit	Delete
648-92-1872	Blotchet-Halls	Reginald	503 745-6402	55 Hillsdale Bl.	Corvallis	OR	97330	-1	Edit	Delete
672-71-3249	Yokomoto	Akiko	415 935-4228	3 Silver Ct.	Walnut Creek	CA	94595	-1	Edit	Delete
712-45-1867	del Castillo	Innes	615 996-8275	2286 Cram Pl. #86	Ann Arbor	MI	48105	-1	Edit	Delete
722-51-5454	DeFrance	Michel	219 547-9982	3 Balding Pl.	Gary	IN	46403	-1	Edit	Delete

Figure 4-14. Page-by-page representation of data records

> **REMARK** *A change in data is possible only if the table has a column identified as PRIMARY KEY (usually with* id *values that identify each record).*

Other Operations

Executing SQL Commands

In database view (see Figure 4-8) you can input SQL commands. With GO the command is then executed for the current database. The SQL command does not have to be terminated with a semicolon, as in mysql. However, a semicolon is necessary if several commands are to be executed simultaneously.

If the command involves *SELECT*, then the results are displayed page by page, like the contents of a table. However, the links EDIT and DELETE function only if the query results come from a single table (no *JOIN*s from several tables) and the *PRIMARY KEY* column of the table is a part of the query results.

> **TIP** *The input field in the default configuration is rather on the small side for SQL commands. In the section on phpMyAdmin configuration above we described how a field can be widened, either by assigning a larger value to the variable* $cfgMaxInputsize *in* config.inc.php *or by editing the file* db_details.php.

> **POINTER** *An introduction to SQL can be found in Chapter 6. There you will learn about the various possibilities for formulating queries, editing data with* UPDATE, *and doing other exciting, though nonetheless relevant, things with databases.*

Executing SQL Commands from a File

Instead of inputting SQL commands, you can input instead the name of a file containing SQL commands. Then phpMyAdmin loads this file and executes the commands contained therein. This procedure can also be used to load a previously executed phpMyAdmin database backup.

> **REMARK**   *If you are working in a test environment under Windows, you will often encounter the error* fopen("\\php2", "r")—Invalid argument. *The cause of this error is that no temporary directory for intermediate storage of the selected file was specified in* php.ini.
>
>   *The solution is simple: Edit the assignment of the variable* upload_tmp_dir *in* php.ini. *The directory given there must already exist.*
>
> ```
> ;change in php.ini (specify a valid directory!)
> upload_tmp_dir = "Q:\tmp";
> ```

SQL Query Generator

If are not thrilled at the prospect of creating your own SQL commands, you can summon the phpMyAdmin genie to your assistance. However, the link QUERY BY EXAMPLE promises more than the query generator actually contains. The form is not particularly intuitive, and it is also rather complex to use. Without a good basic knowledge of SQL you will scarcely be able to link to tables.

Here are some ideas for your first experiments: In the list box USE TABLES you must select those tables affected by the query. (A multiple selection is possible using the Ctrl key.) The button UPDATE QUERY creates an SQL command out of the previous input that is represented in the text field in the bottom right-hand corner (see also Figure 4-15). The text field is well suited for a first check as to whether the generated SQL code is plausible. SUBMIT QUERY terminates the query.

Executing Backups, Saving the Database Structure

In database view of phpMyAdmin (see Figure 4-16) you can generate a number of SQL commands under the topic VIEW DUMP OF DATABASE. You can recreate either the structure of the database (STRUCTURE ONLY) only or the contents as well as the structure (STRUCTURE AND DATA).

Details of this function can be set with three options:

- **ADD DROP TABLE:** Before every *CREATE TABLE* command a *DROP TABLE* command is inserted.

- **SEND:** The resulting SQL commands are not displayed in the web browser, but (like an FTP file) are sent to the browser. In this manner SQL commands can be easily stored in a file.

- **COMPLETE INSERTS:** For every INSERT command phpMyAdmin also specifies the column name, for example in the form *INSERT INTO author (authorID, author) VALUES ('1', 'name')*. Without this option the *INSERT* command would be generated in a more compact form: *INSERT INTO author VALUES ('1', 'name')*.

Database books

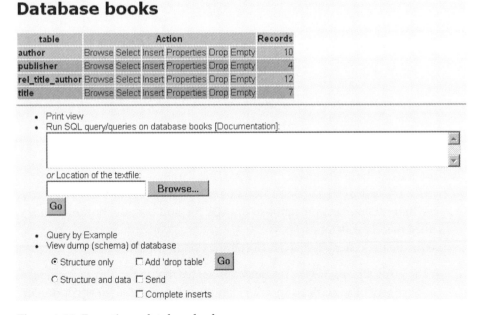

Figure 4-15. Creating SQL commands with the query generator

Database books

table	Action					Records
author	Browse	Select	Insert	Properties	Drop	Empty	10
publisher	Browse	Select	Insert	Properties	Drop	Empty	4
rel_title_author	Browse	Select	Insert	Properties	Drop	Empty	12
title	Browse	Select	Insert	Properties	Drop	Empty	7

- Print view
- Run SQL query/queries on database books [Documentation]:

  or Location of the textfile:

  [Browse...]

  [Go]

- Query by Example
- View dump (schema) of database

  ⦿ Structure only   ☐ Add 'drop table'   [Go]

  ○ Structure and data ☐ Send

  ☐ Complete inserts

Figure 4-16. Executing a database backup

COMPLETE INSERTS are necessary if the data are to be inserted from one table into another that exhibits additional columns or whose arrangement of columns is different from that in the initial table.

CAUTION   *In writing the table data phpMyAdmin 2.1.0 attempts to use the PHP function* set_time_limit *to increase the* timeout *value for the PHP script. If PHP is executed in* safe *mode, however, this leads to the error message* Warning: Cannot set time limit. *This error message, alas, is located between the* INSERT *commands and thus makes the resulting backup file worthless.*

Fortunately, we are in luck, and the solution is simple: Search in the phpMyAdmin script file lib.inc.php *for the function* set_time_limit *and prefix the function with the character @. You thereby achieve the desired result that no error message is displayed if an error occurs in execution of the function.*

REMARK   *The resulting SQL commands are comparable to the result of the MySQL tool* mysqldump. *However, internally, phpMyAdmin cannot access* mysqldump, *but must determine the database structure and the contents of the tables via SQL commands, which is a more complex and error-prone process. In other words, if you use* mysqldump, *you should give precedence to this program over phpMyAdmin. In Chapter 11 we shall go more deeply into* mysqldump.

Database Upload

To read in a database (database uploading), the database must first be created (CREATE DATABASE in the database view of phpMyAdmin). Then in database view you use BROWSE to select the name of the SQL file and execute the commands contained therein with GO.

Unfortunately, many errors can occur in uploading a database.

- The error *fopen—Invalid argument* indicates that in php.ini no path for temporary files has been specified (and that there is also no environment variable from which PHP can determine this path).

- phpMyAdmin 2.1.0 has problems in reading character strings that contain the character #. (Under some circumstances the semicolon character can also cause trouble.) If a new version of phpMyAdmin has not appeared by the time you are reading this, the unofficial version 2.1.0.1 can help: http://eleves.mines.u-nancy.fr/phpMyAdmin/

- The attempt to move large SQL files can lead to an error message due to the permitted file size being exceeded. This value is determined by the variable *upload_max_filesize* in php.ini (the default setting is 2 megabytes).

- The *timeout* error frequently occurs with very large SQL files. The error is due to the fact that there is a limit on the run time (CPU time) of PHP scripts (usually 30 seconds). This makes sense as a rule, since if a PHP script takes longer that that, the cause is often a programming error (for example, an infinite loop). One wishes to avoid such an error bringing down the web server.

  With database uploads, however, the long execution time is legitimate. The *timeout* time is set in the configuration file php.ini (variable *max_execution_time*). Moreover, the *timeout* value can also be set within a PHP script with *set_time_limit()*, which phpMyAdmin attempts to do. However, this works only if PHP is not running in *safe mode* (which is the case as a rule).

When PHP is run on the same computer as that of your Internet service provider, you have, unfortunately, no influence on the file php.ini. (You could, of course, ask your ISP to change certain variables, but experience shows that you are not likely to get far with this approach.) The only solution is usually to break the upload file into smaller pieces and read these in one after the other.

Protecting Individual Tables

Just as you can make backups of entire databases (that is, all of the tables in a database), you can also generate SQL commands for backing up individual tables. The relevant options can be set in the table view of phpMyAdmin. As a further variant you can also save tables in CSV (comma separated values) format. The columns of the table are separated by a character of your choice (usually the semicolon). Such files are useful for importation into a spreadsheet program.

Importing ASCII Tables

What do you do when you have an ASCII file with data that you would like to import into a table? Here, too, phpMyAdmin comes to your assistance. In table view you will find the link INSERT TEXTFILES INTO TABLE. This link leads you to the dialog depicted in Figure 4-17. There you specify the name of the file. Moreover, you can set a number of options that format the ASCII file.

Database mylibrary - table categories

Location of the textfile	J:\FTP\categories.txt Browse...	
Replace table data with file	☐ Replace	The contents of the file replaces the contents of the selected table for rows with identical primary or unique key.
Fields terminated by	;	The terminator of the fields.
Fields enclosed by	☐ OPTIONALLY	Often quotation marks. OPTIONALLY means that only char and varchar fields are enclosed by the "enclosed by"-character.
Fields escaped by	\\	Optional. Controls how to write or read special characters.
Lines terminated by	\r\n	Carriage return: \r Linefeed: \n
Column names		If you wish to load only some of a table's columns, specify a comma separated field list.
[Documentation]		
Submit Reset		

Figure 4-17. ASCII importation of table data

POINTER   *The meaning of the various options is detailed in the description of the command* LOAD DATA *in Chapter 13. Examples of the application of* LOAD DATA, *which can also be used for importing with phpMyAdmin, can be found in Chapter 11.*

NULL *is usually represented in a text file as* \N *(with uppercase* N, *not* n).

Renaming and Copying Tables

At the bottom of the table view you will find the commands RENAME TABLE TO and COPY TABLE TO. With RENAME you can, not surprisingly, rename a table, while COPY duplicates the table to create a new table in the current database. In this process you have a choice of whether to save just the table structure or the data as well. If you would like to copy a table into a different database, then you have merely to specify the new table name in the form *databasename.tablename*.

Additional Administrative Tasks

If you click on HOME at the root of the database tree (left-hand region of the window), you will return to the phpMyAdmin start page. This page contains, among other things, links for several administrative operations:

- SHOW MYSQL RUNTIME INFORMATION shows the status of the MySQL server (corresponds to *SHOW STATUS*). Although the links EDIT and DELETE are shown for the individual values, it is not possible to delete or change the status variables.

- SHOW MYSQL SYSTEM VARIABLES displays the contents of the MySQL variables (corresponds to *SHOW VARIABLES*). As with RUNTIME INFORMATION, changes cannot be made to the variables.

- SHOW PROCESSES shows the current process list (corresponds to *SHOW PROCESSLIST*). Individual processes in the process list can be terminated with KILL. (However, EDIT and DELETE are without effect.)

- RELOAD MYSQL reloads the *mysql* grant database (corresponds to *FLUSH PRIVILEGES*).

KSql (Linux)

Under Linux/Unix you can also use KMySql (to be called KSql in future versions) to create a new database. The program is simple to use, but it does not offer as many options as does phpMyAdmin.

Installation

KMySQL, or KSql, is already included as a regular part of certain Linux distributions, and it can be easily installed (for example, with YaST under SuSE Linux). If KSql is not part of your distribution, you can obtain the program via the Internet from `http://www.ksql.org/`

Forging a Link

If you wish to create a link to a MySQL server for the first time, execute SERVER|ADD SERVER and provide the computer name (or localhost), the desired user name, and optional password. The actual construction of the link is accomplished by a double click on the server entry. (If you do not specify the password, then every time the link is made you will be asked to provide it. If you give an incorrect password, you will have to delete the entire server entry and replace it. There is no opportunity to correct the password.)

Examining Preexisting Data

All databases located on the server together with their tables and columns are represented as a hierarchical tree. To display the contents of a table, simply double click on the table in question. The table will then be displayed in the right-hand region of the window (NEW VIEW). With VIEW|WINDOWIZE you can transform this window region into an independent window and thus view several tables at once.

Editing Data

If you would like to edit the contents of a table, click on the table with the right mouse button and execute EDIT CONTENTS. A new window appears as if by magic, and you can edit existing records. However, you cannot add new data records, nor can you delete existing records.

Executing SQL Queries

In the lower region of the window you can input SQL queries and then execute them with SUBMIT. If you are dealing with *SELECT* queries, the data will be displayed as a NEW VIEW. All commands are stored in a listbox and can be executed again with a double click.

Creating a Database

To create a new database, execute CREATE BASE in the treelike KMySQL database list with the right mouse button and specify the name of the database.

Creating and Editing Tables

Using the context menu (right mouse button on the name of the new database) you arrive at a dialog for designing a new table. There you specify the table name and use ADD to insert the desired columns (see Figure 4-18). You can use the same dialog later to edit the properties of the individual columns, add new columns, and perform other such tasks. KMySQL in its current version does not, alas, offer the possibility of defining indexes or inserting test data.

Generating Forms for PHP Code

With KSql you can also generate forms. To do this, click the database and in the context menu execute NEW FORM. Like the kinkier varieties of sushi, the forms editor requires some getting used to, but after a bit of experimentation its use should become clear. Before the form can be saved, it must be given a name via the context menu. The properties of the form's elements are also set via the context menu.

You cannot do much with your new form right off the bat. However, in combination with the library Kmysqlphp you can create HTML forms complete with PHP code from KSql forms with relatively little effort. Further details on this can be found on the KSql home page.

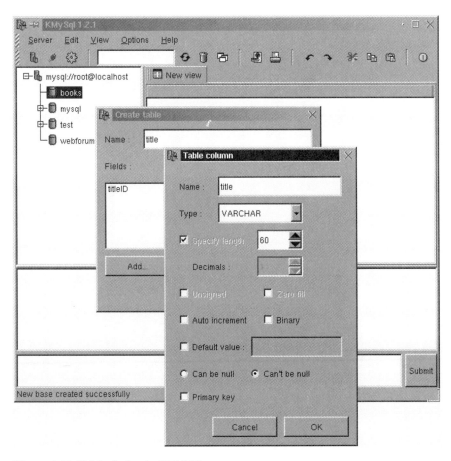

Figure 4-18. Table design in KMySQL

#### CHAPTER 5

Database Design

THE FIRST STAGE IN ANY database application is the design of the database. The design will have a great influence on the efficiency of the application, the degree of simplicity or difficulty in programming and maintenance, and the flexibility in making changes in the design. Errors that occur in the design phase will come home to roost in the heartache of future efforts at correction.

This chapter discusses the fundamentals of relational databases, collects the varieties of data and tables available under MySQL, offers concrete examples of MySQL database structures, shows how indexes enable more efficient table access, and, finally, offers enlightenment on concrete ways that databases and tables can be generated.

Chapter Overview

Introduction

Database design is doubtless one of the greatest challenges in the development of complex database applications. This chapter attempts to provide a first introduction to the topic. But please don't expect any foolproof recipes. Many of the skills in database design are won by experience, and in a single chapter we can transmit only some of the basic principles.

To help in your orientation in this relatively long chapter, here is an overview:

- The following two sections provide basic information. We discuss how to divide data logically among several tables, where the primary goal is to avoid redundancy. The *normalization* process helps in this.

  We also present the data types belonging to MySQL. For example, we answer the question as to what data type should be used for storing amounts of money and for long and short character strings.

- We then go into some more advanced topics: How can searching and sorting tables be speeded up with the help of indexes? What types of tables does MySQL recognize, and which should be used when?

- How are databases and their tables actually generated? The next section introduces various *CREATE* commands, which help in this. (However, it is considerably more convenient to create new tables using instead a user interface such as phpMyAdmin.)

- Theory is all well and good, but at some point we have to roll up our sleeves, put on an apron, and start cooking up some databases of our own. Therefore, the last sections of this chapter offer some concrete examples of the design of databases: for managing a small library, for running a discussion group, and for testing special cases.

> **POINTER** *In this chapter we cannot avoid entirely introducing some SQL commands now and then, although SQL is actually introduced in detail only in the next chapter. (However, it is conversely also impossible to describe SQL without assuming a particular database layout.) You may find it necessary at times to flip back and forth between this chapter and the next.*

Further Reading

There are countless books that deal exclusively, independently of any specific database system, with database design and SQL. Needless to say, there is a variety of opinion as to which of these books are the good ones. Therefore, consider the following recommendations as my personal hit list.

1. Joe Celko: *SQL for Smarties*, Morgan Kaufmann Publishers, 1999. (This is not a book for SQL beginners. Many examples are currently not realizable in MySQL, because MySQL is not sufficiently compatible with ANSI-SQL/92. Nonetheless, it is a terrific example-oriented book on SQL.

2. Judith S. Bowman et al.: *The Practical SQL Handbook*, Addison-Wesley, 1996 (new edition planned for 2001).

3. Michael J. Hernandez: *Database Design for Mere Mortals*, Addison-Wesley, 1997. (The first half is somewhat long-winded, but the second half is excellent and very clearly written.)

4. The MySQL documentation recommends an additional book as an introduction to SQL, though I am not acquainted with it. Martin Gruber: *Mastering SQL*, Sybex, 2000.

5. If you are not quite ready to shell out your hard-earned (or even perhaps ill-gotten) cash for yet another book and you are interested for now in database design only, you may find the compact introduction on the design of relational databases by Fernando Lozano adequate to your needs. See `http://www.edm2.com/0612/msql7.html`

Database Theory

Why is that that authors of books think about nothing (well, almost nothing) but books? The author begs the indulgence of his readers in that the example in this section deals with books. The goal of the section is to create a small database in which data about books can be stored: book title, publisher, author(s), publication date, and so on.

Normal Forms

These data can, of course, be stored without a database, in a simple list in text format, for example, as appears in the Bibliography at the end of this book:

Michael Kofler: *Linux*. Addison-Wesley 2000.

Robert Orfali, Dan Harkey, Jeri Edwards: *Client/Server Survival Guide*. Addison Wesley 1997.

Tobias Ratschiller, Till Gerken: *Web Application Development with PHP 4.0*. New Riders 2000.

This is a nice and convenient list, containing all necessary information. Why bother with all the effort to transform this text (which perhaps exists as a document composed with some word-processing program) into a database?

Needless to say, the reasons are legion. Our list can be easily searched, but it is impossible to organize it in a different way, for example, to create a list of all books by author x or to create a new list ordered not by author but by title.

Our First Attempt

Just think: Nothing is easier than to turn our list into a database table. (To save space we are going to abbreviate the book titles and names of authors.)

Table 5-1 immediately shows itself to be riddled with problems. A first glance reveals that limiting the number of authors to three was an arbitrary decision. What do you do with a book that has four or five authors? Do we just keep adding columns, up to *authorN*, painfully aware that those columns will be empty for most entries?

Table 5-1. A book database: first attempt

title	publisher	year	author1	author2	author3
Linux	Addison-Wesley	2000	Kofler, M.		
Definitive ...	Apress	2000	Kofler, M.	Kramer, D.	
Client ...	Addison-Wesley	1997	Orfali, R.	Harkey, D.	Edwards, E.
Web ...	New Riders	2000	Ratschiller, T.	Gerken, T.	

The First Normal Form

Database theorists have found, I am happy to report, a solution to such problems. Simply apply to your database, one after the other, the rules for the three *normal forms*. The rules for the first normal form are as follows (though for the benefit of the reader they have been translated from the language of database theorists into what we might frivolously call "linguistic normal form," or, more simply, plain English):

- Columns with similar content must be eliminated.

- A table must be created for each group of associated data.

- Each data record must be identifiable by means of a *primary key*.

In our example, the first rule is clearly applicable to the *authorN* columns.

The second rule seems not to be applicable here, since in our example we are dealing exclusively with data that pertain specifically to the books in the database.

Thus a single table would seem to suffice. (We will see, however, that this is not, in fact, the case.)

The third rule signifies in practice that a running index must be used that uniquely identifies each row of the table. (It is not strictly necessary that an integer be used as primary key. Formally, only the uniqueness is required. For reasons of efficiency the primary key should be as small as possible, and thus an integer is generally more suitable than a character string of variable length.)

A reconfiguration of our table after application of the first and third rules might look like that depicted in Table 5-2.

Table 5-2. A book database: first normal form

id	title	publisher	year	author
1	Linux	Addison-Wesley	2000	Kofler, M.
2	Definitive Guide . . .	Apress	2000	Kofler, M.
3	Definitive Guide . . .	Apress	2000	Kramer, D.
4	Client/Server . . .	Addison-Wesley	1997	Orfali, R.
5	Client/Server . . .	Addison-Wesley	1997	Harkey, D.
6	Client/Server . . .	Addison-Wesley	1997	Edwards, E.
7	Web Application . . .	New Riders	2000	Ratschiller, T.
8	Web Application . . .	New Riders	2000	Gerken, T.

Clearly, the problem of multiple columns for multiple authors has been eliminated. Regardless of the number of authors, they can all be stored in our table. Of course, there is no free lunch, and the price of a meal here is rather high: The contents of the columns *title*, *publisher*, and *year* are repeated for each author. There must be a better way!

Second Normal Form

Here are the rules for the second normal form:

- Whenever the contents of columns repeat themselves, this means that the table must be divided into several subtables.

- These tables must be linked by *foreign keys*.

If you are new to the lingo of the database world, then the term *foreign key* probably seems a bit, well, foreign. A better word in everyday English would probably be *cross reference*, since a foreign key refers to a line in a different (hence foreign) table. For programmers the word *pointer* would perhaps be more to the point, while in Internet jargon the term *link* would be appropriate.

In Figure 5-2 we see that data are repeated in practically every column. The culprit of this redundancy is clearly the author column. Our first attempt to give the authors their very own table can be seen in Tables 5-3 and 5-4.

Table 5-3. title *table: second normal form*

titleID	title	publisher	year
1	Linux	Addison-Wesley	2000
2	Definitive Guide . . .	Apress	2000
3	Client/Server . . .	Addison-Wesley	1997
4	Web Application . . .	New Riders	2000

Table 5-4. author *table: second normal form*

authorID	titleID	author
1	1	Kofler, M.
2	2	Kofler, M.
3	2	Kramer, D.
4	3	Orfali, R.
5	3	Harkey, D.
6	3	Edwards, E.
7	4	Ratschiller, T.
8	4	Gerken, T.

In the *author* table the first column, with its running *authorID* values, provides the primary key. The second column takes over the task of the foreign key. It points, or refers, to rows of the *title* table. For example, row 7 of the *author* table indicates that *Ratschiller, T.* is an author of the book with ID *titleID=4*, that is, the book *Web Application* . . . .

Second Normal Form, Second Attempt

Our result could hardly be called optimal. In the *author* table the name *Kofler, M.* appears twice. As the number of books in this database increases, the amount of such redundancy will increase as well, whenever an author has worked on more than one book.

The only solution is to split the *authors* table again and live without the *titleID* column. The information as to which book belongs to which author must be specified in yet a third table. These three tables are shown in Tables 5-5 through 5-7.

Table 5-5. title *table: second normal form*

authorID	titleID	author		
1	Linux	Addison-Wesley	2000	
2	Definitive Guide . . .	Apress	2000	
3	Client/Server . . .	Addison-Wesley	1997	
4	Web Application . . .	New Riders	2000	

Table 5-6. author *table: second normal form*

authorID	author
1	Kofler, M.
2	Kramer, D.
3	Orfali, R.
4	Harkey, D.
5	Edwards, E.
6	Ratschiller, T.
7	Gerken, T.

Table 5-7. rel_title_author *table: second normal form*

authorID	titleID
1	1
2	1
2	2
3	3
3	4
3	5
4	6
4	7

This is certainly the most difficult and abstract step, probably because a table of the form *rel_title_author* has no real-world content. Such a table would be completely unsuited for unautomated management. But then, computers are another matter altogether, being totally without consciousness, regardless of what the nuttier cognitive scientists have to say.

Once a computer has been provided with a suitable program, such as MySQL, it has no trouble at all processing such data. Suppose you would like to obtain a list of all authors of the book *Client/Server* . . . . MySQL would first look in the *title* table to find out what *titleID* number is associated with this book. Then it would search in the *rel_title_author* table for data records containing this number. The associated *authorID* numbers then lead to the names of the authors.

> **REMARK** *It may have occurred to you to ask why in the* rel_title_author *table there is no* ID *column, say,* rel_title_author_ID. *Usually, such a column is omitted, since the combination of* titleID *and* authorID *is already an optimal primary key. (Relational database systems permit such primary keys, those made up of several columns.)*

Third Normal Form

The third normal form has a single rule, and here it is:

- Columns that are not directly related to the primary key must be eliminated (that is, transplanted into a table of their own).

In the example under consideration the column *publisher* appears in the *title* table. The set of publishers and the set of book titles are independent of one another and therefore should be separated. Of course, it should be noted that each title must be related to the information as to the publisher of that title, but it is not necessary that the entire name of the publisher be given. A foreign key (that is, a reference, a pointer, a link) suffices. See Tables 5-8 and 5-9.

Table 5-8. title *table: third normal form*

titleID	title	publisherID	year
1	Linux	1	2000
2	Definitive Guide . . .	2	2000
3	Client/Server . . .	1	1997
4	Web Application . . .	3	2000

The *author* and *rel_title_author* tables remain the same in the third normal form. The completed book database now consists of four tables, as indicated in Figure 5-1.

Table 5-9. publisher *table: third normal form*

publisherID	publisher
1	Addison-Wesley
2	Apress
3	New Riders

If we had paid closer attention to the rules for the first normal form (associated data belong together in a table), we could, of course, have saved some of our intermediate attempts. But that would have diminished the pedagogical value of our example. In fact, in practice it often occurs that only when test data are inserted and redundancies are noticed that it becomes clear how the tables need to be subdivided.

The Bestowal of Names

In our example we have attempted to leave the names of fields unaltered from the beginning (before normalization) right through to the end, so as not to cause more confusion than absolutely necessary. The result is not quite optimal, and it would be worth going back and looking at the complete table structure and reconsidering what names should be given to the various fields. The following points provide some tips on the naming of tables and their columns (fields).

- MySQL distinguishes between uppercase and lowercase in the naming of tables, but not in the naming of columns (see also Chapter 13). Thus it is important to pay attention to this case sensitivity at least in names of tables.

- Of course, field and table names should be as clear as possible. Field names like *author* and *publisher* are not particularly good role models. First of all, they coincide with table names, which can cause confusion, and second, *name* or *authorsName* or *companyName* would have been more precise.

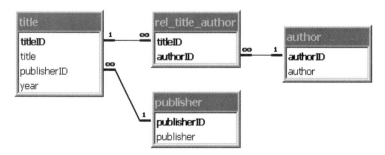

Figure 5-1. The structure of the book database

- A uniform pattern for naming fields will save many errors caused by haste. Whether you prefer *authors_name* or *authorsName*, choose one format and stick with it.

- Likewise, you should consider how to deal with singular and plural forms. In our example I could have named the tables *title*, *author*, and *publisher* just as easily *titles*, *authors*, and *publishers*. There is no rule as to what is right or wrong here, but it is certainly confusing if half of your tables use the singular, and the other half the plural.

- Finally, it is worth thinking about whether field names should provide information about the table. In our example there are fields called *titleID*, *publisherID*, and the like. Fields containing a primary key could as well be called *id*. This would satisfy the uniqueness criterion, since in *SELECT* queries that encompass several tables the table name has often to be provided in any case. (SQL allows the format *tablename.fieldname*.) This could lead to confusing instructions like *WHERE publisher.publisherID = title.publisherID*.

On the other hand, many tables also contain foreign keys, and there the specification of the table name is unavoidable. (In the *title* table, for example, you could not have three columns all labeled *id*.) That would lead to *publisher.id = title.publisherID*, which is also not optimal. (You can see that there is no easy solution that works optimally for all cases.)

POINTER *From* books *another example database was created, namely,* mylibrary. *The design of that database is described later in this chapter. It is better than the* books *database in the sense of the bestowal of names. The database* mylibrary *serves as the basis for many examples in this book.*

More Theory ...

The three normal forms for relational databases were first formulated by the researcher E. F. Codd. They continue to form the basis for a branch of research that is concerned with the formal description of mathematical sets in general and of relational databases in particular.

Depending on what you read, you may come across three additional normal forms, which, however, are of much less significance in practice. The normal forms and their rules are described much more precisely than we have done. However, such descriptions are so teeming with such exotica as entities, attributes, and their ilk that the connection with relational databases can easily be lost.

If you are interested in further details on this topic, then you are encouraged to look into a good book on the subject of database design (see also the suggestions at the beginning of this chapter).

Less Theory ...

I have attempted to present the three first normal forms in as simple and example-oriented a way as possible, but perhaps even that was too theoretical. Actually, the normal forms are not necessarily helpful to database beginners, since the correct interpretation of the rules is often difficult. Here are some rules that will perhaps make those first baby steps less shaky:

- Give yourself sufficient time to develop the database. (If at a later date you have to alter the database design, when the database is already stuffed with real data and there is already client code in existence, changes will take a great deal of time and effort.)

- Avoid giving columns names with numbers, such as *name1*, *name2*, or *object1*, *object2*. There is almost certainly a better solution involving an additional table.

- Immediately supply your database with some test data. Attempt to include as many special cases as possible. If you encounter redundancies, that is, columns in which the same content appears several times, this is usually a hint that you should break your table into two (or more) new tables.

- Try to understand the ideas of relations (see the next section).

- A good database design cannot be obtained before you have had some experience with SQL (see also next chapter). Only when you know and understand the range of SQL queries can you judge the consequences of one or another ways of organizing your data.

- Orient yourself using an example database (from this book or from another book on databases).

> **TIP** *A good example of normalizing a database can be found at the following Internet location:*
>
> `http://www.phpbuilder.com/columns/barry20000731.php3`

Normal Forms: Pro and Con

Normal forms are a means to an end, nothing more and nothing less. Normal forms should be a help in the design of databases, but they cannot replace human reasoning. Furthermore, it is not always a good idea to follow the normal form thoughtlessly, that is, to eliminate every redundancy.

- **Con:** The input of new data, say in a form on a web page, becomes more and more complex as the number of tables among which the data are distributed increases. This is true as much for the end user (who is led from one page to another) as for the programmer.

  Furthermore, for efficiency in queries it is sometimes advantageous to allow for a bit of redundancy. Bringing together data from several tables is usually slower than reading data from a single table. This is true especially for databases that do not change much but that are frequently given complex queries to respond to. (In a special area of databases, the *data warehouses*, redundancy is often deliberately planned for in order to obtain better response times. The purpose of data warehouses is the analysis of complex data according to various criteria. However, MySQL is not a reasonable choice of database system for such tasks anyhow, and therefore we shall not go more deeply into the particular features of this special application area.)

- **Pro:** Redundancy is generally a waste of storage space. You may hold the opinion that in the era of hundred-gigabyte hard drives this is not an issue, but a large database will inevitably become a slow database (at the latest when the database size exceeds the amount of RAM).

  As a rule, databases in normal form offer more flexible query options. (Unfortunately, one usually notices this only when a new form of data query or grouping is required, which often occurs months after the database has become operational.)

Relations

If you want to transform a database into normal form, you have to link a number of tables. These links are called *relations* in database-speak. At bottom, there are three possible relations between two tables:

1 : 1
In a one-to-one relation between two tables, each data record of the first table corresponds to precisely one data record of the second table and vice versa. Such relations are rare, since in such a case the information in both tables could as easily be stored in a single table.

$1:n$

In a one-to-many relation a single record in the first table can correspond to several records in the second table (for example, a vendor can be associated with many orders). The converse may be impossible: A single order cannot, say, be filled by many vendors. Occasionally, one hears of an n-to-1 relation, but this is merely a 1-to-n relation from the opposite point of view.

$n:m$

Here a data record in the first table can be linked to several records in the second table, and vice versa. (For example, several articles can be included in a single order, while the same article may be included in several different orders. Another example is books and their authors. Several authors may have written a single book, while one author may have written several books.)

$1:1$ *Relations*

A one-to-one relation typically comes into being when a table is divided into two tables that use the same primary key. This situation is most easily grasped with the aid of an example. A table containing a corporation's personnel records contains a great deal of information: name, department, date of birth, date of employment, and so on. This table could be split into two tables, called, say, *personnel* and *personnel_extra*, where *personnel* contains the frequently queried and generally accessible data, while *personnel_extra* contains additional, less used and more private, data.

There are two possible reasons for such a division. One is the security aspect: It is simple to protect the table *personal_extra* from general access. (For MySQL this argument is valid only to a limited extent, since access privileges can in any case be set separately for each column of a table.)

The other reason is that of speed. If a table contains many columns, of which only a few are required by most queries, it is more efficient to keep the frequently used columns in a single table. (In the ideal situation the first table would contain exclusively columns of a given size. Such table are more efficient to manage than tables whose columns are of variable size. An overview of the types of tables supported by MySQL can be found later in this chapter.)

The significant disadvantage of such a separation of tables is the added overhead of ensuring that the tables remain synchronized.

$1:n$ *Relations*

One-to-many relations come into play whenever a particular field of a data record can assume a value of another table. The first table is often called the master table, while the second is called the detail table.

The linkage takes place via key fields. The detail table possesses a primary key. In the master table a foreign key field contains references to the records of the detail table. Here are a few examples:

- The normalization example of the previous section (book database): Here there is a one-to-many relation between the *title* and *publisher* tables. Each book title can be associated with one of n possible publishers. The *title* table is therefore the master table, and the *publisher* table is the detail table. Then *publisher.publisherID* is the primary key of the *publisher* table, while *title.publisherID* is the foreign key of the *title* table (see Figure 5-1).

- A business application containing tables with orders: A table contains data on all processed orders. This is the master table. A possible detail table would a table of customers. For each order there is a foreign key referring to the customer who placed the order.

- Discussion groups containing tables with messages: A table contains data on every contribution to a discussion group in place on the web site (title, text, date, author, group, etc.). Two possible detail tables are a group table with a list of all discussion groups, and an author table with a list of all members of the web site who are allowed to make contributions to a discussion.

- A database containing tables of music CDs: A table contains data on every CD in the collection (title, performer, number of disks, etc.): Two possible detail tables are a table containing a list of performers occurring in the database and a recording label table with a list of recording companies.

> **REMARK**   *Often during the creation of a database one attempts to give the same name to fields of two tables that will later be linked by a relation. This contributes to clarity, but it is not required.*
>
> *The table diagrams in this book (such as shown in Figure 5-1) were created with Microsoft Access. For all of the technical drawbacks that Access offers on account of the file/server architecture vis-à-vis MySQL, the user interface is easy to use. There is hardly a program with which relation diagrams can be so quickly drawn. However, Access has the peculiarity of labeling $1 : n$ diagrams with $1 : \infty$. Here 1 denotes the detail table, while ∞ stands for the master table. Often an arrow is used instead of this nomenclature.*

It is also possible for the primary and foreign keys to be located in the same table. Then a data record in such a table can refer to another record in the same table. This is useful if a hierarchy is to be represented. Here are a few examples:

- A table of personnel, in which each employee record (except for that of the top banana) refers to a field containing that individual's immediate supervisor.

- Discussion groups, with tables with messages, in which each message refers to a field containing the next-higher message in the hierarchy (that is, the one to which the current message is responding).

- A music database, containing tables with different types of music. Each style field refers to a field with the name of the genre of which the current style is a subset (for example, bebop within the category jazz, or string quartet within the category of chamber music; see www.amazon.com).

> **REMARK** *Relations within a table indeed allow for a very simple way to store a hierarchy, but the evaluation of such data is more complicated. For example, the query command* SELECT *does not allow for recursion, which is often necessary for the analysis of hierarchical relations. Consider carefully the types of queries that will be applied to your database before you heedlessly implement complex hierarchies based on internal table references.*
>
> *The database* mylibrary *introduced below provides a concrete example of the representation of hierarchies.*

$n : m$ Relations

For $n : m$ relations it is necessary to add an auxiliary table to the two original tables so that the $n : m$ relation can be reduced to two $1 : n$ relations. Here are some examples:

- Normalization example (book database): Here we have an $n : m$ relation between book titles and authors. The relation is established by means of the *rel_title_author* table.

- Business application, tables with orders: To establish a relation between an order and the articles included in the order, the auxiliary table specifies how many of article x are included in order y.

- College administration, list of exams: To keep track of which student has passed which exam and when and with what grade, it is necessary to have a table that stands between the table of students and the table of exams.

Primary and Foreign Keys

Relations depend intimately on primary and foreign keys. This section provides comprehensive information on these two topics and their application. Alas, we cannot avoid entirely a bit of an excursus into SQL commands, which are not formally introduced until the end of this chapter and the chapter following.

Primary Key

The job of the primary key is to locate, as fast as possible, a particular data record in a table (for example, to locate the record with *id=314159* from a table of a million records). This operation must be carried out whenever data from several tables are assembled—in short, very often indeed.

With most database systems, including MySQL, it is also permitted to have primary keys that are formed from several fields of a table. Whether it is a single field or several that serve as primary key, the following properties should be satisfied:

- The primary key must be unique. It is not permitted that two records have the same content in their primary key field.

- The primary key should be compact, and there are two reasons for this: First, for the primary key it is necessary to maintain an index (the primary index) to maximize the speed of search (e.g., for *id=314159*). The more compact the primary field key, the more efficient the management of this index. Therefore, an integer is more suitable than a character string of variable length.

  Second, the content of the primary key field is used as a foreign key in other tables, and there as well it is efficient to have the foreign key as compact as possible. (Relations between tables are established not least to avoid wasted space on account of redundancies. This makes sense only if the use of key fields doesn't take up even more space.)

With most database systems it has become standard practice to use a 32- or 64-bit integer as primary key field, generated automatically in sequence (1, 2, 3, ...) by the database system. Thus neither the programmer nor the user need be concerned how a new and unique primary key value is to be found for each new record.

In MySQL such fields are declared as follows:

```
CREATE TABLE publisher
  (publisherID INT NOT NULL AUTO_INCREMENT,
  othercolumns ... ,
  PRIMARY KEY (publisherID))
```

If we translate from SQL into English, what we have is this: The field *publisherID* is not permitted to contain *NULL*. Its contents are generated by the database (unless another value is explicitly inserted there). The field functions as a primary key; that is, MySQL creates an auxiliary index file to enable rapid search. Simultaneously, it is thereby ensured that the *publisherID* value is unique when new records are input (even if a particular *publisherID* is specified in the *INSERT* command.

For tables in which one expects to make many new entries or changes, one should usually use *BIGINT* (64-bit integer) instead of *INT* (32 bits).

> **REMARK** *The name of the primary key field plays no role. In this book we usually use* id *or* tablenameID. *Often, you will see combinations with* no *or* nr *(for "number") as, for example, in* customerNr.

Foreign Key

The task of the foreign key field is to refer to a record in the detail table. However, this reference comes into being only when a database query is formulated, for example in the following form:

```
SELECT title.title, publisher.publisher FROM title, publisher
WHERE title.publisherID = publisher.publisherID
ORDER BY title
```

With this an alphabetical list of all book titles is generated, in which the second column gives the publisher of the book. The result would look something like this:

title	*publisher*
Client/Server ...	Addison-Wesley
Definitive Guide ...	Apress
Linux	Addison-Wesley
Web Application ...	New Riders

Decisive here is the clause *WHERE title.publisherID = publisher.publisherID*. It is here that the link between the tables is created.

On the other hand, in the declaration of a table the foreign key plays no particular role. For MySQL a foreign key field is just another ordinary table field. There are no particular key words that must be employed. In particular, no index is necessary (there is practically never a search to find the contents of the foreign key). Of course, you would not be permitted to supply the attribute *AUTO_INCREMENT*. After all, you want to specify yourself the record to which the field refers. You need to take care, though, that the foreign key field is of the same data type as the type of the primary key field. Otherwise, the evaluation of the *WHERE* condition can be very slow.

```
CREATE TABLE title
  (othercolumns ... ,
  publisherID INT NOT NULL)
```

Whether you specify the attribute *NOT NULL* depends on the context. In most cases *NOT NULL* is to be recommended in order to avoid at the outset the occurrence of incomplete data. However, if you wish to allow, for example, that in the book database a book could be entered that had no publisher, then you should do without *NOT NULL*.

Referential Integrity

If you delete the author *Kofler* from the *author* table in the example of the normalized database (see Tables 5-6 through 5-9 and Figure 5-1), you will encounter problems in many SQL queries that access the books *Linux* and *Definitive Guide*. The *authorID* number 1 specified in the *rel_title_author* table no longer exists in the *author* table. In database language one would put it like this: The referential integrity of the database has been damaged.

As a database developer it is your responsibility to see that such events cannot happen. Therefore, before deleting a data record you must always check whether there exists a reference to the record in question in another table.

Since one cannot always rely on programmers (and databases often must be altered by hand), many databases have rules for maintaining referential integrity. Such rules test at every change in the database whether any cross references between tables are affected. Depending on the declaration of the foreign key there are then two possible consequences: Either the operation will simply not be executed (error message), or all affected records in dependent tables are deleted as well. Which modus operandi is to be preferred depends on the data themselves.

Under MySQL this point is currently moot, since MySQL does not yet concern itself with referential integrity. But one may hope that this functionality will someday arrive. Therefore (and also to achieve ANSI compatibility to the extent possible), the required SQL key words are already provided.

If MySQL happens to have mastered referential integrity by the time you are holding this book in your hands, then you may presumably declare foreign key fields like this:

```
CREATE TABLE title
  (column1, column2, ... ,
    publisherID INT NOT NULL,
    FOREIGN KEY (publisherID)
      REFERENCES publisher (publisherID) [options]
  )
```

This means that *title.publisherID* is a primary key that refers to *publisher.publisherID*. Possible options are *RESTRICT* and *ON DELETE CASCADE*. They specify how the database system is to respond to possible damage to its referential integrity.

Moreover, this instruction will now be correctly executed; the *FOREIGN KEY* information is ignored, however, and currently not even saved. (At least this latter should change soon: Even if MySQL does not concern itself with maintaining referential integrity, the corresponding table declarations should be maintained. This would be particularly practical for programs for formulating SQL queries and for graphical user interfaces, which then would know how tables are linked with one another.)

Other Indexes

POINTER *The primary index, which is inseparably bound to the primary key, is a special case of an index. Indexes always have the task of speeding up searching and sorting in tables by particular columns. Other indexes supported by MySQL are introduced later in the chapter.*

MySQL Data Types

Now that we have dealt with the first issue in database design, dividing the data among several tables in the most sensible way, in this section we go a level deeper. Here you will find information about the data types that MySQL provides for every field (every column). Should a character string stored in a field be of fixed or variable length? Should currency amounts be stored as fixed-point or floating-point numbers? How are binary objects handled?

This section also deals in part with the attributes that can be specified in the definition of columns to give a supplementary definition to a data type.

POINTER *This section describes the data types, but not the* CREATE TABLE *command, with which tables are actually created. Information on how tables can be created, that is, how the database, having been designed, can actually be implemented, can be found later in this chapter.*

Integers: xxxINT(M)

TINYINT	8-bit integer (1 byte)
SMALLINT	16- bit integer (2 bytes)
MEDIUMINT	24- bit integer (3 bytes)
INT, INTEGER	32- bit integer (4 bytes)
BIGINT	64- bit integer (8 bytes)

With the *INT* data type both positive and negative numbers are generally allowed. With the attribute *UNSIGNED* the range can be restricted to the positive integers.

With *TINYINT* numbers between -128 and $+127$ are allowed. With the attribute *UNSIGNED* the range is changed to 0–255. If one attempts to store a value above or below of the given range, MySQL simply replaces the input with the largest or, respectively, smallest permissible value.

Optionally, in the definition of an integer field the desired column width (number of digits) can be specified, such as, for example, *INT(4)*. This parameter is called *M* (for *maximum display size*) in the literature. It assists MySQL as well as various user interfaces in presenting query results in a readable format.

REMARK *Note that with the* INT *data types the* M *restricts neither the allowable range of numbers nor the possible number of digits. In spite of setting* INT(4), *for example, you can still store numbers greater than* 9999. *However, in certain rare cases (such as in complex queries for the evaluation of which MySQL constructs a temporary table) the numerical values in the temporary tables can be truncated, with incorrect results as a consequence.*

With the attribute *AUTO_INCREMENT* you can achieve that MySQL automatically inserts a number that is 1 larger than the currently largest value in the column when a new record is created for the field in question. However, this attribute is permitted only when the attribute *PRIMARY KEY* or *UNIQUE* is used as well. This condition determines the typical application of *AUTO_INCREMENT*: It is used mostly in the definition of fields that are to serve as the primary key for a table.

The automatic generation of an ID value functions only when in inserting a new data record a specific value or *NULL* is not specified. However, it is possible to generate a new data record with a specific ID value, provided that the value in question is not already in use.

Floating-Point Numbers: FLOAT(M,D) and DOUBLE(M,D)

FLOAT	floating-point number, 8-place precision (4 bytes)
DOUBLE	floating-point number, 16-place precision (8 bytes)
REAL	Synonym for *DOUBLE*

Since version 3.23 of MySQL the types *FLOAT* and *DOUBLE* correspond to the IEEE numerical types for single and double precision that are available in many programming languages.

Optionally, the number of digits in *FLOAT* and *DOUBLE* values can be set with the two parameters M and D. In that case, M specifies the number of digits before the decimal point, while D gives the number of places after the decimal point.

The parameter M does no more than assist in the formatting of numbers; it does not limit the permissible range of numbers. On the other hand, D has the effect of rounding numbers when they are stored. For example, if you attempt to save the number 123456.789877 in a field with the attribute *DOUBLE(6,3)*, the number stored will, in fact, be 123456.790.

> **REMARK** *MySQL expects floating-point numbers in international notation, that is, with a decimal point, and not a comma (which is used in a number of European countries). Results of queries are always returned in this notation, and very large or very small values are expressed in scientific notation (e.g., 1.2345678901279e+017).*
>
> *If you have your heart set on formatting floating-point numbers differently, you will have either to employ the function* FORMAT *in your SQL queries (though this function is of use only in the thousands groupings) or to carry out your formatting in the client programming language (that is, in PHP, Perl, etc.).*

Fixed-Point Numbers: DECIMAL(P, S)

DECIMAL(p, s)	fixed-point number, saved as a character string; arbitrary number of digits (one byte per digit + 2 bytes overhead)
NUMERIC, DEC	synonym for *DECIMAL*

The integer type *DECIMAL* is recommended when rounding errors caused by the internal representation of numbers as *FLOAT* or *DOUBLE* are unacceptable, perhaps with currency values. Since the numbers are stored as character strings, the storage requirement is much greater. At the same time, the possible range of values is smaller, since exponential notation is ruled out.

The two parameters *P* and *S* specify the total number of digits (*precision*) and, respectively, the number of digits after the decimal point (*scale*). The range in the case of *DECIMAL(6,3)* is from 9999.999 to −999.999. This bizarre range results from the apparent fact that six places are reserved for the number plus an additional place for the decimal point. When the number is positive, the place for the decimal point can be used to store another digit. If *P* and *S* are not specified, then MySQL automatically uses $(10, 0)$, with the result that positive integers with eleven digits and negative integers with ten digits can be stored.

Date and Time: DATE, TIME, and DATETIME

DATE	date in the form '2001-12-31', range 1000-01-01 to 9999-12-31 (3 bytes)
TIME	time in the form '23:59:59', range $\pm 838 : 59 : 59$ (3 bytes)
DATETIME	combination of *DATE* and *TIME* in the form '2001-12-31 23:59:59' (8 bytes)
YEAR	year 1900–2155 (1 byte)

With the *DATE* and *DATETIME* data types only a limited amount of type checking takes place. Values between 0 and 12 for months, and between 0 and 31 for days, are generally allowed. However, it is the responsibility of the client program to provide correct data. (For example, 0 is a permissible value for a month or day, in order to provide the possibility of storing incomplete or unknown data.) As for the question that may have occurred to you—Why is it that *DATETIME* requires eight bytes, while *DATE* and *TIME* each require only three bytes?—the answer is that I have no idea.

MySQL returns results of queries in the form 2001-12-31. However, with *INSERT* and *UPDATE* it manages to deal with other formats, provided that the order year/month/day is adhered to and the values are numeric. If the year is given as a two-digit number, then the following interpretation is made: 70–99 becomes 1970–1999, while 00–69 becomes 2000–2069.

If query results are to be specially formatted, there are several MySQL functions available for processing date and time values. The most flexible of these is *DATE_FORMAT*, whose application is demonstrated in the following example:

```
SELECT DATE_FORMAT(birthdate, '%Y %M %e') FROM students
2000   September 3
2000   October 25
 ...
```

Time of the Most Recent Change: TIMESTAMP(M)

TIMESTAMP	date and time in the form 20011231325959 for times between 1970 and 2038 (4 bytes)

Among the data types for date and time, *TIMESTAMP* plays a particular role. Fields of this type are automatically updated whenever the record is altered, thereby reflecting the time of the last change. Fields of type *TIMESTAMP* are therefore usually employed only for internal management, not for the storage of "real" data, though such is possible.

For the automatic *TIMESTAMP* updating to function, either no explicit value is assigned to the field, or else the value *NULL*. In both cases MySQL itself inserts the current time.

In the declaration of a *TIMESTAMP* column the desired column width is specified. The *TIMESTAMP* values that then result from queries will be truncated. (In the case of $M = 8$, for example, the result will be a date without the time). Internally, however, the values continue to be stored in their complete form.

REMARK *Many database operations with particular client libraries (for example, with MyODBC) function only when each table of the database displays a* TIMESTAMP *column. The time of the last update is often needed in the internal administration of data.*

Character Strings

CHAR(n)	character string with specified length, maximum 255 characters (n bytes).
VARCHAR(n)	character string with variable length, maximum n characters ($n < 256$). Storage requirement: one byte per character (actual length) + 1.
TINYTEXT	character string with variable length, maximum 255 characters ($n + 1$ bytes).
TEXT	character string with variable length, maximum $2^{16} - 1$ characters ($n + 2$ bytes).
MEDIUMTEXT	character string with variable length, maximum $2^{24} - 1$ characters ($n + 3$ bytes).
LONGTEXT	character string with variable length, maximum $2^{32} - 1$ characters ($n + 4$ bytes).

With *CHAR* the length of a character string is strictly specified. For example, *CHAR(20)* demands 20 bytes in each record, regardless of the length of the character string actually stored. (Blank characters at the beginning of a character string are eliminated before storage. Short character string are extended with blanks. These blank characters are automatically deleted when the data are read out, with the result that is impossible to store a character string that actually has blank characters at the end.)

In contrast, the length of a character string of type *VARCHAR* or one of the four *TEXT* types is variable. The storage requirement depends on the actual length of the character string.

Although *VARCHAR* and *TINYTEXT*, both of which can accept a character string up to length 255 characters, at first glance seem equivalent, there are, in fact, several features that distinguish one from the other:

- The maximum number of characters in *VARCHAR* columns must be specified (in the range 0 to 255) when the table is declared. Character strings that are too long will be unceremoniously, without warning, truncated when they are stored.

  In contrast, with *xxxTEXT* columns one cannot specify a maximal length. (The only limit is the maximal length of the particular text type.)

- In *VARCHAR* columns, as with *CHAR* columns, blank characters are deleted from the beginning of a character string. (This behavior is ANSI compliant only for *CHAR* columns, not for *VARCHAR* columns. This behavior may change in future versions of MySQL.)

With *xxxTEXT* columns character strings are stored exactly as they are input.

- In MySQL 3.22 only *VARCHAR* columns can be indexed (and not *xxxTEXT* columns). This restriction was lifted in MySQL 3.23.

Columns of type *TEXT* can optionally be given the attribute *BINARY*. They then behave essentially like *BLOB* columns (see below). The attribute *BINARY* can be useful when you store text (and not binary objects): What you achieve is that in sorting it is exclusively the binary code of the characters that is considered (and not a particular sorting table). Thus case distinction is made (which otherwise would not be the case). The internal management of binary character strings is simpler and therefore faster than is the case with garden-variety character strings.

> **REMARK** *MySQL currently provides only for character strings employing an 8-bit character set. For such character sets there are numerous sorting tables available that can be selected at compilation of MySQL as well as at the startup of the server.*
>
> *Unicode character strings or other character sets in which characters are coded in several bytes are currently not supported directly. Nonetheless, there are several sorting tables for multibyte character sets available (see the chapter "MySQL Server Functions" in the MySQL documentation). Unicode support is planned for future versions of MySQL.*

Binary Data

TINYBLOB	binary data, variable length, max 255 bytes.
BLOB	binary data, variable length, max $2^{16} - 1$ bytes.
MEDIUMBLOB	binary data, variable length, max $2^{24} - 1$ bytes.
LONGBLOB	binary data, variable length, max $2^{32} - 1$ bytes.

For the storage of binary data there are four *BLOB* data types at your service, all of which display almost the same properties as the *TEXT* data types. (Recall that "BLOB" is an acronym for "binary large object.") The only difference is that text data are usually compared and sorted in text mode (case-insensitive), while binary data are sorted and compared according to their binary codes. But even this distinction can be eliminated if you provide your *TEXT* fields with the attribute *BINARY*.

> **REMARK** *There is considerable disagreement as to whether large binary objects should even be stored in a database. The alternative would be to store the data (images, for example) in external files and provide links to these files in the database.*
>
> *The advantage to using BLOBs is the resulting integration into the database (more security, simpler backups). The drawback is the usually significant slowdown. It is particularly disadvantageous that large and small data elements—strings, integers, etc.—on the one hand and BLOBs and long texts on the other must be stored all mixed together in a table file. The result is a slowdown in access to all of the data records.*
>
> *Note as well that BLOBs in general can be read only as a whole. That is, it is impossible to read, say, the last 100 kilobytes of an 800 kilobyte BLOB. The entire BLOB must be transmitted.*

Enumerations: ENUM, SET

ENUM	select one from at most 65,535 character strings (1 or 2 bytes)
SET	combine at most 255 character strings (1–8 bytes)

MySQL offers the two special enumeration types *ENUM* and *SET*. With *ENUM* you can manage a list of up to 65,535 character strings, ordered by a running index. Then, in a field, one of these character strings can be selected.

In queries involving comparison of character strings there is no case distinction. In addition to the predefined character strings, an empty character string can also be stored in a field (as well as *NULL*, unless this has been excluded via *NOT NULL*).

Such a field is then handled like any other character string field. The following commands show how a table with an *ENUM* enumeration is generated and used. In the field *color* of the table *testenum* one of five predefined colors can be stored.

```
CREATE TABLE testenum
  (color ENUM ('red', 'green', 'blue', 'black', 'white'))
INSERT testenum VALUES ('red')
SELECT * FROM testenum WHERE color='red'
```

SET uses a similar idea, though here arbitrary combinations are possible. Internally, the character strings are ordered by powers of 2 (1, 2, 4, 8, etc.), so that a bitwise combination is possible. The storage requirement is correspondingly larger (one bit per character string). At most 63 character strings can be combined (in which case the storage requirement is 8 bytes).

For a combination of several character strings to be stored in one field these must be given separated by commas (and with no blank characters between strings). The order of the strings is irrelevant and is not considered. In query results combinations are always specified in the order in which the set was defined.

```
CREATE TABLE testset
  (fontattr SET ('bold', 'italic', 'underlined'))
INSERT testset VALUES ('bold,italic')
```

In queries with the operator "=" an exact comparison is made of the entire combination. The result is that only those records are returned for which the combination corresponds exactly. Thus if in *testset* only the above-inserted record is stored with *'bold,italic'*, then the following query returns no result:

```
SELECT * FROM testset WHERE fontattr='italic'
```

In order to locate records in which an attribute has been set (regardless of its combination with other attributes), the MySQL function *FIND_IN_SET* can be used. This function returns the position of the sought character string within the set (in our example, 1 if *'bold'* is found, 2 for *'italic'*, etc.):

```
SELECT * FROM testset WHERE FIND_IN_SET('italic', fontattr)>0
```

> **TIP** ENUM *and* SET *values are represented internally as integers, not as character strings. If you wish to determine the internally stored value via a query, simply use* SELECT x+0 FROM table, *where* x *is the column name of the* ENUM *or* SET *column. It is also permitted to store numeric values with* INSERT *and* UPDATE *commands.*

> **REMARK** *The contents of* ENUM *and* SET *fields are not alphabetically sorted, but are maintained in the order in which the character strings for selection were defined. The reason for this is that MySQL works internally with numeric values associated to the character strings. If you would like an alphabetic sorting, you must transform the string explicitly into a character string, for example, via* SELECT CONCAT(x) AS xstr . . . ORDER BY xstr.

> **TIP** *If you would like to determine the list of all admissible character strings for an* ENUM *or* SET *field (in a client program, for example), you must summon* DESCRIBE tablename columnname *to your aid. This SQL command returns a table in which the field* columnname *is described. The column* Type *of this table contains the* ENUM *or* SET *definition. In Chapter 8 you will find an example for the evaluation of this information (in the programming language PHP).*

Indexes

If you are searching for a particular record in a table or would like to create a series of data records for an ordered table, MySQL must load *all* the records of the table. The following lines show some of the relevant *SELECT* commands (details to follow in the next chapter):

```
SELECT column1, column2 ... FROM table WHERE column3=12345
SELECT column1, column2 ... FROM table ORDER BY column3
SELECT column1, column2 ... FROM table WHERE column3 LIKE 'Smith%'
SELECT column1, column2 ... FROM table WHERE column3 > 2000
```

With large tables performance will suffer under such everyday queries. Fortunately, there is a simple solution to cure our table's performance anxiety: Simply use an index for the affected column (in the example above, for *column3*).

An index is an auxiliary file with sorted cross references to the data records of a table. (Thus a database index functions like the index in this book. The index saves you the trouble of reading the entire book from one end to the other to find out where a particular topic is covered.)

In principle, an index can be created for each field of a table, up to a maximum of sixteen indexes per table. (MySQL also permits indexes for several fields simultaneously. That makes sense if sorting is frequently carried out according to a combination of fields, as in *country='Austria' AND city='Graz'*).

> **CAUTION** *Indexes are not a panacea! They speed up access to data, but they slow down each alteration in the database. Every time a data record in changed, the index must be updated. This drawback can be ameliorated to some extent with various SQL commands by means of the option* DELAY_KEY_WRITE. *The effect of this option is that the index is not updated with each new or changed record, but only now and then.* DELAY_KEY_WRITE *is useful, for example, when many new records are to be inserted in a table as quickly as possible.*
>
> *A further apparent disadvantage of indexes is that they take up additional space on the hard drive. (Internally, in addition, B trees are used for managing the index entries.)*
>
> *Therefore, use indexes only for those columns that will often be searched and sorted. Indexes remain largely useless when the column contains many identical entries. (In such cases you might ask yourself whether the normalization of the database has been optimally carried out.)*

Types of Index

All indexes are not alike, and in this section we discuss the various types of indexes.

Ordinary Index

The only task of an ordinary index (defined via the key word *INDEX*) is to speed up access to data.

> **TIP** *Index only those columns that you require in conditions (*WHERE column= . . . *) or for sorting (*ORDER BY column*). Index, if possible, columns with compact data (for example, integers). Do not index columns that contain many identical values. (For example, it makes little sense to index a column with 0/1 or Y/N values.)*

Restrictions

MySQL cannot use indexes where inequality operators are used (*WHERE column
!=* . . .).

Likewise, indexes cannot be used for comparisons where the contents of the
column are processed by a function (*WHERE DAY(column)=* . . .).

With *JOIN* operations (that is, in uniting data from various tables) indexes are
of use only when primary and foreign keys refer to the same data type.

If the comparison operators *LIKE* and *REGEXP* are used, an index is of use
only when there is no wild card at the beginning of the search pattern. With *LIKE*
'abc%' an index is of use, but with *LIKE '%abc'* it is not.

Finally, indexes are used with *ORDER BY* operations only if the records do not
have to be previously selected by other criteria. (Unfortunately, an index rarely
helps to speed up *ORDER BY* with queries in which the records are taken from
several tables.)

Unique Index

With an ordinary index it is allowed for several data records in the indexed field to
refer to the same value. (In a table of personnel, for example, the same name can
appear twice, even though it refers to two distinct individuals.)

When it is clear from context that a column contains unique values,
you should then define an index with the key word *UNIQUE*. This has two
consequences. One is that MySQL has an easier time managing the index; that is,
the index is more efficient. The other is that MySQL ensures that no new record
is added if there is already another record that refers to the same value in the
indexed field. (Often, a *UNIQUE* index is defined for this reason alone, that is, not
for access optimization, but to avoid duplication.)

Primary Index

The primary index mentioned again and again in this chapter is nothing more
than an ordinary *UNIQUE* index. The only peculiarity is that the index has the
name *PRIMARY*. (You can tell that a primary index is an ordinary index because
MySQL uses the first *UNIQUE* index of a table as a substitute for the missing
primary index.)

Combined Indexes

An index can cover several columns, as in *INDEX(columnA, columnB)*. A peculiarity of such indexes is that MySQL can selectively use such an index. Thus when a query requires an index for *columnA* only, the combined index for *INDEX(columnA, columnB)* can be used. This holds, however, only for partial indexes at the beginning of the series. For instance, *INDEX(A, B, C)* can be used as index for *A* or *(A, B)*, but not as index for *B* or *C* or *(B,C)*.

Limits on the Index Length

In the definition of an index for *CHAR* and *VARCHAR* columns you can limit an index to a particular number of characters (which must be smaller than the maximum number of characters allowed in this field). The consequence is that the resulting index file is smaller and its evaluation quicker than otherwise. In most applications, that is, with character strings representing names, perhaps ten to fifteen characters altogether suffice to reduce the search set to a few data records.

With *BLOB* and *TEXT* columns you must institute this restriction, where MySQL permits a maximal index length of 255 characters.

Full-Text Index

An ordinary index for text fields helps only in the search for character strings that stand at the beginning of the field (that is, whose initial letters are known). On the other hand, if you store texts in fields that consist of several, or possibly very many, words, an ordinary index is useless. The search must be formulated in the form *LIKE '%word%'*, which for MySQL is rather complex and with large data sets leads to long response times.

In such cases it helps to use a full-text index. (This is a relatively new addition to MySQL, which was first available in version 3.23.23.) With this type of index MySQL creates a list of all words that appear in the text. In *SELECT* queries one can search for records that contain one or more words. This is the query syntax:

```
SELECT * FROM table
WHERE MATCH(column1, column2) AGAINST('word1', 'word2', 'word3')
```

Then all records will be found for which the words *word1*, *word2*, and *word3* appear in the columns *column1* and *column2*.

> **POINTER** *The use of a full-text index and the associated search and sort possibilities are among the most advanced MySQL techniques and will not be discussed in detail until Chapter 12.*

Query and Index Optimization

Realistic performance estimates can be made only when the database has been filled with a sufficient quantity of test data. A test database with several hundred data records will usually be located entirely in RAM after the first three queries, and all queries will be answered quickly with or without an index. Things become interesting when tables contain well over 1000 records and when the entire size of the database is larger than the total RAM of the MySQL server.

In making the decision as to which columns should be provided with indexes, one may sometimes obtain some assistance from the command *EXPLAIN SELECT*. This is simply an ordinary *SELECT* command prefixed with the key word *EXPLAIN*. Instead of the *SELECT* being simply executed, MySQL places information in a table as to how the query was executed and which indexes (to the extent that they exist) came into play.

Here are some pointers for interpreting the table created by *EXPLAIN*. In the first column appear the names of the tables in the order in which they were read from the database. The column *type* specifies how the table is linked to the other tables (*JOIN*). This functions most efficiently (i.e., quickly) with the type *system*, while more costly are the types *const*, *eq_ref*, *ref*, *range*, *index*, and *ALL* (*ALL* means that for each record in the next higher table in the hierarchy all records of this table must be read. That can usually be prevented with an index. Further information on all *JOIN* types can by found in the MySQL documentation.)

The column *possible_keys* specifies which indexes MySQL can access in the search for data records. The column *key* specifies which index MySQL has actually chosen. The length of the index in bytes is given by *key_len*. For example, with an index for an *INTEGER* column the number of bytes is 4. Information on how many parts of a multipart index are used is also given by *key_len*. As a rule, the smaller *key_len* is, the better (that is, the faster).

The column *ref* specifies the column of a second table with which the linkage was made, while *rows* contains an estimate of how many records MySQL expects to read in order to execute the entire query. The product of all the numbers in the *rows* column allows one to draw a conclusion as to how many combinations arise from the query.

Finally, the column *extra* provides additional information on the *JOIN* operation, for example *using temporary* when MySQL must create a temporary table in executing a query.

POINTER   *Though the information proffered by* EXPLAIN *is often useful, the interpretation requires a certain amount of MySQL and database experience. You will find further information in the MySQL documentation.*

Example 1

This query produces an unordered list of all books with all their authors. All *ID* columns are equipped with primary indexes.

```
USE mylibrary
EXPLAIN SELECT * FROM titles, rel_title_author, authors
  WHERE rel_title_author.authID = authors.authID
  AND rel_title_author.titleID = titles.titleID
```

table	type	possible_key	key_len	ref	rows
titles	ALL	PRIMARY		23	
rel_title_author	ref	PRIMARY PRIMARY	4	titles.titleID	1
authors	eq_ref	PRIMARY PRIMARY	4	rel_title_author.authID	1

This means that first all records from the *titles* table are read, without using an index. For *titles.titleID* there is, in fact, an index, but since the query considers all records in any case, the index is not used. Then with the help of the primary indexes of *rel_title_author* and *authors* the links to the two other tables are made. The tables are thus optimally indexed, and for each part of the query there are indexes available.

Example 2

Here the query produces a list of all books (together with their authors) that have been published by a particular publisher. The list is ordered by book title. Again, all *ID* columns are equipped with indexes. Furthermore, in the *titles* table *title* and *publID* are indexed.

```
EXPLAIN SELECT title, authName
FROM titles, rel_title_author, authors
WHERE titles.publID=1
  AND titles.titleID = rel_title_author.titleID
  AND authors.authID = rel_title_author.authID
ORDER BY title
```

table	type	key	key_len	ref	rows	Extra
titles	ref	publID	5	const	9	where used; Using filesort
rel_title_author	ref	PRIMARY	4	titles.titleID	1	Using index
authors	eq_ref	PRIMARY	4	rel_title_author. authID	1	

To save space in this example we have not shown the column *possible_keys*. The interpretation is this: The tables are optimally indexed; that is, for each part of the query there are indexes available. It is interesting that the title list (*ORDER BY title*) is apparently sorted externally, although there is an index for the *title* column as well. The reason for this is perhaps that the *title* records are first selected in accordance with the condition *publID=1* and the *title* index can then no longer be applied.

Example 3

This example uses the same *SELECT* query as does Example 2, but it assumes that *titles.publID* does not have an index. The result is that now all records of the *titles* table must be read, and no index can be used.

table	type	key	key_len	ref	rows	Extra
titles	ALL				23	where used; Using filesort
rel_title_author	ref	PRIMARY	4	titles.titleID	1	Using index
authors	eq_ref	PRIMARY	4	rel_title_author. authID	1	

MySQL Table Types

Up till now we have tacitly assumed that all tables have been set up as MyISAM tables. That has been the default behavior since MySQL 3.23, and it holds automatically if you do not explicitly demand a different type of table when the table is generated. This section provides a brief overview of the different types of table recognized by MySQL, their properties, and when they should be used.

- **MyISAM—Static:** These tables are used when all columns of the table have fixed, predetermined size. Access in such tables is particularly efficient. This is true even if the table is frequently changed (that is, when there are many *INSERT, UPDATE*, and *DELETE* commands). Moreover, data security is quite high, since in the case of corrupted files or other problems it is relatively easy to extract records.

- **MyISAM—Dynamic:** If in the declaration of a table there is also only a single *VARCHAR, xxxTEXT*, or *xxxBLOB* field, then MySQL automatically selects this table type. The significant advantage over the static MyISAM variant is that the space requirement is usually significantly less: Character strings and binary objects require space commensurate with their actual size (plus a few bytes overhead).

  However, it is a fact that data records are not all the same size. If records are later altered, then their location within the database file may have to change. In the old place there appears a hole in the database file. Moreover, it is possible that the fields of a record are not all stored within a contiguous block within the database file, but in various locations. All of this results in increasingly longer access times as the edited table becomes more and more fragmented, unless an *OPTIMIZE TABLE* or an optimization program is executed every now and then (myisamchk; see Chapter 11).

- **MyISAM—Compressed:** Both dynamic and static MyISAM tables can be compressed with the auxiliary program myisamchk. This usually results in a shrinkage of the storage requirement for the table to less than one-half the original amount (depending on the contents of the table). To be sure, thereafter every data record must be decompressed when it is read, but it is still possible under some conditions that access to the table is nevertheless faster, particularly with a combination of a slow hard drive and fast processor.

  The decisive drawback of compressed MyISAM tables is that they cannot be changed (that is, they are read-only tables).

- **ISAM:** The ISAM table type is the precursor of MyISAM. ISAM tables exhibit a host of disadvantages with respect to MyISAM tables. Perhaps the most significant of these is that the resulting files are not independent of the operating system. Thus in general, an ISAM table that was generated by MySQL under operating system x cannot be used under operating system y. (Instead, you must use mysqldump and mysql to transfer it to the new operating system.) In general, there is no longer any good reason to use ISAM tables (unless, perhaps, you are using an antiquated version of MySQL).

- **BDB (Berkeley_DB):** The most significant feature of BDB tables is that they permit transactions. It is only when BDB tables are used that the SQL commands *BEGIN*, *COMMIT*, and *ROLLBACK* are available.

  However, this advantage brings with it a greater cost in management overhead; that is, access to and changes in BDB tables are somewhat slower than with MyISAM tables. A further significant drawback is that BDB tables have existed for only a relatively brief period (since version 3.23.15). Thus this table type is not uniformly stable and mature. In addition, certain MySQL functions such as full-text index currently are not available for MyISAM tables.

  Moreover, BDB tables differ from MyISAM tables in a number of small details. Here are two of them: BDB tables must have a primary key (this is, of course, usually to be recommended with MyISAM tables, but it is not required). *SHOW TABLE STATUS* returns less information with BDB tables than with MyISAM tables.

  Practical information on the use of BDB tables and transaction commands appears in Chapter 12.

- **InnoDB:** The InnoDB table type is even newer than the type BDB: The source code has been available since version 3.23.34, while a precompiled binary version (MySQL-Max) has existed since version 3.23.37. The concerns about stability that apply to BDB hold to an even greater extent for InnoDb.

  InnoDB tables support transactions, as do BDB tables. Moreover, a locking concept similar to the one for Oracle databases is used (*row-level locking*). One may generally expect from InnoDB tables, once it is mature, not only a high degree of data security, but also increased speed. Further information on the use of this table type can be found in Chapter 12.

- **Gemini:** The Gemini table type just became available in beta version as this book was being readied for printing. According to information from the MySQL development team, the introduction of this table type is planned for one of the 3.23.n versions. Like InnoDB tables, Gemini tables will support transactions and row-level locking.

- **MERGE:** This table type is also rather new (available since version 3.23.25). These are essentially a virtual union of several existing MyISAM tables all of which exhibit identical column definitions. A MERGE table composed of several tables can have some advantages over a single, large, MyISAM table, such as a higher read speed (if the tables are distributed over several hard drives) or a circumvention of the maximum file size in a number of operating systems (for example, 2 gigabytes for Linux; 2.2 for 32-bit processors). Among the disadvantages are that it is impossible to insert data records into MERGE tables (that is, *INSERT* does not function). Instead, *INSERT* must be applied to one of the subtables.

- **HEAP:** HEAP tables exist only in RAM (not on the hard drive). They use a *hash index*, which results in particularly fast access to individual data records.

  In comparison to normal tables HEAP tables present a large number of functional restrictions, of which we mention here only the most important: No *xxxTEXT* or *xxxBLOB* data types can be used. Records can be searched only with = or <=> (and not with <, >, <=, >=). *AUTO_INCREMENT* is not supported. Indexes can be set up only for *NOT NULL* columns.

  HEAP tables should be used whenever relatively small data sets are to be managed with maximal speed. Since HEAP tables are stored exclusively in RAM, they disappear as soon as MySQL is terminated. The maximum size of a HEAP table is determined by the parameter `max_heap_table_size`, which can be set when MySQL is launched.

Temporary Tables: With most of the table types listed above there exists the possibility of creating a table on a temporary basis. Such tables are automatically deleted as soon as the link with MySQL is terminated. Furthermore, temporary tables are invisible to other MySQL links (so that it is possible for two users to employ temporary tables with the same name without running into trouble).

Temporary tables are not a separate table type unto themselves, but rather a variant of the types that we have been describing. Temporary tables are often created automatically by MySQL in order to assist in the execution of *SELECT* queries.

Temporary tables are not stored in the same directory as the other MySQL tables, but in a special temporary directory (under Windows it is usually called `C:\Windows\Temp`, while under Unix it is generally `/tmp` or `/var/tmp` or `/usr/tmp`). The directory can be set at MySQL launch.

> **REMARK** *Often, temporary tables are generated that are of type* HEAP. *However, this is not a necessary combination. Note, however, that nontemporary* HEAP *tables are visible to all MySQL users until they are deleted.*

Table Files

MySQL databases are stored as directories, and tables are stored as files. (The location for the database directories can be prescribed at MySQL launch. Under

Unix/Linux `/var/lib/mysql` is often used, while under Windows it is usually `\Program Files\mysql\data`.)

The following list presents the most important file identifiers that are used for table files:

`tablename.frm`	table structure (data type of columns, indexes, etc.)
`tablename.MYD`	MyISAM table files
`tablename.MYI`	MyISAM indexes (all indexes of the table)
`tablename.db`	BDB tables (data and all indexes)
`tablename.gmd`	Gemini table data
`tablename.gmi`	Gemini indexes (all indexes for the table)

InnoDB tables are stored in special files without a particular identifier. Thus various tables from different databases are housed in a single file. The name and location of the InnoDB files can be determined from the MySQL configuration file `my.cnf`.

Creating Databases, Tables, and Indexes

In the course of this chapter you have learned a great deal about database design. But building castles in the air is one thing, and assembling the plans and materials for real-world construction quite another. We now confront the question of how a database and its tables are actually built. As always, there are several ways of going about this task:

- Genuine SQL pros will not shrink before the prospect of doing things the old-fashioned way and typing in a host of *CREATE TABLE* commands in `mysql`. However, the complicated syntax of this command is not compatible with the creative character of the design process. Nonetheless, SQL commands are often the only way to achieve certain features of tables.

- For beginners in the wonderful world of database construction (and for all who do not enjoy making their lives more complicated than necessary) the graphical user interfaces offer more convenience in the development of a database. Some of these programs (for example, phpMyAdmin and kSQL) have been introduced in the previous chapter.

In this chapter only the *CREATE TABLE* variant is considered. All of our examples refer to the little book database *books*, which in the portion of this chapter dealing with theory was introduced for the purpose of demonstrating the normalization process.

REMARK   *Regardless of the tool that you choose to work with, before you begin, the question of access rights must be clarified. If MySQL is securely configured and you do not happen to be the MySQL administrator, then you are not permitted to create a new database at all.*

The topics of access privileges and security are not dealt with until Chapter 7. If you are responsible for the security of MySQL, then you should probably concern yourself with this issue before you create your new database. If there is an administrator, then please ask him or her to set up an empty database for you and provide you with a user name and password.

POINTER   *This section proceeds on the assumption that the new database will be created on the local computer, which is plausible if one is creating a new application. What happens, then, when a web application will run on the Internet service provider's computer? How do you transport the database from the local computer to that of the ISP? How can you, should the occasion arise, create a new database directly on the ISP's computer? Such questions will be discussed in their own section of Chapter 12.*

POINTER   *There is yet another path to a MySQL database: the conversion of an existing database from another system. Fortunately, there are quite a few converters available, and they can be found at the MySQL web site, which at last sighting was at the following address:*

```
http://www.mysql.com/downloads/contrib.htm
```

In this book only two variants will be considered, namely, conversion of databases in the format of Microsoft Access or of Microsoft SQL Server. This topic is dealt with in Chapter 10.

Creating a Database (CREATE DATABASE)

Before you can create tables for your database, you must first create the database itself. The creation of a database results in an empty directory being created on the hard drive. The following *USE* command makes the new database the default database for all further SQL commands.

```
CREATE DATABASE books
USE books
```

> **REMARK** *The commands given here can be executed, for example, in the MySQL monitor* mysql. *(Please recall that in* mysql *you must follow each command with a semicolon.)*
>
> *A complete syntax reference for the SQL commands introduced here can be found in Chapter 13.*

Creating Tables (CREATE TABLE)

For the four tables of our example database we require four *CREATE TABLE* commands. Each of these commands contains a list of all fields (columns) with the associated data type and attributes. The syntax should be immediately clear. The definition of the primary index is effected with *PRIMARY KEY*, where all columns that are to be included in the index are specified in parentheses. Of interest here is the table *rel_title_author*, in which the primary index spans both columns.

```
CREATE TABLE author (
    authorID     INT                NOT NULL    AUTO_INCREMENT,
    author       VARCHAR(60)        NOT NULL,
    PRIMARY KEY  (authorID))
CREATE TABLE publisher (
    publisherID  INT                NOT NULL    AUTO_INCREMENT,
    publisher    VARCHAR(60)        NOT NULL,
    PRIMARY KEY  (publisherID))
CREATE TABLE rel_title_author (
    titleID      INT                NOT NULL,
    authorID     INT                NOT NULL,
    PRIMARY KEY  (titleID, authorID))
```

```
CREATE TABLE title (
    titleID       INT           NOT NULL   AUTO_INCREMENT,
    title         VARCHAR(120)  NOT NULL,
    publisherID   INT           NOT NULL,
    year          INT           NOT NULL,
    PRIMARY KEY   (titleID))
```

Editing a Table Design (ALTER TABLE)

It is fortunate indeed that you do not have to recreate your database from scratch every time you wish to modify its design, say to add a new column or change the data type or default value of a column. The command *ALTER TABLE* offers sufficient flexibility in most cases. It is also good to know that MySQL is capable in most cases of preserving existing data (even if the data type of a column is changed). Nevertheless, it is a good idea to maintain a backup copy of the table in question.

The following example shows how the maximal number of characters in the *title* column of the *title* table is reduced to 100 characters. (Titles longer than 100 characters will be truncated.) The first line of code shows how to make a backup of the original table (which is a good idea, since we might lose some data if titles are truncated).

```
CREATE TABLE titlebackup SELECT * FROM title
ALTER TABLE title CHANGE title title VARCHAR(100)
NOT NULL
```

Something that might be a bit confusing with our use of the *ALTER TABLE* command is the threefold appearance of the name *title*. The first usage refers to the table, while the second is the name of the column before the change, and the third the new, in this case unchanged, name of the column.

Inserting Data (INSERT)

Normally, data are inserted into the database via a client program (which, it is to be hoped, is convenient and easy to use). Since you, as developer, are responsible in most cases for the code of these programs, it would not hurt for us to take a peek at the *INSERT* command. (Additional commands for inserting, changing, and deleting data can be found in the next chapter.)

```
INSERT INTO author VALUES ( '1', 'Kofler M.')
INSERT INTO author VALUES ('2', 'Kramer D.')
```

```
  ...
INSERT INTO publisher VALUES ('1', 'Addison-Wesley')
INSERT INTO publisher VALUES ('2', 'Apress')
  ...
INSERT INTO title VALUES ('1', 'Linux', '1', '2000')
INSERT INTO title VALUES ('2', 'Definitive Guide to Excel VBA', '2', '2000')
  ...
INSERT INTO rel_title_author VALUES ('1', '1')
INSERT INTO rel_title_author VALUES ('2', '1')
INSERT INTO rel_title_author VALUES ('2', '2')
  ...
```

You can also edit several records at once:

```
INSERT INTO rel_title_author VALUES ('1', '1'), ('2', '1'), ('2', '2'), ...
```

Creating Indexes (CREATE INDEX)

Indexes can be created via the *CREATE TABLE* command or else later with an *ALTER TABLE* or *CREATE INDEX* command. The syntax for describing the index is the same in all three cases. The following three commands show three variants for providing the *title* column of the *title* table with an index. The index received the name *idxtitle*. (Of course, only one of the three commands can be executed. If you try a second command, MySQL will inform you that an index already exists.)

```
CREATE TABLE title (
  titleID ... , title ... , publisherID ... , year ... , PRIMARY KEY ... ,
  INDEX idxtitle (title))
CREATE INDEX idxtitle ON title (title)
ALTER TABLE title ADD INDEX idxtitle (title)
```

SHOW INDEX FROM tablename produces a list of all defined indexes. Existing indexes can be eliminated with *DROP INDEX indexname ON tablename*.

If you wish to reduce the number of significant characters per index in the index to the first 16 characters, the syntax looks like this:

```
ALTER TABLE title ADD INDEX idxtitle (title(16))
```

Example *mylibrary* (Library)

Writers of books frequently not only write books, but read them as well (as do many other individuals who do not write books), and over time, many of these readers acquire a significant collection of books, sometimes so many that they lose track of what's what and what's where. After a hopeless effort at bringing order to the author's domestic library, he created the database *mylibrary*. See Figure 5-2 for an overview of the structure of the *mylibrary* database.

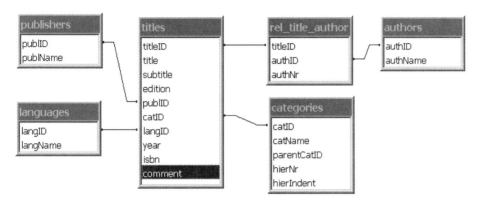

Figure 5-2. Structure of the mylibrary *database*

The main purpose of this database is to store the titles of books together with their authors and publishers in a convenient format. The database will additionally offer the convenient feature of allowing books to be ordered in various categories.

> **TIP** *If you happen to be a victim of the compulsion to collect something, you can use* mylibrary *as a basis for your own database. You should have little trouble in converting this database into one for CDs, MP3 files, stamps, scientific articles, postal and e-mail addresses, Barbie dolls, birthdays and other noteworthy dates, and so on.*

Basic Design

Titles, Authors, and Publishers

Just as in the *books* database, here there are three tables in which book titles, name of authors, and names of publishers are stored: *titles*, *authors*, and *publishers*.

The $n : m$ relation between *titles* and *authors* is created via the table *rel_title_author*. Here the sequence of authors for a given book can be specified in the field *authNr* (that is, the first, second, third, etc., author). This is practical above all if the database is to store the names of scientific publications, where it is not always a good idea to list the authors in alphabetical order. However, *authNr* can be left empty (that is, *NULL*) if you are not interested in such supplemental information.

In general, in the *library* database it is permitted to store the value *NULL* in many of the columns. Thus it is possible to store a book title quickly without bothering to specify the publisher or year of publication. Perfectionists in database design would, of course, frown on such practice, but on the other hand, too many restrictions often lead to the result that data simply do not get catalogued. From this point of view it is practical to allow the publisher, say, to be indicated for some books without it being mandatory that it be given for all.

Categories and Languages

The table *categories* enables the construction of a hierarchical category list in which the books can be ordered. (Details on this table appear in the following section.) The table *languages* contains a list with the languages in which the books have appeared. Thus for each title the language can be stored as well.

Dealing with (Author) Names

In *mylibrary* names are generally stored in a field where the surname must be given first (to take a random example, *Kofler Michael*, and not *Michael Kofler*). This is the usual ordering for sorting by name.

A quite different approach would be to save surnames, given names, and even initials and titles, in separate fields (for example, *firstname*, *lastname*, and perhaps even *middlename*, etc.). Several fields are, of course, more trouble to manage than a single field, but in return a greater flexibility is achieved as to how the name can be displayed. This is important, for example, if the data are to be used for personalizing letters or e-mail messages.

Independent of the internal storage, there is clearly a problem in that many people (myself included, alas) now and again input the surname and given name in the wrong order. One falsely input name will be practically untraceable in the database.

Therefore, it is important that the user interface always show and receive names in a uniform order and that the desired order—best indicated by an example—be shown in the input form. Be sure to label the input fields in a clear and unambiguous way (for example, use "family name" or "surname" and not "last name").

Data Types

All tables are provided with an *AUTO_INCREMENT* column, which also serves as the primary index. Most fields possess the attribute *NOT NULL*. Exceptions are those fields that describe the properties of the title. Thus *NULL* is allowed for *subtitle, edition, publID, catID, langID, year, isbn,* and *comment.*

Column name	Data type
All ID fields	*INT*
authors.authName	*VARCHAR(60)*
categories.catName	*VARCHAR(60)*
categories.hierNr	*INT*
categories.hierIndent	*TINYINT*
languages.langName	*VARCHAR(40)*
publishers.publName	*VARCHAR(60)*
titles.title and *.subtitle*	*VARCHAR(100)*
titles.year	*INT*
titles.edition	*TINYINT*
titles.isbn	*VARCHAR(20)*
titles.comment	*VARCHAR(255)*

Hierarchical Categorization of the Books

The table *categories* helps in ordering books into various categories (technical books, children's books, etc.). To make the *library* more interesting from the point of view of database design, the field *parentCatID* will be represented hierarchically. Here is an example: Figure 5-3 shows how the hierarchy represented in Table 5-10 can be depicted with respect to the database.

> **REMARK**   *In the development of applications* parentCatID=NULL *must be treated as a special case.*

Table 5-10. Database representation of the hierarchy in Figure 5-3

catID	catName	parentCatID
1	Computer books	11
2	Databases	1
3	Programming	1
4	Relational Databases	2
5	Object-oriented databases	2
6	PHP	3
7	Perl	3
8	SQL	2
9	Children's books	11
10	Literature and fiction	11
11	All books	NULL

Hierarchy Problems

Let me state at once that although the representation of such hierarchies looks simple and elegant at first glance, they cause many problems as well. (That this example nonetheless uses hierarchies has, of course, pedagogical purposes: It allows us to demonstrate interesting SQL programming techniques. Even though the representation of hierarchies in this example is somewhat artificial, there are many database applications where the use of hierarchies is unavoidable.)

All books
    Computer books
        Databases
            Object-oriented databases
            Relational Databases
            SQL
        Programming
            Perl
            PHP
    Children's books
    Literature and fiction

Figure 5-3. Example data for the categories *table*

> **POINTER**   *In point of fact, this chapter is supposed to be dealing with database design and not with SQL, but these two topics cannot be cleanly separated. There is no point in creating a super database design if the capabilities of SQL do not suffice to extract the desired data from the database's tables.*
>
> *If you have no experience with SQL, you should dip into the following chapter a bit. Consider the following instructions as a sort of "advanced database design."*

Almost all problems with hierarchies have to do with the fact that SQL does not permit recursive queries:

- With individual queries it is impossible to find all categories lying above a given category in the hierarchy.

  Example: The root category is called *Relational Databases* (*parentCatID=2*). You would like to create a list that contains *Computer Books* → *Databases* → *Relational Databases*.

  With *SELECT * FROM categories WHERE catID=2* you indeed find *Databases*, but not *Computer Books*, which lies two places up the hierarchy. For that you must execute an additional query *SELECT * FROM categories WHERE catID=1*. Of course, this can be accomplished in a loop in the programming language of your choice (Perl, PHP, etc.), but not with a single SQL instruction.

- It is just as difficult to represent the entire table in hierarchical form (as a tree). Again, you must execute a number of queries.

- It is not possible without extra effort to search for all books in a higher category.

  Example: You would like to find all books in the category *Computer Books*.

  With *SELECT * FROM titles WHERE catID=1* you find only those titles directly linked to the category *Computer Books*, but not the titles in the categories *Databases, Relational Databases, Object-oriented databases*, etc. The query must be the following: *SELECT * FROM titles WHERE catID IN (1, 2 . . .)*, where *1, 2 . . .* are the ID numbers of the subordinate categories. The actual problem is to determine these numbers.

- In the relatively simple representation that we have chosen it is not possible to associate the same subcategory with two or more higher-ranking categories.

Example: The programming language *SQL* is linked in the above hierarchy to the higher-ranking category *Databases*. It would be just as logical to have a link to *Programming*. Therefore, it would be optimal to have *SQL* appear as a subcategory of both *Databases* and *Programming*.

- There is the danger of circular references. Such references can, of course, appear only as a result of input error, but where there are human beings who input data (or who write programs), there are certain to be errors. If a circular reference is created, most database programs will find themselves in an infinite loop. The resolution of such problems can be difficult.

None of these problems is insuperable. However, hierarchies often lead to situations in which to answer a relatively simple question involves executing a whole series of SQL queries, and that is often a slow process. Many problems can be avoided by doing without genuine hierarchies (for example, by allowing at most a two-stage hierarchy) or if supplementary information for a simpler resolution of hierarchies is provided in additional columns or tables (see the following section).

Optimization (Efficiency Versus Normalization)

If you have taken to heart the subject of normalization of databases as presented in this chapter, then you know that redundancy is bad. It leads to unnecessary usage of storage space, management issues when changes are made, etc.

Yet there are cases where redundancy is quite consciously sought in order to increase the efficiency of an application. The *mylibrary* database contains many examples of this, which we shall discuss here rather fully.

This section should make clear that database design is a multifaceted subject. There are usually several ways that lead to the same goal, and each of these paths is, in fact, a compromise of one sort or another. Which compromise is best depends largely on the uses to which the database will be put: What types of queries will occur most frequently? Will data be frequently changed?

Authors' Names in the titles Table

The authors' names are stored in the *authors* table in normalized form. However, it will often happen that you wish to obtain a list of book titles, and with each book title you would like to list all of that book's authors, such as in the following form:

Client/Server Survival Guide by Robert Orfali, Dan Harkey, Jeri Edwards
Definitive Guide to Excel VBA by Michael Kofler, David Kramer
Linux by Michael Kofler
Web Application Development with PHP 4.0 by Tobias Ratschiller, Till Gerken

There are now two possible ways of proceeding:

- **Variant 1:** The simplest and thus most often chosen route is first to execute an SQL query to determine the desired list of titles, without the corresponding authors. Then for each title found a further SQL query is formulated to determine all the authors of that title. Now, however, twenty-one SQL queries were necessary to obtain a list with twenty book titles. The following lines show the requisite pseudocode. The bits in pointy brackets cannot be executed in SQL; they must be formulated in a client programming language (Perl, PHP, etc.).

```
SELECT titleID, title FROM titles WHERE ... ⟨for each titleID⟩
  SELECT authName FROM authors, rel_title_author
  WHERE rel_title_author.authID = authors.authID
  AND rel_title_author.titleID = ⟨titleID⟩
  ORDER BY authNR
```

- **Variant 2:** Another possibility is to include all the data in a single query:

```
SELECT titles.titleID, title, authName
FROM titles, rel_title_author, authors
WHERE rel_title_author.titleID = titles.titleID
AND rel_title_author.authID = authors.authID
ORDER BY title, rel_title_author.authNr, authName
```

You thereby obtain, however, a list in which each book title appears as many times as it has authors (see Table 5-11).

Table 5-11. Query result in the mylibrary *database*

titleID	title	authName
3	Client/Server Survival Guide	Edwards E.
3	Client/Server Survival Guide	Harkey D.
3	Client/Server Survival Guide	Orfali R.
2	Definitive Guide to Excel VBA	Kofler Michael
2	Definitive Guide to Excel VBA	Kramer David
1	Linux, 5th ed.	Kofler Michael
9	MySQL & mSQL	King T.
9	MySQL & mSQL	Reese G.
9	MySQL & mSQL	Yarger R.J.
4	Web Application Development with PHP 4.0	Gerken Till
4	Web Application Development with PHP 4.0	Ratschiller Tobias

At this point you can use some client-side code to create the list of books by collecting authors' names for books with the same *titleID* number and displaying the book title only once.

The significant disadvantage of this modus operandi is that it is relatively difficult to represent the results in page format (for example, with twenty titles per page). Of course, you can limit the number of result records in the *SELECT* query with *LIMIT*, but you don't know in advance how many records will be required to obtain twenty titles (since it depends on the number of authors per title).

This problem can be circumvented if first a query is executed by which only the *titleID* values are determined. The second query then uses these *titleID* values. Unfortunately, MySQL does not permit nested *SELECT* queries, and therefore either the *titleID* list must be processed by the client program in the second query (*WHERE titleID IN(x, y, . . .*) or a temporary table must be used.

- **Solution:** From the standpoint of efficiency the second variant is significantly better than the first, but even it is not wholly satisfying. The most efficient solution would be to provide a column *authorsList* in the *titles* table, in which the list of authors is stored for each title.

  Such a column is no substitute for the *authors* table, which will be used and reused (for example, to search for all books on which a particular author has worked, or to store additional information about an author). The column *authorsList* must be updated each time a new title is stored or an old one is changed. It is much more burdensome that now title records must also be updated when changes in the *authors* table are made (such as when a typo in an author's name is corrected): a classical redundancy problem.

  You now have the choice between redundancy and efficiency. Which variant is better for your application depends on the size of the database, whether it will be used primarily in read-only mode for queries or frequently altered, what type of queries will be used most frequently, etc. (In our realization of *mylibrary* we have done without *authorsList*.)

Hierarchical Order in the categories Table

The necessity will continually arise to display the *categories* table in hierarchical representation similar to that of Figure 5-3. As we have already mentioned, such processing of the data is connected either with countless SQL queries or complex client-side code. Both of these are unacceptable if the hierarchical representation is needed frequently (for example, for a list box in a form).

A possible solution is provided by the two additional columns *hierNr* and *hierIndent*. The first of these gives the row number in which the record would be located in a hierarchical representation. (The assumption is that data records are sorted alphabetically by *catName* within a level of the hierarchy.) The second of these two columns determines the level of indentation. In Table 5-12 are displayed for both of these columns the values corresponding to the representation in Figure 5-3.

Table 5-12. categories *table with* hierNr *column*

catID	catName	parentCatID	hierNr	hierIndent
1	Computer books	11	1	1
2	Databases	1	2	2
3	Programming	1	6	2
4	Relational Databases	2	4	3
5	Object-oriented databases	2	3	3
6	PHP	3	8	3
7	Perl	3	7	3
8	SQL	2	5	3
9	Children's books	11	9	1
10	Literature and fiction	11	10	1
11	All books	NULL	0	0

A simple query in mysql proves that this arrangement makes sense. Here are a few remarks on the SQL functions used: *CONCAT* joins two character strings. *SPACE* generates the specified number of blank characters. *AS* gives the entire expression the new name *category*. The result of the query is displayed in Figure 5-4.

```
SELECT CONCAT(SPACE(hierIndent*2), catName) AS category
FROM categories ORDER BY hierNr
```

You may now ask how the numerical values *hierIndent* and *hierNr* actually come into existence. The following example-oriented instructions show how a new data record (the computer book category *Operating systems*) is inserted into the table.

1. The data of the higher-ranking initial record (that is, *Computer books*) are known: *catID=1, parentCatID=0, hierNr=1, hierIndent=1*.

2. (a) Now we search within the *Computer books* group for the first record that lies in the hierarchy immediately after the record to be newly

inserted (here this is *Programming*). See Figure 5-3. All that is of interest in this record is *hierNr*.

Here is a brief explanation of the SQL command:

WHERE parentCat_ID=1 finds all records that are immediately below *Computer books* in the hierarchy (that is, *Databases* and *Programming*).

catName>'Operating Systems' restricts the list to those records that occur after the new record *Operating Systems.*

ORDER BY catname sorts the records that are found.

LIMIT 1 reduces the result to the first record.

```
SELECT hierNr FROM categories
WHERE parentCatID=1 AND catName>'Operating Systems'
ORDER BY catName
LIMIT 1
```

The query just given returns the result *hierNr=6.* It is thereby clear that the new data record should receive this hierarchy number. First, however, all existing records with *hierNr>=6* should have their values of *hierNr* increased by 1.

(b) It can also happen that the query returns no result, namely, when there are no entries in the higher-ranking category or when all entries come before the new one in alphabetic order. (This would be the case if you wished to insert the new computer book category *Software Engineering.*)

In that case you must search for the next record whose *hierNr* is larger than *hierNr* for the initial record and whose *hierIndent* is less than or equal to *hierIndent* of the initial record. (In this way the beginning of the next equal- or higher-ranking group in the hierarchy is sought.)

```
category
All books
  Computer books
    Databases
      Object-oriented databases
      Relational Databases
      SQL
    Programming
      Perl
      PHP
  Children's books
  Literature and fiction
```

Figure 5-4. Query result to display the hierarchy in mylibrary

```
SELECT hierNr FROM categories
WHERE hierNr>1 AND hierIndent<=1
ORDER BY hierNr LIMIT 1
```

This query returns the result 9 (that is, *hierNr* for the record *Children's books*). The new record will get this hierarchy number. All existing records with *hierNr>=9* must have their *hierNr* increased by 1.

(c) If this query also returns no result, then the new record must be inserted at the end of the hierarchy list. The current largest *hierNr* value can easily be determined:

```
SELECT MAX(hiernr) FROM categories
```

3. To increase *hierNr* of the existing records the following command is executed (for case 2a):

```
UPDATE categories SET hierNr=hierNr+1 WHERE hiernr>=6
```

4. Now the new record can be inserted. For *parentCatID* the initial record *catID* will be used. Above, *hierNr=6* was determined. Here *hierIndent* must be larger by 1 than was the case with the initial record.

```
INSERT INTO categories (catName, parentCatID, hierNr, hierIndent)
VALUES ('Operating systems', 1, 7, 2)
```

The description of this algorithm proves that inserting a data record is a relatively complex and costly process. (A concrete realization of the algorithm can be found in the form of a PHP script in Chapter 8.) It is much more complicated to alter the hierarchy after the fact. Imagine that you wish to change the name of one of the categories in such a way as to change its place in the alphabetical order. This would affect not only the record itself but many other records as well. For large sections of the table it will be necessary to determine *hierNr*. You see, therefore, that redundancy is bad.

Nevertheless, the advantages probably outweigh the drawbacks, above all because changes in the category list will be executed very infrequently (and thus the expenditure of time becomes insignificant), while queries to determine the hierarchical order, on the other hand, must be executed frequently.

Searching for Lower-Ranked Categories in the categories Table

Suppose you want to search for all *Databases* titles in the title table. Then it would not suffice to search for all titles with *catId=2*, since you also want to see all the titles relating to *Relational databases, Object-oriented databases,* and *SQL* (that is, the titles with *catID* equal to 4, 5, and 8). The totality of all these categories will be described in the following search category group.

There are two problems to be solved: First, you must determine the list of the *catID* values for the search category group. For this a series of *SELECT* queries is needed, and we shall not go into that further here. Then you must determine from the *titles* table those records whose *catID* numbers agree with the values just found. Since MySQL, alas, does not support sub*SELECT*s, for the second step a temporary table will be necessary.

Thus in principle the title search can be carried out, but the path is thorny, with the necessity of several SQL queries and client-side code.

The other solution consists in introducing a new (redundant) table, in which are stored all records lying above each of the *categories* records. This table could be called *rel_cat_parent*, and it would consist of two columns: *catID* and *parentID* (see Table 5-13). We see, then, for example, that the category *Relational Databases (catID=4)* lies under the categories *All books, Computer books,* and *Databases (parentID=11, 1, 2)*.

Table 5-13. Some entries in the rel_cat_parent *table*

catID	parentID
1	11
2	1
2	11
3	1
3	11
4	1
4	2
4	11
. . .	. . .

The significant drawback of the *rel_cat_parent* table is that it must be synchronized with every change in the *categories* table. But that is relatively easy to take care of.

In exchange for that effort, now the question of all categories ranked below *Databases* is easily answered:

```
SELECT catID FROM rel_cat_parent
WHERE parentID=2
```

If you would like to determine all book titles that belong to the category *Databases* or its subcategories, the requisite query looks like the following. The key word *DISTINCT* is necessary here, since otherwise, the query would return many titles with multiplicity.

```
SELECT DISTINCT titles.title FROM titles, rel_cat_parent
WHERE (rel_cat_parent.parentID = 2 OR titles.catID = 2)
  AND titles.catID = rel_cat_parent.catID
```

We are once more caught on the horns of the efficiency versus normalization dilemma: The entire table *rel_cat_parent* contains nothing but data that can be determined directly from *categories*. In the concrete realization of the *mylibrary* database we decided to do without *rel_cat_parent*, because the associated PHP example (see Chapter 8) in any case does not plan for category searches.

Searching for Higher-Ranked Categories in the categories Table

Here we confront the converse question to that posed in the last section: What are the higher-ranking categories above an initial, given, category? If the initial category is *Perl* (*catID=7*), then the higher-ranking categories are first *Programming*, then *Computer books*, and finally, *All books*.

When there is a table *rel_cat_parent* like that described above, then our question can be answered by a simple query:

```
SELECT CONCAT(SPACE(hierIndent*2), catName) AS category
FROM categories, rel_cat_parent
WHERE rel_cat_parent.catID = 7
  AND categories.catID = rel_cat_parent.parentID
ORDER BY hierNr
```

The result is seen in Figure 5-5.

```
category
All books
  Computer books
    Programming
```

Figure 5-5. Query result in search for higher-ranking categories

On the other hand, if *rel_cat_parent* is not available, then a series of *SELECT* instructions must be executed in a loop *categories.parentCatID* until this contains the value 0. This process is demonstrated in the PHP example program categories.php (see Chapter 8).

Indexes

All the *mylibrary* Tables are supplied with a *PRIMARY* index for the *ID* column. Additionally, the following usual indexes are defined:

Table	Column	Purpose
authors	*author*	search/sort by author's name
categories	*catName*	search by category name
	hierNr	hierarchical sort of the category list
publishers	*publName*	search/sort by publisher's name
titles	*title*	search/sort by book title
	publID	search by titles from a particular publisher
	catID	Search by titles from a particular category
	isbn	search by ISBN

Example *myforum* (Discussion Group)

Among the best-loved MySQL applications are guest books, discussion groups, and other web sites that offer users the possibility of creating a text and thereby adding their own voices to the web site. The database *myforum* creates the basis for a discussion group. The database consists of three tables:

- *forums* contains a list of the names of all discussion groups. Furthermore, each group can be assigned a particular language (English, German, Zemblan, etc.).

- *users* contains a list of all users registered in the database who are permitted to contribute to discussions. For each registered user a login name, password, and e-mail address are stored. (One can imagine extending this to hold additional information.)

- *messages* contains all the stored contributions. These consist of a *Subject* row, the actual text, *forumID*, *userID*, and additional management information. This table is the most interesting of the three from the standpoint of database design.

The structure of the *myforum* database is depicted in Figure 5-6

Data Types

All three tables are equipped with *AUTO_INCREMENT* columns, which also serve as primary index. In general, all fields have the attribute *NOT NULL*.

Column name	Data type
All ID fields	*INT*
forums.forumname	*VARCHAR(80)*
forums.language	*ENUM('german', 'english', 'zemblan')*
messages.subject	*VARCHAR(80)*
messages.msgText	*TEXT*
messages.level	*INT*
messages.timest	*TIMESTAMP*
messages.orderstr	*VARCHAR(128), BINARY*
users.username	*VARCHAR(30)*
users.email	*VARCHAR(120)*
users.password	*VARCHAR(30)*

Hierarchies Among Messages

As we have already seen in the case of the *mylibrary* database there is a battle in *myforum* in dealing with hierarchies. A significant feature of discussion groups is that the discussion thread is represented in a hierarchical list. The hierarchy is the result of the fact that each contribution can elicit a response. A discussion among the five participants Antony, Banquo, Coriolanus, Duncan, and Edmund (*A*, *B*, *C*, *D*, and *E* for short) might look like that depicted in Figure 5-7.

Here as illustration a description of the content is added to the title line (*subject*) of each contribution. In reality, the title line of a response is usually simply the letters *Re:* together with the original title line (e.g., *Re: How do I . . .*).

A representation in database format might look like that shown in Table 5-14. It is assumed here that the five participants *A* through *E* have *userID* numbers 201 through 205. The messages of the thread have *msgID* numbers that begin with 301. (In practice, it is natural to expect that a thread will not exhibit sequential

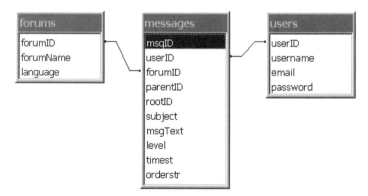

Figure 5-6. Structure of the myforum *database*

msgID numbers. More likely, other threads will break into the sequence.) The table is sorted chronologically (that is, in the order in which the messages were posted).

Table 5-14. messages *table with records of a discussion thread*

msgID	userID	subject	parentID	timest
301	201	How do I . . .	0	2001-01-17 12:00
302	202	first answer	301	2001-01-17 18:30
303	201	thanks	302	2001-01-17 19:45
304	204	second answer	301	2001-01-18 3:45
305	201	I don't . . .	304	2001-01-18 9:45
307	205	third answer	303	2001-01-18 19:00
306	204	the same . . .	305	2001-01-18 22:05
308	203	better suggestion	302	2001-01-19 10:30

The hierarchy is expressed via the column *parentID*, which refers to the message up one level in the hierarchy. If *parentID* has the value 0, then the contribution is one that began a new thread.

Optimization

From the standpoint of normalization, *parentID* is sufficient to express the hierarchy. However, this slick table design makes some frequently occurring queries difficult to answer:

• What are all the messages in this discussion thread?

• How should the messages be sorted? (A glance at Table 5-14 shows that a chronological sorting is not our goal.)

```
A: How do I sort MySQL tables? (17.1.2001 12:00)
  B: first answer (1.17.2001 18:30)
    A: thanks (1.17.2001 19:45)
    C: better suggestion (1.19.2001 10:30)
  D: second answer (1.18.2001 3:45)
    A: I don't understand (1.18.2001 9:45)
    D: the same explanation, but more extensive (1.18.2001 22:05)
  E: third answer (1.18.2001 19:00)
```

Figure 5-7. A discussion thread

- How far should each message be indented if the messages are to be represented hierarchically?

To answer the first question it is necessary to search (in a recursive loop) through all *parentID/ msgID* pairs. With long threads this will require a large number of *SELECT* queries. Of course, each of these queries can be quickly executed, but taken together, they represent a considerable degree of inefficiency.

Recursion also comes into play in the second question: A sorting by the time stored in *timest* leads to our goal, but the answers must be sorted by group for each branch of the hierarchical tree and inserted at the correct place in the list.

The answer to the third question is achieved by following the *parentID* pointer back to the start of the discussion thread.

To increase efficiency we must back off from our wishful goal of zero redundancy. We shall add three new columns:

- *rootID* refers to the original message that begins the discussion thread and thus makes it possible to answer the first question easily.

- *orderstr* contains a binary concatenation of the *timest* times of all higher-ranking messages. As we shall soon see, this character string can be used for sorting messages within a thread.

- *level* specifies the level of the hierarchy and thus immediately answers the third question.

Having absorbed these new columns into our database, we have a new representation of our database, as depicted in Table 5-15. In comparison with Table 5-14 you can see in the column *timest* that now there are only three digits, which should correspond to the internal binary representation. (In fact, four bytes are used, which permits 256 different values. For greater clarity we have used three-digit numbers here.)

While the meaning of the contents of the columns *rootID* and *level* is clear, that of *orderstr* might be a bit more opaque. In this binary column is stored a binary seqence of *TIMESTAMP* values of all higher-ranking messages. This simple measure ensures that associated groups of messages are not separated during sorting.

Pluses and Minuses

The obvious advantage of the three additional columns is the increased efficiency in displaying the messages. Since the reading operation occurs much more frequently than the writing operation in a discussion forum, reading efficiency has a correspondingly high status in the design of our database. (Furthermore, saving a new data record is efficient and not at all problematic. The values for

Table 5-15. messages table with records of a discussion thread

msgID	userID	subject	parentID	timest	rootID	level	orderstr
301	201	How . . .	0	712	0	0	712
302	202	first . . .	301	718	301	1	712718
303	201	thanks	302	719	301	2	712718719
304	204	second . . .	301	803	301	1	712803
305	201	O don't . . .	304	809	301	2	712803809
307	205	third . . .	303	819	301	1	712819
306	204	the same . . .	305	822	301	3	712803809822
308	203	better . . .	302	910	301	2	712718910

the three supplementary columns can be easily determined for a response from the associated higher-ranking message. If the message begins a new thread, then *rootID* and *level* are 0, while *orderstr* contains the binary representation of the current time.)

The single drawback is the additional storage space required for the three columns. However, in comparison to the typical storage requirement of a message with several lines of text, this additional storage requirement can be considered negligible. (The maximum length of *oderstr* is limited to 128 characters. That is, at most 32 hierarchical levels can be represented.)

Due to the nature of discussion groups, the additional disadvantages due to redundancy, that is, the problems of subsequent changes in data, are insignificant. Changes in existing messages are not anticipated, and neither are additions and deletions after the fact, which would have the effect of changing the sequence of messages.

> **REMARK** *Please note that the* orderstr *character string is based on* TIMESTAMP *values, which change only once per second. If it should chance that two messages are received at the same second, the sort order could become confused.*

Indexes

All *myforum* tables are supplied with a *PRIMARY* index for the *ID* column. Furthermore, the following usual indexes are defined:

Table	Column	Purpose
users	*userName*	search for user name (at login)
messages	*orderStr*	sort messages in discussion order
	forumID	search for messages in a discussion group
	rootID	search for messages in a thread

The PHP example for *myforum* does not provide for searching for messages. For such a search a full-text index covering the columns *subject* and *msgText* is recommended.

Example *exceptions* (Special Cases)

When you begin to develop an application with a new database, programming language, or API that is unfamiliar to you it is often practical to implement a simple test database for quickly testing various special cases. For the work on this book, as well as for testing various APIs and various import and export tests, the database *exceptions* was used. Among the tables of this database are the following:

- Columns with most data types supported by MySQL, including *xxxTEXT*, *xxxBLOB*, *SET*, and *ENUM*.

- *NULL* values.

- Texts and BLOBs with all possible special characters.

- All 255 text characters (code 1 to 255).

The following paragraphs provide an overview of the tables and their contents. The column names indicate the data type (thus the column *a_blob* has data type *BLOB*). The *id* column is an *AUTO_INCREMENT* column (type *INT*). In all the columns except the *id* column the value *NULL* is allowed.

test_blob

With the *test_blob* table you can test the use of binary data (import, export, reading and storing a client program, etc.).

Columns: *id*, *a_blob*.

Contents: A record (*id=1*) with a 512-byte binary block. The binary data represent byte for byte the codes 0, 1, 2, . . . , 255, 0, 1, . . . , 255.

test_date

With this table you can test the use of dates and times.

Columns: *id, a_date, a_time, a_datetime, a_timestamp.*

Content: A data record (*id=1*) with the values *2000-12-07, 09:06:29, 2000-12-07 09:06:29*, and *20001207090649.*

test_enum

With this table you can test the use of *SET* and *ENUM.*

Columns: *id, a_enum,* and *a_set* (with the character strings 'a', 'b', 'c', 'd', 'e').

Content:

id	a_enum	a_set
1	a	a
2	e	b,c,d
3		
4	NULL	NULL

test_null

With this table you can test whether *NULL* (first record) can be distinguished from an empty character string (second record).

Columns: *id, a_text.*

Content:

id	a_text
1	NULL
2	
3	'a text'

test_order_by

With this table you can test *ORDER BY* and the character set in use (including sort order). The table consists of two columns: *id* and *a_char.* The column *id* contains sequential numbers from 1 to 255, while *a_char* contains the associated character code. An index was deliberately not defined for the column *a_char.*

Content:

id	a_char
...	
65	'A'
66	'B'
...	

importtable1, importtable2, exporttable

These three tables contain test data for importation and exportation of text files. A description of the tables as well as numerous possibilities for import and export by MySQL can be found in Chapter 11.

CHAPTER 6

SQL

THIS CHAPTER PROVIDES AN INTRODUCTION to the database language *Structured Query Language*, or SQL for short. This language is used primarily to formulate instructions to a database system, including queries and commands to change or delete database objects. The most important of these commands are *SELECT*, *INSERT*, *UPDATE*, and *DELETE*, and these are the main attractions in this chapter, which aims to instruct in large part by presenting many examples.

Chapter Overview

Preparations

SELECT, INSERT, UPDATE, and *DELETE,* as well as several additional commands, together form the *Data Manipulation Language* (DML), a subset of SQL.

There is also the *Data Definition Language* (DDL), with which the design of a database can be altered. Some commands of this type were introduced as examples in the last chapter.

> **POINTER** *SQL commands for setting the security mechanisms of MySQL, which belong among the DDL command set, are presented in Chapter 5*
>
> *Commands for controlling the transaction mechanisms are described in Chapter 12. Furthermore, in Chapter 13 is to be found a complete reference for all SQL commands.*

All of the examples presented in this chapter are based on our example databases. Most of the examples use the database *mylibrary*, which was introduced in Chapter 5. All of the example databases can be found on the web site for this book, available for downloading (`www.kofler.cc`; see Appendix B). If you wish to try out these databases for yourself, then you must download them to your own test environment.

> **TIP** *Which database is involved in a particular example will be clear from the line* USE databasename *that appears at the beginning of the example or the beginning of the section in question.*

The best way of testing simple SQL commands is to use the MySQL monitor `mysql`. This program can be launched under Unix/Linux with the command `mysql`. Under Windows you can simply double click on the program in Explorer. You will find it in the directory `mysql/bin`. (Please note that you must terminate `mysql` commands with a semicolon. We shall not indicate the semicolon in this chapter, because it is required only by `mysql`, and not by other client programs. That is, it is not part of the MySQL syntax. Additional information on the `mysql` monitor can be found in Chapter 4.)

When you get to the point of editing multiline SQL commands you will find that the level of comfort and convenience afforded by mysql goes into a steep decline. A possible alternative is to save the SQL command in a small text file and then read the command into mysql with the command *SOURCE*. Another possibility is to use phpMyAdmin, which offers direct input of SQL queries and provides in addition some aids in the formulation of queries (see the end of this chapter). The greatest advantage of phpMyAdmin is that the results of a query are displayed in a reader-friendly tabular format.

For diehard Emacs fans there are extension files available on the Internet for a MySQL mode, which also provides a convenient environment for formulating and executing SQL commands.

> **POINTER** *In this book we generally write SQL commands and key words in uppercase letters, reserving lowercase for the names of databases, tables, and columns. Sometimes we use a mixed format (e.g.,* columnName*). MySQL is largely case-insensitive. The exception is in the names of databases and tables, where case distinction is made. With names for such objects you must hew to the straight and narrow path of exactitude with regard to case. Details on naming rules can be found in Chapter 13.*

Simple Queries (*SELECT*)

Here is a simple database query: *SELECT * FROM table*. This query returns all data records of the table specified. The asterisk indicates that the query is to encompass all the columns of the table. (See Figure 6-1.)

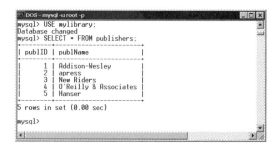

Figure 6-1. First SQL experiments in MySQL monitor mysql

```
USE mylibrary
SELECT * FROM publishers
```

publID	publName
1	Addison-Wesley
2	Apress
3	New Riders
4	O'Reilly & Associates
5	Hanser

> **REMARK** SELECT *can be used without reference to a database or to tables, for example, in the form* SELECT 2*3, *in which case* SELECT *returns its result in the form of a small table (one column, one row). This is used relatively often to determine the content of MySQL variables or functions (as in, say,* SELECT NOW()*, to determine the current time).*

Determining the Number of Data Records (Lines)

Perhaps you do not have a craving to view your data records in gruesome detail, but would like merely to determine how many records there are in one of your tables. For that, you can use the following query:

```
SELECT COUNT(publID) FROM publishers
```

COUNT(publID)
5

In this query you could specify, instead of *publID*, any column of the table (or * for all columns). In any case, MySQL optimizes the query and returns only the *number* of records, without actually reading them.

Column Restriction

Often, you are not interested in all the columns of a table. In such a case you must specify the columns explicitly (instead of using the asterisk).

```
SELECT publName FROM publishers
```

publName
Addison-Wesley
Apress
New Riders
O'Reilly & Associates
Hanser

> **TIP** *If a query is going to return a large number of data records, you should get accustomed to the idea of specifying explicitly only those columns of interest (instead of taking the lazy person's route of simply typing an asterisk). The reason is that MySQL (unnecessary data extraction), the client program (memory usage), and the network (unnecessary data transfer) work significantly more efficiently if the data set to be processed is limited to the absolute minimum.*

Limiting the Number of Resulting Records

You can limit not only the number of columns in a query result, but also the number of data records. Imagine that your *title* table contains the names of 100,000 books, but you would like to access only the first ten of these (for example, to display in an HTML document). To query the remaining 99,990 records would be a gross squandering of CPU time, memory, and network capacity. To avoid such a scenario, you can limit the number of records returned with *LIMIT n*. The following command returns two records from the *titles* table:

```
SELECT title FROM titles LIMIT 2
```

title
Client/Server Survival Guide
Definitive Guide to Excel VBA

To return the next two records, execute a new query, but this time with *LIMIT offset, n*. Here *offset* specifies the number of the record at which access to the table is to begin. (Warning: The enumeration of data records begins with 0. An *offset* of *n* skips the first *n* records and, since counting begins with 0, starts processing at record number *n*.)

```
SELECT title FROM titles LIMIT 2, 2
```

title
Linux
Web Application Development with PHP 4.0

Sorting Results

SELECT returns its results in no particular order. If you would like your list of results ordered, then you must request this explicitly via *ORDER BY column.* The following command returns an alphabetically ordered list of the authors in the *books* database.

```
SELECT authName FROM authors ORDER BY authName
```

authName
Bitsch Gerhard
Darween Hugh
Date Chris
DuBois Paul
Edwards E.
Garfinkel Simon
Gerken Till
Harkey D.
Holz Helmut
...

If you would like the reverse order, then you must add the key word *DESC* (for *descending*) to *ORDER BY,* as in, for example, *ORDER BY authName DESC.*

In sorting by character string the order is determined by the character set chosen at the startup of MySQL. This of particular importance when the character strings contain special characters outside of the ASCII character set. Information on selecting the character set for sorting can be found in Chapter 12.

> **REMARK** *In point of fact, the sequence of* SELECT *results, even without* ORDER BY, *is not random, but it depends rather on the order in which the records are stored in the table. However, you probably have no influence on this order. Therefore, do not expect that* SELECT *results will have a particular order. In the case of new tables, query results usually are returned ordered by increasing* id *number (if* id *is an* AUTO_INCREMENT *field). But as soon as records are altered or deleted, the ordering is ruined. Do not rely on it!*

> **TIP** *If you require your data records to be returned in a random order, then use* ORDER BY RAND(). *For example, to choose two records from a table at random, use* ORDER BY RAND() LIMIT 2.
>
> *Note, however, that* ORDER BY RAND() LIMIT n *without additional conditions is a very costly operation. For each record in the table a random number must be generated. Then all the random numbers are sorted so that the first* n *records can be returned.*

Selecting Data Records by Conditions (WHERE, HAVING)

Often, it is not all of the records in a table that are of interest, but only those that satisfy one or more conditions. Such conditionals are introduced with *WHERE*. In our first example we wish to display the names of only those authors whose surname starts with one of the letters L through Z:

```
SELECT authName FROM authors WHERE authName>='L'
```

author
Orfali R.
Pohl Peter
Ratschiller Tobias
Reese G.
...

In our second example we employ the operator *LIKE* to compare character strings. The query determines all authors whose names contain the sequence of letters "er." With the operator *LIKE* the character % serves as a placeholder for an arbitrary character string.

```
SELECT authName FROM authors WHERE authName LIKE '%er%'
```

author
Bitsch Gerhard
Gerken Till
Kofler Michael
Kramer David
Pohl Peter
Ratschiller Tobias
Schmitt Bernd
Yarger R.J.

> **CAUTION** *Comparisons with* LIKE *can be very slow when they are applied to large tables. All the data records must be read and analyzed. It is impossible to use indexes to optimize such queries.*

Comparisons with a large number of values can be carried out easily with *IN*:

```
SELECT authID, authName FROM authors
WHERE authID IN (2, 7, 12)
```

authID	authName
hline 2	Kramer David
7	Gerken Till
12	Yarger R.J.

> **REMARK** *Instead of formulating conditionals with* WHERE, *you could instead use* HAVING. *The* WHERE *conditionals are executed first, while* HAVING *conditionals are used only on intermediate results (returned by* WHERE). *The advantage of* HAVING *is that the conditions can also be applied to calculated fields (for example, to* SUM(columnXy) *in a* GROUP BY *query). An example appears in the section after next.*
>
> HAVING *conditionals are less easily optimized for MySQL than* WHERE *conditionals, and they should be avoided if an equivalent* WHERE *is possible.*

> **REMARK** *Please note that the conditional* colname = NULL *is not permitted. If you are searching for records that contain* NULL, *you must work with* ISNULL(colname).

Queries with Related Tables

Up to now all of our examples with *SELECT* have been applied to the search for records from a single table. However, with relational databases we are usually dealing with a number of related tables. Therefore, we are usually interested in applying a *SELECT* command to combine data from several tables.

For this we will use the *JOIN* syntax. The importance of the *JOIN* syntax is indicated by the fact that it is not treated along with *SELECT* in the MySQL documentation but is handled separately.

JOINs *Across Two Tables*

A first attempt to create a list of all book titles (column *title*) together with their publishers (column *publName*) from the tables *titles* and *publishers* is a colossal failure:

```
USE mylibrary
SELECT title, publName FROM titles, publishers
```

title	publName
Client/Server Survival Guide	Addison-Wesley
Definitive Guide to Excel VBA	Addison-Wesley
Linux	Addison-Wesley
Web Application Development with PHP 4.0	Addison-Wesley
Client/Server Survival Guide	Apress
Definitive Guide to Excel VBA	Apress
Linux	Apress
Web Application Development with PHP 4.0	Apress
Client/Server Survival Guide	New Riders
Definitive Guide to Excel VBA	New Riders
Linux	New Riders
Web Application Development with PHP 4.0	New Riders
...	

MySQL returns a list of all possible combinations of titles and publishers. In our relatively small database we can pick ourselves up from this minicatastrophe without too much damage. But imagine a database with 10,000 titles and 500 publishers, resulting in 5,000,000 combinations.

If queries spanning several tables are to return sensible results, precise information must be given as to how the data from the different tables are to be joined together. One possibility for formulating this connection is offered by *WHERE*. Since the linking field *publID* occurs in both tables, we must use the form *table.column* to indicate precisely which field is meant.

```
SELECT title, publName FROM titles, publishers
WHERE titles.publID = publishers.publID
```

title	publName
Linux, 5th ed.	Addison-Wesley
Definitive Guide to Excel VBA	Apress
Client/Server Survival Guide	Addison-Wesley
Web Application Development with PHP 4.0	New Riders
MySQL	New Riders
MySQL & mSQL	O'Reilly & Associates
...	

There are quite a few additional ways of arriving at the same result. One variant consists in creating the table list with *LEFT JOIN* and then forming the linking connection with *ON*:

```
SELECT title, publName
  FROM titles LEFT JOIN publishers
    ON titles.publID = publishers.publID
```

Another variant makes use of the key word *USING*, in which the common linking field is specified. However, this variant assumes that the linking field (in this case *publisherID*) has the same name in both tables. That is, of course, not always the case.

```
SELECT title, publName
  FROM titles LEFT JOIN publishers
USING (publID)
```

JOINs *Across Three or More Tables*

Things become a bit more confusing when the query must examine data from more than two tables. The following query returns a list of all book titles with all their authors. (Books with several authors occur in this list with multiplicity.)

```
SELECT title, authName
  FROM titles, rel_title_author, authors
WHERE titles.titleID = rel_title_author.titleID
  AND authors.authID = rel_title_author.authID
ORDER BY title
```

title	author
A Guide to the SQL Standard	Date Chris
A Guide to the SQL Standard	Darween Hugh
Alltid den där Annette	Pohl Peter
Client/Server Survival Guide	Orfali R.
Client/Server Survival Guide	Harkey D.
Client/Server Survival Guide	Edwards E.
Definitive Guide to Excel VBA	Kofler Michael
Definitive Guide to Excel VBA	Kramer David
Excel 2000 programmieren	Kofler Michael
Jag saknar dig, jag saknar dig	Pohl Peter
LaTeX	Kopka Helmut
Linux für Internet und Intranet	Holz Helmut
Linux für Internet und Intranet	Schmitt Bernd
Linux für Internet und Intranet	Tikart Andreas
Linux, 5th ed.	Kofler Michael
Maple	Kofler Michael
Maple	Komma Michael
Maple	Bitsch Gerhard
...	

Our next example is somewhat more complex: Here we generate a list of publishers and their authors. (Thus the query determines which authors write for which publishers.) The connection between publishers and authors is made via the tables *title* and *rel_title_author*, so that altogether, four tables are brought into play.

New in this query is the SQL key word *DISTINCT*. It has the effect that equivalent data records are output only once. Since there are authors in the *mylibrary* database who have written several books (for the same publisher), the simple joining of these tables would result in many combinations in which an author and publisher combination occurred with multiplicity.

```
SELECT DISTINCT publName, authName
  FROM publishers, titles, rel_title_author, authors
WHERE titles.titleID = rel_title_author.titleID
  AND authors.authID = rel_title_author.authID
  AND publishers.publID = titles.publID
ORDER BY publName, authName
```

publName	authName
Addison-Wesley	Bitsch Gerhard
Addison-Wesley	Darween Hugh
Addison-Wesley	Date Chris
Addison-Wesley	Edwards E.
Addison-Wesley	Harkey D.
...	
Apress	Kofler Michael
Apress	Kramer David
New Riders	DuBois Paul
New Riders	Gerken Till
New Riders	Ratschiller Tobias
...	

Syntax Variants

If you read about the details of *FROM* under the description of the *SELECT* syntax in the MySQL documentation, you may find your head spinning from the large number of (almost) identical variants. Here is a brief overview:

JOIN without condition (combination of all possibilities)

(1) *FROM table1, table2*

(2) *FROM table1 JOIN table2*

(3) *FROM table1 CROSS JOIN table2*

(4) *FROM table1 INNER JOIN table2*

(5) *FROM table1 STRAIGHT_JOIN table2*

Option (5) is distinguished from the other four in that there the order of data extraction from the tables is not optimized by MySQL. In (1) and (4) MySQL tries on its own to find an optimal sequence for access to the data. Variant (5) is then to be recommended when you have doubts as to MySQL's ability to optimize its performance.

JOIN (with condition)

(1) *FROM table1, table2 WHERE table1.xyID = table2.xyID*

(2) *FROM table1 LEFT [OUTER] JOIN table2 ON table1.xyID = table2.xyID*

(3) *FROM table1 LEFT [OUTER] JOIN table2 USING (xyID)*

(4) *FROM table1 NATURAL [LEFT [OUTER]] JOIN table2*

With option (1) only those fields that are identical are considered in joining the two tables. With (2) and (4), on the other hand, for every record of the first (left) table a result record is generated, even when the linked field contains *NULL*. For example, if the *titles* table is used for *table1*, and the *publishers* table for *table2*, then *LEFT JOIN* will return even those titles for which no publisher name has been stored. (The key word *OUTER* is optional and has no effect on the function.)

The variants with *USING* and *NATURAL* work only when the *ID* fields in both tables have the same name. In the case of *NATURAL*, like-named fields in both tables are used for joining. For *NATURAL* to work, the *ID* fields must have the same name and type. Furthermore, there must be no other like-named fields.

WARNING *Please note that with* LEFT JOIN *the order of the tables is significant.*

- titles LEFT JOIN publishers *returns titles that have no publisher, but no publishers that have not published a single title.*

- publishers LEFT JOIN titles *returns, contrariwise, publishers that have yet to publish a title, but no titles that do not have an associated publisher.*

In contrast to many other SQL dialects, MySQL recognizes no FULL JOIN, *which would return all such combinations.*

Grouped Queries, Aggregate Functions

The data records for our books, stored in the *mylibrary* database, are assigned to various categories. If you require information as to which categories contain which books, then you will find the following query helpful. (Warning: Books that have not been assigned to a category will not appear at all. If you wish to see all books, then you must execute *FROM titles LEFT JOIN categories ON titles.catID = categories.catID*.)

```
USE mylibrary
SELECT catName, title FROM titles, categories
WHERE titles.catID = categories.catID
ORDER BY catName, title
```

catName	title
Children's books	Alltid den där Annette
Children's books	Jag saknar dig, jag saknar dig
Computer books	LaTeX
Computer books	Linux, 5th ed.
Computer books	Maple
Databases	Client/Server Survival Guide
Databases	Visual Basic Datenbankprogrammierung
Programming	Definitive Guide to Excel VBA
Programming	Visual Basic
SQL	A Guide to the SQL Standard

If you wish to determine only how many books there are in each category, you can put the fingers of both hands to work and begin counting in the list just produced: two children's books, three computer books not more precisely categorized, two books on databases, and so on.

It has probably crossed your mind that there may be a more automated way of doing this: *GROUP BY name* creates in the resulting list a group for each member of the specified column. With *GROUP BY catName* in the above query a single row is made out of the two entries with *catName='Children's books'*. Which title is shown depends on the sort order, if any.

We see that with *GROUP BY* alone we do not accomplish much (unless we merely wanted to generate a list of all the categories, but there are easier ways of accomplishing that). However, in connection with *GROUP BY*, SQL supports *aggregate functions*. This means that in the column list at the beginning of a *SELECT* you can use functions like *COUNT, SUM, MIN,* and *MAX.* It is when these functions are brought into play that *GROUP BY* finally becomes a useful tool, as is demonstrated by the following example: We shall count (*COUNT*) how many entries are associated with each category.

New here is also the use of the key word *AS*, whereby the second column in the query is given the name *nrOfItems*. Without *AS* the column would have the name *'COUNT(itemID)*, which not only would be a bit confusing, but would increase the amount of typing each time the column was referenced (e.g., in *ORDER BY*).

```
SELECT catName, COUNT(title) AS nrOfItems
FROM titles, categories
WHERE titles.catID = categories.catID
GROUP BY catname
ORDER BY catname
```

catName	nrOfItems
Children's books	2
Computer books	3
Databases	2
Programming	2
SQL	1

Altering Data (*INSERT, UPDATE,* and *DELETE*)

> **TIP** *MySQL novices are in danger of getting burned by the* UPDATE *and* DELETE *commands by applying them to the entire table, thereby changing or deleting more records than intended. If you launch* mysql *with the option* --i-am-a-dummy, *then the risk of accidental damage is reduced considerably:* mysql *refuses to execute* UPDATE *and* DELETE *commands without a* WHERE.

Executing a Backup

Before you start playing around with your database, you should consider backing up individual tables or perhaps the whole database, so that after you make a mess of things you can restore the database to its original pristine condition.

Creating Copies of a Table

The following instruction creates a new table with the name *newtable* and copies all the data records of *table* into the new table. The column definitions of the new table are identical to those of the old one, but there are some occasional differences. For example, the attribute *AUTO_INCREMENT* is lost. Moreover, in the new table no indexes are created.

```
CREATE TABLE newtable SELECT * FROM table
```

Restoring Tables

With the given commands, first all data records of the original table *table* are deleted. Then the records that were saved into *newtable* are copied back into *table*. (The original *AUTO_INCREMENT* values remain untouched during the copying back and forth.)

```
DELETE FROM table
INSERT INTO table SELECT * FROM newtable
```

If you no longer require the backup data, you can simply delete *newtable*.

```
DROP TABLE newtable
```

Backup of a Table (Since Version 3.23.25)

Starting with MySQL version 3.23.25 a backup copy of a table can be made even more easily and more quickly.

```
BACKUP TABLE table TO '/tmp/backups'
```

Instead of *'/tmp/backups'* you can specify an existing directory into which the files are to be copied. To recreate the table, execute *RESTORE TABLE*.

```
RESTORE TABLE table FROM '/tmp/backups'
```

Making a Backup of an Entire Database

With the program mysqldump (under Windows it is mysqldump.exe) you can create an ASCII backup file of a complete database. Note, please, that you cannot execute mysqldump from within mysql, but rather you must launch it as a free-standing program in a shell or DOS window. (The program will be described in detail in Chapter 11.)

```
user$ mysqldump -u loginame -p --opt dbname > backupfile
Enter password: xxx
```

Restoring a Database

There is no counterpart to mysqldump for reading in a saved database. Instead, you will have to rely on our old friend the SQL monitor mysql, where you give the backup file as input source. The database *dbname* must already exist.

```
user$ mysql -u loginname -p dbname < backupfile
Enter password: xxx
```

Of course, you can also recreate the database in interactive mode:

```
user$ mysql -u root -p
Enter password: xxx
Welcome to the MySQL monitor ...
mysql> CREATE DATABASE dbname; -- if dbname does not yet exist
mysql> USE dbname;
mysql> SOURCE backupfile;
```

Inserting Data Records (INSERT)

With *INSERT* you can add a new record to a table. After the name of the table there must appear first a list of the column names and then a list with the values to be inserted. (Columns with a default value, columns that can be *NULL*, and *AUTO_INCREMENT* columns do not have to be specified.)

In the following example a new data record is saved in the table *titles* in the *mylibrary* database. Only two columns (*title* and *year*) will be specified. All remaining columns are taken care of by MySQL: A new *AUTO_INCREMENT* value is placed in *titleID*, and in the other columns the requisite default value or *NULL*. (This process is allowed only because when the *titles* table was created a default value was specifically provided for and *NULL* was specified as a permissible value.)

```
USE mylibrary
INSERT INTO titles (title, year)
VALUES ('MySQL', 2001)
```

One may do without naming the columns if values for all columns (including default and *AUTO_INCREMENT* columns) are given and the order of the columns is followed exactly. In the case of *titles* there are quite a few columns: *titleID, title, subtitle, edition, publID, catID, langID, year, isbn,* and *comment.*

For some columns the value *NULL* is given. In most cases MySQL actually stores the value *NULL*. The only exception here is the column *titleID*, into which MySQL automatically places a new ID number. Instead of *NULL* you can specify an explicit ID number. However, this will result in an error is this number is already being used by another record. (There is one further column type in which MySQL places a value on its own if *NULL* is given: In *TIMESTAMP* columns, instead of *NULL* the current date and time are stored.)

```
INSERT INTO titles
VALUES (NULL, 'deleteme', ' ', 1, NULL, NULL, NULL, 2001, NULL, NULL)
```

Another syntax variant enables several new records to be inserted with a single command:

```
INSERT INTO table (columnA, columnB, columnC)
VALUES ('a', 1, 2), ('b', 12, 13), ('c', 22, 33), ...
```

INSERT *with Related Tables*

If you are dealing with related tables, then normally insertion of records is not accomplished with a single *INSERT* command. For example, to store a book record in the *mylibrary* database, new records must be stored in at least the tables *titles* and *rel_title_author*. If the new book was written by an author or authors whose names have not yet been stored in the database, or if it was published by a publisher that is currently unknown to the database, then new data records will also have to be added to the tables *publishers* and *authors* (see also Figure 5-2).

However, now we have the problem that not all the data for the insert command are known at the outset. To store a book published by a new publisher, the *publID* of the publisher must be given in the *titles* table. This is an *AUTO_INCREMENT* value, which is generated by MySQL only when the new publisher is stored in the database.

There must, then, be a way to access the last-generated *AUTO_INCREMENT* value. And indeed there is. The function for this is *LAST_INSERT_ID()*, which returns the *AUTO_INCREMENT* value of the last *INSERT* command. This function has effect only within the current connection. That is, *AUTO_INCREMENT* values that may have arisen through the *INSERT* commands of other database users are ignored.

The following lines show how a book with a good deal of new information (three new authors, a new publisher) is stored. The book in question is the following: Randy Yarger, George Reese, Tim King: *MySQL & mSQL.* O'Reilly 1999.

```
INSERT INTO publishers (publName) VALUES ('O''Reilly & Associates')
SELECT LAST_INSERT_ID()
    4 <--- publisherID for the publisher

INSERT INTO authors (authName) VALUES (('Yarger R.J.')
SELECT LAST_INSERT_ID()
    12 <--- authorID for the first author

INSERT INTO author (author) VALUES (('Reese G.')
SELECT LAST_INSERT_ID()
    13 <--- authorID for the second author

INSERT INTO author (author) VALUES (('King T.'')
SELECT LAST_INSERT_ID()
    14 <--- authorID for the third author

INSERT INTO titles (title, publID, year)
VALUES ('MySQL & mSQL', 4, 1999)
SELECT LAST_INSERT_ID()
    9 <--- titleID for the book

INSERT INTO rel_title_author
VALUES (9, 12), (9, 13), (9,14)
```

In practice, you will not, of course, input these commands manually. That would be terribly boring, and the probability of error would be high. Rather, the insertions will be made in program code by way of a user interface. The code will concern itself not only with the evaluation and reevaluation of the *ID* values, but will ensure that authors and publishers who already appear in the database are not stored again by mistake.

Altering Data Records (UPDATE)

With *UPDATE* you can change individual fields of an existing database. The usual syntax of this command is the following:

```
UPDATE tablename
SET column1=value1, column2=value2, ...
WHERE columnID=n
```

Thus individual fields of a record specified by its *ID* value are changed. In the following example we change the title of the Linux book (*titleID=1*):

```
USE mylibrary
UPDATE titles SET title='Linux, 5th ed.' WHERE titleID=1
```

If *UPDATE* is used without *WHERE*, then the change is instituted for all data records (so beware!). The following command, for example, would change the publication date of all books to the year 2001:

```
UPDATE titles SET year=2001
```

With certain restrictions calculations are permissible in *UPDATE* commands. Let us suppose that the price of the book was stored in the *title* table. Then it would be easy to increase all prices by five percent:

```
UPDATE title SET price=price*1.05
```

Deleting Data Records (DELETE)

There can be little doubt that the syntactically simplest command of this section is *DELETE*. All records selected with *WHERE* are simply deleted. Here it is not required to specify the columns (indeed, it is not possible), since in any case the entire data record is made to disappear without a trace. The following instruction deletes a single record from the *title* table:

```
USE mylibrary
DELETE FROM titles WHERE titleID=8
```

> **CAUTION** *If* DELETE *is executed without a* WHERE *condition, then all the records of the table will be deleted. There is no "undo" possibility.*
> *The table itself with its definition of columns, indexes, etc., remains intact. If you wish to delete the table itself, then you must execute the command* DROP TABLE.

Creating New Tables

You can store the result of a query directly in a new table. (In practice, this path is often followed in order to store the results of a complex query temporarily.) To do this you simply specify the name of a new table with *CREATE TABLE* and insert an ordinary *SELECT* command at the end of the instruction. The following instruction copies all titles with *catID=1* (category *Computer books*) into the new table *computerbooks*.

```
USE mylibrary
CREATE TABLE computerbooks
SELECT * FROM titles WHERE catID=1
```

From then on the new table is available. With *SELECT* you can convince yourself that indeed the desired data are in the table.

```
SELECT title FROM computerbooks
```

title
Linux, 5th ed.
LaTeX
Mathematica
Maple
Practical UNIX & Internet security

When the time comes that you no longer have any need of the table *computerbooks*, you will not find yourself in the situation of Woody Allen in the film *Crimes and Misdemeanors*, who, you may recall, felt compelled to hire a hit man to rid him of an unwanted mistress. In the case of an unwanted table you can easily delete it by giving a command:

```
DROP TABLE computerbooks
```

Advanced SQL

This section contains a collection of small SQL examples that go somewhat beyond the elementary level of the other examples in this chapter. The goal is to give you, dear reader, an idea of some of the possibilities that the world of SQL opens to you. Experts in SQL will not find these examples particularly advanced, but for those who wish to dive more deeply into the depths of SQL there is no lack of a relevant secondary literature.

Determining the Number of Authors (mylibrary)

In the *mylibrary* database the association between the tables *titles* and *authors* is effected by means of the table *rel_title_author*. Yet it can happen that no author is associated with individual entries in the *titles* table. The following query determines the number of authors associated with each of the *titles* entries.

The key point here is the use of *LEFT JOIN* (instead of simply enumerating the tables with *FROM*). This ensures that the result list also contains titles that do not have authors. The result is sorted by the number of authors, so that books with many authors are named first.

```
USE mylibrary

SELECT title, COUNT (authID) AS authCount
FROM titles LEFT JOIN rel_title_author USING(titleID)
GROUP BY titles.titleID
ORDER BY authCount DESC, title
```

title	authCount
Client/Server Survival Guide	3
Maple	3
MySQL & mSQL	3
A Guide to the SQL Standard	2
Definitive Guide to Excel VBA	2
Practical UNIX & Internet security	2

   . . .

Searching for a Title Without an Author (mylibrary)

From the query we have just formulated it is but a small step to find a title for which no author has been saved. The query finds a single title, which apparently got itself into the database during a test.

```
USE mylibrary
SELECT title, COUNT(authID) AS authCount
FROM titles LEFT JOIN rel_title_author USING(titleID)
GROUP BY titles.titleID
HAVING authCount=0
ORDER BY title
```

title
dummy

> **REMARK** *Please note especially that here* HAVING *(and not* WHERE*) must be used.* WHERE *is valid only for conditionals that affect the original data, but* authCount *arose from a calculation with an aggregate function.*

Searching for Invalid Records in $1 : n$ Relations (mylibrary)

In the ideal case all records in the *titles* table should contain either the name of a publisher in *publID* or else the value *NULL*. But what would happen if somehow a publisher were accidentally deleted? Then there would be *titles* data records that would refer with their *publID* to a nonexistent publisher in the database. (Analogous problems can exist with all other links to other tables. With the *titles*, problems can exist with relation to the fields *catID* and *langID*. The following query does not find all the *titles* records with invalid cross references, but only those with a problem with *publID*. The purpose here is to demonstrate the principle of how to find such records.)

The following query joins the tables *titles* and *publishers* via the linking field *publID*. With *LEFT JOIN* those titles are included for which this link leads to no result. There can be two reasons for this: Either *titles.publID* contains the value *NULL* (which is permissible) or there is no correspondence to *titles.publID* in the *publishers* table (and thus an error has been found). The two *ISNULL* conditionals are necessary so that in fact, only those records are displayed for which the second (error-ridden) reason holds.

The query finds in *titles* only a single record (which was inserted precisely for this purpose).

```
SELECT title, titles.publID, publishers.publID
FROM titles LEFT JOIN publishers
ON titles.publID=publishers.publID
WHERE ISNULL(publishers.publID)
  AND NOT(ISNULL(titles.publID))
```

title	publID	publID
deleteme	99	NULL

Searching for Invalid Records in $n : m$ Relations (mylibrary)

Somewhat more complex is a search involving $n : m$ relations (such as, for example, with the title/author relation). Now there are three sources for error:

- Titles that refer via *rel_title_author* to nonexistent authors.

- Authors that refer via *rel_title_author* to nonexistent titles.

- Entries in *rel_title_author* where both *titleID* and *authID* refer to invalid records. (If the search for illegal records begins with existing authors or titles, then this third source of error will go undetected.)

To simulate these error conditions, three invalid data records have been inserted into *rel_title_author*. (The following instruction assumes that there exists an author with *authID=1* and a title with *titleID=1*, and no title or author with ID number 9999.)

```
INSERT INTO rel_title_author (titleID, authID)
VALUES (1,9999), (9999,1), (9999, 9999)
```

The following query refers to the first error (title with author IDs that do not exist in the database). It is interesting in this query that the link between *titles* and *rel_title_author* is effected with an ordinary *JOIN*, while that between *rel_title_author* and *authors* is done with *LEFT JOIN* (otherwise, the missing authors would not be included and thus would not be not found). The result is not very surprising: The title *Linux* with *titleID=1* refers to an author with *authID=9999*, which doesn't exist.

```
SELECT title, rel_title_author.titleID, rel_title_author.authID
FROM titles, rel_title_author
LEFT JOIN authors
ON rel_title_author.authID=authors.authID
WHERE titles.titleID=rel_title_author.titleID
  AND ISNULL(authors.authID)
```

title	titleID	authID
Linux, 5th ed.	1	9999

The symmetric command for the second error case looks like this:

```
SELECT authName, rel_title_author.authID, rel_title_author.titleID
FROM authors, rel_title_author
LEFT JOIN titles
ON rel_title_author.titleID=titles.titleID
WHERE authors.authID=rel_title_author.authID
  AND ISNULL(titles.titleID)
```

authName	authID	titleID
Kofler Michael	1	9999

The query for the third error case consists of two *LEFT JOINs*, one from *rel_title_author* to *authors*, and the other from *rel_title_author* to *titles*.

```
SELECT rel_title_author.authID, rel_title_author.titleID
FROM rel_title_author
LEFT JOIN titles
    ON rel_title_author.titleID=titles.titleID
LEFT JOIN authors
```

```
    ON rel_title_author.authID=authors.authID
WHERE ISNULL(titles.titleID) AND ISNULL(authors.authID)
```

authID	titleID
9999	9999

Instead of the three queries just formulated, we can get by with only one. For this to work all the data in all three tables must be considered. Furthermore, in the conditional we will need to use *AND* and *OR*. (In practice, it is often more useful to split the query into three parts, because then one can tailor one's response to the different types of error.)

```
SELECT rel_title_author.authID, rel_title_author.titleID,
authName, title
FROM rel_title_author
LEFT JOIN titles
    ON rel_title_author.titleID=titles.titleID
LEFT JOIN authors
    ON rel_title_author.authID=authors.authID
WHERE ISNULL(titles.titleID) OR ISNULL(authors.authID)
```

authID	titleID	authName	title
9999	1	NULL	Linux, 5th ed.
1	9999	Kofler Michael	NULL
9999	9999	NULL	NULL

One of the most important results of this example should be your realization of the universal applicability of *JOIN* operations.

Correcting Data

Of course, it helps in correcting data to be able to determine which data are corrupt. It would be even better if one could correct errors automatically as soon as they were found. Alas, as a rule, errors must be corrected manually. For example, if a book title refers to a nonexistent author because of an error in *rel_title_author*, then it will not do simply to delete this entry. It must first be determined whether the author list for the book is, in fact, in error. It may be that a new author (or only a new reference in *rel_title_author* to an existing author) has to be incorporated into the database.

Even with the best SQL command you cannot automate such tasks. However, SQL is a good aid in searching through the database for errors and listing them in a readable format as a basis for manual correction to follow.

When the problem is only the syntactic correctness of data (and you have no possibility of tracking the error to its source and then manually recreating the data), you can, of course, simply delete erroneous data (for example all records in *rel_title_author* that refer to a nonexistent author or title).

Since MySQL 3.23.*n* and all earlier versions do not, unfortunately, offer the possibility of accessing data in several tables in *DELETE* commands (no sub*SELECT*s), you must carry out such tasks in an external programming language (in Perl, for example). There you first determine with *SELECT* the list of erroneous data records and then delete them with *DELETE* commands. An example of this modus operandi can be found in Chapter 9.

Temporary Tables as a Substitute for subSELECTs (myforum)

Most database systems recognize so-called sub*SELECT*s, that is, nested *SELECT* queries, at least to a certain extent. To search for book titles whose *publID* refer to a nonexistent publisher one could use a query in the following form:

```
SELECT * FROM titles
WHERE publID NOT IN
  (SELECT publID FROM publishers)
```

In MySQL through version 3.23.*n* such queries are, sad to tell, impossible. In many cases this restriction can be circumvented with well thought out *JOIN* operations (though this way of proceeding is not always particularly intuitive):

```
USE mylibrary

SELECT titles.*
FROM titles LEFT JOIN publishers
ON titles.publID=publishers.publID
WHERE ISNULL(publishers.publID) AND NOT(ISNULL(titles.publID))
```

The query presented above for searching for invalid data provides further examples for this process.

Unfortunately, *JOIN* operations cannot always replace sub*SELECT*s. This is particularly true when the resulting record list is to be sorted other than by the selection criterion of the query used.

In the following example an alphabetically ordered list is to be created for those writers who contributed the last ten messages in the *myforum* database. With a sub*SELECT* the query would look like this:

```
SELECT DISTINCT userName FROM users
WHERE userID IN
(SELECT userID FROM messages
ORDER BY timest DESC
LIMIT 100)
ORDER BY userName
```

userName
kofler
test
testaccount
. . .

To be sure, with the direct connection between *users* and *messages* you can achieve the same result, but a sort by *userName* is impossible. You must sort by *timest*. It is particularly annoying that in this query *DISTINCT* doesn't work at all. That is, if there were a writer who had written the last hundred messages, that name would appear with multiplicity. (*DISTINCT* works only if the result list is sorted by *userName*.)

```
SELECT DISTINCT userName FROM users, messages
WHERE users.userID = messages.userID
ORDER BY timest DESC LIMIT 10
```

userName
test
test
kofler
test
kofler
testaccount
testaccount
. . .

The only possible solution without sub*SELECT*s consists in employing a temporary table for intermediate results. As table type we use *HEAP*. Thus a temporary table is set up in RAM only (not on the hard drive), which is much faster.

```
CREATE TEMPORARY TABLE tmp TYPE=HEAP
SELECT userID, timest FROM messages
ORDER BY timest DESC
LIMIT 10
```

The contents of the temporary table are now linked to *users*.

```
SELECT DISTINCT userName FROM users, tmp
WHERE users.userID = tmp.UserID
ORDER BY userName
```

userName
kofler
test
testaccount
...

The temporary table can now be deleted:

```
DROP TABLE tmp
```

Further Examples

> **POINTER**   *Further examples of SQL commands can be found in Chapter 5, where we have indicated a number of complications arising in database design. Moreover, there are many further examples lurking in the code examples of Chapters 8 and 10.*

CHAPTER 7

Security

IT IS A FACT OF life, or at least of human social organization, that not all information is intended to be made available to all individuals. Thus with MySQL a database is generally set up in such a way that not everyone can see all of the data (let alone change or delete it). In order to protect data from prying eyes (or unauthorized tampering), MySQL provides a dual access system. The first level determines whether the user has the right to communicate with MySQL at all. The second level determines what actions (such as *SELECT, INSERT, DROP*) are permitted for which databases, tables, or columns.

This chapter describes rather extensively the access system of MySQL, both its internal management and the tools that can assist you in changing access privileges.

Chapter Overview

Introduction

Normally, it is undesirable to allow everyone to execute all database operations. To be sure, there must be one, or perhaps even several, administrators who have wide-ranging powers. However, it would be a great security risk to allow all users to act as they please in altering records or even deleting entire databases.

There can be many different degrees of access rights. In a company with an employee database, for example, it may make sense to allow all employees to read part of the database (for example, to find someone's telephone number), while other parts remain invisible (such as personnel records).

MySQL offers a finely meshed system for setting such access privileges. In the MySQL documentation this system is called the *access privilege system*, while the individual lists of the system are called *access control lists* (ACLs). The management of these lists is carried out internally in the tables of the *mysql* database, which will be described in detail.

Setting the Access Privileges

There are several ways to set access privileges:

- You can change *mysql* directly with *INSERT* and *UPDATE* commands.

- You can use the SQL commands *GRANT* and *REVOKE*, which offer greater convenience.

- You can use the Perl script mysql_setpermission.pl. This script is even easier to use than *GRANT* and *REVOKE*, though it assumes, of course, that you have a Perl installation up and running.

- You can use an administration program with a graphical user interface. (However, as I was writing this chapter in October 2000 I had not yet found a program that would carry out this task to my satisfaction.)

User Name, Host Name, and Password

MySQL's access system has two phases. In the first phase the question is whether the user is permitted to make a connection to MySQL at all. (Such does not imply the right to read or alter any databases, but nevertheless, such access provides the capability to pass SQL commands to MySQL. Then MySQL decides, based on its security settings, whether this command should actually be executed.)

While you are probably accustomed to providing a user name and password to enter the operating system of a multiuser computing system, MySQL evaluates a third piece of information: the name of the computer (host name) from which you are accessing MySQL. Since MySQL's entire security system is based on this informational triple, it seems not inappropriate to take a few moments now to explain what is going on.

User Name

The user name is the name under which you announce your presence to MySQL. The management of user names by MySQL has nothing to do with login names managed by the operating system. It is, of course, possible, and indeed, it is often advisable, to use the same name for both purposes, but management of each of these names is independent of the other. There is no mechanism to synchronize these operations (such that, for example, a new MySQL user name is generated when the operating system generates a new user name).

The user name can be up to sixteen characters in length, and it is case-sensitive. In principle, such names do not have to be composed exclusively of ASCII characters. But since different operating systems handle special characters differently, such characters often lead to problems and therefore should be avoided.

Password

What holds for user names holds for passwords as well. There is no relation between the MySQL password and that for the operating system, even if they are identical. (Within MySQL passwords are stored in encrypted form, which allows passwords to be checked, but does not allow reconstruction of a password. Even if an attacker should gain access to the *user* table of MySQL, there is no way for the villain to determine the passwords themselves.

Passwords, like user names, are case-sensitive. More than sixteen characters are allowed. Special characters outside of the ASCII character set are possible, but are not recommended.

> **CAUTION** For security reasons do not use the same password for MySQL as for the operating system!
>
> *MySQL passwords must often be supplied in plain text in script files, configuration files, and programs. Thus they are in danger of being intercepted. If an attacker who acquires such a password were to gain access not only to your database, but also discovers that the same password allows entry into the operating system, the villain will be very happy indeed.*

Host Name

The host name specifies the computer on which the MySQL server is running. If that is not the local computer, then the connection is created with the protocol TCP/IP. The host name can also be given as an IP number (e.g., 192.168.23.45).

Default Values

If no other parameters are given in establishing a MySQL connection, then under Unix/Linux the current login name is given as user name, while under Windows it is the character string *ODBC*. As password an empty character string is passed. The host name is *localhost*.

You can easily test this. Launch the program mysql and execute the command *status*. The current user name is displayed in the line *current user*. The following commands were executed under Linux:

```
kofler:~ > mysql
Welcome to the MySQL monitor.
mysql> status
mysql Ver 9.38 Distrib. 3.22.32, for suse-linux (i686)
 ...
Current user: kofler@localhost
 ...
```

If in establishing a connection you must provide a user name other than the login name and a password, then the start of mysql looks like this:

```
kofler:~ > mysql -u surveyadmin -p
Enter password: xxx
Welcome to the MySQL monitor.
mysql> status
mysql Ver 9.38 Distrib. 3.22.32, for suse-linux (i686)
 ...
Current user: surveyadmin@localhost
 ...
```

> **REMARK** *MySQL recognizes the term* anonymous user. *This expression comes into play when any user name is permitted in establishing a connection to MySQL. (In the default configuration this is precisely what is allowed.) In this case* status *shows as* current user *the user name used when the connection was established, but internally an empty character string is used as user name. This is important primarily for the evaluation of additional access privileges. Further background information is contained in later in this chapter, where the inner workings of the access system are discussed.*

When a PHP script establishes the connection to the database and no other user name is supplied within `mysql_connect()` (or `mysql_pconnect()`), then what is used as user name is the name of the account under which the PHP interpreter is executed. (As a rule, this is the same account under which Apache is also executed. Thus for security reasons most Unix/Linux systems use the account *nobody*, which has few privileges.)

Default Security Setting

If you have newly installed MySQL on a test system, then you are starting out with an immensely insecure default setting. It is interesting to note that this default setting depends on the operating system. Under Windows the setting is even more insecure than under Unix and Linux.

Unix/Linux

The user *root* on the local system (host name *localhost* or *computername*) has unlimited rights. The *root* user is not secured with a password (that is, every user on the local system can access MySQL as *root*). Furthermore, all users on the local system are permitted to access MySQL without a password; in contrast to *root*, these users have no rights whatsoever (they can't even execute a *SELECT* command).

Windows

The user *root* has unlimited rights, and this is independent of whether *root* is coming from the local system or from an external computer in the network. Moreover, all users on the local system (but not from an external computer) have unrestricted rights. Finally, anyone can log in (any user name, any host name), although the user, at least in this case, has no rights. Here as well there are no passwords.

CAUTION *To make things perfectly clear: According to the MySQL default installation under Unix/Linux anyone with access to the local system can connect to MySQL as* root *and do whatever he or she wants with your databases. Under windows it is not even necessary to use the local computer: A connection as* root *is possible over a network. In the next section, on first aid, you will learn how with a little effort you can replace this default setting with something more restrictive.*

REMARK *For those with little experience with Unix/Linux,* root *under Unix/Linux plays somewhat the same role as* Administrator *under Windows, that is, a superuser with almost unrestricted privileges. However, be advised that user names under MySQL have no connection with the login names for the operating system. Thus* root *has so many privileges under MySQL because the MySQL default setting was chosen, not because under Unix/Linux* root *has such privileges. It would have been possible to choose a name other than* root *for the MySQL user with administrative access rights.*

Test Databases

Regardless of the operating system under which MySQL is installed, any user who connects to MySQL can create test databases. The only condition is that the name of the database must begin with the letters *test* (under Unix/Linux it must begin with *test_*). Please note that not only can every MySQL user create such a database, in addition, every user can read, alter, and delete all data in such a database. In fact, anyone can delete the entire database. In short, the data in *test* databases are completely unprotected.

> **POINTER** *Tables 7-3, 7-4, and 7-6 depict this default setting. To understand these figures it is necessary that you understand the* mysql *table functions* user *and* db, *which are described in this chapter.*

First Aid

Perhaps you are not quite ready to immerse yourself in the depths of SQL access management. In that case, this section provides a bit of first aid advice.

Protecting the MySQL Installation Under Unix/Linux

The following commands assume that MySQL has been freshly installed and that no changes have been made to the default access privileges.

root *Password for Local Access*

With the following two commands you can secure *root* access with a password *xxx*. (Instead of *xxx*, you should, of course, provide the password of your choice.)

```
root# mysqladmin -u root -h localhost password xxx
root# mysqladmin -u root -h computername password xxx
```

Instead of *computername* you should give the name of the local computer (which you can determine with the command hostname).

No Local Access Without Password

Please note that in accordance with the MySQL default settings, a MySQL connection can be made from the local computer with any user name other than *root*. In contrast to the *root* connection such connections are, to be sure, provided with no privileges, but nonetheless they represent a security risk. (For example, such users have unrestricted access to *test* databases.)

However, here simple password security with mysqladmin is impossible, since there is no user name to which the password can be assigned. However, you can delete the two relevant entries in the *user* table of the *mysql* database. The necessary commands look like this:

```
root# mysql -p
Enter password: xxx
Welcome to the MySQL monitor. ...
mysql> USE mysql;
Database changed
mysql> DELETE FROM user WHERE user='';
Query OK, 2 rows affected (0.00 sec)
mysql> FLUSH PRIVILEGES;
Query OK, 0 rows affected (0.01 sec)
mysql> exit
```

Please note that in the future you will have to provide the password to execute mysql and mysqladmin (option -p) that was defined with mysqladmin at the beginning of this section. *FLUSH PRIVILEGES* is necessary so that the changes carried out directly in the *mysql* database become effective. (MySQL keeps a copy of the *mysql* database in RAM, for speed optimization, which is updated via *FLUSH PRIVILEGES*. Instead of executing *FLUSH PRIVILEGES*, you can exit mysql and instead execute mysqladmin reload.)

Protecting the MySQL Installation Under Windows

The way of proceeding under Windows is very similar to that under Unix/Linux. However, the default configuration under Windows is even more insecure, for which reason a bit more work is necessary.

Furthermore, using the commands mysql and mysqladmin is more complex (in particular, when you wish to pass parameters). The simplest way of proceeding is first to open a command window (START|PROGRAMS|ACCESSORIES|COMMAND PROMPT) and there use cd to make the bin\ directory of the MySQL installation the current directory. (Hint: You will save some typing if you move the directory via *Drag-&-Drop* from Explorer into the command window.)

> **TIP** *In the following, for the sake of clarity, we shall always launch* mysql *anew in order to carry out the individual security measures. If you wish to execute all of the security measures at once, you will, of course, not have to quit* mysql *each time.*

root *Password for Local Access*

With the following command you can secure *root* for the local computer with a password (where instead of *xxx* you provide the password of your choice).

```
Q:\> cd 'Q:\Program Files\mysql\bin'
Q:\ ... \bin> mysqladmin -u root -h localhost password xxx
```

No root *Access from External Computers*

The following commands prevent *root* access from external computers.

```
Q:\ ... \bin> mysql
Welcome to the MySQL monitor.
mysql> USE mysql;
mysql> DELETE FROM user WHERE user='root' AND host='%';
Query OK, 1 row affected (0.00 sec)
mysql> FLUSH PRIVILEGES;
Query OK, 0 rows affected (0.01 sec)
```

Fewer Privileges for Local Users

In the default setting local users have unrestricted rights, even if they do not register as *root*. The following command deletes all privileges for non*root* access.

```
mysql> REVOKE ALL ON *.* FROM ''@localhost;
Query OK, 1 row affected (0.00 sec)
mysql> REVOKE GRANT OPTION ON *.* FROM ''@localhost;
Query OK, 1 row affected (0.00 sec)
mysql> FLUSH PRIVILEGES;
Query OK, 0 rows affected (0.01 sec)
```

No Local Access Without a Password

Local users can still access universally visible databases (for example, those whose name begins with *test_*). If it is not your wish that anyone with access to the local computer can register without a password, you can do without the above command and instead simply forbid local access without a password.

```
mysql> DELETE FROM user WHERE user='' AND host='localhost';
Query OK, 1 row affected (0.00 sec)
mysql> FLUSH PRIVILEGES;
Query OK, 0 rows affected (0.01 sec)
```

From now on administrative tasks are possible only as *root* under *localhost*. Therefore, you must use the commands `mysql` and `mysqladmin` with the options `-u root` and `-p`.

No Access from External Computers Without a Password

In the default setting anyone can register with MySQL from an external computer. This access comes with no privileges, but nonetheless it should be prevented. Here are the necessary commands:

```
mysql> DELETE FROM user WHERE host='%' AND user='';
Query OK, 1 row affected (0.00 sec)
mysql> FLUSH PRIVILEGES;
Query OK, 0 rows affected (0.01 sec)
```

WinMySQLadmin Users

If you specified a user name and password at the initial launch of WinMySQLadmin, then the program has an additional user with unrestricted privileges (like those of *root*). In the following it is assumed that the user name is *namexy*.

User *namexy* is secured by a password, but this password is stored in plain text in the file `Windows\my.ini`. Anyone who is permitted to work at the computer and knows a bit about MySQL can easily obtain unrestricted access to MySQL. You have three options for closing this security loophole:

- Delete the user *namexy*.

- Delete the password line in `Windows\my.ini`.

- Restrict the privileges of this user.

The first two of these options are not ideal, because the program WinMySQLadmin can then be used only with severe restrictions. A workable compromise consists in setting the privileges of *namexy* in such a way that the most important administrative tasks are possible, but alteration of data is forbidden.

```
mysql> REVOKE INSERT, UPDATE, DELETE, DROP, FILE, ALTER
    > ON *.* FROM mk@localhost;
Query OK, 1 row affected (0.00 sec)
mysql> REVOKE GRANT OPTION ON *.* FROM mk@localhost;
Query OK, 1 row affected (0.00 sec)
mysql> FLUSH PRIVILEGES;
Query OK, 0 rows affected (0.01 sec)
```

> **REMARK** *From this point on,* mysql *commands will be shown without the* mysql> *prompt.*

Setting Access Without a Password

Perhaps you were too restrictive in securing MySQL and now would like to provide general access on the local computer (and possibly to a set of particular other computers as well) without the necessity of providing a user name and password. Then simply execute in mysql the following command:

```
GRANT USAGE ON *.* TO ''@localhost
```

Perhaps you would like to give the users some more privileges. Then in the command given above replace *USAGE* by a list containing, for example, *SELECT, INSERT, UPDATE*, etc. (A list of all possible privileges that are available under MySQL appears in the next section.)

Creating a New Database and User

Among the bread-and-butter tasks of a database administrator is setting up a new database and making it available to a user (who then can insert tables and fill them with data).

This task is easily fulfilled. You have merely to execute the following two commands with mysql. The result is the creation of the database *forum*, to which the user *forumadmin* has been granted unrestricted access. (If you execute the commands in mysql, do me and yourself a favor and do not forget to terminate the commands with a semicolon.)

```
CREATE DATABASE forum
GRANT ALL ON forum.* TO forumadmin IDENTIFIED BY 'xxx'
```

It is often useful to create a second access to the database, one with fewer privileges (and therefore with fewer security risks).

```
GRANT SELECT, INSERT, UPDATE, DELETE ON forum.*
  TO forumuser IDENTIFIED BY 'xxx'
```

Creating New Users

After the database that we have just created, *forum*, has been in operation for a while, it turns out that another individual, operating from another computer, requires unrestricted access to this database. The following command gives user *forumadmin2* on computer *uranus.sol* full privileges:

```
GRANT ALL ON forum.* TO forumadmin2@uranus.sol IDENTIFIED BY 'xxx'
```

If you wish to allow *forumadmin2* to sign in from any computer, then the command looks like this:

```
GRANT ALL ON forum.* TO forumadmin2@'%' IDENTIFIED BY 'xxx'
```

If you wish to go so far as to allow *forumadmin2* access to all databases (and not just *forum*), the command is as follows:

```
GRANT ALL ON *.* TO forumadmin2@uranus.sol IDENTIFIED BY 'xxx'
```

In comparison to *root*, the only privilege that *forumadmin2* does not possess is the right to change access privileges. But a small change remedies the situation:

```
GRANT ALL ON *.* TO forumadmin2@uranus.sol
IDENTIFIED BY 'xxx' WITH GRANT OPTION
```

Granting the Right to Create One's Own Database

When there are many users each with his or her own databases (for example, on the system of an Internet service provider), it becomes increasingly burdensome for the administrator to create yet another database for a particular user. In such cases it would be a good idea to give this user the right to create databases. In order to prevent a jungle of databases from appearing with no clue as to which belongs to whom, it is usual practice to allow a user to create only databases that begin with that user's user name. That is, a user named, say, *kofler*, is allowed to create databases named, say, *kofler_test, kofler_forum, kofler1, koflerXy*, etc., but no databases whose names do not begin with *kofler*.

In the following the way to proceed will be demonstrated for a user with the remarkable user name *username*. If this user is not yet known to MySQL, then first it must be created:

```
GRANT USAGE ON *.* TO username@localhost IDENTIFIED BY 'xxx'
```

Then, sad to tell, you must wrestle with an *INSERT* command, since the more convenient *GRANT* command does not, alas, permit wild cards in the specification of database names. Therefore, the necessary changes in the database *db* must be made directly.

```
INSERT INTO mysql.db (Host, Db, User, Select_priv, Insert_priv,
  Update_priv, Delete_priv, Create_priv, Drop_priv, Grant_priv,
  References_priv, Index_priv, Alter_priv)
VALUES ('localhost', 'username%', 'username', 'Y', 'Y', 'Y', 'Y',
  'Y', 'Y', 'N', 'Y', 'Y','Y')
```

For these changes to become effective, *FLUSH PRIVILEGES* must finally be executed.

```
FLUSH PRIVILEGES
```

Honey, I Forgot the root Password!

What do you do if you have forgotten the *root* password for MySQL (and there is no other MySQL user with sufficient administrative privileges and a known password to restore the forgotten password)?

Fear not, for I bring you glad tidings. MySQL has thought about this possibility. The way to proceed is this: Terminate MySQL (that is, the MySQL server mysqld) and then restart it with the option --skip-grant-tables. You thereby achieve that the tables with access privileges is not loaded. You can now delete the encrypted password for *root*, terminate MySQL, and then restart without the given option. Now you can give the *root* user a new password.

The following example is based on MySQL under SuSE Linux, although the same procedure is possible under other configurations (though with slight variations). In each case we assume that you have system administrator privileges on the operating system under which MySQL is running.

The first step is to terminate MySQL:

```
root# /sbin/init.d/mysql stop
```

Under Red Hat Linux this script is located in the directory /etc/rc.d/init.d. Alternatively, you can use kill under Unix/Linux to terminate the MySQL daemon (that is, the program mysqld). All open files will be closed, which ensures that all databases remain in a consistent state. (However, avoid kill -9, which will terminate mysqld at once, without giving the program the opportunity to terminate open operations.) Under Windows you end MySQL in the Service Manager (CONTROL PANEL| ADMINISTRATIVE TOOLS|SERVICES).

In the second step you relaunch mysqld via safe_mysqld (a launch script for mysqld) with the option --skip-grant-tables. The option --user specifies the account under which mysqld should be executed. The option --datadir tells where the MySQL databases can be found. Here the same setting as with a normal MySQL launch should be used. (The precise instruction depends on the system configuration.)

```
root# startproc /usr/bin/safe_mysqld --user=mysql \
        --datadir=/var/mysql --skip-grant-tables
```

Now you can use mysql to delete the *root* password.

```
root# mysql -u root
Welcome to MySQL monitor.
mysql> USE mysql;
Database changed.
mysql> UPDATE user SET password=''
    > WHERE user='root' AND host='localhost';
Query OK, 1 row affected (0.00 sec)
```

After restarting MySQL you can again take over administration as *root* (and the first thing you should do is to create a new password and memorize it).

```
root# /sbin/init.d/mysql restart
```

> **CAUTION** *The procedures described here can, of course, be used by an attacker who wishes to spy on your data or manipulate it somehow. The only (fortunately, not easily achieved) condition is to acquire Unix/Linux root access. This shows how important it is not only to secure MySQL, but also the computer on which MySQL is running. (This topic, security under Unix/Linux/Windows, is, like any number of other topics, beyond the scope of this book.)*

The Internal Workings of the Access System

You are perhaps, dear reader, sorely tempted to skip over this foundational section, especially since the management of access privileges is rather complicated. However, I strongly suggest that you gird up your loins and make the effort to read through the description of the *mysql* tables. Regardless of the means that you use for setting up security on your system, it is helpful first to understand the inner workings of the system itself. This holds even for the case that you yourself are not the manager of access privileges, but that they are managed by a system administrator. It is only when you understand how it all works that you will be able to tell your system administrator just what your needs are.

Fundamentals

Two-Tiered Access Control

Access control for MySQL databases is managed in two tiers: In the first tier it is merely checked whether the user has the right to establish a connection to MySQL. This is accomplished by the evaluation of three pieces of information: user name, host name, and password.

Only if a connection can be established does the second level of access control come into play, which involves every single database command. For example, if a *SELECT* is executed, MySQL checks whether the user has access rights to the database, the table, and the column. If an *INSERT* is executed, then MySQL tests whether the user is permitted to alter the database, the table, and finally the column.

Privileges

How, then, does MySQL manage the information as to which commands can be executed? For this MySQL uses tables in which are stored *privileges*. If a user, let us call her *athena*, has a *SELECT* privilege for the database *owls*, then she is permitted to read all the data in *owls* (but not to change it). If *athena* has a global *SELECT* privilege, then it holds for all databases saved under MySQL. The privileges recognized by MySQL are displayed in Table 7-1.

The *Grant* privilege indicates that a MySQL user can dispense access privileges. (This is most easily accomplished with the SQL command *GRANT*, whence the name of the privilege.) However, the ability to dispense privileges is limited to the privileges possessed by the grantor. That is, no user can give privileges to another that he or she does not already possess.

Table 7-1. MySQL Privileges

For tables	
Select	may read data (*SELECT* command)
Insert	may insert new records (*INSERT*)
Update	may change existing records (*UPDATE*)
Delete	may delete existing records (*DELETE*)
Index	may create and delete indexes for tables
Alter	may rename tables and change their structure (*ALTER*)
For databases, tables, and indexes	
Create	may create new databases and tables
Drop	may delete existing databases and tables
Grant	may give privileges to other users
References	currently not in use
For file access	
File	may read and change files in the local file system
For MySQL administration	
Process	may list and terminate MySQL processes (*processlist, kill*)
Reload	may execute various commands (*reload, refresh, flush-xxx*)
Shutdown	may terminate MySQL

CAUTION Grant *is an often overlooked security risk. For example, a test database is created to which all members of a team have unrestricted access. To this end all the privileges in the relevant entry in the* db *table are set to* Y *(the* db *table will be described a bit later).*

A perhaps unforeseen consequence is that everyone who has unrestricted access to this test table can give unrestricted access privileges (either to him- or herself or to other MySQL users) for other databases as well!

MySQL users with the *File* privilege may use SQL commands for direct access to the file system of the computer on which the MySQL server is running, for example, with the command *SELECT . . . INTO OUTFILE name* or the command *LOAD DATA* or with the function *LOAD_FILE*.

In the case of file access, it is necessary, of course, to pay heed to the access privileges of the file system. (Under Unix/Linux the MySQL server normally runs under the *mysql* account. Therefore, only those files that are readable by the Unix/Linux user *mysql* can be read.) Nevertheless, the *File* privilege is often a considerable security risk.

> **REMARK** *In the MySQL documentation you will encounter (in the description of the* GRANT *command, for instance) the privileges* All *and* Usage. All *indicates that all privileges are to be granted (set to* Y*). Usage has the opposite meaning: All privileges are withheld.*

Global Privileges Versus Object Privileges

In MySQL privileges can be chosen to be either global or related to a particular object. Global indicates that the privilege is valid for all MySQL objects (that is, for all databases, tables, and columns of a table).

The management of object-related privileges is somewhat more difficult, but it is also more secure. Only thus can you, for example, achieve that a particular MySQL user can alter a particular table, and not all tables managed under MySQL. An assumption in the use of object-related privileges is that the corresponding global privileges are not set. (What is globally allowed cannot be withheld at the object level.)

This hierarchical idea is maintained within the object privileges as well. First it is checked whether access to an entire database is allowed. Only if that is not allowed is it then checked whether access to the entire table named in the SQL command is allowed. Only if that is forbidden is it then checked whether perhaps access to individual columns of the table is allowed.

The mysql *Database*

It is not surprising that the management by MySQL of access privileges is carried out by means of a database. This database has the name *mysql,* and it consists of several tables, responsible for various aspects of access privileges.

> **REMARK** *It is sometimes not entirely a simple matter to distinguish among the various uses to which the word "MySQL" is put. In this book we attempt to use different type styles to obtain some degree of clarity:*
>
> - *MySQL: the database system as a whole.*
>
> - mysqld: *the MySQL server (MySQL daemon).*
>
> - mysql: *the MySQL monitor (a type of command interpreter).*
>
> - *mysql: the database for managing MySQL access privileges.*

The Tables of the Database mysql

The database *mysql* contains six tables (five in earlier versions) of which five are for managing access privileges. These five tables are often referred to as *grant* tables. The following list provides an overview of the tasks of these six tables:

- *user* controls who (user name) can access MySQL from which computer (host name). This table also contains global privileges.

- *db* specifies which user (user name) can access which databases.

- *host* extends the *db* table with information on the permissible host names (those that are not present in *db*).

- *tables_priv* specifies who can access which tables of a database.

- *columns_priv* specifies who can access which columns of a table.

- *func* enables the management of UDFs (*user-defined functions*); this is still undocumented.

> **REMARK** *When you newly install MySQL, the default values of* user *and* db *depend on the operating system. The contents of these two tables are displayed in Tables 7-3, 7-4, and 7-6, which appear further later. The effect of these settings was discussed earlier. (The tables* host, tables_priv, *and* columns_priv *start off life empty.)*

> **REMARK** *In MySQL's two-tiered access system the table* user *is solely responsible for the first level (that is, for the connection to MySQL). For the second tier (that is, access to specific objects: databases, tables, and columns) it is the tables* db, host, tables_priv, *and* columns_priv *that are responsible, in addition to* user.
>
>   *The tables* db, host, tables_priv, *and* columns_priv *come into play in this order when the privileges for their respective tiers are set to* N *(which stands for "No"). In other words, if the* SELECT *privilege is granted to a user in* user, *then the other four tables will not be consulted in checking the permissibility of a* SELECT *command executed by that user.*
>
>   *The result is that if fine distinctions in access privileges are to be made, the global privileges in the* user *table must be set to* N.

Example

Before we attempt to describe the individual tables in detail, we present an example: Let us suppose that a particular MySQL user, let us call him *zeus*, is to be allowed to read a particular column of a particular table, and nothing else. Then *zeus* (user name, host name, password) must be entered in the *user* table. There all of *zeus*'s global privileges will be set to *N*.

Furthermore, *zeus* (user name, host name) must be registered in the *columns_priv* table as well. There it must also be specified which column *zeus* is permitted to access (database name, table name, column name). Finally, there the *Select* privilege (and only this privilege) must be activated. In the tables *db*, *host*, and *tables_priv* no entries for *zeus* are necessary.

The Table user

The *user* table (see Table 7-2) fulfills two tasks: It alone regulates who has any access at all to MySQL. Secondly, global privileges can be granted through this table.

Table 7-2. Structure of the user *table*

Field	Type	Null	Default
Host	char(60)	No	
User	char(16)	No	
Password	char(16)	No	
Select_priv	enum('N', 'Y')	No	N
Insert_priv	enum('N', 'Y')	No	N
Update_priv	enum('N', 'Y')	No	N
Delete_priv	enum('N', 'Y')	No	N
Create_priv	enum('N', 'Y')	No	N
Drop_priv	enum('N', 'Y')	No	N
Reload_priv	enum('N', 'Y')	No	N
Shutdown_priv	enum('N', 'Y')	No	N
Process_priv	enum('N', 'Y')	No	N
File_priv	enum('N', 'Y')	No	N
Grant_priv	enum('N', 'Y')	No	N
References_priv	enum('N', 'Y')	No	N
Index_priv	enum('N', 'Y')	No	N
Alter_priv	enum('N', 'Y')	No	N

Access Control

For control over who can connect to MySQL there are three necessary identifiers—as we have mentioned already several times—that must be evaluated: user name, host name, and password. Here we shall say a few words about how this information is stored in the fields *User*, *Host*, and *Password*.

- **User Name:** Access control is case-sensitive. In the *User* field no wild cards are allowed. If the *User* field is empty, then any user name is permitted for accessing MySQL. Then the user is considered to be an anonymous user.

This means that in the second tier of access control the actual user name is not used, but rather an empty character string.

- **Host Name:** The host name can be given either as a name or as an IP number. Here the wild cards _ (an arbitrary character) or % (zero or more characters) are permitted, for example, *192.168.37.%* or *%.myfavoriteen-terprise.com*. In the case of IP numbers the forms (which are equivalent to those of the first example) *192.168.37.0/255.255.255.0* and *192.168.37.0/24* are permitted. If the host name is given simply as the character %, the a connection can be made from any computer. To enable access to users on the local computer, specify the host name *localhost*. As with the user name, the host name is case-sensitive.

- **Password:** The password must be encrypted with the SQL function *PASSWORD*. It is not possible to store a password in plain text. Furthermore, wild cards are not allowed. If the password field remains empty, then a connection can be made with no password whatsoever. (An empty password field thus does not mean that an arbitrary password can be given.)
  Be thou once more warned: For reasons of security you should never use as your MySQL password a password that you use to gain admittance to the operating system.

It often happens that in making a connection to MySQL several records match the given login data. If, for example, you log in as *root* from the local computer under the default settings of the *user* table for Windows, then all four entries would match. MySQL then decides in favor of the most nearly exact description (thus in this case for *root/localhost* and not for *' '/%).*). The reason for this is that with an exact match in the login one can expect more in the way of access privileges.

In order to speed up the selection of the correct record, the *user* table is sorted internally by MySQL. Here the field *Host* serves as the first sort criterion, and *User* as the second. In sorting, those character strings without the wild cards _ and % are given priority. Empty character strings and the character string % come in last in the sort order. Tables 7-3 and 7-4 show the default settings for the *user* table in their respective internal sort orders.

Privileges

In addition to MySQL access control, the *user* table also has the responsibility for global privileges. To this end there are fourteen fields that take part, which can be set to *Y* or *N*. Since *Y* stands for "yes," this setting means that the associated privilege is set globally for the MySQL user (for all databases, tables, and columns).

Contrariwise, *N* means "no" (or *non* in French, *nein* in German, *nyet* in Russian; you get the idea), and so such a setting means that the operation in question is not allowed globally, and therefore the tables *db*, *host*, *tables_priv*, and *columns_priv* will be consulted for object-specific privileges.

Default Setting

As we described in the introduction to this chapter, after installation of MySQL there are various default settings of the *user* table that depend on the particular operating system. Tables 7-3 and 7-4 give these settings (for MySQL version 3.23.*n*). The last line in Table 7-4 is maintained only if at the first launch of WinMySQLadmin a name and password for a new user have been given.

Table 7-3. Default setting for the user *table under Unix/Linux*

Host	User	Password	Select_priv	Insert_priv	Xxx_priv
localhost	root		Y	Y	Y ...
computer name	root		Y	Y	Y ...
localhost			N	N	N ...
computer name			N	N	N ...

Table 7-4. Default setting for the user *table under Windows after a new user has been registered with WinMySQLadmin*

Host	User	Password	Select_priv	Insert_priv	Xxx_priv
localhost	root		Y	Y	Y ...
localhost			Y	Y	Y ...
%	root		Y	Y	Y ...
%			N	N	N ...
localhost	*username*	1930448230873237	Y	Y	Y ...

The db and host Tables

The db Table

The *db* table (see Table 7-5) contains information on which databases a particular user is permitted to read, edit, and delete. The function of this table is easy to understand: If user *u* located at computer *h* wishes to access database *d* by executing a *SELECT* command and does not possess a global *Select* privilege, then MySQL pores over the *db* table and looks for the first *User/Host/Db* entry for the triple *u/h/d*. (As we saw in the case of the *user* table, uniquely identifying entries take precedence over those with wild cards. The entries are case-sensitive.) If a matching entry is found, then it must then only be checked as to whether the column *Select_priv* contains the value *Y*.

Table 7-5. Structure of the db *table*

Field	Type	Null	Default
Host	char(60)	No	
Db	char(64)	No	
User	char(16)	No	
Select_priv	enum('N', 'Y')	No	N
Insert_priv	enum('N', 'Y')	No	N
Update_priv	enum('N', 'Y')	No	N
Delete_priv	enum('N', 'Y')	No	N
Create_priv	enum('N', 'Y')	No	N
Drop_priv	enum('N', 'Y')	No	N
Grant_priv	enum('N', 'Y')	No	N
References_priv	enum('N', 'Y')	No	N
Index_priv	enum('N', 'Y')	No	N
Alter_priv	enum('N', 'Y')	No	N

> **REMARK** *In order for security control to be executed quickly, MySQL maintains various* mysql *tables presorted in RAM. However, that has the consequence that direct changes in these tables become active only when MySQL is ordered to reread these tables with* FLUSH PRIVILEGES *or* `mysqladmin reload`.

Practically the same rules as in the *user* table hold for the settings of *User* and *Host* in the *db* table. The only exception relates to the *Host* column: If this remains empty, then MySQL evaluates the *host* table as well (see below under "The *host* Table").

Default Setting

After installation of MySQL all users (those who are able to access MySQL) are permitted to set up, edit, and delete databases whose names begin with *test_*. (Under Windows the underscore in the database name is not required.) This default setting is supposed to allow a nonbureaucratic testing of MySQL without the beleaguered system administrator having to set up such databases.

An obvious problem with this arrangement is that anyone with access to MySQL has the right to create a database and stuff it with data and then stuff it some more until the computer's hard drive is full.

Table 7-6 shows the default setting for the *db* table. Please note in particular that for *test* databases all privileges except for the *Grant* privilege are set. This exception is important, so that the privileges from the *test* databases cannot be transferred to other databases.

Table 7-6. Default setting of the db *table under Unix/Linux*

Host	Db	User	Select_priv	Insert_priv	Xxx_priv	Grant_priv
%	test_%		Y	Y	Y ...	N

> **REMARK** *Have you understood the privileges system of MySQL? Then see whether you can answer the following question:*
>
> *Can a MySQL user create and edit a* test *database even if all global privileges are set to* N*?*
>
> *The answer is yes, of course. If all the global privileges are set to* N*, then the object-specific privileges are consulted (where every database that begins with* test *is considered an object). This is precisely the concept of the privilege system of MySQL.*

The host Table

The *host* table (see Table 7-7) is an extension of the *db* table if the latter's *Host* field is empty. In this case entries for the database in question are sought in the *host* table. If an entry that matches the computer name is found there, the privilege settings in *db* and *host* are joined with a logical *AND* (that is, privileges must be granted in both tables).

The *host* table is brought into play relatively rarely. (As a rule, the settings of the *db* table meet all requirements.) This is also expressed in the fact that the commands *GRANT* and *REVOKE*, introduced below, do not affect the *host* table. Thus the *host* table is empty in the default setting.

Table 7-7. Structure of the host *table*

Field	Type	Null	Default
Host	char(60)	No	
Db	char(64)	No	
Select_priv	enum('N', 'Y')	No	N
Insert_priv	enum('N', 'Y')	No	N
...			
Alter_priv	enum('N', 'Y')	No	N

The tables_priv *and* columns_priv *Tables*

With the tables *tables_priv* (see Table 7-8) and *columns_priv* (see Table 7-9) privileges can be set for individual tables and columns, respectively. For *Host* and *User* the same rules hold as in the *user* table. In the fields *Db*, *Table_name*, and *Column_name*, on the other hand, no wild cards are permitted. All the fields except *Column_name* are case-sensitive.

Table 7-8. Structure of the tables_priv *table*

Field	Type	Null	Default
Host	char(60)	No	
Db	char(64)	No	
User	char(16)	No	
Table_name	char(64)	No	
Grantor	char(77)	No	
Timestamp	timestamp(14)	Yes	
Table_priv	set1	No	
Column_priv	set2	No	

In the undocumented column *Grantor* is stored information as to who has given the access rights (for example, *root@localhost*).

Table 7-9. Structure of the columns_priv *table*

Field	Type	Null	Default
Host	char(60)	No	
Db	char(64)	No	
User	char(16)	No	
Table_name	char(64)	No	
Column_name	char(64)	No	
Timestamp	timestamp(14)	Yes	
Column_priv	set2	No	

Unlike the tables described above, these tables have their privileges managed by two sets. (Sets are a peculiarity of MySQL; see also Chapter 5. With sets an arbitrary combination of all character strings specified by set definitions can be stored.) The two sets for *tables_priv* and *columns_priv* look like this:

```
set1: SET('Select', 'Insert', 'Update', 'Delete', 'Create', 'Drop',
          'Grant', 'References', 'Index', 'Alter')
set2: SET('Select', 'Insert', 'Update', 'References')
```

Here *set2* contains only those privileges that hold for individual columns. (The *Delete* privilege is missing, because only an entire data record can be deleted, not an individual field of a record. This field can, of course, be set to *NULL*, 0, or ' ', but for that the *Update* privilege suffices.)

It is my sad duty to report that it is not documented as to when in the table *tables_priv* the field *Table_priv* is to be used and when the field *Column_priv*. If one considers how the fields are changed by the SQL command *GRANT*, one may venture the following hypothesis:

- Privileges that relate to the entire table are stored in the field *Table_priv*.

- Privileges that relate to individual columns are stored in the field *Column_priv*, as well as in the *tables_priv* and *columns_priv* tables. The *tables_priv* table is to a certain extent a conglomeration of all privileges for which there are additional details in the *columns_priv* table (perhaps divided over several data records). The reason for this is probably the idea that evaluating both tables leads to simplification or increased speed for MySQL.

If you are in doubt, use the commands *GRANT* and *REVOKE* for setting column privileges. Have a look at the MySQL documentation. Perhaps since this was written the *Columns_priv* field has received a better treatment.

The tables *tables_priv* and *columns_priv* are empty in the default setting.

Tools for Setting Access Privileges

One can edit the tables of a database (assuming, of course, that you have the appropriate access privileges) with the usual SQL commands *INSERT*, *UPDATE*, and *DELETE*. However, that is a tiring and error-prone occupation. It is much more convenient to use the commands *GRANT* and *REVOKE*, which are the centerpiece of this section. Further alternatives for particular tasks are the MySQL tool mysqladmin as well as the Perl script mysql_setpermission.

> **CAUTION**   *MySQL maintains, for reasons of speed optimization, copies of the* mysql *tables in RAM. Direct changes to the tables are effective only after they are explicitly reread by MySQL via the SQL command* FLUSH PRIVILEGES *or the external program* mysqladmin reload. *(With* GRANT *and* REVOKE *this rereading takes place automatically.)*

Changing Access Privileges with GRANT and REVOKE

The syntax of the *GRANT* and *REVOKE* commands is as follows:

```
GRANT privileges
ON [database.]table
TO user@host [IDENTIFIED BY 'password']
[WITH GRANT OPTION]
REVOKE privileges
ON [database.]table
FROM user@host
```

If you wish to change the access privileges for all the tables of a database, the correct form to use is *ON database.**. If you wish to alter global privileges, then specify *ON *.**. It is not allowed to use wild cards in database names.

For *user* you can specify ' ' to indicate all users on a particular computer (for example, ' '@*computername*). On the other hand, for *host* you must use '%' (for example, *username*@'%').

Depending on their function, these commands change the *mysql* tables *user*, *db*, *tables_priv*, and *columns_priv*. (The *host* table remains untouched.)

> **POINTER** *The complete syntax of* GRANT *and* REVOKE *are given in Chapter 13. However, you can get a fairly good feel for these commands from the following examples.*

Enabling Access to a Database

The following command gives the user *juno* on the local computer the right to read and alter data in all tables of the database *library*. If *juno@localhost* is unknown to the *user* table of the *mysql* database, then this name is added without a password. (If there is already a *juno@localhost*, then the password is not changed.)

```
GRANT SELECT, INSERT, UPDATE, DELETE
ON library.* TO juno@localhost
```

Prohibiting Changes in a Database

The next command takes away from *juno* the right to make changes to *library*, but *juno* retains the right to read the database using *SELECT* (assuming that the command of the previous example was just executed).

```
REVOKE INSERT, UPDATE, DELETE
ON library.* FROM juno@localhost
```

Enabling Access to Tables

With the following command the user *apollo* on the local computer is given the right to read data from the table *authors* in the database *library* (but not to alter it):

```
GRANT SELECT ON library.authors TO apollo@localhost
```

Enabling Access to Individual Columns

The access privileges for *diana* are more restrictive than those for *apollo*: She is permitted only to read the columns *title* and *subtitle* of the table *books* in the database *library*.

```
GRANT SELECT(title, subtitle) ON library.books TO diana@localhost
```

Granting Database Access to All Local Users

All users on the local computer can read and edit data in the *mp3* database:

```
GRANT SELECT, INSERT, DELETE, UPDATE ON mp3.* TO ''@localhost
```

Registering New Users

All users with the computer name **.myorganization.com* are permitted to link to MySQL if they know the password *xxx*. The privilege *USAGE* means that all global privileges have been set to *N*. The users thereby at first have no privileges whatsoever (to the extent that so far no individual databases, tables, or columns have been made accessible to all users who can log into MySQL).

```
GRANT USAGE ON *.* TO ''@'%.myorganization.com' IDENTIFIED BY 'xxx'
```

The following command gives the user *admin* on the local computer unrestricted privileges: All privileges (including *Grant*) are set.

```
GRANT ALL ON *.* TO admin@localhost IDENTIFIED BY 'xxx'
WITH GRANT OPTION
```

POINTER *An additional example for changing access privileges can be found in this chapter under the heading "First Aid."*

Viewing Access Privileges with SHOW GRANTS

If you have lost track of which privileges a particular user has, the command *SHOW GRANTS* is just what you need. (This command has been available only since MySQL version 3.23.04.)

```
mysql> SHOW GRANTS FOR juno@localhost;
  Grants for juno@localhost:
  GRANT SELECT ON library.* TO 'juno'@'localhost'
1 row in set (0.00 sec)
```

Changing a Password with `mysqladmin`

The program `mysqladmin` carries out various administrative tasks (see also Chapter 11). Although this program does not offer any immediate assistance in managing access privileges, it does offer two applications that seem to fit into this chapter.

Changing a Password

You can use *GRANT* to change the password of a previously registered user. However, *GRANT* can be used only when at the same time access privileges are to be changed. If all you want to do is to change a password, then `mysqladmin` is a simpler alternative:

```
> mysqladmin -u juno -p password newPW
Enter password: oldPW
```

The above command changes the password for the user *juno* on the computer *localhost*. Please note that the new password is passed as a parameter, while the old password is entered on request. (This order, first the new and then the old, is rather unusual.)

Reading in New `mysql` Tables

For speed enhancement, MySQL loads *mysql* into RAM at startup. The disadvantage of this modus operandi is the following: If you change *mysql* directly using the *INSERT, UPDATE,* or *DELETE* commands, MySQL simply ignores these changes until you execute either the SQL command *FLUSH PRIVILEGES* or `mysqladmin` reload:

```
> mysqladmin -u root -p reload
Enter password: xxx
```

It is not necessary to use `mysqladmin reload` if you wish to change access privileges with *GRANT* or *REVOKE*. In those cases the altered tables are automatically read into RAM.

Viewing Access Privileges with `mysqlaccess`

Here we note that `mysqlaccess` is a Perl script that summarizes the access privileges of MySQL users. Thus `mysqlaccess` has a function similar to that of *SHOW GRANTS*, but with more features. It gives information as to which entries in the *mysql* tables are used for access, and it indicates security loopholes. This script is therefore useful if you need to get an overview of MySQL access privileges. It is also very practical in administering an older version of MySQL in which *SHOW GRANTS* is not available (versions prior to 3.23.04).

> **REMARK** *Information on using* `mysqlaccess` *can be obtained by executing the script with the option* `--help` *or* `--howto`.
> *The script* `mysqlaccess` *is not included with all MySQL distributions. To execute* `mysqlaccess` *Perl must be installed on the local computer.*

Our first example shows how *juno* is able to access the database *library*:

```
user@linux:~ > mysqlaccess juno library
Password for MySQL superuser root: xxx
```

Sele	Inse	Upda	Dele	...	Alte	Host,User,DB
Y	N	N	N	...	N	localhost,juno,library

In our second example it is determined who (user name ***) is permitted to access the *mysql* database:

```
user@linux:~ > mysqlaccess '*' mysql
Password for MySQL superuser root: xxx
```

Sele	Inse	Upda	Dele	...	Alte	Host,User,DB
Y	Y	Y	Y	...	Y	localhost,root,mysql
N	N	N	N	...	N	localhost,juno,mysql
N	N	N	N	...	N	localhost,ANY_NEW_USER,mysql

Changing Access Privileges with `mysql_setpermission`

If you find the commands *GRANT* and *REVOKE* too burdensome for standard tasks (such as giving a user access to a database), you may instead use the Perl script `mysql_setpermission`. The script is very simple to use, though the number of possible operations is small. (In particular, it is not possible to restrict privileges that have already been granted.)

> **REMARK** *The script* `mysql_setpermission` *assumes that Perl is installed on your computer together with the DBI and MySQL modules. (Under SuSE the packages* `perl`, `perl-dbi`, *and* `mysqperl` *are required.)*

The following example shows how with `mysql_setpermission` the database *webforum* is set up for the user *forumadmin*. As always, inputs are shown in boldface.

```
user@linux:~ > mysql_setpermission -u root
Password for user root to connect to MySQL: xxxx
What would you like to do:
  1. Set password for a user.
  2. Add a database + user privilege for that database.
   - user can do all except all admin functions
  3. Add user privilege for an existing database.
   - user can do all except all admin functions
  4. Add user privilege for an existing database.
   - user can do all except all admin functions + no create/drop
  5. Add user privilege for an existing database.
   - user can do only selects (no update/delete/insert etc.)
  0. exit this program

Make your choice [1,2,3,4,5,0]: 2

Which database would you like to add: webforum
The new database webforum will be created
What user name is to be created: forumadmin
user name = forumadmin
Would you like to set a password for [y/n]: y
What password do you want to specify for : newPW
Type the password again: newPW
We now need to know from what host(s) the user will connect.
Keep in mind that % means 'from any host' ...
```

```
The host please: localhost
Would you like to add another host [yes/no]: n
Okay we keep it with this ...
The following host(s) will be used: localhost.

That was it ... here is an overview of what you gave to me:
The database name  : webforum
The user name      : forumadmin
The host(s)        : localhost

Are you pretty sure you would like to implement this [yes/no]: y
Okay ... let's go then ...
Everything is inserted and mysql privileges have been reloaded.
```

With `mysqlacces` you can quickly check which privileges `mysql_setpermission` has granted (in our example, all except *Reload, Shutdown, Process,* and *File*).

```
user@linux:~ > mysqlaccess forumadmin webforum
Password for MySQL superuser root: xxx
```

Sele	Inse	Upda	Dele	Crea	Drop	Relo	Shut
Y	Y	Y	Y	Y	Y	N	N

Proc	File	Gran	Refe	Inde	Alte	Host,User,DB
N	N	Y	Y	Y	Y	localhost,forumadmin,webforum

System Security

Up to this point we have dealt in this chapter with issues of security as they apply directly to MySQL. In reality, of course, your data within a MySQL database are only as secure as the underlying operating system. (It is assumed that MySQL is running under an operating system that is equipped with security mechanisms. Security under Windows 9x/ME is a contradiction in terms, and it is to be hoped that no one will get the wild idea of running a public MySQL server under Windows 9x/ME.)

To secure your MySQL database system you should begin by asking the following questions:

- Are there security loopholes that would place an attacker in a position to log in as *root* (Unix/Linux) or with administrator privileges (Windows NT/2000)?

- Are the logging files secured? There, for example, the passwords can be found in plain text.

- Are script files containing passwords in plain text adequately secured? (And if full-fledged security is impossible, is it ensured that the user name/password combination in these files is provided with minimal access privileges? Is it ensured that the given password can really be used only for this MySQL login, that for convenience the same password as for *root* was not used?)

An additional issue concerns the data within a database. You should prepare yourself for the worst-case scenario—the possibility that an attacker gains access to your data—by encrypting key information within the database:

- If you store login information in the database (for example, the login information for users of your web site), then do not store the passwords in plain text, but only as MD5 check sums. These check sums are sufficient to verify a password. (The drawback is that a forgotten password cannot be restored from the check sum.)

- If you store even more sensitive data (credit card information, say, to take a particularly relevant example), such data should be encrypted. You should ask whether MySQL is a suitable database system for managing such data. If you store such critical data, you should engage security experts to make your system as secure as possible. Anything less should be considered gross negligence.

Note that MySQL itself can present a security risk that can be used for access to the entire operating system. For example, a MySQL user with *File* privileges can read and alter files in the local file system. The extent of this ability depends on how the file system itself is secured (access privileges for directories and files) and under what account the MySQL server (and thus mysqld) is running.

In no case should the server be run as *root* under Unix/Linux or with administrator privileges under Windows, since then every MySQL user with *File* privileges would have the run of the entire file system.

Under Unix/Linux you can use ps -axu to ensure that mysqld is not executed under *root*. You may also use the following entry in /etc/my.cnf:

```
# file /etc/my.cnf
[mysqld]
user = mysql
```

POINTER *A nice example of what can happen when* mysqld *is executed as* root *is shown by the text located at* http://www.dataloss.net/papers/how.defaced.apache.org.txt, *where it is described how the web server of* apache.org *was attacked in May 2000.*

TIP *If you set up MySQL as a database server only within a local network (that is, so that it is inaccessible from outside) and you use an IP packet filter as a fire wall, then as an additional security measure you should close the IP port 3306. You thereby achieve that the MySQL server cannot be addressed directly from outside the network.*

Internet access over dynamic web sites is still possible in spite of all security measures, since dynamic web sites are generated from the locally running web server (which in turn calls a script interpreter). The MySQL server is thus addressed locally, and external communication is accomplished not via port 3306, but via the HTTP protocol (normally port 80). If there is a security loophole there, then closing port 3306 will not be of any help.

POINTER *We may sum up by saying that one can achieve genuine security of MySQL only if one has a deep understanding of the operating system itself, and this cannot be discussed here, not least because I myself know too little about such issues, especially in regard to security mechanisms under Windows NT/2000.*

Further information can be found in the chapter "The MySQL access privilege system" in the MySQL documentation. Furthermore, there are many books on operating systems—completely independent of MySQL—that deal with the topics of administration and security.

Part III

Programming

CHAPTER 8

PHP

PHP STANDS FOR *PHP HYPERTEXT PREPROCESSOR* (A recursive abbreviation typical of Unix-world shenanigans). PHP is a script programming language for HTML pages. The code embedded in an HTML file is executed by the server. (The *Active Server Pages* of Microsoft also follow this plan.)

When a programming language is brought into play with MySQL, that language is almost always PHP. The reason for this is that MySQL offers almost ideal conditions for building dynamic web sites: simple deployment, high speed, unbeatable price (free).

This chapter is a long one, in justice to the high status of PHP. It provides, first of all, general programming techniques, and it then demonstrates the cooperation of the "dream team" PHP and MySQL with several examples. (All the examples can be tested on line at www.kofler.cc.)

Chapter Overview

Programming Techniques

> **POINTER** *Information on the installation of PHP is located in Chapter 2.*
> *The examples in this section are based on the database* mylibrary, *which*
> *was introduced in Chapter 5. A compact reference of all MySQL functions of*
> *PHP can be found in Chapter 15.*

Establishing a Connection to the Database

To create a connection one usually uses the PHP function *mysql_pconnect,* to
which three parameters are passed: the computer name (host name) of the
MySQL server, the MySQL user name, and the password. If MySQL is running on
the same computer as the PHP script (that is, on *localhost*), then the computer
name does not have to be given.

```
$connId = mysql_pconnect("localhost", "username", "xxx");
```

This function returns an identification number for the connection. This
number will be needed in the future only if you have more than one connection
to MySQL open. (As long as there is only one connection to MySQL, this is the
default connection. The ID number thus does not have to be given in calling
various *mysql_xxx* functions.)

Problems with Establishing the Connection

If problems occur in establishing the connection, the variable *connId* will contain
the value *FALSE.* Moreover, *mysql_pconnect* sends an error message to the web
server, so that in the resulting HTML document a rather unattractive error
message appears for you to behold. To avoid this error message it is necessary to
place the @ character before *mysql_pconnect.* (In general, this character prevents
error messages from being displayed in calls to PHP functions.)

If you would like to supply the PHP code for the connection with a readable
error message, you might write code something like the following:

```
$connId = @mysql_pconnect("localhost", "username", "xxx");
if ($connID == FALSE) {
echo "<p><b>I regret to inform you that a connection to the database
  cannot be established at this time.
```

```
  Please try again later. Perhaps you will have better luck.\n";
echo "</body></html>\n"; // close HTML Document!
exit(); // end PHP Script
}
```

Selecting the Default Database

As soon as a connection is established you can use various *mysql_xxx* functions to execute SQL commands and do a lot of other neat stuff as well. To avoid having to specify the desired database over and over, you can use *mysql_select_db* to select the default database (*mysql_select_db* corresponds to the SQL command *USE*).

```
mysql_select_db("mylibrary");
```

Specifying the MySQL user Name and Password in an Include File

You should always avoid storing a user name and password in plain text in a file that is accessible over the web. Of course, visitors to your site should in principle never obtain a glimpse of the source text of a PHP file, since the PHP code is evaluated by the web server and is no longer visible in the resulting HTML document. But configuration errors have been known to occur by which the PHP file in raw form is revealed to a web surfer.

An additional security risk is that the file might be read not via HTTP but via anonymous FTP. (That would also be the result of a configuration error. The directory for anonymous FTP should be completely separate from that with HTML files. Yet such configuration errors occur frequently.)

Thus to avoid allowing strangers to tumble onto your password too easily (but also so as not to have to write this information in every PHP script, which would entail a great deal of work if the MySQL password were to change), the MySQL login information is usually stored in its own file. For the examples of this section the password file has the name mylibraryconnect.inc.php, and it looks like this:

```php
<?php
  // <website-root-dir>/_private/mylibraryconnect.inc.php
    $mysqluser="user";       // user name for MySQL access
    $mysqlpasswd="xxx";      // password
    $mysqlhost="localhost";  // name of the computer on which MySQL is running
?>
```

The best place to store this file depends on the configuration of the web server. On my web site this file is located in the directory htdocs/_private/. The directory _private is secured by .htaccess. Therefore, loading the file with `http://www.mysite.com/_private/mylibraryconnect.inc.php` is possible only if the HTTP user name given in `.htaccess` and the associated encrypted password stored in the authentication file are given.

> **CAUTION** *Be absolutely certain that the include file cannot be accessed by anonymous FTP.*
>
> *Be sure that all include files end with* `*.php`. *Thus do not use, say,* `name.inc`, *but* `name.inc.php`. *This ensures that the file will be executed by the PHP interpreter during an HTTP access in every case (for example, if an attacker guesses the* `.htaccess` *user name and associated password).*
>
> *Be sure that it is impossible via anonymous FTP to display a PHP file on your web server in such a way that this file then can be read over the web server. If there is an FTP directory called* `incoming`, *then this directory must not also be accessible over the web server (for example, as* `http://www.mysite.com/ftp/incoming`). *If that were the case, then an attacker could write a simple PHP script that reads your include file and outputs the contents of the variables. (To do this, the attacker would have to know the name of the include file and names of the variables, but they just might be guessed. Often, examples are taken directly from various books, and there are not that many MySQL books.)*

> **REMARK** *If you can upload files outside the web-site root directory (this depends on your ISP), this is another rather safe place for include files. That is, you could create a* `private` *directory completely outside the directory for web files that are externally accessible. Again, be sure that this location cannot be accessed by anonymous FTP. (If it can, this would be an administrative failure on the part of your ISP.)*

We return now to the PHP file in which the connection to MySQL is to be established. There an *include* must be used to load the file with the password information.

```
include("../../_private/mylibraryconnect.inc.php");
$connID = @mysql_pconnect($mysqlhost, $mysqluser, $mysqlpasswd);
```

Depending on the directories in which the PHP script and the include file are located relative to each other, you will have to change the path information in the *include* command.

Building the Connection in the Include File

If an include file is used, then one should make full use of its advantages. If you wish to create a connection to MySQL from several different PHP files, it makes sense to store all of the code for creating the connection together with error checking in the include file.

The following model assumes that the function *mylibrary_connect* is executed before any HTML headers or the like are created in the PHP script file. Of course, other ways of proceeding are possible, but take care that the resulting HTML document is in any case complete (that is, inclusive of HTML header and with closure of all open HTML tags).

```php
<?php
// <website-root-dir>/_private/mylibrary-connect.inc.php
function connect_to_mylibrary() {
  $mysqluser="useruser"; // user name
  $mysqlpasswd="xxx"; // password
  $mysqlhost="localhost"; // name of the computer of which MySQL is running
  $connID = @mysql_pconnect($mysqlhost, $mysqluser, $mysqlpasswd);
  if ($connID) {
    mysql_select_db("mylibrary"); // set default database
    return $connID;
  }
  else {
    echo "<!DOCTYPE HTML PUBLIC \"-//W3C//DTD HTML 4.0//EN\">
      <html><head>
      <title>Sorry, no connection ... </title>
      <body><p>Sorry, no connection to database ... </body>
      </html>\n";
    exit(); // terminate PHP interpreter
    }
  }
?>
```

Introductory Example

The following miniscript (see also Figure 8-1) makes use of the function called *connect_to_mylibrary* introduced above to establish a connection to MySQL, and it then determines the number of data records stored in the table *titles*. (The two functions *mysql_query* and *mysql_result* are introduced in the following sections.)

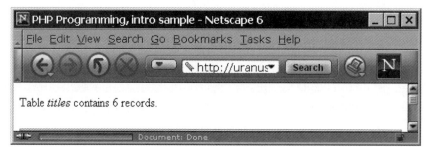

Figure 8-1. PHP introductory example

```
<!-- php/general/intro.php -->
<?php
  include("../../_private/mylibraryconnect.inc.php");
  $connID = connect_to_mylibrary();
?>
<!DOCTYPE HTML PUBLIC "-//W3C//DTD HTML 4.0//EN">
<html><head><title>PHP Programming, intro sample</title>
</head><body>
<?php
  $result = mysql_query("SELECT COUNT(*) FROM titles");
  echo "<P>Table <I>titles</I> contains ",
    mysql_result($result, 0, 0),
    " records.\n";
?>
</body></html>
```

mysql_connect *Versus* mysql_pconnect

PHP provides two functions for creating a connection to MySQL. One is the function *mysql_pconnect*, which we have already discussed, and the other is the function *mysql_connect*. The advantage of *mysql_pconnect* is that an attempt is made to reactivate an earlier connection with the same host name, user name, and password. This proceeds more quickly than establishing a completely new connection. In such a case the connection is called *persistent*. (Establishing a connection to MySQL usually is rapid in any case, and thus the time savings from a persistent connection are not enormous. On the other hand, with other database systems a persistent connection is absolutely necessary.)

Persistent connections are possible only if PHP is used as a module of the web server (and not in the CGI versions, which is the rule under Windows).

Persistent connections are managed by a thread. They are reused when the combination of host name, user name, and password coincides with an existing (but not currently in use) connection.

Regardless of how your web server is configured, you can always use *mysql_pconnect*. If recycling a connection is impossible, then a new connection is established. That is, *mysql_pconnect* does not result in any disadvantage vis-à-vis *mysql_connect*.

The only argument against *mysql_pconnect* is the resulting large number of open connections. On a frequently visited web server *mysql_pconnect* leads to many connections to MySQL being opened that then are not closed. On the one hand, this results in a large storage requirement, and on the other, the number of connections is limited by the MySQL variable *max_connections* (default setting is 100). Before you change *max_connections*, however, you should read about the topic "tuning." For example, there is an increase in the number of file descriptors needed by mysqld. (The MySQL variable *max_used_connections* informs you as to the maximum number of simultaneous connections that have been established hitherto. The content of this variable can be determined with *SHOW STATUS*.)

> **CAUTION** *The term "persistent" might lead one to think that the MySQL connection remains established when a PHP script is changed. That is not the case. In fact, it is quite the opposite.*
>
> *As a rule, after a change from one PHP page to another, a different MySQL connection is used (which has opened another script).*
>
> *Therefore, you may not depend on any connection-specific information (such as the current database) surviving a page change. In particular, you cannot execute SQL transactions over several pages.*
>
> *Do not depend on temporary tables being deleted at the end of a script. Temporary tables are indeed automatically deleted at the close of a connection by MySQL, but the life span of persistent connections is not foreseeable and is, as a rule, much longer than the time during which your script is being executed. You should delete temporary tables explicitly with* DROP TABLE *at the end of a script.*

Closing the Connection

With *mysql_close* you can explicitly close a connection to MySQL. Usually, this is not done, because at the end of a PHP script the connection is automatically closed in any case. However, this command can have practical use if your script addresses several MySQL connections or runs for a long period of time, in which case connections should not be open longer than is absolutely necessary.

Executing SQL Commands

To execute an SQL command you pass it as a character string to the function *mysql_query*. If the command is not to be applied to the current database, then you can use *mysql_db_query* to provide the name of the intended database. With each of these functions the ID number of the connection (that is, the return value of *mysql_pconnect*) can be passed as the optional last parameter if there is more than one connection to MySQL.

```
$result = mysql_query("SELECT COUNT(*) FROM titles");
$result = mysql_db_query("mylibrary", "SELECT COUNT(*) FROM titles");
```

With *mysql_query* any type of SQL command can be executed: queries with *SELECT*; changes to data with *INSERT, UPDATE,* and *DELETE*; changes to the database structure with *CREATE TABLE*; and so on.

> **REMARK** *An SQL command may not be terminated with a semicolon. It is not possible to give several commands at once. If you wish to execute several commands, then they must be given separately with* mysql_query.

Return Value ($result)

If an SQL command can be correctly executed, then *mysql_query* returns a nonzero value. If a query was involved, then the return value of *mysql_query* is a reference to a PHP resource (for example, a character string of the form *"Resource id #2"*. This return value can then be inserted into various other functions (for example, *mysql_fetch_row*) to evaluate the individual fields of a table. In the examples of this chapter the return value is usually stored in a variable with the name *result*. (Working with *SELECT* results will be described in detail in the next section.)

On the other hand, if an SQL command cannot be executed, then *mysql_query* returns the result *FALSE* (i.e., 0). Moreover, an error message is displayed, which you may suppress by executing *mysql_query* with the @ prefixed. (The cause of the error can be determined by evaluating *mysql_errno* and *mysql_error*. Further information on error evaluation can be found further below.)

Metainformation on Query Results

After *INSERT*, *UPDATE*, and *DELETE* commands (and all other commands that change data records) you can determine with *mysql_affected_rows* how many records were changed. This function is also helpful after *CREATE TABLE . . . SELECT . . .* for determining how many records were inserted into the new table.

Moreover, you can determine with *mysql_insert_id* after an *INSERT* command which *AUTO_INCREMENT* value was used for inserting the last new record.

```
$n = mysql_affected_rows(); // number of changed records
$new_id = mysql_insert_id(); // ID number of the last AUTO_INCREMENT record
```

On the other hand, if you have executed a *SELECT* query with *mysql_query*, you can use the functions *mysql_num_rows* and *mysql_num_fields* to determine the number of resulting data records and columns, respectively.

```
$rows = mysql_num_rows($result); // number of records
$cols = mysql_num_fields($result); // number of columns
```

> **REMARK** *Please note the various parameters that the functions we have been discussing take:*
>
> - *In the case of* mysql_affected_rows *and* mysql_insert_id *no parameter should be given. (Optionally, the ID number of the MySQL connection can be given, that is,* $connID, *if you follow the nomenclature of the examples of this chapter.)*
>
> - *On the other hand,* mysql_num_rows *and* mysql_num_fields *expect as parameter the ID number of the query (that is,* $result),

Releasing Query Results

PHP stores query results until the end of the script. If you wish to release these results sooner (for example, because you wish to execute a large number of queries in a script and do not wish to use more memory than necessary), you can release the query result early with *mysql_free_result*. This is particularly to be recommended when there is a loop in your script that executes SQL queries.

```
mysql_free_result($result);
```

Evaluating SELECT *Queries, Representing Tables*

If you execute a *SELECT* query with *mysql_query*, then as result you obtain a reference to a table with *rows* rows and *cols* columns:

```
$result = mysql_query("SELECT * FROM titles");
$rows = mysql_num_rows($result);
$cols = mysql_num_fields($result);
```

This holds as well for two special cases:

- If the query returns only a single value (for example, *SELECT COUNT(*) FROM table*), then the table has only one row and one column.

- If the query does not return any result at all (for example, if there are no records that correspond to a *WHERE* condition), then the table has zero rows. This case can be identified only by evaluating *mysql_num_rows*.

Only if the SQL query was syntactically incorrect or there was a problem with communication with MySQL will you receive no result at all (that is, the return value of *mysql_query* is *FALSE*).

Access to Individual Table Fields

The simplest, but also the slowest, access to individual fields of a table is offered by *mysql_result*. You simply provide the desired row and column numbers in two parameters. (Numbering begins with 0, as with all PHP MySQL functions.) Instead of the column number you can give the column name (or the alias name if in the SQL query you have worked with *AS alias*).

```
$item = mysql_result($result, $row, $col);
```

It is considerably more efficient to evaluate the result by rows. There are three functions for this:

```
$row = mysql_fetch_row($result);
$row = mysql_fetch_array($result);
$row = mysql_fetch_object($result);
```

- *mysql_fetch_row* returns the record in the form of a simple array. Access to the columns is accomplished with *$row[$n]*.

- *mysql_fetch_array* returns the record in the form of an associative array. Access to the columns is accomplished with *$row["colname"]*. The column name must be given in case-sensitive form.

- *mysql_fetch_object* returns the record as an object. Access to the columns is accomplished with *$row->colname*.

A feature that all three of these functions have in common is that with each call the next record is automatically returned (or *FALSE* if the end of the list of records has been reached). If this given order is to be altered, then the currently active data record can be changed with *mysql_data_seek*.

```
mysql_data_seek($result, $rownr);
```

Column Names and Other Metainformation

If you have processed valid queries and wish to display the results, what you need are not only the data themselves, but also metainformation about the nature of the data: the names of the columns, their data types, and so on.

The function *mysql_field_name* returns the name of the specified column. The function *mysql_field_table* tells in addition from what table the data come (this is important in queries that collect data from several tables). The function *mysql_field_type* gives the data type of the column in the form of a character string (for example, *"BLOB"*). The function *mysql_field_len* gives the maximum length of a column (especially of interest with the data types *CHAR* and *VARCHAR*).

```
$colname = mysql_field_name($result, $n);
$tblname = mysql_field_table($result, $n);
$typename = mysql_field_type($result, $n);
$collength = mysql_field_len($result, $n);
```

Yet more detailed information about a column is given by *mysql_field_flags* and *mysql_fetch_field*: The function *mysql_field_flags* returns a character string in which the most important attributes of the column are given (for example, *"not_null primary_key"*). The properties are separated by a space. Evaluation proceeds most simply with the function *explode.*

On the other hand, *mysql_fetch_field* returns an object that partially provides the same information as the character string of *mysql_field_flags*. Evaluation proceeds in the form *colinfo->name, colinfo->blob*, etc. (A complete table of all object properties can be found in the API reference in Chapter 15.)

```
$colflags = mysql_field_flags($result, $n);
$colinfo = mysql_fetch_field($result, $n);
```

Example: Displaying SELECT Results as a Table

The following example (see also Figure 8-2 shows how the result of a simple query (*SELECT * FROM titles*) can be displayed in an HTML table. The code for table output resides in the function *show_table*, which is defined at the beginning of the PHP script. The resulting table has the absolute minimum of bells and whistles. To be sure, background color and the like could yield a more cogent presentation, but that is not the theme of this book. (Any book on HTML will inform you of the necessary HTML tags that you would have to add to the code.)

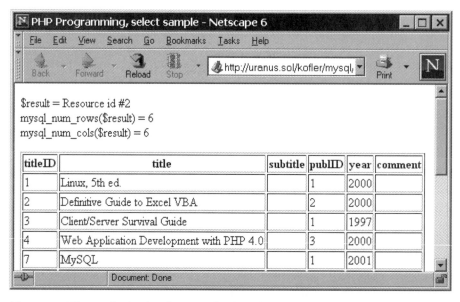

Figure 8-2. The result of a simple query displayed as a table

> **TIP** *Independent of questions of layout you should take one further detail into consideration: In the display of numbers, right justification often gives a clearer presentation than left justification. You can determine the data type of each column and set the justification accordingly.*

```
<!DOCTYPE HTML PUBLIC "-//W3C//DTD HTML 4.0//EN">
<!-- php/general/select.php -->
<?php

include("../../_private/mylibraryconnect.inc.php");
$connID = connect_to_mylibrary();
```

```php
// displays the result of a query as an HTML table
function show_table($result)
{
  if(!$result) {
    echo "<p>Error in SQL statement.\n"; return;
  }
  $rows = mysql_num_rows($result);
  $cols = mysql_num_fields($result);
  if($rows>0) {
    echo "<table border=1>";
    echo "<tr>";
    // column headings
    for($i=0; $i<$cols; $i++) {
      echo "<th>", htmlentities(mysql_field_name($result, $i)),
          "</th>";
    }
    echo "</tr>";
    // table content
    while($row = mysql_fetch_row($result)) {
      echo "<tr>";
      for($i=0; $i<$cols; $i++) {
          echo "<td>", htmlentities($row[$i]), "</td>";
      }
      echo "</tr>\n";
    }
    echo "</table>";
  }
}
?>
<!-- start of the HTML document -->
<html><head>
<title>PHP Programming, SELECT sample</title>
</head><body>
<?php
  // execute SQL query
  $result = mysql_query("SELECT * FROM titles");

  // display metainformation
  $rows = mysql_num_rows($result);
  $cols = mysql_num_fields($result);
  echo "<p>\$result = $result\n",
    "<br>mysql_num_rows(\$result) = $rows\n",
    "<br>mysql_num_cols(\$result) = $cols\n";
```

```
  // display HTML table with result
  echo "<p>\n";
  show_table($result);
?>
</body></html>
```

> **POINTER** *When a query returns many results it is not a good idea simply to display all the results. It is better to divide the results over several pages. Furthermore, the user should be given the option of jumping from one page to the next (and back again). An example of a pagewise representation of* SELECT *queries can be found in this chapter.*

Changes to Data (INSERT, UPDATE, DELETE)

There are no MySQL functions included in PHP for changing data. All alterations must be made with *mysql_query* in the form of SQL commands (*INSERT, UPDATE, DELETE*, etc.). This means as well that all data (BLOBs included) must be transmitted as character strings.

If you insert records into tables with *AUTO_INCREMENT*, you can determine the last *AUTO_INCREMENT* value generated by MySQL with the function *mysql_insert_id*, which we have already mentioned.

The following lines show how a new book title, together with its two authors, can be stored in the *mylibrary* database. Please note that three *ID* values must be temporarily stored, which then must be inserted together in the *rel_title_author* table. It is assumed that the publisher of this book (here Addison-Wesley) is already stored in the database with *publID=1*.

```
mysql_query("INSERT INTO titles (title, publID, year)
    VALUES ('A Guide to the SQL Standard', 1, 1997)");
$titleID = mysql_insert_id();
mysql_query("INSERT INTO authors (authName)
    VALUES ('Date Chris')");
$author1ID = mysql_insert_id();
mysql_query("INSERT INTO authors (authName)
    VALUES ('Darween Hugh')");
$author2ID = mysql_insert_id();
mysql_query("INSERT INTO rel_title_author (titleID, authID, authNr)
    VALUES ($titleID, $author1ID, 1),
        ($titleID, $author2ID, 2)");
```

> **POINTER** *In practice, that is, when data are input interactively, the storing of new input is somewhat more complicated. For example, it must be checked whether an author already exists. If so, the ID of that author must be stored in* rel_title_author. *If not, a new author must be inserted. (Or was there perhaps a typo? To minimize this possibility, similar names in sound or appearance can be displayed.) An extensive example will be presented in the next section.*

Character Strings, BLOBs, DATEs, SETs, ENUMs, and NULL

This section describes how to deal with various data types that in practice present a number of difficulties. Coping with *NULL* will also be covered. This section deals separately with storing, altering, and output of data.

Altering Data

To alter data in a database the corresponding SQL commands must be passed as character strings to *mysql_query*. In constructing such character strings there is no difference between the rules for MySQL (see Chapter 13). That is, dates and times must be passed in the syntax prescribed by MySQL.

The starting point for the following discussion of various data types is the variable *data*, which contains the data to be stored. The contents of this variable should be formed into an *INSERT* command, which is stored temporarily in the variable *sql*. In the simplest case it works like this:

```
$sql = "INSERT INTO tablename VALUES('$data1', '$data2', ... );
```

Of course, you can put *sql* together piece by piece:

```
$sql = "INSERT INTO tablename VALUES(";
$sql .= "'$data1', ";
$sql .= "'$data2', ";
 ...
$sql .= ")";
```

- **Dates and Times:** To format a date or time in accordance with the MySQL rules, you can summon to your aid the PHP functions *date* and *strftime*. If data are the result of user input, you should carry out the usual validation tests. (MySQL carries out only very superficial validation and is perfectly happy to store data that cannot possibly refer to a real date or time.)

- **Timestamps:** PHP and MySQL timestamps are really the same thing, but they are formatted differently. In the case of PHP timestamps we are dealing simply with a 32-bit integer that gives the number of seconds since 1/1/1970. MySQL, on the other hand, expects timestamps in the form *yyyyddmmhhmmss* or *yyyy-dd-mm hh:mm:ss*.

  As a rule, timestamps are used to indicate the time of the last change. In this case you simply pass *NULL*, and MySQL takes care of the correct storage automatically.

  ```
  $sql .= "NULL";
  ```

  On the other hand, if you wish to store a PHP timestamp as a MySQL timestamp, then you should rely on MySQL *FROM_UNIXTIME* in the *INSERT* or *UPDATE* command.

  ```
  $data = time(); // data contains the current time as a Unix timestamp
  $sql .= "FROM_UNIXTIME(" . $data . ")";
  ```

- **Character Strings and BLOBs:** If BLOBs or special characters appear in a character string, then there are frequently problems with quotation marks. SQL requires that the characters ', ", \, and the zero byte be prefixed by a backslash.

  The usual way of quoting character strings that may contain special characters is via the PHP function *addslashes*. This function replaces the character with code 0 by \0 and prefixes the characters ', ", \, with a backslash. Please do not forget to place the result inside single quotes, so that SQL realizes that it is dealing with a character string.

  ```
  $sql .= "'" . addslashes($data) . "'";
  ```

  An alternative to this is to transmit such data in hexadecimal form. PHP offers the convenient function *bin2hex*, which transforms character strings of arbitrary length into hexadecimal. The hexadecimal character string must not be placed within single quotes.

  ```
  $sql .= "0x" . bin2hex($data);
  ```

There is a drawback to this modus operandi: For each byte of data, two bytes are transmitted to MySQL by PHP, thus almost double the number of bytes that are absolutely necessary.

> **REMARK** *If the data to be stored come from an HTML form and the PHP configuration variable* magic_quotes_gpc *is set to* on *(which is usual), then the data are already quoted. In this case there should be no additional quotation. Further information on* magic quotes *appears at the end of this section.*

- **NULL:** If *data* contains no data (*isset($data)==FALSE*) and this condition is to be stored in the database as *NULL*, then the following is recommended:

```
$sql .= isset($data) ? "'$data'" : "NULL";
```

Please note that within the SQL character command you do not set *NULL* in single quotes as if it were a character string.

Reading Data

The starting point of this section is again the variable *data*, which contains a data field that results from a query. For example, *data* could be filled as follows:

```
$result = mysql_query("SELECT ... ");
$row = mysql_fetch_row($result);
$data = $row[0];
```

Timestamps

The variable *data* contains timestamps as a character string of the form 20001231235959. In PHP you cannot get very far with this. If you wish to work further with a timestamp value in PHP, you should employ the MySQL function *UNIX_TIMESTAMP* and formulate the *SELECT* query accordingly. Then *data* contains (for the above data) the value 978303599.

```
SELECT ... , UNIX_TIMESTAMP(a_timestamp) FROM ...
```

Date

In a *DATETIME* column, *data* contains a character string of the form 2000-12-31 23:59:59. In a *DATE* column the time specification is lacking. In many instances it is most practical for the further processing of dates in PHP to use the function *UNIX_TIMESTAMP* here as well. You can achieve a desired format with the MySQL function *DATE_FORMAT*. With the following instruction *data* receives a character string of the form *'December 31 2001'*.

```
SELECT ... , DATE_FORMAT(a_date, '%M %d %Y')
```

Time

In a *TIME* variable *data* contains a character string of the form 23:59:59. If you do not wish to extract hours, minutes, and seconds from this character string, then you might use the MySQL function *TIME_TO_SEC*, which returns the number of seconds since 00:00:00. You can also use any of a number of additional MySQL functions for processing times. Caution: *UNIX_TIMESTAMP* does not work for *TIME* columns.

> **POINTER** *You will find an overview of the functions provided by MySQL for processing dates and times in Chapter 13.*

Character Strings and BLOBs

PHP fortunately has (in contrast to C) no problems with truly binary data. That is, even 0-bytes within a character string are readily processed. Thus *data* truly contains all the data from the database in one-to-one correspondence.

> **CAUTION** *Do not forget that in general, you cannot output character strings directly with* echo *into an HTML document. If the character string contains special characters like <, >, ', ", or characters outside of the 7-bit ASCII character set, you must replace these characters by the corresponding HTML code via the function* htmlentities.

NULL

When a data field contains *NULL*, then *isset($data)* returns the value *FALSE*. Similar tests could be carried out, depending on the data type, with *is_numeric*, *is_string*, etc. Please note, however, that tests on character strings with the function *empty* do not lead to correct results: With *NULL* as well as with an empty character string, *empty* returns the result *TRUE*.

Determining the Elements of an ENUM/SET

Working with *ENUM*s and *SET*s causes no difficulties: The values are passed in both directions as simple character strings. Note that with *ENUM*s, no additional spaces are allowed between comma-separated character strings.

Often, one wishes to display in an HTML input form all character strings of an *ENUM* or *SET* from which a selection is to be made (in a list box, for example). To do this you must determine with the SQL command *DESCRIBE tablename columnname* the definition of this field.

```
DESCRIBE test_enum a_enum
```

Field	Type	Null	Key	...
a_enum	enum('a','b','c','d','e')	YES		...

The column *Type* of the result table contains the required information. In the following code lines the character strings *enum('a','b','c')* and *set('a','b','c')* will be abbreviated via *ereg* to *'a','b','c'*. The function *str_replace* removes the single quotation marks, and then *explode* forms *a,b,c* into an array, which is stored in the variable *fieldvalues*. Then the *while* loop displays the values in the HTML document. You can use similar code to create an HTML form with radio buttons or a list box using *SET* or *ENUM*.

```
$result = mysql_query("DESCRIBE test_enum a_set");
$row = mysql_fetch_object($result);
$fieldtype = $row->Type; // enum( ... ) or set( ... )
ereg("\\((.*)\\)", $row->Type, $tmp); // xyz('a','b','c')
// --> 'a','b','c'
$tmp = str_replace("'", "", $tmp[1]); // 'a','b','c' --> a,b,c
$fieldvalues = explode(",", $tmp);

// a, b, c display in rows
while($i = each($fieldvalues)) {
echo "<br>", htmlentities($i[1]), "\n";
}
```

> **POINTER** *The code directly above assumes that no commas appear within the* SET *and* ENUM *character strings. If there are, then the decomposition (pedagogically less intuitive, but syntactically more stable) can be expressed as follows:*

```
ereg("('(.*)')", $row->Type, $tmp);
$fieldvalues = explode("','", $tmp[2]);
```

Magic Quotes (PHP)

Although this is not a book on PHP, we should mention that *magic quotes* cause difficulties for many PHP programmers in the evaluation of forms and in saving the resulting data. Thus it does not seem out of place here to include a brief description of this peculiarity of PHP.

The significance of *magic quotes* is that under particular circumstances the PHP interpreter alters character strings that are read in from an external data source (data from GET/POST forms, cookies, SQL queries, etc.).

In the process, the special characters ', ", \, and the 0-byte are replaced by \', \", \\, and \0, respectively. (This operation can be carried out manually with the PHP function *addslashes*.) In many cases this automatic alteration simplifies the processing of character strings, but often it leads to confusion and chaos.

PHP recognizes three *magic quote* modes, which are set in `php.ini`.

- *magic_quotes_gpc*: GPC stands for get/post/cookie. That is, when a variable is set, data from these three sources are changed. Note that this affects all data in a form that are processed in PHP scripts.

- *magic_quotes_run-time*: When this variable is set, PHP in most cases quotes those character strings that come from external data sources (for example, from MySQL).

- *magic_quotes_sybase*: The character ' is quoted by doubling it (that is, by ' ' instead of by \'). However, this holds only when one of the other two *magic_quote* configuration variables is set.

Magic Quote Default Setting

In the default setting of PHP 4.0, *magic_quotes_gpc* is set to *On*, while the two other modes are *Off*. This setting has the following consequences for programming:

- Data transmitted from forms can be used in *INSERT* commands without alteration. The critical characters ', ", and \ are already quoted.

```
$sql = "INSERT ... VALUES('$formVar')";
```

- If you compare data in a form with data from an SQL query, you must first free the form data from backslash characters with the PHP function *stripslashes()*.

```
if(stripslashes($formVar) == $sql_result_row[0]) ...
```

On the other hand, if you make the comparison not in PHP, but with MySQL (as part of a *WHERE* conditional), then no extra measures are required:

```
$sql = "SELECT ... WHERE authorsName = '$formVar'";
```

- If you wish to display the form data in an HTML document (or in a new form, say to allow corrections to be made), then you must first delete the quotation marks with *stripslashes* and then quote anew (and differently!) all HTML-specific special characters with *htmlentities*:

```
echo htmlentities(stripslashes($formVariable));
```

TIP *Before you begin developing your own code, you should certainly determine which* magic quote *settings hold on your ISP's server.*

Determining and Changing Magic Quote Modes in a PHP Script

To some extent you can determine or change the three configuration variables in the code of your PHP script:

- *magic_quotes_gpc: get_magic_quotes_gpc()* determines the current status. A change cannot be made.

- *magic_quotes_run-time: get_magic_quotes_runtime()* determines the current status; *set_magic_quotes_runtime()* changes it.

- *magic_quotes_sybase:* The status can be neither determined nor altered.

Turning Off Magic Quotes

If you develop code in which a large amount of data is read from forms and is later replaced in the same or another form, then it can make sense to remove any quoting carried out by PHP right at the start of the script.

The following loop encompasses all variables that came into the script via *<form method="POST" . . . >*. However, only their copies in the PHP array *HTTP_POST_VARS* will be changed. Analogously, you can, of course, also deal with *get* or *cookie* variables. You simply replace *HTTP_POST_VARS* by *HTTP_GET_VARS* or *HTTP_COOKIE_VARS*.

```
if($HTTP_POST_VARS and get_magic_quotes_gpc()) {
  while($i = each($HTTP_POST_VARS)) {
    $tmp = stripslashes($i[1]);
    ${$i[0]} = $tmp; // alter the variable
    $HTTP_POST_VARS[$i[0]] = $tmp; // alter HTTP_POST_VARS
  }
}
```

Error Checking

All *mysql_xxx* functions return *FALSE* if an error occurs during execution. You obtain information as to the nature of the error by evaluating the functions *mysql_errno* (returns the error number) and *mysql_error* (error message).

```
$result=mysql_query($sql);
if(!$result) {
  echo "<P>error: ", mysql_errno(),
  ": " . htmlentities(mysql_error()), ".\n";
}
```

One always must reckon with the reality of errors, and in particular in the execution of SQL commands that alter data. One possible source of error is in the connection to the MySQL server.

In the development of PHP scripts the function *mysql_query_test* is often very useful in searching for the cause of the error. It is meant as a replacement for *mysql_query*, displaying every executed SQL command in blue. If an error occurs, then an error message will be displayed as well.

```
function mysql_query_test($sql) {
  echo "<p><font color=0000ff>SQL:", htmlentities($sql), "</font>\n";
  $result = mysql_query($sql);
```

```
  if($result) return($result);
  echo "<p><font color=ff0000>Error: ", htmlentities(mysql_error()),
    "</font>\n";
  die();
}
```

> **POINTER** *A list of all error messages can be found in the files* errmsg.h *and* mysqld_error.h. *Both files are part of the source-code package for MySQL. Since many MySQL users install only the binary distribution of MySQL, a list of these error messages in included in Appendix A.*

Example: Library Management (*mylibrary*)

The example of this section is based on the database *mylibrary*, which was introduced in Chapter 5. It shows how a few PHP pages can be used to input book information into a database and then to search the database. Our example consists of the following files:

mylibraryconnect.inc.php	auxiliary functions (including database login)
find.php	search for authors/titles
simpleinput.php	simple input of new book titles
input.php	convenient input of new book titles
categories.php	management of the hierarchical category list

The script files are independent of one another. Within each script the transmittal of session information is carried out as necessary via URL variables (that is, *name.php?variable=xxx*) or by formula fields. (URL stands for *Uniform Resource Locator* and denotes addresses like http://www.company.com/page.html.)

Auxiliary Functions (mylibraryconnect.inc.php)

The file _private/mylibraryconnect.inc.php contains several auxiliary functions that either have already been introduced in the section on programming techniques or else are not of particular interest from the point of view of database programming. The following enumeration gives a brief description. If you want to read the source code, the files can be found, together with the other example files, on my web site.

1. *connect_to_mylibrary()* creates the connection to MySQL. If the connection cannot be made, an error message is displayed. Before the function is called, no HTML code is to be generated, since the error message represents a complete HTML page (including the HTML header).

2. *show_table($result)* displays the result of a *SELECT* query as a table.

3. *build_href($url, $query, $name)* creates an HTML link of the form *<a href="$url?$query">htmlentities($name)</a>*.

4. *mysql_query_test($sql)* displays an SQL command, executes it, and displays an error message if necessary. This function returns the query result, and thus can be implemented just like *mysql_query*, and moreover, it greatly simplifies debugging.

Book Search (`find.php`)

The file `find.php` helps in locating authors and books in the *mylibrary* database. To do this, the initial letters of the title or of the author are entered into the search form (see Figure 8-3).

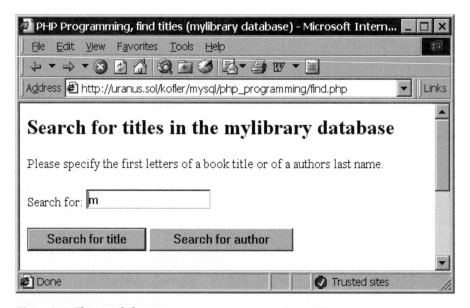

Figure 8-3. The search form

In the search results (see Figures 8-4 and 8-5) authors and publishers are executed as links, so that it is quite simple to find all the books of a given author or all books put out by a particular publisher.

If search results do not fit on a page, then one can leaf page by page through the results. (The number of titles per page is set in the program by the variable *$pagesize* to 5. This value can easily be increased.)

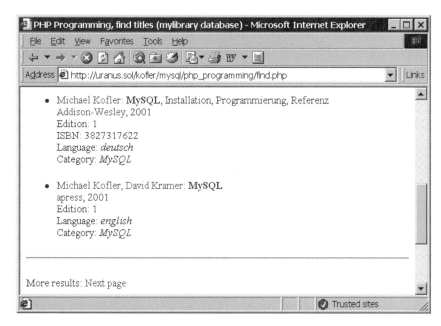

Figure 8-4. Results of a search for book titles beginning with the letter M

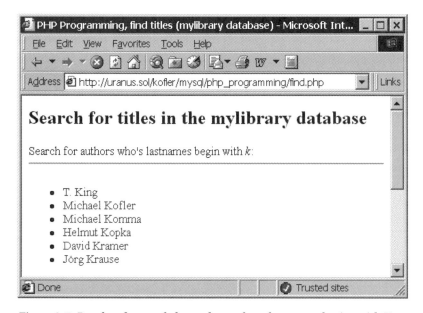

Figure 8-5. Results of a search for authors whose last name begins with K

Problems of Efficiency in the Representation of Search Results

The file find.php divides long lists of book titles into several pages. To this end *SELECT* is called with *LIMIT pagesize * (pagenr-1), pagesize*. Unfortunately, there are two factors that make the paged representation of *SELECT* results inefficient:

1. Generally, you would like to report on each page of the results the number of additional pages. But to do this you need to know how many records the query returns. This can be easily determined via *SELECT COUNT(. . .)*, but if your query is complex, then the twofold execution—once with *SELECT COUNT* for the number and then with *SELECT LIMIT* for the results of the current page—is very inefficient.

   There is, alas, no optimal solution to this problem. One approach would be always to search for *pagesize+1* results. If *pagesize+1* results are actually found, it is then clear that there are more results (at least one, perhaps more). The program then displays *pagesize* results together with a MORE button, which indicates that there are additional results, but without telling how many. This is efficient, but not very elegant (find.php follows this strategy).

   Another possibility is to execute *SELECT* for the first page without *COUNT* and without *LIMIT* (or at least with a relatively high *LIMIT* value). The advantage is that with a single query you determine both the number of all data records (via *mysql_num_rows*) and the desired result records. The disadvantage is that if the query returns a large number of results, then all the records are transmitted from MySQL to PHP, even though relatively few records are actually to be displayed. This is probably even less efficient than two *SELECT* queries.

   If you decide to determine the number of result records (by whatever means), than you should do this only for the first result page. For all further pages you should store this information in a session or transmit it further as part of the link.

2. The second problem is that for each page, the entire *SELECT* query with somewhat altered *LIMIT* parameters must be executed anew. Of course, the *LIMIT* clause prevents all the result records from being transmitted each time from MySQL to PHP, but depending on the query type, the cost is the same at least for MySQL. (This holds especially for queries that join information from several tables with *JOIN*, that sort or group the results, or that contain complex *WHERE* conditionals that cannot be resolved directly with the help of an index.)

   Again, there is no perfect solution. Many programming languages offer the possibility of temporarily storing intermediate results, but not PHP. (Theoretically, you can store the query results in a new table, but then how and when will this table be deleted? Perhaps the user will be satisfied with the first search results anyhow, and then it would be excessively costly to construct a new table.)

The only generally valid recommendation is this: Display as many results per page as possible and thus avoid the user having to do too much paging. (If your main goal is to achieve the maximum number of page accesses, then of course, this is not the optimal recipe. In find.php the number of titles per page is limited for a different reason to five: The example database contains relatively few titles, and with *pagesize=25* you would scarcely have the chance to formulate a query that would yield that many results.)

Program Structure

The starting point for the program is the search form displayed in Figure 8-3. To evaluate the form's input we again call find.php. The search results and the page references again refer to find.php. In this case information such as the search item and the current page number are passed as part of the link (find.php?sqlType=author& ...).

In find.php, therefore, we must first analyze how the script was called: If no data are transferred, then find.php simply displays the empty form. But if there are predefined variables, then the program forms a corresponding SQL query and then displays the result of the search.

Code Outline

The following lines give an overview of the code in find.php, which should help in orientation for the following extensive description.

```
<!-- php/mylibrary/find.php -->
<?php

// insert auxiliary function
include("../../_private/mylibraryconnect.inc.php");

// define additional auxiliary functions (see description
// in the next section)
function last_name_last($x) { ... }

// establish link to the database
$connID = connect_to_mylibrary();

?>

<!-- start of the HTML document -->
<!DOCTYPE HTML PUBLIC "-//W3C//DTD HTML 4.0//EN">
```

```
<html><head>
<html><head>
<title>PHP Programming, find titles (mylibrary database)</title>
</head><body>
<h2>Search for titles in the mylibrary database</h2>

<?php
    // Main-Code
    //initialize $pagesize, validate $page
    // if called without parameters:
    // display form
    // initialize $sql, $sqlcreate, $sqllimit
    // if there are form variables:
    // form SQL query corresponding to form input (--> $sql)
    // if there are URL variables:
    // form SQL query corresponding to the URL variables(--> $sql)
    // if the variable $sql is not empty
    // execute SQL query
    // display results
    // if $page>1 or if there are additional results
    // display links to other pages with search results
?>

</body></html>
```

> **POINTER** *The function* last_name_last *places the first word in a character string at the end. This turns the database-specific* "Kennedy John F." *into the more readable* "John F. Kennedy". *The code for this function and for the inverse function* last_name_first *appear in the next section.*

Form Variables

- *formSearch* contains the search character string (that is, the initial letters of the author or title sought).

- *formSubmitTitle* contains *"Search for title"* if the user clicks on the button for title search.

- *formSubmitAuthor* contains *"Search for author"* if the user clicks on the button for author search.

URL Variables

- *sqlType* contains *"title"* if the HTTP address contains further variables for the display of search results for a title search.

- *authID* contains the *ID* number of an author if a title by this author is to be displayed.

- *publID* contains the *ID* Number of a publisher if a title put out by that publisher is to be displayed.

- *search* contains the search character string if the title with these initial letters is to be displayed.

- *page* contains the page to be displayed. (The program code ensures that values less than zero and larger than 100 cannot be passed.)

Main Code: Displaying the Form

If *sqlType* is empty (that is, if data were not passed via the HTTP address) and if either no form data or impermissible form data are at hand (that is, an empty search string), then the form is displayed.

```
if(empty($sqlType) &&
  (empty($HTTP_POST_VARS) ||
    ($HTTP_POST_VARS and empty($formSearch))))) {
?>
<form method="POST" action="./find.php">
<p>Please specify the first letters of a book title or
  of an author's last name.
<p>Search for:
<input name="formSearch" size=20 maxlength=20>
<p>
<input type="submit" value="Search for title" name="formSubmitTitle">
<input type="submit" value="Search for author"
  name="formSubmitAuthor">
</form>
<?php
  } // end of if ( ... )
```

Forming the SQL Command for Title or Author Search

In the following our task is to formulate an SQL command for a search for a book title or author. Regardless of the database to which this query will be referred, several variables must be initialized.

The variable *pagesize* specifies how many titles can be displayed per page. If the variable *page* contains a value, this value specifies which page will be the next to be displayed. This variable is imported via the HTTP address and contains within it the risk of misuse. (Even if an evil-minded user specifies input.php?page=10000000000 as HTTP address, the program should react in a reasonable manner and not display links to the previous 9999999999 pages.) The permissible range for *page* will therefore be limited to the range 1–100.

```
// number of titles per page
$pagesize = 5;
// validate page variable
if($page>100)
  $page=100;
elseif($page<1)
  $page=1;
elseif(!is_numeric($page))
  unset($page);
```

In *sql* the *SELECT* command for the title or author search is formed. If a title is the search object, then a title search takes place in five steps:

- The database *tmpTitleIDs* is deleted if it already exists (for example, because the script was broken off during its previous execution due to an error and was not executed to the end).

- With a *SELECT* query the *titleID* numbers of the sought titles (only for the page to be displayed) are returned. These results are stored in the temporary table *tmpTitleIDs*.

- In a second query the detailed information (that is, book title, subtitle, category, etc.) for each *titleID* number is determined from the tables *titles*, *categories*, *languages*, etc.

- In a third query the tables *titles*, *rel_title*, and *authors* are consulted to determine the authors for each title.

- After the evaluation of all these data the temporary table *tmpTitleIDs* is deleted.

At first, a title query proceeds only to the second step. In *sql*, therefore, only the command for the generation of the *tmpTitleIDs* table is temporarily stored. The beginning and end of this command are the same: It is the part of the command for the generation of the temporary table (*CREATE TEMPORARY ...*) and the part for limiting the search results to one page (*LIMIT ...*). To avoid redundant code these parts of the SQL command are placed in advance in the variables *sqlcreate* and *sqllimit*.

> **POINTER**   *The reason for working here with a temporary table and thereby determining title and author details separately is discussed in Chapter 5.*
> *The temporary table is very small: It contains at most* pagesize *ID numbers. To optimize speed, the table type* HEAP *is chosen. This ensures that the table is generated exclusively in RAM.*

```php
// predefine variables
$sql = "";

$sqlcreate = "CREATE TEMPORARY TABLE tmpTitleIDs TYPE=HEAP ";

if(isset($page))
  $sqllimit = "LIMIT " . (($page-1) * $pagesize) . "," .
    ($pagesize + 1);
else
  $sqllimit = "LIMIT " . ($pagesize + 1);
```

Creating SQL Queries from Form Data

If form data are available, then the following lines create the SQL command on that basis. First the user input is separated from the PHP magic quotes. Then the special characters <, >, ", %, *, _, and \ are eliminated. The one remaining problematic special character, namely, the apostrophe, is permissible, since it can appear in names (e.g., *O'Reilly*).

```php
// formulate SQL command from form data
if(isset($HTTP_POST_VARS) && isset($formSearch)) {
  //remove < > " % _ * \ from $formSearch
  $search = trim(stripslashes($formSearch));
  $remove = "<>\"_%*\\";
  for($i=0; $i<strlen($remove); $i++)
    $search = str_replace(substr($remove, $i, 1), "", $search);
```

Depending on whether the search is for an author or a title, the program displays a brief text about the content of the search and then constructs *sql* according to one of the two following patterns. Note, please, that in the case of an author search a relatively high limit (not *pagesize*) is used. This is because the program anticipates more than one page in the search result only in the case of a title search.

```
SELECT authName, authID FROM authors
WHERE authName LIKE 'abc%'
ORDER BY authName LIMIT 100

CREATE TEMPORARY TABLE tmpTitleIDs TYPE=HEAP
SELECT titleID FROM titles " .
WHERE title LIKE 'abc%'
ORDER BY title LIMIT 21
```

Here is the PHP code for assigning this command to the variable *sql*:

```
if($search=="")
  unset($search);
else {
  // search for authors
  if($formSubmitAuthor) {
    echo "<p>Search for authors whose family names begin with <i>",
        htmlentities($search), "</i>:\n";
    $sqlType = "author";
    $sql =
        "SELECT authName, authID FROM authors " .
        "WHERE authName LIKE '" . addslashes($search) . "%' " .
        "ORDER BY authName LIMIT 100";
  }
  // search for titles
  else {
    echo "<p>Search for titles beginning with <i>",
        htmlentities($search), "</i>:\n";
    $sqlType = "title";
    $sql = $sqlcreate .
        "SELECT titleID FROM titles " .
        "WHERE title LIKE '" . addslashes($search) . "%' " .
        "ORDER BY title " . $sqllimit;
  }
}
```

Creating SQL Queries from URL Variables

One can deduce the existence of URL variables from the variable *sqlType*. In the current form *sqlType=title* is specified exclusively in the HTTP address, but perhaps in an extension of find.php another search would be possible.

Three possible search criteria can be passed in the form of URL variables: *authID* (title by a particular author), *publID* (title from a particular publisher), or *search* (title with particular initial letters).

In the search for titles by a particular author a query first determines and then displays the name of the author. This query also serves for validation of *authID*. If the query returns no result (or more than one), then there is something other than a unique valid ID value to be dealt with. In this case a brief error message is displayed. Otherwise, the name of the author is displayed in the "usual" way of writing it (given name followed by family name), and an SQL command is created according to the following format:

```
CREATE TEMPORARY TABLE tmpTitleIDs TYPE=HEAP
SELECT titles.titleID
FROM titles, rel_title_author
WHERE rel_title_author.authID = '$authID'
  AND titles.titleID = rel_title_author.titleID
ORDER BY title LIMIT 21
```

The search for titles of a particular publisher is accomplished with almost the same pattern, but now no *JOIN* is necessary. The search for titles with particular initial letters proceeds as in the similar case involving form data.

```
elseif($sqlType=="title") {// else to: if( ... ) {sql form data }
  // authID contains a value: Search for titles by this author
  if($authID) {
    $result =
      mysql_query("SELECT authName FROM authors " .
                  "WHERE authID='$authID' LIMIT 2");
    if(mysql_num_rows($result)!=1)
      echo "<p>Sorry, ID number for author seems to be invalid.\n";
    else {
      echo "<p>Titles written by <i>",
        htmlentities(last_name_last(mysql_result($result, 0, 0))),
        "</i>:\n";
      $sql = $sqlcreate .
        "SELECT titles.titleID " .
        "FROM titles JOIN rel_title_author " .
        "WHERE rel_title_author.authID = '$authID' " .
```

```
                    " AND titles.titleID = rel_title_author.titleID " .
                    "ORDER BY title " . $sqllimit;
          }
          mysql_free_result($result);
        }
        // publID contains a value: search for titles of this publisher
        elseif($publID) {
          $result =
            mysql_query("SELECT publName FROM publishers " .
                          "WHERE publID='$publID' LIMIT 2");
          if(mysql_num_rows($result)!=1)
            echo "<p>Sorry, ID number for publisher seems to be ",
                  "invalid.\n";
          else {
            echo "<p>Titles published by <i>",
                mysql_result($result, 0, 0), "</i>:\n";
            $sql = $sqlcreate .
                "SELECT titleID FROM titles " .
                "WHERE publID = '$publID' " .
                "ORDER BY title " . $sqllimit;
          }
          mysql_free_result($result);
        }
        // search contains search character string: search for titles with these
        // initial letters
        elseif($search) {
          echo "<p>Titles beginning with <i>",
            htmlentities($search), "</i>:\n";
          $sql = $sqlcreate .
            "SELECT titleID FROM titles " .
            "WHERE title LIKE '" . addslashes($search) . "%' " .
            "ORDER BY title " . $sqllimit;
        }
        if($page>1)
          echo "Page $page\n";
      } // end of elseif($sqlType=="title")
```

Displaying Results of an Author Search

The last part of find.php is responsible for executing the command stored in *sql* and displaying the result. This is relatively uncomplicated when the search is for authors. The names are transformed with *last_name_last* into a more readable format. Furthermore, *build_href* is used to represent the name as an HTTP link. As search strings *sqlType= title* and *authID=n* are passed.

```
if(!empty($sql)) {
  if($sqlType=="author") {
    // display results for author search
    $result = mysql_query($sql);
    if(!$result or !mysql_num_rows($result))
      echo "<p>No results.\n";
    else {
      echo "<hr><ul>\n";
      while($row = mysql_fetch_object($result)) {
        echo "<li>",
          build_href("./find.php",
                     "sqlType=title&authID=$row->authID",
                     last_name_last($row->authName)),
          "</li>\n";
      }
      echo "</ul>\n";
    }
  }
}
```

Displaying Results of a Title Search

From the point of view of database programming the code for the representation of book titles is much more interesting. With *DROP TABLE* the table *tmpTitleIDs* is deleted (which can exist only if the script was previously executed and did not terminate due to an error). Then the table is rebuilt with the command contained in *sql*. If the query contained in *sql* has returned results, two additional queries are executed. The first determines the detailed information for each title:

```
SELECT titles.titleID AS titleID, titles.title AS title,
       titles.subtitle AS subtitle, titles.edition AS edition,
       titles.year, titles.isbn, titles.comment,
       publishers.publName AS publisher, publishers.publID,
       categories.catName AS category, languages.langName AS language
FROM titles JOIN tmpTitleIDs
LEFT JOIN categories ON titles.catID = categories.catID
LEFT JOIN languages ON titles.langID = languages.langID
LEFT JOIN publishers ON titles.publID = publishers.publID
WHERE titles.titleID = tmpTitleIDs.titleID
```

A result is the unification of data from five tables. In three cases a *LEFT JOIN* is used, so that title records are created even if any of the fields *catID, langID,* and *publID* contain the value *NULL*.

```
elseif($sqlType=="title") {
  // there should not be any tmpTitleIDs---but let's be certain
  mysql_query("DROP TABLE IF EXISTS tmpTitleIDs");
  // create temporary table tmpTitleIDs
  mysql_query($sql);
  if(!mysql_affected_rows()) {
    echo "<p>No results.\n";
  }
  else {
    // query for the detailed title data
    $result1 = mysql_query
      ("SELECT titles.titleID AS titleID, " .
       ... (see above)
       "WHERE titles.titleID = tmpTitleIDs.titleID");
```

The second query determines a list of all *titleID* values and the associated author names. Please observe that this list can contain several entries for each *titleID* value (since there can be several authors for a given title).

```
SELECT tmpTitleIDs.titleID, rel_title_author.authID,
       authName AS author
FROM authors, rel_title_author, tmpTitleIDs
WHERE authors.authID = rel_title_author.authID
  AND rel_title_author.titleID = tmpTitleIDs.titleID
ORDER BY rel_title_author.authNr, authName
```

In the query an $n : m$ relation is created between the *titleID* in the *tmpTitleIDs* table and the *authID* values in the *author* table. The entries are sorted by *authNr* and *authName*. Thereby it is achieved that in the later formation of the author list the first author is indeed given first for each title. Only if no differentiation is possible based on *authNr* (because, for example, the field contains *NULL*) is an alphabetical order imposed.

```
    // query for authors
    $result2 = mysql_query
      ("SELECT tmpTitleIDs.titleID, rel_title_author.authID, " .
       ... (see above)
       "ORDER BY rel_title_author.authNr");
```

The results contained in *result2* are now brought into an array, where *titleID* is used as key. If there are several authors for a *titleID*, then the names are separated by commas. The author names are formatted with *build_href* as HTTP links, which later provide the user with a convenient way to search for all the titles of this author.

```
// enter author names in the field authors[]
while($row = mysql_fetch_object($result2)) {
    // separate authors by commas
    if($authors[$row->titleID])
      $authors[$row->titleID] .= ", ";
    $tmp = build_href("./find.php",
                      "sqlType=title&authID=$row->authID",
                      last_name_last($row->author));
    $authors[$row->titleID] .= $tmp;
}
```

After all data have been collected and the author list has been prepared, we may begin with the output of titles. In *publref* a publisher name is formatted as an HTTP link (similar to what was just done with author names). Then comes an almost interminable *echo* command, which looks quite complicated, because most of the title fields can be empty.

```
// display title
echo "<hr><ul>\n";
$titlecount=0;
while($row = mysql_fetch_object($result1)) {
    $titlecount++;
    if($titlecount<=$pagesize) {
      if($row->publisher)
          $publref = build_href("./find.php",
                    "sqlType=title&publID=$row->publID",
                    $row->publisher);
      echo "<p><li>", $authors[$row->titleID], ": ",
        "<b>", htmlentities($row->title), "</b>",
        $row->subtitle ?
          ", " . htmlentities($row->subtitle) . " " : "",
        $row->publisher || $row->year ? "<br>" : "",
        $row->publisher ? $publref : "",
        $row->year ? ", " . htmlentities($row->year) . " " : "",
        $row->edition ?
          "<br>Edition: " . htmlentities($row->edition) .
          " " : "",
        $row->isbn ?
```

```
                "<br>ISBN: " . htmlentities($row->isbn) . " " : "",
              $row->language ?
                "<br>Language: <i>" . htmlentities($row->language) .
                "</i> " : "",
              $row->category ?
                "<br>Category: <i>" . htmlentities($row->category) .
                "</i> " : "",
              $row->comment ?
                "<br>Comment: <i>" . htmlentities($row->comment) .
                "</i> " : "",
              "</li>\n";
        }
    }
    echo "</ul>\n";
```

All that remains is to delete the temporary table *tmpTitleIDs*:

```
} // end of the else block to if(!mysql_affected_rows())
// delete temporary table
mysql_query("DROP TABLE IF EXISTS tmpTitleIDs");
```

Links to Previous Pages and to the Next Page

If the displayed page number is greater than 1 or if more titles were found than were displayed (*$titlecount>$pagesize*), then a row with links to additional pages with search results is displayed (see Figure 8-6).

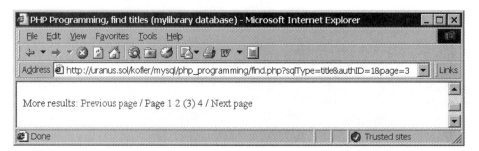

Figure 8-6. Links to additional pages with search results

Since for reasons of efficiency the total number of search results is not determined, near the top only a link to the next page (*$page+1*) is displayed. Near the bottom links to pages 1 through (*$page-1*) are displayed. Since the page *$page* is currently being shown, it does not make sense to display a link to this page. This number of pages is placed in parentheses for clarity. In addition to the page numbers the two links PREVIOUS PAGE and NEXT PAGE are displayed.

```php
    // display links to additional search results
    if(isset($page) or $titlecount>$pagesize) {
      echo "<hr>\n";
      $query = "sqlType=title";
      $query .= isset($authID) ? "&authID=$authID" : "";
      $query .= isset($publID) ? "&publID=$publID" : "";
      $query .= isset($search) ?
          "&search=" . urlencode($search) : "";
      echo "<p>More results: ";
      // links to previous pages
      if(isset($page) and $page>1) {
        echo build_href("./find.php",
                          $query . "&page=" . ($page-1),
                          "Previous page");
        echo " / Page ";
        for($i=1; $i<$page; $i++) {
          if($i>1) echo " ";
          echo " ",
              build_href("./find.php", $query . "&page=" . $i, $i);
        }
      }
      // place current page in parentheses
      if($page>1) echo " ";
      else      echo "Page ";
      echo "<b>($page)</b> ";
      // links to the next page
      if($titlecount>$pagesize) {
        if(isset($page)) echo " ";
        else        $page=1;
        echo build_href("./find.php",
                          $query . "&page=" . ($page+1),
                          ($page+1)), " / ";
        echo build_href("./find.php",
                          $query . "&page=" . ($page+1),
                          "Next page");

      }
      echo "\n";
    }
  }
}
```

Ideas for Improvements

The search options in this example are rather limited. The following list contains some ideas for improvements:

- Search criteria: Search for all books from publisher *x* that appeared between *year1* and *year2*. Limit the search results to books in a particular language.

- Category search: Search for all books in a given category and all subcategories.

- Sort possibility: Sort by year of publication, category, publisher, etc. (In find.php sorting is always by title.)

- Full-text search: Search by words that appear in the title, subtitle, commentary, or list of authors.

Simple Input of New Books (simpleinput.php)

This section shows a minimalist input form for new books (see Figure 8-7). A new book title together with a list of authors can be specified in only two input fields. Then the script tests whether any of the authors input are already stored in the database. All as yet unknown authors are inserted with *INSERT*. Then the new title is stored, as well as the required entries in *rel_title_author* for linking a title and its authors.

The script simpleinput.php does not enable input of subtitles, publishers, category, and so on. It is as good as useless in support of input error correction. The input of special characters can lead to problems. Boy, are we in trouble! Therefore, in the next section, where we introduce the script input.php, we will add all of these missing features as well as increase the convenience factor in input and allow for error correction.

The great advantage of simpleinput.php vis-à-vis input.php is its simplicity. The code is readable and easy to understand. Once you have understood simpleinput.php, you have a good foundation for what lies ahead, namely, wading through the much more extensive and sinuous highways and byways of input.php.

Program Structure, Code Outline

The structure of the script simpleinput.php is relatively simple. First some auxiliary functions are loaded from mylibraryconnect.inc.php, and the connection to the database is established. The next lines begin the resulting HTML document.

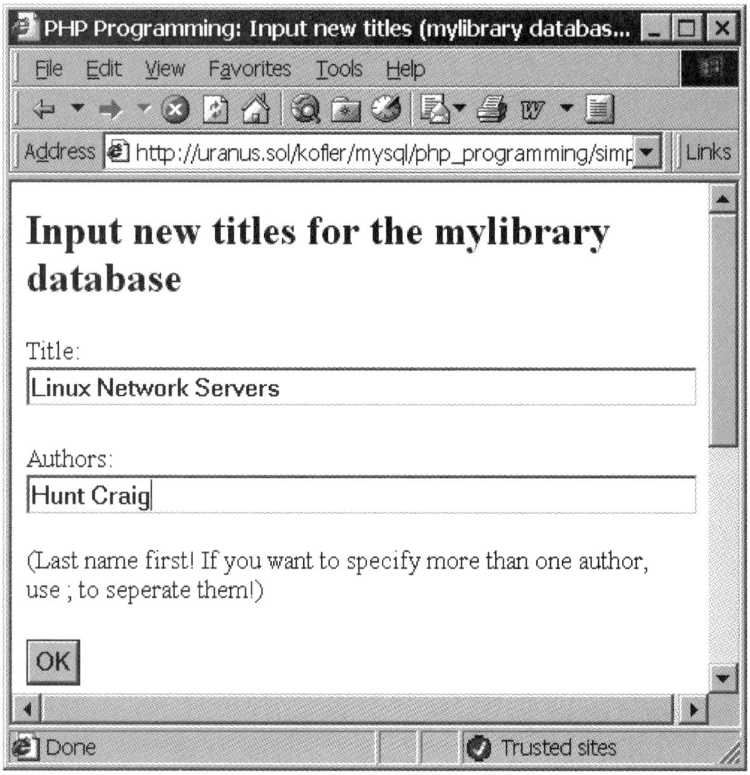

Figure 8-7. Simple book title input

The script is responsible for both the display of the form and the evaluation of the form data. Therefore, the section *Main-Code* begins with the evaluation of several form variables. If these variables are empty, then all that happens is that the next form is displayed. If the input is incomplete, an error message is dispatched and the form is displayed again so that input can be completed. If correct input is offered, then the data are stored in the database. In this case, too, an empty form is again displayed, so that additional data can be input.

```
<!-- php/mylibrary/simpleinput.php -->
<?php
  // read in auxiliary functions
  include("../../_private/mylibraryconnect.inc.php");
  // establish connection to database
  $connID = connect_to_mylibrary();
?>
<!-- start of the HTML document -->
<!DOCTYPE HTML PUBLIC "-//W3C//DTD HTML 4.0//EN">
<html><head>
<title>PHP Programming: Input new titles (mylibrary database)</title>
```

```
</head><body>
<h2>Input new titles for the mylibrary database</h2>
<?php
  // Main-Code
  //evaluation of the form, store new record if any
   ...
?>
<!-- Form -->
<form method="POST" action="./simpleinput.php">
  <p>Title:
  <br><input name="formTitle" size=60 maxlength=80
              value="<?php echo htmlentities($formTitle); ?>">
  <p>Authors:
  <br><input name="formAuthors" size=60 maxlength=100
              value="<?php echo htmlentities($formAuthors); ?>">
  <br>(Last name first! If you want to specify more than
     one author, use ; to separate them)
  <p><input type="submit" value="OK" name="formSubmit">
</form>
</body></html>
```

Form Variables

When the script for the evaluation of the form input is invoked, three variables receive the contents of the form fields:

- *formSubmit* contains *"OK"*.

- *formTitle* contains the title of the book to be stored.

- *formAuthors* contains the semicolon-separated list of authors.

Main Code (Store a Title)

The code for evaluating the form is executed only if the form variables contain data. In this case it is first checked whether the input is complete, that is, whether both a title and author(s) were input. If that is not the case, then a brief error message is displayed and the form is again displayed with the partial data. The variables *formTitle* and *formAuthors* are then freed of any magic quote characters, so that the form is ready for additional input.

```
if($formSubmit) {
  // check for completeness of the form
  if(empty($formTitle) or empty($formAuthors)) {
    echo "<p>Please specify title and at least one author.\n";
    // remove magic quotes
    if(get_magic_quotes_gpc()) {
      $formTitle = stripslashes($formTitle);
      $formAuthors = stripslashes($formAuthors);
    }
  }
}
```

The rest of the code, for storing the new record, is contained in the ensuing *else* block. The author character string is transformed by *explode* into an array, which then is run through a loop. For each author name a check is made as to whether that author already appears in the database. If that is the case, then the ID number is stored in the array *authIDs*. Otherwise, the new author is inserted into the database with *INSERT*. The ID number of the author is then determined with the function *mysql_insert_id*.

```
else {
  $authCount=0;
  $authorsArray = explode(";", $formAuthors);
  // loop over all authors
  while($i = each($authorsArray)) {
    $author = trim($i[1]);
    if($author) {
      // is the author already known to the database?
      $result =
        mysql_query("SELECT authID FROM authors " .
                    "WHERE authName = '$author'");
      if(mysql_num_rows($result))
        $authIDs[$authCount++] = mysql_result($result, 0, 0);
      // author is not known --> insert author
      else {
        mysql_query("INSERT INTO authors (authName) " .
                    "VALUES('$author')");
        $authIDs[$authCount++] = mysql_insert_id();
      }
    }
  } // end of the author loop
```

A further *INSERT* command is then invoked to store the title. The resulting ID number is then used in constructing the SQL command by which the relation between the book title and its authors is established.

```
// store title
mysql_query("INSERT INTO titles (title) VALUES ('" .
            trim($formTitle) . "')");
$titleID=mysql_insert_id();
// establish title/author relation
$sql = "INSERT INTO rel_title_author " .
  "(titleID, authID, authNr) VALUES ";
for($i=0; $i<$authCount; $i++) {
  if($i!=0) $sql .= ",";
  $sql .= "($titleID, $authIDs[$i], $i)";
}
mysql_query($sql);
```

The SQL command has the following form:

```
INSERT INTO rel_title_author (titleID, authID, authNr)
VALUES (titleID, authorID1, 1), (titleID, authorID2, 2) ...
```

To finish, a message is displayed (in a very sloppy manner, without checking the return value *mysql_query*) that the data were stored and that input of the next data record may now be begun. In order that an empty form be displayed, the variables *formTitle* and *formAuthors* are cleared.

```
    echo "<p>Your last input has been saved.\n",
         "<br>You may now continue with the next title.\n";
    $formTitle = $formAuthors = "";
  } // end of the else block for storing data
} // end of the if block for form evaluation
```

Convenient Input of New Book Data (input.php)

The input form introduced in the last section was a minimalist enterprise in every sense. (If it were music, it would be by Philip Glass.) The script input.php offers more in the way of input possibilities, more convenience, and more data security. The price for all of these added features is rather more complex code, that is, code that is closer to a real-world application than was our previous example simpleinput.php.

Operating Instructions

Title input takes place in two phases. In the first phase only the initial letters of the author and publisher names may be input (see Figure 8-8).

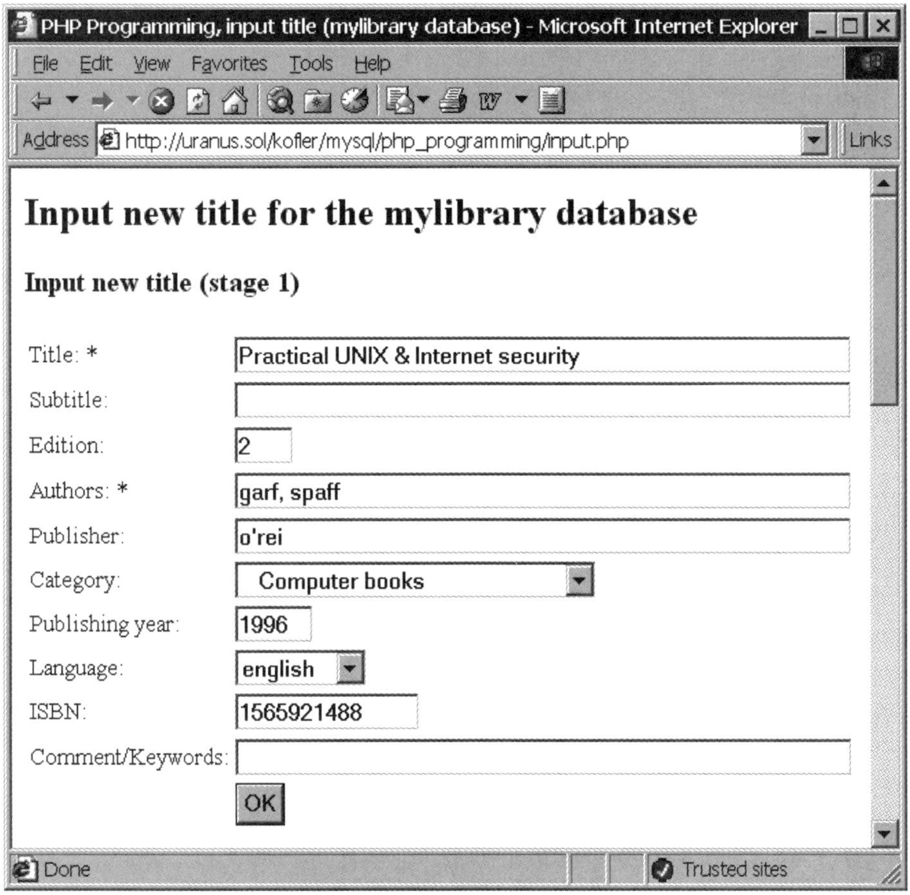

Figure 8-8. Input of a new book title (phase 1)

The script `input.php` searches the database for similar names and then in the second phase presents them as suggestions (see Figure 8-9). This can save the user a bit of typing, but the true benefit is the possible prevention of adding misspelled names to the database.

The script `input.php` expects author names in their customary (unless you are Hungarian, Chinese, . . .) order of given name followed by family name, and then it takes care of storing it in the form specific to the database, namely, family name, then given name).

The script recognizes existing authors even if the name is input in the incorrect order. Thus, for example, if you input (horror of horrors!) *King Stephen* instead of *Stephen King* and this particular author happens to be in the database already, then the program recognizes the existing name and does not store the "new" name, this time in the incorrect order. Needless to say, this technique of error correction does not work with new names. If the given and family names of an author are incorrectly input in reverse order, that author will be stored incorrectly.

In Figure 8-9 it is apparent that the script has correctly recognized the first author *Simon Garfinkel* and publisher from the initial letters. The second author (*Gene Spafford*) was not found in the database, and so this name must be input in full.

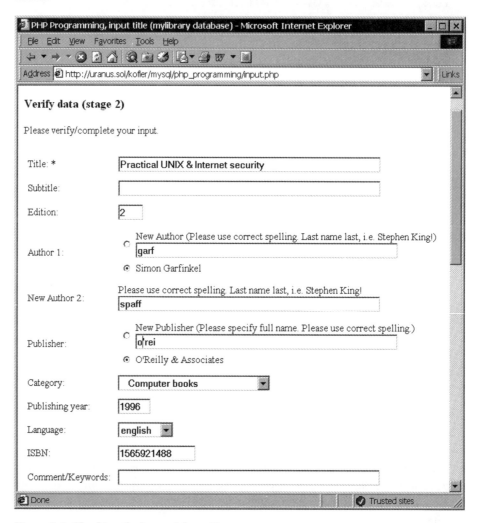

Figure 8-9. Checking the input (phase 2)

In addition, the first validation of the input now takes place. Was an integer greater than zero given as edition number? Is the year of publication believable (that is, not greater than the current year plus 1)? If input errors are suspected, the HTML document displays red warnings, such as, for example "Publishing year needs to be either empty or a 4-digit integer number not larger than 2002."

The validation process is repeated in connection with phase two. Furthermore, it is checked whether an option was selected in the case that the user had a choice in the selection of the publisher or author names. If errors are detected, then an error message is displayed and the form is displayed again so that corrections can be entered.

Assumptions

In order for this script to function correctly, or even at all, the PHP configuration variable *track_vars* must be set in php.ini to *ON* in versions prior to 4.0.3. (This is generally the default setting. Since PHP 4.0.3 the setting in the configuration file is not checked, and *track_vars* is always considered as being set to *ON*.) The effect of *track_vars* is that variables from forms (get and post operations) and cookies as well as environmental and server variables can be read from the PHP arrays *HTTP_*_VARS* (where the asterisk is replaced by one of *GET, POST, COOKIE, ENV, SERVER*).

Program Structure

The script input.php begins with the definition of a number of functions, whose code will be described at the end of this section. But first let us consider these functions' functionality:

- *sql_str* prepares a character string for use in an SQL command (*addslashes*, within single quotation marks).

- *str_or_null* returns *NULL* or an SQL-suitable character string (*sql_str($x)*).

- *num_or_null* returns *NULL* or an integer.

- *last_name_first("John F. Kennedy")* returns *"Kennedy John F."*. The function transforms a name from given name first format to the database-specific format of given name last.

- *last_name_last("Kennedy John F.")* returns *"John F. Kennedy"*. This represents the inverse function to *last_name_first*.

- *build_select_list* generates a selection list for a form from an SQL query.

- *build_categories_select* generates a hierarchical selection list for a form from the *categories* table.

- *show_publisher_options* evaluates the publisher name and displays a list of similar names in the form. The function is called between input phases 1 and 2.

- *restore_publisher_options* again displays the publisher list. The function called in input phase 2 must be repeated due to input errors.

- *show_authors_options* and *restore_authors_options* fulfill the analogous tasks for the author names.

- *validate_stage1* and *_stage2* check the input data and display error messages as required.

- *save_data* stores the input data in the database.

Code Outline

The main code begins with an evaluation of the form data (if such are available). Depending on the result, these data are again displayed (for completion or correction), or the data are stored and a new form is displayed for input of the next data record.

```php
<!-->php/mylibrary/input.php
<?php

// read in auxiliary functions
include("../../_private/mylibraryconnect.inc.php");

// define new functions
function sql_str($x) { ... }
function str_or_null($x) { ... }
function num_or_null($x) { ... }
function last_name_first($x) { ... }
function last_name_last($x) { ... }
function build_select_list($formname, $sql, $defaultitem) { ... }
function build_categories_select($defaultitem) { ... }
function show_publisher_options($publname) { ... }
function restore_publisher_options($formvars) { ... }
function show_authors_options($formAuthors) { ... }
function restore_authors_options($formvars) { ... }
function validate_stage1($formvars) { ... }
function validate_stage2($formvars) { ... }
function save_data($formvars) { ... }

// establish connection to the database
$connID = connect_to_mylibrary();

?>

<!-- HTML-Header -->
<!DOCTYPE HTML PUBLIC "-//W3C//DTD HTML 4.0//EN">
<html><head>
```

```
<title>PHP Programming, input title (mylibrary database)</title>
</head><body>
<h2>Input new title for the mylibrary database</h2>

<?php

// Main-Code
//eliminate \', \", \\ and \0 from form variables
// $stage=1;
// if there are form data from phase 1:
// validate data;
// $stage=2; (--> Phase 2)
// if there are form data from phase 2:
// validate data;
// if OK: store data; $stage=1; (--> next input)
// otherwise: display error message, $stage=2; (--> correction)
// if $stage==1:
// display form phase 1
// otherwise
// display form phase 2

?>
```

Form Variables: Phase 1

If the script is called with form data from phase 1, then the following variables are assigned values:

- *formSubmit1* contains *"OK"*.

- *formTitle* and *formSubtitle* contain book title and subtitle.

- *formAuthors* contains a comma- or semicolon-separated list of author names.

- *formEdition* contains the edition number.

- *formCategory* contains the ID number of the selected category.

- *formYear* contains the publication year of the book.

- *formLanguage* contains the ID number of the language of the book.

- *formISBN* contains the ISBN number.

- *formComment* contains a comment or key words.

All variables except for *formAuthors* and *formTitle* may be empty.

Form Variables: Phase 2

- *formSubmit2* contains *"OK"*.

- *formTitle, formSubtitle, formEdition, formCategory, formYear, formLanguage, formISBN, formComment* have the same meaning as above.

- *formAuthorsCount* specifies the number of authors displayed.

- *formAuthorType<n>* specifies how author *n* was handled: 1 means that the author is already known. 2 means that the author is unknown and no similar author names were found. 3 means that the author was not found exactly, but one or more authors with the same initial letters were found. These authors are displayed as options.

- *formAuthor<n>* contains the input name of *n*.

- *formAuthorRadio<n>* contains either *"new"*, if the radio button by the text field was clicked, or the ID number of an existing author if the option for that author was clicked (only for the case *formAuthorType<n>=3*).

- *formAuthorNames<n>* contains a semicolon-separated list of all authors found (only in the case *formAuthorType<n>=3*).

- *formAuthorIDs<n>* contains a semicolon-separated list of all found authors (only in the case *formAuthorType<n>=3*).

- *formPublType* tells whether a publisher was specified and whether this publisher is already known: 0 means no publisher; 1 means known publisher; 2 means unknown publisher; 3 means a list of publishers.

- *formPublisher* contains the name of the publisher.

- *formPublRadio* contains either *"new"* or the ID number of an existing publisher (only in the case *formAuthorType<n>=3*).

- *formPublNames* and *formPublID*s have the same meaning as *formAuthorNames* and *ID*s.

Main Code

The backslash characters normally inserted by PHP before ' and " have proved themselves to be burdensome in this program. For the complex form evaluation and generation of new forms it is truly unpleasant always to have to be thinking about *stripslashes*. Therefore, the following loop strips all *magic quotes* from all form variables.

```
if($HTTP_POST_VARS and get_magic_quotes_gpc()) {
  while($i = each($HTTP_POST_VARS)) {
    $tmp = stripslashes($i[1]);
    ${$i[0]} = $tmp; // change form variables
    $HTTP_POST_VARS[$i[0]] = $tmp; // change HTTP_POST_VARS array
  }
}
```

Data Validation, Changeover Between Input Phases 1 and 2

Depending on whether form data are present from phase 1 or phase 2, a more or less thorough validation of the data and their eventual storage takes place. The result of the validation process determines the content of the variable *stage*. This variable then determines in the rest of the program how the formula is displayed.

If data from phase 1 are present, then it is ensured that at least the author field has been filled in. If that is the case, then a changeover to phase 2 takes place. Otherwise, the input form for phase 1 is displayed anew.

```
// if $formSubmit1 and $formSubmit2 are empty
$stage=1;
// evaluation of form data from phase 1
if($formSubmit1) {
  // in the author list replace, by ;
  $formAuthors = str_replace(",", ";", $formAuthors);
  // check whether formAuthor contains data (other than ";" and " "):
  // if formAuthor is empty, remain at phase 2
  if(!trim(str_replace(";", "", $formAuthors))) {
    echo "<br><font color=ff0000>You must specify ",
      "<i>authors</i> in stage 1.</font>\n";
    $stage=1;
  }
  // otherwise, change over to phase 2
  // possible display of error messages via validate_stage1()
  else {
    validate_stage1($HTTP_POST_VARS);
    $stage=2;
  }
}
```

If the form data come from phase 2, then the function *validate_stage2* is summoned. If no errors occur, then the data are stored with *save_data*. Then all of the input variables are reset. First *stage* is reset to 1; that is, an empty form is displayed for input of the next book title. If errors occurred in the validation process, then it remains at *stage=2*; that is, the form is displayed again in its current state.

> **REMARK** *The list of form data from phase 2 is very large and difficult to understand (since the number of authors is variable, and thus there are variables like* formAuthor1, formAuthor2*). Therefore, instead of passing long lists of variables to the functions* validate_stage2 *and* save_data, *the entire array* HTTP_POST_VARS *is passed.*

```
// evaluation of form data from phase 2
if($formSubmit2) {
  // basic validation; then store data
  // or display input form again for corrections
  if(validate_stage2($HTTP_POST_VARS)) {
    save_data($HTTP_POST_VARS);
    echo "<p>Last input has been saved.\n";
    // input of next record
    $stage=1;
    // reset form variables
    $formTitle = $formSubtitle = $formYear = $formISBN="";
    $formAuthors = $formPublisher = $formCategory = "";
    $formComment = $formLanguage = $formEdition = "";
  } else
    // display form again for corrections
    $stage=2;
}
```

Displaying the Form for Input Phase 1

The HTML code for the form is given directly, for the most part. There are only a few embedded PHP functions for displaying the content of variables and creating the hierarchical category list box (function *build_categories_select*) and the language list box (function *build_select_list*). Within the form a table is used to achieve a somewhat pleasing appearance. In the following, only the more interesting code lines are given.

```
if($stage==1) {
?>
<h3>Input new title (stage 1)</h3>
<form method="POST" action="./input.php">
<table>
<tr><td>Title: *
    <td><input name="formTitle" size=60 maxlength=80
          value="<?php echo htmlentities($formTitle); ?>"></tr>
<tr><td>Subtitle: ... (as above)
<tr><td>Edition: ...
<tr><td>Authors: *
    <td><input name="formAuthors" size=60 maxlength=100
          value="<?php echo htmlentities($formAuthors); ?>"></tr>
<tr><td>Publisher:
    <td><input name="formPublisher" size=60 maxlength=100
  value="<?php echo htmlentities($formPublisher); ?>"></tr>
<tr><td>Category:
    <td><?php build_categories_select($formCategory); ?></tr>
<tr><td>Publishing year: ...
<tr><td>Language:
    <td><?php build_select_list("formLanguage",
              "SELECT langID, langName FROM languages " .
              "ORDER BY langName", $formLanguage); ?></tr>
<tr><td>ISBN: ...
<tr><td>Comment/Keywords: ...
<tr><td>
    <td><input type="submit" value="OK" name="formSubmit1"></tr>
</table>
</form>
```

Displaying the Form for Input Phase 2

For most of the input fields the code for input phase 2 is simply a repetition of that for phase 1. What is new is the processing of authors and publisher. If a form from phase 1 was just displayed (that is, *if($formSubmit1)*), then the input is evaluated with *show_authors_options* or *show_publisher_options*. Similar names in the database are then displayed in the form in radio button fields.

If just previously a form in phase 2 was displayed (during the evaluation of which input errors were detected that now must be corrected), then the radio button fields from the form just displayed must be restored. The functions *restore_authors_options* and *restore_publishers_options* access the data that have been stored in hidden fields of the form.

```php
<?php
if($stage==2) {
?>
<h3>Verify data (stage 2)</h3>
<form method="POST" action="./input.php">
<table cellpadding=5>
<tr><td>Title: *
    <td><input name="formTitle" size=60 maxlength=80
               value="<?php echo htmlentities($formTitle); ?>"></tr>
<tr><td>Subtitle:
<tr><td>Edition:
<?php
if($formSubmit1)
  show_authors_options($formAuthors);
else
  restore_authors_options($HTTP_POST_VARS);
if($formSubmit1)
  show_publisher_options($formPublisher);
else
  restore_publisher_options($HTTP_POST_VARS);
?>
<tr><td>Category:
<tr><td>Publishing year:
<tr><td>Language:
<tr><td>ISBN:  ...
<tr><td>Comment/Keywords: ...
<tr><td>
    <td><input type="submit" value="OK" name="formSubmit2"></tr>
</table>
</form>
```

sql_str, str_or_null, num_or_null: *SQL Auxiliary Functions*

In formulating SQL commands, character strings must always be given in single quotation marks. Special characters must be preceded by a backslash. Distinction must be made between a number or character string and *NULL* according to whether a PHP variable is empty or not. The following three functions are helpful in this regard.

```php
//mark ', ", and \, place character strings in '
function sql_str($x) {
  return "'" . addslashes($x) . "'";
}
```

```php
// returns SQL-suitable character string or NULL
function str_or_null($x) {
  if(trim($x)=="")
    return("NULL");
  else
    return(sql_str(trim($x)));
}
// returns integer or NULL
function num_or_null($x) {
  if(empty($x))
    return("NULL");
  else
    return($x);
}
```

last_name_first, last_name_last: *Functions for Name Processing*

In databases names must generally be stored with family name first so that searching and sorting by family name can proceed in as simple a manner as possible. However, people are not, at least the last time we checked, computers. In many cultures they are accustomed to writing given name first, and they are inclined to write the name in that order.

The function *last_name_first* assumes that the character string passed as parameter contains a name in the given-name-first format. This function places the family name (the part of the character string after the last space character) at the beginning of the string. The string is unchanged if it consists of a single word or if it ends with a period. (Since usually only given names are abbreviated with a period, in this case the assumption is made that the character string already appears in the form suitable for storage in the database. This safety measure is designed to recognize names that are input in the form in the incorrect order.)

```php
// "John F. Kennedy" --> "Kennedy John F."
function last_name_first($x) {
  $x = trim($x);
  // no change if ends with a period
  if(substr($x, -1) == ".") return($x);
  // no change if there is no space character
  if(!$pos = strrpos($x, " ")) return($x);
  // place last word at the head of the character string
  return(trim(substr($x, $pos+1) . " " . substr($x, 0, $pos)));
}
```

The function *last_name_last* is more or less the inverse function. As parameter is given a character string in the database-specific ordering (with family name at the head). The first word is then placed at the end of the string.

```
function last_name_last($x) {
  $x = trim($x);
  // no change if there is no space character
  if(!$pos = strpos($x, " ")) return($x);
  // place first word at the end of the string
  return(trim(substr($x, $pos+1) . " " . substr($x, 0, $pos)));
}
```

build_select_list: *Function to Create a List Box for the Form*

The function *build_select_list* expects as its first parameter the name of the list box, and as the second parameter it wants an SQL query, while for the third parameter the ID number of the default entry for the list box is required. The result of the SQL query must contain the ID value in the first column and in the second, a character string from the table (here, for example, the name of the language). From this information the function creates the HTML code for the list box (see Figure 8-10). The following lines show how the function is called.

```
build_select_list("formLanguage",
  "SELECT langID, langName FROM languages " .
  "ORDER BY langName", "");
```

The resulting HTML code looks as follows. Please note especially that although the character strings are displayed (in Figure 8-10 the names of languages), it is their ID numbers that are stored with *value= . . . .* The ID numbers are much better suited than character strings for further processing of the selection.

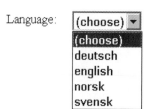

Figure 8-10. list box for languages

```
<select name="formLanguage" size=1>
<option value="none">(choose)
<option value="2"> deutsch
<option value="1"> english
<option value="4"> norsk
<option value="3"> svensk
</select>

function build_select_list($formname, $sql, $defaultitem) {
  $result = mysql_query($sql);
  echo '<select name="', $formname, '" size=1>';
  echo '<option value="none">(choose)';
  while($row=mysql_fetch_row($result)) {
    echo "<option ";
    if($defaultitem==$row[0]) echo "selected ";
    echo "value=\"$row[0]\"> ", htmlentities($row[1]), "\n";
  }
  echo "</select>\n";
  mysql_free_result($result);
}
```

build_categories_select: *Creating a Hierarchical List Box*

The function *build_categories_select* is related to the function just introduced, though it is less broadly applicable. The function evaluates the *categories* table and then creates a hierarchical list box (that is, the list entries are indented according to their place in the hierarchy; see Figure 8-11). For indentation nonbreaking space characters are used (HTML code). As single parameter the ID number of a default category can be passed to the function.

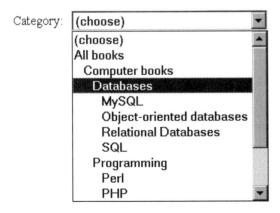

Figure 8-11. Hierarchical list box for selecting the book category

```
function build_categories_select($defaultitem) {
  $result =
    mysql_query("SELECT catID, catName, hierIndent " .
                "FROM categories " .
                "ORDER BY hierNr");
  echo '<select name="formCategory" size=1>';
  echo '<option value="none">(choose)';
  while($row=mysql_fetch_object($result)) {
    echo "<option ";
    if($defaultitem==$row->catID) echo "selected ";
    echo "value=\"$row->catID\">",
      $row->hierIndent>0 ?
        str_repeat("   ", $row->hierIndent) : "",
      htmlentities($row->catName), "\n";
  }
  echo "</select>\n";
  mysql_free_result($result);
}
```

show_publisher_options: *Function for Evaluating the Publisher Name*

The function *show_publisher_options* is invoked to display the input fields for the publisher name in the second form. The parameter *publname* contains the publisher name provided in the first form. Now an attempt is made to find the name that was input in the *publishers* table. If this does not succeed, then a list of similar names is sought. For this purpose the character string is reduced to at most six characters. Then a *SELECT* query is used to find all publisher names that begin with these letters.

```
function show_publisher_options($publname) {
  // if no name was given thus far, display an empty input field
  $publname=trim($publname);
  if($publname=="") {
    echo '<tr><td>Publisher: ',
      '<td><input name="formPublisher" size=60 maxlength=100',
      ' value=""></tr>', "\n";
    echo '<input type=hidden name="formPublType" value=0>', "\n";
    return;
  }
  // is this publisher known?
  $result = mysql_query("SELECT publName FROM publishers " .
                "WHERE publName = " . sql_str($publname) . " LIMIT 2");
```

```
if(mysql_num_rows($result)==1) {
  $known_publisher = 1;
  $publname = mysql_result($result, 0, 0);
  mysql_free_result($result);
}
// search for similar names
else {
  if(strlen($publname<7))
    $publpattern = $publname . '%';
  else
    $publpattern = substr($publname, 0, 6) . '%';
  $result =
    mysql_query("SELECT publID, publName FROM publishers " .
                "WHERE publName LIKE " . sql_str($publpattern) .
                " ORDER BY publName LIMIT 20");
}
```

In connection with this analytical phase the result is displayed. There are three variants:

- The publisher was found. The name is displayed in an input field titled *Known publisher.*

- The publisher was not found, and there were no similar names found as well. Apparently, we are dealing with a new publisher. The name is again shown in an input field, but this time the title is *New publisher.* Furthermore, a message is displayed to the effect that input must be in the correct format.

- The publisher was not found, but there were found publishers with the same initial letters. In this case both an input field and radio button list with all publishers found is displayed. (The length of this list is limited by *LIMIT 20* in the *SELECT* query.) The user now has the opportunity to specify a new publisher name in detail or to select one of the options offered (see Figure 8-12). To keep the form readable, in this case the options are displayed as a table.

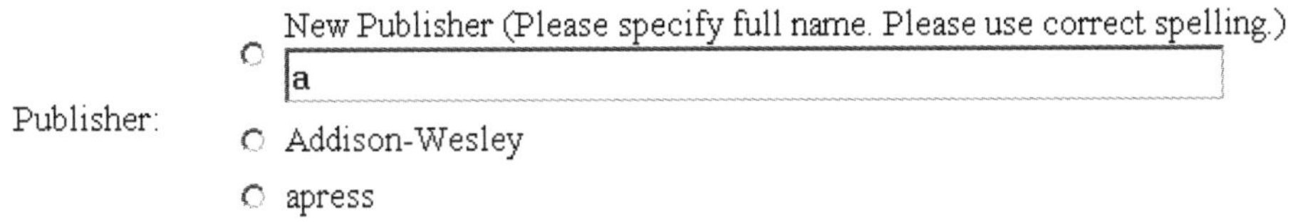

Figure 8-12. Selection or new input of a publisher name in the second input phase

```
// display input field/radio-button options in form
// case 1: publisher is known
if($known_publisher) {
  echo "<tr><td>Known Publisher:\n",
    '<td><input name="formPublisher" size=60 maxlength=100 ',
    'value="', htmlentities($publname), '">', "\n</tr>\n";
  echo '<input type=hidden name="formPublType" value=1>', "\n";
}
else {
  // case 2: publisher unknown, no similar publishers found
  if(!mysql_num_rows($result)) {
    echo "<tr><td>New Publisher:\n",
        '<td>Please specify full name. Please use correct spelling.',
        '<br><input name="formPublisher" size=60 maxlength=100 ',
        'value="', htmlentities($publname), '">', "\n</tr>\n";
    echo '<input type=hidden name="formPublType" value=2>', "\n";
  }
  // case 3: publisher unknown, but similar publishers found
  else {
    echo "<tr><td>Publisher:\n",
        "<td><table cellpadding=2\n";
    echo '<tr><td><input type=radio name="formPublRadio"
            value="new">',
        '<td>New Publisher (Please specify full name. Please use ',
        'correct spelling.) ', "\n",
        '<input name="formPublisher" size=60 maxlength=100 ',
        'value="', htmlentities($publname), '"></tr>', "\n";
    // display list of similar publishers
    $publNames="";
    $publIDs="";
    while($row=mysql_fetch_object($result)) {
        echo '<tr><td><input type=radio name="formPublRadio" ',
          mysql_num_rows($result)==1 ? 'checked ' : '',
          'value="', $row->publID, '"><td>',
          $row->publName, "</tr>\n";
        $publNames .= ";" . $row->publName;
        $publIDs .= ";" . $row->publID;
    }
    echo "</table>\n</tr>\n";
    // place information about input fields in hidden form fields
    echo '<input type=hidden name="formPublType" value=3>', "\n";
    echo '<input type=hidden name="formPublNames" value="',
        htmlentities(substr($publNames, 1)), '">', "\n";
    echo '<input type=hidden name="formPublIDs" value="',
```

```
          substr($publIDs, 1), '">', "\n";
    }
    mysql_free_result($result);
  }
}
```

At the end of the input options information is stored in three hidden form fields as to whether the input name is known (*formPublType*). If options with similar publisher names were displayed, then a list of these names and ID numbers is stored. In this way the input form can be recreated if necessary with *restore_publisher_options*. (This will be necessary if the phase 2 form must be displayed again due to an input error having been discovered in one or another field.) The following lines show the HTML code corresponding to Figure 8-12, including the hidden fields:

```
<tr><td>Publisher:
    <td>
    <table cellpadding=2>
    <tr><td><input type=radio name="formPublRadio" value="new">
        <td>New Publisher (Please specify full name. Please use
            correct spelling.)
        <input name="formPublisher" size=60 maxlength=100 value="a">
    </tr>
    <tr><td><input type=radio name="formPublRadio" value="1">
        <td>Addison-Wesley</tr>
    <tr><td><input type=radio name="formPublRadio" value="2">
        <td>Apress</tr>
    </table>
</tr>
<input type=hidden name="formPublType" value=3>
<input type=hidden name="formPublNames"
      value="Addison-Wesley;Apress">
<input type=hidden name="formPublIDs" value="1;2">
```

restore_publisher_options: *Restoring the Publisher Selection Fields*

The function *restore_publisher_options* is called if the form displayed in phase 2 of the input process must be shown again (due to the discovery of an input error). The form variables *formPublisher* (from the input field) and *formPublRadio* (selected options), as well as *formPublType*, *formPublNames*, and *formPublIDs* (hidden fields), are used to restore the form to its last displayed condition.

From the point of view of database programming the code is not particularly interesting, for which reason we shall refrain from presenting all of the gory details. However, the passing of parameters is worth a bit of a look. Instead of passing a long list of all the variables, the function is called with the array *HTTP_POST_VARS* as parameter. In the function, all the form variables contained in this array are copied to local variables with *extract*.

```
function restore_publisher_options($formvars) {
  extract($formvars);

   ...
}
```

show_authors_options *and* restore_authors_options: *Author Input*

The functions *show_authors_options* and *restore_authors_options* take on the same tasks as the *publisher* functions that we have just described, although this time it is for the input of author names. There are two significant differences:

- In the input form in phase 1 several authors can be input. Therefore, *show_authors_options* decomposes the character string *formAuthors* into its components and then treats each author separately.

- With all the author names the order of names is reversed. (The program expects input in the form *Stephen King*, and then it searches the database for *King Stephen*.) Just to be on the safe side the author table searches for names in both forms, so that the author will be found even if the input was in the incorrect order.

```
function show_authors_options($formAuthors) {
  // decompose formAuthors into individual author names
  $authArray = explode(";", $formAuthors);
  $authCount = 0;
  // loop over all the authors
  while($i = each($authArray)) {
    $known_author = 0;
    $author = trim($i[1]);
    if($author) {
      $authCount++;
      // author perhaps has the given name first
      // but authorDB is in database format
      $authorDB = last_name_first($author);
      // search for names (with authorDB)
      $result1 =
        mysql_query("SELECT authName FROM authors " .
```

```
            "WHERE authName = " . sql_str($authorDB) .
            " LIMIT 2");
    if(mysql_num_rows($result1)==1) {
        $known_author=1;
        $authorDB = mysql_result($result1, 0, 0);
        $author = last_name_last($authorDB);
    }
    // search again for names (with author)
    else {
        $result2 =
            mysql_query("SELECT authName FROM authors " .
                    "WHERE authName = " . sql_str($author) .
                    " LIMIT 2");
    ...
```

The rest of the code for *show_authors_options* is very similar to that of *show_publisher_options*, for which reason we do not show it here. The same holds for *restore_authors_options*.

validate_stage1 *and* _stage2: *Functions for Data Validation*

In *validate_stage1* it is checked that a title was input, that the input field for the edition is either empty or contains an integer greater than 0, and that the input field for the year of publication is either empty or contains an integer that is not larger than one plus the current year. (Publishers often give the following year as publication date for a book that appears in the last three months of the year.)

The function *validate_stage2* calls on *validate_stage1*. Moreover, the function validates the input for author and publisher names. It must be ensured that either a character string was input or one of the options was selected.

save_data: *Function for Storing the New Data Record*

From the database programming viewpoint we are again in interesting territory with the function *save_data*. The data input in the form should now be stored in the database.

In the first step it is checked whether the input publisher already appears in the database. If this is the case, then the ID number of the record is temporarily stored in *publID*. (The ID number will be needed later to store the *title* data record.) If the publisher is as yet unknown, then an *INSERT* command is employed to insert it into the table. Now *publID* is determined via *mysql_insert_id*. Things are simpler if the user has clicked on one of the radio buttons. Then the form variable *formPublRadio* already contains the ID number. Finally, there is the possibility that no publisher was specified in the form. In that case, *publID* is deleted with *unset*. (The *titles* table allows the storage of records without a publisher. Likewise, most of the other columns of the *titles* table are optional, and may contain *NULL*.)

```
function save_data($formvars) {
  extract($formvars);
  // search for or store publisher
  $formPublisher = trim($formPublisher);
  if(($formPublType<3 or
      ($formPublType==3 and $formPublRadio=="new"))
    and !empty($formPublisher)) {
    // is the publisher already known to the database?
    $result =
      mysql_query("SELECT publID FROM publishers " .
                  "WHERE publName = " . sql_str($formPublisher));
    if(mysql_num_rows($result))
      $publID = mysql_result($result, 0, 0);
    // publisher is not yet known; store it
    else {
      mysql_query("INSERT INTO publishers (publName) " .
                  "VALUES(" . sql_str($formPublisher) . ")");
      $publID = mysql_insert_id();
    }
    mysql_free_result($result);
  }
  // radio button with known publisher was selected
  elseif($formPublType==3 and $formPublRadio!="new") {
    $publID = $formPublRadio;
  }
  // no publisher was specified
  else
    unset($publID);
```

A similar process is repeated for each of the authors. Since the relevant information is specified in variables such as *formAuthor1* and *formAuthor2*, in the author loop first the values must be extracted from these variable (!) variable names. To this end the PHP syntax *${'name'}* is employed to determine the content of the specified variables in the nested parentheses.

```
  // loop over all authors
  $authCount=0;
  for($i=1; $i<=$formAuthorsCount; $i++) {
    $newID = "none";
```

```
// extract form variables
$author = ${'formAuthor' . $i};
$authorRadio = ${'formAuthorRadio' . $i};
$authorType =${'formAuthorType' . $i};
$author = trim($author);
// author name in database-specific format
$authorDB = last_name_first($author);
```

In the following lines the ID number of the author is determined (variable *newID*). To accomplish this, the author is searched for in the database in both formats (given name followed by family name and conversely). If the name is not found, then it is inserted into the database as a new author with *INSERT*.

```
// author from text field
if($author and $authorType<3 or $authorRadio=="new") {
  // is the author already known to the database?
  $result =
    mysql_query("SELECT authID FROM authors " .
                "WHERE authName = " . sql_str($authorDB) .
                " OR authName = " . sql_str($author));
  if(mysql_num_rows($result))
    $newID = mysql_result($result, 0, 0);
  // the author is unknown: insert into database
  else {
    mysql_query("INSERT INTO authors (authName) " .
                "VALUES('" . sql_str($authorDB) . ")");
    $newID = mysql_insert_id();
  }
  mysql_free_result($result);
}
// radio button with known author was chosen
elseif ($authorRadio!="new")
  $newID = $authorRadio;
```

The variable *newID* is inserted into the field *authIDs*, which contains all the authors of the new book title. Here it must be ensured that the same author is not inserted twice due to improper input.

```
// each author must be inserted only once into the authIDs
for($j=0; $j<sizeof($authIDs); $j++)
  if($authIDs[$j]==$newID) {
    $newID="none"; break;
  }
```

```
    // insert newID in authIDs
    if($newID!="none") {
      $authIDs[$authCount]=$newID;
      $authCount++;
    }
  } // end of the loop over author names
```

Only one *INSERT* command is required in order to enter the new book into the *titles* table, but because of the numerous columns it is rather substantial. To create the command the functions *str_or_null* and *num_or_null* are called on, which return the content of the respective variable or else *NULL* if the variable is empty.

```
    // store book title
    if($formCategory=="none") unset($formCategory);
    if($formLanguage=="none") unset($formLanguage);
    mysql_query("INSERT INTO titles (title, subtitle, " .
                " edition, publID, catID, langID, year, " .
                " isbn, comment) VALUES (" .
                sql_str(trim($formTitle)) . ", " .
                str_or_null($formSubtitle) . ", " .
                num_or_null($formEdition) . ", " .
                num_or_null($publID) . ", " .
                num_or_null($formCategory) . ", " .
                num_or_null($formLanguage) . ", " .
                num_or_null($formYear) . ", " .
                str_or_null($formISBN) . ", " .
                str_or_null($formComment) . ")");
    $titleID = mysql_insert_id();
```

Finally, the relation between the book title and the authors must be created. For this the *INSERT* command is assembled in the variable *sql*:

```
    // store entries in rel_title_author
    $sql = "INSERT INTO rel_title_author " .
      "(titleID, authID, authNr) VALUES ";
    for($i=0; $i<$authCount; $i++) {
      if($i!=0) $sql .= ",";
      $sql .= "($titleID, $authIDs[$i], $i)";
    }
    mysql_query($sql);
  }
```

Room for Improvement

The script input.php does quite a bit, yet one can think of a number of ways in which it could be improved.

- The program does not check whether the book title that is input perhaps already exists in the database. Such a control is not trivial to implement, because a comparison of titles alone is not sufficient. For example, there might certainly be more than one computer book with the title *MySQL*. Thus all additional information such as subtitle, publisher, edition, authors, all of which is subject to error, must be taken into consideration. A possible solution would be to display a list of all books with the same or similar titles in the second input phase to lessen the danger of a duplicate being inserted. (If all titles were consistently accompanied by their ISBN numbers, then a test for uniqueness would be easy. But in our program such input is optional.)

- In comparing author names one can use the function *SOUNDEX*. This MySQL function returns the same value for similar-sounding English words (e.g., *Green* and *Greene*). In this way possible typographical errors in author input can be repaired before it is too late. However, there is an assumption that the *authors* table is equipped with an additional *soundex* column in which all like-sounding names have been stored for existing authors. (It would be too costly to execute the *SOUNDEX* for all existing authors each time a comparison needs to be made.)

- There should be better protection of *save_data* against errors. It is relatively unlikely, based on the prior validation, that a problem will occur in storing a name, but an error can be caused externally, for example, from a locking problem. In general, after every call to *mysql_query* a check against possible errors should be carried out.

- A relatively obvious lack in the input form is that the number of authors is fixed in the first phase and cannot be changed in the second phase.

- Finally, there is an inconsistency in that with input.php there is the possibility of storing new titles, authors, publishers, etc., but these data cannot be changed.

All of these goals are realizable, but they would make the code even more complex than it is already and begin to make this less of a demonstration example and more of a real-world application.

Managing the Book Categories (categories.php)

Each title in *mylibrary* can be associated with a category of books. This section is devoted to introducing a PHP page for managing these categories. With this page you will be able to create new categories and delete existing ones.

From the user's point of view this management takes place over two pages: The initial page (see Figure 8-13) shows a hierarchical list of all the categories. You can select a category in order to insert subcategories (INSERT link) or delete one (DELETE link). If a category is deleted, then all of its subcategories are automatically deleted as well. Deletion is possible only if there is no book in the database that is associated with the category in question. Warning: Deletion takes place with no warning and no "undo" option.

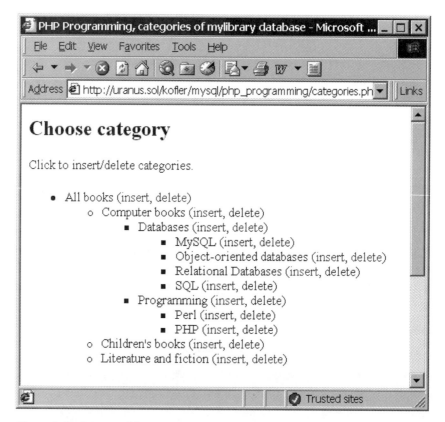

Figure 8-13. Select or delete a category

The form for input of a new category appears in Figure 8-14. Only the part of the hierarchy that applies to the selected entry (shown in boldface) is displayed. It is possible to input several new subcategories at one time (separated by a semicolon).

Figure 8-14. Adding the category Visual Basic *in the group* All books|Computer books|Programming

Code Outline

The script categories.php begins with two auxiliary functions: *insert_new_category* stores a new category in the database; *delete_category* deletes a category and all of its subcategories. These two functions are described at the end of this section.

We now present the code for representing the hierarchical list of all categories as well as the representation and evaluation of a form for input of new categories. The following outline should provide orientation inside of categories.php.

```
<!-- php/mylibrary/categories.php -->
<?php
  // read in auxiliary functions
  include("../../_private/mylibraryconnect.inc.php");

  // define new functions
  function insert_new_category($catID, $newcatName) { ... }
  function delete_category($catID) { ... }
```

```
    // establish connection to database
    $connID = connect_to_mylibrary();
?>

<!-- start of the HTML document -->
<!DOCTYPE HTML PUBLIC "-//W3C//DTD HTML 4.0//EN">
<html><head>
<title>PHP Programming, categories of mylibrary database</title>
</head><body>
<?php
    // Main-Code
    // if deleteID==n: delete category
    // if isempty(catID): display hierarchical list of all categories
    // else: - evaluate form data, insert new categories
    //       - display hierarchical list of the selected category
    //       - display form for input of a new category
php?>
</body></html>
```

URL Parameters

There are at most two variables that can be passed to the page as part of the address:

- *catID* contains the ID number of the selected category (into which the new subcategory is to be inserted).

- *deleteID* contains the ID number of the category that is to be deleted.

Form Variables

If the page used to evaluate form results is to be called, then two more variables are added to this list:

- *submitbutton* contains *"OK"*.

- *subcategories* contains a character string with the new category to be added.

Main Code

The code for the PHP page begins with a test of both parameters that may have been passed: *deleteID* and *catID*. If *deleteID* is the ID number of exactly one record in *categories*, then *delete_category* is called to delete this category. (The test should ensure that no wild cards are smuggled in as *deleteID* so that more will be deleted than was intended.)

A similar test is carried out for *catID*. If this test is passed successfully, then the variable *validCatID* is set to *TRUE*.

```
// test whether deleteID refers to exactly one categories record
if($deleteID) {
  $result = mysql_query("SELECT catID FROM categories " .
                        "WHERE catID='$deleteID'");
  // delete category
  if(mysql_num_rows($result)==1)
    delete_category($deleteID);
}
// test whether catID refers to an existing record
if($catID) {
  $result =
    mysql_query("SELECT catID FROM categories WHERE catID='$catID'");
  if(mysql_num_rows($result))
    $validCatID=TRUE;
}
```

Display Hierarchical List of All Categories

If *catID* is invalid or was not even passed, then a hierarchical list of all categories is displayed. For indenting the list the HTML tag *<ul>* is used. For each category the contents of the variable *lastIndent* is compared to the value of *hierIndent* from the database. If the indentation depth has changed, then the corresponding number of *<ul>* or *</ul>* tags are output.

For each category a link to the insertion of a new record (with *?catID=n*) or to the deletion of the category is displayed (with *?deleteID=n*). These links are assembled via the auxiliary function *build_href*.

```
if(!$validCatID) {
  echo "<h2>Choose category</h2>\n";
  echo "<p>Click to insert/delete categories.\n";
  // query over all categories
  $result = mysql_query("SELECT catName, catID, hierIndent " .
                        "FROM categories ORDER BY hierNr");
  // evaluate query result
  echo "<p>\n";
  $lastIndent=-1;
  while($row=mysql_fetch_object($result)) {
```

```
        // <ul>'s for the next hierarchy level
        if($row->hierIndent > $lastIndent)
          echo "<ul>\n";
        // </ul>'s, to get out of the last valid hierarchy level
        if($row->hierIndent < $lastIndent)
          for($i=$row->hierIndent; $i<$lastIndent; $i++)
            echo "</ul>\n";
        $lastIndent = $row->hierIndent;
        // display category name as well as insert and delete links
        echo "<li>",
          htmlentities($row->catName), " (",
          build_href("./categories.php", "catID=$row->catID", "insert"),
          ", ",
          build_href("./categories.php", "deleteID=$row->catID",
                    "delete"),
          ")",
          "</li>\n";
      }
      // close all <ul>'s still open
      for($i=-1; $i<=lastIndent; $i++)
        echo "</ul>\n";
  }
```

Inserting New Categories

The *else* that begins here runs almost to the end of the PHP file. It is not the entire category list that should be displayed, but a particular category into which new subcategories may be added (see Figure 8-14).

However, this code segment is executed only if form results are to be evaluated. To accomplish this, the variable *subcategories* is decomposed into an array containing all the new categories to be inserted. They are inserted into the database with *insert_new_category*. The variable *count* keeps track of how often this is successfully accomplished. A brief message reports on the result.

```
else {// to if(!validCatID)
  echo "<h2>Insert new categories</h2>\n";
  // evaluate form data (insert new subcategories)
  if($subcategories){
    $subcatarray = explode(";", $subcategories);
    $count=0;
    while($i = each($subcatarray)) {
      $newcatname = trim($i[1]);
      $count += insert_new_category($catID, $newcatname);
```

```
    }
  if($count)
    echo "<p>$count new categories have been inserted ",
      "into the categories table.\n";
}
```

Representing a Branch of the Hierarchical Tree

The following lines of code have the purpose of displaying the category described by *catID* together with its super- and subcategories (see Figure 8-14). The purpose, then, is to display a small segment of the entire hierarchical tree.

In the first step three arrays (*catNames, catIDs, parentCatIDs*) are constructed, which contain the higher levels of the hierarchy (*catNames[0]*, i.e., *all books*; *catNames[1]*, e.g., *Computer books*; *catNames[2]*, e.g., *Programming*, etc. (see Figure 8-14). The arrays are then filled with the data of the current record described by *catID*. Thereafter, a loop follows *parentCatIDs* back to the root of the hierarchy.

After these data have been determined they are displayed in a loop (indented as required by means of <*ul*>). The current category is treated in the same manner, except that it is displayed in boldface type.

```
// determine data of the current category (catID)
$result =
  mysql_query("SELECT * FROM categories WHERE catID='$catID'");
$row = mysql_fetch_object($result);
$maxIndent = $row->hierIndent;
$catNames[$maxIndent] = $row->catName;
$catIDs[$maxIndent] = $row->catID;
$parentCatIDs[$maxIndent] = $row->parentCatID;

// loop to determine the data of the next higher category
for($i=$maxIndent-1; $i>=0; $i--) {
  $result = mysql_query("SELECT * FROM categories " .
                "WHERE catID='" . $parentCatIDs[$i+1] . "'");
  $row = mysql_fetch_object($result);
  $catNames[$i] = $row->catName;
  $catIDs[$i] = $row->catID;
  $parentCatIDs[$i] = $row->parentCatID;
}

// display next higher category
for($i=0; $i<$maxIndent; $i++) {
  echo "<ul><li>", htmlentities($catNames[$i]), "</li>\n";
}
```

```
// display current category
echo "<ul><li><b>", htmlentities($catNames[$maxIndent]),
  "</b></li>\n";
```

To give a view as to which subcategories already exist, all existing subcategories of *catID* are determined and displayed. The categories are supplied with a DELETE link, so that incorrectly inserted categories can be deleted.

```
// display all subcategories of catID together with a delete link
$result =
  mysql_query("SELECT catName, catID FROM categories " .
                "WHERE parentCatID='$catID' ORDER BY catName");
echo "<ul>\n";
if(mysql_num_rows($result)) {
  while($row=mysql_fetch_object($result)) {
    echo "<li>", htmlentities($row->catName), " (",
      build_href("./categories.php",
                "catID=$catID&deleteID=$row->catID",
                "delete") .
      ")</li>\n";
  }}
else {
  echo "(No subcategories yet.)\n";
}
echo "</ul>\n";
```

Finally, all open *<ul>* tags must be closed:

```
// close hierarchical category list
for($i=0; $i<=$maxIndent; $i++) {
  echo "</ul>\n";
}
```

Input Form for New Categories

The input form for new categories consists merely of a text field (*subcategories*) and a "submit" button. The *action* link refers again to categories.php, where additionally, the current *catID* number is transmitted. This has the effect that as result of the input the reduced hierarchical tree and the form are shown. Thus the result of the input is immediately visible (in the form of additional subcategories). Moreover, additional categories can be immediately input.

```
echo "<form method=\"POST\" ",
    "action=\"./categories.php?catID=$catID\">\n";
echo "<p>Insert new sub-categories to ",
  "<b>$catNames[$maxIndent]</b>. <br>You may add several ",
  "subcategories at once. <br>Use ; to separate ",
  "your entries.\n";
echo "<p><input name=\"subcategories\" size=60 maxlength=80>\n";
echo "<input type=\"submit\" value=\"OK\"",
    " name=\"submitbutton\">\n";
echo "</form>\n";
```

The PHP code ends with a link that leads back to the complete category list. The closing curly brace ends the long *else* block following *if(!validCatID)*.

```
// link back to complete category list
echo "<p>Back to full ",
  build_href("./categories.php", "", "categories list") . ".\n";
}
```

insert_new_category: *Function to Save a New Category*

The function *insert_new_category* adds a new category to the table *categories*. The ID number (*catID*) of the category to which the new category (*newcatName*) is to be subordinated must be passed as parameter.

The function assumes that *catID* is valid. With *newcatName* a test is made as to whether the character string is empty or whether perhaps the new category already exists as a subcategory of *catID*. If either case obtains, the function is immediately terminated.

```
function insert_new_category($catID, $newcatName) {
  // $catID: category into which the new subcategory is to be inserted
  // $newcatName: name of the new subcategory

  // terminate if newcatName is empty
  if(!$newcatName) return(0);

  // test whether the category already exists
  $result = mysql_query("SELECT catID FROM categories " .
              "WHERE parentCatID=$catID " .
              " AND catName='$newcatName'");
  if(mysql_num_rows($result)) return(0);
  mysql_free_result($result);
```

Now comes the actualization of the insertion algorithm that was explained in detail in Chapter 5. Briefly, the position of the new category within the hierarchical category list is found (that is, the *hierNr* value for the new category).

```
// (1) get information on the higher-ranking category
$result =
  mysql_query("SELECT * FROM categories WHERE catID='$catID'");
$base=mysql_fetch_object($result);
mysql_free_result($result);
// (2a) search for the category below $newcatName
$result =
  mysql_query("SELECT hierNr FROM categories " .
              "WHERE parentCatID='$base->catID' " .
              "" AND catName>'$newcatName' " .
              "ORDER BY catName LIMIT 1");
if(mysql_num_rows($result)) {
  $newhierNr = mysql_result($result, 0, 0);
  mysql_free_result($result);
}
// (2b) search for the start of the next category group
else {
  $result =
    mysql_query("SELECT hierNr FROM categories " .
                "WHERE hierNr>'$base->hierNr' " .
                " AND hierIndent<='$base->hierIndent' " .
                "ORDER BY hierNr LIMIT 1");
if(mysql_num_rows($result)) {
  $newhierNr = mysql_result($result, 0, 0);
  mysql_free_result($result);
}
  // (2c) search for the maximal hierNr in the table
  else {
    $result =
      mysql_query("SELECT MAX(hierNr) FROM categories");
    $newhierNr = mysql_result($result, 0, 0)+1;
    mysql_free_result($result);
  }
}
```

Once *hierNr* has been determined, this value is increased by 1 for all existing records with the same or higher *hierNr*, so as to make room for the new record. Then the new record is inserted.

```
// (3) increase hierNr for all categories below $newcatName
mysql_query("UPDATE categories SET hierNr=hierNr+1 " .
              "WHERE hiernr>=$newhierNr");

// (4) insert new category
mysql_query("INSERT INTO categories " .
              " (catName, parentCatID, hierNr, hierIndent) " .
              "VALUES ('$newcatName', $catID, $newhierNr, " .
                 ($base->hierIndent+1) . ")");
return(1); }
```

> **REMARK** *To save on resources, in this function and the next function to be introduced,* delete_category, *all SQL query results will be released with* mysql_free_result. *This makes sense because within the function a number of queries are executed and because the function can be called a number of times during the lifetime of the script (for example, if several new categories are to be added at one time).*

delete_category: *Function to Delete an Existing Category*

As parameter to the function *delete_category* the ID number of the category to be deleted is passed. Within the function it is determined whether there are any subcategories to this category. If that is the case, then *delete_category* is called recursively to delete these subcategories. During this process a running total of return values is calculated, where 1 indicates that the category was able to be deleted, and 0 that it could not be. This allows a simple determination to be made as to whether all the subcategories were deleted. If that is not the case, then the function is terminated.

```
function delete_category($catID) {
  // search for subcategories of catID
  // and delete them with recursive calls to delete_category
  $result =
    mysql_query("SELECT catID FROM categories " .
                "WHERE parentCatID='$catID'");
  $rows = mysql_num_rows($result);
  $deletedRows = 0;
  while($row=mysql_fetch_row($result)) {
    $deletedRows += delete_category($row[0]);
  }
```

```
mysql_free_result($result);

// if not all subcategories could be deleted,
// then the category catID cannot be deleted
if($deletedRows != $rows)
  return(0);
```

Then a test is made as to whether there are book titles that belong to the category that is to be deleted. In such a case the category cannot be deleted. If there are such titles, an error message is output that gives the name of the category and the number of associated titles.

```
// are there titles that belong to catID?
$result = mysql_query("SELECT COUNT(titleID) FROM titles " .
              "WHERE catID='$catID'");
// yes, the category may not be deleted;
// display error message
if($nrOfTitles = mysql_result($result, 0, 0)) {
  mysql_free_result($result);
  $result =
    mysql_query("SELECT catName FROM categories " .
              "WHERE catID='$catID'");
  $catName = mysql_result($result, 0, 0);
  mysql_free_result($result);
  echo "<br>Category <b>$catName</b> is used in $nrOfTitles ",
    "titles. You cannot delete it and its parents.\n";
  return(0);
}
```

Otherwise, there is nothing to stop the hand of destruction: The category can now be deleted.

```
// delete category
mysql_query("DELETE FROM categories WHERE catID='$catID'");
return(1);
}
```

> **REMARK** *Deleting categories can result in holes in the sequence of* hierNr *values in the* categories *table. Thus you may not assume that the difference of two* hierNr *values represents the number of categories of intermediate records.*

Ideas for Improvements and Extensions

The three PHP pages displayed do not, unfortunately, represent a complete user interface to the *mylibrary* database. The following list presents some of the most pressing improvements that might be made.

- Altering existing records (for example, to correct typographical errors in title, author, or publisher names; change the association title $\leftrightarrow$ publisher or title $\leftrightarrow$ category).

- Delete existing records (title, author, publisher, etc.), with queries that ensure that no empty cross references remain.

- Unification of duplicates (for example, if an author has been stored two or three times due to a typographical error).

- management of the table *languages*.

None of these points represents a difficult problem, but the amount of programming required is rather large. To keep the code readable, the various auxiliary functions should be organized on a modular plan.

However, one may ask the question whether such an HTML-based user interface is worth the effort. If the user interface were to be developed with a free-standing programming language (C++, Visual Basic, Delphi, for example), then the amount of work would not be much greater, but one could achieve greater ease of use and perhaps even greater speed.

Example: Discussion Forum (myforum)

The example of this section shows how a discussion forum managed by its users can be realized with several PHP script files and the database *myforum* introduced in Chapter 5.

POINTER *As with all the examples in this book, we are interested more in explicating programming techniques than in producing a polished application. If your ambitions range in the direction of creating a web discussion forum, it would be worthwhile looking into the numerous off-the-shelf solutions available. The two currently most popular PHP scripts for discussion forums (or "fora" for all you Latinate purists out there), namely phorum and fforum, can be found at the following addresses:*

http://www.phorum.org/
http://fumanchi.tabu.uni-bonn.de/forum/

Assumptions

Our example assumes PHP 4.0 for session management. The session variables are discussed in the following sections.

How to Run It

From the user's viewpoint the portals leading to the discussion forum are opened by a login dialog (see Figure 8-15). One need not log in if one wishes only to read the postings. For this purpose a direct link to all forums is offered. A login is, however, required for those wishing to post messages. But first it is necessary to establish a *myforum* account (see Figure 8-16). (If you would like to try out the example on my web site, you can save yourself the trouble of establishing an account by logging in under the name *test* with the password *secret*.)

With or without registration you arrive at the page forumlist.php, in which all discussion forums are listed for your perusal (each with the language of the forum indicated). At the start of the page is displayed the user name of the current login (or *anonymous*). See Figure 8-17.

Figure 8-15. Login dialog for the myforum *discussion forum*

On the page forumread.php (see Figure 8-18) the last fifty messages to have been posted are displayed. The most current discussion threads are displayed at the start of the page. Within the thread appears the place in the sequence in which each article was posted (oldest article first).

Individual messages are displayed by means of the script forummessage.php (see Figure 8-19). If there are several replies to a given message, then the entire thread (a list of all messages together with their texts) can be displayed on a single page with forumthread.php (see Figure 8-20).

The script forumwrite.php (see Figure 8-21) assists in composing a new message or responding to an existing one.

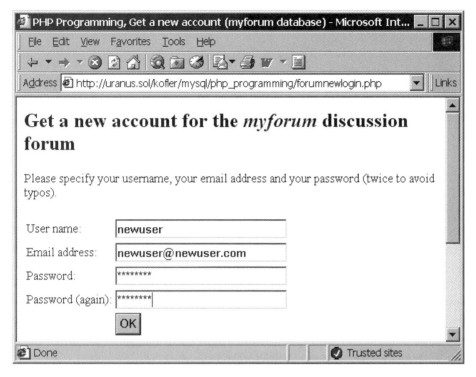

Figure 8-16. Establishing a new myforum *account*

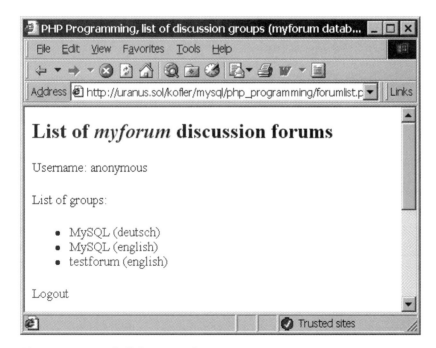

Figure 8-17. List of all discussion forums

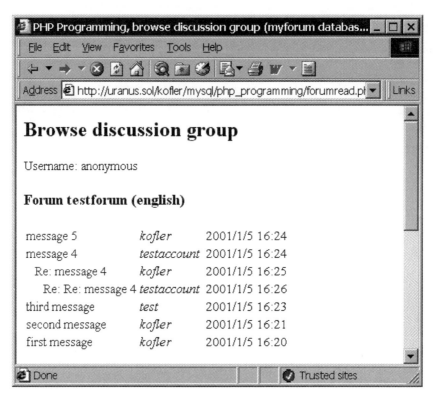

Figure 8-18. List of all postings to testforum

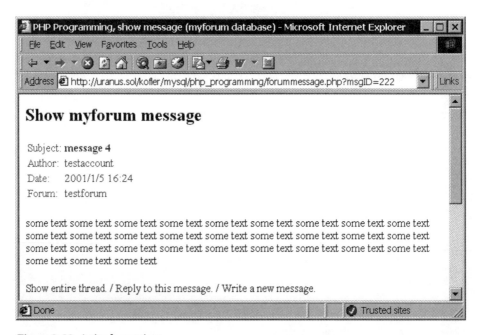

Figure 8-19. A single posting

Figure 8-20. An entire discussion thread

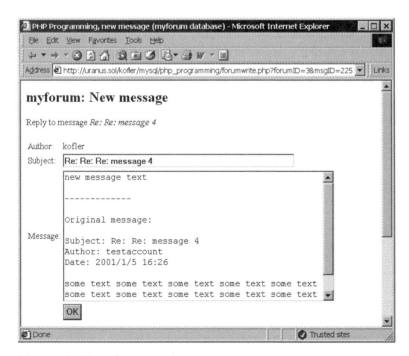

Figure 8-21. Form for composing a message

Overview of the Program Code

Our example consists of the following files:

`myforumconnect.inc.php`	auxiliary functions (including database login)
`forumlogin.php`	login to the forum
`forumnewlogin.php`	new registration
`forumlist.php`	display list of all discussion groups
`forumread.php`	display list of titles of all messages
`forumthread.php`	display discussion thread
`forummessage.php`	display discussion message
`forumwrite.php`	compose message
`forumlogout.php`	unregister

Managing a Session

Passing information about who has registered (variables *sesUserID* and *sesUser-Name*) between the script files is managed by means of a PHP-4.0 session. Otherwise, the passing of information between the script files is carried out with URL parameters.

Since the required code is in more or less the same form in all the script files, it is described here in one place. At the beginning of each script the function *session_register* is executed in order to declare the session variables.

```
session_register("sesUserID", "sesUserName");
```

If the client permits cookies (that is, in the user's browser), then all of this happens automatically; that is, the content of the session variables continues to be available when a switch is made to a new page.

On the other hand, if cookies are not allowed, then an identification number for the session must be passed as part of the URL at each page change. In many cases (and depending on the options under which PHP was compiled) PHP itself takes care of this. In order to ensure that management of the session functions dependably in all circumstances, the evaluation of the constant *SID* and a bit of hand operation are necessary. The constant *SID* contains a character string of the form *PHPSESSID=3ff5* . . . . This character string must be specified as a URL parameter at each change between PHP scripts. To avoid constant queries of the form *if(SID)* . . . , the two variables *sid1* and *sid2* are defined on the basis of *SID*.

```
if(SID) {
  $sid1 = "?" . SID;
  $sid2 = "&" . SID; }
```

In what follows, *sid1* (first URL parameter) or *sid2* (additional URL parameter) can simply be attached to URL character strings, for example, as follows:

```
// page change to forumlist.php
header("Location: ./forumlist.php$sid1");

// write link to page forumwrite.php in the HTML document
$query = "forumID=$row->forumID&msgID=$row->msgID" . $sid2;
echo "<p>",
  build_href("./forumwrite.php", $query, "Reply to this message"),
  ".\n";
```

> **REMARK** *If PHP 4.0 is not available to you, you must specify with all links the two session variables* sesUserID *and* sesUserName *as supplementary URL parameters. This requires many small changes in the script files presented here. The variables are initialized in* forumlogin.php *and* forumnewlogin.php, *cleared in* forumlogout.php, *and used in all other scripts.*

Auxiliary Functions in `myforumconnect.inc.php`

The file `myforumconnect.inc.php` contains several auxiliary functions. The most important of these is *connect_to_myforum,* which establishes the connection to MySQL. The functions are almost identical to those of `mylibraryconnect.inc.php`, for which reason we do not describe them here.

Registration (`forumlogin.php`)

The script `forumlogin.php` displays a simple form in which a login name and password can be given (see Figure 8-15). The evaluation of the form variables *formUser* and *formPassword* also takes place in this script.

```
<?php // php/myforum/forumlogin.php

//read in standard functions
include("../../_private/myforumconnect.inc.php");

// establish connection to database
$connID = connect_to_myforum();

// declare session variables
session_register("sesUserID", "sesUserName");
if(SID) {
  $sid1 = "?" . SID;
  $sid2 = "&" . SID; }
```

If the *users* database contains the character string pair, then the sessions variables *sesUserID* and *sesUserName* are initialized. Then the PHP function *header* is used to effect a change to the page forumlist.php. (In order for *header* to work, no HTML output can occur before this function. For this reason the HTML header is output relatively late in forumlogin.php.)

```
// evaluate form data
if($formSubmit) {
  $result =
    mysql_query("SELECT userID, userName FROM users " .
                "WHERE userName = '$formUser' " .
                " AND password = PASSWORD('$formPassword')");
  // ok, user recognized
  if(mysql_num_rows($result)==1) {
    $sesUserID = mysql_result($result, 0, 0);
    $sesUserName = mysql_result($result, 0, 1);
    // change to page forumlist.php
    header("Location: ./forumlist.php$sid1");
    exit;
  }
}
?>
```

The remainder of the code serves to display the input form and some links and additional information.

```
<!DOCTYPE HTML PUBLIC "-//W3C//DTD HTML 4.0//EN">
<html><head>
<title>PHP Programming, forum login (myforum database)</title>
</head><body>
<h2>Login to the <i>myforum</i> discussion forum</h2>
<form method="POST" action="./forumlogin.php">
```

```
<?php
// display error message is login fails
if($formSubmit and empty($userID))
  echo "<p><font color=ff0000>User name or password ",
    "is invalid. Please try again.</font>\n";
?>
<p>Please specify your user name and password. ...
<p><table>
<tr><td>User name:
    <td><input name="formUser" size=30 maxlength=30>
<tr><td>Password:
    <td><input type="password" name="formPassword" size=30
        maxlength=30>
<tr><td>
    <td><input type="submit" value="Login" name="formSubmit">
</table>
</form>
</body></html>
```

Registering a New User (forumnewlogin.php)

In the form forumnewlogin.php a new user for *myforum* can be defined (see
Figure 8-16). A user name, e-mail address, and (twice to avoid typos) password
are required.

```
<?php // php/myforum/forumnewlogin.php
// read in standard functions
include("../../_private/myforumconnect.inc.php");
// establish connection to database
$connID = connect_to_myforum();
// declare session variables
session_register("sesUserID", "sesUserName");
if(SID) {
  $sid1 = "?" . SID;
  $sid2 = "&" . SID; }
```

The actual program code begins with the evaluation of the form variables
formUser, formEMail, formPassword1, and *formPassword2.* The first thing to
occur is a check as to whether the name is already in use. If that is the case, then
the variable *wrongName* is set to 1 (for the purpose of a later error message to be
displayed). Additionally, a test is made as to whether an e-mail address was given
(without verifying its format) and whether the two passwords are identical.

```
// evaluate form variables
if($formSubmit=="OK") {
  $formUser = trim($formUser);
  $formEMail = trim($formEMail);
  $formPassword1 = trim($formPassword1);
  $formPassword2 = trim($formPassword2);

  // is the user name available?
  if($formUser) {
    $result =
      mysql_query("SELECT userID, userName FROM users " .
                     "WHERE userName = '$formUser' ");
    if(mysql_num_rows($result)==1)
      $wrongName = 1; // name is in use
  }
  else
    $wrongName = 1;// no name was given whatsoever
  // was an e-mail address given?
  if(!$formEMail)
    $wrongEMail=1;
  // do the passwords agree?
  if($formPassword1=="" or $formPassword1!=$formPassword2)
    $wrongPassword=1;
```

If no formal errors are detected, then the new user is stored in the *user* database with an *INSERT*. Then the session variables *sesUserID* and *sesUserName* are initialized and the page forumlist.php displayed.

```
  // ok?
  if(!($wrongName || $wrongPassword || $wrongEMail)) {
    // store user name and password, determine ID,
    mysql_query("INSERT INTO users (user name, email, password) " .
                   "VALUES ('$formUser', '$formEMail', " .
                   " PASSWORD('$formPassword1'))");
    $sesUserID = mysql_insert_id();
    $sesUserName = stripslashes($formUser);
    // page change to forumlist.php
    header("Location: ./forumlist.php$sid1");
    exit;
  }
}
?>
```

The remaining code serves to display the form and any error messages that might be required:

```
<!DOCTYPE HTML PUBLIC "-//W3C//DTD HTML 4.0//EN">
<html><head>
<title>PHP Programming, Get a new account (myforum database)</title>
</head><body>
<h2>Get a new account for the <i>myforum</i> discussion forum</h2>

<form method="POST" action="./forumnewlogin.php<?php echo $sid1;?>">
<p>Please specify your user name ...

<?php

// display error messages
if($wrongName) echo " ... ";
if($wrongEMail) echo " ... ";
if($wrongPassword) echo " ... ";

?>

<p><table>
<tr><td>User name:
    <td><input name="formUser" size=30 maxlength=30
        value=<?php echo "\"$formUser\""; ?> >
<tr><td>Email address:
    <td><input name="formEMail" size=30 maxlength=30
        value=<?php echo "\"$formEMail\""; ?> >
<tr><td>Password:
    <td><input type="password" name="formPassword1" size=30
        maxlength=30 value=<?php echo "\"$formPassword1\""; ?> >
<tr><td>Password (again):
    <td><input type="password" name="formPassword2" size=30
        maxlength=30 value=<?php echo "\"$formPassword2\""; ?> >
<tr><td>
    <td><input type="submit" value="OK" name="formSubmit">
</table>
</form>

</body></html>
```

Possibilities for Expansion

Verifying an e-mail address: The easiest improvement to implement is to send a initial access code to the specified e-mail address (optimally in the form of an HTTP link). You could use a random number, for example, that is generated at the time of registration and stored in the user table until the user first accesses the account.

Display List of All Discussion Groups (forumlist.php)

The script forumlist.php displays a list of all discussion groups defined in the table *forums* (see Figure 8-17). The list is determined by means of a simple *SELECT* instruction and represented in the form of links that refer to the script forumread.php.

```php
<?php // php/myforum/forumlist.php

// read in standard functions
include("../../_private/myforumconnect.inc.php");

// establish connection to database
$connID = connect_to_myforum();

// declare session variables
session_register("sesUserID", "sesUserName");

if(empty($sesUserID))
  $sesUserName = "anonymous";
if(SID) {
  $sid1 = "?" . SID;
  $sid2 = "&" . SID; }

?>
<!DOCTYPE HTML PUBLIC "-//W3C//DTD HTML 4.0//EN">
<html><head>
<title>PHP Programming, list of discussion groups
      (myforum database)</title>
</head><body>
<h2>List of <i>myforum</i> discussion forums</h2>

<?php

echo "<p>Username: $sesUserName\n";

// display list of all discussion groups
echo "<p>List of groups:\n";
echo "<ul>\n";
$result =
  mysql_query("SELECT forumID, forumName, language FROM forums " .
              "ORDER BY forumName, language ");
while($row=mysql_fetch_object($result)) {
  echo "<li>",
    build_href("./forumread.php",
               "forumID=$row->forumID" . $sid2,
               "$row->forumName ($row ->language)"), "\n"; }
echo "</ul>\n";

// link to the logout script
```

```
echo "<p><a href=\"./forumlogout.php$sid1\">Logout</a>\n";

?>

</body></html>
```

Message List of a Discussion Group (forumread.php)

From the viewpoint of database programming the script forumread.php must be considered one of the most interesting modules of this example. Its task consists in displaying the fifty most recent messages of a discussion group (see Figure 8-18). If the discussion group contains more than that number of messages, then forumread.php enables the user to leaf pagewise through the messages.

The problem in representing the list of messages is that the pagewise division of the list results in the separation of discussion threads. (A recent message can arise as the reaction to a much older thread.)

To clarify the situation we present Figure 8-22, which shows three discussion threads with 17 messages altogether from users A–G. The threads are ordered chronologically (the newest thread first), and within the threads the messages are ordered hierarchically based on who was responding to whom.

Thread 3	G	*18.1.2001 21:00*
Re: Thread 3	B	*19.1.2001 15:30*
Re: Re: Thread 3	A	*19.1.2001 16:45*
Re: Re: Thread 3	C	*19.1.2001 17:30*
Re: Thread 3	E	*19.1.2001 19:00*
Thread 2	E	*17.1.2001 18:00*
Re: Thread 2	A	*18.1.2001 10:45*
Re: Re: Thread 2	B	*18.1.2001 10:55*
Re: Re: Re: Thread 2	F	*20.1.2001 22:05*
Re: Thread 2	C	*18.1.2001 19:00*
Thread 1	A	*17.1.2001 12:00*
Re: Thread 1	B	*17.1.2001 18:30*
Re: Re: Thread 1	A	*17.1.2001 19:45*
Re: Re: Thread 1	C	*19.1.2001 10:30*
Re: Thread 1	D	*18.1.2001 3:45*
Re: Re: Thread 1	A	*18.1.2001 9:45*
Re: Re: Re: Thread 1	D	*18.1.2001 22:05*

Figure 8-22. Hierarchical representation of three threads (ordered by flow of the discussion)

Many discussion forums simply do not display the message hierarchy with the pagewise display of messages. The advantage of this is that such a solution is easy to implement, and the messages can be ordered according to their creation dates. However, the flow of the discussion is lost (see Figure 8-23 with the ten most current messages from Figure 8-22 ordered by creation time).

Re: Re: Re: Thread 2	F	*20.1.2001 22:05*
Re: Thread 3	E	*19.1.2001 19:00*
Re: Re: Thread 3	C	*19.1.2001 17:30*
Re: Re: Thread 3	A	*19.1.2001 16:45*
Re: Thread 3	B	*19.1.2001 15:30*
Re: Re: Thread 1	C	*19.1.2001 10:30*
Re: Re: Re: Thread 1	D	*18.1.2001 22:05*
Thread 3	G	*18.1.2001 21:00*
Re: Thread 2	C	*18.1.2001 19:00*
Re: Re: Thread 2	B	*18.1.2001 10:55*

Figure 8-23. Flat representation of the ten most recent messages from Figure 8-22 (ordered by time of creation)

In Figure 8-24, on the other hand, an attempt is made to retain the hierarchy. In the most current thread this effort has brought success. In the two older threads the messages are properly indented, but the flow of the discussion is incomplete due to missing messages. The order of messages still corresponds to the thread structure, but the result is confusing.

Nonetheless, we have chosen this solution for forumread.php, because it seemed a reasonable compromise. (The number of messages per page is 50, and this number can be reset if it is so desired. Of course, the larger this value, the less often will there be dangling threads.) For threads that cannot be completely displayed on a page the link *(show entire thread)* is displayed, which leads to the script forumthread.php. There the entire thread is displayed regardless of its length.

> **REMARK** *Some discussion forums offer the possibility of expanding and contracting threads dynamically. This would be the most elegant solution, of course. However, in practice the entire page must be reloaded every time the level of the representation is changed, which leads to annoying delays.*
>
> *There is probably no truly perfect solution for HTML-based discussion forums. Forums that are very active are better off being organized as news groups, for which there are programs for reading threads.*

Thread 3	G	18.1.2001 21:00
Re: Thread 3	B	19.1.2001 15:30
Re: Re: Thread 3	A	19.1.2001 16:45
Re: Re: Thread 3	C	19.1.2001 17:30
Re: Thread 3	E	19.1.2001 19:00
(show entire thread)		
Re: Re: Thread 2	B	18.1.2001 10:55
Re: Re: Re: Thread 2	F	20.1.2001 22:05
Re: Thread 2	C	18.1.2001 19:00
(show entire thread)		
Re: Re: Thread 1	C	19.1.2001 10:30
Re: Re: Re: Thread 1	D	18.1.2001 22:05

Figure 8-24. Hierarchical representation of the most recent ten messages (ordered according to the discussion flow)

URL Variables

Two URL variables can be passed to forumread.php:

- *forumID* determines the forum whose messages are to be displayed.

- *page* specifies the page that is to be displayed.

Program Code

The program code begins with the by now well-known initialization instructions. If *forumID* is empty, the script is terminated and instead, forumlist.php is displayed.

```php
<?php // php/myforum/\{forumread.php}

// read in standard functions, create connection to database
include("../../_private/myforumconnect.inc.php");
$connID = connect_to_myforum();

// declare session variables
session_register("sesUserID", "sesUserName");
if(empty($sesUserID))
  $sesUserName = "anonymous";
if(SID) {
  $sid1 = "?" . SID;
  $sid2 = "&" . SID; }
```

```
// if forumID is empty, display forumlist.php
if(empty($forumID)) {
  header("Location: ./forumlist.php$sid1" );
  exit; }

?>
```

Validating ForumID

The following lines contain the HTML header. Then a *SELECT* query checks whether *forumID* refers to an existing discussion forum. In the *SELECT* query *LIMIT* is used to ensure that no wild cards are passed in *forumID*. If *forumID* is valid, then the name of the forum is displayed.

```
<!DOCTYPE HTML PUBLIC "-//W3C//DTD HTML 4.0//EN">
<html><head>
<title>PHP Programming, browse discussion group
      (myforum database)</title>
</head><body>
<h2>Browse discussion group</h2>

<?php
echo "<p>Username: $sesUserName\n";

// links forumID to a discussion group
$forumID = trim($forumID);
$result = mysql_query("SELECT forumName, language FROM forums " .
                      "WHERE forumID='$forumID' LIMIT 2");
if(!$result or mysql_num_rows($result)!=1) {
  echo "<p><font color=ff0000>ID number of forum seems ",
    "to be invalid.</font> Please choose a forum in the ",
    "<a href=\"./forumlist.php$sid1\">forum list</a>.\n";
  echo "</body></html>\n";
  exit;
}
// display name of the forum
$row = mysql_fetch_object($result);
echo "<h3>Forum $row->forumName ($row->language)</h3>\n";
mysql_free_result($result);
```

SQL Query for Determining the Message Text

The page size is determined by the variable with the unsurprising name *pagesize*. If a valid page number was not specified, then the page number is set to 1.

```
$pagesize = 50;
if(!$page or !(is_numeric($page)) or $page<0 or $page>100)
  $page=1;
```

In the following the list of message titles to be displayed is determined. To effect this, first the temporary table *tmpMsgIDs* with the *msgID* numbers of the desired page is generated. The variable *moremessages* is later evaluated to build into the HTML page a link to the next page with additional messages.

```
mysql_query("DROP TABLE IF EXISTS tmpMsgIDs");
mysql_query("CREATE TEMPORARY TABLE tmpMsgIDs TYPE = HEAP " .
            "SELECT msgID FROM messages " .
            "WHERE forumID = $forumID " .
            "ORDER BY timest DESC " .
"LIMIT " . ($pagesize*($page-1)) . ", " . ($pagesize+1));
if(mysql_affected_rows() > $pagesize)
$moremessages=1;
```

In a second query the data *msgID, subject, level, rootID, timest,* and *username* are determined for all messages contained in *tmpMsgIDs*. What is rather unconventional is the sorting of the messages: With *ORDER BY LEFT(orderstr, 4) DESC* we achieve that the creation time of the thread is used as the first sort criterion. New threads are displayed at the head of the list. As a second sort criterion *orderstr* is used. This results in the messages being sorted hierarchically based on the flow of the discussion (see also Chapter 5, where the design of the *myforum* database is discussed.

```
$result =
  mysql_query("SELECT messages.msgID, subject, level, rootID, " .
              " DATE_FORMAT(timest, '%Y/%c/%e %k:%i') AS timest, " .
              " username " .
              "FROM messages, users, tmpMsgIDs " .
              "WHERE messages.msgID = tmpMsgIDs.msgID " .
              " AND messages.userID = users.userID " .
              "ORDER BY LEFT(orderstr, 4) DESC, orderstr");
// delete temporary table
mysql_query("DROP TABLE tmpMsgIDs");
```

Display Message List

The following loop displays the results of the above query. Each message is represented as an HTML link on the page forummessage.php. If a thread cannot be completely displayed (that is, if the first message of the thread cannot be displayed), then instead a link to forumthread.php is inserted, so that the entire thread can be displayed.

```
$oldthreadID = 0; // helps in recognizing a new thread
if(mysql_num_rows($result)) {
  echo "<table>\n";
  while($row=mysql_fetch_object($result)) {
    // link to the entire thread
    if($row->rootID!=0 and $row->rootID!=$oldthreadID) {
      $query = "rootID=$row->rootID" . $sid2;
      echo "<tr><td>",
        build_href("./forumthread.php", $query,
                   "(show entire thread)"),
        "<td><td>\n";
    }
    // display subject, username, and date of the message
    $query = "msgID=$row->msgID" . $sid2;
    echo "<tr><td>",
      $row->level ?
        str_repeat("   ", $row->level) : "",
      build_href("./forummessage.php", $query, $row->subject),
      "<td><i>", htmlentities($row->username), "</i>",
      "<td> $row->timest \n";
    // update oldthreadID (for recognizing a new thread)
    if($row->rootID==0)
      $oldthreadID=$row->msgID;
    else
      $oldthreadID=$row->rootID;
  }
  echo "</table>\n";
}
```

Links to Other Pages

The program code ends with the output of links to later and earlier messages and to the form for input of a new message:

```
echo "<p><hr>\n";

// are there new messages?
if($page>1) {
  $query = "forumID=$forumID&page=" . ($page-1) . $sid2;
  echo build_href("./forumread.php", $query, "Show newer messages.");
  if($moremessages) echo " / ";
}
```

```
// are there further (i.e., older) messages?
if($moremessages) {
  $query = "forumID=$forumID&page=" . ($page+1) . $sid2;
  echo build_href("./forumread.php", $query, "Show older messages.");
}
echo "\n";

// link to forumwrite.php (compose new message)
if($page>1 or $moremessages)
  echo " / ";
$query = "forumID=$forumID" . $sid2;
echo build_href("./forumwrite.php", $query, "Write a new message"),
  ".\n";

?>

</body></html>
```

Representation of Message Text (forummessage.php)

In forumread.php the title of each message is linked to forummessage.php (see Figure 8-25). This script displays not only the message text, but also links for creating a reply and for the display of the complete thread (see Figure 8-19). The message to be displayed is passed to the script via the URL variable *msgID*.

Once again, the program code begins with our tried and true initialization. If *msgID* is empty, then the script is terminated, and instead, forumlist.php is displayed.

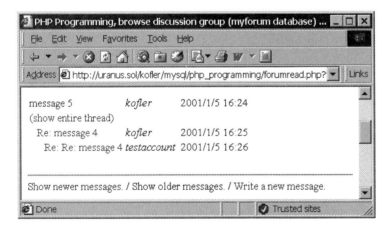

Figure 8-25. Representation of messages via forumread.php

```php
<?php // php/myforum/forummessage.php

// read in standard functions, establish connection to database
include("../../_private/myforumconnect.inc.php");
$connID = connect_to_myforum();

// declare session variables
session_register("sesUserID", "sesUserName");
if(empty($sesUserID))
  $sesUserName = "anonymous";
if(SID) {
  $sid1 = "?" . SID;
$sid2 = "&" . SID; }
// is $msgID empty? --> goto forumlist.php
if(empty($msgID)) {
  header("Location: ./forumlist.php$sid1");
exit; }

?>

<!-- start of html document if no connection error has happened -->
<!DOCTYPE HTML PUBLIC "-//W3C//DTD HTML 4.0//EN">
<html><head>
<title>PHP Programming, show message (myforum database)</title>
</head><body>
<h2>Show myforum message</h2>
```

The heart of the code begins with a test as to whether *msgID* actually refers to a message. If the *SELECT* is successful, then all the data are retrieved that will need to be displayed (*subject, msgText,* etc.):

```php
<?php

$msgID = trim($msgID);
$result =
  mysql_query("SELECT msgID, rootID, subject, msgText, " .
              " username, forumName, messages.forumID, " .
              " DATE_FORMAT(timest, '%Y/%c/%e %k:%i') AS timest " .
              "FROM messages, users, forums " .
              "WHERE msgID='$msgID' " .
              " AND messages.userID = users.userID " .
              " AND messages.forumID = forums.forumID " .
              "LIMIT 2");
if(!$result or mysql_num_rows($result)!=1) {
  echo "<p><font color=ff0000>ID number of message seems ",
    "to be invalid.</font> Please choose a forum in the ",
    "<a href=\"./forumlist.php$sid1\">forum list</a>.\n";
```

```
  show_copyright();
  echo "</body></html>\n";
  exit;
}
```

If all goes well, then first the message header (author, date, etc.) is displayed as a table, followed by the message itself. Please note in particular how the PHP function *nl2br* transforms line breaks in the message text into HTML line breaks and how *str_replace* replaces sequences of blank characters by nonbreaking HTML spaces with the code * * (important for the representation of indented program code!):

```
// show message
$fnt1s = "<font color=B02020>"; // font 1 start
$fnt1e = "</font>"; // font 1 end
$fnt2s = "<font color=303030>"; // font 2 start
$fnt2e = "</font>"; // font 2 end
$row = mysql_fetch_object($result);
echo "<table>\n";
echo "<tr><td>$fnt1s Subject:$fnt1e<td><b>", $fnt2s,
  htmlentities($row->subject), $fnt2e, "</b>\n";
echo "<tr><td>$fnt1s Author:$fnt1e<td>", $fnt2s,
  htmlentities($row->username), $fnt2e, "\n";
echo "<tr><td>$fnt1s Date:$fnt1e<td>",
  "$fnt2s$row->timest$fnt2e\n";
echo "<tr><td>$fnt1s Forum:$fnt1e<td>", $fnt2s,
  htmlentities($row->forumName), $fnt2e, "\n";
echo "</table>\n";
$msg = nl2br(htmlentities($row->msgText));
$msg = str_replace(" ", "  ", $msg);
echo "<p>$msg\n";
```

Links to forumthread.php and forumwrite.php are displayed at the bottom of the page:

```
// link to forumthread.php (display entire thread)
if($row->rootID)
  $query = "rootID=$row->rootID" . $sid2;
else
  $query = "rootID=$row->msgID" . $sid2;
echo "<p>",
  build_href("./forumthread.php", $query, "Show entire thread"),
  ".\n";
```

```
// link to forumwrite.php (reply to message)
$query = "forumID=$row->forumID&msgID=$row->msgID" . $sid2;
echo " / ",
  build_href("./forumwrite.php", $query, "Reply to this message"),
  ".\n";

// link to forumwrite.php (compose new message)
$query = "forumID=$row->forumID" .$sid2;
echo " / ",
  build_href("./forumwrite.php", $query, "Write a new message"),
  ".\n";
?>
</body></html>
```

Displaying a Thread (forumthread.php)

The script forumthread.php is to some extent a combination of forumread.php and forummessage.php: With it all messages of a thread—first the titles and then the actual text—are displayed on a single HTML page. This makes it possible to read the entire thread without having to jump back and forth between pages.

The URL variable *rootID* is passed to the script. After a brief test as to whether this variable contains reasonable data, a *SELECT* query is employed to read all the messages of the thread:

```
<?php // php/myforum/forumthread.php
  ...
$result =
  mysql_query("SELECT messages.msgID, subject, msgText, " .
              " level, rootID, username, forumName, " .
              " DATE_FORMAT(timest, '%Y/%c/%e %k:%i') AS timest " .
              "FROM messages, users, forums " .
              "WHERE (messages.rootID = '$rootID' " .
              " OR messages.msgID = '$rootID') " .
              " AND messages.userID = users.userID " .
              " AND messages.forumID = forums.forumID " .
              "ORDER BY orderstr");
  ...
```

Otherwise, the script contains no code that is not similar to code that we have already described elsewhere. Therefore, we shall not include it here.

Contributing to a Discussion (forumwrite.php)

The script forumwrite.php enables the user to compose a new message in a discussion group or to reply to an existing message (see Figure 8-21). The program code is responsible both for the display of the form and for the evaluation of the form data.

Variables

The script expects two URL variables as parameters:

- *forumID* contains the ID number of the discussion forum.

- *msgID* contains the ID number of the message that is to be replied to. If *msgID* is absent, the script assumes that a new message is being composed (that is, a new thread is to be created).

The form data are read from the following variables:

- *formForumID* and *formMsgID* contain the ID numbers of the forum and the message that is to be replied to. (Both variables are represented in the form with *<input type="hidden" . . . >*.)

- *formSubject* contains the title of the message.

- *formText* contains the message text.

Auxiliary Functions

The code begins with the definition of two auxiliary functions. The text of an existing message is passed to *reply_text*. This function prefixes to the text a header block with the name of the original author and the date. (If you wish, you can optimize *reply_text* by executing a line break in the function and then indenting each line with the character ">".)

```php
<?php // php/myforum/forumwrite.php
// read in standard functions
include("../.._private/myforumconnect.inc.php");

//auxiliary function to quote an existing message
function reply_text($txt, $subject, $author, $date) {
  return("\n\n-------------\n\nOriginal message:\n\n" .
        "Subject: $subject\nAuthor: $author\n" .
        "Date: $date\n\n$txt");
}
```

From the point of view of database programming the function *insert_new_message* is much more interesting. To this function the following are passed in order to store the new message in the *messages* table: the ID number of the original message (or 0), the ID number of the forum, the ID number of the user, the message header, and the actual message text.

If 0 was not passed in *parentID*, then the function first returns information about the original message, which it stores in the variables *orderstr*, *level*, and *rootID*. Of particular interest is *orderstr*, which with the help of the PHP function *bin2hex* is transformed into hexadecimal format:

```php
// auxiliary function for storing a message
function insert_new_message($parentID, $forumID, $userID,
                    $msgSubject, $msgText) {
  if($parentID) {
    $result =
      mysql_query("SELECT * FROM messages WHERE msgID=$parentID");
    $row = mysql_fetch_object($result);
    $level = $row->level+1;
    $orderstr = bin2hex($row->orderstr);
    $rootID = $row->rootID;
    if(!$rootID) // if rootID=0 use msgID as rootID for new message
      $rootID = $row->msgID;
  }
  else {
    $level=0; // new message: level=rootID=parentID=0
    $rootID=0;
    $parentID=0;
  }
```

If the maximal hierarchical level within a thread has not been reached, then the character string *orderstr* is now extended by the hexadecimal code of the current timestamp value.

```php
// create orderstr character string (append Hex.code of the current timestamp);
maximum level = 31
if($level<=31) {
  $tmp = dechex(time());
  if(strlen($tmp)<8)
    $tmp = str_repeat(" ", 8-strlen($tmp));
  $orderstr = "0x" . $orderstr . $tmp;
}
else {
  $level=31;
  $orderstr = "0x" . $orderstr; }
```

The data, after having been thus prepared, must now be stored:

```
mysql_query("INSERT INTO messages (forumID, parentID, rootID, " .
             "userID, subject, msgText, level, orderstr) " .
             "VALUES($forumID, $parentID, $rootID, $userID, " .
             " '" . addslashes($msgSubject) . "', " .
             " '" . addslashes($msgText) . "', " .
             " $level, $orderstr)");
}
```

Main Code

The main code begins, as always in this example, with establishing the connection to the database and the initialization of the session variables.

```
// main code
$connID = connect_to_myforum();
session_register("sesUserID", "sesUserName");
if(SID) {
  $sid1 = "?" . SID;
  $sid2 = "&" . SID; }
```

Storing a Message

When the script for evaluating form data is called, first a test is made as to whether *formMsgID* actually refers to an existing message. If that is the case, then the message is stored with the function *insert_new_message*, which was described above. Then a shift to page forumread.php is carried out, where the new message is to be displayed.

```
if($formSubmit=="OK" and $formSubject
  and $formText and $formForumID
  and $sesUserID) {
  // is formMsgID (if specified) a valid ID number?
  $invalidMsgID=0;
  if($formMsgID) {
    $result =
      mysql_query("SELECT msgID FROM messages
                   "WHERE msgID = '$formMsgID' " .
                   "LIMIT 2");
    if(!$result or mysql_num_rows($result)!=1)
      $invalidMsgID=1;
  }
```

```
  // store message
  if(!$invalidMsgID)
    insert_new_message($formMsgID, $formForumID, $sesUserID,
                       trim(stripslashes($formSubject)),
                       trim(stripslashes($formText)));
  // display new message in forumread.php
  header("Location: ./forumread.php?forumID=$formForumID$sid2");
  exit;
}
?>
```

Display Form

The remaining code is responsible for displaying the form. First, however, some tests are necessary: Does *sesUserID* contain an ID number? If not, the user is taken to the login form. Is *msgID* correct? If not, an error message is displayed. Otherwise, the query results are stored temporarily so that later the form controls can be initialized. Is *forumID* correct? If not, again an error message is displayed.

```
<!DOCTYPE HTML PUBLIC "-//W3C//DTD HTML 4.0//EN">
<html><head>
<title>PHP Programming, new message (myforum database)</title>
</head><body>
<h2>myforum: New message</h2>

<?php
// does sesUserID contain a value?
if(empty($sesUserID)) ... display error message --> forumlogin.php
// copy form variables in forumID and msgID
if($formForumID) {
  $forumID = $formForumID;
  $msgID = $formMsgID;
}
// determine original message (for reply)
if($msgID) {
  $result =
    mysql_query("SELECT msgID, msgText, subject, level, rootID, " .
                " DATE_FORMAT(timest,'%Y/%c/%e %k:%i') AS timest," .
                " forumID, username " .
                "FROM messages, users " .
                "WHERE msgID = '$msgID' " .
                " AND messages.userID = users.userID " .
                "LIMIT 2");
```

```php
  // was msgID invalid?
  if(!$result or mysql_num_rows($result)!=1) {
    .. display error message, exit
  }
  // store query result
  $row = mysql_fetch_object($result);
  $forumID = $row->forumID;
  $oldMsg = $row->msgText;
  $oldSubject = $row->subject;
  $oldLevel = $row->level;
  $oldRoot = $row->rootID;
  $oldOrderstr = $row->orderstr;
  $oldAuthor = $row->username;
  $oldDate = $row->timest;
}
// determine name of the forum
$result = mysql_query("SELECT forumID, forumName FROM forums " .
                      "WHERE forumID = '$forumID' " .
                      "LIMIT 2");
// was forumID invalid?
if(!$result or mysql_num_rows($result)!=1) {
  ... display error message, exit
}
$forumID = mysql_result($result, 0, 0);
$forumName = mysql_result($result, 0, 1);
// form header
if($msgID)
  echo "<p>Reply to message <i>", htmlentities($oldSubject),
      "</i>\n";
else
  echo "<p>New message for forum <i>", htmlentities($forumName),
    "</i>\n";
// auxiliary variables for displaying the form
$actionscript = "./forumwrite.php$sid1";
$newsubject = "";
if($formSubmit)
  $newsubject = htmlentities(stripslashes($formSubject));
elseif($msgID) {
  $newsubject = "Re: " . $oldSubject;
  if(strlen($newsubject)>78)
    $newsubject = substr($newsubject, 0, 78);
}
```

```
$newtext="";
if($formSubmit)
  $newtext = htmlentities(stripslashes($formText));
elseif($msgID)
  $newtext = reply_text($oldMsg, $oldSubject, $oldAuthor, $oldDate);

// display form
?>
<form method="POST" action="<?php echo $actionscript;?>">
<table>
<tr><td>Author:
    <td> <?php echo htmlentities($sesUserName); ?>
<tr><td>Subject:
    <td> <input name="formSubject" size=60 maxlength=78
          value="<?php echo htmlentities($newsubject); ?>">
<tr><td>Message:
    <td> <textarea name="formText" rows=12 cols=50><?php
        echo htmlentities($newtext); ?></textarea>
<tr><td>
    <td><input type="submit" value="OK" name="formSubmit">
<input type="hidden" name=formForumID value="<?php echo $forumID;?>">
<input type="hidden" name=formMsgID value="<?php echo $msgID;?>">
</table></form>
</body></html>
```

Leaving the Forum (forumlogout.php)

The logout script has the sole task of deleting the session variables. Then the login page forumlogin.php is again displayed:

```
<?php // php/myforum/forumlogout.php
session_register("sesUserID", "sesUserName");
unset($sesUserID);
unset($sesUserName);
header("Location: ./forumlogin.php");
exit;
?>
```

Possibilities for Extension

In addition to the suggestions for detailed improvements and extensions mentioned as the individual script files were presented, there are, needless to say, a number of major features that could be added or improved:

- **Administrative Tasks:** For the administrator of the forum there should be the simple option of generating new discussion groups or terminating existing ones, deleting individual messages, and so on. At present this is possible only via directly accessing the *myforum* database.

- **Moderated Forum:** Experience has shown that open discussion groups with a great deal of activity tend to have a small number of relevant messages littered with a large quantity of garbage. A moderated forum can rescue the situation: Every message must be approved by the moderator before it is posted.

- **E-Mail Notification of Replies:** An individual who posts a message to a forum is usually interested in the reactions to that posting. Instead of having to check daily (or even more often for the nervous Nellies and Nelsons among us) to see whether any responses have been posted, the poster of the original message might enjoy receiving notification by e-mail of any replies. This would enable the poster to fire off a rapid (but not, please, rabid) reply.

- **Multilingual Guidance:** In the *forums* table a language is specified for each discussion group. However, all the instructions for all of the forums are in English. Wouldn't it be nice if all of the links, form titles, and so on, appeared in the language of the discussion?

- **Search Option:** Currently, the forum offers no possibility of searching. It would be desirable to have a key-word search (full-text search) either for *Subject* lines only or for the full text of the message, as well as a search for authors (for example, display all messages posted by a particular author).

- **Personalization:** In addition to the name of the user other information could be stored, for example, a default discussion group, desired parameters (such as the number of messages to be displayed per page), and so on. It would be more complicated to implement an option whereby messages that had been read could be marked as such or marked not to be displayed again.

TIP   *Let us end with a little tip. There is plenty to invent besides the wheel, which has already been invented, and reinvented. If you would like to practice your PHP and MySQL, then implementing all of these features would be a good exercise. However, if your goal is to create a stable and reliable discussion forum as quickly as possible, then your time might be better spent in seeking out tested solutions:*

```
http://www.phorum.org/
http://fumanchi.tabu.uni-bonn.de/forum/
```

#### CHAPTER 9

Perl

FOR MANY YEARS PERL HAS been the best-beloved scripting language in the Unix/Linux universe. Moreover, Perl continues to play an important role as a programming language for CGI scripts, by which dynamic web sites can be realized. This chapter gives a brief introduction to MySQL database access with Perl and shows by means of a few examples the large bandwidth of possible applications.

Chapter Overview

Programming Techniques

> **POINTER** *This chapter assumes that Perl and the modules* DBI *and* DBD::mysql *are installed on your computer and that they are functioning properly. An introduction to the installation procedure can be found in Chapter 2.*
>
> *Further information on both Perl modules can be found in the official MySQL documentation (the chapter "Client Tools and APIs"). Furthermore, the command* perldoc *nets you extensive on-line help.*
>
> ```
> perldoc DBI
> perldoc DBI::FAQ
> perldoc DBD::mysql
> ```
>
> *HTML versions of these three help pages can be found at, for example,* http://www.perldoc.com/cpan
>
> *Links to additional Internet pages with information on database programming with Perl and DBI can be found at my home page:* http://www.kofler.cc/mysql
>
> *Finally, a compact reference to DBI functions and methods can be found in Chapter 15.*

The Modules DBI and DBD::mysql

Access to MySQL is carried out in Perl via the modules *DBI* and *DBD::mysql*. (The abbreviation "DBI" stands for *database interface*, while "DBD" stands for *database driver*.) *DBI* is a general interface for database programming, independent of particular database systems. Thus DBI can be used for database programming with Oracle, DB/2, etc. Ideally, the code is the same in every case; that is, you can switch database systems without changing the Perl code (with the exception of *datasource* character strings for establishing the connection).

DBD::mysql is used by *DBI* to communicate with MySQL. (There exist comparable driver modules for a host of other database systems.) Which driver module *DBI* must use is determined by the character string specified when the connection is established (method *connect*). Therefore, the instruction *use DBI* at the beginning of the Perl script suffices for incorporating the DBI module.

Although *DBI* actually follows a process that is independent of the database, *DBD:: mysql* makes available a number of MySQL-specific functions. The reason for this is that DBI constitutes the greatest common denominator of all database systems, and thus is relatively small. The use of MySQL-specific functions simplifies MySQL programming with Perl considerably, but leads, of course, to the result that the code can be ported to another database system only with difficulty.

DBI and *DBD* are object-oriented modules. For this reason most of their functions are available in the form of methods, which are applied to objects (which in Perl are represented by so-called *handles*). For example, *DBI->connect* returns a handle to a *database* object (which is usually stored in the variable *$dbh*). Various functions that affect the database can now be executed as methods of this object, for example, *$dbh->do("INSERT . . . ")*, for executing an SQL command.

Establishing a Connection to the Database

The connection is established with the DBI method *connect*. The first parameter to this method is a character string specifying the type of the database and the name of the computer (or *localhost*). The syntax of the character string can be deduced from the following example. The next two parameters must contain the user name and password.

A fourth, optional, parameter can be used to specify numerous attributes. For example, *'RaiseError'=>1* has the effect that the Perl script is broken off with an error message if the connection to the database cannot be established. (A list of the possible attributes can be found in Chapter 15. Further information on error-handling can be found in this chapter.)

```
use DBI;
$datasource = "DBI:mysql:database=mylibrary;host=localhost";
$user = "root";
$passw = "xxx";
$dbh = DBI->connect($datasource, $user, $passw,
  {'RaiseError' => 1});
```

Specifying the Configuration File

In the *datasource* character string you may also specify the name of a configuration file in which the user name, password, and possible additional connection options are specified. This is particularly practical under Unix/Linux if such configuration files are stored in the home directories of the users. (Information on creating configuration files can be found in Chapter 14.)

In the following example the option *mysql_read_default_file* specifies the location of the configuration file (relative to the home directory from the environment variable *HOME*).

The option *mysql_read_default_group* specifies the group *[mygroup]* within the configuration file. If this option is not used, then *connect* automatically evaluates the group *[client]*. The second and third parameters to the method *connect* are both specified as *undef*, to make it clear that the user name and password are specified in another location.

```
$datasource = "DBI:mysql:database=mylibrary;" .
    "mysql_read_default_file=$ENV{HOME}/.my.cnf;" .
    "mysql_read_default_group=mygroup";
$dbh = DBI->connect($datasource, undef, undef, {'RaiseError' => 1});
```

The associated configuration file ˜/.my.cnf might look like the following:

```
[mygroup]
user=root
password=xxx
host=uranus.sol
```

Please note that access rights to this file are set in such a way that only the user is allowed to read it.

REMARK   *Under Windows I was unable to evaluate a configuration file with* DBI->connect(). *Perhaps this function is available only under Unix/Linux (though such is not explicitly documented).*

Terminating the Connection

All accesses to the database are attained via the variable *$dbh* (or from variables derived from it). When the connection to the database is no longer needed, it should be closed with *disconnect*.

```
$dbh->disconnect();
```

Persistent Connections

Unlike the case of MySQL functions for PHP, in the case of the Perl DBI module there is no possibility of making use of persistent connections in order to minimize the time for repeated establishment of a connection to the database.

If you execute CGI Perl scripts via the Apache module *mod_perl* (which is recommended for reasons of efficiency), you achieve by use of the Perl module *Apache::DBI* that MySQL connections remain after the script has ended and are reused when another script requires the same type of MySQL connection. To use the module you have merely to insert *use Apache::DBI* before all *use DBI* commands in your script. No other changes are necessary. (*Apache::DBI* replaces the *connect* method of *DBI* with its own version.) Additional information on *Apache::DBI* can be found at the following location: `http://www.perldoc.com/cpan/Apache/DBI.html`

Executing SQL Commands

SQL Commands Without Record List as Result

SQL commands that do not return a list of records are generally executed by means of *do*:

```
$n = $dbh->do("INSERT INTO authors (authName) " .
              "VALUES ('New author')");
```

Normally *do* returns the number of altered data records. Other possible return values are as follows:

- *"0E0"* means that no record has been changed. This character string can be changed into a number by means of an arithmetic operation (i.e., *$n+=0*).

- −1 means that the number of changed records is unknown.

- *undef* means that an error has occurred.

Determining AUTO_INCREMENT Values

After *INSERT* commands it is frequently necessary to determine the *AUTO_INCREMENT* value of the newly inserted data record. For this task the attribute *mysql_insertid* of *DBD::mysql* is helpful:

```
$id = $dbh->{'mysql_insertid'};
```

> **REMARK** *The attribute* mysql_insertid *is not portable; that is, it is available only for MySQL databases. In porting the code to another database system you will have to find another way of proceeding.*

SELECT *Queries*

SQL commands that do return a list of records (typically *SELECT* commands) cannot be executed with *do*. Instead, the query must first be prepared with *prepare*. (Many database servers will compile the query or execute other operations. However, with MySQL that is not the case.)

The return value of *prepare* is a *statement handle*, which must be used for all further operations with the query, even for the method *execute*, in order actually to execute the query. (If an error occurs in the execution of the query, the return value is *undef*.)

```
$sth = $dbh->prepare("SELECT * FROM titles LIMIT 5");
$sth->execute();
```

Then the resulting records can be output with *$sth*, about which we shall have more to say in the next section. When the evaluation is complete, the resources bound to *$sth* should be released with *finish*.

```
$sth->finish();# delete query object
```

SQL Queries with Wild Cards for Parameters

It often happens that the same type of query needs to be executed over and over with varying parameters (*WHERE id=1*, *WHERE id=3*, etc.). In such cases *DBI* offers the possibility of replacing the parameters in *prepare* by a question mark, which serves as a wild card. Each question mark corresponds to a parameter, whose value must subsequently be specified with *execute*. Note that in *execute* the correct order of the parameters must be adhered to. The following lines demonstrate how to proceed:

```
$sth = $dbh->prepare("SELECT * FROM titles " .
               "WHERE catID=? AND publID=?");
$sth->execute(1, 1);    # title with catID=1 and publID=2
 ...                     # evaluate results
$sth->execute(1, 2); # title with catID=1 and publID=2
 ...                     # evaluate results
$sth->finish();         # delete query object
```

In working with wild cards a few points should be noted: First of all, wild cards must be given in SQL commands unquoted (even if it is a character string). Secondly, the value passed to *execute* by the *DBI* module is dealt with automatically with *quote*, which places character strings in single quotation marks and prefixes a backslash to the apostrophe and backslash characters. If you wish to pass *NULL* to an SQL command, you must specify the value *undef*, which *quote* turns into *NULL*.

If you execute the commands

```
$sth = $dbh->prepare("INSERT INTO publishers (publName)" .
                     "VALUES (?)");
$sth->execute("O'Reilly");
```

with Perl, then it is the following SQL command that is actually executed in MySQL:

```
INSERT INTO publishers (publName) VALUES ('O\'Reilly')
```

This example shows that *prepare* and *execute* are suitable not only for *SELECT* queries, but also for any SQL queries that need to be executed a number of times.

> **REMARK** *This procedure is not only elegant, but with many database servers it is also efficient. Namely, the command is temporarily stored on the server with* prepare. *Thereafter, only the parameters need to be transmitted to the server. However, MySQL does not implement this type of optimization.*

> **TIP** *Wild cards can also be used when SQL commands are executed with* do. *This does not contribute to increased speed, but it does generally improve readability, since* DBI *takes care of both single quotation marks and* quote:

```
$dbh->do("INSERT INTO table (cola, colb) VALUES (?, ?),
   undef, ($data1, $data2)");
```

Evaluating SELECT Queries

Provided that no error occurs in a query (test by *if(defined($sth))*), the resulting records can be read via the *statement handle* (i.e., *$sth*). There are several different methods for accomplishing this.

Reading Data Records with `fetch` alias `fetchrow_array`

The two equivalent methods *fetch* and *fetchrow_array* return an array with the values of the next record. Within the array the vale *NULL* is expressed by *undef.* When the end of the record list is reached or if an error occurs, the array is empty. (To distinguish between these two cases *$sth->err()* must be evaluated.) The following lines execute a query and display the results line by line. Here *NULL* is represented as a character string *<NULL>*.

```
$sth = $dbh->prepare("SELECT * FROM titles LIMIT 5");
$sth->execute();
while(@row = $sth->fetchrow_array()) {# process all records
  foreach $field (@row) {# each field
    if(defined($field)) {# test for NULL
      print "$field\t";
    } else {
      print "<NULL>\t";
    }
  }
  print "\n";
}
$sth->finish();
```

The evaluation of the columns in a *foreach* loop is rather the exception. To be sure, the individual columns could also be selected in the form *$row[n]*, where *n=0* must be specified for the first column. A further variant consists in assigning all the columns at once to the variables in question. Then, of course, the correct order of the variables must be heeded.

```
($titleID, $title, ... ) = @row;
```

Selecting Individual Values

It is often clear from the outset that a query will return only a single value (e.g., *SELECT COUNT(*) FROM . . .*). In this case neither a loop over all records nor an evaluation of all elements of an array is necessary. Instead, simply assign *fetchrow_array* to a scalar variable:

```
$sth = $dbh->prepare("SELECT COUNT(*) FROM titles");
$sth->execute();
$result = $sth->fetchrow_array();
print "$result\n";
$sth->finish();
```

> **CAUTION**   *According to the DBI documentation, in the scalar context (e.g.,*
> *$field = $sth->fetchrow_array()), fetchrow_array should return the contents*
> *of the first column. However, tests with the available version have revealed*
> *that $field contains, to the contrary, the value of the last column. There*
> *should be no problem when there is only one column.*
>
> *But in addition the scalar evaluation of* fetchrow_array *is not quite*
> *unproblematic. There are now three reasons for which $field can contain*
> *the value* undef: *The column contains* NULL *in the record in question, the*
> *last record was reached, or an error has occurred.*

Instead of the code given above you could use the following shorthand version:

```perl
$result = $dbh->selectrow_array("SELECT COUNT(*) ... ");
```

Binding Columns to Variables

In processing a *SELECT* command, instead of transmitting every data record manually in variables, you can automate this step and at the same time increase the efficiency and readability of your program a bit. To do this you bind the column of the query with *bind_col* to individual variables. Each time that *fetchrow_array* is executed, the associated variables contain the value of the new record. It is necessary that *bind_col* be executed after *execute*. The return value of *bind_col* is *false* if an error occurs. Please note that column numbering begins with 1 (not, as is usual in Perl, with 0).

```perl
$sth = $dbh->prepare("SELECT titleID, title FROM titles");
$sth->execute();
$sth->bind_col(1, \$titleID);
$sth->bind_col(2, \$title);

while($sth->fetchrow_array()) {
  print "$title $titleID\n";
}
$sth->finish();
$dbh->disconnect();
```

Instead of binding the variables individually, you can do this for all columns at once with *bind_columns*. Please observe the correct sequence and number of variables.

```perl
$sth->bind_columns(\$titleID, \$title);
```

Determining the Number of Data Records

The *DBI* module provides no possibility of determining the number of records returned by a *SELECT* command. (This has to do with the fact that with many database servers the records are transmitted to the module only when they are needed.) If you wish to know how many resulting records there are, you have the following options:

- You can count during the evaluation. (This variant is ruled out if you wish to know the number of records in advance.)

- You can execute the second query with *SELECT COUNT(*)* . . . . Depending on the application this can be relatively costly.

- You may use the *DBI* method *fetchall_arrayref* (see below). Thereby all resulting records are transmitted together into a local array, so that the number can easily be determined.

- You may use the method *$sth->rows()*. This method can be evaluated after *execute()*. At first glance this seems the obvious solution, but it has, in fact, a number of drawbacks.

  Firstly, the method is not portable. (According to the *DBI* documentation, *rows* may be used to determine the altered records, say after *UPDATE* or *DELETE*, but not for investigating records read with *SELECT*.)

  Secondly, the method is itself available in conjunction with the *DBD::mysql* driver only when queries are evaluated without the attribute *mysql_use_result*. That is indeed the default setting, but it is not always particularly efficient.

Determining Column Names and Other Metainformation

If you wish to program a generally valid function for representing tables, you need not only the data themselves, but also metainformation about the data (column names, data types, etc.). This information is made available by *DBI* via various attributes of *$sth*:

- *$sth->{'NUM_OF_FIELDS'}* returns the number of columns.

- *$sth->{'NAME'}* returns a pointer to an array with the names of all columns. The same holds for *$sth->{'NAME_lc'}* and *$sth->{'NAME_uc'}*, but with the names all in lowercase or uppercase, respectively.

- *$sth->{'NULLABLE'}* returns a pointer to an array whose values tell whether a column can contain *NULL*.

- *$sth->{'PRECISION'}* and $sth->{'SCALE'} return pointers to arrays with the maximum number of characters and the number of decimal places, respectively.

- *$sth->{'TYPE'}* returns a pointer to an array with numerical values that permit one to determine the data types of the columns.

The following loop demonstrates the evaluation of this information:

```
$sth = $dbh->prepare("SELECT * FROM testall");
$sth->execute();
for($i=0; $i < $sth->{'NUM_OF_FIELDS'}; $i++) {
  print @{$sth->{'NAME'}}[$i] . " " .
        @{$sth->{'TYPE'}}[$i] . "\n";
}
```

> **POINTER** DBD::mysql *makes available some additional attributes with MySQL-specific information. These attributes are presented in their own subsection of this chapter, together with other MySQL-specific (and therefore nonportable) extensions of the* DBI *module.*

Reading Data Records with fetchrow_arrayref

The functioning of *fetchrow_arrayref* is similar to that of *fetchrow_array*. The sole difference is that now pointers (references) to arrays instead of the arrays themselves are returned. This method returns *undef* if the end of the data list is reached or an error has occurred.

```
while(my $arrayref = $sth->fetchrow_arrayref()) {
  foreach $field (@{$arrayref}) {
    ... as before
}
```

Reading Data Records with fetchrow_hashref

The method *fetchrow_hashref* returns an associative array (*hash*) with the values of the next data record. It returns *undef* if the end of the record list has been reached or an error has occurred.

Access to the individual columns is effected with *$row->{'columnname'}*. In providing the *columnname* attention must be paid to case-sensitivity. The following lines demonstrate its application:

```
$sth = $dbh->prepare("SELECT title, titleID FROM titles LIMIT 5");
$sth->execute();
while($row = $sth->fetchrow_hashref()) {
  print "$row->{'title'}, $row->{'titleID'}\n";
}

$sth->finish();
$dbh->disconnect();
```

If *fetchrow_hashref* is called with the optional parameter *"NAME_lc"* or *"NAME_uc"*, then all the hash keys are transformed into lowercase or uppercase, respectively.

Reading All Data Records with fetchall_arrayref

A drawback of all the access methods described above is that the data records must be read sequentially, and thereafter they are no longer available. It is thus impossible to move about to your heart's content in the list of data records. (Depending on the database system this has at least the advantage that it is miserly with resources. Under MySQL, *fetchall_arrayref* does not exhibit this drawback because in any case all records that are found are immediately transmitted to the client. Please note, though, that this can be avoided by using the attribute *mysql_use_result*. More about *mysql_use_result* can be found further along in this section.)

If you wish to access all data records in an arbitrary order and to do so multiple times, you could output the entire result of the query *fetchall_arrayref*. As result you obtain an array with pointers to the individual records, which themselves are arrays. Access to an individual element is then accomplished via *$result->[$row][$col]*, where the indices begin with 0.

```
$sth = $dbh->prepare("SELECT titleID, title FROM titles");
$sth->execute();
$result = $sth->fetchall_arrayref();
print "$result->[2][5]\n"; # third record, sixth column
$sth->finish();
$dbh->disconnect();
```

The number of records and columns can be determined as follows:

```
$rows = @{$result};
$cols = @{$result->[0]};
```

An optional parameter can be passed to *fetchall_arrayref*, which influences both the columns to be read and the organization of the data. The following command reads only the first, fourth, and last columns:

```
$result = $sth->fetchall_arrayref([0,3,-1]);
```

The following command reads all columns, but returns a pointer to an array that contains pointers to hashes. Access to individual elements is via *$result->[$row]->{'columnname'}*, as in, for example, *$result->[3]->{'titleID'}*.

```
$result = $sth->fetchall_arrayref({});
```

Our last example again returns hashes, but this time only for columns with the names *titleID* and *title*.

```
$result = $sth->fetchall_arrayref({titleID=>1, title=>1});
```

In general, it makes better sense to limit the number of columns already in the *SELECT* command, instead of waiting until *fetchall_arrayref* to do so, after all the data have been extracted from the database. The method *fetchall_arrayref* can be executed only once per query. If you would like to execute the method more than once, you must execute *execute* before each call.

If the query has returned no result, then *fetchall_arrayref* returns a pointer to an empty array. If an error occurs during data selection, then *$result* contains all data read to that point. If in any event you are working without *'RaiseError' => 1*, then after *fetchall_arrayref*, you should see to it that *$sth->err()* is evaluated.

> **TIP** *Instead of the three methods* prepare, execute, fetchall_arrayref, *you can also use the shorthand form* $dbh->selectall_arrayref($sql).

Character Strings, BLOBs, DATEs, SETs, ENUMs, and NULL

Altering Data

To alter data records in your database you must transmit the relevant SQL commands as character strings to *do*. The structure of this character string must conform to the syntax of MySQL (see Chapter 13).

The starting point for the following discussion of the various data types is the variable *data*, which contains the data to be stored. The contents of this variable should be placed in an *INSERT* command, which is stored temporarily in the variable *sql*. In the simplest case it goes like this:

```
$sql = "INSERT INTO tablename VALUES('$data1', '$data2', ... );
```

- **Dates and Times:** To format a date or time according to the MySQL official regulations, you must use the corresponding Perl function or module (for example, *gmtime()* or *TIME::Local*).

- **Timestamps:** Perl and MySQL timestamps have the same meaning, but have different formats. A Perl timestamp (function *time()*) is simply a 32-bit integer that gives the number of seconds since 1/1/1970. MySQL, on the other hand, expects a timestamp in the form *yyyyddmmhhmmss* or *yyyy-dd-mm hh:mm:ss*.

  As a rule, timestamps are used to mark the time of the last change. In such a case you simply pass *NULL*, and MySQL automatically takes care of proper storage:

  ```
  $sql .= "NULL";
  ```

  On the other hand, if you would like to store a Perl timestamp as a MySQL timestamp, then you should use the MySQL function *FROM_UNIXTIME* in your *INSERT* or *UPDATE* command.

  ```
  $data = time(); // data contains the current time as a Unix timestamp
  $sql .= "FROM_UNIXTIME(" . $data . ")";
  ```

- **Character Strings and BLOBs:** If special characters occur in a character string or BLOB, then there are frequently problems with quotation. SQL requires that the single-quote, double-quote, 0-byte, and backslash characters be prefixed by a backslash.

  If you place value on the portability of your Perl code, then you should use the method *$dbh->quote()* for quoting character strings. This method not only adds \ or \0 to the character string, but it also encloses the character string in single quotation marks. Thus *$dbh->quote('ab'c')* returns *'ab\'c'*. (If you execute an SQL command with wild cards, *quote()* will be used automatically.)

```
$sql .= $dbh->quote($data);
```

In putting together SQL commands the Perl construct *qq{}*, which returns the specified character string, is often useful. Within *qq{}*, variables are replaced by their contents (but not quoted). The advantage of *qq{}* over a direct concatenation of character strings with *$sql="INSERT ... "* is that within *qq{}* the single- and double-quote characters may be used:

```
$data = $dbh->quote($data);
$sql = qq{INSERT INTO table (col1, col2, col3)
          VALUES ($data, 'abc', PASSWORD("abc"))};
```

- ***NULL:*** I am pleased to be able to inform you, dear reader, that *$dbh->quote()* also treats the value *undef* correctly and in this case returns *NULL* (without a single quote).

```
$sql .= $dbh->quote($data);
```

If you do not wish to use *quote()*, then you might try the following:

```
$sql .= defined($data) ? "'$data'" : "NULL";
```

Please note that within an SQL character command you do not place *NULL* in quotation marks as if it were a character string.

Reading Data

The starting point for the following considerations is the variable *$data*, which contains a data field. For example, *$data* can be initialized as follows:

```
$sth = $dbh->prepare("SELECT * FROM titles");
$sth->execute();
@row = $sth->fetchrow_array();
$data = $row(0);
```

- **Timestamps:** Timestamps in the form of a character string of the form 20001231235959 are contained in *data*. This won't get you very far in Perl. If you want to work with the timestamp value in Perl, then use the MySQL function *UNIX_TIMESTAMP* and formulate the corresponding *SELECT* query. Then for the above date *data* contains the value 978303599.

```
SELECT ... , UNIX_TIMESTAMP(a_timestamp) FROM ...
```

- **Date:** For a *DATETIME* column, *data* contains a character string of the form 2000-12-31 23:59:59. For *DATE* columns the time information is lacking. For the further processing of dates in Perl it is practical in many cases here, too, to use the function *UNIX_TIMESTAMP*. You can obtain any format you like with the MySQL format *DATE_FORMAT*. The following instruction results in *data* containing a character string of the form *'December 31 2001'*.

```
SELECT ... , DATE_FORMAT(a_date, '%M %d %Y')
```

- **Time:** For a *TIME* column *data* contains a character string of the form 23:59:59. If you do not wish to extract hours, minutes, and seconds from this character string, then the MySQL function *TIME_TO_SEC* can be used to return the number of seconds since 00:00:00. Additionally, you can, of course, use any of the numerous MySQL functions for processing times. Warning: *UNIX_TIMESTAMP* does not work for *TIME* columns.

POINTER *In Chapter 13 you will find an overview of the MySQL functions for processing and converting dates and times.*

- *NULL:* Since *$data* is as yet undefined, it contains *undef*. Whether *$data* contains *NULL* can most easily be determined with the Perl function *defined($data)*. (Do not compare *$data* with *" "* or *0* to detect *NULL*. Both comparisons return *True*, though preceded by a Perl warning.)

- **Character Strings and BLOBs:** Perl, in contrast to C, has no difficulties with truly binary data; that is, even zero-bytes within a character string are correctly handled. Thus *data* truly contains the exact data from the database.

> **TIP**   *If you wish to output character strings read from tables into HTML documents, as a rule you must use the function* encode_entities *from the module* HTML::Entities. *The function* escapeHTML *from the module* CGI *can be used only if you are certain that the database contains no characters other than those of the 7-bit ASCII character set.*

> **REMARK**   *If problems arise in reading large BLOBs because the maximum amount of data per field is limited, then this limit can be set (before* execute*) with* $dbh->{'LongReadLen'}=n. *The value* n *specifies the maximum number of bytes.*
>   *Warning: 0 means that long fields will not be read at all. In this case* $data *contains the value* undef, *which cannot be distinguished from* NULL.

Determining Elements of an ENUM or SET

The use of *ENUM*s and *SET*s presents no problems in and of itself: The values are passed in both directions as simple character strings. Note that with *ENUM*s no empty spaces are permitted between the comma-separated items.

When in a Perl program you wish to display the character strings of an *ENUM* or *SET* for selection (in an HTML listbox, for example), you must determine the definition of this field with the SQL command *DESCRIBE tablename columnname*.

```
USE exceptions
DESCRIBE test_enum a_enum
```

Field	Type	Null	Key	...
a_enum	enum('a','b','c','d', 'e')	YES		...

The column *Type* of the result table contains the required information. In the following lines of code the character string *enum('a', 'b', 'c')* will first be decomposed step by step and then displayed line by line. (The algorithm assumes that the *SET* or *ENUM* character string contains no commas.)

```
$sth = $dbh->prepare("DESCRIBE test_enum a_set");
$sth->execute();

$row = $sth->fetchrow_hashref();
$tmp = $row->{'Type'};              # enum( ... ) or set( ... )
($tmp) = $tmp =~ m/\((.*)\)/;       # xyz('a','b','c') --> 'a','b','c'
$tmp =~ tr/'//d;                    # 'a','b','c' --> a,b,c
@enums = split(/,/, $tmp);          # @enums[0]=a, @enums[1]=b ...

foreach $enum (@enums) {            # output all values
  print "$enum\n";
}
```

DBD::mysql-*specific Methods and Attributes*

Whereas the *DBI* module represents the greatest common denominator of all database APIs, *DBD::mysql* contains as well various MySQL-specific functions. Their application leads to Perl code that can be transferred to other database systems only with difficulty. However, such code is often more efficient.

> **POINTER**   *This section introduces only the most important MySQL-specific methods and attributes. A complete reference of* DBD::mysql *extensions can be found in Chapter 13.*

Using rows *to Determine the Number of Records Found with* SELECT

The method *$sth->rows()*, which was mentioned previously, is, in fact, not MySQL-specific. But only with the *DBD::mysql* driver does this method return, after *execute*, the number of records found. This holds only if queries are executed without the attribute *mysql_use_result*.

Determining the AUTO_INCREMENT *Value*

The *$dbh* attribute *mysql_insertid* has also been mentioned. It enables you to determine the *AUTO_INCREMENT* value of the most recently inserted data record after an *INSERT* command.

```
$id = $dbh->{'mysql_insertid'};
```

Determining Additional Column Information

DBI makes a number of *$sth* attributes available that make it possible to determine information about the columns of a *SELECT* result (for example, *$sth-> {'NAME'}*). *DBD::mysql* adds some additional attributes, such as *'MYSQL_IS_BLOB'*, to establish whether a column contains *BLOB*s; or *'MYSQL_TYPE_NAME'*, to determine the name of the data type of the column.

mysql_store_result *Versus* mysql_use_result

If a *SELECT* command is executed with *prepare* and *execute*, then usually, *DBD::mysql* calls the C function *mysql_store_result*. This means that all the data records found have been transmitted at once to the client and retained there in memory until *$sth->finish()* is executed.

If between *prepare* and *execute* you set the attribute *mysql_use_result* to 1, then *DBD::mysql* uses the C function *mysql_use_result* for transmitting the records. This means that records are brought from the server to the client only when they are needed. In particular, in processing large amounts of data the RAM requirement can be greatly lowered on the client side. (This advantage is lost if you use *fetchall_arrayref*.)

```
$sth = $dbh->prepare("SELECT * FROM table");
$sth->{'mysql_use_result'}=1;
$sth->execute();
```

	mysql_store_result (default)	**mysql_use_result**
$sth->rows();	returns the number of records found	returns 0 or the number of records transmitted thus far
Locking	minimal *READ-LOCK* time	if locking is used, the table is blocked until the last record is read
Client Memory Requirement	all found records are stored at the client	only one record stored at the client at one time
Speed	access to the first record comparatively slow (since all records are transmitted to the client); very fast thereafter	access to the first record very rapid, further access slower than with *mysql_store_result*

Error-Handling

There are several possibilities for Perl-script error-handling. The most convenient way (especially during program development) is to specify the option *{' RaiseError' =>1}* in establishing the connection. The result is that an error message is automatically displayed at each error. Additionally, the Perl program is terminated immediately. (This holds not only for errors during the connection, but also for all additional errors that occur in the execution of DBI methods.)

For many administrative tasks this sort of error-handling is sufficient. However, once you employ Perl for programming dynamic web pages, the immediate termination of a script (and the display of a usually cryptic error message) is quite the opposite of what one might call user-friendly.

You can achieve more refined error-handling by turning off *DBI*'s automatic response to errors and executing *connect()* with *{' PrintError' =>0}*. Now you must consistently evaluate the two DBI methods *err()* and *errstr()*. The first of these contains the error number, or 0 if no error has occurred, while *errstr()* contains the error text corresponding to the last error to have occurred.

> **REMARK** *DBI methods return* undef *if an error has occurred. However, individual DBI methods sometimes also return* undef *in the course of their normal operation (such as when a data field contains* NULL*). For this reason a simple evaluation of the return value is usually insufficient.*

The methods *err()* and *errstr()* can also be applied to the DBI handles *$dbh* and *$sth* (depending on the context in which the method that caused the error was executed). Immediately after the connection has been established, *err()* or *errstr()* must be applied to *DBI* (since *$dbh* cannot be used after an unsuccessful connection attempt).

Example

The following lines show error-handling for Perl DBI code. In this example the reaction to an error is always that the script is terminated, but of course, you can execute other instructions. Note particularly how *err()* and *errstr()* are applied to the objects *DBI*, *$dbh*, and *$sth*.

The code contains something particular to MySQL: With the *SELECT* command, error-handling occurs only after *execute*. With many other database systems an error can be recognized after *prepare* (but not with MySQL).

```
$datasource = "DBI:mysql:database=exceptions;host=localhost;";
$user = "root";
$passw = "xxx";
$dbh = DBI->connect($datasource, $user, $passw,
  {'PrintError' => 0});
if(DBI->err()) {
  print "error with connection: " . DBI->errstr() . "\n";
  exit(); }
$dbh->do("INSERT INTO neu.autotest (data) VALUES (1)");
if($dbh->err()) {
  print "error with INSERT command: " . $dbh->errstr() . "\n";
  exit(); }
$sth = $dbh->prepare("SELECT * FROM test_blob");
$sth->execute();
if($sth->err()) {
  print "error with SELECT execute: " . $sth->errstr() . "\n";
  exit(); }
while(my $hashref = $sth->fetchrow_hashref()) {
  if($sth->err()) {
    print "error with SELECT fetch: " . $sth->errstr() . "\n";
    exit(); }
  print length($hashref->{'a_blob'}) . "\n";
}
$sth->finish();
$dbh->disconnect();
```

Logging (trace)

If you suspect that the cause of an error is not in your code, but in MySQL, *DBI*, or *DBD::mysql* (or if you have no idea as to the cause of the error), it can help to display internal DBI logging information or to write it to a file. This is enabled by *trace()*, which, like *err()* and *errstr()*, can be applied to all *DBI* objects (including *DBI* itself).

Expected as parameters are the desired logging level (0 = none, 9 = maximal logging) and an optional file name. Without a file name the logging data are sent to *STDERR* (under Windows to the standard output *STDOUT*).

```
DBI->trace(2); # activate logging globally for the DBI module
$sth->trace(3, 'c:/dbi-trace.txt'); # logging only for $sth methods
```

Example: Deleting Invalid Data Records (*mylibrary*)

After months-long experiments with the database *mylibrary* a variety of invalid records have accumulated. This is a scenario well known to most database developers, and one often forgets to clean house after the testing is complete.

In the case of the *mylibrary* database the script `delete-invalid-entries.pl` offers help in most cases. It takes care of the following cases:

- For book titles whose *publID* refers to a nonexistent publisher, *publID* is set to *NULL.*

- For book titles whose *catID* refers to a nonexistent category, *catID* is set to *NULL.*

- In the table *rel_title_author* all entries that refer to nonexistent book titles or authors are deleted. (This can result in titles without authors or authors without titles remaining. Such records are not deleted by the script.)

Of course, the script could be enlarged to include other tests, such as for checking the hierarchy within the *categories* table or for searching for invalid *langID* entries in the *titles* table.

> **POINTER**   *The SQL commands that appear in the script for searching for incorrect data are described extensively in Chapter 6.*

Program Code

The script begins as usual with establishing a connection to the database. If an error occurs (then or later), the script, on account of *{'RaiseError' => 1}*, is simply terminated with an error message.

```perl
#!/usr/bin/perl -w
# delete-invalid-entries.pl

use strict;
use DBI;

# declare variables
my($datasource, $user, $passw, $dbh, $sth, $row);

# establish connection to the database
$datasource = "DBI:mysql:database=mylibrary;host=localhost;";
$user = "root";
$passw = "xxx";
```

```
$dbh = DBI->connect($datasource, $user, $passw,
  {'RaiseError' => 1});
```

The *SELECT* query finds all titles for which *publID* contains an invalid value (that is, a value that does not exist in the *publishers* table). In the following loop *publID* is set to *NULL* with *UPDATE* for all of the defective records found.

```
# (1a) search for invalid publID entries in the title table
$sth =
  $dbh->prepare("SELECT title, titleID " .
                "FROM titles LEFT JOIN publishers " .
                " ON titles.publID=publishers.publID " .
                "WHERE ISNULL(publishers.publID) " .
                " AND NOT(ISNULL(titles.publID))");
$sth->execute();
# set publID of the affected records to NULL
while($row = $sth->fetchrow_hashref()) {
  print "set publID=NULL for title: $row->{'title'}\n";
  $dbh->do("UPDATE titles SET publID=NULL " .
           "WHERE titleID=$row->{'titleID'}");
}
$sth->finish();

# (1b) search for invalid catID entries in the title table
# ... code analogous to (1a)
```

A little more complex is the query for searching for invalid entries in the *rel_title_author* table. Such entries are simply deleted in the following loop. The *print* commands display the affected data records on the computer monitor, where the operator *?* is used to replace *undef* by *NULL*.

```
# (2) search for invalid authID or titleID entries in the
# rel_title_author table
$sth =
  $dbh->prepare("SELECT authName, title, rel_title_author.authID, " .
                " rel_title_author.titleID " .
                "FROM rel_title_author " .
                "LEFT JOIN titles " .
                " ON rel_title_author.titleID=titles.titleID " .
                "LEFT JOIN authors " .
                " ON rel_title_author.authID=authors.authID " .
                "WHERE ISNULL(titles.titleID) " .
                " OR ISNULL(authors.authID)");
$sth->execute();
```

387

```
# delete the affected entries in the rel_title_author table
while($row = $sth->fetchrow_hashref()) {
  print "delete rel_title_author entry:\n";
  print " title = ",
    defined($row->{'title'}) ? $row->{'title'} : "NULL", "\n";
  print " author = ",
    defined($row->{'authName'}) ? $row->{'authName'} : "NULL", "\n";
  $dbh->do("DELETE FROM rel_title_author " .
           "WHERE authID=$row->{'authID'} " .
           " AND titleID=$row->{'titleID'}");
}
$sth->finish();

# Program end
$dbh->disconnect();
```

CGI Example: Book Management (*mylibrary*)

Access to the database looks the same in CGI scripts as it does in Perl programs, which for administrative purposes are usually executed as *stand alone*. One must, however, note in the output of data from the database that special characters in character strings are coded with *encode_entities* according to the HTML syntax.

This section introduces two small Perl programs that access the *mylibrary* database.

- mylibrary-simpleinput.pl enables the input of new book titles.

- mylibrary-find.pl enables the search for book titles.

> **POINTER**   *An interesting tool for Perl–CGI programmers is* mysqltool. *This is a collection of CGI scripts for the administration of MySQL databases (comparable with phpMyAdmin). It can be found at the following address:*
>
> http://www.dajoba.com/projects/mysqltool/

Book Search (mylibrary-find.pl)

The script mylibrary-find.pl assists in locating books in the *mylibrary* database. The initial letters of the title are given in the search form. Clicking the OK button leads to an alphabetical list of all titles found, together with their authors, publisher, and year of publication (see Figure 9-1).

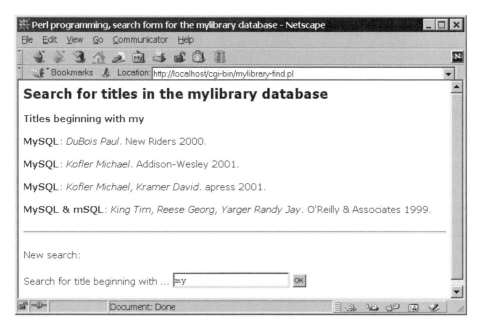

Figure 9-1. Searching for Book Titles

Program Structure

The script mylibrary-find.pl looks after the display of a simple form as well as the evaluation of that form (including the display of search results). The method *param()* of the *CGI* is used to evaluate the form variable *formSearch*.

Program Code

The code begins with the declaration of modules and variables. The combination of *strict* and *my* helps in discovering typographical errors in variable names; *DBI* enables access to the database; *CGI* assists in the output of HTML structures; *CGI::Carp* displays error messages in the resulting HTML document, which is especially practical in searching for errors; *HTML::Entities* contains the function *encode_entities*, with which special characters are translated into HTML syntax.

```perl
#!/usr/bin/perl -w
# mylibrary-find.pl

use strict;
use DBI;
use CGI qw(:standard);
use CGI::Carp qw(fatalsToBrowser);
use HTML::Entities;
```

```
# declaration of variables
my($datasource, $user, $passw, $dbh, $search, $sql, $sth, $result,
  $rows, $i, $row, $authors);
```

Establishing the connection to the database offers nothing new over our previous examples in this chapter. If an error occurs, an error message (in the form of an HTML document) is displayed and the script is terminated. If the connection succeeds, then the HTML document is opened with several methods from the *CGI* module.

```
# establish connection to the database
$datasource = "DBI:mysql:database=mylibrary;host=localhost;";
$user = "root";
$passw = "xxx";
$dbh = DBI->connect($datasource, $user, $passw,
  {'PrintError' => 0});

# display error message if required and terminate the script
if(DBI->err()) {
  print header(),
    start_html("Sorry, no database connection"),
    p("Sorry, no database connection"), end_html();
  exit();
}

# open HTML Document
print header(),
    start_html("Perl programming, search form for the ",
               "mylibrary database"), "\n",
    h2("Search for titles in the mylibrary database"), "\n";
```

Evaluate Form, Display Search Results

If the script is called with form data, then the form variable *formSearch* is evaluated with *param*. The special characters _ and % are removed from the character string. If the variable *search* is not empty, then in *sql* an extensive *SELECT* command is assembled and executed. The results are transmitted with *fetchall_arrayref* into a two-dimensional array.

```
# process form data
$search = param('formSearch');
# remove characters _ and %
$search =~ tr/%_//d;
if($search) {
```

```
print p(), b("Titles beginning with ", encode_entities($search));
# title search
$sql = "SELECT titles.titleID, titles.title, titles.year, " .
       " publishers.publName, authors.authName " .
       "FROM titles, authors, rel_title_author " .
       "LEFT JOIN publishers " .
       " ON titles.publID = publishers.publID " .
       "WHERE titles.titleID = rel_title_author.titleID " .
       " AND authors.authID = rel_title_author.authID " .
       " AND title LIKE '$search%' " .
       "ORDER BY title, titleID, authName " .
       "LIMIT 100";
$sth = $dbh->prepare($sql);
$sth->execute();
$result = $sth->fetchall_arrayref({});
$sth->finish();
```

The evaluation of the array begins with a test as to whether any book titles were found at all. The following loop is somewhat complicated by the fact that book titles with several authors should be displayed only once, with all of the authors. Therefore, in *authors* a character string of all the authors is assembled. When the last record in *result* is reached or if the next record refers to a *titleID* other than the current record, then the book title is displayed.

```
# were any titles found?
$rows = @{$result};
if($rows==0) {
  print p(), "Sorry, no titles found."; }
# display titles
else {
  # loop over all records
  for($i=0; $i<$rows; $i++) {
    $row = $result->[$i];
    # create author list
    if($authors) {$authors .= ", ";}
    $authors .= $row->{'authName'};
    # output title if arrived at the last record
    # in result or if titleID for the next record refers to
    # another value
    if($i==$rows-1 ||
        $row->{'titleID'} != $result->[$i+1]->{'titleID'}) {
        print p(),
          b(encode_entities($row->{'title'})), ": ",
```

```
            i(encode_entities($authors)), ". ",
            encode_entities($row->{'publName'}), " ",
            $row->{'year'}, ".";
         $authors = "";
       }
     }
     print p(), hr(), p(), "New search:", p();
   }
}
```

Display Form

```
# display form
print start_form(),
    p(), "Search for title beginning with ... ",
    textfield({-name => 'formSearch', -size => 20,
                -maxlength => 20}), " ",
    submit({-name => 'formSubmit', -value => 'OK'}),
    end_form();
print end_html();

# end of program
$dbh->disconnect();
```

Ideas for Improvements

The code as it stands permits only a search based on the initial letters of a title. It would be desirable, of course, to allow a search by author(s), categories, and so on, ideally in the form of a full-text search. (A somewhat more refined example of book search in *mylibrary* was presented in Chapter 8, where PHP was used as the programming language. That program offers pagewise representation of the search results as well as cross references between results, for example to display all titles written by a particular author.)

Simple Input of New Books (mylibrary-simpleinput.pl)

This section presents a minimalist input form for new books (see Figure 9-2). In two input fields are placed the new book title and a list of authors. The script then tests which if any of the authors are already stored in the database. All as yet unknown authors are added with *INSERT*. Then the new title is stored as well as the requisite entries in *rel_title_author* for relating title and authors.

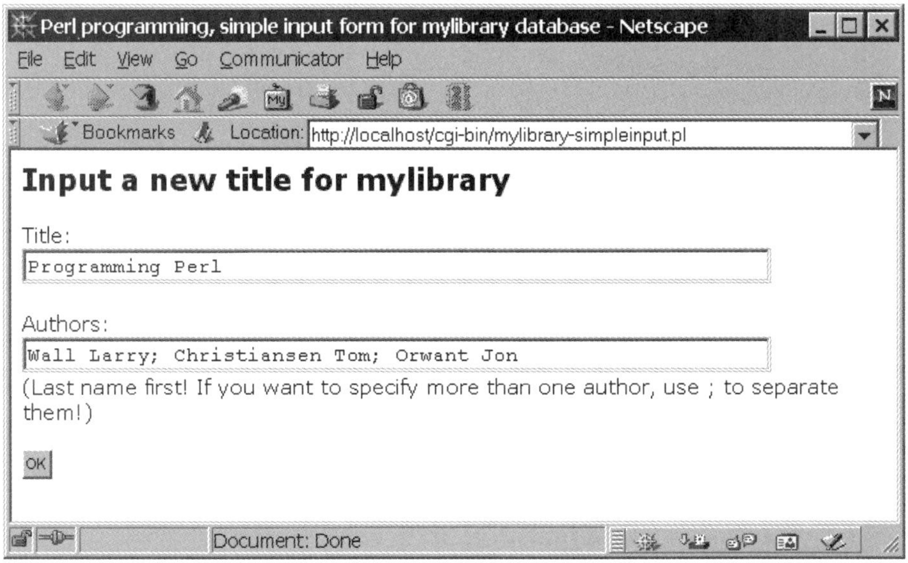

Figure 9-2. Simple Book Title Input

Program Structure

The script `mylibrary-simpleinput.pl` displays a simple form and then evaluates it when OK is clicked. The method *param()* of the *CGI* module is used to transmit the two form variables: *formTitle* with the title, and *formAuthors* with the list of authors.

Program Code

As with `mylibrary-find.pl` the code begins with the declaration of modules and variables:

```perl
#!/usr/bin/perl -w
# mylibrary-simpleinput.pl

use strict;
use DBI;
use CGI qw(:standard);
use CGI::Carp qw(fatalsToBrowser);
# Declaration of variables
my($datasource, $user, $passw, $dbh, @row,
  $formTitle, $formAuthors, $titleID, $authID, $author);
```

The next lines of code are similar to those of the script `mylibrary-find.pl`, which we have just seen, and so we do not reproduce the code.

```
# establish connection to the database
  ... as in mylibrary-find.pl
# if an error occurs, display error message and terminate script
  ... as in mylibrary-find.pl
# begin HTML document
  ... as in mylibrary-find.pl
```

Storing a Book Title and Its Authors

If the script is called with form data (these are located in *param()*), there follows a quick test as to whether a title and author list have been specified. If that is not the case, then an error message is displayed. The program is continued below with the redisplay of the form.

```
# evaluate form data
if(param()) {
  $formTitle = param('formTitle');
  $formAuthors = param('formAuthors');

  # title and authors were specified
  if($formTitle eq "" || $formAuthors eq "") {
    print p(), b("Please specify title and at least one author!"); }
```

For storing the book title in the *titles* table the *INSERT* command with one parameter is passed to *do*. As parameter *$formTitle* is passed. The effect of this way of proceeding is that *$formTitle* (with a minimal amount of typing) is placed in single quotation marks and all special characters are handled correctly.

```
  # form data seem to be correct; store them
  else {
    # store title
    $dbh->do("INSERT INTO titles (title) VALUES (?)",
             undef, ($formTitle));
    $titleID = $dbh->{'mysql_insertid'};
```

The list of authors is processed in a *foreach* loop. For each author a test is made as to whether the author already resides in the *authors* table. If that is indeed the case, then *authID* is read from the *authors* table. Otherwise, the new author is stored, and with *mysql_insertid* the new *authID* value is determined. Finally, the combination of *titleID* and *authID* must be stored in the table *rel_title_author*.

```
   # store authors
   foreach $author (split(/;/, $formAuthors)) {
     # does the author already exist?
     @row = $dbh->selectrow_array("SELECT authID FROM authors " .
                       "WHERE authName = " .
                       $dbh->quote($author));
     # yes: determine existing authID
     if(@row) {
        $authID = $row[0]; }
     # no: store new author and determine new authID
     else {
        $dbh->do("INSERT INTO authors (authName) VALUES (?)",
                undef, ($author));
        $authID = $dbh->{'mysql_insertid'};
     }
     # store entry in rel_title_author table
     $dbh->do("INSERT INTO rel_title_author (titleID, authID) " .
              "VALUES ($titleID, $authID)");
   }
```

In the HTML document a brief announcement is made that the new title was successfully stored. Then the form variables are deleted so that the next title can be input in the form.

```
   # feedback
   print p(), "Your last input has been saved.";
   print br(), "You may now continue with the next title.";
   # delete form variables (to prepare for the next input)
   param(-name=>'formTitle', -value=>'');
   param(-name=>'formAuthors', -value=>'');
  }
}
```

Displaying the Form

The remaining lines of code serve to display the form and close the HTML document:

```
print start_form(),
   p(), "Title:",
   br(), textfield({-name => 'formTitle', -size => 60,
                    -maxlength => 80}),
   p(), "Authors:",
```

```
        br(), textfield({-name => 'formAuthors', -size => 60,
                         -maxlength => 100}),
        br(), "(Last name first! If you want to specify more ",
              "than one author, use ; to separate them!)",
        p(), submit({-name => 'formSubmit', -value => 'OK'}),
        end_form();
print end_html();

# end of program
$dbh->disconnect();
```

Ideas for Improvements

The script mylibrary-simpleinput.pl does not permit one to specify subtitle, publisher, category, etc. Furthermore, it is as good as completely unprotected against input errors. It is impossible to make changes to titles already stored. Thus there is enormous potential to improve this script! (A much more satisfactory input form was presented in Chapter 8. There, to be sure, the programming language PHP was used. Nonetheless, many of the techniques employed there could easily be ported to Perl.)

CHAPTER 10

MyODBC

ODBC IS NOT A PROGRAMMING language, but rather a database interface that is well liked in Microsoft circles. MyODBC makes it possible to address MySQL via ODBC. That means that under Windows popular products and programming languages such as Access, Excel, Visual Basic, and VBA can be used for working with MySQL databases.

This chapter uses several examples to show some of the possibilities and limits of MyODBC under Windows, and it demonstrates some of the necessary programming techniques for ADO programming based on MyODBC.

The last two sections of this chapter have to do with ODBC only tangentially, but their content places them in this Windows-specific chapter. First, `MyVbQL.dll` is introduced, which is an object library that permits access to MySQL without MyODBC and ADO. This results in fewer compatibility problems and in many cases is more efficient. Second, the use of `mssql2mysql` is discussed. This is a database converter from the Microsoft SQL server to MySQL.

Chapter Overview

Fundamentals

ODBC (open database connectivity) is a popular mechanism under Windows for standardized access to a great variety of database systems. The only condition on ODBC for it to be used to access MySQL is in the installation of MyODBC, the ODBC driver for MySQL.

> **POINTER** *This chapter is based on the assumption that you have installed MyODBC as described in Chapter 2.*
>
> *The Spartan official documentation for MyODBC can be found in a separate chapter of the MySQL documentation ("MySQL ODBC Support"), as well as in the* Readme *file of the MyODBC installation files.*
>
> *There are also several MyODBC mailing lists, which can be read very conveniently with the help of, for example, Geocrawler (*www.geocrawler.com, *under* MAILING LISTS|DATABASES|MYODBC*).*

Determining the MyODBC Version Number

To determine whether MyODBC is installed on your computer (and in what version), execute START|SETTINGS|CONTROL PANEL|ADMINISTRATIVE TOOLS|DATA SOURCES (ODBC) and search in the DRIVERS dialog sheet of the ODBC dialog for the MyODBC driver (see Figure 10-1).

A Small Glossary from the World of Microsoft Databases

If you are new to the world of Microsoft databases, then ODBC is not the only abbreviation that is going to confuse you. Here is a brief overview:

- **OLE-DB:** OLE-DB is the successor to ODBC, thus again an interface for providing unified access to various database systems. For MySQL there is at present, sad to say, no mature OLE-DB driver. However, there is an ODBC interface for OLE-DB, by means of which all ODBC-compatible databases without their own OLE-DB drivers can be addressed. As a MySQL programmer you generally have nothing to do directly with OLE-DB, since you use ADO for the actual programming.

- **ADO (ActiveX Data Objects):** ADO is a collection of objects that are used in the programming languages Visual Basic, VBA, Delphi, etc., for creating

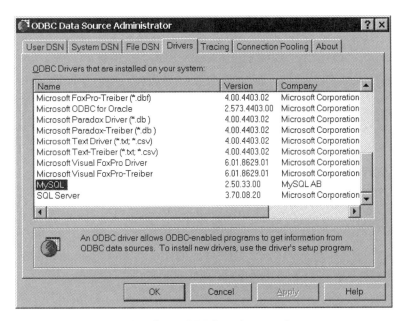

Figure 10-1. Determining the MyODBC version number

database programs. ADO stands between the programming language and OLE-DB. For programmers the object-oriented ADO library offers much more convenience than direct access to the database via OLE-DB functions. Later in the chapter, we provide information on ADO programming with Visual Basic for accessing MySQL databases.

- **MDAC (Microsoft Data Access Components):** MDAC is the general term for the countless Microsoft database components and libraries (including ADO and OLE-DB). Various MDAC versions are installed as parts of Windows, Office, Internet Explorer, etc. The most current versions can be found (at no cost) at the following address:

  http://www.microsoft.com/data/download.htm

- **DAO, RDO:** DAO and RDO are like ADO libraries for database programming. These are precursors to ADO and are now supported by Microsoft only half-heartedly. DAO and RDO are not discussed further in this book.

- **DSN (Data Source Name):** With many programs with an ODBC interface (e.g., Access, Excel) you cannot directly select a database. Instead, you must have previously defined a DSN for the database in the ODBC manager. Access to the database then proceeds via the DSN. (If you access MySQL via a programming language, you can create the database access without a DSN as well. Later on, we will show both variants, that is, access with and without a DSN.)

Setting Up a DSN for a MySQL Database

DSNs are usually set up in the ODBC administrator dialog. (Many Windows programs themselves provide dialogs for this purpose, but they are no improvement.) You launch the ODBC administrator dialog in the system control, under Windows 2000, for example, with START|SETTINGS|CONTROL PANEL|ADMINISTRATIVE TOOLS|DATA SOURCES (ODBC). There you have the choice among three DSN types: user, system, and file DSNs.

- **User-DSNs:** These are available only to the user who has defined the DSN. (During MyODBC installation a user DSN with the name *sample-MySQL* is automatically set up.) However, with this DSN the correct database name must first be employed before the DSN can be used.

- **System-DSNs:** These DSNs are available to all users of the computer. With both user and system DSNs the settings are managed internally by ODBC.

- **File-DSNs:** Here we are dealing with individual files with the identifier *.dsn, in which all setting data are stored in ASCII format. These files are usually stored in the directory Program Files\Common Files\ODBC\Data Sources. File DSNs are more transparent to some extent, because it is clear what information is stored where. However, MyODBC is currently incapable of generating file DSNs, so that this option does not come into question. (After the configuration is ended, various error messages appear.)

> **TIP** *If you wish to access more than one MySQL database, you must make use of the corresponding number of DSNs.*

The definition of a new DSN begins with clicking on the ADD button in the User DSN or System DSN dialog sheet. There appears a dialog in which you can choose from among various ODBC drivers. The correct choice in our case is, of course, MySQL. A double click now leads into an extensive dialog (see Figure 10-2), in which you must make the following settings:

- **Windows DSN Name:** Here is where you specify the name of the DSN (that is, under what name the data source can be addressed by ODBC programs). Select a name that is connected to the database name and the use to which the DSN is to be put.

- **MySQL Host (Name or IP):** Here you give the name or IP number of the computer on which MySQL (i.e., the server) is running. If it is the local computer, then give *localhost*.

- **MySQL Database Name:** Here you give the name of the MySQL database (for example, *mylibrary*, if you wish to access the database used for many examples in this book).

- *User* and *Password*: Of course, the access system described in Chapter 7 holds for MyODBC as well. (If you have begun to read the book at this point and are unable to achieve a MyODBC connection, then inadequate access privileges is the most likely cause of the difficulty.)

  In the fields *User* and *Password* you can input the user name and password for access to the database. However, whether you should actually do this is another question entirely. First, you provide access to the database to anyone who can use the DSN. Second, the password is not encrypted and can therefore easily be discovered.

  To circumvent this security risk, you can leave both fields empty. Then every time you or someone else wishes to use this DSN to obtain a connection to MySQL, the dialog pictured in Figure 10-2 appears. While this is very practical, in that name and password can be input, it is very confusing for the average user. It is not clear that user name and password are indeed to be entered, and it is possible that the poor user will stumble around in the other input fields of this dialog, which can lead to errors that will be difficult to unravel.

- **Port:** Here is where the IP port can be specified, in case it should be other than 3306. In most cases this field is left empty.

  If MySQL is running on a computer other than the one on which MyODBC is running and there is a fire wall between the two computers, then port 3306 must be opened. Otherwise, no communication between MySQL and MyODBC will be possible.

- **SQL Command on Connect:** Here an SQL command can be given that is to be executed immediately upon establishment of the connection. In rare cases this can be used to create a temporary table or set a variable (*SET*). As a rule, this field is left empty.

- **Options:** The remainder of the dialog is filled with a large number of options. We shall discuss some of these in the course of this chapter. Options with the identifier *(exp.)* are in the nature of experimental options and should, as a rule, not be used (except for testing purposes). At this point we will simply give a brief description of the most important options.

  ○ **Return Matching Rows:** Alas, it is not documented exactly how this option works. All that is certain is that this option must be set for MyODBC to be able to function in combination with a number of programs (including Microsoft Access and Visual Basic/VBA with ADO).

- **Don't Prompt on Connect:** This option prevents the dialog displayed in Figure 10-2 from being displayed before each connection. (Even if this option is activated, the dialog will appear if the login is unsuccessful on account of an incorrect or missing user name or password.)
- **Simulate ODBC 1.0:** In many situations MyODBC behaves according to the rules of ODBC 1.0. This option must be set if MyODBC is used with Microsoft Access 2.0.
- **Change BIGINT into INT:** Most Microsoft libraries are unable to deal with 64-bit integers. This option has the effect that MySQL *BIGINT* fields are automatically reduced to 32 bits upon transmittal. This option is necessary in particular for ADO programming with Visual Basic/VBA. Be thou warned, however: The most-significant 32 bits will be lost.
- **Force Use of Named Pipes:** This option results in *named pipes* (instead of TCP/IP) being used in communication between client and server. This is possible only under Windows NT/2000.

> **POINTER** *A bit (a very small bit, sad to relate) of additional information on MyODBC options together with some tips on how to use them can be found in the file* readme *that is provided with the MyODBC installation files.*

If at a later point you wish to change the settings of a DSN, simply reopen the ODBC administration dialog. A double click on the DSN (or the button CONFIGURE) leads again to the dialog depicted in Figure 10-2.

Access

Access and MySQL are two programs that are fundamentally different from each other. Access has a very well developed user interface, which simplifies the design of databases as well as the development of database programs. Unfortunately, Access is as slow as molasses outdoors in Moscow in winter if more than three or four users wish to access the database simultaneously. Furthermore, Access is extremely unsuited for Internet applications.

In comparison, MySQL is incomparably more efficient and secure in multiuser operation. Here the problem is in using the darn thing: Although there exists a variety of user interfaces to MySQL, at present, none of these offers the convenience of Access.

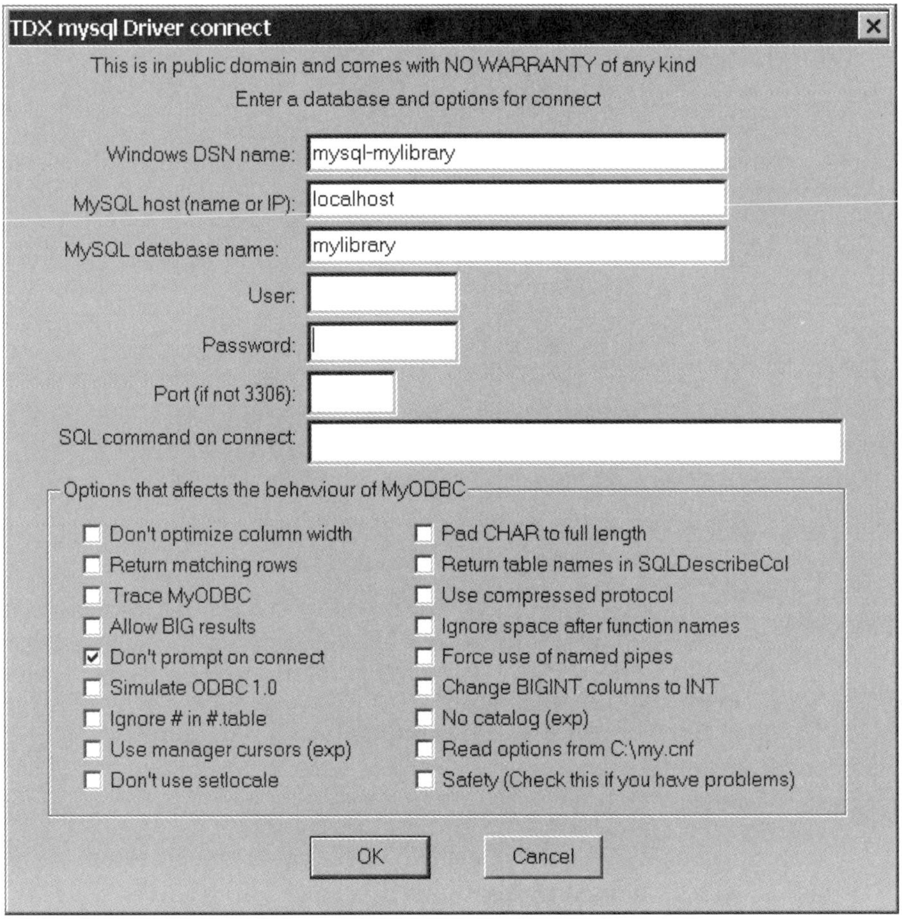

Figure 10-2. Configuration dialog of a MySQL DSN

Taking all of this into consideration, it seems a good idea to try to combine the best of both worlds. Even though there are many restrictions and limitations, the potential applications of Access in combination with MySQL are quite numerous:

- Access tables can be exported to MySQL and there processed further.

- MySQL tables can be imported to Access or a link to the tables can be created and the data further processed.

- Data from Access and MySQL databases can be combined.

- You can develop the design of a new database in Access and then export the entire database to MySQL.

- You can use Access as an interface for changing the contents of MySQL tables.

- You can develop complex queries in Access and then place the SQL code in your scripts.

- You can create and print database reports.

- You can develop VBA code in Access for automatically processing data from MySQL databases in Access.

- You can create diagrams of database structures. (All such diagrams in this book were created in this manner.)

> **REMARK**   *This section assumes that you are familiar with Access. An introduction to Access would be beyond the scope of this book. All procedures described in this section were tested with Access 2000.*

Problems

Don't let your hopes soar too high. Access was never conceived as an interface to MySQL and will not become one in the future. Thus it is not surprising that a number of difficulties exist in stretching Access into the Procrustean bed of an interface to MySQL:

- There are several data types that are available either only in Access or only in MySQL. In import/export such data types can create trouble. For example, MySQL *ENUM*s and *SET*s are turned into simple text fields upon importation. There are also problems to be had with single-precision *FLOAT*s. In general, you should use *DOUBLE* floating-point numbers if you plan on working with Access.

  You should generally count on having to change various attributes of a MySQL table as a result of importing it into Access and later exporting it back to MySQL.

- MySQL presently offers no way of creating links between tables. Relations (including rules for ensuring referential integrity) that are easily constructed in Access are lost upon exportation to MySQL.

- The SQL dialect of MySQL and that of Access are not quite identical. Thus it can happen that SQL queries developed in Access will function in MySQL only after some minor adjustments.

Assumptions

- If you wish to change data from linked MySQL tables in Access, the option *Return Matching Rows* must be set in the definition of the DSN. If you are working with Access 2.0, you will also need the option *Simulate ODBC 1.0*.

- Furthermore, all linked MySQL tables must be equipped with a *TIMESTAMP* field so that data can be altered. (You don't need to concern yourself with the care and feeding of this field, since both MySQL and Access automatically store the time of the last change. Access requires this information to distinguish altered data from unaltered data.)

- All MySQL tables must be equipped with a primary index (usually an *INT* field with the property *AUTO_INCREMENT*).

- In the MyODBC documentation one may find the occasional remark that working with Access 2000 is possible only if the latest version of MDAC has been installed. However, that holds only for older versions of MySQL and MyODBC. Beginning with MySQL 3.23.*n* and MyODBC version 2.50.33 the MDAC update is no longer required.

- A significant source of problems is the existence of incompatible data types:
  - MySQL tables use *DOUBLE* instead of *FLOAT* and *DATETIME* instead of *DATE*.
  - Avoid *BIGINT*, *SET*, and *ENUM*.
  - Access has occasional problems with *BLOB*s and believes that it is dealing with OLE objects. It is usually better to represent such columns in MySQL as *TEXT* with the attribute *BINARY*.

> **TIP** *If you develop queries in Access and then wish to use the SQL code in MySQL, you will frequently find yourself in a compatibility quagmire. (The SQL dialect of Access is different from that in MySQL.) Here is how you can solve this problem: Work with linked tables, and in Access execute the following command (while the window for query formulation is open):* QUERY|SQL SPECIFIC|PASS-THROUGH. *You thereby let Access know in no uncertain terms that the program should hold more rigorously to SQL standards.*

TIP *If you are working in Access with linked tables and if after an alteration in a data record you see #deleted displayed, then one of the above conditions has not been satisfied.*

Importing and Exporting Tables

Imported Tables Versus Linked Tables

If you wish to process MySQL data in Access, then you have two possibilities: You can first import the table(s) into Access and then do the processing, or else you can merely create a link between Access and the MySQL tables.

- With linked tables you can insert or alter data, although the table will then be managed by MySQL. Here Access serves simply as the interface. A change in the table's properties (insertion or deletion of a column, for example) is not possible with linked tables. The principal advantages are that the creation of links proceeds very quickly (independent of the size of the tables) and the data remain with MySQL (where they are well cared for).

- There are no restrictions on imported tables as they pertain to changes in the table design. Since the tables are now stored in an Access database file, you can carry out all the operations provided by Access. However, there can be problems if you later attempt to return the table(s) to MySQL, since not all of the Access data types can be transformed to MySQL data types without further ado.

Importing MySQL Tables into Access

The first step is either to open an existing Access database or to create a new (empty) database. Then you execute FILE|GET EXTERNAL DATA|IMPORT and in the file selection dialog you choose ODBC as file type. As if by magic the dialog SELECT DATASOURCE appears. In the dialog sheet MACHINE DATA SOURCES all the user and system DSNs are enumerated. Select the DSN of your choice. As a rule, there will now appear the dialog shown in Figure 10-2, in which you have merely to provide the user name and password.

If the connection to MySQL can be established, then the next dialog (see Figure 10-3) shows a list of all tables in the database specified by the DSN. There you can mark several tables at once (mouse button and Ctrl). The importation is initiated with OK, which can take a bit of time if the tables are large. (Access creates a local copy of the tables and stores them in an Access database file.)

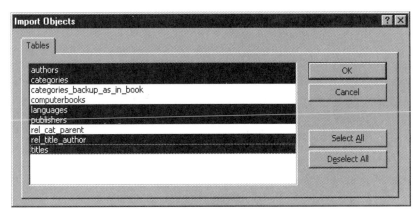

Figure 10-3. Selection of the tables to be imported into Access

Creating Links to MySQL Tables

The way to create a database link is the same as with the importation of a MySQL table. The only difference is that this time you begin with the Access menu command FILE|GET EXTERNAL DATA|IMPORT|LINK TABLES.

> **CAUTION** *If you change the properties of a table in MySQL (for example, if you add a new column), then you must delete the links to this table in Access and recreate them, so that Access knows that the changes have been made.*

Exporting Access Tables to MySQL

If you have imported a table from MySQL to Access and then changed it, or if you have developed an entire database in Access and then wish to transport it to MySQL, then you have to go in the opposite direction.

To do this you mark the table in the Access database window, execute the command FILE|EXPORT, and choose the file type ODBC. In the EXPORT dialog you can specify the name of the table under MySQL. (As a rule, you can use the name being used under Access simply with an OK.) Now comes the familiar selection of the DSN. And that does it!

In principle, exportation functions acceptably well, but usually there is some additional manual work required. The following list gives some of the basic problems with exportation.

- All indexes defined in Access are lost (including the primary index).

- The Access column property *Required* is not translated into the MySQL attribute *NOT NULL.*

- The Access column property *Autonumber* is not translated into the MySQL attribute *AUTO_INCREMENT*.

- The translation of data types is not always optimal. For example, *Currency* is translated to *DOUBLE* (MySQL). Here *DECIMAL* would be preferable. In general, you should check your MySQL tables carefully for such losses in translation.

Unfortunately, there is no possibility in Access to export several tables simultaneously. Thus if you wish to export an entire database, you must repeat the steps outlined above for each table.

Converter: Access → MySQL (exportsql.txt)

Due to the problems, enumerated in the previous section, that arise in the export of individual tables from Access to MySQL, Pedro Freire has programmed a converter that writes an entire Access database to a file *.sql, which then can be input with mysql. The quality of this converter is considerably better than ODBC Export, which is integrated into Access. This free program, exportSQL.txt, can be obtained at the following address:

http://download.sourceforge.net/mirrors/mysql/Downloads/Contrib/exportsql.txt

The method for exporting is documented in the program code. Here is a summary:

- Load the database to be exported into Access.

- With Alt+F11 switch into the VBA editor, there insert a new module (INSERT|MODULE), and copy the entire file exportsql.txt into the module (see the link above).

  You can work in the VBA editor only if you are working with an Access 2000 database. If the database was created with an earlier version of Access, then you must open a new module in the database window and insert the code into this module.

- Change the export options in the program code. This involves a block of constants (*Private Const name* = . . .) that control certain parameters of the exportation process. As a rule, you will have to change only the two constants *ADD_SQL_FILE* and *DEL_SQL_FILE*, which specify the names of the file into which the export files are to be written.

- Begin exporting with F5. (In the macro dialog you must select the procedure *exportSQL*.)

- During the exportation process you may see displayed some warning messages relating to incompatibilities between Access and MySQL data types, which you must approve by clicking OK. The warnings will appear as well in the resulting files. (The affected lines begin with *#Warning.*)

- In MySQL generate an empty new database (with *CREATE DATABASE*).

- Execute the SQL command specified in esql_add.txt. You can best accomplish this with mysql:

```
> mysql -u root -p databasename < q:\tmp\esql_add.txt
Enter password: xxxxx
```

If errors occur, you may have to alter esql_add.txt in a text editor. In some situations some small changes in the program code of the converter may be necessary.

Before making a new attempt, you must delete any existing data. For this the second file esql_del.txt will be of help.

```
> mysql -u root -p databasename < q:\tmp\esql_del.txt
Enter password: xxxxx
```

Problems

- Access permits a number of special characters in table and column names that MySQL does not allow. The following changes in the program code (indicated in boldface) will permit exportSQL.txt automatically to replace these characters by _:

```
Private Function conv_name(strname As String) As String
  ...
  Select Case Mid$(str, I, 1)
    Case " ", Chr$(9), Chr$(10), Chr$(13), "-", ")", "("
  ...
```

- In those countries where floating-point numbers are formatted with a comma for the decimal point (MySQL is clueless about this) the following remedy is available:

```
Sub exportSQL()
  ...
```

```
Select Case crs.Fields(cfieldix).Type
  ...
Case Else
  sqlcode = sqlcode & conv_str(str(crs.Fields(cfieldix).Value))
```

- *PRIMARY KEY* columns must have the attribute *NOT NULL* in MySQL. However, exportsql.txt does not guarantee this condition, and that can lead to problems. The solution is to edit the column definitions of the export file esql_add.txt in a text editor.

> **REMARK** *I have sent these ideas for changes to the author of* exportSQL.txt. *Perhaps there is already an improved version as you are reading these lines. Here we have described version 2.0.*

Converter: MySQL → Access (importsql.txt)

As the inverse of exportsql.txt, we have importsql.txt, which, however, I have not tested in detail:

```
http://www.netdive.com/freebies/importsql/module.txt
```

MyAccess

MyAccess offers a simple user interface to the above-described basic functions (importing, exporting, developing and executing SQL queries), based, however, on its own code (that is, not on the converters that we have presented). MyAccess is a commercial tool, but there is a free evaluation version, whose only limitation is that each time you launch it, a dialog appears asking you to register it. Access to MyAccess is at the following address:

```
http://www.accessmysql.com/
```

Data Analysis with Excel

Excel is of interest to users of MySQL primarily as a tool for data analysis. Thanks to MyODBC you can import MySQL data into an Excel worksheet and there perform analyses, create graphics, and so on. In Figure 10-4 you can see, as an example, a pivot table that for the *mylibrary* database tells which publisher has published how many books in a given category. (Because of the relatively small number of data records the result is, of course, not very informative. But if *mylibrary* contained a large number of books, then this table would allow you to determine easily which publishers specialize in which subjects.)

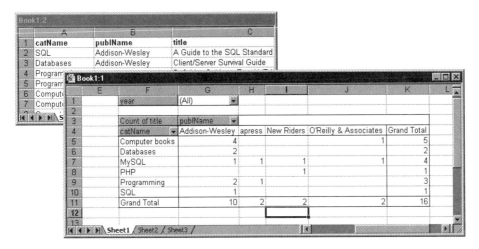

Figure 10-4. Excel pivot table

POINTER *If you use the macro programming language VBA, which is included in Excel, then a broader range of options is open to you, particularly if your goal is to automate or simplify the steps discussed here. A brief introduction to database access via VBA (or Visual Basic) will be given later in the chapter.*

Importing Data with MS Query

Whether you wish to insert MySQL data directly into an Excel worksheet (command DATA|GET EXTERNAL DATA|NEW DATABASE QUERY) or to create a pivot table or chart based on external data, Excel will launch the auxiliary program MS Query. This program functions as the interface between Excel and any external database, and it assists in the setting of import and query parameters.

In this program you select the DSN in the dialog CHOOSE DATA SOURCE. At that point the QUERY WIZARD appears, which assists in the creation of a database query. In the first step you select the required tables or table fields (see Figure 10-5). In the next two steps you can specify the filter criteria (corresponding to *WHERE* conditions) and the sort order.

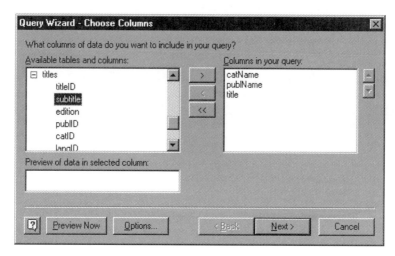

Figure 10-5. Selecting the desired columns in MS Query

If these specifications suffice for executing the query, you can now terminate MS Query with FINISH. Usually, however, it is preferable first to click on the option VIEW DATA OR EDIT QUERY. In this case the query is displayed by MS Query in a way such that it can be optimized (see Figure 10-6). In particular, any relations between the tables that MS Query has not recognized on its own can be established. To accomplish this you simply *Drag&Drop* the ID fields from one table to the other. A dialog appears in which you can set the relational properties.

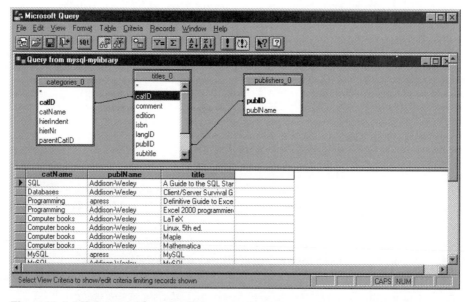

Figure 10-6. MS Query with option VIEW DATA OR EDIT QUERY

> **TIP** *Excel frequently has difficulties with the importation of information about data. You can solve some of these problems with the help of the SQL function* CONCAT. *To format a column with this function, open the dialog* EDIT COLUMN *in MS Query with a double click on the column in question. In the input field* FIELD *you set the expression present there in* CONCAT(…). *For example, from* table.birthdate *you would produce* CONCAT(table.birthdate).

ADO Programming and Visual Basic/VBA

Introduction

In this section we describe access to MySQL databases via program code, where we use Visual Basic or VBA as our programming language. We use ADO as our database library. The actual access to the database is effected by means of MyODBC, where between ADO and MyODBC we have OLE-DB and the ODBC driver for OLE-DB. Thus we have the following relationship: VB/VBA → ADO → OLE-DB → ODBC driver for OLE-DB → MyODBC → MySQL.

If MySQL is running on a computer as a Visual Basic program, then the first five stages of this communication chain take place on the client computer. It is MySQL that communicates over the network with the MySQL server.

> **REMARK** *In this book we are assuming that the reader has basic knowledge of ADO. If you know nothing much about ADO, do not know what* Connection *and* Recordset *objects are or the purpose of bound controls, then you should consult the literature on ADO programming before you read further, since we are not making much ado about nothing.*
>
> *The code presented here was developed with MyODBC 2.50.36, Visual Basic 6, and ADO 2.5. The code should function as well with VBA 6 and ADO 2.1 (Office 2000), except as it involves ADO controls.*
>
> *Of course, you can also work with a scripting variant of Visual Basic, for example, if you wish to develop Active Server Pages (ASP) or programs for the Windows Scripting Host (WSH). In that case you must leave out* As typename *in the variable declaration and create ADO objects according to* Set conn = CreateObject("ADODB.Connection").

> **POINTER** *On the page "Contributed Software" of the MySQL web site there is also an OLE-DB driver for MySQL (MyOLEDB). However, I have been unable to find documentation for this driver or to ascertain the current state of this project. For this reason I have not given a description of it:*
>
> http://www.mysql.com/downloads/contrib.html

Assumptions and Limitations

- **MySQL-Tables:** Tables that you wish to alter via ADO *Recordsets* or in bound controls (*Insert, Update, Delete*) must have a primary index and a *TIMESTAMP* column.

- **MyODBC Options:** In the configuration of a DSN the options *Return matching rows* and *Change BIGINT into INT* must be selected. If the connection is made without a DSN, then instead, the equivalent setting *Options=16386* must be specified.

- **No Server-Side Cursor:** MyODBC currently does not support server-side cursors. This means that with ADO you can use only client-side cursors. For this you must execute the instruction *res.CursorLocation = adUseClient* before *rec.Open*. (Without this instruction ADO attempts to open the *Recordset* automatically with a server-side cursor. This works as well, but you are unable to edit data and can move through the *Recordset* only with *MoveNext*.)

  This does not represent a great limitation in itself, as both ADO and the Visual Basic controls are in any case optimized for use with a client-side cursor. However, a client-side cursor means that in opening a *Recordset* all data are transferred at once to the client.

  Therefore, if you open a *Recordset* on the basis of *SELECT * FROM table*, the entire table is transported into the *Recordset* object before the program is continued. With large tables this can cost considerable time and memory, and it is a burden on MySQL and on the network. So consider how you formulate your queries and limit if possible the list of records with *WHERE* or *LIMIT*.

- **Changing Data with Recordsets and Bound Controls:** If the above conditions have been satisfied, you can use *Recordsets* and bound controls to read, display, and alter data.

This last point can often cause problems. Storing altered data (whether via a *Recordset* object or a bound control) functions properly in many simple cases, but in more complex applications it often leads to problems that are difficult to resolve. (These problems do not always have to do with MySQL/MyODBC, but with the vagaries of OLE-DB/ADO. Many experienced ADO programmers therefore do without bound controls, even if a Microsoft database system is used as the data source.

For this reason you will continually find in MySQL newsgroups and mailing lists the recommendation to use *Recordset*s and bound controls exclusively for reading or displaying data. If you wish to alter data, then formulate a traditional SQL command (*UPDATE . . .*) and execute it with *conn Execute*. Even if I have demonstrated both methods in this chapter (both the convenient editing of data with a *Recordset* object and the variant with SQL commands), I recommend the latter variant.

- **Speed:** Because of the many layers and libraries between Visual Basic and MySQL, and also because of the wretched speed in the processing of character strings with Visual Basic, solutions using Visual Basic and MySQL tend to be rather slow. Better performance is promised by the *MyVbQL* library, which establishes a direct connection between Visual Basic and MySQL (without ODBC).

Visual Basic and MySQL: Applications

If you use VB/VBA/WSH/ASP, etc. (that is, a Microsoft programming language) for the development of free-standing database solutions, then you will presumably be doing this in the future in combination with a Microsoft database system. The combination of Visual Basic and MySQL functions acceptably in principle, but it is not always the best solution, on account of a number of compatibility problems.

> **POINTER**   *Please note that MySQL, contrary to popular opinion, is free for open source applications, including dynamic web sites, no matter whether they are developed with Visual Basic or some other programming language. On the other hand, if you wish to develop a commercial bookkeeping program that builds on MySQL, then your clients must have a MySQL license. Take another look at Chapter 1 or in the Internet:*
>
> ```
> http://www.mysql.com/doc/L/i/Licensing_and_Support.html
> ```

The combination of Visual Basic and MySQL can be recommended especially if you have anyhow used MySQL (for example for a web site) and now wish to develop tools for maintenance or analysis that will run under Windows or if you frequently convert data between the MySQL and Windows worlds.

Example Programs

As in the other chapters of this book, for this chapter, too, all of the more extensive examples can be found at my web site (www.kofler.cc). These examples assume Visual Basic version 6. Furthermore, the examples assume the existence of the *mylibrary* database, which must have been previously installed. Please note that at the start of the program (usually in *Form_Load*) the connection parameters (computer name, user name, password) must be set as required by your system. In the example programs the computer name is *localhost*, the user name is *root*, and the password is *uranus*.

Establishing the Connection

Establishing the Connection with a DSN

The following lines show a code outline for establishing a connection to MySQL based on a DSN and for executing a simple *SELECT* query. The resulting record list can then be processed with the properties and methods of the *rec* object.

```
Dim conn As Connection
Dim rec As Recordset
Set conn = New Connection
conn.ConnectionString = "DSN=mysql-mylibrary"
conn.Open
Set rec = New Recordset
rec.CursorLocation=adUseClient
rec.Open "SELECT * FROM tablename", conn
   ...    'process record list
rec.Close 'close record list
conn.Close 'terminate connection
```

The only really interesting code line is the one for setting the *ConnectionString* property. In the simplest case you simply specify the DSN. Optionally, you can also specify the user name and password. These parameters must be separated by semicolons. The *ConnectionString* character string looks like this:

```
conn.ConnectionString = "DSN=mysql-mylibrary;UID=root;PWD=xxx"
```

Connection Without DSN

DSN=name	DSN
UID=name	user name for the MySQL connection
PWD=password	password for the MySQL connection

Establishing the Connection Without a DSN

With Visual Basic you can also establish a connection to a MySQL database without previously having defined a DSN. (This is particularly practical if you wish to develop a program to access an arbitrary MySQL database.) The *ConnectionString* character string looks like this:

```
conn.ConnectionString = "Provider=MSDASQL;Driver=MySQL;" & _
  "Server=localhost;UID=username;PWD=xxx; database=databasename;" & _
  "Option=16386"
```

ConnectionString *parameters (Connection Without DSN)*

Provider=MSDASQL	name of the ODBC driver for OLE-DB (Microsoft Data Access SQL)
Driver=MySQL	name of the MySQL-ODBC driver
Server=name	name or IP address of the computer on which MySQL is running
UID=name	user name for the MySQL connection
PWD=password	password for the MySQL connection
Database=name	name of the database
Prompt=noprompt/complete	display MyODBC dialog is connection fails
Option=n	MyODBC options

Prompt=complete leads to the program automatically displaying the dialog depicted in Figure 10-2. This dialog can be used, for example, to provide a missing or incorrect password. Moreover, an arbitrary character string must be specified in the field WINDOWS DSN NAME so that the dialog can be exited.

Since the dialog is not particularly user-friendly (the many choices are more confusing than helpful), it is better to do without *Prompt=complete*. (The default setting is *noprompt*.)

Instead, execute *On Error Resume Next* before establishing the connection and test after establishing the connection whether an error has occurred. If this is the case, display your own dialog, in which the user can input other connection parameters as necessary and from which the program can then construct a new *ConnectionString* character string.

Options enables the setting of a number of MyODBC connection options. The required value is determined from the sum of the values of the individual options, which are listed in the MyODBC Readme file. For Visual Basic/ADO programs, the value 16384+2 must be specified, according to the MyODBC documentation. This corresponds to the options *Return matching rows* and *Change BIGINT into INT*.

Establishing the Connection with DataEnvironment

If you are working with Visual Basic Professional or Enterprise version 6, then you have *DataEnvironment* available for setting connection properties.

In the properties dialog for the *Connection* object choose, in the dialog sheet PROVIDER, the entry MICROSOFT OLE-DB PROVIDER FOR ODBC DRIVERS. You can then choose, in the dialog sheet CONNECTION (see Figure 10-7), an already defined DSN or assemble an equivalent character string with the required connection properties with the button BUILD. (This button leads to the familiar ODBC dialogs and finally to the MyODBC dialog depicted in Figure 10-2. However, the result of the setting is copied as a character string into the *DataEnvironment* dialog, where it can be edited as necessary.)

In the further program code you can now access the *Connection* object. (The following lines assume that the *DataEnvironment* object have the name *DE* and the *Connection* the name *Conn*.)

```
Dim rec As Recordset
Set rec = New Recordset
If DE.Conn.State = adStateClosed Then
  DE.Conn.Open
End If
rec.CursorLocation=adUseClient
rec.Open "SELECT * FROM database", DE.Conn
  ...
```

The *DataEnvironment* helps not only in setting the connection data, but also in the development of SQL queries. With the SQL generator you have a convenient tool for this purpose. You can then access the query in code via the *Command* object.

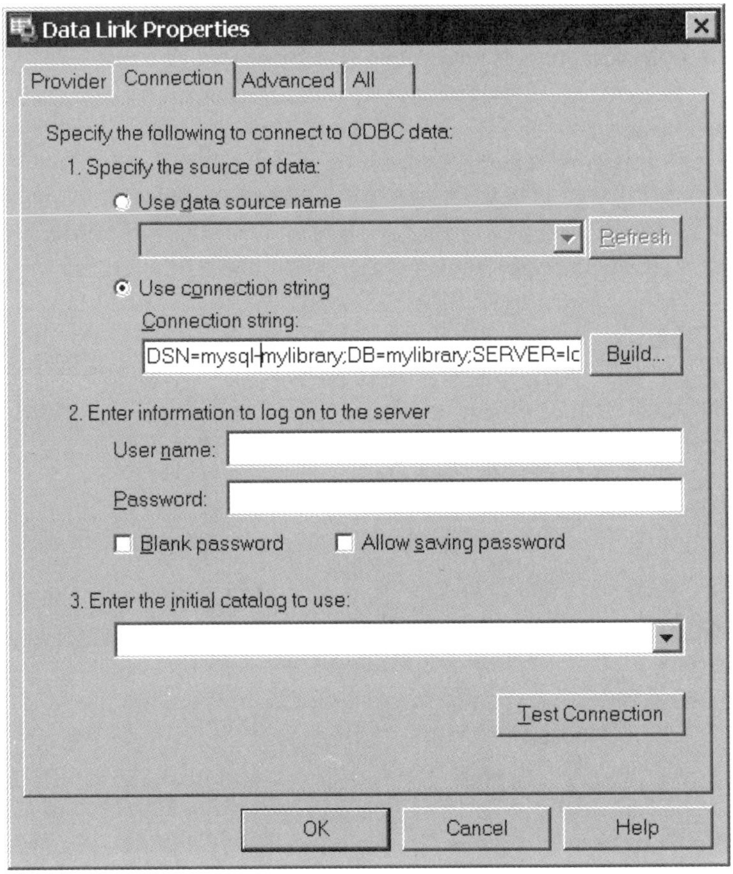

Figure 10-7. DataEnvironment Dialog *for setting the connection properties*

Connection Properties

The *ConnectionString* parameters described in this section represent only a small part of the available parameters. For those parameters that are not specified, ADO/ODBC simply uses various default settings.

Sometimes, it is useful to know how these parameters are set. The property *ConnectionString*, which is changed in establishing the connection (and then no longer contains the character string originally set), provides our first overview. Here most of the parameters are collected into a sort of superparameter *Extended Properties*.

```
conn.ConnectionString = "Provider=MSDASQL;Driver=MySQL;Server= ... "
conn.Open
Debug.Print conn.ConnectionString
  Provider=MSDASQL.1;Extended Properties="DSN=;DB=books;
    SERVER=localhost;UID=root;PWD=uranus;PORT=;OPTION=;STMT=;"
```

Considerably more information is provided by the *Properties* enumeration of the *Connection* object. Moreover, the values saved there can be more easily extracted:

```
Debug.Print conn.Properties("Max Columns in Index")
   16
```

A complete list of all properties and their values can be obtained with the following loop:

```
Dim p As Property
For Each p In conn.Properties
  Debug.Print p.Name & " = " & p.Value
Next
```

And here is the output (squeezed into two columns to save space):

```
Accessible Procedures = False
Accessible Tables = True
Active Sessions = 0
Active Statements = 0
Asynchable Abort = False
Asynchable Commit = False
Autocommit Isolation Levels = 256
Catalog Location = 1
Catalog Term = database
Catalog Usage = 13
Column Definition = 1
Connect Timeout = 15
Connection Status = 1
Current Catalog = books
Data Source =
Data Source Name =
Data Source Object Threading
  Model = 1
DBMS Name = MySQL
DBMS Version = 3.23.23-beta
Driver Name = myodbc.dll
Driver ODBC Version = 02.50
Driver Version = 2.50.33
Extended Properties =
  DSN=;DB=books;
  SERVER=localhost;UID=root;
  PWD=xxxx;PORT=;OPTION=;STMT=;
File Usage = 0
General Timeout =
GROUP BY Support = 3
Heterogeneous Table Support = 0
Identifier Case Sensitivity = 8

Initial Catalog =
Integrity Enhancement Facility
  = False
Isolation Levels = 256
Isolation Retention = 0
Like Escape Clause = N
Locale Identifier = 1031
Location =
Max Columns in Group By = 0
Max Columns in Index = 16
Max Columns in Order By = 0
Max Columns in Select = 0
Max Columns in Table = 0
Maximum Index Size = 120
Maximum Row Size = 0
Maximum Row Size Includes
  BLOB = True
Maximum Tables in SELECT = 32
Mode =
Multiple Parameter Sets = False
Multiple Results = 1
Multiple Storage Objects = False
Multi-Table Update = False
NULL Collation Order = 8
NULL Concatenation Behavior = 0
Numeric Functions = 16777215
OLE DB Services = -7
OLE DB Version = 02.00
OLE Object Support = 1
Open Rowset Support = 0
ORDER BY Columns in Select List
  = False
```

```
Outer Join Capabilities = 121              = True
Outer Joins = F                   Schema Term = owner
Output Parameter Availability = 4   Schema Usage = 0
Pass By Ref Accessors = True        Server Name = localhost via T
Password =                          Special Characters =
Persist Security Info =               ÇüáâåçêëèïîìÄ
Persistent ID Type = 4              SQL Grammar Support = 1
Prepare Abort Behavior = 2          SQL Support = 259
Prepare Commit Behavior = 2         Stored Procedures = False
Procedure Term = procedure          String Functions = 491519
Prompt = 4                          Structured Storage = 1
Provider Friendly Name =            Subquery Support = 0
  Microsoft OLE DB Provider         System Functions = 7
  for ODBC Drivers                  Table Term = table
Provider Name = MSDASQL.DLL         Time/Date Functions = 106495
Provider Version = 02.50.4403.6     Transaction DDL = 0
Quoted Identifier Sensitivity = 4   User ID =
Read-Only Data Source = False       User Name = user
Reset Datasource =                  Window Handle =
Rowset Conversions on Command
```

Programming Techniques

Recordsets *with Client-Side Cursors*

Recordset objects are opened on the basis of an existing *Connection* object (see the previous section). In all the examples in this chapter the variable name for this object is *conn*.

Since ADO provides a server-side cursor as the default cursor position, a client-side cursor must be set before the *Open* method. The following lines demonstrate how this is done:

```
Dim rec As Recordset
rec.CursorLocation = adUseClient 'client-side cursor
rec.Open "SELECT ... FROM ... WHERE ... ", _
      conn, adOpenStatic, adLockReadOnly
```

We note the following about the parameters of *Open*: In the first parameter the SQL code is expected, in the second the *Connection* variable. The third parameter describes the desired cursor type. Since for client-side cursors only the type *adOpenStatic* is supported, it doesn't matter what is given here. The fourth parameter specifies whether the data in the *Recordset* are read-only (*adLockReadOnly*) or whether changes are permitted (*adLockOptimistic*). ADO provides the locking types *adLockPessimistic* and *adLockBatchOptimistic* as well, which, however, I have not tested.

With the *Open* method all the data encompassed by the SQL query are transmitted to the program. (This can take considerable time with large data sets.) You can then apply all *Recordset* properties and methods to run through the data (*MoveNext*, etc.), to search (*Find*), to sort locally (*Sort*), to change (*column="new value": rec.Update*), etc.

Null, Dates and Times, and Suchlike

The following list describes how various MySQL data types are represented in ADO *Recordset*s.

- **Null:** The value *Null* in a column of a *Recordset* can be determined with *IsNull(rec!column)*.

- **Date/Time:** Columns in the MySQL formats *DATE, TIME, DATETIME*, and *TIMESTAMP* are automatically transformed into the Visual Basic data type *Date*. Please exercise caution with *TIME* values: These values are supplemented with the current date. (For example, from 9:00 you may get 2001/3/17 9:00.)

- **BLOBs:** *BLOB*s are transformed into *Byte* arrays. Access to individual bytes is effected in the manner *rec!a_blob(n)*, where *n=0* addresses the first byte. A *Byte* array can be interpreted by Visual Basic as a character string. However, again caution is advised: Since internally, Visual Basic works with Unicode, a *BLOB* with 512 bytes corresponds in Visual Basic to a character string with 256 Unicode characters. For bytewise evaluation of the character string the Visual Basic functions *AscB, ChrB, LenB, MidB, LeftB, RightB, InStrB*, etc., must be used.

- **Decimal:** Columns in the MySQL format *DECIMAL* are metamorphosed into the Visual Basic data type *Decimal*, which is not to be confused with *Currency*. It is to be thought of more as a subtype of *Variant*.

- **Sets/Enums:** Columns in the MySQL formats *SET* and *ENUM* are transformed into garden-variety character strings.

Determining the AUTO_INCREMENT Number After the Insertion of a Data Record

It often occurs that after the insertion of a new data record into a table you require the *ID* number of that record (that is, the value of the *AUTO_INCREMENT* column for the primary index). Unfortunately, this cannot be read from the *Recordset* with which the record was inserted. The solution to this conundrum is to determine the ID number via *SELECT LAST_INSERT_ID()*. To accomplish this, you would do well to add the following function to your program:

```
Private Function LastInsertedID()
  Dim rec As New Recordset
  rec.CursorLocation = adUseClient
  rec.Open "SELECT LAST_INSERT_ID()", conn
  LastInsertedID = rec.Fields(0)
End Function
```

Recordset *with Server-Side Cursor*

Initially, I wrote that MyODBC does not support server-side cursors. I should modify that assertion to mention that there is a single exception: You can open a *Recordset* with a server-side cursor with the properties *CursorType = adForwardOnly* and *LockType = adLockReadOnly*. You can thereby move through and read all the records of the query with *MoveNext*.

No changes in the data are permitted. No navigation method other than *MoveNext* is allowed. You cannot use *Bookmarks*. You cannot determine the number of records. (To do this, formulate a query with *SELECT COUNT(*) FROM table*.)

In spite of all these restrictions, in a few cases it can make sense to use a server-side cursor, namely, when large quantities of data are to be read sequentially. The drawbacks of the client-side cursor are thereby avoided (namely, that all the records are transmitted at once to the client.)

Possible Recordset *Properties*

ADO provides for an almost endless number of combinations of properties of a *Recordset*. But the *Recordset* does not always contain the properties requested by *Open*. If a given driver does not support a particular cursor type, then ADO automatically chooses another.

As a way of testing which properties a *Recordset* actually possesses you can use the program Cursortypes.vbp (see Figure 10-8). With a click of the mouse you can set the desired properties. The program then opens the *Recordset*, determines the actual properties, and then displays them. (Note, please, that the results of the program are not always correct for server-side cursors. In particular, the *Recordset* method *Supports(. . .)* returns completely incorrect results.)

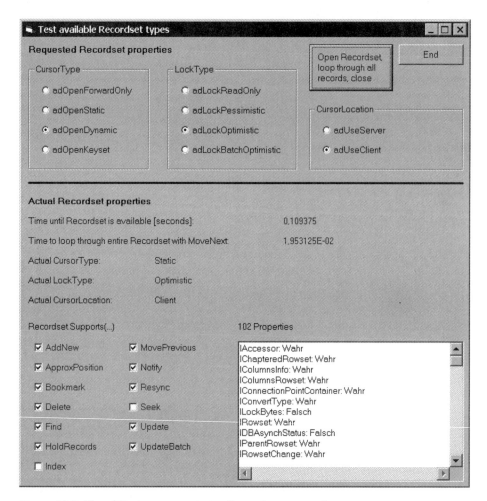

Figure 10-8. Visual Basic program to test Recordset *properties*

Executing SQL Commands

ADO *Recordsets* can simplify your dealings with query results, but it is often necessary to execute SQL commands directly. To do this, use the *Execute* method of the *Connection* object.

```
conn.Execute "INSERT INTO table (a, b) VALUES ('x', 'y')"
```

As with other programming languages, with Visual Basic you also run into the problem that you have to format various data in conformity with the rules of MySQL. In the following you will find some auxiliary functions to help you in this task.

- **Floating-Point Numbers:** With floating-point numbers you must take into account that Visual Basic normally formats such numbers according to the country for which the language has been customized (for example, in Germany one has 3,14159265 instead of 3.14159265). If your program is to function equally well everywhere in the known universe, you should transform your floating-point numbers into character strings with the Visual Basic function *Str*.

- **Date:** The following *Format* instruction formats the date contained in *x* in accord with MySQL conventions:

```
Format(x, "'yyyy-mm-dd Hh:Nn:Ss'")
```

Character Strings: *Quote* places a backslash character before the backslash and before the single- and double-quote characters, and it replaces the byte code 0 with \0:

```
Function Quote(tmp)
  tmp = Replace(tmp, "\", "\\")
  tmp = Replace(tmp, """", "\""")
  tmp = Replace(tmp, "'", "\'")
  Quote = Replace(tmp, Chr(0), "\0")
End Function
```

- **Binary Data:** *HexCode* transforms a byte array of arbitrary length into a hexadecimal character string of the form *0x0102031232*.

```
Function HexCode$(bytedata() As Byte)
  Dim i&
  Dim tmp$
  tmp = ""
  For i = LBound(bytedata) To UBound(bytedata)
    If bytedata(i) <= 15 Then
      tmp = tmp + "0" + Hex(bytedata(i))
    Else
      tmp = tmp + Hex(bytedata(i))
    End If
  Next
  HexCode = "0x" + tmp
End Function
```

HexCodeStr functions in principle like *Hexcode*, except that it expects data bytewise in a character string. (Please note that Visual Basic operates with Unicode character strings.)

```
Function HexCodeStr$(bytedata$)
  Dim i&, b&
  Dim tmp$
  tmp = ""
  For i = 1 To LenB(bytedata)
    b = AscB(MidB(bytedata, i, 1))
    If b <= 15 Then
      tmp = tmp + "0" + Hex(b)
    Else
      tmp = tmp + Hex(b)
    End If
  Next
  HexCodeStr = "0x" + tmp
End Function
```

Bound Database Controls

Visual Basic offers several controls that can be bound directly to database queries (to *Recordset* objects). Within the control the contents of the *Recordset* (or perhaps only of the currently active data record) are displayed. Such controls offer a great savings in effort in the representation of database queries. Some controls even offer the possibility of altering data directly. In the ideal case, one can program a database interface with a minimal amount of code. See Figure 10-9.

In reality, things do not always go so smoothly. In general, you must take care in your work with MyODBC that for bound controls, too, you work with a client-side cursor. Furthermore, the alteration of data does not always function reliably, so that (except in well-tested special cases) one is advised not to use this feature.

Apart from that, the use of bound controls is independent of whether you use a Microsoft database system or MySQL as the data source. Additional information on using bound controls can be found in any book on database programming with Visual Basic.

Example: authors Column for the titles Table

In Chapter 5 we described a possible extension for the *titles* table of the *mylibrary* database, whereby the table would be equipped with an additional *authors*

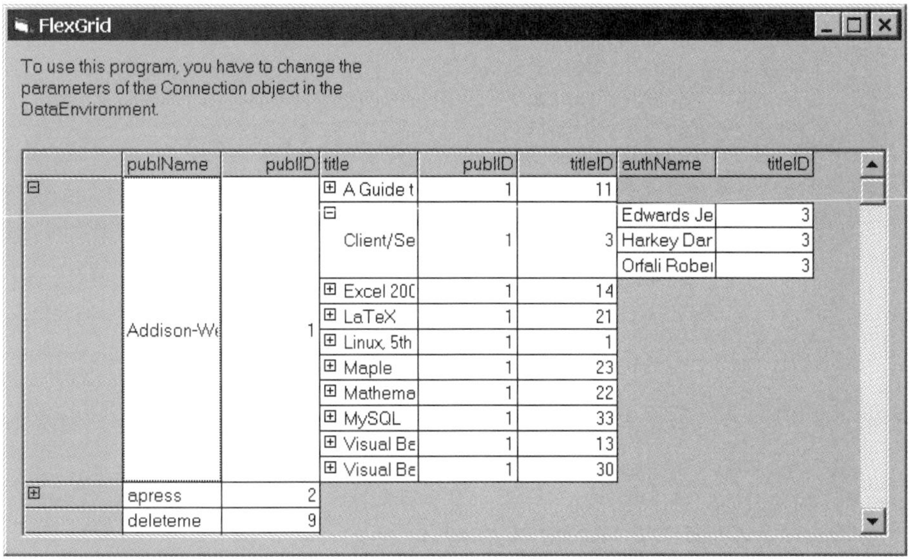

Figure 10-9. Visual Basic example program with the MSHFlexGrid for representing data from the mylibrary *database*

column in which the authors' names would be stored (see Figure 10-10). To be sure, this is redundant, but it will speed up read access to the database.

Figure 10-10. Visual Basic example program for changing the titles *table*

The example program presented here shows how the *authors* column can be filled with data. For this we simply run through all the *titles* records, determine the authors for each book, combine the authors into a character string, and store them.

> **REMARK** *Our program assumes that the* titles *table has been enlarged to include an (as of yet empty)* authors *column of type* VARCHAR(255) *and a* TIMESTAMP *column.*
>
> ```
> ALTER TABLE titles ADD authors VARCHAR(255)
> ALTER TABLE titles ADD timest TIMESTAMP
> UPDATE titles SET timest=UNIX_TIMESTAMP()
> ```

Variant 1: Changing Data with Read/Write Recordsets

All of the code is contained in the event procedure *Command2a_Click*. This procedure assumes that the global variable *conn* creates the connection to the database (*Connection* object).

In the program two *Recordset*s are opened. One of them, *titles*, refers directly to the like-named table and enables changes to it (*LockingType=adLockOptimistic*). The second, *authors*, contains a list of all *titleID* values and their authors. The *Recordset* is sorted locally after being read in (property *Sort*), and apart from the database, in order not to put unnecessary demands on resources.

The following loop runs through all the *titleID* values of the *titles Recordset*. With *Find* the associated authors in the *authors Recordset* are determined and joined into the character string *authors_str*. This character string is then stored.

```
' example program authors_for_titles\form1.frm
Private Sub Command2a_Click()
  Dim authors_str
  Dim titles As New Recordset
  Dim authors As New Recordset
  ' titles Recordset: read/write
  titles.CursorLocation = adUseClient
  titles.Open "SELECT titleID, authors FROM titles", _
              conn, adOpenStatic, adLockOptimistic
  ' authors Recordset: readonly, disconnected
  authors.CursorLocation = adUseClient
  authors.Open "SELECT titleID, authname " _
              "FROM authors, rel_title_author " & _
              "WHERE authors.authID=rel_title_author.authID", _
              conn, adOpenStatic, adLockReadOnly
  authors.Sort = "titleID, authname"
  Set authors.ActiveConnection = Nothing
```

```
  ' loop over all titles
  While Not titles.EOF
    authors_str = ""
    ' loop over all authors of this title
    authors.MoveFirst
    authors.Find "titleID=" & titles!titleID
    While Not authors.EOF
      If authors_str <> "" Then authors_str = authors_str + "; "
      authors_str = authors_str & authors!authName
      authors.MoveNext
      authors.Find "titleID=" & titles!titleID
    Wend
    ' store author list
    If authors_str <> "" Then
      titles!authors = authors_str
      titles.Update
    End If
    titles.MoveNext
  Wend
End Sub
```

Variant 2: Changing Data with conn.Execute

In our second variant the *authors Recordset* is opened just as in variant 1. The
structure of the loop is a bit different in how it finds all the authors of the current
titleID value. The authors are stored temporarily in the variable *authors_str*.

What is new in comparison to variant 1 is the instruction *conn.Execute*, with
which the list of authors is stored in the *titles* table with the help of an *UPDATE*
command. The function *Quote* is necessary to ensure that the SQL command is
correct even when the author name has special characters such as '.

```
Private Sub Command2b_Click()
  Dim authors_str, titleID
  Dim authors As New Recordset

  ' authors Recordset: client-side, readonly, disconnected
  authors.CursorLocation = adUseClient
  authors.Open "SELECT titleID, authname " & _
               "FROM authors, rel_title_author " & _
               "WHERE authors.authID=rel_title_author.authID " & _
               "ORDER BY titleID, authName", _
               conn, adOpenStatic, adLockReadOnly
  authors.Sort = "titleID, authname"
```

```
      Set authors.ActiveConnection = Nothing
   ' loop over all titles (titleID)
   While Not authors.EOF
     titleID = authors!titleID
     authors_str = ""
     ' search for all authors of the current titleID value
     authors_str = ""
     Do While Not authors.EOF
       ' at the next titleID jump out of the inner loop
       If authors!titleID <> titleID Then
         Exit Do
       End If
       ' add the author name to authors_str
       If Not IsNull(authors!authName) Then
         If authors_str <> "" Then authors_str = authors_str + "; "
         authors_str = authors_str & authors!authName
       End If
       authors.MoveNext
     Loop

     ' store author list
     If authors_str <> "" Then
       conn.Execute "UPDATE titles " & _
                    "SET authors = '" & Quote(authors_str) & "'" & _
                    "WHERE titleID=" & titleID
     End If
   Wend
End Sub

' place \ before ', ", and \ , replace Chr(0) by \0
Private Function Quote(tmp)
  tmp = Replace(tmp, "\", "\\")
  tmp = Replace(tmp, """", "\""")
  tmp = Replace(tmp, "'", "\'")
  Quote = Replace(tmp, Chr(0), "\0")
End Function
```

Example: Adding a New Book Title to the mylibrary Database

With the following example program you can store a new book title in the
mylibrary database. The book title consists of the title itself, one or more authors,
and a publisher (see Figure 10-11). The program does not test whether the authors

or publisher already exists in the database. The goal of this program is simply to demonstrate the principal methods of inserting data into linked tables.

Figure 10-11. Visual Basic example program for inserting a new book title

Variant 1: Changing Data with Read/Write Recordsets

At the beginning of the procedure four *Recordset* objects are opened, with whose help the data are to be stored. Without *LIMIT 1* the *SELECT* statement would retrieve all matching *Recordset*s. But we are not interested in these (we want only to change data here), so this would be a waste of time. What we want is an ADO object pointing to this table, and to get one, we have to execute a *SELECT* statement. The use of *LIMIT 1* thus speeds things up for us. (If you would like to improve the efficiency of the code, you should define the four *Recordset* variables globally and open them in *Form_Load*. You thereby avoid the *Recordset*s having to be opened for each storage event.)

The commands for storing the data from the three text fields *txtPublisher*, *txtTitle*, and *txtAuthors* are easy to understand. Worthy of note is the use of the auxiliary function *LastInsertedID()*, described above, for determining the most recently added *AUTO_INCREMENT* value.

```
' insert_new_title\form1.frm
Private Sub SaveData_WithRecordsets()
  Dim i&, titleID&, authID&, publID&
  Dim authors_array
  Dim authors As New Recordset, titles As New Recordset
  Dim publishers As New Recordset, rel_title_author As New Recordset
  ' open Recordsets
  authors.CursorLocation = adUseClient
  titles.CursorLocation = adUseClient
  publishers.CursorLocation = adUseClient
```

```
  rel_title_author.CursorLocation = adUseClient
  authors.Open "SELECT * FROM authors LIMIT 1", _
    conn, adOpenStatic, adLockOptimistic
  titles.Open "SELECT * FROM titles LIMIT 1", _
    conn, adOpenStatic, adLockOptimistic
  publishers.Open "SELECT * FROM publishers LIMIT 1", _
    conn, adOpenStatic, adLockOptimistic
  rel_title_author.Open "SELECT * FROM rel_title_author LIMIT 1", _
    conn, adOpenStatic, adLockOptimistic

  ' store publisher (if given)
  If Trim(txtPublisher) <> "" Then
    publishers.AddNew
    publishers!publName = Trim(txtPublisher)
    publishers.Update
    publID = LastInsertedID()
  End If

  ' store book title (with publID reference as needed)
  titles.AddNew
  titles!Title = Trim(txtTitle)
  If publID <> 0 Then titles!publID = publID
  titles.Update
  titleID = LastInsertedID()

  ' store authors and make entries in rel_title_author
  authors_array = Split(txtAuthor, ";")
  For i = LBound(authors_array) To UBound(authors_array)
    authors.AddNew
    authors!authName = Trim(authors_array(i))
    authors.Update
    authID = LastInsertedID()
    rel_title_author.AddNew
    rel_title_author!titleID = titleID
    rel_title_author!authID = authID
    rel_title_author.Update
  Next
End Sub

Private Function LastInsertedID() ... see heading "Programming Techniques"
```

Variant 2: Changing Data with conn.Execute

In our second variant the code is more like that to which you are accustomed in MySQL programming with languages such as PHP or Perl: You need to cobble together the SQL commands painstakingly, taking care to treat special characters correctly. (For this the auxiliary function *Quote* will be used.) The structure of the code is otherwise like that of the first variant.

```
Private Sub SaveData_WithSQLCommands()
  Dim i&, titleID&, authID&, publID&
  Dim authors_array
  ' store publisher (if given)
  If Trim(txtPublisher) <> "" Then
    conn.Execute "INSERT INTO publishers (publName) " & _
                 "VALUES ('" & Quote(Trim(txtPublisher)) & "')"
    publID = LastInsertedID()
  End If

  ' store book title (with publID as needed)
  conn.Execute "INSERT INTO titles (title, publID) " & _
               "VALUES ('" & Quote(Trim(txtTitle)) & "', " & _
                       IIf(publID <> 0, publID, "NULL") & ")"
  titleID = LastInsertedID()

  ' store authors and add entries to rel_title_author
  authors_array = Split(txtAuthor, ";")
  For i = LBound(authors_array) To UBound(authors_array)
    conn.Execute "INSERT INTO authors (authName) " & _
                 "VALUES ('" & Quote(Trim(authors_array(i))) & "')"
    authID = LastInsertedID()
    conn.Execute "INSERT INTO rel_title_author " & _
                 " (titleID, authID) " & _
                 "VALUES (" & titleID & ", " & authID & ")"
  Next
End Sub

Private Function Quote(tmp) ... see heading "Programming Techniques"
```

Visual Basic Programming Without ADO and MyODBC

The ADO programming based on MyODBC introduced in the previous section functions in principle, but it is not particularly efficient and quickly presses MyODBC to its limits. This section offers as an alternative the object library *MyVbQL*. This library, developed in Visual Basic, offers Visual Basic programmers more direct access to MySQL. To this end the *MyVbQL* objects *MYSQL_CONNECTION*, *MYSQL_RS*, *MYSQL_FIELD*, and *MYSQL_ERR* display functionality similar to that of the ADO objects *Connection*, *Recordset*, *Field*, and *Error*, without, however, there being any need to worry about the compatibility of the methods and properties.

The DLL and underlying Visual Basic code can be found on the Internet:

```
http://www.icarz.com/mysql/
```

For its part, *MyVbQL* builds on the library libmySQL.dll, which is part of the MySQL client package for Windows. Access to MySQL via *MyVbQL* takes place according to the following scheme: Visual Basic → MyVbQL Object library → libmySQL.dll → MySQL.

In comparison to ADO/ MyODBC, *MyVbQL* code is faster, as a rule. However, there are some drawbacks as well:

- The time for establishing the connection is somewhat longer (particularly if MySQL is running on another computer under another operating system), which is unsatisfactory above all for ASP applications.

- *MyVbQL* currently does not support BLOBs.

- *MyVbQL* is not ADO-compatible. It therefore takes some effort to convert existing ADO code to *MyVbQL*.

- The *MYSQL_RS* object cannot be used as the data basis for bound database controls, which makes the use of database controls in combination with *MyVbQL* impossible.

- The included documentation for *MyVbQL* is (still) in the nature of a simple reference. The use of *MyVbQL* therefore assumes some background in Visual Basic and databases.

Installation

In order for *MyVbQL* to be able to be used, the two DLLs MyVbQL.dll and libmysql.dll must be installed on the computer (for example, in the Windows system directory). Both files are located in MyVbQL.zip on the web site cited above.

With MyVbQL.dll we are dealing with an ActiveX DLL. Therefore, it must be registered in the Windows registration database. This takes place automatically as soon as the library is transformed for the first time via PROJECT|REFERENCES into a Visual Basic project. (Registration also proceeds automatically if you install the program *MyTool*, which likewise is available at the web site cited above.)

The file libmysql.dll is a traditional DLL. It should be located either in the Windows system directory or in the directory of the Visual Basic development environment or in the directory of the compiled Visual Basic program.

Application

In order to use *MyVbQL* in your own Visual Basic project you must simply create a reference to the library. As soon as the library is registered, you will find it under the name *MySQL Visual Basic API* in the dialog PROJECT|REFERENCES. If the library has not yet been registered, then use the button BROWSE in order to load the DLL. You can then use the four *MYSQL_xxx* objects as you would normal Visual Basic objects.

Example

Again we shall use as an example the program that stores a character string with all the authors belonging to a given book title in the *authors* column of the *titles* table.

For establishing the connection you create an object of type *MYSQL_CONNECTION* and pass the computer name, user name, password, and database name to the method *OpenConnection*:

```
' authors_for_titles_myvbql\form1.frm
' establish connection to MySQL
Dim conn As New MYSQL_CONNECTION
Private Sub Command1_Click()
  conn.OpenConnection "localhost", "root", "xxx", "mylibrary"
  Command2.Enabled = True
End Sub
```

In *Command2_Click* of the procedure for changing the *titles* a loop is executed over all titles with the *MYSQL_RS* object. In the second *MYSQL_RS* object *authors* all the authors belonging to this title are determined for each *titleID* number found, and they are collected into a character string. This character string is then stored in the *titles* table. Thus the *MYSQL_RS* object *titles* is used not only for reading, but also for changing data.

MYSQL_RS objects are derived with the method *Execute* from the *MYSQL_CONNECTION* object. Access to individual fields of the current record is effected with *rs.Fields("columnName").Value* (instead of *rs!columnName* as with ADO). To change data, simply assign a new value to the *Value* property of the affected column and store the changes with the *Update* method. (You can also insert a new record with *AddNew* or delete one with *Delete*, but these are not demonstrated in our example.)

```
' change column authors in table titles
Private Sub Command2_Click()
  Dim authors_str, titleID
  Dim titles As MYSQL_RS
  Dim authors As MYSQL_RS

  ' titles Recordset to loop through all titles and
  ' to change the authors column
  Set titles = conn.Execute( _
    "SELECT titleID, authors FROM titles")

  ' loop through titles
  While Not titles.EOF
    titleID = titles.Fields("titleID").Value

    ' authors Recordset to read authors per titleID
    Set authors = conn.Execute( _
      "SELECT authname FROM authors, rel_title_author " & _
      "WHERE authors.authID=rel_title_author.authID " & _
      "  AND rel_title_author.titleID = " & titleID & " " & _
      "ORDER BY authName")

    ' loop through authors
    authors_str = ""
    Do While Not authors.EOF
      ' build string with authors names
      If Not IsNull(authors.Fields("authName").Value) Then
        If authors_str <> "" Then authors_str = authors_str + "; "
        authors_str = authors_str & authors.Fields("authName").Value
      End If
      authors.MoveNext
    Loop
    authors.CloseRecordset

    ' save authors field in titles RS
    If Len(authors_str) > 254 Then _
      authors_str = Left(authors_str, 254)
    titles.Fields("authors").Value = authors_str
    titles.Update
    titles.MoveNext
  Wend
  titles.CloseRecordset
  MsgBox "done"
End Sub
```

Converter: Microsoft SQL Server $\longrightarrow$ MySQL

If up to now you have managed a database with the Microsoft SQL Server (or the MSDE, that is, the Microsoft Data Engine) and are considering porting it to MySQL, there are two main ways of bringing your data into a MySQL database.

- Summon Access to your assistance. First, import the table into an empty Access database, and then export it to MySQL.

- Use the VBA/Visual Basic script `mssql2mysql` (developed in my first version). The program should generally enable a more exact copy of the database structure, since there is no intermediate Access step. The remainder of this section is related to this program. The program can also be seen as a further example of ADO database programming with MySQL, although for reasons of space we omit the source code.

> **POINTER** *Converters between MySQL and a number of other databases (dBase, FoxPro, mSQL) can be found at the following address:*
>
> `http://www.mysql.com/downloads/contrib.html`

Properties of `mssql2mysql`

- freely obtainable (GPL)

- copies an entire database, that is, all user-defined tables (structure, indexes, data)

- automatically changes the name of a table or column if the name is not allowable in MySQL (for example, *My table* becomes *My_table*)

- changes Unicode character strings into ANSI character strings or BLOBs

- generates either a text file with SQL commands or executes the required commands directly

Restrictions

- In MySQL, currently unavailable or incompatible database attributes cannot be copied (views, stored procedures, foreign keys, user-defined data type, access privileges, etc.).

- The program is relatively slow. (For example the conversion of the 2.8-megabyte *Northwind* database took about 80 seconds on a computer with a 400-megabyte Pentium II processor.)

  This slowness is determined above all by the very slow Visual Basic string functions. If you have Visual Basic 6 available, you can actually compile the program, but the resulting improvement in speed is scarcely measurable.

How to Use It

The text file mssql2mysql is available over the Internet:

```
http://www.kofler.cc/mysql/
```

To execute the code, use either Visual Basic 6 or a program with VBA 6 support (for example, Excel 2000, Word 2000, Access 2000).

- **Visual Basic 6:** If you are working with Visual Basic 6, begin a new standard project and insert the entire code into the code window of a form. Then start the program with F5.

- **VBA:** If you are working with a VBA 6 compatible program, switch with Alt+F11 into the VBA development environment, insert a new, empty, module, and copy the code into this module. Then with F5 open the dialog for macro execution and execute the procedure *main*.

Setting Parameters

All the parameters of the conversion process are controlled by a number of constants, which can be found at the beginning of the code. The first five constants describe the database on the Microsoft SQL server. The login to the database can be effected either via the security system integrated into Windows NT/2000 or by the explicit specification of user name and password.

```
Const MSSQL_SECURE_LOGIN = True 'login type (True for NT Security)
Const MSSQL_LOGIN_NAME = "" 'username ("" for NT Security)
Const MSSQL_PASSWORD = "" 'password (""for NT Security)
Const MSSQL_HOST = "mars" 'computer ("(local)" for localhost)
Const MSSQL_DB_NAME = "pubs" 'database name
```

OUTPUT_TO_FILE specifies whether the program should generate a text file with SQL commands or whether the commands should be executed at once.

The first variant has the advantage that if problems arise, the text file can be directly edited.

```
Const OUTPUT_TO_FILE = 0     '1 write file,
                             '0 execute SQL commands at once
```

If you have decided for *OUTPUT_TO_FILE=1*, you must specify the name of the resulting file in *OUTPUT_FILENAME*.

```
Const OUTPUT_FILENAME = "c:\export.sql"
```

With *OUTPUT_TO_FILE=0* you must specify all parameters so that a connection to MySQL can be created. For this there must be sufficient access privileges so that *CREATE DATABASE*, etc., can be executed.

```
Const MYSQL_USER_NAME = "root"'username
Const MYSQL_PASSWORD = "uranus" 'password
Const MYSQL_HOST = "localhost" 'computer name or "localhost"
```

Finally, we mention a few conversion options.

- *NEW_DB_NAME* enables the name of the new MySQL database to be given. If the constant remains empty, the new database keeps the same name as the SQL server database.

- *UNICODE_TO_BLOB* specifies whether *UNICODE* character strings should be transformed into BLOBs (*True*) or ANSI character strings (*False*). The second variant makes sense if Unicode data types were used in the SQL server database, but within them no special characters were used outside of the ANSI character set.

- *DROP_DATABASE* specifies whether at the beginning of the conversion any existing MySQL database with the same name should be deleted.

- *MAX_RECORDS* specifies how many records per table should be converted. Here 0 means that all data records should be converted. This option is practical for first carrying out a quick test and, for example, converting only ten records per table. Only after it has been verified that all is well is the entire database converted.

```
Const NEW_DB_NAME = ""         'MySQL database name
Const UNICODE_TO_BLOB = False  'Unicode --> BLOBs?
Const DROP_DATABASE = True     'begin with DROP database?
Const MAX_RECORDS = 0          '0: convert all data
```

Part IV

Administration, MySQL for Pros

#### CHAPTER 11

Administration

IN THIS CHAPTER WE DELVE into the most important topics on the subject of database administration: backups, logging files, migration of databases from one computer to another (or from one version of MySQL to a newer one), importation of text files into a database, exportation of data from a database.

Chapter Overview

Basic Administration

This section collects information on the elementary aspects of administration and refers the reader to other places in this book where additional details are to be found.

> **POINTER** *Some additional topics related to administration of MySQL are discussed in the following chapters:*
>
> - *Chapter 4: Use of* mysql, *phpMyAdmin, etc.*
>
> - *Chapter 7: Access controls,* mysql *databases*
>
> - *Chapter 12: BDB tables, compiling MySQL, replication*
>
> - *Chapter 14: reference to* mysqld, mysql, mysqladmin, *etc.*

Basic Server Configuration

Setting the Root Password

A fresh installation leaves MySQL completely unprotected. As soon as you begin to use MySQL for storing data, you should secure MySQL with a password. Under Unix/Linux the following commands suffice. (As *computername* the complete network name of the computer must be given.)

```
root# mysqladmin -u root -h localhost password xxx
root# mysqladmin -u root -h computername password xxx
```

The process is somewhat more complicated under Windows, since the default configuration is even more insecure.

> **POINTER** *The MySQL access system was described in detail in Chapter 7. In particular, in the section "First Aid" you will find a concrete introduction to securing MySQL under both Windows and Unix/Linux.*

Personalizing the MySQL Server

If you have followed the installation instructions presented in Chapter 2, then the MySQL server should be running mysqld and should be functioning without any problems for most applications. But if you have particular wishes, say you need a particular sort order or wish to optimize performance, then you can specify a number of options for mysqld.

> **POINTER** *Tips on using another sort order can be found in the first section of Chapter 12*
>
> *A description of how you can compile MySQL yourself and set it up under Linux appears in Chapter 12. There you will also find an explanation of how you can launch* mysqld *securely (in the account* mysql *and not in the account* root*).*
>
> *A reference to the most important options for* mysqld *can be found in Chapter 14.*

Configuration File for Setting Options

Both at launch of mysqld and during the execution of administrative tools it is tiresome always having to specify the same old options. Therefore, one may specify these options in a configuration file:

Validity	Windows	Unix/Linux
global options (for both mysqld and administrative tools)	C:\my.cnf, Windows\my.ini	/etc/my.cnf
user-specific options (only for administrative tools)		~/.my.cnf

The server-specific options in the configuration file begin with the line [mysqld]. The following options indicate that MySQL is to be executed under the account *mysql* (this makes sense only under Unix/Linux), that /tmp/mysql.sock is to be used as socket file (again only under Unix/Linux), and that in sorting of tables a German alphabetic sort order is to be used.

```
# Example of the server-specific part of
# /etc/my.conf and Windows\my.ini
[mysqld]
user       = mysql
socket     = /tmp/mysql.sock
default-character-set = german1
```

> **POINTER** *Information on the evaluation and syntax of configuration files as well as a reference to the most important options of MySQL tools and* mysqld *can be found in Chapter 14.*

Restarting the MySQL Server

Changes in configuration files become effective only after a restart of the affected program. This holds, of course, for the MySQL server as well. Thus, if you change server-specific options, you must restart the server (which is to be avoided as much as possible with a running system).

Under Windows you execute the restart most simply via WinMySQLadmin. (If you are working under NT/2000, you can also use the system administration services dialog.)

Under Unix/Linux you can use the appropriate Init-V script for restarting, which you typically execute first with the parameter *stop* and then with the parameter *start*.

```
Red Hat: root# /etc/rc.d/init.d/mysqld stop
         root# /etc/rc.d/init.d/mysqld start

SuSE:    root# /sbin/init.d/mysql stop
         root# /sbin/init.d/mysql start
```

Using Administrative Tools

With MySQL you get a number of administrative tools (such as mysqladmin and myisamchk), some of which are described in some detail in this chapter. A common feature of all these tools is that they are command-oriented programs. That is, there is no graphical user interface, and the tool is used with options and commands.

Under Unix/Linux the tools are executed in a shell window, while under Windows they are executed in a DOS window. (Chapter 4 contains tips on the optimal configuration of the DOS window as well as the proper setup of the Windows system variable *PATH*.)

Most of the administrative tools can be used with their full functionality only if you sign in as *root* and provide your password. To do this you specify the options -u and -p at launch of mysqld. For example, with the following command all active logging files are closed and reopened (with the result that in update protocols the sequential file ending is increased by 1).

```
root# mysqladmin -u root -p flush-logs
Enter password: ******
```

> **REMARK** *Some of the commands described in this and the next chapter, generally those involving Perl scripts, are currently available only under Unix/Linux, and not under Windows.*

Creating a Database Structure (mysqlshow)

The command mysqlshow helps in obtaining a quick overview of the databases, tables, and columns managed by MySQL. If the command is executed without parameters, it simply returns a list of all databases managed by MySQL. If a database is specified, then mysqlshow shows a list of the tables contained within that database. If a table is specified in addition to the database, then mysqlshow displays a list of the columns of that table, including its properties (data type, default value, etc.).

In the last parameter the wild cards _ and % can be used to filter the indicated data. The same information obtained with mysqlshow can also be obtained with various variants of the SQL command *SHOW*. The advantage of mysqlshow is that the program is well suited for the automation of administrative tasks.

```
> mysqlshow -u root -p
Enter password: xxx
Databases:
  books
  myforum
  mylibrary
  mysql
  test
  ...
```

```
> mysqlshow -u root -p mysql
Enter password: xxx
Database: mysql
Tables:
  columns_priv
  db
  host
  tables_priv
  user

> mysqlshow -u root -p books author
Enter password: xxxxxx
Database: books Table: author Rows: 10
```

Field	Type	Null	Key	Default	Extra	Privileges
authorID	int(11)		PRI		auto_increment	select, ...
author	varchar(60)					select, ...

Executing Administrative Commands (mysqladmin)

As the name of the program implies, mysqladmin assists in the execution of a variety of administrative tasks:

- Create and delete databases

- Change a user's password

- Input again the privileges database *mysql*

- Update database and logging files (clear buffer or intermediate storage)

- Determine status information and variables of the MySQL server

- List and store MySQL Processes

- Test connection to MySQL server (*ping*)

- Shut down the MySQL server (*shutdown*)

The following examples demonstrate a few possible applications:

```
> mysqladmin -u root -p create mynewdatabase
Enter password: xxx

> mysqladmin -i 5 ping
mysqld is alive
mysqld is alive

  ...
```

```
> mysqladmin status
  Uptime: 435152   Threads: 2      Questions: 26464   Slow queries: 3
  Opens: 140       Flush tables: 1 Open tables: 0      Queries per second avg: 0.061
> mysqladmin -u root -p processlist
Enter password: xxx
  Id    User   Host       db      Command   Time   State   Info
  1     ODBC   localhost  books3  Sleep     7
  196   root   localhost          Query     0               show processlist
  ...
```

Each time `mysqladmin` is called, only one operation can be executed. Most `mysqladmin` operations can be carried out as well with SQL commands (for example, with `mysql` or with a client program). The advantage of `mysqladmin` is that the program is easily adapted to the automation of administrative tasks.

> **POINTER** *Additional examples of the use of* mysqladmin *in connection with the setting of privileges, access, and passwords can be found in Chapter 7.*
> *A reference to all* mysqladmin *options and commands can be found in Chapter 14.*

Backups

Backups are doubtless one of the most important tasks of a database administrator. MySQL offers a variety of methods for executing a backup.

- The classical way, so to speak, uses the command `mysqldump`. This command returns a file with SQL commands for generating the tables of the database and filling them anew with data. Backups using `mysqldump` are comparatively slow, but they offer maximal portability. Therefore, `mysqldump` is used for database migration (for example, to transfer a database created under MySQL $3.22n$ for use with MySQL $3.23n$).

  The command `mysql` is used to recreate the database.

- Significantly faster is simply to copy the database directories at the system level. This is quite efficient and secure if the MySQL server is stopped for this purpose. However, if the server is to continue running, then it must be ensured that during the copying process no changes are allowed to be made in the database. This task is taken care of by the script `mysqlhotcopy`.

  To recreate the database it is necessary merely to copy the backed-up directory into the MySQL database directory.

- One can use logging files in combination with regular backup files for incremental backups. However, that is practicable only as long as the number of changes in the database is not too large. Backup strategies based on logging files are not handled in this section, but in the section on logging.

- Another variant of securing data is replication. This mechanism allows a database to be synchronized on two different computers. For databases that are changed frequently this can result in a high demand on communication between the computers. If you really want nothing more than to keep two copies of your database on two different hard drives, then it is more efficient to mirror a hard drive using RAID. Replication is not dealt with in this section, but in Chapter 12.

Hot Backups

Both the execution of mysqldump and the copying of database directories can take place while the database is in operation. However, the integrity of the backup is ensured only if *read lock* is executed during the backup for the affected tables.

The result is, on the one hand, that the backup can be executed only when the table is not blocked by a *write lock*. On the other hand, no client can access the tables during the execution of the backup. Since the backup of large databases can take a relatively long time (especially if you use mysqldump), blocking is quite burdensome.

To circumvent this problem, commercial database systems offer *hot backup* mechanisms that permit a backup while the system is running without the complete blocking of entire tables. MySQL is currently incapable of this (despite the promises of mysqlhotcopy). The backup options are supposed to be greatly improved with version 4.0.

Securing Databases (mysqldump)

The command mysqldump returns a long list of SQL commands required for the exact recreation of a database. Normally, the program returns a *CREATE TABLE* command for each table in order to generate the table together with its indexes, as well as numerous *INSERT* commands (one for each record). The following example shows the result of mysqldump for the *author* table of the *books* database presented in Chapter 5.

```
> mysqldump -u root -p books author
Enter password: xxx
# MySQL dump 8.9
# Host: localhost Database: books
# Server version   3.23.32
# Table structure for table 'author'
CREATE TABLE author (
  authorID int(11) NOT NULL auto_increment,
  author varchar(60) NOT NULL,
  PRIMARY KEY (authorID));
# Dumping data for table 'author'
INSERT INTO author VALUES (1,'Kofler M.');
INSERT INTO author VALUES (2,'Kramer D.');
 ...
```

Provided that the option --tab is not used, mysqldump displays the list of commands on the monitor. Usually, however, it makes more sense to direct the output to a file using > filename.

> **CAUTION**   *When output is redirected to a file under Windows one has the problem that the line* Enter password *will be entered into the target file. When the file is later read, a syntax error will occur, since* Enter password *is not an SQL command. This is not a pretty error. However, the data can be input without difficulties. If you wish to avoid the error message, you must either delete the line with a text editor after the file has been dumped, or else specify the password directly with the option* --password=xxx, *which is insecure.*
>
> *Under Unix/Linux this error does not occur, because a distinction is made between the channel for standard output and that for error messages. The line* Enter password *is normally displayed via the error channel on the monitor, while the SQL commands are stored by the output channel in the file.*

Backup of All Databases

The following command creates a backup of all databases managed by MySQL (provided that the user has *root* access) and stores these in a single file. During the backup the database is blocked for all write operations.

```
> mysqldump -u root --password=xxx --opt --all-databases > backup.sql
```

Syntax of mysqldump

The general syntax of mysqldump is the following:

```
mysqldump [options] dbname [tables] > backup.sql
```

If no tables are specified, then mysqldump writes all the tables of the database into the file backup.sql. Optionally, the backup can be limited to specific tables. If you wish to back up more than one database or even all of them, then the following syntax variants are what you use:

```
mysqldump [options] --databases dbname1 dbname2 ...
mysqldump [options] --all-databases
```

The details of the backup can be controlled by an impressive number of options. A reference to all the options appears in Chapter 14. To execute a simple backup, a single option usually suffices, --opt, which has the following effect:

- During the backup *read lock* is executed for all tables.

- The resulting backup file is as small as possible (one *INSERT* command for all records of the table).

- The resulting file contains *DROP TABLE* commands to delete existing tables when the database is restored.

- All features of the database are retained (including MySQL-specific features that could interfere with migration to a different database system).

REMARK *Perhaps you are aware that there is also a command* mysqldumpslow. *This command has nothing to do with* mysqldump, *but helps in the evaluation of a special logging file in which all SQL commands that took a particularly long time to execute are recorded.*

Restoring a Database (mysql)

There is no direct inverse operator for mysqldump, simply because the old workhorse mysql is completely satisfactory for this purpose.

> **REMARK** *Tables are automatically recreated in the type that they previously possessed. Thus* mysqldump *and* mysql *are well suited as tools for securing data independent of table type (MyISAM, BDB, etc.).*
> *The re-creation of a database works even if you use a different (newer) version of MySQL.*

Restoring a Single Database

If backup.sql contains only a single database, then the restore command looks like this:

```
> mysql -u root -p databasename < backup.sql
Enter password: xxx
```

The database *databasename* must already exist. If that is not the case, then you can easily create it with mysqladmin create databasename.

Restoring Several Databases

If several databases were backed up with mysqldump, then backup.sql contains the requisite *CREATE DATABASE* commands for creating the databases anew if they do not yet exist. There is no necessity to create the databases first. You also do not need to specify a database when mysql is called.

```
root# mysql -u root -p < backup.sql
Enter password: xxx
```

mybackup

The Perl script mybackup is currently not included with MySQL. However, you can find it on the Internet: http://www.mswanson.com/mybackup/
The script mybackup uses mysqldump. The advantage over mysqldump is that the backup files (one per database) are written into a specified directory and there immediately compressed with gzip.

Fast Backups (`mysqlhotcopy`)

For a considerable time, the Perl script `mysqlhotcopy` has been provided with the Unix/Linux version of MySQL. This script is supposed to help in improving the speed of backups executed with `mysqldump`. The basic idea of the program is first to execute a *read lock* for the specified databases and then with *FLUSH TABLES* to ensure that the database files are actually in their current versions. Then the database files are directly copied.

CAUTION   *The documentation says that* `mysqlhotcopy` *is an alpha version, that is, a version in its earliest test phase. Nonetheless,* `mysqlhotcopy` *seems sufficiently reliable, but you must decide for yourself whether you want to entrust the security of your data to* `mysqlhotcopy`. *Furthermore, it is not out of the question that some of the options described here will change before* `mysqlhotcopy` *becomes a mature product.*

TIP   *The documentation to this script is obtained with the following command. Instead of* /usr/bin *you may have to give another path.*

```
user$ perldoc /usr/bin/mysqlhotcopy
```

Making a Backup

In the simplest case the use of `mysqlhotcopy` is as follows:

```
root# mysqlhotcopy dbname1 dbname2 dbname3 backup/
```

With this the databases *dbname1*, *dbname2*, *dbname3*, are copied into the specified backup directory. (This backup directory must already exist.) Each database is copied into a subdirectory named for the database.

Options

The following list gives merely the most important options. A full description of all the options can be found in the documentation.

- --allowold overwrites existing backup files.

- --keepold archives existing backup files into the directory dbname_old. If this directory already exists, then its contents are overwritten.

- --flushlog has the effect that MySQL changes made in the databases after the backup are written to a new logging file. This option makes sense only if the logging files are to be used for an incremental backup.

- --noindices copies for (My)ISAM tables only the actual data, not the index files. (More precisely, the first two kilobytes of the index files are copied. This makes possible an uncomplicated, though slow, restoration of the index files with myisamchk -r. But the backup can be executed more quickly, because fewer data must be copied.)

The options -u, -p, -P, and -S, as well as --user=, --password=, --port=, and --socket= function as they do with all MySQL tools, but with one exception. In the case of -p the password must be given here (while all other tools provide interactive password input, which is more secure).

Restoring a Database

To restore a database you simply copy the entire database directory into MySQL's data directory. If you execute this operation as *root*, you must then specify the owner of the database files with chown. (The owner must have the same account under which mysqld is running, usually *mysql*.)

```
root# chown -R mysql.mysql /usr/local/mysql/var/data/dbname
```

> **CAUTION** *If the database to be restored already exists, the files involved in an operational MySQL cannot simply be overwritten. First execute* DROP DATABASE.
>
>   *It is possible to recreate data only if the version of MySQL that is running is compatible with the version under which the backup was executed. This is the case with the various MySQL versions 3.23n. However, it is not guaranteed that a backup executed with MySQL 3.23 will be able to be restored with MySQL 4.0. (With each change in the main version number the format of database files can conceivably change.).*

Database Migration

The term "migration" applied to databases denotes the transport of a database from one system to another. There are many reasons that can account for the migratory instinct appearing in a database:

- Installation of a new database server

- Transfer of a development system (for example, on a local computer) to a production system (on the ISP's computer)

- A MySQL update (for example, from version 3.22 to 3.23).

- A change in database system (for example, from Microsoft SQL Server to MySQL)

Transfer of Databases Between MySQL Systems

Migration between MySQL systems is generally carried out with the backup tools `mysqldump` and `mysql`, which we have previously described.

If the tables are in MyISAM format and compatible versions of MySQL are running on both computers (say, 3.23n), then the migration can be effected by simply copying the database files. This holds beginning with version 3.23 even if MySQL is running under different operating systems.

MySQL guarantees compatibility of database files within a principal version (for example, from 3.23.32 to 3.23.33), but not between principal versions (3.22 to 3.23, 3.23 to 4.0, etc.).

The main advantage of direct copying as opposed to the use of `mysqldump`/`mysql` is, of course, the much greater speed. Note, however, that you must recreate all the indexes with `myisamchk` if MySQL on the other computer uses a different character set (that is, a different sort order).

> **TIP** *If you wish to change only the format of database files, say from MyISAM to BDB, then you do not need to go through the migration process. The command* ALTER TABLE tblname TYPE=newtype *will be adequate to meet your needs. If you wish to convert a large number of tables, then under Unix/Linux the Perl script* `mysql_convert_table_format` *will save you a great deal of effort. (The script assumes that a connection to the MySQL server can be established.)*

TIP *If you carry out the migration with* mysqldump/mysql, *then you do not necessarily have to create (possibly enormous) files. You can pass the output of* mysqldump *directly to* mysql.

The following command demonstrates the usual way of proceeding. It assumes that the command is executed on the computer with the source database and transports the data to a second computer (hostname destinationhost). *There the database in question must already exist, and the access privileges must allow access to the source computer.*

For space considerations the command is broken over two lines.

```
root# mysqldump -u root --password=xxx --opt sourcedb | \
      mysql -u root --password=yyy -h destinationhost dbname
```

POINTER *A special case of migration, namely setting up a database on an ISP, is described at the end of this chapter. The usual problem in doing this is the possession of inadequate access privileges to the ISP computer.*

MySQL Update from Version 3.22 to Version 3.23

In updating from version 3.22 to 3.23 you must use mysqldump and mysql for transferring the tables. There are also some details to keep track of:

- If you wish to transfer the database *mysql* with access privileges, then you must update this database with the script mysql_fix_privilege_tables. (In MySQL 3.23 certain *mysql* tables were extended with additional columns that were unavailable in version 3.22.)

- If you want a foreign sort order, say *german*, then you must recreate all the indexes (myisamchk -r -q). The sort order has changed in certain details.

- If you have been working with ISAM tables, then a transfer to tables of type MyISAM is to be recommended. For conversion execute *ALTER TABLE tblname TYPE=MYISAM* or use the Perl script mysql_convert_table_format (only under Unix/Linux). (The script assumes that a connection to the database can be established.)

> **TIP** *If it is necessary to transfer tables from MySQL 3.23 to the older version 3.22 (for example, because MySQL 3.22 is still running on your ISP's server), then you must use* mysqldump *without the options* --opt *and* --full.

> **POINTER** *A list of further details that distinguish MySQL 3.22 from 3.23 can be found in the MySQL documentation at the end of the chapter "Installing MySQL."*

Changing the Database System

For migrating to MySQL from another database system or vice versa there is no universal solution. Almost every database system offers a tool, comparable to mysqldump, that represents the contents of the database as an SQL file. The problem is that the resulting files are seldom precisely compatible (for example, due to different column types or lack of ANSI SQL/92 conformity). With *Find and Replace* you can solve some of these problems. Under Unix/Linux the tools awk and sed can be helpful.

For some database systems you will find converters for migration to MySQL at the following address: http://www.mysql.com/downloads/contrib.html

If you are working under Windows, then ODBC is often helpful. For example, you can use Access to import a database of an ODBC-compatible system and then to export it to MySQL. Do not expect, however, that all the details of the definition of the columns will remain intact.

> **POINTER** *Information of the use of MyODBC, the ODBC driver for MySQL, can be found in Chapter 10. There you will also find a description of how to move databases between MySQL and Access. Finally, you will also find there a converter from Microsoft SQL Server to MySQL.*

Importing and Exporting Text Files

Sometimes, the contents of a table should be written as efficiently as possible into an ASCII file or read from such a file. MySQL offers several ways of doing this:

- The SQL command *LOAD DATA* reads in a text file and transfers the contents into a table.

- With `mysqlimport` there is a command available that is equivalent to *LOAD DATA*. It is especially well suited for automating the importation of a script file.

- The SQL command *SELECT . . . INTO OUTFILE* writes the result of a query into a text file.

- If you wish to automate exportation with a script, then the command `mysqldump` is to be recommended. Its functionality is similar to that of *SELECT . . . INTO OUTFILE*.

- In many cases you can use the universal tool `mysql` for implementing text or HTML exportation.

If none of the above commands suits your needs, then you will have to write your own script to assist you in importing or exporting. The programming language Perl was made for such tasks.

Special Characters in the Imported or Exported File

A common feature of *LOAD DATA*, *SELECT . . . INTO OUTFILE*, `mysqlimport`, and `mysqldump` is the set of options for handling special characters in a text file. There are four options for this purpose, which as SQL commands look like this:

```
FIELDS TERMINATED BY 'fieldtermstring'
       ENCLOSED BY 'enclosechar'
       ESCAPED BY 'escchar'
LINES TERMINATED BY 'linetermstring'
```

- *fieldtermstring* specifies the character string that separates the columns within the row (for example, a tab character).

- *enclosechar* specifies a character that is permitted to appear in the text file before and after individual entries (usually a single or double quote character for character strings). If an entry begins with this character, then that character is deleted at the beginning and end. (The end of a column is recognized by *fieldtermstring*.)

- *escchar* specifies the escape character that is to be used to indicate special characters (the default is the backslash). This is necessary if special characters appear in character strings of the text file that are also used for separating rows or columns. Moreover, MySQL expects ASCII code 0 in the form \0 (where the backslash is to be replaced by *escchar*).

- *linetermstring* specifies the character string with which a row is terminated. With DOS/Windows text files the character string '\r\n' must be used.

Working with Character Strings, Numbers, Dates, and BLOBs

For all the commands introduced in this section there is a data format that must be followed exactly. In particular, for importation you must hold to the format expected by MySQL. For exportation you have somewhat more leeway, in that you can use SQL functions for formatting data in the *SELECT* command (such as *DATE_FORMAT* for formatting dates and times).

Moreover, there are four options that you can use to determine how rows and columns should be separated and how character strings and special characters should be indicated. (Details can be found in Chapter 13 under *LOAD DATA* and *SELECT . . . INTO OUTFILE.*

- **Numbers:** For very large and very small numbers in the *FLOAT* and *SINGLE* formats one has the use of scientific notation in the form *-2.3e-037*.

- **Character Strings:** Strings are not changed in importation and exportation (ANSI format, one byte per character). Special characters contained in the character string are marked by default with the backslash in order to distinguish these from the characters used for separation (e.g., tab, *carriage return, linefeed,* etc.).

- **BLOBs:** Binary objects are treated byte for byte like character strings. Neither in importing nor exporting is there the possibility of using hexadecimal character strings (0x123412341234 . . .).

- **Date and Time:** Dates are treated as character strings of the form *2001-12-31*, and times as character strings of the form *23:59:59*. Timestamp values are considered integers of the form *20001231235959*.

- **NULL:** The treatment of *NULL* is problematic. The following text assumes that the backslash is used as the escape character for special characters and the double quote character for indicating a character string. If you use other characters (options *FIELDS ESCAPED BY '?' ENCLOSED BY '?'*), then you will have to reconfigure the following paragraphs.

  In exporting with escape characters, *NULL* is represented by \N. In exporting without escape characters *NULL* is simply represented by the four characters *NULL*. However, *NULL* or \N is placed between double quote characters (though not if they are in a text or BLOB field) and can therefore be distinguished from character strings.

  In importing with escape characters MySQL accepts *NULL*, \N, and *"\N"* as *NULL*. However, *"NULL"* is interpreted as a character string (consisting of the four characters *NULL*).

CAUTION   *If you neither use escape characters for special characters nor employ enclose characters for character strings in importing and exporting, then the condition* NULL *cannot be distinguished from the character string* NULL.

In the character string \N *the N must be uppercase. Note that* \n *is the newline character.*

Importing with `LOAD DATA INFILE`

The syntax of *LOAD DATA* is as follows:

```
LOAD DATA [loadoptions] INFILE 'filename.txt' [duplicateoptions]
  INTO TABLE tablename [importoptions] [IGNORE ignorenr LINES]
  [(columnlist)]
```

The result is that the file `filename.txt` is imported into the table *tablename*. There are various options (see the reference in Chapter 13) that can be given, as well as the column names for the table.

Example 1

The table *importtable1* consists of five columns: one *AUTO_INCREMENT* column (*id*) and the columns *a_double*, *a_datetime*, *a_time*, and *a_text*.

The column name refers to its data type. The Windows text file `import1.txt` is to be imported into this table. (Here ↪ represents a tab character):

```
12.3        ↪   12/31/1999   ↪   17:30   ↪   text
-0.33e-2    ↪   2000/12/31   ↪   11:20   ↪   "text in quotes"
1,23        ↪   31.12.2001   ↪   0:13    ↪   "german text with äöü"
```

The import command looks like this:

```
USE exceptions
LOAD DATA INFILE 'c:\import1.txt'
INTO TABLE importtable1
FIELDS TERMINATED BY '\t'
    ENCLOSED BY '\"'
LINES TERMINATED BY '\r\n'
(a_number, a_date, a_time, a_string)
```

A *SELECT* command demonstrates that the importation was only partially successful. In both the first and third lines the date has been incorrectly interpreted. Moreover, in the third line the decimal number with the German comma for a decimal point has caused problems; namely, the part to the right of the decimal point has gone missing. In sum, take care to obey the MySQL formatting rules to the letter when preparing a file for importation.

```
SELECT * FROM importtable1
```

id	a_number	a_datetime		a_time	a_string
1	12.3	0000-00-00	00:00:00	17:30:00	text
2	-0.0033	2000-12-31	00:00:00	11:20:00	text in quotes
3	1	2031-12-20	01:00:00	00:13:00	german text with äöü

Example 2 (BLOB, NULL)

The starting point for our second example is the table *importtable2* with columns *id* and *a_blob*. The second column is allowed to contain *NULL*.

The following Unix text file is to be imported into this table (again, ↪ represents a tab character):

```
1  ↪ NULL
2  ↪ "NULL"
3  ↪ \N
4  ↪ "\N"
5  ↪ \n
6  ↪ "\n"
7  ↪ 0x414243
8  ↪ "0x414243"
9  ↪ blob blob
10 ↪ "blob blob"
```

The text file is imported with the following command. (By default, the backslash serves as escape character, and the tab sign as column separator.)

```
USE exceptions

TRUNCATE importtable2

LOAD DATA INFILE '/tmp/import2.txt'
INTO TABLE importtable2
FIELDS ENCLOSED BY '\"'
```

In order to analyze the result of the importation in more detail, we shall use *SELECT* * to look into the additional columns *LENGTH(a_blob)* and *ISNULL*. This enables us to distinguish the state *NULL* (length *NULL*) from the character string *NULL* (length 4).

```
SELECT *, LENGTH(a_blob) FROM importtable2
```

id	a_blob	LENGTH(a_blob)	ISNULL(a_blob)
1	NULL	NULL	1
2	NULL	4	0
3	NULL	NULL	1
4	NULL	NULL	1
5		1	0
6		1	0
7	0x414243	8	0
8	0x414243	8	0
9	blob blob	9	0
10	blob blob	9	0

We see that in the first six records *NULL* was treated correctly in only the first, third, and fourth records. In the second record the character string *"NULL"* was stored, while in the fifth and sixth records a newline character was stored.

The attempt to read in a hexadecimal number as a binary object fails. Both times, 0x414243 is interpreted as the character string "0x414243" (and not, as intended in record 7, as hex code for the character string "ABC").

CSV Import

Sometimes, one wishes to import data into MySQL from a spreadsheet program like Excel. Such programs generally offer the possibility to store tables in CSV (comma-separated values) format. In principle, the importation of such files proceeds effortlessly. For files that were created with Excel under Windows, suitable import options look like this:

```
FIELDS TERMINATED BY ',' ENCLOSED BY '\"'
LINES TERMINATED BY '\r\n'
```

In practice, importation usually runs into trouble with the formatting of dates (usually in the form 12/31/2001, about which MySQL is clueless). In particular, with Microsoft software the automatic country-specific formatting of numbers can cause problems, when, for example, Excel suddenly represents a decimal number with a comma instead of a period for the decimal point. In such cases one can get help from a special import script for MySQL (or else you can program your own export filters for Excel).

Importing with `mysqlimport`

If you wish to execute *LOAD DATA* not as an SQL command but through an external program, then MySQL offers the tool `mysqlimport`. (It relies on *LOAD DATA*.)

```
mysqlimport databasename tablename.txt
```

The command reads the specified file into a like-named table of the database *databasename*. (The table name is thus taken from the file name, with the file identifier being eliminated. Thus `mysqlimport db1 authors.txt` imports the data into the table *authors* of the database *db1*.)

Please note that the file normally is read from the file system of the MySQL server. If you are working at another computer and wish to read a file that is located there, you must use the option `--local`. The options `--fields-terminated-by`, `--fields-enclosed-by`, `--fields-escaped-by`, and `--lines-terminated-by` correspond to the SQL options described at the beginning of this section. These options should be placed in quotation marks, for example, `"--fields-enclosed-by=+"`.

To carry out the importation demonstrated in the previous section (example 2) with `mysqlimport`, the file to be imported must first be renamed to correspond with the table name in `importtable2.txt`. Then the following command is necessary:

```
root# mysqlimport --local "--fields-enclosed-by=\"" \ exceptions /tmp/importtable2.txt
```

Under Windows (that is, for importing a Windows text file) the command would look like this (broken into two lines for reasons of space):

```
> mysqlimport --local "--fields-enclosed-by=\"" "--lines-terminated-by=\r\n"
    exceptions c:\importtable2.txt
```

Exporting with SELECT ... INTO OUTFILE

With the command *SELECT . . . INTO OUTFILE* we are dealing with a garden-variety *SELECT*, where before the *FROM* part, *INTO OUTFILE* is used to specify a file name and several possible options.

```
SELECT [selectoptions] columnlist
INTO OUTFILE 'filename.txt' exportoptions
FROM ... WHERE ... GROUP BY ... HAVING ... ORDER BY ... LIMIT ...
```

The result of the query is thus stored in the file `filename.txt`. With *exportoptions* various options can be specified for dealing with special characters (see the reference in Chapter 13).

Example

The following example assumes that there exists a table *exporttable* in the current database that has the following contents (note in particular the field *a_char* in the second data record):

```
SELECT * FROM exporttable
```

id	a_char	a_text	a_blob	a_date	a_time	...
1	char char	text text	blob blob	2001-12-31	12:30:00	
2	' " \ ; +	adsf	NULL	2000-11-17	16:54:54	

...	a_timestamp	a_float	a_decimal	a_enum	a_set
	20001117164643	3.14159	0.012	b	e,g
	20001117165454	-2.3e-037	12.345	b	f,g

The data types of the columns are taken from the column names. The following lines show the result of an *OUTFILE* exportation without special options. The tab character is again indicated by a hooked arrow. The resulting file has only two lines, which for reasons of space are here distributed over four lines:

```
SELECT * INTO OUTFILE '/tmp/testfile.txt'
FROM exporttable
1 ↪ char char ↪ text text ↪ blob blob ↪ 2001-12-31 ↪ 12:30:00 ↪ 20001117164643
  ↪ 3.14159 ↪ 0.012 ↪ b ↪ e,g
2 ↪ ' " \\ ; + ↪ adsf ↪ \N ↪ 2000-11-17 ↪ 16:54:54 ↪ 20001117165454
  ↪ -2.3e-037 ↪ 12.345 ↪ b ↪ f,g
```

In the second attempt a semicolon is used as column separator. All fields are enclosed at beginning and end with a double quote character. As escape character the backslash is used (the default setting). Of particular interest is the behavior with the field *a_char*.

```
' " \ ; +
```

becomes

```
"' \" \\ ; +".
```

The semicolon within the character string remains untouched, since it is clear on account of the double quote character where *a_char* ends. However, the double quote becomes a backslash to ensure that the character is not misinterpreted at the end of the character string.

Please note also that *NULL* is represented as \N, and in fact, without being enclosed in double quotes.

```
SELECT * INTO OUTFILE '/tmp/testfile.txt'
FIELDS TERMINATED BY ';' ENCLOSED BY '\"'
FROM exporttable

1;"char char";"text text";"blob blob";"2001-12-31";"12:30:00";
20001117164643;3.14159;0.012;"b";"e,g"

2;"' \" \\ ; +"; "adsf";\N;"2000-11-17";"16:54:54";
20001117165454;-2.3e-037;12.345;"b";"f,g"
```

In our third attempt a semicolon is again used as a column separator. The plus sign (+) is used as optional field identifier (that is, only with character strings, dates, times, and BLOBs, and not with numbers). Finally, the exclamation mark (!) is used as escape character. Again the most interesting feature is the transformation of *a_char*:

```
' " \ ; +
```

becomes

```
+' " \ ; !++
```

```
SELECT * INTO OUTFILE '/tmp/testfile.txt'
FIELDS TERMINATED BY ':' OPTIONALLY ENCLOSED BY'+' ESCAPED BY '!'
FROM exporttable
```

Now *NULL* becomes *!N* (that is, for *NULL*, too, the changed escape character is used).

```
1;+char char+;+text text+;+blob blob+;+2001-12-31+;+12:30:00+; 20001117164643;
   3.14159;0.012;+b+;+e,g+

2;+' " \ ; !++;+adsf+;!N;+2000-11-17+;+16:54:54+; 20001117165454;
   -2.3e-037;12.345;+b+;+f,g+
```

Basically, we have that the data stored in an ASCII file with *LOAD DATA* can be read again into a table unchanged if the same options are used as with *SELECT . . . INTO OUTFILE*.

Exporting with `mysqldump`

As an alternative to *SELECT . . . INTO OUTFILE* there is the auxiliary program `mysqldump`. This program is actually primarily a backup program (see also earlier in this chapter and the references in Chapter 13).

The program `mysqldump` always stores entire tables (and not the result of a particular *SELECT* query). A further difference is that `mysqldump` normally does not return a text file with the raw data, but entire *INSERT* commands. The resulting file can then later be read in with `mysql`. To use `mysqldump` for text exportation you must specify the option `--tab`.

```
mysqldump --tab=verz [options] databasename tablename
```

With `--tab` a directory is specified. In this directory `mysqldump` stores two files for each table: `tablename.txt` and `tablename.sql`. The `*.txt` file contains the same data as after *SELECT . . . INTO OUTFILE*. The `*.sql` file contains a *CREATE TABLE* command, which allows the table to be recreated.

As with `mysqlimport`, the representation of special characters can be controlled with four options: `--fields-terminated-by`, `--fields-enclosed-by`, `--fields-escaped-by`, and `--lines-terminated-by`. These options are analogous to the SQL options described at the beginning of this section. They should be set in quotation marks (for example, `"--fields-enclosed-by=+"`).

```
C:\> mysqldump -u root -p --tab=c:\tmp "--fields-enclosed-by=\"" exceptions exporttable
Enter password: ******
```

Exporting with `mysql` *in Batch Mode*

The universal tool `mysql` can be used to execute SQL commands in batch mode and store the results in a text file. In contrast to `mysqldump`, `mysql` is distinguished in that the resulting file is actually more or less readable—for human beings, that is. (However, there is no attempt to make the file suitable for a later reexportation.)

```
> mysql -u root --password=xxx --batch "--execute=SELECT * FROM TITLE;"
        databasename > output.txt
```

With the option --execute the SQL command is passed, where the entire option must be placed in quotation marks. In the resulting text file output.txt the columns are separated by tab characters. The first line contains the column headings.

Exchanging Rows and Columns

If a table has many columns, then mysql returns very long rows, which can be difficult to interpret. In this case, instead of --batch you can use the option --vertical. Then each record is divided over several lines, where in each row only one data item is given (this command must be typed on one line).

```
> mysql -u root --password=xxx --vertical
    "--execute=SELECT * FROM titles;" mylibrary > c:\tmp\test.txt
```

The resulting file looks like this:

```
*************************** 1. row ***************************
titleID: 1
  title: Linux, 5th ed.
subtitle: NULL
edition: NULL
 publID: 1
  catID: 1
 langID: NULL
   year: 2000
   isbn: NULL
comment: NULL
*************************** 2. row ***************************
titleID: 2
  title: Definitive Guide to Excel VBA
subtitle: NULL
edition: NULL
 ...
```

Generating HTML Tables

If instead of --batch the option --html is used, then mysql generates an HTML table with column headers (see Figure 11-1). However, the resulting file does not contain any HTML headers. Note as well that `mysql` does not deal with coding of characters outside of the 7-bit ASCII character set.

```
> mysql -u root --password=xxx --html
      "--execute=SELECT * FROM titles;" mylibrary > c:\tmp\test.html
```

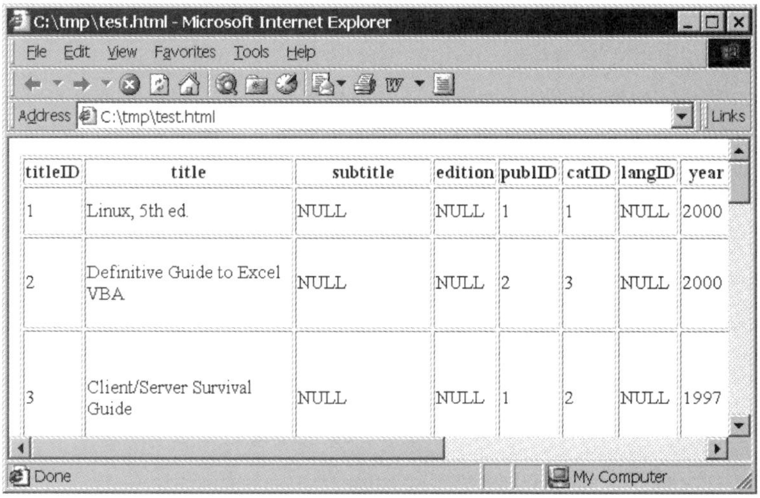

Figure 11-1. A table generated with `mysql`

Logging

The term "logging" generally denotes the recording of each change in a database. (As you will see in the course of this section there are other items that can be recorded as well.) Thus, if a MySQL client program executes the following command:

```
INSERT INTO mydatabase.mytable (col1, col2) VALUES (1, 'xy')
```

then MySQL changes the table *mydatabase.mytable* accordingly. If logging is activated, then the command is also saved as ASCII text in a logging file.

> **POINTER**   *In the MySQL documentation you will find information on the subject of logging in the chapters titled "Maintaining a MySQL installation" and "Solving some common problems."*

Why Logging?

There are various goals that can be achieved through logging:

- **Security:** It is not possible to execute backups uninterruptedly. Thus, for example, if you make a backup one night, and then the next day your hard drive crashes, all that day's changes would be lost. If you have a logging file (naturally, on a different hard drive), then you can recreate the lost data.

  Logging files also help in determining who has used the database when, at what times an unusually large number of failed attempts to access MySQL were made, etc.

- **Monitoring:** Normally, you know only the current state of the data. If your tables contain *TIMESTAMP* columns, then the time of the last change can easily be determined. But it is impossible to determine who made this change. If such information is important for your system, if it should be possible to find out who changed what data when, then you can activate an expanded logging protocol that will capture this additional information.

- **Optimization:** Often, it is difficult to determine which queries are most burdensome to a database system. Therefore, MySQL offers the possibility to log all queries whose execution takes a particularly long time.

Drawbacks

In the default setting almost all logging variants are deactivated. (The only exception is the logging of errors.) The main reason for this deactivation is speed: Logging slows down the operation of MySQL considerably (only, of course, if data are altered frequently).

The second drawback is the tendency of logging files rapidly to consume more and more space on your hard drive. In particular, with database systems in which data are frequently altered, logging files often require significantly more space than the actual database.

Logging Changes to the Database

The standard form of logging—the logging of changes to a database—is activated by the line log-update in the configuration file. MySQL must then be restarted so that the change can become effective.

```
# in /etc/my.cnf or Windows\my.ini
[mysqld]
log-update
```

MySQL now generates a new file, *hostname*.001, in the directory in which the database directories are located. (Instead of *hostname* the name of the computer is given.) All changes are logged in this file. The contents of this file might look something like this:

```
# /usr/local/mysql/libexec/mysqld, Version: 3.23.32-log
# at 010208 8:01:00
use mylibrary;
SET timestamp=981615751;
INSERT INTO titles (title) VALUES ('new book');
SET timestamp=981615944;
INSERT INTO TITLES (title) VALUES ('yet another new book');
 ...
```

MySQL also logs all changes to the database structure (thus, for example, the generation of a new table, adding a new column).

MySQL logs only actual changes. An *UPDATE* that leaves the data unchanged will not be logged.

> **CAUTION** *In the case of ASCII importation of data with* LOAD DATA *only the command itself is logged, not the changes to the database. The logging file can therefore be used for a backup only if the underlying import file is still available.*

Beginning New Logging Files

When you stop and restart the MySQL server, the server automatically begins to fill the next logging file with data (*hostname*.002, .003, etc.). A change in the logging file can, of course, be effected without a server restart, and in fact, with the SQL command *FLUSH LOGS* or with mysqladmin flush-logs.

A suitable time to begin filling new logging files is after the execution of a complete backup. (The new logging file can help later to reconstruct all changes that occurred after the backup.)

Restoring a Database on the Basis of a Logging File

If, perish the thought, misfortune should visit you, then the reconstruction of your database begins with the last full backup to restore the database. Then you employ all your logging files made since the last backup. The SQL commands contained therein are simply executed with mysql. (Be careful to follow the correct order. The oldest logging file must be executed first.)

```
root# mysql -u root -p < hostname.031
root# mysql -u root -p < hostname.032
root# mysql -u root -p < hostname.033
```

Determining the Location of the Logging File

You can determine the location of the logging file yourself. (For reasons of security and speed the logging files should be located on a different hard drive from that on which the database resides.) For this you specify the file name with the option *log-update*. MySQL extends the file name with *.nnn* (that is, with a three-digit running integer).

Please make sure that the MySQL server, which under Unix/Linux is usually executed as user *mysql*, has writing privileges in the specified directory (here /var/log/mysql).

```
# in /etc/my.cnf or Windows\my.ini
[mysqld]
log-update = /var/log/mysql/updates
```

Extended Logging

If you wish not only the changes to be logged, but the time and user (*user@host*) as well, then specify the option *log-long-format*. The supplementary information is indicated in the file as commentary (character #).

```
# in /etc/my.cnf or Windows\my.ini
[mysqld]
log-long-format
```

Binary Logging

Logging files are usually produced in text format. In order to save time and space you can instead use a binary format. To do this you specify log-bin instead of log-update in the configuration file. If a file name is not specified, the logging files are created in the database directory. They have the name *hostname-bin.nnn*. Moreover, a list of binary logging files is stored in the file *hostname-bin.index*.

> **REMARK** *In principle, it is possible to use both* log-bin *and* log-update. *Then logging takes place simultaneously in text and binary modes. This is, of course, particularly slow, but it can serve as a test mode if you do not entirely trust binary logging. (This feature is still relatively new and therefore not as well tested as other features of MySQL.)*

With binary logging the time of each change, the client thread ID number, and certain other parameters are recorded. (If you wish to know which users are hidden behind these ID numbers, you must activate a further logging file with the option log, in which each login to the MySQL server is recorded.)

Logging files can be viewed with mysqlbinlog logfile. If you use the option -s or --short, then only the relevant SQL commands are displayed, and not the additional comments.

To recreate a database on the basis of binary logging files you use the following command:

```
root# mysqlbinlog logfile | mysql -u root -p
```

Logging and Transactions

> **CAUTION** *If you employ a table type that supports transactions, you must use binary logging. With traditional logging you will find* BEGIN, COMMIT, *and* ROLLBACK *simply ignored (that is, not logged). All other SQL commands will be logged at once. Therefore, even those SQL commands withdrawn by* ROLLBACK *will remain in the log.*
>
> *On the other hand, with binary logging, changes will be logged only when the transaction has been completed with* COMMIT.

Logging Files for Various Table Types

The logging procedure described in this section works for all table types (it is independent of type). However, some table types require their own logging files.

For example, if you are working with BDB tables, then the file log.0000000001 is automatically generated in the database directory. The small amount of available information on the topic of BDB is collected in Chapter 12.

Logging Errors, Logins, and Slow Queries

Logging Errors

MySQL automatically logs each launch and shutdown of the MySQL server as well all server error messages in the file hostname.err in the database directory (Windows: mysql.err). There is no option whereby this error logging can be prevented. It appears to be equally as impossible to set the location of the log file.

Logging Logins and Operations

With the option log you can enable the logging of each connection to MySQL as well as every command. If you do not specify a file name, then MySQL creates the file hostname.log in the database directory. The resulting file is not for the purpose of restoring data but for keeping track of which users are looking at and changing what data, etc.

```
# in /etc/my.cnf or Windows\my.ini
[mysqld]
log
```

The following lines show a small section of such a log:

```
/usr/local/mysql/libexec/mysqld, Version: 3.23.32-log, started with:
Tcp port: 3306 Unix socket: /tmp/mysql.sock
```

Time	Id	Command	Argument
010208 13:35:03	1	Connect	root@localhost on test
	1	Query	show databases
	1	Query	show tables
	1	Field List	importtest
	1	Query	load data infile ...
010208 13:35:39	2	Connect	user@localhost on testmigration
	2	Query	show databases
	2	Field List	authors
010208 13:49:56	1	Query	select * from titles
010208 13:50:01	1	Query	select * from authors

Logging Slow Queries

If MySQL is becoming painfully slow due to the burden of complex queries, it is often useful to undertake an analysis to find out which *SELECT* queries are actually causing the greatest delays. To do this, use the option `log-slow-queries`. Then MySQL will create a logging file with the name *hostname*-slow.log. All queries whose execution takes longer than ten seconds will be logged. (You can change the time limit by setting the variable `long_query_time`.)

```
# in /etc/my.cnf or Windows\my.ini
[mysqld]
log-slow-queries
set-variable = long_query_time=5
```

Administration of Logging files

Logging files are like children: It is easier to create them than to take care of them, and furthermore, they grow on you. And just as children will take over your life if you aren't careful, your logging files will very quickly fill even the largest hard drive if you don't take prophylactic measures. So here is a bit of advice:

- Do not log more than is absolutely necessary.

- Use binary format if possible for update logs.

Update Logs

With `mysqladmin flush-logs` or the SQL command *FLUSH LOGS* you achieve that MySQL closes the currently active logging file and begins a new update logging file (with a new running number).

You have unrestricted access to all update logging files with the exception of the currently active file. You can thus move these files to another directory, compress them, and even delete them (for example, if they exceed a certain age or if they are older than the last complete backup). Under Unix/Linux you can develop a cron job to automate this task.

Logins and Slow Queries

With logging files for logins and operations (option `log`) and for slow queries (option `log-slow-queries`) there is a problem in that there is only one file, which gradually grows larger and larger. The MySQL documentation recommends that you simply rename these files while MySQL is running and then execute `mysqladmin flush-logs` or *FLUSH LOGS*:

```
root# cd logpath
root# mv hostname.log hostname.log.old
root# mv hostname-slow.log hostname-slow.old
root# mysqladmin flush-logs
```

The `*.old` files can now be compressed and eventually deleted.

Error Logging

Alas, neither `mysqladmin flush-logs` nor *FLUSH LOGS* has any effect on the logging file for error messages (`hostname.err`). Therefore, it is impossible to manipulate this file while MySQL is running. If this file becomes too large (which is seldom the case), you must stop MySQL, rename the file, and then restart MySQL.

Maintenance of MyISAM Tables

The command `myisamchk` is, in a sense, a universal tool for the maintenance of MyISAM tables. With this command you can accomplish the following:

- Check the integrity of MyISAM tables.

- Repair damaged MyISAM table files (e.g., after a power outage).

- Release unused storage space in MyISAM files.

- Recreate the index to MyISAM tables (for example, after a change in the sort order of the MySQL server).

Instead of `myisamchk` you can also use the following SQL commands:

- *ANALYZE TABLE* provides information about internal index management.

- *CHECK TABLE* tests the table file for errors in consistency.

- *OPTIMIZE TABLE* optimizes the use of storage space in tables.

- *REPAIR TABLE* attempts to repair defective tables.

These commands currently work only for MyISAM tables. However, it is possible that their effectiveness will someday extend to other types of tables. The advantage of the SQL commands over myisamchk is that you do not need to worry about the MySQL server and myisamchk interfering with each other. The disadvantage is that the MySQL server must be running (which may be problematic after a crash), that under some circumstances not all errors can be corrected, that there are fewer options for control of the process, and that the SQL commands are somewhat slower in their execution.

An extension to myisamchk is the command myisampack, with which MyISAM tables can be compressed. In this way a great deal of space can be saved. However, only read access to such tables is then possible. At the end of this section we shall have more to say about myisampack.

> **POINTER** *A reference to all options of* myisamchk *and* myisampack *can be found in Chapter 14. Further information on the use of* myisamchk *can be found in the MySQL documentation, in the chapter "Maintaining a MySQL Installation."*

Using myisamchk

The syntax of the myisamchk command is as follows:

```
myisamchk [options] tablename1 tablename2 ...
```

The table names are given as complete file names, either with or without the ending *.MYI (but, surprisingly, not with *.MYD). Depending on the options specified, however, both MyISAM files, that is, name.MYD (data) and name.MYI (indexes), are analyzed or changed.

To check on the integrity of all tables in the database *mydatabase* you should execute the following command. (You must, of course, replace /usr/local/mysql/var with your actual database directory.)

```
root# myisamchk /usr/local/mysql/var/mydatabase/*.MYI
```

You can use myisamchk independently of the MySQL server (the server may be running, but it does not have to be). If the server is running, then mysqladmin flush-tables or the SQL command *FLUSH TABLES* must be executed first.

> **CAUTION** *If* myisamchk *actually changes MyISAM files and not just checks them, it must be ensured that the MySQL server does not change any data during this time.*
>
> *Therefore, you must execute if necessary the SQL command* LOCK TABLES *with* mysql, *followed by* myisamchk, *and then, finally,* UNLOCK TABLES. *You must not leave* mysql *during this time, since otherwise, the* LOCKs *would end.*

Speed Optimization, Memory Usage

In the case of large tables the analysis, and even more the repair, of tables is a very costly operation. The speed of myisamchk depends greatly on the amount of available RAM.

The memory usage of myisamchk is set by four variables. In the default setting, myisamchk requires about three megabytes of RAM. If you have more memory to squander, then you should raise the values of the appropriate variables, since then myisamchk will execute much more quickly for large tables. The MySQL documentation recommends the following values:

```
root# myisamchk  -O sort_buffer_size=xM -O key_buffer_size=xM \
                 -O read_buffer_size=1M -O write_buffer_size=1M ...
```

Here x should represent about one-fourth of available RAM (e.g., 64 MB on a 256-MB computer).

Furthermore, for repairing database files myisamchk requires a huge amount of space on the hard drive (among other reasons, because a copy of the database file is first made). A copy of the file is placed in the directory specified by the environment variable TMPDIR. You can also specify this directory via --tmpdir.

Shrinking and Optimizing MyISAM Tables

The MyISAM table driver attempts, normally, to keep table files as small as possible. However, if you delete a large number of records from your tables or if you often carry out changes to records with columns of variable size (*VARCHAR, xxxTEXT, xxxBLOB*), then the optimization algorithm runs up against its limit. In the worst case the database files are significantly larger than necessary. Moreover, the data are scattered throughout the file, which slows down access to the database.

The following command provides some assistance. It regenerates the database file and optimizes the index file in view of providing the speediest access to the database. With the options --set-character-set and --character-sets-dir the character set is specified for the sort order. (You must be dealing with the same character set with which the MySQL server is running.) The effect of --check-only-changed is that only those tables are processed that were changed since the last processing by myisamchk. (For space reasons the command has been split using a backslash over several lines.)

```
root# myisamchk --recover --check-only-changed --sort-index \
      --analyze --set-character-set=german1 \
      --character-sets-dir=charsetpath databasepath/*.MYI
```

> **TIP** *If you would like to check the performance of* myisamchk, *create a test database and then delete at random about half of the data records:*
> ```
> DELETE FROM testtable WHERE RAND()>0.5
> ```

Repairing MyISAM Tables

For me, this section is largely of a theoretical nature, because fortunately, I have thus far had no problems with corrupt MyISAM tables. Corrupted files can arise when the database is stopped by a power failure, when MySQL or the operating system crashes, or if MySQL or the MyISAM table driver contains errors (which is not improbable in the case of developmental versions of MySQL).

Damaged MyISAM files make themselves known in MySQL service by error messages like *Index-file/Record-file/Table is crashed* or *No more room in index/record file*. In such a case myisamchk will not, of course, be able to work a miracle. Data that for some reason are no longer available or have been overwritten cannot be restored. However, myisamchk can repair the database to the extent that at least all other records can again be read.

```
root# myisamchk --recover --set-character-set=german1 \
      --character-sets-dir=charsetpath databasepath/*.MYI
```

If you suspect that only the index file has been affected, then execute myisamchk with the additional option --quick (which is considerably faster). In this case myisamchk regenerates the index file.

In particularly difficult cases, that is, when myisamchk --recover fails, you can attempt recovery with --safe-recover. However, that will take much longer than --recover.

If MySQL is running with a character set other than the standard latin1, you must specify the character set for sorting with the options --character-sets-dir and --set-character-set.

Restoring or Creating a New MyISAM Index

If you change the character set of the MySQL server (for which a restart is necessary), then you must generate new indexes for all your tables. The command for doing so looks like this:

```
root# myisamchk --recover --quick --set-character-set=german1 \
      --character-sets-dir=charsetpath databasepath/*.MYI
```

Compressing MyISAM Tables (myisampack)

If you exclusively read (but do not change) large tables, then it is a good idea to compress your files. Not only does this save space, but in general, it speeds up access (since larger portions of the table can reside in the file buffer of the operating system).

```
root# myisampack databasepath/*.MYI
```

Although with myisampack the identifier *.MYI is specified for the index file, the command changes only the data file *.MYD. To uncompress compressed table files you should execute myisamchk with the option --unpack.

ISP Database Administration

Up to now we have assumed that you have installed MySQL on your own computer and have unrestricted access to the server. And indeed, this is the usual starting point for every database administrator.

However, with MySQL the situation can be a bit different. Often, your database is located on the computer of an Internet service provider. There you have almost no administrative privileges. That is, the ISP administers MySQL on its own. (If you have a responsible ISP, it will automatically carry out backups of your databases, but don't count on it.) Nonetheless, you will have to carry out certain administrative tasks:

- Create new databases (provided that the ISP permits this).

- Execute backups. (Even if your ISP does this regularly, it is good to be able to be responsible for your own data.)

- Execute a database upload. (For example, you have developed a database application on your own computer and now wish to transfer the completed database to the ISP computer.)

Working via telnet/ssh

Administration is at its simplest when your ISP provides you with telnet access (or ssh access, which would be more secure). Then you can log into the ISP's computer and use all of the commands introduced in this chapter. Needless to say, with commands such as mysqldump you can access only your own databases. But that should suffice. For moving files between your local computer and that of the ISP, you can use ftp.

Unfortunately, only few ISPs offer their clients access via telnet or ssh (or only for a large additional fee), since this means extra work for the ISP and greater security risks.

Working via phpMyAdmin

Probably the most popular solution to this administrative problem is offered by phpMyAdmin, a collection of PHP scripts installed in a www directory on the ISP's computer. In principle, phpMyAdmin is suited for all the administrative tasks mentioned above. In practice, however, there are problems in two areas:

- There are often problems with database uploading if certain special characters are used in the database.

- For PHP scripts—and thus for phpMyAdmin as well—there is a time limit. If the execution of a script exceeds the allotted time, the script is automatically terminated. In most cases this limit represents a sensible protective measure against programmer error (such as infinite loops), but unfortunately, this limit makes the backup or upload of a large database impossible.

Implementing Custom PHP Scripts for Administration

Instead of working with phpMyAdmin you can, of course, program your own PHP scripts for administration and store them in a directory on your web site. For example, you can execute a backup of a database with a PHP file of the following design:

```
<?php system("/usr/bin/mysqldump --host=hostname --user=username " .
             "--password=xxx dbname > backup.sql"); ?>
```

Instead of /usr/bin you may have to specify a different path (for example, /usr/local/bin). In some circumstances things will work without a path name being specified. As *hostname* you can use *localhost* if the web server and MySQL are running on the same computer.

After you have loaded the page via your web browser (and thereby executed the script), you can transfer the file backup.sql, which is located in the same directory as the script, to your computer, again via the web browser or FTP.

Conversely, for an upload you first transfer via FTP the file upload.sql generated on your computer into the directory in which your PHP administration scripts are located. Then you execute a script via your web browser according to the following pattern:

```
<?php system("/usr/bin/mysql --host=hostname --user=username " .
            "--password=xxx dbname < upload.sql"); ?>
```

For the upload to succeed the specified database must already exist. If that is not the case, you can first create the database with `mysqladmin` (which you also execute in the PHP script via *system*).

If you have previously created `upload.sql` with `mysqldump`, then the database at the ISP may not contain the tables defined in `upload.sql`. If necessary, you must insert some *DROP TABLE IF EXISTS* commands in `upload.sql`.

In comparison to phpMyAdmin, the advantage of this way of proceeding is that no time is lost in the transfer of the database files over the Internet. Instead, the upload file is read from the local computer, or the download file is written there. However, this does not change anything in regard to the time limit for PHP scripts. Of course, you can transport somewhat larger databases with the method presented here than with phpMyAdmin, but sooner or later you will find yourself nose to nose with the PHP time limit.

> **POINTER** *Do not forget to secure access to the directory with your administrative scripts with* `.htaccess`. *The use of* `.htaccess` *is described in Chapter 2.*

Custom Perl Scripts for Administration

What works with PHP works also, of course, with Perl, and often better. The advantage of Perl is that in the execution of CGI scripts there is often no time limit. (But this depends on the provider.)

In Perl, too, there is a *system* function for calling external commands. In the lines below there is also code added that evaluates and displays the return value of this function. The `mysqldump` and `mysql` commands look exactly the same in the PHP scripts presented above. Even the preparatory work is identical.

```
#!/usr/bin/perl -w
use CGI qw(:standard);
use CGI::Carp qw(fatalsToBrowser);
print header(), start_html("Backup");
if(system("/usr/bin/mysqldump --host=hostname --user=username " .
          "--password=xxx dbname > backup.sql")) {
  print p(), "failed", end_html(); }
else {
  print p(), "done", end_html(); }
```

MySQL for Pros

AS INDICATED BY THE TITLE, this chapter is directed at the advanced MySQL user. Among the topics covered in this chapter are international customizing of MySQL (in particular setting the sort order); the use of full-text indexes; compilation of MySQL, use of BDB, InnoDB, and Gemini tables (transactions); as well as the setting up of a replication system.

Chapter Overview

International Customization, Character Sets

In the default setting of the binary distribution of MySQL (which is included in most Linux distributions) MySQL delivers error messages in English, uses the `latin1` character set (ISO-8859-1), and sorts texts according to the Swedish rules. For applications in the English-speaking world this default setting is as it should be. (The peculiarities of the Swedish sorting rules have to do with characters outside of the 7-bit ASCII character set and do not affect the sorting of normal English text.)

Error Messages in Other Languages

If you wish to have your MySQL server deliver its error messages in a language other than English, say German or French, then you have merely to set the option `language` in one of the configuration files. The language selected is also used for entries in the error logging file `hostname.err`.

MySQL currently supports about twenty languages. A glance at the directory `mysql/share/` will tell you their names. If, for example, you find German error messages more to your liking than the English ones, then make the following change in the MySQL configuration file:

```
# in windows\my.ini or /etc/my.cnf
[mysqld]
language = german
```

> **TIP** *Do not forget that you must restart the server for the changes to take effect. If MySQL does not find the file with the error messages, you can also give the entire path name with* language, *as, for example (under Windows),* Q:/Program Files/mysql/share/german

Default Sort Order (Swedish)

With MySQL the character set not only determines the relationship between characters and their codes, but also influences the way that character strings are compared and sorted. Other SQL functions, those for which a case distinction is made, are influenced as well by the character set.

In the default setting MySQL uses the ISO-8859-1 character set with Swedish sort order. This default setting is practicable only if you are storing English or, of course, Swedish texts in your database.

The following commands demonstrate how you can test the influence of the character set on some elementary SQL commands. Please note how *UCASE* transforms *abcäå* correctly into uppercase characters, but not *öüêõ*. A comparison between *a* and *ä* returns 0 (i.e., *false*).

```
SELECT UCASE('abc äöü âêõ')
  ABC Äöü Âêõ
SELECT 'a'='A', 'a'='ä', 'ä'='Ä', 'ö'='Ö', 'ü'='Ü'
 'a'='A'    'a'='ä'    'ä'='Ä'    'ö'='Ö'    'ü'='Ü'
  _____
   1          0          1          1          1
```

Recall the database *exceptions* that we created in Chapter 5 to check the sort order of MySQL. The table *test_order_by* of this test database has with 255 records, with columns *id*, which contains character codes, and *a_char*, which contains the characters that match these codes. The result of the following query is here presented not in the usual columnar format, but in comma-separated rows. Various special characters and nonrepresentable characters were deleted from the result (and replaced by ...).

Please note that some variants of the letter A have been placed between A and B, while Å, Ä, and Ö appear after Z (corresponding to the Swedish sort order).

```
USE exceptions
SELECT a_char FROM test_order_by
WHERE id>31
ORDER BY a_char
!, ", #, $, %, &, ', (, ), *, +, ,, -, ., /, 0, 1, 2, 3, 4, 5, 6, 7,
8, 9, :, ;, <, =, >, ?, @,
A, a, À, Á, Â, Ã, À, á, â, ã, B, b, C, c, Ç, ç, D, d, …, …, E, e, È,
É, Ê, Ë, è, é, ê, ë, F, f, G, g, H, h, I, i, Ì, Í, Î, Ï, ì, í, î, ï,
J, j, K, k, L, l, M, m, N, n, Ñ, ñ, O, o, Ò, Ó, Ô, Õ, ò, ó, ô, õ, P,
p, Q, q, R, r, S, s, T, t, U, u, Ù, Ú, Û, ù, ú, û, V, v, W, w, X, x,
Y, y, Ü, Ý, ü, ý, Z, z, [, Å, å, \, Ä, Æ, ä, æ, ], Ö, ö, …,
ƒ, …, Š, …, Ž, …, š, …, ž, Ÿ, …, …, …, ÿ, …
```

Setting the Sort Order

If you prefer a different sort order, you must change the option `default-character-set` in the MySQL configuration file (in the following example this is done for the German sort order). You will find a *.conf file for each supported character set in the directory `mysql/share/charsets`. If MySQL cannot find this directory, you must specify the location with the option `character-sets-dir`.

```
# in windows\my.ini or /etc/my.cnf
[mysqld]
character-sets-dir = Q:/Program Files/mysql/share/charsets
default-character-set = german1
```

For the settings to become effective the server must be restarted.

> **REMARK**   *The option* default-character-set *is not particularly well named. It does not set the character set, but rather a combination of character set and sort order. For example, if you wish to set* german1, *then the ISO-8859-1 character set will be used as in the default setting, but with a different sort order.*

> **REMARK**   *At present, MySQL can cope only with 1-byte character sets. The setting of the character set holds for all tables and all clients. It is impossible to set the sort order for each table (or database). In particular, you as MySQL user have no say in the sort order: Only the MySQL administrator can change it. (In other words, if MySQL is running at the site of an ISP, you will have to make do with the sort order in force there.)*

Resetting Indexes

Of course, the character set influences the sort order of table indexes. Therefore, you must reset all the table indexes after a change in the character set. Under Unix/Linux the command looks like this:

```
root# myisamchk --recover --quick --set-character-set=german1 \
        --character-sets-dir=charsetpath mysqlpath/data/*/*.MYI
```

You must, of course, adapt the desired character set, the path to the character set files, and the path to the database files to your own circumstances. On my test system the complete command looks like this:

```
root# myisamchk --recover --quick --set-character-set=german1 \
     --character-sets-dir=/usr/local/mysql/share/mysql/charsets \
     /usr/local/mysql/var/*/*.MYI
```

> **POINTER**   *While* myisamchk *is being executed the server must not make any changes in the database. (The easiest way to ensure this condition is to stop the server.) Further information on* myisamchk *is to be found in Chapter 11.*

Client Configuration

The MySQL server informs its clients as to which character set it is using. However, the problem often occurs that the client (e.g., mysql) needs the character set table but cannot find it. In most cases the following lines in the MySQL configuration file solves the problem:

```
# in Windows\my.ini or /etc/my.cnf
[mysql]
character-sets-dir = Q:/Program Files/mysql/share/charsets
```

If you are working under Windows with MyODBC, you must copy the character set files into the directory C:\mysql\share\charsets. (You may need to create this directory.) MyODBC is not capable of evaluating the MySQL configuration files, and therefore always looks in this predefined place for the character set files.)

Tests with default-character-set=german1

In what follows the SQL test commands will be executed once again. It turns out that *UCASE* now transforms *ö* and *ü* correctly and that *a* and *ä* are viewed as equivalent for the purpose of sorting. Furthermore, the sort position of some letters has been changed.

```
SELECT UCASE('abc äöü åêõ')
  ABC ÄÖÜ ÅÊÕ
SELECT 'a'='A', 'a'='ä', 'ä'='Ä', 'ö'='Ö', 'ü'='Ü'
```

'a'='A'	'a'='ä'	'ä'='Ä'	'ö'='Ö'	'ü'='Ü'
1	1	1	1	1

```
USE exceptions
SELECT a_char FROM test_order_by
WHERE id>31
ORDER BY a_char
```

```
!, ", #, $, %, &, ', (, ), *, +, ,, -, ., /, 0, 1, 2, 3, 4, 5, 6, 7, 8,
9, :, ;, <, =, >, ?, @,
A, a, À, Á, Â, Ã, Ä, Å, Æ, à, á, â, ã, ä, å, æ, B, b, C, c, Ç, ç, D, d, E, e,
È, É, Ê, Ë, è, é, ê, ë, F, f, G, g, H, h, I, i, Ì, Í, Î, Ï, ì, í, î, ï, J, j,
K, k, L, l, M, m, N, n, Ñ, ñ, O, o, Ò, Ó, Ô, Õ, Ö, Ø, ò, ó, ô, õ, ö, ø, P, p, Q, q,
R, r, S, s, …, T, t, U, u, Ù, Ú, Û, Ü, ù, ú, û, ü, V, v, W, w, X, x, Y, y, …, …, Z, z,
Š, …, š, …, ž, Ÿ, ÿ
```

Full-Text Search, Full-Text Index

If you are using SQL to search for a word in a character string, the query is often posed in the following form:

```
SELECT * FROM table WHERE column LIKE '%word%'
```

This query indeed achieves its goal. The only question is, when? There are few queries that are more time-consuming for MySQL to answer than this. (What is worse is searching for several words, perhaps in several columns.) It is not only that all the records of the table must be read. Additionally, many character string comparisons must be made. A traditional index cannot help you here.

Unfortunately, what is most difficult for the computer is simple for the user, who has become accustomed to using an Internet search machine to input a number of search terms without having to deal with complex search criteria.

If you wish to be able to process such queries efficiently in MySQL, you need a *full-text index*. This is a particular type of index, one that creates a list of all words that appear in a column of a table. MySQL has supported this type of index since version 3.23.23.

> **POINTER** *Further information on the topic of full-text indexes and full-text search can be found in the MySQL documentation in the chapter "MySQL Internals."*

Generating a Full-Text Index

To provide an existing table with a full-text index you should execute the following command. You may specify arbitrarily many *xxxTEXT* and *(VAR)CHAR* columns.

```
ALTER TABLE tablename ADD FULLTEXT (columnname1, columnname2)
```

Of course, new tables can also be generated at once with a full-text index:

```
CREATE TABLE tablename (col1, col2, FULLTEXT (col1, col2))
```

Full-Text Search

For a full-text search the SQL expression *MATCH AGAINST* is used:

```
SELECT * FROM table
WHERE MATCH (columnname1, columnname2) AGAINST ('word1 word2 word3')
```

The result is that all data records are found in which at least one of the three words *word1, word2, word3* is contained. The list of columns in *MATCH* must correspond exactly to the one with which the index was generated.

The expression *MATCH (columns) AGAINST (' words')* can be used not only in the *WHERE* condition, but also in other parts of a *SELECT* query. *MATCH* returns a value whose size is in direct relation to the degree of agreement of the search criteria with the data record. Words that appear seldom in the table have a higher value with *MATCH*. Likewise, words have a higher value if they appear in a short text or if they appear several times in a text.

MATCH returns 0 if none of the words is found or if the search text appears in very many records and thus can be ignored. (Words of three letters or fewer are generally ignored, and the search is case-insensitive.) *MATCH* works well with large tables, but with small tables it often returns results that are difficult to evaluate.

For the following example the column *title* of the table *titles* from the *mylibrary* database is equipped with a full-text index. Then the ten best hits of the search for *excel* or *basic* are returned.

```
USE mylibrary
ALTER TABLE titles ADD FULLTEXT (title)
SELECT title, MATCH (title) AGAINST ('excel basic') AS fulltextmatch
FROM titles
WHERE MATCH (title) AGAINST ('excel basic')
ORDER BY fulltextmatch DESC
LIMIT 10
```

title	fulltextmatch
Microsoft Excel 2000 Visual Basic for Applications	4.1628470025601
Visual Basic	2.7304086712709
Visual Basic Datenbankprogrammierung	2.7000560462937
VBA-Programmierung mit Excel 7	1.6664204590726
Definitive Guide to Excel VBA	1.6478956734678
Excel 2000 programmieren	1.6478956734678
Excel 2000 Formulas	1.6478956734678
Excel 2000 For Windows For Dummies	1.6297782459791
Microsoft Excel 2000 Power Programming with VBA	1.6120549671889
Microsoft Excel 2000: Step by Step	1.389070650218

In the above query the *WHERE* condition is actually unnecessary, since *LIMIT 10* limits the list of results. However, the *WHERE* condition makes the query significantly more efficient, since from the outset only records with *fulltextmatch>0* are considered. (Otherwise, first all records are returned, and only then are all records sorted, after which most of them are then discarded.)

Please note as well that it is unfortunately not possible to formulate the condition as *WHERE fulltextmatch*. No alias names are allowed in the *WHERE* clause.

Full-Text Search over Several Tables

A full-text search can be defined only for a single table. Since it is in the nature of relational databases that data are distributed over several tables, this restriction can be rather a painful one. For example, with the *mylibrary* database it would be practical to search for author and title simultaneously. The search *excel kofler*, for example, should return my book on Excel that is stored in the database.

The apparent solution consists in simply equipping all the tables with a full-text index and then in the query specifying *MATCH* expressions for each index. However, the resulting queries are relatively inefficient (especially with large data sets).

```
USE mylibrary
ALTER TABLE titles ADD FULLTEXT (title)
ALTER TABLE authors ADD FULLTEXT (authName)
SELECT title, authname FROM titles, authors, rel_title_author
WHERE titles.titleID = rel_title_author.titleID
  AND authors.authID = rel_title_author.authID
  AND MATCH (title) AGAINST ('excel kofler')
  AND MATCH (authName) AGAINST ('excel kofler')
```

title	authname
VBA-Programmierung mit Excel 7	Kofler Michael
Excel 2000 programmieren	Kofler Michael
Definitive Guide to Excel VBA	Kofler Michael

If *titles* contained, say, 100 thousand titles and *authors* as many author names, then the above query would be somewhat slow despite the full-text index. It would be more efficient to store the relevant data in a single table. In the following example *titles* must be expanded to include an *authors* column with author names. It is precisely this that was suggested in Chapter 5 as a possible change in database design.

The following example assumes that the table has been changed as suggested and that the *authors* column has been filled with data. In this case a full-text index can be defined for both columns.

```
USE mylibrary
ALTER TABLE titles ADD FULLTEXT (title, authors)
```

The following query now returns all titles that either were written by *kofler* or are about *excel* (thus more titles than anticipated):

```
SELECT title, authors FROM titles
WHERE MATCH (title, authors) AGAINST ('excel kofler')
```

title	authors
VBA-Programmierung mit Excel 7	Kofler Michael
MySQL	Kofler Michael
Linux, 5th ed.	Kofler Michael
Excel 2000 programmieren	Kofler Michael
Definitive Guide to Excel VBA	Kofler Michael; Kramer David
...	

It therefore makes sense to order the results by relevance:

```
SELECT title, authors FROM titles
WHERE MATCH (title, authors) AGAINST ('excel kofler')
ORDER BY MATCHtitle, authors) AGAINST ('excel kofler') DESC
LIMIT 5
```

title	authors
VBA-Programmierung mit Excel 7	Kofler Michael
Excel 2000 programmieren	Kofler Michael
Definitive Guide to Excel VBA	Kofler Michael; Kramer David
Excel 2000 Formulas	NULL
Excel 2000 For Windows For Dummies	NULL

Limitations

- A full-text search is based on complete words. Every little alteration (plural, conjugational endings) is considered another word. This makes searches more difficult. (It could be worse: At least there is no case distinction.)

  To find all relevant records, then, variants must be specified in *AGAINST* (e.g., *AGAINST('book books')*).

  In the sense of a full-text search a *word* is a piece of text consisting of letters, numbers, and the single quote and underscore characters. Such accented letters as é and ü are also considered letters.

- Words must be at least four letters long to be considered. Thus an abbreviation like SQL cannot be searched for.

- The words in the search expression are joined by a Boolean OR. Other Boolean operators, like AND, are not possible.

- A full-text search is limited to a single table. (Possible ways of circumventing this limitation were described above.)

- Currently, full-text search is available only for MyISAM tables (and not for BDB, InnoDB, and Gemini tables).

- Creating a full-text index is slow. This affects not only the initial setup of the index, but also all further changes in the table.

- Full-text searching is a relatively new MySQL feature, and thus not completely mature. Frequent reports of problems appear on the MySQL mailing list (from little nitpicking stuff all the way up to the server crashing).

A Peek at MySQL 4.0

Although MySQL 4.0 was not ready as this text was being written, the MySQL documentation already provides information about the proposed extensions for full-text search in some detail.

Many changes relate to the internal management of the index. From the outside these changes will be noticeable in increased speed (both in creating the index and in searching). Furthermore, there are also proposed extensions that affect the search string (that is, the character string in *AGAINST*):

+word   This word must be contained in the record. Thus
        AGAINST(' +word1 +word2') amounts to a Boolean
        AND for the two search criteria.

-word   This word must not be contained in the data record.

<word   This word is given a lower valuation.

>word   This word is given a higher valuation.

~word   This word is to be ignored.

Compiling MySQL

MySQL is available in binary form for most operating systems (that is, already compiled). Therefore, compiling MySQL yourself is necessary only if you are not satisfied with the options that were chosen when the binary package was compiled or if you wish to use particular table types or other features of MySQL that are not included by default in the compiled version.

> **REMARK**   *The following lines describe the compilation and running of MySQL 3.23.37 under SuSE Linux 7.1. It is assumed that the compiler and other development tools have already been installed.*
>
> *The procedure described here should also work in principle for recent versions of MySQL and for most other Unix operating systems. Tips for compilation under Windows and other operating systems can be found in the MySQL documentation.*

Code for the Table Types BDB, InnoDB, and Gemini

Since version 3.23.34 the source code for MySQL has contained the driver for the new table types BDB, InnoDB, and Gemini, to the extent that they are available for a particular operating system. Here is the situation as of version 3.23.37:

- **Unix code:** including BDB and InnoDB, but still without Gemini

- **Windows code:** none of the new table drivers

According to the promises of the MySQL development team, code for Unix/Gemini, Windows/BDB, and Windows/InnoDB will be available in the very nearest future—probably before this book has reached your hands. Please note, however, that these new table types cannot yet be compiled under all Unix dialects and that they do not function equally reliably.

> **CAUTION**   *The code for the table types BDB/InnoDB/Gemini is not as mature and stable as that for MyISAM tables. You would do well to wait until the MySQL team declares the new table drivers* stable *before using them in a production system.*

Compilation of MySQL

Preparations

If you have already installed MySQL, you should stop execution, back up all databases, and then deinstall MySQL.

You will find the source code for MySQL at www.mysql.com/downloads under *Source downloads*. With tar you unpack the code into the directory ./mysql-*version* and shift into this directory:

```
root# tar xzf mysql-version.tar.gz
root# cd mysql-version
```

The installation scripts provide for a group mysql and a user mysql that belongs to this group. If that is not the case, then you must set up users and groups:

```
root# groupadd mysql
root# useradd -g mysql mysql
```

If under SuSE the user mysql already exists, but not the group mysql, then instead of useradd you should execute usermod:

```
root# groupadd mysql
root# usermod -g mysql mysql
```

Configuration Tasks

The next task is to execute the script ./configure. This script checks whether all conditions for compilation are satisfied and creates the make files for the ensuing compilation. The script recognizes automatically whether MySQL should be compiled with BDB support.

As its name suggests, configure is also responsible for setting the compilation options. You may view a practically interminable list of options with configure --help. Further information on the meaning of the most important of these options can be found in the MySQL documentation. (For most of the options configure chooses suitable default settings if you do not specify a setting yourself.)

Directories

With the following options you can specify where the various MySQL files should be installed. In the default setting MySQL is installed in /usr/local and various subdirectories. However, this is impractical, because MySQL files and other operating system files get all mixed up with one another. It is then possible only by dint of excruciating labor that one may separate out the MySQL files. (A script for a proper deinstallation does not exist. Therefore, for deinstallation you must delete all MySQL files, and that is, of course, simpler if all MySQL files reside in a particular directory.)

It thus makes sense to set another base directory with --prefix. However, it then requires considerable effort to get MySQL scripts like mysql_install_db and safe_mysqld to run. These programs often fail to locate files or directories and can be convinced to cooperate only with (often undocumented) options.

`--prefix`	specifies the directory for all files that do not depend on the operating system or system architecture (e.g., database files, documentation). As default directory `/usr/local` is used. Almost all further directories are relative to `--prefix`, which in the following will be denoted by *prefix*.
`--exec-prefix`	specifies the directory for files that are system- or architecture-dependent (in particular, all program files). As default directory *prefix*/ is used.
`--bindir`	specifies the directory for program files for all users (default: *execprefix*/bin).
`--sbindir`	specifies the directory for the system program files (default: *execprefix*/sbin).
`--libdir`	specifies the location for libraries (default: *execprefix*/lib).
`--localstatedir`	specifies the location for database files (default: *prefix*/var).
`--mandir, --infodir`	specifies the location for man and info pages (default: *prefix*/man and *prefix*/info).
`--with-unix-socket-path`	specifies the location of the file mysql.sock, which under Unix/Linux is used for local communication between client and server (default: /tmp).

Libraries

A further question has to do with types of libraries. MySQL can be compiled with either dynamic or static libraries. The static variant has the advantage that the resulting programs run somewhat faster and suffer fewer compatibility problems if the programs are later run on a computer with a different Linux distribution. The two options are as follows:

```
--with-client-ldflags=-all-static
--with-mysqld-ldflags=-all-static
```

Table Drivers

By default MySQL is compiled only with table drivers that have reached a certain level of maturity. If you would like to fool around with some of the less-stable table drivers, then you must specify the necessary options:

`--with-berkeley-db`

    specifies that BDB table drivers are to be compiled with MySQL

`--with-innodb`

    specifies that InnoDB table drivers are to be compiled with MySQL

`--with-gemini`

    specifies that Gemini table drivers are to be compiled with MySQL

Compilation and Installation

To compile you must first execute `configure` with the necessary options and follow that by `make`. (The compilation will take several minutes, the precise amount of time depending, of course, on your processor and its speed.) Finally, `make install` copies all files to their intended locations. Here we have used `/usr/local/mysql` as the base directory.

```
root# mkdir /usr/local/mysql
root# ./configure --prefix=/usr/local/mysql --with-berkeley-db --with-innodb
root# make
root# make install
```

The script `mysql_install_db` then creates the database *mysql* with the default setting for MySQL access management as well as the test database *test*. With `--basedir` the same directory must be specified as with `--prefix`. The directory for the databases is specified by `--ldata` (by default `/usr/local/var` is used, and indeed, this is independent of the options `--prefix` and `--basedir`).

```
root# ./scripts/mysql_install_db --basedir=/usr/local/mysql  \
   >                             --ldata=/usr/local/mysql/var
```

The following two commands establish *mysql* as the owner and the group with access to all MySQL files. This is necessary so that MySQL can be executed by the user *mysql* (which is definitely to be recommended for reasons of security).

Please note that you can execute the two commands in this form only if all MySQL files are located in their own directory (option --prefix).

```
root# chown -R mysql /usr/local/mysql/
root# chgrp -R mysql /usr/local/mysql/
```

Starting, Testing, and Stopping MySQL Manually

The first launch of MySQL should now succeed with the following two commands. The script safe_mysqld should launch MySQL with maximum security.

```
root# cd /usr/local/mysql/
root# ./bin/safe_mysqld --user=mysql
```

The cd command is important here! The directory from which the launch should take place is determined by safe_mysqld. All the remaining commands in this section assume that the MySQL installation directory is the current directory.

If there are problems, you can attempt to specify the installation directory and the directory for the database files with the options --basedir and --datadir. This will be necessary particularly if the databases are not located in the directory ./var relative to the installation directory.

If no errors occur, then you can now start the MySQL monitor (./bin/mysql) and test whether an attempt to establish a client/server connection succeeds. If problems arise, then check with ps -ax as to whether the MySQL server mysqld is actually running.

A further possible source of error is the socket file /tmp/mysql.sock. This file is generated automatically when the MySQL server is launched and is then deleted at program termination. Convince yourself that this file actually exists and determine where it is located. (The directory /tmp is the default location.) If needed, you can use /etc/my.cnf to inform both server and client as to where this file is to be generated.

```
root# ./bin/mysql
Welcome to the MySQL monitor. Commands end with ; or \g.
Your MySQL connection id is 1 to server version: 3.23.37
mysql> status
./bin/mysql Ver 11.15 Distrib 3.23.37, for pc-linux-gnu (i686)
  ...
```

```
Current user:          root@localhost
Current pager:         stdout
Using outfile:         ' '
Server version:        3.23.37
Protocol version:      10
Connection:            Localhost via UNIX socket
Client characterset:   latin1
Server characterset:   latin1
UNIX socket:           /tmp/mysql.sock
 ...
```

To terminate MySQL you use `mysqladmin shutdown`. (If you have already instituted MySQL access protection, you will have to give your user name and password.)

```
root# ./bin/mysqladmin shutdown
```

Automatically Starting and Shutting Down MySQL

To have MySQL start up automatically when Linux is started, a start and stop script must be built into the init-V process. Unfortunately, the way of doing this is a bit different in some details for each Unix and Linux variant. In each case we start with the script `mysql.server`, included in the distribution, which you will find in the directory `share/mysql` (relative to the MySQL installation directory). For its part, `mysql.server` makes use of the script `safe_mysqld`, of which we have already made mention.

Under SuSE you copy this file into the directory `/etc/init.d` and rename it as `mysql`.

```
root# cp ./share/mysql/mysql.server   /etc/init.d/mysql
root# chmod u+x /etc/init.d/mysql
```

In `/etc/init.d/mysql` you will have to change both lines to correspond to the correct settings of the base and data directories. If you have stuck to the configuration of this section, then the following settings are required:

```
# changes in /etc/init.d/mysql
 ...
datadir=/usr/local/mysql/var
basedir=/usr/local/mysql
```

For MySQL to be executable not as Linux user *root* but as user *mysql* you must create the file /etc/my.cnf (should it not already exist) and add at least the following three lines:

```
# file /etc/my.cnf
[mysqld]
user     = mysql
```

It should now be possible to start and stop MySQL via this script. Give it a try!

```
root# /etc/init.d/mysql start
Starting mysqld daemon with databases from /usr/local/mysql/var
root# /etc/init.d/mysql stop
Killing mysqld with pid 29489
010203 15:09:57 mysqld ended
```

You have now only to set up the directories to the left of /etc/init.d/rc?.d so that MySQL can be automatically started and stopped by a change in the run level.

```
root# ln -s /etc/init.d/mysql /etc/init.d/rc2.d/S99mysql
root# ln -s /etc/init.d/mysql /etc/init.d/rc3.d/S99mysql
root# ln -s /etc/init.d/mysql /etc/init.d/rc5.d/S99mysql
root# ln -s /etc/init.d/mysql /etc/init.d/rc2.d/K10mysql
root# ln -s /etc/init.d/mysql /etc/init.d/rc3.d/K10mysql
root# ln -s /etc/init.d/mysql /etc/init.d/rc5.d/K10mysql
```

> **CAUTION** *Please convince yourself with the following command that* mysqld *is being executed not by* root *but by* mysql. *(It is a great security risk to execute* mysqld *as* root.*)*
>
> ```
> root# ps -axu | grep mysqld
> mysql ... /usr/local/mysql/libexec/mysqld ...
> ```

For speed enhancement mysqld will automatically be started several times and is therefore displayed several times by ps. You need have no fear that mysqld will therefore use n times the necessary amount of memory specified by ps or top. For the most part, memory is shared by all mysqld processes.

In a very few cases it can be worthwhile to execute several MySQL servers on the same computer. Of course, the server must be installed in several different directories. At startup of the server the script mysqld_multi, which is described in the MySQL documentation in the chapter "MySQL Utilities," is helpful.

Configuration Details

Setting Up /etc/my.cnf

As described in Chapter 14, both the MySQL server and most clients use the file /etc/my.cnf. However, this file does not yet exist. The correct configuration of this file not only can optimize the efficiency of the server, but also can help to avoid many communications problems between client and server. (Make certain in particular that the path specifications of the socket file are correct.) The following lines represent a minimal variant for /etc/my.cnf:

```
# pattern for /etc/my.cnf
# server configuration
[mysqld]
user        = mysql
port        = 3306
socket      = /tmp/mysql.sock
# general client configuration
[client]
port        = 3306
socket      = /tmp/mysql.sock
# special for mysql (monitor)
[mysql]
character-sets-dir = /usr/local/mysql/share/mysql/charsets
```

> **TIP** *The pattern for* /etc/my.cnf *for various application scenarios can be found in the files* ./share/mysql/my*.cnf. *These files are very helpful primarily in performance optimization.*
>
> *Please note that the line* user=mysql *in the section* [mysqld] *is missing from these files. Add this line so that* mysqld *will not be executed as* root.

Simplifying Access to MySQL Files

At this point all of the MySQL files are still located in /usr/local/mysql. This means that administration programs like mysql and mysqladmin must always be called with their complete path name, that man help texts are not accessible via man, and so on. In principle, there are two ways of circumventing this problem:

- You can specify the paths to the bin, man, info, and lib directories in environment variables or configuration files (*PATH, MANPATH, INFOPATH,* and *INFODIR,* /etc/ld.so.conf).

- You can copy the MySQL files into the directory in which they are found by the system in its current configuration. (The problem is that many files are now at locations where Linux cannot "see" them, and we have either to change the configuration to make the files visible to Linux, or else move the files to other locations.)

Both variants are associated with a certain amount of work, but the first variant promises fewer problems with later updates. (It is easy to forget that one has to copy the MySQL files again.)

With SuSE Linux the variables *PATH*, *MANPATH*, *INFOPATH*, and *INFODIR* are set in /etc/profile. These settings are effective only after a new login.

The paths to dynamic libraries (in particular, to the file libmysqlclient, which is used by several external programs) are set in /etc/ld.so.conf. There you simply add an additional line with /usr/local/mysql/lib/mysql. For this setting to become effective, ldconfig must be executed.

After all these settings have been made (and you have assured yourself that the MySQL server is running), you should carry out some tests withPHP, Perl, etc., to ensure that their libraries can actually communicate with MySQL. (If there is a problem, the most likely sources of error are unfindable libmysqlclient libraries and the MySQL socket file.)

Transactions

Transactions are not available under the default MySQL table type MyISAM. If you would like to use transactions, then you must employ BDB, InnoDB, or Gemini tables. However, these three table types are not yet fully mature and also are not available to MySQL under all operating systems.

Why Transactions?

Transactions can help to make database systems more efficient and more secure.

- Transactions ensure that a group of SQL commands that are introduced with *BEGIN* and terminated with *COMMIT* are executed either completely or not at all. Even if the power goes off during the operation, the computer crashes, or some other catastrophe intervenes, it cannot happen that only a part of the commands are executed.

The grouping of several commands is necessary, for example, if you wish to transfer funds from one account into another. It must not be permitted for the funds to be removed from the first account without being deposited in the second.

- Transactions also ensure that data are not simultaneously altered by other users. With MyISAM tables you can achieve this result with *LOCK*s, but with the drawback that the entire table is blocked from all clients.

- Transactions make life easier on the programmer. A transaction can be interrupted at any time, which simplifies error protection.

- After a crash BDB/InnoDB/Gemini tables can very quickly be brought into a consistent state. The sort of complex repair that is necessary for MyISAM tables via `myisamchk` is unnecessary.

Drawbacks of Transactions

- Under normal conditions table operations are slower in tables with transaction support than with MyISAM tables, because there is higher management overhead.

  However, there is an exception to this rule: If transaction support permits you to avoid *LOCK* commands (which affect the entire table), then the overall speed of your database application can be increased. This is above all the case if several clients undertake many changes in the database.

- As we have mentioned already a number of times, the new table types—BDB/InnoDB/Gemini—are not yet completely mature. (The BDB driver is in the best shape at this moment. While relatively new in MySQL, it has been used for years in other projects.)

- To some extent these table types do not yet support all of the properties and data types that are available with MyISAM tables.

> **NOTE** *Please note that within a database table various table types can be used. If you need transactions only for a certain table in your database, then it suffices to declare that one table as a BDB/InnoDB/Gemini table.*

Assumptions

In order for transactions to be usable under MySQL you will need a version of MySQL that supports the new table types. This is not currently the case with the standard version.

- **MySQL-Max:** The most convenient variant is simply to install the MySQL-Max server. This is a precompiled MySQL server with support for BDB,

InnoDB, and Gemini tables. However, the MySQL-Max version is at present available for only a few operating systems, and some of these versions do not support all three new table types. Information on the installation of the MySQL-Max version can be found in Chapter 2.

- **MaxSQL:** This variant was announced with great fanfare in the summer of 2000 as a new version of MySQL. According to the announcement it was to be a complete package containing MySQL with BDB support. However, all is quiet on the MaxSQL front, and www.maxsql.com has been unreachable for quite a while. Perhaps MySQL-Max is in fact what MaxSQL was supposed to have been.

The third variant consists simply in compiling MySQL yourself.

The following SQL command allows you to check which table types your MySQL version supports. (For the table type MyISAM there is no variable. This type is supported by all MySQL versions since 3.23.n.)

```
SHOW VARIABLES LIKE 'have_%'
```

Variable_name	Value
have_bdb	YES
have_gemini	NO
have_innodb	YES
have_isam	YES
have_raid	NO
have_ssl	NO

If *DISABLED* is displayed for individual table drivers, then this type is in fact supported, but there are configuration problems. More information can generally be found in the MySQL logging file *hostname*.err .

BEGIN, COMMIT, *and* ROLLBACK

After you have created a table of type BDB, InnoDB, or Gemini you have not yet accomplished much of anything. To make use of the advantages offered by transactions you must introduce them with *BEGIN* and end with *COMMIT*. This will cause all SQL commands after the *BEGIN* to be executed. Instead of *COMMIT* you can undo the entire transaction with *ROLLBACK*.

Currently, there is no table driver that permits multilevel (i.e., nested) transactions. If you introduce a new transaction with *BEGIN* while a previous transaction is still open, the open transaction will be terminated with a *COMMIT*.

Transactions are automatically terminated by the following commands (as with *COMMIT*): *ALTER TABLE, CREATE INDEX, DROP DATABASE, DROP TABLE, RENAME TABLE, TRUNCATE.*

Transactions are managed by the client. If the connection is lost while a transaction is open, all open changes are canceled (as with *ROLLBACK*).

The extent to which open transactions block read or write access to a table depends on the implementation of the transaction support.

Autocommit Mode

MySQL is usually run in autocommit mode (*AUTOCOMMIT=1*). This means that all SQL commands that are not prefaced by *BEGIN* as a transaction are executed immediately.

If you execute the SQL command *SET AUTOCOMMIT=0*, then this autocommit mode is switched off. This means that *all* SQL commands are considered one big transaction. The transaction can be finalized with *COMMIT* or *ROLL-BACK*. Then a new transaction begins automatically. (You do not need to execute a *BEGIN*. This convenience alone is often enough to convince one to use *SET AUTOCOMMIT=0*.)

An important consequence of *AUTOCOMMIT=0* is that if the connection is interrupted (whether accidentally or on purpose), all SQL commands that have not been confirmed with *COMMIT* are undone.

Note as well that with *AUTOCOMMIT=0* very long transactions can arise if you do not regularly execute *COMMIT* or *ROLLBACK*. Many table drivers do not handle long transactions well; that is, locking problems can arise that have a negative effect on efficiency. Because of its architecture, the InnoDB table driver does better than average with such transactions.

> **NOTE** AUTOCOMMIT *mode is relevant only for tables with transaction support. SQL commands applied to other table types (e.g., MyISAM) are executed at once, independently of* AUTOCOMMIT *as well as of* BEGIN/COMMIT/ROLLBACK.

BDB Tables

BDB stands for "Berkeley Databases." This is an open source library for storing data in tables. BDB is not in and of itself a complete database system, which is achieved only in combination with MySQL. (There are other systems besides MySQL that support BDB functions.)

> **POINTER** *The use of BDB tables is described in the MySQL documentation in the chapter "MySQL table types." Further information on BDB (independent of MySQL) can be found at* http://www.sleepycat.com/

Limitations

- BDB Tables are not available under all operating systems supported by MySQL.

- BDB Tables must be equipped with a primary key column. MySQL will generate such columns itself if you do not do so (in which case they are hidden).

- Certain MySQL functions (e.g., full-text indexes, full-text search) are not yet available for BDB tables.

- BDB does not allow nested transactions.

- *SELECT COUNT(*) FROM table* is significantly slower than with MyISAM tables, since BDB does not manage an internal record counter.

- During a transaction, operations are partially blocked for other clients. In your programming you must figure that under some conditions *SELECT* commands will not return results immediately (as with a write *LOCK*). Furthermore, it can happen that transactions making changes to a table can be interrupted by MySQL (equivalent to *ROLLBACK*).

- During a transaction it is not only the immediately affected records to which access is withheld from other clients, but records stored nearby as well. (Internally, page-level locking is used, which means that all records in the same page of memory are affected.)

Generating BDB Tables

In order to generate BDB tables you use the command *CREATE TABLE*, which was discussed in Chapter 5. The only special feature here is that you must specify *TYPE=BDB*.

```
CREATE DATABASE testbdb
USE testbdb
CREATE TABLE table1 (colA INT AUTO_INCREMENT, colB INT,
            PRIMARY KEY (colA)) TYPE=BDB
INSERT INTO table1 (colB) VALUES (5)
```

If you now take a glance into the database directory, you will see that the table file exhibits the identifier .db (and not the MyISAM table identifier *.MYD). Note that the path to the database directory is dependent on your installation.

```
root# ls /usr/local/mysql/var/testbdb/
table1.db table1.frm
```

Converting Tables from MyISAM to BDB

You can easily change existing tables from MyISAM to BDB (or vice versa). To do this, use the command *ALTER TABLE*.

```
ALTER TABLE tblname TYPE=BDB
```

> **TIP** *Most MySQL user interfaces (e.g., phpMyAdmin) are not able to generate BDB tables. But not to worry! Simply generate a run-of-the-mill table and then change the table type with* ALTER TABLE.
> *As soon as the table type has been set, then most user interfaces can again be used unrestrictedly (even for changes in the table design).*

If you wish to change the type of a large number of tables, then under Unix/Linux you can use the script mysql_convert_table_format. If you do not specify a name of the table, then all the tables in the database will be converted.

```
mysql_convert_table_format [options] --type=BDB dbname [tablename]
```

The following example shows the conversion of all tables in the database *mylibrary*.

```
root# mysql_convert_table_format --user=root --password=xxx
```

Error Protection in Programming

If you use transactions, then the probability of receiving certain error messages from the server is increased.

- While a transaction is open, another client cannot carry out any operations (whether within its own transaction or not) on data records affected by the open transaction. (This holds as well for records that are stored on the same memory page, since BDB uses page-level locking.)

Example:

- ○ Client A executes *BEGIN* and then *INSERT INTO table VAL-UES ('a', 'b')*.

- ○ Client B attempts to execute *SELECT * FROM table*. This command, however, is blocked until client A completes its transaction with *COMMIT* or *ROLLBACK*.

Many clients (e.g., mysql) wait endlessly until open transactions are ended (that is, there is no timeout). However, other clients may report a timeout error (or other error).

Solution: End your transactions as soon as possible.

- Any transaction can be terminated due to deadlock problems. (The BDB table driver automatically recognizes deadlock situations, that is, the case where two transactions each block the other. To avoid an endless blockade, one of the client transactions will be interrupted.)

Update Logging

MySQL can log changes in a database in both text and binary modes. If you are working with transactions, you should use the binary variant, since only this variant handles transactions correctly. (In update logging in text mode, commands that were canceled with *ROLLBACK* are also logged.)

Logging Transactions

If you have configured MySQL in such a way that logging files are generated for incremental backups (*update logs*), then these logging files are valid for all table types, including BDB tables.

Moreover, the internal administration of BDB requires its own transaction logging files. When BDB is run for the first time, MySQL places the logging file log.0000000001 in the database directory. As suggested by its name, after a time, log.0000000002 is automatically created, and so on. The directory for the BDB logging files can be set with the option bdb-log-dir.

The MySQL documentation has not a word to say about the significance of these logging files. In the BDB documentation as well, at www.sleepycat.com, you will find no information about why such logging files are needed or what they are used for.

The SQL command *SHOW LOGS* gives information about which logging files are currently in use (status: *IN USE*). These logging files must not be deleted (all others apparently can be).

```
SHOW LOGS
 File                                   Type   Status
 /usr/local/mysql/var/log.0000000001    BDB    IN USE
```

InnoDB Tables

The first version of the InnoDB table driver has been available since version 3.23.34a. Like BDB tables, InnoDB tables also support transactions. Internally, however, InnoDB tables are managed completely differently. For example, the InnoDB table driver uses a different locking algorithm, which promises greater speed for quasi-simultaneous database accesses. The author of the table driver places great value on matching the features of his driver to those of Oracle. It should be possible to restore InnoDB tables after a crash quickly to a consistent state (which was not yet the case in version 3.23.37).

Since InnoDB was still in beta version as these lines were being written, it is difficult to say how far InnoDB has met the hopes and expectations of its author. In any event, InnoDB was developed with great diligence and could well quickly become one of the most attractive table formats alongside MyISAM.

> **POINTER** *The use of InnoDB tables is described rather extensively in the MySQL documentation, in the chapter "MySQL Table Types." Further information, including many technical details, can be found at* http://www.innobase.fi/

Limitations

- Individual data records in InnoDB tables can currently not exceed about 8 kilobytes (including *TEXT/BLOB* columns). Furthermore, neither prefix indexes nor indexes for *TEXT/BLOB* columns are possible. Finally, you cannot use full-text indexes for InnoDB tables. More complete compatibility with MyISAM tables should be achieved in the near future.

- *DROP DATABASE, CHECK TABLE*, and *TRUNCATE* do not yet work. Nor is it possible to generate temporary InnoDB tables. (These features should also be implemented soon.)

- There is currently no possibility of executing hot backups.

- Since InnoDB possesses its own locking algorithm based on transactions, the MySQL command *LOCK TABLE* must not be executed for InnoDB tables. This command is executed by MySQL outside of the control of the InnoDB table driver. Therefore, this can confuse the locking management and in the worst case lead to deadlock (in which two or more processes wait eternally for one another).

- While with most MySQL table drivers each table is stored in its own file, which grows or shrinks as required, the InnoDB table driver stores all data and indexes in a *tablespace*, comprising one or more files that must be created before first use. These files cannot later be enlarged or contracted. This complicates considerably the administration of the storage for InnoDB tables.

First Tests with InnoDB Tables

As we have already mentioned, all InnoDB tables (regardless of database of origin) are stored in one large file, together with their indexes. This file represents a sort of virtual storage, which is managed by the InnoDB driver itself.

Before InnoDB tables can be created for the first time, the directory for all InnoDB files (option innodb_data_home_dir) must be set in the MySQL configuration file. Usually, one uses the same directory as for MyISAM database files (under Linux often /var/lib/mysql). Furthermore, you must specify the file name of an InnoDB file (innodb_data_file_path) with a size specification.

```
# settings in /etc/my.cnf or windows\my.ini
[mysqld]
innodb_data_home_dir = /var/lib/mysql
innodb_data_file_path = testib:10M
```

Then the MySQL server must be restarted. The InnoDB driver then generates automatically the 10-MB data file /var/lib/mysql/testib. Moreover, two logging files with the names ib_logfile0 and ib_logfile1 are created. (These steps are also logged in the MySQL logging file *hostname*.log.) As soon as you have executed the first commands with InnoDB tables, another file, ib_arch_log_0000000000, is generated in addition to the logging files.

Creating InnoDB Tables

From now on you can generate as many InnoDB tables as you like, which can be placed in existing databases or in new ones. In the following example a database is created, and within it a new InnoDB table:

```
CREATE DATABASE innotest
USE innotest
CREATE TABLE table1 (colA INT AUTO_INCREMENT, colB INT,
PRIMARY KEY (colA)) TYPE=InnoDB
INSERT INTO table1 (colB) VALUES (10)
```

The following commands provide an overview of the files that now exist. The actual data are located in testib. The file innotest/table1.frm contains merely the definition of the table layout (in the same binary format as for all other MySQL tables).

```
root# cd /var/lib/mysql
root# ls -l ib* testib
-rw-rw---- 1 mysql mysql 25088 ib_arch_log_0000000000
-rw-rw---- 1 mysql mysql 5242880 ib_logfile0
-rw-rw---- 1 mysql mysql 5242880 ib_logfile1
-rw-rw---- 1 mysql mysql 10485760 testib
root# ls -l innotest/
-rw-rw---- 1 mysql mysql 8578 table1.frm
```

Changing a Table Type

You can easily change existing tables from MyISAM to InnoDB (and, of course, from InnoDB to MyISAM). To accomplish this you use the command *ALTER TABLE*.

```
ALTER TABLE tblname TYPE=InnoDB
```

If you wish to change a large number of tables, then you will want to use (under Unix/Linux) the script mysql_convert_table_format. If you do not specify a table name, then all tables of the database will be converted.

```
mysql_convert_table_format [opt] --type=InnoDB dbname [tablename]
```

Trying Out Transactions

To try out transactions you must establish two connections to the database. The simplest way to do this is to execute the monitor mysql in two windows. Then execute commands first in one window and then in the other. The following examples assume that there is a table *table1* in the database *innotest*, in which there is a record. (In practice, of course, you will have several records, but for the purposes of this demonstration a single record suffices.)

At time point 1 (as indicated in the right-hand column of Table 12-1) the contents of *table1* look different to the two different connections. For connection A the record with *colA=1* already has *colB=11*. Since this transaction has not actually been executed, connection B sees *colB=10* for the same record.

At time point 2, B begins a transaction, in which *colB* of the data record with *colA=1* is to be increased by 3. The InnoDB table driver recognizes that it cannot execute this command at this time, and it blocks B, which then waits until A completes its transaction.

At time point 3, A completes its transaction with *COMMIT*, whereby *colB* attains the definitive value 11. And now B's *UPDATE* command can be completed.

At time point 4, A sees *colB=11*. For B things look as though *colB* already had the value 14.

Now B cancels its transaction. Then at time point 5 both A and B see the value actually stored, namely *colB=11*.

> **REMARK** *Of course, you can try out this example with other table types that support transactions. The result of the commands will be the same (if you maintain the sequence of execution). However, it can happen that blocking comes at other places. For example, if you use BDB tables, then the* SELECT *command begun by B at time point 1 will be executed only at time point 3.*

Locking Behavior

The InnoDB table driver generally takes care of all necessary locking operations on its own, as soon as you execute your transactions. However, there are cases where the default behavior of InnoDB is not optimal. In such cases InnoDB offers several possibilities of having its locking behavior altered.

Table 12-1. Coordinating transactions

Connection A	Connection B	Time point
USE innotest	USE innotest	
SELECT * FROM table1 *colA colB* 1 10		
BEGIN		
UPDATE table1 SET colB=11 WHERE colA=1		
SELECT * FROM table1 *colA colB* 1 11	SELECT * FROM table1 *colA colB* 1 10	1
	BEGIN UPDATE table1 SET colB=colB+3 WHERE colA=1	2
COMMIT		3
SELECT * FROM table1 *colA colB* 1 11	SELECT * FROM table1 *colA colB* 1 14	4
	ROLLBACK	
SELECT * FROM table1 *colA colB* 1 11	SELECT * FROM table1 *colA colB* 1 11	5

SELECT LOCK IN SHARE MODE

A peculiarity of InnoDB is that *SELECT* commands are immediately executed even on blocked records. The results returned do not consider the possibility of open transactions of other clients (see connection B at time point 1 in the example above), and thus return potentially outmoded data.

If you execute the *SELECT* with the key word *LOCK IN SHARE MODE*, then you achieve that when the command is executed it is held pending until all transactions already begun have been terminated (of course, only to the extent that these transactions affect result records of the *SELECT* command). Thus if in the above example B were to issue the command

```
SELECT * FROM table1 LOCK IN SHARE MODE
```

at time 1, then a result would be displayed only when the transaction begun by A had been completed (time point 3).

If *SELECT . . . LOCK IN SHARE MODE* is executed within a transaction, then additionally, all result records for all other clients will be locked until the end of the transaction. Such a lock is called a *shared lock*, whence the key word *SHARE*. With a shared lock you are assured that the records read during your transactions are not being changed or deleted by other clients.

With a shared lock, locked records can continue to be read by all clients, even if other clients are also using *SELECT LOCK IN SHARE MODE*. Any attempt by a client to change such records leads to the client being blocked until your transaction is completed.

SELECT FOR UPDATE

The key words *FOR UPDATE* also represent an extension of the normal *SELECT*. With this all result records are provided an *exclusive lock*.

With an exclusive lock, locked records cannot be changed by other clients. They can continue to be read by all clients with a normal *SELECT* command, but not with *SELECT . . . LOCK IN SHARE MODE*. The difference between a shared lock and an exclusive lock therefore relates only to whether other clients can execute *SELECT . . . LOCK IN SHARE MODE*.

INSERT, UPDATE, DELETE

All three of these commands have the effect that changed records are locked by an exclusive lock.

Deadlocks

According to the documentation, InnoDB recognizes deadlock situations automatically (that is, situations in which two or more processes block one another, each waiting for the other to finish, ad infinitum). If the InnoDB table driver recognizes a deadlock, then a *ROLLBACK* is executed for the process that triggered the deadlock.

CAUTION *In no case should you execute a* LOCK TABLE *for an InnoDB table. This command is executed at the MySQL level, without the InnoDB table driver hearing about it. The consequence can be a deadlock of which InnoDB never becomes aware.*

Deadlocks that InnoDB doesn't know about can also arise when SQL commands affect both InnoDB tables and other tables as well. In order for the clients not to have to wait forever in such cases, the maximum wait time (in seconds) can be placed in the MySQL configuration file with set-variable = innodb_lock_wait_timeout=n. *If this limit is passed, then the entire transaction is interrupted with* ROLLBACK.

POINTER *An extensive description of the InnoDB locking mechanism (with more technical details and background information) can be found in the MySQL documentation.*

Tablespace Administration

If you wish to know how much free storage space remains in the InnoDB data file (in the *tablespace*, that is), then simply execute the command *SHOW TABLE STATUS* for any database that contains InnoDB tables. The amount of free space (which applies to all InnoDB tables together) is given in the comment column.

```
SHOW TABLE STATUS FROM innotest
```

Name	Type	Row_format	...	Comment
table1	Innobase	Fixed		InnoDB free: 6144 kB
table2	Innobase	Fixed		InnoDB free: 6144 kB
table3	MyISAM	Fixed		
...				

InnoDB files cannot be enlarged. If you require more space, you must specify additional files together with their size in the MySQL configuration file with the option innodb_data_file_path. After a restart of MySQL all of these files constitute the new tablespace.

```
# settings in /etc/my.cnf or windows\my.ini
[mysqld]
innodb_data_home_dir = /var/lib/mysql
innodb_data_file_path = testib:10M;testib2:10M
```

An enlargement of the tablespace is thus rather simple. However, there is no provision for shrinking the space. The only way to do this is to export the tables with mysqldump, regenerate a smaller tablespace from scratch, and then reimport the tables.

Logging Files

InnoDB logs all changes into logging files with the names ib_logfile0, ib_logfile1, etc. The purpose of these logging files is to enable large transactions. On the other hand, the logging files are used as well to recreate the InnoDB data after a crash.

If MySQL is properly configured and has adequate memory allotment, then most of the data needed at any one time should fit in RAM. For reasons of speed optimization the InnoDB table driver makes changes in data at first only in RAM, and not in the actual data files (that is, in the tablespace). Changed pages in the tablespace are transferred only now and then to the hard drive. However, every change in the data is logged into the logging file immediately, so that in the case of a crash the tablespace can be recreated.

The InnoDB logging files are filled in order. When the last file is full, the InnoDB driver begins to write data to the first logging file. Thus the total size of all the logging files limits the maximum amount of tablespace changes that can be stored temporarily in RAM.

The proper sizing of the logging files has a great influence on the speed of MySQL/InnoDB. A collection of the most important options and variables can be found in Chapter 14, while tips on the proper setup can be found in the MySQL documentation, in the chapter "MySQL Table Types/InnoDB."

> **REMARK** *The InnoDB logging files are intended only for internal data management, and not for backups. If you need a log of all changes in data since a particular point in time (since the last full backup, say), you must use MySQL's binary logging (which is independent of InnoDB); see Chapter 11.*

Gemini Tables

The Gemini table driver offers features similar to those of the InnoDB table driver:

- Transactions

- Row-level locking

- Automatic restoration of databases after a crash

A particular feature is that all four isolation levels defined in the ANSI-SQL/92 standard are supported.

As these lines were written there was not yet an official version of the Gemini table driver. The little information collected here was determined from a Gemini beta version from Nusphere (using MySQL 3.23.36) and is also based on the available beta documentation. It is by no means out of the question that some details will change by the time the Gemini table driver is released.

> **POINTER** *The Gemini table driver was developed by the firm Nusphere. Further information can be found in the MySQL documentation in the chapter "MySQL Table Types," as well as on the Internet:* http://www.nusphere.com

Limitations

- Individual records in Gemini tables can currently not exceed 32 kilobytes.

- *DROP DATABASE, BACKUP*, and *RESTORE TABLE*, as well as *FLUSH TABLES*, do not work. Nor is it possible to generate temporary Gemini tables.

- Full-text indexes cannot be used in Gemini tables. In general, the length of indexes is limited to 230 bytes (that is, in *TEXT/BLOB* fields only the first 230 bytes are considered).

Creating Gemini Tables and Changing Table Type

Unlike our experience with InnoDB, the first experiments with Gemini could be carried out without changes to the MySQL configuration files. While there are numerous mysqld options and variables with Gemini (see Chapter 14), these serve only speed and security optimization. The only condition for generating Gemini tables is that you have a version of mysqld with Gemini support.

Gemini tables can be created in any database. To do this you use the command *CREATE TABLE* with the option *TYPE=Gemini*.

You can also change an existing table to type Gemini. For this you employ the command *ALTER TABLE*.

```
ALTER TABLE tblname TYPE=Gemini
```

If you have a large number of tables to change, then you should use (under Unix/Linux) the script `mysql_convert_table_format`. If you do not specify a table name, then all tables of the database will be converted.

```
mysql_convert_table_format [opt] --type=Gemini dbname [tablename]
```

Locking Behavior

The Gemini table driver usually sees to all necessary locking operations once you execute a transaction.

INSERT, UPDATE, DELETE

Records that have been changed with *INSERT, UPDATE,* or *DELETE* are locked from other clients with an *exclusive lock* until the end of the transaction. This means that all other clients are forbidden to change these data. Furthermore, such data records (in particular, their previous state before you have terminated your transaction) can be read with *SELECT* only if these clients use the isolation level *READ UNCOMMITTED* in their transactions (see the next heading).

SELECT FOR UPDATE

With the key words *FOR UPDATE*, which can be placed at the end of a *SELECT* command, all result records can be provided with an *exclusive lock*. These results are thereby locked to all clients in the same way as if they had already been changed with *INSERT, UPDATE,* or *DELETE*.

SELECT

An ordinary *SELECT* command can also be used to lock records with exclusive locks, namely, when the *SELECT* command is executed in a transaction with isolation level *REPEATABLE READ* or *SERIALIZABLE*.

Isolation Levels for Transactions

Before the start of a transaction the *isolation level* can be defined. For this the following command is available:

```
SET [SESSION|GLOBAL] TRANSACTION ISOLATION LEVEL
    READ UNCOMMITTED | READ COMMITTED |
    REPEATABLE READ | SERIALIZABLE
```

The scope and period of validity of this command are set by the optional key words *SESSION* and *GLOBAL:*

- If *SET TRANSACTION* is executed without *SESSION/GLOBAL,* then the setting holds only for the next transaction (that is, from the next *BEGIN* command. All further commands will be executed in the default setting for the isolation degree (usually *READ COMMITTED*).

- The key word *SESSION* has the effect that the setting holds until the connection is terminated.

- With *GLOBAL* the default setting of the MySQL server is changed. The new default setting holds only for new connections, not for already active connections (including the connection of the client that executed the command).

The isolation level influences the manner in which *SELECT* commands are executed within a transaction. The following list orders the isolation levels by increasing degree of exclusivity. This means that with *READ UNCOMMITTED* you achieve the greatest access speed (no mutual blocking), while with *SERIALIZABLE* you attain the greatest security against simultaneous changes in data by other clients.

- ***READ UNCOMMITTED:*** *SELECT* reads the latest valid data. Any transactions of other clients that are running are not heeded. The data read are not blocked for other processes. (Thus it can happen that the data read will be out of date or even nonexistent when other processes complete their transactions.)

- ***READ COMMITTED:*** If data queried by *SELECT* are blocked by other clients (that is, by exclusive locks), then *SELECT* waits until all other transactions that could affect the data are complete. Then all data queried by *SELECT* are blocked until they have been completely read. This ensures that no part of the data can be changed by another transaction during the reading of the data. However, this blocking of the data holds only until the end of the *SELECT* command, and not to the end of the transaction.

  It can thus transpire that data that you have read can be changed by other clients before your transaction is complete.

- **REPEATABLE READ:** As with *READ COMMITTED* there is a wait until the end of the transactions of other processes. Then the records that have been read are locked for other processes until the end of the transaction.

  This ensures that the data read by you are not changed by another client before your transaction is complete. It can happen that during this time period new records are inserted. (If you execute *SELECT * FROM table WHERE colA<10*, you obtain all records that satisfy the condition *colA<10* at that point in time. However, it is possible that another process has inserted additional records in the table before the end of your transaction that also satisfy the condition *colA<10*.)

- **SERIALIZABLE:** As with *READ COMMITTED* there is a wait for the end of the transactions of other processes. Then all tables from which records were read are completely locked. This ensures that nothing is changed in any of the affected tables until your transaction is complete. However, this blocks all other clients.

The maximum wait time for locked records is determined by the `mysqld` option `gemini_lock_wait_timeout`. The default setting is 10 seconds. After this time period the transaction is broken off with *ROLLBACK*.

> **REMARK** *For the Gemini table driver* READ COMMITTED *is the default setting.*
>
> *Since the locking of many records in the three* READ *isolation levels makes considerable demands on RAM, in such cases* SERIALIZABLE *should be used.*
>
> *The Gemini table driver can manage transactions correctly only if Gemini tables are the only type of tables accessed during the transaction.*
>
> *In the beta version of Gemini the isolation levels described here do not function exactly as advertised. However, one may expect that these problems will be resolved before the final version.*

Replication

Replication makes it possible to synchronize two or more MySQL servers running on different computers.

Different database systems employ differing methods of establishing replication. If you are familiar with replication from another database system, you should not expect MySQL to exhibit the exact same properties.

MySQL currently supports master/slave replication exclusively. There is one master system (*read/write*). This system is responsible for all changes to data.

Additionally, there is one or more slave systems (*read-only*) on which, perhaps after a brief delay, exactly the same data are available as on the master system.

The exchange of data between the master and slaves is accomplished via binary logging files belonging to the master. The slaves remain in constant contact with the master and synchronize their databases by taking the requisite SQL commands from these logging files.

Replication functions even when the computers are running under different operating systems. (For example, the master can be running under Linux and a slave under Windows.)

> **POINTER**   *In addition to the information of this section, in Chapter 13 you will find a reference to all SQL commands for running replication (Chapter 13 provides an overview), and in Chapter 14 there is a reference to all* mysqld *options related to replication.*
>
> *Further information can be found in the MySQL documentation, the chapter called "Replication in MySQL." The following article is also worth reading:* http://www.phpbuilder.com/columns/tanoviceanu20000912.php3

Why Replication?

There are two reasons that argue in favor of setting up a replication system: security and speed.

Security

Thanks to replication, your database is available on several computers. If a slave computer goes off line, the entire system can continue to run without interruption. (A new slave system can automatically synchronize itself.)

If the master computer goes off line, then the preservation of the data can be taken over by a slave computer. Alternatively, the entire system can be reconfigured so that a slave computer takes over the role of the master. In either case, though, the entire system is only partially (that is, *read-only*) available.

If you are considering replication for reasons of security only, you should also consider a RAID system, whereby the contents of two (or more) hard drives are synchronized. A RAID system is simpler to set up than a MySQL replication system. However, it protects only against a hard-drive crash, and not against an operating system crash, power outage, or the like.

Speed

If the speed of a database system is limited primarily by many read-only queries (and not by a large number of alterations to the data), then a replication system can gain you great savings in time: The expensive queries are divided among several slave systems, while the master system is used exclusively or primarily for updates. (Of course, part of the theoretical increase in speed is lost due to the increased communication overhead.)

Please note that you can gain speed only if the programming of the client is compatible with your system. The client programs must divide your queries according to a load-balancing procedure (or simply at random) among all available slave systems. MySQL itself provides no mechanism for this purpose.

If your interest in replication is motivated by performance problems, you should consider alternative performance-enhancing measures, in particular, better hardware (in the following order: more RAM, faster hard drive, a RAID system, a multiprocessor system).

Limitations

- Replication is a relatively new feature of MySQL (available since version 3.23.15), and therefore still exhibits some growing pains. For this book replication was tested on version 3.23.33. All earlier versions exhibit significant errors, and there are probably some serious problems in version 3.23.33 that had not yet been discovered when this book went to press.

  The documentation on a number of aspects of replication is still unsatisfactory (in particular as it relates to administration of replication systems, error-correction, and the application of relevant SQL commands).

- MySQL currently supports replication only in the form of a master/slave system. All changes in data must be carried out on a single master system. The slave systems can be used only for database queries (*read-only*).

  It is not currently possible for a slave system to take over the role of the master if it should go out of service. Thus replication can produce a system that is secure against breakdowns for database queries, but not for alterations to the data. (An automatic master/slave role change is planned for MySQL version 4.0.)

  Furthermore, it is impossible to synchronize changes to several systems. (This leads to problems with *AUTO_INCREMENT* values. Further problems can arise from the fact that replication requires a certain amount of time.) It is therefore impossible to execute changes in a MySQL database on a notebook computer and later bring these into balance with the master system.

- The replication system does not work properly with several SQL commands:
  - *RAND:* Random numbers generated with *RAND* cannot be synchronized. Every copy of the data contains a different value. To circumvent this problem, you may use *RAND* with a pseudorandom parameter (for example, with the current timestamp value of your client program).
  - *LOAD DATA INFILE:* Data balancing works only if the imported file on the server is available during replication.
  - *LOAD LOCAL DATA INFILE:* This command is simply not supported at all.

Setting Up the Replication Master System

Setting Up the Replication User

The first step consists in setting up a new user on the master system that is responsible for communication between master and client. This user requires the *FILE* privilege (for access to the binary logging files). Instead of *slavehostname*, specify the complete computer name or IP number of the slave computer. For security reasons you should use as password a combination of characters that is in use neither in the operating system nor in the database.

```
GRANT FILE ON *.* TO replicuser@slavehostname IDENTIFIED BY 'xxx'
```

If the replication system is to have several slaves, then you must execute *GRANT* for all the slave computers. Alternatively, you can permit access for all computers in the local system (*replicuser@'%.netname'*). This simplifies administration, though at the cost of introducing an unnecessary security risk.

Shutdown

Next, the MySQL server must be shut down. Under Unix/Linux you use an init-V script (for example, `/sbin/init.d/mysql stop`), while under Windows you use WinMySQLadmin.

If you have been using binary logging, then back up all of the logging files (if you need these files) and then delete all binary logging files from the logging directory including `hostname-bin.index`. (For replication to function correctly, the binary logging files must be newly initialized at the start of replication.)

Creating a Snapshot

Now you create a copy (called a *snapshot*) of all the databases. You will need this snapshot for the installation of the initial state of all the databases on the slave computers.

Under Windows use WinZip or another compression program; under Unix/Linux your best bet is to use `tar`. (If you have enough space on your hard drive, you may simply copy the database directory to another location.)

```
root# cd mysql-data-dir
root# tar czf snapshot.tgz database1/ database2/ database3/
```

With `tar` you cannot, unfortunately, use * to include all databases, because in the MySQL database directory there are usually many logging files that should not be installed on the slave system.

Server Configuration

In order for the MySQL server to be able to function as a replication master there are two small changes that have to be made to the configuration file. The first is to associate to the server a unique ID number using the option `server-id`. (Every computer in the replication system must be so designated.) The second is to activate binary logging with the option `log-bin`.

```
# master configuration
# in /etc/my.cnf or windows\my.ini
[mysqld]
log-bin
server-id=1
```

Then restart the server. (You can now use the server. All changes to the database will now be recorded in the binary logging file. As soon as a slave system goes on line, it will automatically synchronize its database based on the logging files.)

> **TIP** *A brief description of additional master options can be found in the* `mysqld` *reference in Chapter 14. For example, you can restrict the replication to individual databases (option* `binlog-do-db`*) or exclude several databases from the replication (*`binlog-ignore-db`*).*

Setting Up the Replication Slave System

Setting Up the Databases (Snapshot)

If the MySQL server is already running on a slave system, you must stop it. Then copy the database files of the snapshot into the database directory (with WinZip or tar xzf). Make sure that the files can be read and written by the MySQL server. Under Unix/Linux you do this by executing chown mysql.mysql.

Configuration File

With the slave system as well the configuration file must be changed a bit. With server-id each slave system also obtains a unique identification number. With master-host, master-user, and master-password you specify how the slave system is related to the master.

```
# slave configuration
# in /etc/my.cnf or windows\my.ini
[mysqld]
server-id=2
master-host=masterhostname
master-user=replicuser
master-password=xxx
default-character-set = <as for the master>
```

> **REMARK**   *Please be sure that the same character set is specified in the configuration files of all the slaves (option* default-character-set*) as for the master.*
>
> *The logging of all changes (i.e., update logging) is not necessary for the slaves and should be deactivated for speed optimization.*
>
> *A short description of additional slave options can be found in the* mysqld *option reference in Chapter 14.*

Now the slave system can be brought on line. Start the server. If problems arise, look at the error log (file *hostname*.err).

First Test

With `mysql` create a connection to the master system and add a new data record to the table of your choice. Then use `mysql` to establish a connection to a slave system and test whether the new record appears there. If that is the case, then rejoice, for your replication system is working already. (Of course, you could also generate and then delete new tables and even entire databases. The slave system understands and carries out these commands as well.)

Take a look, too, into the logging file *hostname*`.err` on the slave system (`mysql.err` under Windows). There you should see entries on the status of the replication, for example in the following form:

```
010215 17:00:39 Slave: connected to master
  'replicuser@mars.sol:3306', replication started in log
  'FIRST' at position 4
 ...
```

As a further test you can shut down the slave system, make changes in the master system, and then start up the slave system again. The databases on the slave system should be automatically synchronized within a couple of seconds.

The File `master.info`

At the initial startup of replication the slave system will have the file `master.in` added to its database directory. In this file MySQL keeps track of which binary logging file is currently being used, to what point this file has been evaluated, how the master can be contacted (host name, user name, password), etc. This file is absolutely necessary for the operation of replication. The MySQL documentation naturally emphatically recommends that you not mess around with this file.

```
mars-bin.001
418
mars.sol
replicuser
xxx
3306
60
```

> **REMARK** *As soon as* master.info *exists, further changes to the configuration file are ignored (insofar as they affect settings in* master.info*). I could not determine whether this behavior constitutes a feature or a bug. The content of* master.info *can also be determined with the SQL command* SHOW SLAVE STATUS. *Changes can be carried out with* CHANGE MASTER TO. *Both of these commands will be described in the SQL reference in Chapter 13.*

Security Considerations

The *FILE* privilege for the replication user represents a security risk. What is most grievous is that the user name and password generally appear in plain text in the configuration files on the slave computers ((/etc/my.cnf or windows\my.ini). These configuration files can be read by any user on these computers. Moreover, there is a replication user not only on the master system, but on all the slaves as well.

In other words, anyone with a replication system on his computer can read the configuration file, can register as replication user on all the computers, and, thanks to the *FILE* privilege, read and write files. The extent of this user's file access depends on the additional configuration settings of the MySQL server. If the server is running under its own account (which is usual under Unix/Linux), then at least the access security of the operating system comes into play. Nonetheless, the danger is great that an attacker will find a way to make use of the *FILE* privilege.

There is no easy cure to this problem. A replication user with the *FILE* privilege is unavoidable; the slave system must know its user name and password; the global configuration file must be readable by all users (otherwise, it can no longer be used for configuration of client programs).

The only possible starting point is the file in which the options master-user and master-password are specified. Remove these two options from the global configuration file and add them to a new configuration file extra.cnf. (The options must be given in the group [mysqld].) Make sure that this file can be read only by the MySQL account. Under Unix/Linux execute the following command as well:

```
root# chown mysql.mysql extra.cnf
root# chmod 600 extra.cnf
```

Then change the script with which MySQL is started (under SuSE Linux, for example, /sbin/init.d/mysql) by adding the additional start option --defaults-extra-file */dir*/extra.cnf. The option defaults-extra-file must appear before all other options. This option cannot be given in the global configuration file. You have thereby achieved that the name and password of the replication user can no longer be determined so easily.

The user name and password are contained in plain text on all the slave computers in the file master.info. Therefore, be sure that this file as well can be read only by the owner (that is, by the MySQL account).

Replication and Transactions

Surprisingly, given how new all of this is, transactions based on BDB tables also function in combination with replication. The only condition is that the master system support BDB tables. This is not, however, necessary for the slave systems. Transactions would not improve security there, but it would slow down access to the data. BDB tables on the master are automatically generated on the slave as MyISAM tables.

Transactions are executed on the slave only if they are completed on the master via *COMMIT*. On the other hand, if transactions are recalled (*ROLLBACK*), then the affected SQL command is neither logged in the binary logging file nor executed on the slave system.

Client Programming

If the goal of a replication system is to ensure against system failure or to increase speed by dividing up the queries among several systems, then changes are necessary to the client as well.

In establishing the connection a distinction must be made as to whether data are going to queried only or whether changes are required as well. If *INSERT*, *UPDATE*, or *DELETE* commands are to be executed, then a connection to the master system must be made.

On the other hand, if data are to be queried only, then the connection should be made to the server that is currently the least burdened. Since the client program as a rule has no way of determining this, the *Connect* function should randomly select a computer from a predetermined list of computer names or IP numbers and attempt to make a connection. If this does not succeed (because this server is currently unreachable), then the *Connect* should make an attempt to connect to another server.

Random Server Selection

The following example in the programming language PHP assumes that you wish to read (and not alter) data and to select the server randomly to improve efficiency. To do this you define in *mysqlhosts[ ]* an array of all the server names (or IP addresses) and use *rand(min, max)* to select an element of the array.

   After the connection has been established the single query mysql_list_dbs is executed (corresponding to the SQL command *SHOW DATABASES*).

```
<html><head><title>test</title></head><body>
<?php
  $mysqlhosts[0]="venus.sol"; // list of all servers of the
  $mysqlhosts[1]="mars.sol";// replication system
  $mysqlhost=$mysqlhosts[rand(0,1)]; // select server randomly
  $mysqluser="user"; // user name
  $mysqlpasswd="xxx";// password
  $connID=mysql_pconnect($mysqlhost, $mysqluser, $mysqlpasswd);
  $result=mysql_list_dbs();
  echo "<p>Databases at $mysqlhost<p>\n";
  while($row = mysql_fetch_row($result)) {
    echo "<br><i>$row[0]</i>\n"; }
?>
</body></html>
```

Crashproof Server Selection

The starting point for our second example is similar. However, now our goal is to make the connection process immune to a connection failure. The following lines demonstrate a possible procedure whereby at most ten connection attempts are made.

```
  $tries=0;
  while($tries<10 && !$connID) {
    $mysqlhost=$mysqlhosts[rand(0,1)];
    $connID = @mysqld endedysqluser, $mysqlpasswd);
    $tries++;
  }
  if(!$connID) {
    echo "<p>Sorry, no database server found.\n";
    echo "</body></html>";
    exit();
  }
```

Part V

Reference

#### CHAPTER 13

SQL Reference

THIS CHAPTER GIVES AN OVERVIEW of the SQL operators, functions, and commands available under MySQL. My goal in organizing the information in this chapter was to give you, dear reader, a compact overview of the most important and useful syntax variants.

Please note that MySQL boasts countless extensions as well as, alas, certain shortcomings with respect to the ANSI-SQL/92 standard.

Chapter Overview

Syntax

We begin with a brief section describing the syntax of object names, character strings, dates and times, and binary data.

Object Names

Names of objects—databases, tables, columns, etc.—can be at most 64 characters in length. Permitted characters are all the alphanumeric characters of the character set used by MySQL as well as the characters _ and $. However, for reasons of practicality it is a good idea to limit oneself to the alphanumeric ASCII characters and the underscore.

Table names that do not refer to the current database must have the database name prefixed to them. Likewise, the name of a column must be extended by the name of the table and that of the database if the column name alone fails to provide a unique identification (such as in queries in which several like-named columns in different tables appear):

- **Table names:** *tablename* or *db.tablename*

- **Column names:** *colname* or *tblname.colname* or *dbname.tblname.colname*

Case Sensitivity

The following objects are listed according to whether they do or do not exhibit case sensitivity:

- **Case Sensitivity:** Database names, table names, alias names

- **No Case Sensitivity:** SQL commands and functions, column names, index names

CAUTION *MySQL stores databases in directories and tables in files. Whether case sensitivity is observed in the naming of databases and tables depends not on MySQL but on the operating system. Particular caution is called for if a MySQL application is developed under Windows and the finished code ported to Unix/Linux. While Windows tolerates sloppiness in the use of upper- and lowercase, Unix/Linux always makes case distinctions. SQL instructions that function under Windows can thus produce unexpected problems under Unix/Linux.*

Thus it is a good idea to name databases and tables according to an established plan (in this book they are always written lowercase).

Character Strings

MySQL currently supports only 8-bit character sets (and not multibyte character sets like Unicode). Character strings can be enclosed in single or double quotes. The following two expressions are equivalent in MySQL (though only the single-quote variant conforms to the ANSI-SQL/92 standard).

```
'character string'
"character string"
```

If a quotation mark should happen to be part of the character string, then there are various ways of expressing this:

```
"abc'abc"      means    abc'abc
"abc""abc"     means    abc"abc
"abc\'abc"     means    abc'abc
"abc\"abc"     means    abc"abc
'abc"abc'      means    abc"abc
'abc''abc'     means    abc'abc
'abc\"abc'     means    abc"abc
'abc\'abc'     means    abc'abc
```

Within a character string the special characters provided by the prevailing character set are allowed (for example, äöüßáàéő if you are working with the default character set ISO-8859-1 (Latin-1)). However, some special characters must be specially coded:

Quoting of Special Characters Within a Character String

\0   0 character (Code 0)

\b   backspace character (Code 8)

\t   tab character (Code 9)

\n   newline character (Code 10)

\r   carriage return character (Code 13)

\"   double quote character (Code 34)

\'   single quote character (Code 39)

\\   backslash (Code 92)

If x is not one of the above-mentioned special characters, then $\backslash x$ simply returns the character x. If a character string is to be stored as a BLOB (binary object), then the 0 character as well as the single quote, double quote, and backslash must be given in the form \0, \', \", and \\.

Instead of indicating special characters in character strings or BLOBs by the backslash escape character, it is often easier simply to specify the entire object using hexadecimal notation. MySQL accepts hex codes of arbitrary length in SQL commands in the following form: 0x4142434445464748494a.

However, MySQL is incapable of returning the result of a query in this form. (If you are working with PHP, then that programming language offers a convenient function for this purpose: *bin2hex*.)

> **POINTER** *If two character strings are to be concatenated, then you must use the function* CONCAT. *(The operator + will not serve the purpose.) In general, MySQL provides a broad range of functions for working with character strings.*

Numbers

Decimal numbers are written with a period for the decimal point and without a thousands separator (thus 27345 or 2.71828). One may also use scientific notation (6.0225e23 or 6.626e-34) for very large or very small numbers.

MySQL can also interpret hexadecimal numbers prefixed by 0x. Depending on the context, the number is interpreted as a character string or as a 64-bit integer.

```
SELECT 0x4142434445464748494a
       ABCDEFGHIJ
SELECT 0x41 + 0
       66
```

Automatic Transformation of Numbers and Character Strings

In carrying out an operation on two different data types, MySQL makes every attempt to find a compatible data type. Integers are automatically changed into floating-point numbers if one of the operators is a floating-point number. Character strings are automatically changed into numbers if the operation involves a calculation. (If the beginning of the character string cannot be interpreted as a number, then MySQL calculates with 0.)

```
SELECT   '3.14abc' + 1
         4.14
```

Date and Time

MySQL represents dates as character strings of the form *2001-12-31*, and times in the form *23:59:59*. With the data type *DATETIME* both formats are simply concatenated, yielding, for example, *2001-12-31 23:59:59*. In dealing with values in *TIMESTAMP* columns MySQL leaves out all spaces, hyphens, and colons. In our example we would have *20011231235959*.

```
USE exceptions
SELECT * FROM test_date
```

id	a_date	a_time	a_datetime	a_timestamp
1	2000-12-07	09:06:29	2000-12-07 09:06:29	20001207090649

In storing dates MySQL is quite flexible: Both numbers (e.g., *20011231*) and character strings are accepted. Hyphens are allowed in character strings, or they can simply be done without. If a year is given but no century is specified, then MySQL automatically uses the range 1970–2069. Therefore, MySQL accepts the following character strings for a *DATETIME* column: `'2001 12 31'`, `'20011231'`, `'2001.12.31'`, and `'2001&12&31'`.

> **REMARK** *In storing dates, MySQL carries out only an incomplete check as to whether the date is possible. Thus, for example, it is possible to store* `'2001-2-29'` *in a date field, even though 2001 was not a leap year.*
>
> *The date* `'0000-00-00'` *has a special meaning. This value is officially allowed as a date in MySQL. MySQL uses this value itself when it recognizes a date as patently incorrect (e.g.,* `'2001-2-32'`*).*

Binary Data

Binary data that are to be stored in *BLOB* fields are dealt with in SQL commands like character strings; see above. (However, there are differences in sorting.)

Comments

There are three ways of supplying comments in SQL commands:

```
SELECT 1 # comment
SELECT 1 /* comment */
SELECT 1 -- comment since MySQL 3.23
```

539

Comments that begin with # or with -- (there must be a space after the --)
hold until the end of the line. Comments between /* and */ can extend over
several lines, as in C. Nesting is not allowed.

If you wish to write SQL code that makes use of some of the peculiarities
of MySQL yet remains compatible as much as possible with other dialects, a
particular variant of the comment is often useful:

```
SELECT /*! STRAIGHT_JOIN */ col FROM table ...
```

With the MySQL-specific *SELECT* extension *STRAIGHT_JOIN* will be executed
only by MySQL; all other SQL dialects will consider this a comment.

A variant of this enables differentiation among various MySQL dialects:

```
CREATE /*!32302 TEMPORARY */ TABLE ...
```

In this case the keyword *TEMPORARY* is processed only if the command is
executed by MySQL 3.23.02 or a more recent version.

Semicolons at the End of SQL Commands

Be careful with semicolons!

> **CAUTION** *On the basis of your experience with the MySQL monitor (that
> is, the program* mysql*) you have probably become accustomed to placing a
> semicolon at the end of SQL commands. Even phpMyAdmin deals properly
> with such semicolons (in particular, to separate several SQL commands
> from each other). However, the following must be observed:* Neither
> ANSI-SQL nor the SQL dialect of MySQL allows semicolons at the end of
> an instruction or for separating commands!

Semicolons are thus merely a peculiarity of *mysql* and phpMyAdmin. If you
send SQL commands to MySQL in other programs (or in program code), they
must appear without semicolons. Likewise, it is generally not permitted to send
several commands at once. If you wish to execute several commands, you must
send them one at a time (e.g., in a loop).

Operators

MySQL Operators

	Arithmetic Operators
+, -, *, /	basic arithmetic
%	mod (remainder of integer division)

	Bit Operators
|	binary OR
&	binary AND
~	binary negation (inverts all bits)
<<	shift bits left (multiplication by 2^n)
>>	shift bits right (division by 2^n)

	Comparison Operators
=	equality operator
<=>	equality operator, permitting comparison with *NULL*
!=, <>	inequality operator
<, >, <=, >=	comparison operators
IS [NOT] NULL	*NULL* comparison
BETWEEN	range membership (e.g., *x BETWEEN 1 AND 3*)
IN	set membership (e.g., *x IN (1, 2, 3)* or *x IN ('a', 'b', 'c')*)
NOT IN	set membership (e.g., *x NOT IN ('a', 'b', 'c')*)

	Pattern Comparison
[NOT] LIKE	simple pattern comparison (e.g., *x LIKE 'm%'*)
[NOT] REGEXP	extended pattern comparison (e.g., *x REGEXP '.*x$'*)

	Binary Comparison
BINARY	identifies operand as binary (e.g., *BINARY x = y*)

	Logical Operators
!, NOT	negation
||, OR	logical OR
&&, AND	logical AND

Arithmetic Operators, Bit Operators

Arithmetic operators for which one of the operands is *NULL* generally return *NULL* as result. In MySQL a division by zero also returns the result *NULL*.

Comparison Operators

Comparison operators normally return 1 (corresponding to *TRUE*) or 0 (*FALSE*). Comparisons with *NULL* return *NULL*. The two exceptions are the operators <=> and *IS NULL*, which even in comparison with *NULL* return 0 or 1:

```
SELECT NULL=NULL, NULL=0
  NULL, NULL
SELECT NULL<=>NULL, NULL<=>0
  1, 0
SELECT NULL IS NULL, NULL IS 0
  1, 0
```

In comparing character strings with <, <=, >, >=, as well as with *BETWEEN* (and, of course, with all sorting operations), the character set in force when MySQL was launched plays a decisive role. In the default setting the character set is Latin-1 (ISO-8859-1) with Swedish sort order.

The following examples show that the default behavior of MySQL is not always what you would expect. Thus, for example, *UCASE* (for changing characters to uppercase) does not apply to all special characters. Character comparison, however, works much better:

```
SELECT UCASE('abc äöüÿ åêõ')
  ABC Äöüÿ Åêõ
SELECT 'a'='A', 'a'='ä', 'ä'='Ä', 'ö'='Ö', 'ü'='Ü'
```

'a'='A'	'a'='ä'	'ä'='Ä'	'ö'='Ö'	'ü'='Ü'
1	0	1	1	1

In sorting, Swedish rules are in effect. Here we do not display the result of the query by columns in order to save space. Various special characters and unrepresentable characters have been omitted from the result (and replaced by ...).

```
USE exceptions
SELECT a_char FROM test_order_by
WHERE id>31
ORDER BY a_char
```

!, ", #, $, %, &, ', (,), *, +, ,, -, ., /, 0, 1, 2, 3, 4, 5, 6, 7, 8, 9, :, ;, <,
=, >, ?, @, A, a, À, Á, Â, Ã, à, á, â, ã, B, b, C, c, Ç, ç, D, d, …, E, e, È, É,
Ê, Ë, è, é, ê, ë, F, f, G, g, H, h, I, i, Ì, Í, Î, Ï, ì, í, î, ï, J, j, K, k, L, l,
M, m, N, n, Ñ, ñ, O, o, Ò, Ó, Ô, Õ, ò, ó, ô, õ, P, p, Q, q, R, r, S, s, T,
t, U, u, Ù, Ú, Û, ù, ú, û, V, v, W, w, X, x, Y, y, Ü, Ý, ü, ý, Z, z, [, Å,
å, \, Ä, Æ, ä, æ,], Ö, ö, ^, _, `, {, |, }, ~, …, •, …, f, … ,Š, ‹, Œ,
…, ž, … ,', ', ", ", …, š, ›, œ, …, ž, Ÿ, …, £, …, ß, …, ÿ, …

If you need to store and sort characters outside of the ASCII character set,
see Chapter 12, in which the setting of the character set at launch of MySQL
is discussed.

> **CAUTION**   *If you are using the monitor* mysql.exe *under Windows, it runs
> in a DOS environment, which has its own character set, which is not
> compatible with that of MySQL. For this reason, SQL commands with
> special characters seem to be executed incorrectly in* mysql.exe. *In reality,
> MySQL is working correctly, but because of the DOS character set—which is
> valid for* mysql.exe—*incorrect character codes for such special characters
> as* åäê *are transmitted to the MySQL server.*

Pattern Matching with LIKE

MySQL offers two operators for pattern comparison. The simpler, and ANSI-
compatible, of these is *LIKE*. As with normal character string comparison there is
no case distinction. In addition, there are two wild cards:

_   an arbitrary character

%   arbitrarily many (even 0) characters (but not for *NULL*)

```
SELECT 'MySQL' LIKE '%sql'
      1
```

If the character _ or % is itself to be used in the search pattern, then a
backslash must be prefixed to it, as in, for example, *'50%' LIKE '%\%'* (returns
1). If instead of the backslash another character is to be used in order to preserve
the wild-card effect of _ or %, then this character can be specified with *ESCAPE*:
'50%' LIKE '%&%' ESCAPE '&' (likewise returns 1).

> **REMARK** *Please note that carrying out pattern comparisons in a query involving a large table is very slow. This holds for LIKE and even more so for REGEXP.*

Pattern Matching with REGEXP

Considerably wider scope in the formulation of a pattern is offered by *REGEXP* and the equivalent command *RLIKE*. The relatively complicated syntax for the pattern corresponds to the Unix commands grep and sed. The essential features of the syntax are presented here.

REGEXP *Search Patterns*

	Definition of the Pattern x
abc	character string *abc*
(abc)	character string *abc* (made into a group)
[abc]	one of the characters *a, b, c*
[a-z]	one of the characters *a–z*
[^abc]	none of these characters (any others)
.	any character
	Appearance of the Pattern x
x	expression x must appear once
$x\,|\,y$	expression x or y must appear once
$x?$	expression x must appear at most once
$x*$	expression x may appear arbitrarily often (including not at all)
$x+$	expression x may appear arbitrarily often (but at least once)
$x\{n\}$	expression x must appear exactly n times
$x\{,n\}$	expression x may appear at most n times
$x\{n,\}$	expression x must appear at least n times
$x\{n,m\}$	expression x must appear at least n and at most m times
^	wild card for the beginning of a character string
\$	wild card for the end of a character string
$\backslash x$	special character x (e.g., \\\$ for \$)

As with *LIKE* there is no case distinction. Please note that *REGEXP* is successful when the search pattern is found somewhere within the character string. The search pattern is thus not required to describe the entire character string, but only a part of it. If you wish to encompass the entire character string, then you must use ^ and $ in the search pattern.

```
SELECT 'abcabc' REGEXP 'abc','abcabc' REGEXP 'cb'
      1, 0
SELECT 'abcabc' REGEXP '[a-c]+', 'abcabc' REGEXP '^abc$'
      1, 0
SELECT 'abcabc' REGEXP '(abc)2'
      1
```

> **POINTER** *A large number of additional examples can be found in the appendix to the MySQL documentation. A complete description can be obtained under Unix/Linux with* man 7 regex. *This can also be found on the Internet, for example, at* http://linux.ctyme.com/man/alpha7.htm

Binary Character String Comparison

Character strings are normally compared without case being taken into consideration. Thus 'a' = 'A' returns 1 (true). If you wish to execute a binary comparison, then you must place *BINARY* in front of one of the operands. *BINARY* is a *cast* operator; that is, it alters the data type of one of the operands (in this case it changes a number or character string into a binary object). *BINARY* can be used both for ordinary character string comparison and for pattern matching with *LIKE* and *REGEXP*.

```
SELECT 'a'='A', BINARY 'a' = 'A', 'a' = BINARY 'A'
      1, 0, 0
SELECT 'abcabc' REGEXP 'ABC', 'abcabc' REGEXP BINARY 'ABC'
      1, 0
```

Logical Operators

Logical operators likewise return 0 or 1, or *NULL* if one of the operands is *NULL*. This holds also for *NOT*; that is, *NOT NULL* again returns *NULL*.

MySQL Data Types

Integers

TINYINT	8-bit integer (1 byte)
SMALLINT	16-bit integer (2 bytes)
MEDIUMINT	24-bit integer (3 bytes)
INT, INTEGER	32-bit integer (4 bytes)
BIGINT	64-bit integer (8 bytes)

Floating-Point Number

FLOAT	floating-point number, 8-place precision (4 bytes)
DOUBLE	floating-point number, 16-place precision (8 bytes)
REAL	synonym for *DOUBLE*
DECIMAL(p, s)	fixed-point number, stored as string; arbitrary number of places (1 byte per digit + 2 bytes overhead)
NUMERIC, DEC	synonyms for *DECIMAL*

Date, Time

DATE	date in the form `'2001-12-31'`, range `1000-01-01` to `9999-12-31` (3 bytes)
TIME	time in the form `'23:59:59'`, range $\pm$`838:59:59` (3 bytes)
DATETIME	combination of *DATE* and *TIME* in the form `'2001-12-31 23:59:59'` (8 bytes)
YEAR	year 1900–2155 (1 byte)
TIMESTAMP	date and time in the form 20011231235959 for times between 1970 and 2038 (4 bytes)

Character Strings (ANSI)

CHAR(n)	string with preset length, max 255 characters (*n* bytes)
VARCHAR(n)	string with variable length, max *n* characters ($n < 256$) memory requirement: 1 byte per character (actual length) + 1
TINYTEXT	string with variable length, max 255 characters ($n + 1$ bytes)
TEXT	string with variable length, max $2^{16} - 1$ characters ($n + 2$ Byte)
MEDIUMTEXT	string with variable length, max $2^{24} - 1$ characters ($n + 3$ bytes)

LONGTEXT	string with variable length, max $2^{32} - 1$ characters ($n + 4$ bytes)

Binary Data

TINYBLOB	binary data with variable length, max 255 bytes
BLOB	binary data with variable length, max $2^{16} - 1$ bytes
MEDIUMBLOB	binary data with variable length, max $2^{24} - 1$ bytes
LONGBLOB	binary data with variable length, max $2^{32} - 1$ bytes

Other

ENUM	enumeration of max 65535 character strings (1 or 2 bytes)
SET	enumeration of max 255 character strings (1–8 bytes)

Command Overview (Thematic)

In the following section SQL commands will be listed in alphabetical order. As a supplementary aid to orientation we provide here a systematic overview:

Database Queries, Data Manipulation

SELECT	queries existing data records (data search)
INSERT	inserts a new record
REPLACE	replaces an existing record
UPDATE	changes an existing record
DELETE	deletes selected records
TRUNCATE TABLE	deletes all records
LOAD DATA	inserts records from an ASCII file

Transactions (Only for Some Table Types)

BEGIN	begins a group of SQL commands
COMMIT	confirms all executed commands
ROLLBACK	cancels all executed commands

Generate Databases/Tables, Change Database Design

ALTER TABLE	changes individual columns of a table, adds indexes, etc.
CREATE DATABASE	creates a new database
CREATE FUNCTION	includes a function programmed in C/C++ into MySQL
CREATE INDEX	creates a new index for a table
CREATE TABLE	creates a new table
DROP DATABASE	deletes an entire database
DROP INDEX	deletes an index
DROP TABLE	deletes an entire table
RENAME TABLE	renames a table

Table Management (General)

BACKUP TABLE	copies table files into a backup directory
FLUSH TABLES	closes all table files and then reopens them
LOCK TABLE	blocks tables for (write) access by other users
RESTORE TABLE	restores a table that has been backed up with *BACKUP*
UNLOCK TABLES	releases a table that has been locked with *LOCK*

Management of MyISAM Tables

ANALYZE TABLE	returns information about internal index management
CHECK TABLE	tests the table file for consistency
OPTIMIZE TABLE	optimizes memory usage in tables
REPAIR TABLE	attempts to repair errors in table files

Management of BDB Tables

SHOW LOGS	shows which BDB logging files are in use

Information on the Database Structure, Other Management Information

DESCRIBE	corresponds to *SHOW COLUMNS*
EXPLAIN	explains how a *SELECT* command is executed internally
SHOW	gives information on databases, tables, fields, etc.

Administration, Access Privileges, etc.

FLUSH	empties MySQL intermediate storage or inputs it anew
GRANT	gives out additional access privileges
KILL	terminates a process
REVOKE	restricts access privileges
SET	changes the contents of MySQL system variables
SHOW	shows the MySQL status, system variables, processes, etc.
USE	changes the active database

Replication

CHANGE MASTER TO	changes replication settings in `master.info` (slave)
LOAD TABLE FROM	copies a table from master to slave (slave)
PURGE MASTER LOGS	deletes old logging files (master)
RESET MASTER	deletes all logging files (master)
RESET SLAVE	reinitializes `master.info` (slave)
SET SQL_LOG_BIN=0/1	deactivates/activates binary logging (master)
SHOW MASTER LOGS	returns a list of all binary files (master)
SHOW MASTER STATUS	gives the current logging file (master)
SHOW SLAVE STATUS	displays the contents of `master.info` (slave)
SLAVE START/STOP	starts or ends replication (slave)

Command Reference (Alphabetical)

ALTER TABLE *tblname tbloptions*

ALTER TABLE can be used to change various details of the structure of a table. In the following we present an overview of the syntax variants.

In the syntactically simplest form that we shall show here, *ALTER TABLE* changes the table options. The possible options are described in *CREATE TABLE*. The command can be used, for example, to change the type of a table (e.g., from MyISAM to BDB).

ALTER TABLE *tblname* ***ADD*** *newcolname coltype coloptions*
    [FIRST | AFTER existingcolumn]

This command adds a new column to a table. The definition of the new column takes place as with *CREATE TABLE*. If the position of the new column is not specified with *FIRST* or *AFTER*, then the new column will be the last column of the table.

ALTER TABLE *tblname* ***ADD INDEX*** *[indexname] (indexcols . . .)*
ALTER TABLE *tblname* ***ADD FULLTEXT*** *[indexname] (indexcols . . .)*
ALTER** [IGNORE]* ***TABLE *tblname* ***ADD UNIQUE*** *[indexname] (indexcols . . .)*
ALTER** [IGNORE]* ***TABLE *tblname* ***ADD PRIMARY KEY*** *(indexcols . . .)*

These commands create a new index for a table. In no *indexname* is specified, then MySQL simply uses the name of the indexed column.

The optional keyword *IGNORE* comes into play if several identical fields are discovered in the creation of a *UNIQUE* or primary index. Without *IGNORE* the command will be terminated with an error, and the index will not be generated. With *IGNORE* such duplicate records are simply deleted.

ALTER TABLE *tblname* ***ALTER*** *colname* ***SET DEFAULT*** *value*
ALTER TABLE *tblname* ***ALTER*** *colname* ***DROP DEFAULT***

This command changes the default value for a column or table or deletes an existing default value.

ALTER TABLE *tblname* ***CHANGE*** *oldcolname newcolname coltype coloptions*

This command changes the default value for a column in a table or deletes an existing default value. The description of the column proceeds as with *CREATE*

TABLE, which you may refer to. If the column name is to remain unchanged, then it must be given twice (that is, *oldcolname* and *newcolname* are identical). Even if *ALTER TABLE* is used only to change the name of a column, both *coltype* and *coloptions* must be completely specified.

ALTER TABLE *tblname* **DROP** *colname*
ALTER TABLE *tblname* **DROP INDEX** *indexname*
ALTER TABLE *tblname* **DROP PRIMARY KEY**

This command deletes a column, an index, or the primary index.

ALTER TABLE *tblname* **MODIFY** *colname coltype coloptions*

This command functions like *ALTER TABLE . . . CHANGE* (see above). The only difference is that the column cannot be changed, and thus the name needs to be given only once.

ALTER TABLE *tblname* **RENAME AS** *newtblname*

This command renames a table. See also *RENAME TABLE*.

ANALYZE TABLE *tablename1, tablename2, . . .*

ANALYZE TABLE performs an analysis of the indexed values of a column. The results are stored, and in the future this speeds up index access to data records a bit. Currently (version 3.23.*n*), this works only for MyISAM tables.

    ANALYZE TABLE can be used only with tables of type *MyISAM*. Instead of this command the external program `myisamchk -a tblfile` can be used.

BACKUP TABLE *tblname* **TO** *'/backup/directory'*

BACKUP TABLE copies the files for the specified table into a backup directory. The table can be recreated with *RESTORE TABLE*.

BEGIN

If you are working with BDB tables, you can introduce a new transaction with *BEGIN*. The following SQL commands can then be confirmed with *COMMIT* or revoked with *ROLLBACK*. (All changes to tables are executed only via *COMMIT*.) Further information and examples on the topic of transactions can be found in Chapter 12.

CHANGE MASTER TO *variable=value*

With this command you can change settings saved in `master.info`. The command can be used only for slave computers in a replication system. It recognizes the following variable names:

MASTER_HOST	specifies the hostname or IP number of the master computer
MASTER_USER	specifies the username used for communication with the master computer
MASTER_PASSWORD	specifies the associated password
MASTER_PORT	specifies the port number of the master computer (normally 3306)
MASTER_LOG_FILE	specifies the current logging file on the master computer
MASTER_LOG_POS	specifies the current read position within the logging file on the master computer

CHECK TABLE *tablename1, tablename2 . . . [TYPE=QUICK]*

CHECK TABLE tests the internal integrity of the database file for the specified table. Any errors that are discovered are not corrected. Currently (version 3.23.*n*), this functions only for MyISAM tables.

   CHECK TABLE can be used only for tables of type *MyISAM*. Instead of this command the external program `myisamchk -m tblfile` can be used.

COMMIT

COMMIT completes a transaction initiated with *BEGIN* and stores all changes in the database. (Instead of executing *COMMIT*, you can cancel the pending changes with *ROLLBACK*.) *BEGIN/COMMIT/ROLLBACK* function only if you are working with BDB tables. Further information and examples on transactions can be found in Chapter 12.

CREATE DATABASE *dbname*

CREATE DATABASE generates the specified database. (More precisely, an empty directory is created in which tables belonging to the new database can be stored.) Note that database names are case-sensitive. This command can be executed only if the user has sufficient access privileges to create new databases.

CREATE FUNCTION *fnname RETURNS datatype SONAME libraryname*

CREATE FUNCTION makes it possible to bring a function in an external library into MySQL. If you believe that this means that you can simply equip MySQL with a variety of new functions, you are sadly mistaken: The syntax of *CREATE FUNCTION* is simple, but the problem is that first the code for the function must be written in C or C++ and then compiled into a library. This requires a degree of background knowledge about how functions work in MySQL (and, of course, the requisite tools, like compilers). Further information on creating MySQL functions can be found in a chapter of the MySQL documentation devoted to this subject.

CREATE *[UNIQUE\FULLTEXT]* **INDEX** *indexname ON tablename (indexcols . . .)*

CREATE INDEX enlarges an existing database to include an index. As *indexname* the name of the column is generally used. *CREATE INDEX* is not a free-standing command, but merely an alternative form of *ALTER TABLE ADD INDEX/UNIQUE,* which you should see for details.

CREATE *[TEMPORARY]* **TABLE** *[IF NOT EXISTS] tblname*
   (colname1 coltype coloptions reference,
      colname2 coltype coloptions reference . . .
      [, index1, index2 . . .]
)
   [tbloptions]

CREATE TABLE generates a new table in the current database. If a database other than the current one is to be used, the table name can be specified in the form *dbname.tblname.* If the table already exists, an error message results. There is no error message if *IF NOT EXISTS* is used, but in this case the existing table is not affected and no new table is created.

   If the keyword *TEMPORARY* is used (as of version 3.23), then the table that is created is a temporary one. If a temporary table is created and a like-named, but nontemporary, table already exists, the temporary table is created without an error message. The old table is preserved, but it is masked by the temporary table. If you want your temporary table to exist only in RAM (for increased speed), you must also specify *TYPE = HEAP*.

- *colname:* Name of the column.

- *coltype:* Data type of the column. A list of all MySQL data types (*INT, TEXT,* etc.) appears in the previous section.

- *coloptions:* Here several attributes (options) can be specified:

  - **NOT NULL | NULL:** *NOT NULL* indicates that no *NULL* values may be stored in the column, and thus the column may not have empty cells. (By default, columns are created with the attribute *NULL.*)

- ○ **DEFAULT** *defaultval:* *DEFAULT* specifies a default value that is then stored if no value is specified.
  - ○ **AUTO_INCREMENT:** *AUTO_INCREMENT* indicates that MySQL inserts a unique numerical value for each new record (ideal for primary key fields).
  - ○ **PRIMARY KEY:** *PRIMARY KEY* signifies that the field is to be used as a primary key. (MySQL creates a *UNIQUE* index for the field. The field must have the attribute *NOT NULL.*)

- *reference:* MySQL provides various key words for the declaration of foreign keys in keeping track of referential integrity, e.g., *REFERENCES tblname (idcol).* These key words are currently ignored, however. We must wait and see when these key words will actually be supported by MySQL. A description can be found in the MySQL documentation.

- *index: KEY* or *INDEX* defines a usual index spanning one or more columns. *UNIQUE* defines a unique index (that is, in the column or columns no identical values or groups of values can be stored). With both variants an arbitrary index name may be given for the internal management of the index. *PRIMARY KEY* likewise defines a *UNIQUE* index. Here, however, the index name is predefined: It is, not surprisingly, *PRIMARY.* With *FULLTEXT,* finally, an index is declared for full-text search (since MySQL 3.23.23).

  - ○ *KEY | INDEX [indexname] (indexcols . . .)*
  - ○ *UNIQUE [INDEX] [indexname] (indexcols . . .)*
  - ○ *PRIMARY KEY (indexcols . . .)*
  - ○ *FULLTEXT (indexcols . . .)*

  Again, certain key words may be used here that are currently ignored by MySQL and are therefore not described here (e.g., *FOREIGN KEY,* *CHECK(expr)*).

- *tbloptions:* Here various table options can be specified, though here we shall exhibit only the most important of them. Not all options are possible with every table type. Information on the different table types and their variants (MyISAM static, dynamic, or compressed) can be found in Chapter 5. BDB, InnoDB, and Gemini tables were described in Chapter 12.

  - ○ *TYPE = ISAM | MYISAM | HEAP | BDB | MERGE | INNODB | GEMINI*
  - ○ *ROW_FORMAT= default | dynamic | static | compressed*
  - ○ *AUTO_INCREMENT = n:* *AUTO_INCREMENT* gives the initial value for the counter for an *AUTO_INCREMENT* column (e.g., 100000 if you wish to have six-digit integers).
  - ○ *CHECKSUM = 0 | 1:* *CHECK_SUM=1* has the effect that a check sum is stored for each data record, which helps in reconstruction if the database is damaged.

- ○ *COMMENT = 'comment'.*
- ○ *PACK_KEYS = 0 | 1: PACK_KEYS=1* results in a smaller index file. This speeds up read access, but slows down changes.
- ○ *DELAY_KEY_WRITE = 0 | 1: DELAY_KEY_WRITE=1* results in indexes not being updated each time a change to a record is made. Rather, they are updated every now and then.

The *CREATE TABLE* syntax contains some duplication. For example, a primary index can be declared in two different ways, either as an attribute of a column (*coloptions*) or as an independent index (*index*). The result is, of course, the same. It is up to you to decide which form you prefer.

Example

```
CREATE TABLE test    (id INT NOT NULL AUTO_INCREMENT,
                      data INT NOT NULL,
                      txt VARCHAR(60),
                      PRIMARY KEY (id))
```

Additional examples can be found in Chapter 5, under the topic database design.

CREATE *[TEMPORARY]* **TABLE** *[IF NOT EXISTS] tblname*
    [(colname1 coltype coloptions reference,
      colname2 coltype coloptions reference . . .
      [, key1, key2 . . .]
)]
    [tbloptions]
    *[IGNORE | REPLACE]***SELECT** *. . . ***

With this variant of the *CREATE TABLE* command a table is filled with the result of a *SELECT* command. The individual columns of the new table take their types from the data types of the *SELECT* command and thus do not have to be declared explicitly. A declaration is necessary only for individual columns to which a particular property is to be given (e.g., *PRIMARY KEY (id)*). There is also the possibility of defining an additional *AUTO INCREMENT* column.

The key words *IGNORE* and *REPLACE* specify how MySQL should behave if several records with the same value are placed by the command into a *UNIQUE* column. With *IGNORE* the existing record is retained, and new records are ignored. With *REPLACE* existing records are replaced by the new ones. If neither option is used, an error message results.

This command provides the simplest mechanism in MySQL for copying complete tables (see the first example).

Examples

```
CREATE TABLE backuptable SELECT * FROM table
CREATE TEMPORARY TABLE tmp
  SELECT id, authname FROM authors WHERE id<20
```

DELETE *[deleteoptions]* **FROM** *tablename*
    [WHERE condition]
    [LIMIT maxrecords]

DELETE deletes the records in a table encompassed by *condition*.

- *deleteoptions:* Currently, the only available option is *LOW_PRIORITY*. This option has the effect that the data records are deleted only when all read operations are complete. (The goal of this option is to avoid having *SELECT* queries unnecessarily delayed due to *DELETE* operations.)

- *condition:* This condition specifies which records are to be deleted. For the syntax of *condition* see *SELECT*.

- *maxrecords:* With *LIMIT* the maximum number of records that may be deleted is specified.

If *DELETE* is executed without conditions, then all records of the table are deleted (so be careful!). Internally, the much more efficient *TRUNCATE* is used. This has the drawback that *DELETE* does not return the number of deleted records (but 0 instead). With MySQL 4.0 this should be repaired. *DELETE* without conditions cannot be part of a transaction. If a transaction is open, it is closed with *COMMIT* before the *DELETE* command is executed.

Through version 3.23.*n* MySQL does not recognize sub*SELECT*s with *DELETE*. It is thus impossible to formulate a *DELETE* command that deletes records from table *a* based on data from tables *b*, *c*, etc. In contrast to *SELECT*, here the usual tricks (refined *JOIN* constructions, temporary tables, etc.) are of no avail. Delete operations in which data from several tables are to be considered can therefore currently be carried out only via the detour of another programming language (Perl, for example), where the results of a query can be evaluated so that the corresponding *DELETE* commands can then be executed.

DESCRIBE *tablename [columnname]*

DESCRIBE returns information about the specified table in the current database (or about a particular column of this table). Instead of *columnname* a pattern with the wild cards _ and % can be given. In this case, *DESCRIBE* displays information about those columns matching the pattern. *DESCRIBE* returns the same information as *EXPLAIN* or *SHOW TABLE* or *SHOW COLUMN*.

DROP DATABASE *[IF EXISTS] dbname*

DROP DATABASE deletes an existing database with all of its data. This cannot be undone; so be careful! If the database does not exist, then an error is reported. This error can be avoided with an *IF EXISTS*.

In the execution of this command all files in the directory dbname with the following endings are deleted: .BAK, .DAT, .HSH, .ISD, .ISM, .MRG, .MYD, .MYI, .db, .frm.

DROP FUNCTION *fnname*

DROP FUNCTION deactivates an auxiliary function that was made available to MySQL earlier with *CREATE FUNCTION*.

DROP INDEX *indexname ON tablename*

DROP INDEX removes an index from the specified table. Usually, *indexname* is the name of the indexed column, or else *PRIMARY* for the primary index.

DROP TABLE *[IF EXISTS] tablename1, tablename2, . . .*

DROP TABLE deletes the specified tables irrevocably. The option *IF EXISTS* avoids an error message if the tables do not exist.

EXPLAIN *tablename*

EXPLAIN returns a table with information about all the columns of a table (field name, field type, index, default value, etc.). The same information can be determined as well with *SHOW COLUMNS* or *DESCRIBE*, or via an external program such as mysqlshow.

EXPLAIN SELECT *selectcommand*

EXPLAIN SELECT returns a table with information about how the specified *SELECT* command was executed. These data can help in speed optimization of queries, and in particular in deciding which columns of a table should be indexed. (The syntax of *selectcommand* was described under *SELECT*. An example for the use of *EXPLAIN SELECT* and a brief description of the resulting table can be found in Chapter 5.)

***FLUSH** flushoptions*

FLUSH empties the MySQL internal intermediate storage. Any information not stored already is thereby stored in the database. The execution of *FLUSH* requires the *RELOAD* privilege.

- *flushoptions:* Here one may specify which cache(s) should be emptied. Multiple options should be separated by commas.

  - *HOSTS:* Empties the host cache table. This is necessary especially if in the local network the arrangement of IP numbers has changed.
  - *LOGS:* Closes all logging files and then reopens them. In the case of update logs a new logging file is created, whereby the number of the file ending is increased by 1 (*file.003* → *file.004*).
  - *PRIVILEGES:* Reloads the privileges database *mysql* (corresponds to `mysqladmin reload`).
  - *STATUS:* Sets most status variables to 0.
  - *TABLES:* Closes all open tables.
  - *TABLE[S] tblname1, tblname2, . . . :* Closes the specified tables.
  - *TABLES WITH READ LOCK:* As above, except that additionally, *LOCK* is executed for all tables, which remains in force until the advent of a corresponding *UNLOCK table.*

The *FLUSH* operations can also be executed through the auxiliary program `mysqladmin`.

***GRANT** privileges ON objects*
> *TO users [IDENTIFIED BY ' password']*
> *[WITH GRANT OPTION]*

GRANT helps in the allocation of access privileges to database objects.

- *privileges:* Several privileges may be specified (separated by commas):

  > *ALTER, CREATE, DELETE, DROP, FILE, INDEX, PROCESS, REFERENCES, RELOAD, SELECT, SHUTDOWN, UPDATE.*

  If you wish to set all (or no) privileges, then specify *ALL* (or *USAGE*). (The second variant is useful if you wish to create a new MySQL user to whom as of yet no privileges have been granted.) The *Grant* privilege can be set only via *WITH GRANT OPTION*; that is, *ALL* does not include the *Grant* privilege.

  If the privileges are to hold only for certain columns of a table, then specify the columns in parentheses. For example, you may specify *GRANT SELECT(columnA, columnB).*

- *objects:* Here databases and tables are specified. The following syntax variants are available:

databasename.tablename	Only this table in this database
*databasename.**	all tables in this database
tablename	only this table in the current database
*	all tables of the current database
.	global privileges

Wild cards may not be used in the database names.

- *users:* Here one or more (comma-separated) users may be specified. If these users are not yet known to the *user* table, they are created. The following variants are allowed:

username@hostname	only this user at *hostname*
' *username*' @' *hostname*'	as above, with wild cards
username	this user on all computers
'' @*hostname*	all users on *hostname*
''	all users on all computers

Optionally, with *IDENTIFIED BY* a password in plain text can be specified. *GRANT* encrypts this password with the function *PASSWORD* before it is entered in the *user* table.

If the specified user does not yet exist and *GRANT* is executed without *IDENTIFIED BY*, then the new user has no password (which represents a security risk). On the other hand, if the user already exists, then *GRANT* without *IDENTIFIED BY* does not alter the password. (There is thus no danger that a password can be accidentally deleted by *GRANT*.)

It is impossible with *GRANT* to delete privileges that have already been granted (for example, by executing the command again with a smaller list of privileges). If you wish to take away privileges, you must use *REVOKE*.

INSERT *[insertoptions]* **INTO** *tablename [(columnlist)]***VALUES** *(valuelist1),(. . .)*
   . . .
INSERT *[insertoptions]* **INTO** *tablename* **SET** *column1=value1, column2=value2*
   . . .
INSERT *[insertoptions]* **INTO** *tablename [(columnlist)]* **SELECT** . . .

The *INSERT* command has the job of inserting new records into an existing table. There are three main syntax variants. In the first (and most frequently used) of these, new data records are specified in parentheses. Thus a typical *INSERT* command looks like this:

```
INSERT INTO tablename (columnA, columnB, columnC)
VALUES ('a', 1, 2), ('b', 7, 5)
```

The result is the insertion of two new records into the table. Columns that are allowed to be *NULL,* for which there is a default value, or which are automatically filled in by MySQL via *AUTO_IN* do not have to be specified. If the column names (i.e., in *columnlist*) are not given, then in *VALUES* all values must be given in the order of the columns.

With the second variant only one record can be changed (not several simultaneously). Such a command looks like this:

```
INSERT INTO tablename SET columnA='a', columnB=1, columnC=2
```

For the third variant the data come from a *SELECT* instruction.

- *insertoptions*   The behavior of this command can be controlled with a number of global options:

  - *IGNORE* has the effect that the insertion of records with existing values is simply ignored for *UNIQUE KEY* columns. (Without this option the result would be an error message.)
  - *LOW_PRIORITY | DELAYED* have influence over when the insertion operation is carried out. In both cases MySQL delays its storage operation until there are no pending read accesses to the table. The advantage of *DELAYED* is that MySQL returns OK at once, and the client does not need to wait for the end of the saving operation. However, *DELAYED* cannot be used if then an *AUTO_INCREMENT* value with *LAST_INSERT_ID()* is to be determined. *DELAYED* should also not be used if a *LOCK* was placed on the table. (The reason is this: For executing *INSERT DELAYED* a new MySQL thread is started, and table locking uses threads in its operation.)

    The records to be inserted are stored in RAM until the insertion operation has actually been carried out. If MySQL should be terminated for some reason (crash, power outage), then the data are lost.

JOIN

JOIN is not actually an SQL command. This key word is mostly used as part of a *SELECT* command, to link data from several tables. *JOIN* will be described under *SELECT.*

KILL *threadid*

This command terminates a specified thread (subprocess) of the MySQL server. It is allowed only to those users who possess the *PROCESS* privilege. A list of running threads can be obtained via *SHOW PROCESSLIST*. Threads can also be terminated via the external program mysqladmin.

LOAD DATA *[loadoptions] INFILE 'filename' [duplicateoptions]*
    INTO TABLE tablename
    [importoptions]
    [IGNORE ignorenr LINES]
    [(columnlist)]

LOAD DATA reads a text file and inserts the data contained therein line by line into a table as data records. *LOAD DATA* is significantly faster then inserting data by multiple *INSERT* commands.

    Normally, the file *filename* is read from the server's file system, on which MySQL is running. (For this the *FILE* privilege is required. For security reasons the file must either be located in the directory of the database or be readable by all users of the computer.)

- *loadoptions: LOCAL* has the effect that the file *filename* on the local client computer is read (that is, the computer on which the command *LOAD DATA* is executed, not on the server computer). For this no *FILE* privilege is necessary. (The *FILE* privilege relates only to the file system of the MySQL server computer.)

  LOW PRIORITY has the effect that the data are inserted into the table only if no other user is reading the table.

- *filename:* If a file name is given without the path, then MySQL searches for this file in the directory of the current database (e.g., *'bulk.txt'*).

  If the file name is given with a relative path, then the path is interpreted by MySQL relative to the data directory (e.g., *'mydir/bulk.txt'*).

  File names with absolute path are taken without alteration (for example, *'/tmp/mydir/bulk.txt'*).

- *duplicateoptions: IGNORE | REPLACE* determine the behavior of MySQL when a new data record has the same *UNIQUE* or *PRIMARY KEY* value as an existing record. With *IGNORE* the existing record is preserved, and the new records are ignored. With *REPLACE* existing records are replaced by the new ones. If neither of these options is used, then the result is an error message.

- *importoptions:* Here is specified how the data should be formatted in the file to be imported. The entire *importoptions* block looks like this:

  [FIELDS
    [TERMINATED BY ' fieldtermstring']
    [ENCLOSED BY ' enclosechar']
    [ESCAPED BY ' escchar']]
  [LINES TERMINATED BY ' linetermstring']

  - *fieldtermstring* specifies the character string that separates the individual columns within the row (e.g., a tab character).
  - *enclosechar* specifies the character that should stand before and after individual entries in the text file (usually the single or double quote character for character strings). If an entry begins with this character, then that character is removed from the beginning and end. Entries that do not begin with the *enclosechar* character will still be accepted. The use of the character in the text file is thus to some extent optional.
  - *escchar* specifies which character is to be used to mark special characters (usually the backslash). This is necessary if special characters appear in character strings in the text file that are also used to separate columns or rows. Furthermore, MySQL expects the ASCII code null in the form \0, where the backslash is to be replaced as necessary by *escchar* if a character has been specified for *escchar*).
  - *linetermstring* specifies the character string with which rows are to be terminated. With DOS/Windows text files this must be the character string ' \r\n'.

  In these four character strings the following special characters can be specified:

\0	ASCII 0	\t	tab
\b	backspace	\'	singe quote
\n	newline	\"	double quote
\r	carriage return	\\	backslash
\s	blank character		

  Furthermore, the character strings can be given in hexadecimal form (e.g., *0x22* instead of ' \''').

  If no character strings are given, then the following is the default setting:

  FIELDS TERMINATED BY ' \t' ENCLOSED BY '' ESCAPED BY ' \\' LINES TERMINATED BY ' \n'

- *ignorenr:* This value specifies how many lines should be ignored at the beginning of the ASCII file. This is particularly useful if the first lines contain table headings.

- *columnlist:* If the order of the columns in the text file does not exactly correspond to that in the table, then here one may specify which file columns correspond with which table columns. The list of columns must be set in parentheses: for example, *(firstname, lastname, birthdate).*

If *TIMESTAMP* columns are not considered during importation or if *NULL* is inserted, then MySQL inserts the actual time. MySQL exhibits analogous behavior with *AUTO_INCREMENT* columns.

LOAD DATA displays as result, among other things, an integer representing the number of warnings. Unfortunately, there is no way of determining the cause of the warnings (or at least the records or rows that caused the warnings). A typical cause is too many or too few columns in the file to be imported. Excess columns are simply ignored; for missing columns either 0 or an empty character string is inserted. (An incorrect number of columns can also signify that MySQL was unable to locate the exact column boundaries.)

Instead of *LOAD DATA* you can also use the program `mysqlimport`. This program creates a link to MySQL and then uses *LOAD DATA*. The inverse of *LOAD DATA* is the command *SELECT . . . INTO OUTFILE*. With it you can export a table into an ASCII file. Further information and concrete examples can be found in Chapter 11.

LOAD TABLE tablename *FROM MASTER*

This command copies a table in a replication system from master to slave. It is, unfortunately, not documented in what scenario this command might usefully be used: perhaps for the repair of a replication system after errors have been detected. (Under version 2.23.33 the command produces nothing but *access denied* errors.)

LOCK TABLE tablename1 [AS aliasname] locktype, table1 [AS alias2] locktype,

   . . .

LOCK TABLE prevents other MySQL users from executing write or read operations on the specified tables. If a table is already blocked by another user, then the command waits (unfortunately, without a timeout value, thus theoretically forever) until that block is released.

Table *LOCK*s ensure that during the execution of several commands no data are changed by other users. Typically, *LOCK*s are necessary when first a *SELECT* query is executed and then tables are changed with *UPDATE*, where the results of the previous query are used. (For a single *UPDATE* command, on the other hand, no *LOCK* is necessary. Individual *UPDATE* commands are always completely executed by the MySQL server without giving other users the opportunity to change data.)

- *locktype:* Here one of four possible locking types must be specified.
  - ○ *READ:* All MySQL users may read the table, but no one may change anything (including the user who executed the *LOCK* command). A *READ LOCK* is allocated only when the table is not blocked by other *WRITE LOCK*s. (Existing *READ LOCK*s, on the other hand, are no hindrance for new *READ LOCK*s. It is thus possible for several users to have simultaneous *READ LOCK*s on the same table.)
  - ○ *READ LOCAL:* Like READ, except that *INSERT*s are allowed if they do not change existing data records.
  - ○ *WRITE:* The current user may read and change the table. All other users are completely blocked. They may neither change data in the blocked table nor read it. A *WRITE LOCK* is allocated only if the table is not blocked by other *LOCK*s (*READ* or *WRITE*). Until the *WRITE LOCK* is lifted, other users can obtain neither a *READ LOCK* nor a *WRITE LOCK*.
  - ○ *LOW PRIORITY WRITE:* Like WRITE, except that during the waiting time (that is, until all other *READ* and *WRITE LOCK*s have been ended) other users may obtain on demand a new *READ LOCK*. However, this means as well that the *LOCK* will be allocated only when there is no other user who wishes a *READ LOCK*.

Table *LOCK*s can increase the speed with which several database commands can be executed one after the other (of course, at the cost that other users are blocked during this time).

MySQL manages table *LOCK*s by means of a thread, where each connection is associated with its own thread. Only one *LOCK* command is considered per thread. (But several tables may be included.) As soon as *UNLOCK TABLES* or *LOCK* is executed for any other table, then all previous locks become invalid.

For reasons of efficiency it should definitely be attempted to keep *LOCK*s as brief as possible and to end them as quickly as possible by *UNLOCK*. *LOCK*s end automatically when the current process ends (that is, for example, when the connection between server and client is broken).

OPTIMIZE TABLE *tablename*

OPTIMIZE TABLE removes unused storage space from a table file and sees to it that associated data in a data record are stored together. Currently (version 3.23.n), this functions only for MyISAM tables.

OPTIMIZE TABLE should be regularly executed for tables whose contents are continually being changed (many *UPDATE* and *DELETE* commands). Not only is the file made smaller, but access is speeded up. (Alternatively, the program `myisamchk` can be executed.)

PURGE MASTER LOGS TO *'hostname-bin.n'*

This command deletes all binary logging files that are older than the file specified. Execute this command only when you are sure that the logging files are no longer needed, that is, when all slave computers have synchronized their databases. This command can be executed only on the master computer of a replication system. See also *RESET MASTER.*

RENAME TABLE *oldtablename* **TO** *newtablename*

RENAME TABLE gives a new name to an existing table. It is also possible to rename several tables, e.g., *a TO b, c TO d*, etc.

In older versions of MySQL *RENAME TABLE* is not available as a free-standing command. There you must use *ALTER TABLE . . . RENAME AS.*

REPAIR TABLE *tablename1, tablename2, . . . [TYPE = QUICK]*

REPAIR TABLE attempts to repair a defective table file. With the option *TYPE = QUICK* only the index is recreated. Currently (version 3.23.*n*), this functions only for MyISAM tables.

REPAIR TABLE can be used only with *MyISAM* tables. Instead of this command you may also use the external program `myisamchk -r tblfile`. (If *REPAIR TABLE* does not return `OK` as result, then you might try `myisamchk -o`. This program currently offers more repair possibilities than *REPAIR TABLE*.)

REPLACE

REPLACE is a variant of *INSERT*. The only difference relates to new records whose key word is the same as that of an existing record. In this case the existing record is deleted and the new one stored in the table. Since the behavior with duplicates is so clearly defined, *REPLACE* does not have the *IGNORE* option possessed by the *INSERT* command.

RESET MASTER

This command deletes all binary logging files including the index file `hostname-bin.index`. With this command replication can be restarted at a particular time. For this, *RESET SLAVE* must be executed on all slave systems. Before the command is executed it must be ensured that the databases on all slave systems are identical to those of the master system.

If you wish to delete only old (no longer needed) logging files, then use *PURGE MASTER LOGS*.

RESET SLAVE

This command reinitializes the slave system. The contents of master.info (and with it the current logging file and its position) are deleted. This command makes sense only if after some problems the databases are to be set up on the slave based on previous snapshots so that the slave system then can synchronize itself by replication, or when *RESET MASTER* was executed on the master system (so that all logging files are deleted there). In this case first *SLAVE STOP* and then *SLAVE START* should be executed on the slave system.

RESTORE TABLE tblname FROM '/backup/directory'

RESTORE TABLE copies the files of the specified table from a backup directory into the data directory of the current database. *RESTORE TABLE* is the inverse of *BACKUP TABLE*.

REVOKE privileges ON objects FROM users

REVOKE is the inverse of *GRANT*. With this command you can remove individual privileges previously granted. The syntax for the parameters *privileges*, *objects*, and *users* can be read about under the *GRANT* command. The only difference relates to the *Grant* privilege: To revoke this privilege from a user, *REVOKE* can be used in the following form: *REVOKE GRANT OPTION ON . . . FROM . . . .*

Although *GRANT* inserts new users into the *mysql.user* table, *REVOKE* is incapable of deleting this user. You can remove all privileges from this user with *REVOKE*, but you cannot prevent this user from establishing a connection to MySQL. (If you wish to take that capability away as well, you must explicitly remove the entries from the *user* database with the *DELETE* command.)

Please note that in the MySQL access system you cannot forbid what is allowed at a higher level. If you allow x access to database d, then you cannot exclude table $d.t$ with *REVOKE*. If you wish to allow x access to all tables of the database d with the exception of table t, then you must forbid access to the entire database and then allow access to individual tables of the database (with exception of d). *REVOKE* is not smart enough to carry out such operations on its own.

ROLLBACK

ROLLBACK undoes all SQL commands executed since the last *BEGIN*. (Instead of *ROLLBACK*, you can confirm the pending changes with *COMMIT* and thereby finalize their execution.) *BEGIN/COMMIT/ROLLBACK* work only if you are working with BDB tables. Further information and examples on transactions can be found in Chapter 12.

SELECT *[selectoptions] column1 [AS alias1], column2 [AS alias2] . . .*
    [FROM tablelist]
    [WHERE condition]
    [GROUP BY groupfield]
    [HAVING condition]
    [ORDER BY ordercolumn1 [DESC], ordercolumn2 [DESC] . . .]
    [LIMIT [offset,] rows]

SELECT serves to formulate database queries. It returns the query result in tabular form. *SELECT* is usually implemented in the following form:

```
SELECT column1, column2, column3 FROM table ORDER BY column1
```

However, there are countless syntax variants, thanks to which *SELECT* can be used also, for example, for processing simple expressions.

```
SELECT HOUR(NOW())
```

- *selectoptions:* The behavior of this command can be controlled by a number of options:
  - *DISTINCT | ALL* specify how MySQL should behave when a query returns several identical records. *DISTINCT* means that identical result records should be displayed only once. *ALL* means that all records should be displayed (the default setting).
  - *SQL_SMALL_RESULT | SQL_BIG_RESULT* specify whether a large or small record list is expected as result, and they help MySQL in optimization. Both options are useful only with *GROUP BY* and *DISTINCT* queries.
  - *SQL_BUFFER_RESULT* has the effect that the result of a query is stored in a temporary table. This option should be used when the evaluation of the query is expected to range over a long period of time and locking problems are to be avoided during this period.
  - *HIGH_PRIORITY* has the effect that a query with higher priority than change or insert commands will be executed. *HIGH_PRIORITY* should be used only for queries that need to be executed very quickly.
  - *STRAIGHT_JOIN* has the effect that data collected from queries extending over more than one table should be joined in the order of the *FROM* expression. (Without *STRAIGHT_JOIN* MySQL attempts

to find the optimal order on its own. *STRAIGHT_JOIN* bypasses this optimization algorithm.)

- *column:* Here column names are normally given. If the query encompasses several tables, then the format is *table.column.* If a query is to encompass all the columns of the tables specified by *FROM*, then you can save yourself some typing and simply specify *. (Note, however, that this is inefficient in execution if you do not need all the columns.)

  However, instead of column names you may also use general expressions or functions, e.g., for formatting a column (*DATE_FORMAT(. . .)*) or for calculating an expression (*COUNT(. . .)*).

  With *AS* a column can be given a new name. This is practical in using functions, such as *HOUR(column) AS hr*.

  Such an alias name can then be used in most of the rest of the *SELECT* command (e.g., *ORDER BY hr*). The alias name cannot, however, be placed in a *WHERE* clause.

- *tablelist:* In the simplest case there is simply a list (separated by commas) of all tables that are to be considered in the query. If no relational conditions (further below with *WHERE*) are formulated, then MySQL returns a list of all possible combinations of data records of all affected tables.

  There is the possibility of specifying here a condition for linking the tables, for example in the following forms:

  > *table1 LEFT [OUTER] JOIN table2 ON table1.xyID = table2.xyID*
  > *table1 LEFT [OUTER] JOIN table2 USING (xyID)*
  > *table1 NATURAL [LEFT [OUTER]] JOIN*

  An extensive and complete list of the many syntactic synonyms can be found in Chapter 6, where the topic of links among several tables is covered in great detail.

- *condition:* Here is where conditions that the query results must fulfill can be formulated. Conditions can contain comparisons (*column1>10* or *column1=column2*) or pattern expressions (*column LIKE '%xy'*), for example. Several conditions can be joined with *AND*, *OR*, and *NOT*.

  MySQL allows selection conditions with *IN*:

  WHERE id IN(1, 2, 3) corresponds to *WHERE id=1 OR id=2 OR id=3.*
  WHERE id NOT IN (1,2) corresponds to *WHERE NOT (id=1 OR id=2).*

  Unfortunately, MySQL currently (3.23.*n*) allows no sub*SELECT*s, that is, *WHERE id IN(SELECT id FROM othertable).* In many cases this shortcoming can be overcome with clever *JOIN* commands. Otherwise, temporary tables can be of assistance. With MySQL 4.0 this situation should be remedied.

Since MySQL 3.23.23 conditions can be formulated with *MATCH(col1, col2) AGAINST(' word1 word2 word3')*. Thereby a full-text search is carried out in the columns *col1* and *col2* for the words *word1*, *word2*, and *word3*. (This assumes that a full-text index for the columns *col1* and *col2* has been created.)

Conditions can be formulated with *WHERE* or *HAVING*. *WHERE* conditions are applied directly to the columns of the tables named in *FROM*.

HAVING conditions, on the other hand, are applied only after the *WHERE* conditions to the intermediate result of the query. The advantage of *HAVING* is that conditions can also be specified for function results (for example, *SUM(column1)* in a *GROUP BY* query). Conditions that can be equally well formulated with *WHERE* or *HAVING* should be expressed with *WHERE*, because in that case better optimization is possible.

- *groupfield:* With *GROUP BY* you can specify a group column. If the query returns several records with the same values for the group column, then these records are collected into a single new record. Along with *GROUP BY*, in the *column* part of the query so-called aggregate functions are usually placed, with which calculations can be made over grouped fields (e.g., *COUNT, SUM, MIN, MAX*).

- *ordercolumn:* With *ORDER BY* several columns or expressions can be specified according to which the query result should be sorted. Sorting normally proceeds in increasing order (A, B, C, . . . or 1, 2, 3, . . .). With the option *DESC* (for *descending*) you have decreasing order.

- *[offset,] row:* With *LIMIT* the query results can be reduced to an arbitrary selection. This is to be recommended especially when the results are to be displayed pagewise or when the number of result records is to be limited. The position at which the results are to begin is given by *offset* (0 for the first data record), while *row* determines the maximum number of result records.

MySQL does not currently support the formulation *SELECT . . . INTO table*, known in many other SQL dialects. In most cases you can use *INSERT INTO . . . SELECT* or *CREATE TABLE table . . . SELECT . . . .*

SELECT *[selectoptions] columnlist*
INTO OUTFILE *'filename' exportoptions*
[FROM . . . WHERE . . . GROUP BY . . . HAVING . . . ORDER BY . . . LIMIT . . .]

With this variant of the *SELECT* command the records are written into a text file. Here we describe only those options that are specific to this variant. All other points of syntax can be found under *SELECT*.

- *filename:* The file is generated in the file system of the MySQL server. For security reasons the file should not already exist. Moreover, you must have the *FILE* privilege to be able to execute this *SELECT* variant.

- *exportoptions:* Here it is specified how the text file is formatted. The entire option block looks like this:

  [FIELDS
    [TERMINATED BY ' fieldtermstring']
    [[OPTIONALLY] ENCLOSED BY ' enclosechar']
    [ESCAPED BY ' escchar']]
  [LINES TERMINATED BY ' linetermstring']

  - *fieldtermstring* specifies the character string that separates columns within a line (e.g., a tab character).
  - *enclosechar* specifies a character that is placed before and after every entry (e.g., '123' with *ENCLOSED BY ' \' '*. With *OPTIONALLY* the character is used only on *CHAR*, *VARCHAR*, *TEXT*, *BLOB*, *TIME*, *DATE*, *SET*, and *ENUM* columns (and not for every number format, such as *TIMESTAMP*).
  - *escchar* specifies the character to be used to mark special characters (usually the backslash). This is especially necessary when in character strings of a text file special characters appear that are also used for separating data elements.

    If *escchar* is specified, then the escape character is always used for itself (\\) as well as for ASCII code 0 (\0). If *enclosechar* is empty, then the escape character is also used as identifier of the first character of *fieldtermstring* and *linetermstring* (e.g., \t and \n). On the other hand, if *enclosechar* is not empty, then *escchar* is used only for *enclosechar* (e.g., \"), and not for *fieldtermstring* and *linetermstring*. (This is no longer necessary, since the end of the character string is uniquely identifiable due to *enclosechar*.
  - *linetermstring* specifies the character string with which lines are to be terminated. With DOS/Windows text files this must be the character string ' \r\n'.

In the four character strings special characters can be specified, for example, \b for backspace. The list of permissible special characters can be found at the command *LOAD DATA*. Moreover, character strings can be given in hexadecimal notation (such as *0x22* instead of ' \' ').

As with *LOAD DATA* the following is the default setting:

FIELDS TERMINATED BY ' \t' ENCLOSED BY ' ' ESCAPED BY
' \\'
LINES TERMINATED BY ' \n'

If you wish to input files generated with *SELECT . . . INTO OUTFILE* again into a table, then use *LOAD DATA*. This command is the inverse of *SELECT . . . INTO OUTFILE*. Further information and concrete application examples for both commands can be found in Chapter 11.

SELECT *[selectoptions] column*
INTO DUMPFILE *'filename'*
[FROM . . . WHERE . . . GROUP BY . . . HAVING . . . ORDER BY . . . LIMIT . . .]

SELECT . . . INTO DUMPFILE has, in principle, the same function as *SELECT . . . INTO OUTFILE* (see above). The difference is that here data are stored without any characters to indicate column or row division.

 SELECT . . . INTO DUMPFILE is designed for saving a single BLOB object into a file. The *SELECT* query should therefore return precisely one column and one row as result. Should that not be the case, that is, if the query returns more than one data element, then usually (and for some strange reason not always) one receives an error message: *ERROR 1172: Result consisted of more than one row.*

SET *[OPTION] variable=value*

SET is used to modify certain MySQL system variables and options. The optional key word has no influence on the function of this command. For example,

```
SET SQL_LOW_PRIORITY_UPDATES = 0 / 1
```

makes it possible to determine the order in which MySQL executes queries and change commands. The default behavior (1) gives priority to change commands. (This has the effect that a lengthy *SELECT* command will not block change commands, which are usually executed quickly.) With the setting 0, on the other hand, changes are executed only when no *SELECT* command is waiting to be executed.

 SET also offers a convenient way of changing one's password (and saves the relatively more cumbersome manipulation of the access table of the *mysql* database:

```
SET PASSWORD = PASSWORD('newPassword')
```

If you use replication, you can temporarily interrupt binary logging on the master system with *SET SQL_LOG_BIN =0* in order to make manual changes that should not be replicated. *SET SQL_LOG_BIN=1* resumes logging.

 A description of the other (mostly seldom used) setting options can be found in the MySQL documentation in the description of the *SET* command.

SET *@variable = expression*

MySQL permits the management of *user variables*. These variables are identified by the @ symbol before the variable name. These variables are managed separately for each client connection, so that no naming conflicts can arise among various clients. At the termination of the connection the content of such variables disappears.

Instead of *SET* one may also use *SELECT* for variable assignments. The syntax is then *SELECT @variable:=expression* (note that := must be used instead of =).

One may store results of queries in user variables. However, the storage of several values is not possible.

```
SELECT @a:=SUM(colA) FROM table1
```

User variables can be placed, for example, into *WHERE* conditionals.

```
SELECT * FROM table2 WHERE colA>@a
```

SHOW COLUMNS FROM *tablename [FROM databasename] [LIKE pattern]*

SHOW COLUMNS returns a table with information on all columns of a table (field name, field type, index, default value, etc.). With *LIKE* the list of columns can be filtered with a search pattern with the wild cards _ and %. The same information can be obtained with *EXPLAIN tablename* or *DESCRIBE tablename* as well as with the external program mysqlshow.

SHOW CREATE TABLE *tablename*

SHOW CREATE TABLE displays the SQL command with which the specified table can be recreated.

SHOW DATABASES *[LIKE pattern]*

SHOW DATABASES returns a list of all databases managed by MySQL. The list can be filtered with a search pattern with the wild cards _ and %. The same information can also be obtained with the external program mysqlshow.

SHOW GRANTS *FOR user@host*

SHOW GRANTS displays a list of all access privileges for a particular user. It is necessary that *user* and *host* be specified exactly as these character strings are stored in the various *mysql* access tables. Wild cards are not permitted.

SHOW INDEX *FROM table*

SHOW INDEX returns a table with information about all indexes of the given table.

SHOW KEYS

See *SHOW INDEX*

SHOW LOGS

This command shows which BDB logging files are currently being used. (If you are not using BDB tables, the command returns no result.)

SHOW MASTER LOGS

This command returns a list of all binary logging files. It can be executed only on the master computer of a replication system.

SHOW MASTER STATUS

This command shows which logging file is the current one, as well as the current position in this file and which databases are excepted from logging (options `--binlog-do-db` and `--binlog-ignore-db`). This command can be used only on the master computer of a replication system.

SHOW *[FULL]* **PROCESSLIST**

This command returns a list of all running threads (subprocesses) of the MySQL server. If the *PROCESS* privilege has been granted, then all threads are shown. Otherwise, only the user's threads are displayed.

The option *FULL* has the effect that for each thread the complete text of the most recently executed command is displayed. Without this option only the first 100 characters are shown.

The process list can also be determined with the external command `mysqladmin`.

SHOW SLAVE STATUS

This command provides information on the contents of the file `master.info`, which controls replication on the slave system. This command can be executed only on a slave computer in a replication system.

SHOW STATUS

This command returns a list of various MySQL variables that provide information on the current state of MySQL (for example, *Connections, Open_files, Uptime*). A description of all variables can be found in the MySQL documentation under the command *SHOW VARIABLES*. This same information can also be determined with the external program mysqladmin.

SHOW TABLE STATUS

SHOW TABLE STATUS returns information about all tables of the active database: table type, number of records, average record length, *Create_time, Update_time*, etc. The same information can also be determined with the external program mysqlshow.

SHOW TABLES [FROM database] [LIKE pattern]

SHOW TABLES returns a list of all tables of the current (or specified) database. Optionally, the list of all tables can be reduced to those matching the search pattern *pattern* (where the SQL wild cards % and _ are allowed). More information on the construction of individual tables can be obtained with *DESCRIBE TABLE* and *SHOW COLUMNS*. The list of tables can also be retrieved with the external program mysqlshow.

SHOW VARIABLES

This command returns a seemingly endless list of all system variables defined by MySQL together with their values (e.g., *ansi_mode, sort_buffer, tmpdir, wait_timeout*, to name but a very few). A description of all variables can be found in the MySQL documentation under the command *SHOW VARIABLES*.

Many of these variables can be set at launch of MySQL, should the default value be unsuitable for some reason. The list of variables can also be recovered with the external command mysqladmin.

SLAVE START/STOP

These commands start and stop replication (we leave it to the reader to determine which is which). They can be executed only on the slave computer of a replication system. (Under version 3.23.33 the functioning of *SLAVE STOP* is unsatisfactory. The slave waits, and waits, and waits, for this command to be executed. Only when the master is shut down is *SLAVE STOP* finally completed. One suspects that this is not exactly what the designers had in mind. The documentation of this command is unfortunately very sketchy.)

TRUNCATE [TABLE] *tablename*

TRUNCATE has the same functionality as *DELETE* without a *WHERE* condition, that is, the effect is that all records in the table are deleted. This is accomplished by deleting the entire table and then recreating it. (This is considerably faster than deleting each record individually.)

    TRUNCATE cannot be part of a transaction. *TRUNCATE* functions like *COMMIT*; that is, all pending changes are first executed. *TRUNCATE* can also be undone with *ROLLBACK*.

    Up through MySQL 3.23.32 the syntax was *TRUNCATE tablename*. Beginning with version 3.23.33 the optional key word *TABLE* may be given. Beginning with version 4.0 it is anticipated that this key word will be required.

UNLOCK TABLES

UNLOCK TABLES removes all of the user's *LOCK*s. This command holds for all databases (that is, it doesn't matter which database is the current one).

UPDATE *[updateoptions] tablename* **SET** *col1=value1, col2=value2, . . .*
[WHERE condition]
[LIMIT maxrecords]

UPDATE changes individual fields of the table records specified by *WHERE*. Those fields not specified by *SET* remain unchanged. In *value* one can refer to existing fields. For example, an *UPDATE* command may be of the following form:

```
UPDATE products SET price = price + 5 WHERE productID=3
```

    Warning: Without a *WHERE* condition all data records in the table will be changed. (In the above example the prices of all products would be increased by 5.)

- *updateoptions:* Here the options *LOW PRIORITY* and *IGNORE* may be given. The effect is the same as with *INSERT*.

- *condition:* This condition specifies which records are affected by the change. For the syntax of *condition* see *SELECT*.

- *maxrecords:* With *LIMIT* the maximum number of records that may be changed is specified.

USE *databasename*

USE turns the specified database into the default database for the current connection to MySQL. Until the end of the connection (or until the next *USE* command) all table names are automatically assigned to the database *databasename*.

Function Reference

The functions described here can be used in *SELECT* queries are well as in other SQL commands. We begin with a few examples. In our first example we shall join two table columns with *CONCAT* to create a new character string. In the second example the function *PASSWORD* will be used to store an encrypted password in a column. In the third example the function *DATE_FORMAT* will be summoned to help us format a date.

```
SELECT CONCAT(firstname, ' ', lastname) FROM users
  Peter Smith
  ...
INSERT INTO logins (username, userpassword)
VALUES ('smith', PASSWORD('xxx'))

SELECT DATE_FORMAT(a_date, '%Y %M %e')
FROM exceptions.test_date
    2000 December 7
```

> **POINTER** *This section aims to provide only a compact overview of the functions available. Extensive information on these functions can be found in the MySQL documentation. Some of these functions have been introduced at various places in this book by way of example. See the Index for page numbers.*

Arithmetic Functions

ABS(x)	absolute value (nonnegative number)
ACOS(x), ASIN(x)	arcsin and arccos functions
ATAN(x), ATAN2(x, y)	arctangent function
CEILING(x)	rounds up to least integer greater than or equal to x
COS(x)	cosine function (x given in radians)
COT(x)	cotangent function
DEGREES(x)	converts radians to degrees (multiplication by $180/\pi$)
EXP(x)	returns e^x
FLOOR(x)	rounds down to greatest integer less than or equal to x
LOG(x)	natural logarithm (to base e)
LOG10(x)	logarithm to base 10
MOD(x, y)	mod function, corresponds to $x \% y$
PI()	returns 3.1415927
POW(x, y)	returns x^y
POWER(x, y)	like *POW(x, y)*
RADIANS(x)	converts degrees into radians (multiplication by $\pi/180$)
RAND()	returns a random number between 0.0 and 1.0
ROUND(x)	rounds to nearest integer
ROUND(x, y)	rounds to y decimal places
SIGN(x)	returns $-1, 0,$ or 1 depending on the sign of x
SIN(x)	sine function
SQRT(x)	square root
TAN(x)	tangent function
TRUNCATE(x)	removes digits after the decimal point
TRUNCATE(x, y)	retains y digits after the decimal point (*TRUNCATE(1.236439, 2)* returns 1.23)

In general, all functions return *NULL* if provided with invalid parameters (e.g., *SQRT(-1)*).

Comparison Functions

GREATEST(x, y, z, . . .)	returns greatest value or greatest character string
IF(expr, val1, val2)	returns *val1* if *expr* is true; otherwise, *val2*
IFNULL(expr1, expr2)	returns *expr2* if *expr1* is *NULL*; otherwise, *expr1*
INTERVAL(x, n1, n2, . . .)	returns 0 if $x < n1$; 1 if $x < n2$, etc.; all parameters must be integers, and $n1 < n2 < \cdots$ must hold
ISNULL(x)	returns 1 or 0, according to whether *x IS NULL* holds
LEAST(x, y, z, . . .)	returns the smallest value or smallest character string
STRCMP(s1, s2)	returns 1 if *s1* = *s2*; else 0; function is case-sensitive

---

String Processing

Most character string functions can also be used for processing binary data.

Processing Character Strings

CHAR_LENGTH(s)	returns the length of the string *s* (corresponds to *LENGTH*)
CONCAT(s1, s2, s3, . . .)	concatenates the strings
CONCAT_WS(x, s1, s2, . . .)	like *CONCAT*, except that *x* is inserted between each string *sn*; *CONCAT_WS(', ', 'a', 'b', 'c')* returns *'a, b, c'*
ELT(n, s1, s2, . . .)	returns the *n*th string; *ELT(2, 'a', 'b', 'c')* returns *'b'*
EXPORT_SET(x, s1, s2)	creates a string from *s1* and *s2* based on the bit coding of *x*; *x* is interpreted as a 64-bit integer
FIELD(s, s1, s2, . . .)	compares *s* with strings *s1*, *s2* and returns the index of the first matching string; *FIELD('b', 'a', 'b', 'c')* returns 2
FIND_IN_SET(s1, s2)	searches for *s1* in *s2*; *s2* contains a comma-separated list of strings; *FIND_IN_SET('b', 'a,b,c')* returns 2
INSERT(s1, pos, 0, s2)	inserts *s2* into position *pos* in *s1*; *INSERT('ABCDEF', 3, 0, 'abc')* returns *'ABabcDEF'*
INSERT(s1, pos, len, s2)	inserts *s2* at position *pos* in *s1* and replaces *len* characters of *s2* with the new characters; *INSERT('ABCDEF', 3, 2, 'abc')* returns *'ABabcEF'*
INSTR(s, sub)	returns the position of *sub* in *s*;
INSTR('abcde', 'bc')	returns 2
LCASE(s)	changes uppercase characters to lowercase

LEFT(s, n)	returns the first *n* characters of *s*
LENGTH(s)	returns the number of characters in *s*
LOCATE(sub, s)	returns the position of *sub* in *s*; *LOCATE('bc', 'abcde')* returns 2
LOCATE(sub, s, n)	as above, but begins the search for *sub* only at the *n*th character of *s*
LOWER(s)	transforms uppercase characters to lowercase
LPAD(s, len, fill)	inserts the fill character *fill* into *s*, so that *s* ends up with length *len*; *LPAD('ab', 5, '*')* returns '***ab'
LTRIM(s)	removes spaces at the beginning of *s*
MAKE_SET(x, s1, s2 . . .)	forms a new string in which all strings *sn* appear for which in *x* the bit *n* is set; *MAKE_SET(1+2+8, 'a', 'b', 'c', 'd')* returns 'a,b,d'
MID(s, pos, len)	reads *len* characters from position *pos* from the string *s*; *MID('abcde', 3, 2)* returns 'cd'
POSITION(sub IN s)	corresponds to *LOCATE(sub, s)*
REPEAT(s, n)	joins *s* to itself *n* times; *REPEAT('ab', 3)* returns 'ababab'
REPLACE(s, fnd, rpl)	replaces in *s* all *fnd* strings by *rpl*; *REPLACE('abcde', 'b', 'xy')* returns 'axycde'
REVERSE(s)	reverses the string
RIGHT(s, n)	returns the last *n* characters of *s*
RPAD(s, len, fill)	inserts the fill character *fill* at the end of *s*, so that *s* has length *len*; *RPAD('ab', 5, '*')* returns 'ab***'
RTRIM(s)	removes spaces from the end of *s*
SPACE(n)	returns *n* space characters
SUBSTRING(s, pos)	returns the right part of *s* from position *pos*
SUBSTRING(s, pos, len)	as above, but only *len* characters (corresponds to *MID(s, pos, len)*)
SUBSTRING_INDEX(s, f, n)	searches for the *n*th appearance of *f* in *s* and returns the left part of the string up to this position (exclusive); for negative *n* the search begins at the end of the string, and the right part of the string is returned;
	SUBSTRING_INDEX('abcabc', 'b', 2) returns 'abca'
	SUBSTRING_INDEX('abcabc', 'b', -2) returns 'cabc'
TRIM(s)	removes spaces from the beginning and end of *s*
TRIM(f FROM s)	removes the character *f* from the beginning and end of *s*
UCASE(s) / UPPER(s)	transforms lowercase characters to uppercase

Converting Numbers and Character Strings

ASCII(s)	returns the ASCII code of the first character of *s*
BIN(x)	returns the binary code of *x*; *BIN(12)* returns *'1010'*
CHAR(x, y, z, . . .)	returns the string formed from the code *x, y, . . . *; *CHAR(65, 66)* returns *'AB'*
CONV(x, from, to)	transforms *x* from number base *from* to base *to*; *CONV(25, 10, 16)* returns the hexadecimal *'19'*
FORMAT(x, n)	formats *x* with commas for thousands separation and *n* decimal places; *FORMAT(12345.678, 2)* returns *'12,345.68'*
HEX(x)	returns the hexadecimal code for *x*; *x* must be an integer (maximum 64 bits); *HEX* is not able to convert BLOBs or strings into hex code
INET_NTOA(n)	transforms *n* into an IP address with at least four groups; *INET_NTOA(1852797041)* returns *'110.111.112.113' INET_ATON(ipadr)* transforms an IP address into the corresponding 32- or 64-bit integer; *INET_ATON('110.111.112.113')* returns 1852797041
OCT(x)	returns the octal code of *x*
ORD(s)	like *ASCII(s)*, but functions for multibyte character sets
SOUNDEX(s)	returns a string that should match similar-sounding English words; *SOUNDEX('hat')* and *SOUNDEX('head')* both return *'H300'*; extensive information on the SOUNDEX algorithm can be found in the book *SQL for Smarties* by Joe Celko

Encryption of Character Strings

DECODE(crypt, pw)	decrypts *crypt* using the password *pw*
ENCODE(str, pw)	encrypts *str* using *pw* as password; the result is a binary object that can be decrypted with *DECODE*
ENCRYPT(pw)	encrypts the password with the UNIX *crypt* function; if this function is unavailable, returns *ENCRYPT NULL*
MD5(str)	computes the MD5 check sum for the character string
PASSWORD(pw)	encrypts the password with the algorithm that was used for storing passwords in the *USER* table

Date and Time

Using Dates and Times

CURDATE()	returns the current date in the form *'2001-12-31'*
CURTIME()	returns the current time either as a string or number, depending on context; e.g., *'23:59:59'* or 235959 (integer)
DATE_ADD(. . .)	adds a time interval to a starting time; see below
DATE_FORMAT(d, form)	formats *d* according to formatting string *f*; see below
DATE_SUB(. . .)	subtract a time interval from the start time; see below
DAYNAME(date)	returns *'Monday'*, *'Tuesday'*, etc.
DAYOFMONTH(date)	returns the day of the month (1–31)
DAYOFWEEK(date)	returns the day of the week (1 = Sunday through 7 = Saturday)
DAYOFYEAR(date)	returns the day in the year (1–366)
EXTRACT(i FROM date)	returns a number for the desired interval;
	EXTRACT(YEAR FROM '2001-12-31') returns 2001
FROM_DAYS(n)	returns the date *n* days after the year 0;
	FROM_DAYS(3660) returns *'0010-01-08'*
FROM_UNIXTIME(t)	transforms the Unix timestamp number *t* into a date; *FROM_UNIXTIME(0)* returns *'1970-01-01 01:00:00'*
FROM_UNIXTIME(t, f)	as above, but with formatting as in *DATE_FORMAT*
HOUR(time)	returns the hour (0–23)
MINUTE(time)	returns the minute (0–59)
MONTH(date)	returns the month (1–12)
MONTHNAME(date)	returns the name of the month (*'January'*, etc.)
NOW()	returns the current time in the form *'2001-12-31 23:59:59'*
QUARTER(date)	returns the quarter (1–4)
SECOND(time)	returns the second (0–59)
SEC_TO_TIME(n)	returns the time *n* seconds after midnight;
SEC_TO_TIME(3603)	returns *'01:00:03'*
TIME_FORMAT(time, f)	like *DATE_FORMAT*, but for times only
TIME_TO_SEC(time)	returns the seconds since midnight

TO_DAYS(date)	returns the number of days since the year 0
UNIX_TIMESTAMP()	returns the current time as a Unix timestamp number
UNIX_TIMESTAMP(d)	returns the timestamp number for the given date
WEEK(date)	returns week number (1 for the week beginning with the first Sunday in the year)
WEEK(date, day)	as above, but specifies with *day* the day on which the week should begin (0 = Sunday, 1 = Monday, etc.)
WEEKDAY(date)	returns the day of the week (0 = Sunday, 1 = Monday, etc.)
YEAR(date)	returns the year

There are various synonyms for the above functions, *CURRENT_TIMESTAMP*, for example, as an alternative to *NOW()*, which have not been listed. The functions for dealing with dates and times generally assume that the initial data are correct. Thus do not expect a sensible result if you provide the date *'2001-02-31'*.

With all functions that return a time or date (or both) the format of the result depends on the context. Normally, the result is a character string (e.g., *'2001-12-31 23:59:59'*). However, if the function is used in a numerical computation, such as *NOW() + 0*, then the result is an integer of the form *20011231235959*.

> **REMARK** *Several of the functions listed above process Unix timestamps, and there is a MySQL data type for such timestamps. What, then, is a timestamp?*
>
> *In Unix time is counted (at least for timestamps) from 1 January 1970. Each second since then is counted. Since the (signed) integer used for this number was declared as a 32-bit integer, it will overflow in the year 2038. For the time period from 1970 to 2038, then, a timestamp is a practical affair: compact and simple to use. But then what?*
>
> *First of all, there is still one bit in reserve if the timestamp is viewed as an unsigned integer. On this assumption we have until the beginning of the twenty-second century until overflow occurs. But on the other hand, it is expected that in the next few years Unix/Linux will obtain a 64-bit timestamp. At that point, presumably, MySQL will be reconfigured. Because of the increased memory requirement (eight bytes instead of four), all tables will have to migrate to the new format. Presumably, there will be no problems with this, and the year 2000 problem will not repeat itself in 2038 (at least with respect to MySQL).*

Calculating with Dates

DATE_ADD(date, INTERVAL n i) adds *n* times the interval *i* to the starting date *date*. Our first example shows how intelligently the function deals with ends of months (31.12 or 28.2).

> *DATE_ADD(' 2001-12-31 ', INTERVAL 2 month)* returns *' 2002-02-28 '*
> *DATE_ADD(' 2001-12-31 ', INTERVAL '3:30' HOUR_MINUTE)* returns
> *' 2001-12-31 03:30:00 '*

Intervals for DATE_ADD, DATE_SUB, EXTRACT

SECOND	*n*
MINUTE	*n*
HOUR	*n*
DAY	*n*
MONTH	*n*
YEAR	*n*
HOUR_MINUTE	*'hh:mm'*
HOUR_SECOND	*'hh:mm:ss'*
MINUTE_SECOND	*'mm:ss'*
DAY_HOUR	*'dd hh'*
DAY_MINUTE	*'dd hh:mm'*
DAY_SECOND	*'dd hh:mm:ss'*
YEAR_MONTH	*'yy-mm'*

Formatting Dates and Times

DATE_FORMAT(date, format) helps in representing dates and times in other formats than the usual MySQL format. Two examples illustrate the syntax:

> *DATE_FORMAT(' 2001-12-31 ', ' %M %d %Y')* returns
> *' December 31 2001 '*
> *DATE_FORMAT('2001-12-31', ' %D of %M')* returns *'31st of December'*

Names of days of the week, months, etc., are always given in English, regardless of the MySQL language setting (*language* option).

Date Symbols in `DATE_FORMAT, TIME_FORMAT, FROM_UNIXTIME`

%W	day of week	Monday to Sunday
%a	day of week abbreviated	Mon to Sun
%e	day of month	1–31
%d	day of month two-digit	01–31
%D	day of month with ending	1st, 2nd, 3rd, 4th . . .
%w	day of week as number	0 (Sunday)–6 (Saturday)
%j	day in year, three-digit	001–366
%U	week number, two-digit (Sunday)	00–52
%u	week number, two-digit (Monday)	00–52
%M	name of month	January–December
%b	name of month abbreviated	Jan–Dec
%c	month number	1–12
%m	month number, two-digit	01–12
%Y	year, four-digit	2000, 2001, . . .
%y	year, two-digit	00, 01, . . .
%%	the symbol %	%

A few remarks about the week number are in order: *%U* returns 0 for the days from before the first Sunday in the year. From the first Sunday until the following Saturday, it returns 1, then 2, etc. With *%u* you get the same thing, with the first Sunday replaced by the first Monday.

Time Symbols in `DATE_FORMAT, TIME_FORMAT,` *and* `FROM_UNIXTIME`

%S, %s	seconds, two-digit	00–59
%i	minutes, two-digit	00–59
%k	hours (24-hour clock)	0–23
%H	hours, two-digit, 0 to 23 o'clock	00–23
%l	hours (12-hour clock)	1–12
%h, %I	hours, two-digit, to 12 o'clock	01–12
%T	24-hour clock	00:00:00 to 23:59:59
%r	12-hour clock	12:00:00 AM to 11:59:59 PM
%p	AM or PM	AM, PM

GROUP BY *Functions*

The following functions can be used in *SELECT* queries with *GROUP BY*.

```
USE mylibrary
SELECT catName, COUNT(titleID) FROM titles, categories
WHERE titles.catID=categories.catID
GROUP BY catName
ORDER BY catName
```

catName	COUNT(titleID)
Children's books	3
Computer books	5
Databases	2
...	

GROUP BY *Functions*

AVG(expr)	average of *expr*
BIT_AND(expr)	bitwise AND of *expr*
BIT_OR(expr)	bitwise OR of *expr*
COUNT(expr)	number of *expr*
COUNT(DISTINCT expr)	number of different *expr* expressions
MAX(expr)	maximum of *expr*
MIN(expr)	minimum of *expr*
STD(expr)	standard deviation of *expr*
STDDEV(expr)	like *STD(expr)*
SUM(expr)	sum of *expr*

Additional Functions

Miscellaneous

BIT_COUNT(x)	returns number of set bits
COALESCE(list)	returns the first element of the list that is not *NULL*
LOAD_FILE(filename)	loads a file from the local file system

Administrative Functions

BENCHMARK(n, expr)	executes *expr* a total of *n* times and measures the time elapsed
CONNECTION_ID( )	returns the ID number of the current database connection
DATABASE( )	returns the name of the current database
GET_LOCK(name, time)	defines a lock with the name *name* for the time *time* (in seconds)
LAST_INSERT_ID( )	returns the *AUTO_INCREMENT* number most recently generated within the current connection to the database
RELEASE_LOCK(name)	releases the lock *name*
USER( )	returns the name of the current user
VERSION( )	returns the MySQL version number as a string

The two functions *GET_LOCK* and *RELEASE_LOCK* do not execute a lock; that is, neither MySQL nor a database is blocked. These functions serve, rather, for communication between processes. As long as a process has a lock with a particular name defined, no other process can obtain a lock with the same name. The second process in this case receives, with *GET_LOCK*, the return value 0 and therefore knows that currently another process has obtained a lock. (As a rule, the second process must just wait a bit and then try again.)

CHAPTER 14
MySQL Tools

THIS CHAPTER IS A REFERENCE for the options and functions of the most important MySQL tools. We discuss the server `mysqld`, the monitor `mysql`, and the administration tools `mysqladmin`, `myisamchk`, etc.

These tools have a number of common options, and they evaluate configuration files in the same manner. For this reason the chapter begins with a section describing these common properties.

Chapter Overview

Overview

The common feature exhibited by the commands introduced in this section is that they are launched as external programs in a DOS window (Windows) or in a command shell (Unix/Linux). The entire operation of these programs is carried out in text mode and is therefore not what one would term excessively convenient. However, these commands are very well suited for execution in scripts in the automation of administrative tasks.

The following list provides an overview of the commands discussed in this section.

MySQL Server and Included Administration Tools

mysqld*	MySQL server, also known as the MySQL daemon; under Windows there are several variants (mysqld, mysqld-nt, mysqld-opt)
mysql	enables interactive execution of SQL commands
mysqlc	like mysql, but compiled with the Cygnus GNU-C compiler and with the readline library; for Windows only
mysqladmin	assists in various administrative tasks (display status, reinput privileges, execute shutdown, etc.)
mysqldump	saves contents of a MySQL database in an ASCII file
mysqlimport	inputs a table from an ASCII file
mysqlshow	displays information on databases, tables, and columns
mysqlbug	sends (via e-mail) an error message; for Unix/Linux only
myisamchk	checks the integrity of MyISAM table files and repairs them as necessary
myisampack	compresses MyISAM table files for more efficient read-only access

> **POINTER** *The two Perl scripts* mysqlaccess *and* mysql_setpermission *assist in the administration of MySQL access privileges. These scripts were described in Chapter 7, in the discussion of managing access privileges.*
>
> *There are several additional scripts and programs for special tasks, and these were presented in Chapters 11 and 12 (e.g.,* mysqlhotcopy, mysqlbinlog*). However, some of these programs are available only under Unix/Linux.*

> **REMARK** *Most of the commands presented here are compiled programs (**.exe *under Windows). However, others are in script form and can be executed only if a suitable script interpreter is installed (generally Perl). This is usually the case under Unix/Linux. Under Windows it may be that you have to install Perl yourself (see Chapter 2).*

Common Options, Configuration Files

A common feature of the programs described in this chapter is that there are certain options that can be used by almost all of the commands, and these options can be preset in a common configuration file, so as to save typing when the commands are invoked.

Common Options

Various options can be passed to all commands when they are executed. As is usual with Unix/Linux, commands can be prefixed with a hyphen (short form) or two hyphens (full option name). Please note that the short forms of options are case-sensitive.

Common Options of mysql, mysqladmin, mysqld, mysqldump, mysqlimport, myisamchk, myisampack

`--help`	displays a brief operation introduction
`--print-defaults`	displays default values for options; default values can come from configuration files or system variables
`--nodefaults`	causes no configuration files to be read at startup
`--defaults-file=`*filename*	causes only this configuration file to be read at startup
`--defaults-extra-file=`*filename*	first the global configuration file is read, and then *filename*, and finally (only under Unix/Linux) the user-specific configuration file
`--port=`*n*	specifies the TCP/IP port over which communication takes place (usually 3306)
`--version`	displays the version number of the program
`--set-variable` *var=x*	enables setting of the program's variables

Common Options of the MySQL Client Tools

`-u` *un*	`--user=`*username*	determines the username for registration with MySQL
`-p`	`--password`	asks for input of password immediately after start of the command
`-p`*xxx*	`--password=`*xxx*	passes the password directly; in contrast to other options, there can be no space after `-p`; this is more convenient than interactive input of the password, but it can represent a considerable security risk and thus should generally be avoided; under some operating systems any user can see the password by looking at the process list
	`--host=`*hostname*	gives the name of the computer on which the server is running (assumed by default to be *localhost*, that is, the local computer)
`-C`	`--compress`	minimizes the data flow between client and server, by making use of data compression

TIP *For a connection to the MySQL server to be at all possible, the following two options must generally be used at the start of each client command:*

```
> mysql -u username -p
Enter Password: xxxxxx
```

If MySQL is not yet password-secured, then this will work, of course, without a password being specified. Information on user and privilege management in MySQL can be found in Chapter 7.

CAUTION *If you execute MySQL commands under Windows and create a directory with options, then instead of the backslash you should use the forward slash (/). If the file name contains space characters, then put the entire path in quotation marks, as in the following example:*

```
--character-sets-dir="Q:/Program Files/mysql/share/charsets"
```

Configuration Files

If you observe that you are using particular options over and over, you can save these in options files for many of the commands covered in this section. The options are used by mysql, mysqladmin, mysqld, mysqldump, mysqlimport, myisamchk, myisampack, safe_mysqld.

The following list collects the locations where the options files must be stored. At the beginning all options files—those that exist already—are read in the order in which they are listed below. In the case of contradictory settings, the most recently read options file takes precedence. (Whether and what configuration files will be read depends on the options --no-defaults, --defaults-file, and --defaults-extra-file; see above.)

Where Options Files Are Stored

Validity	Windows	Unix/Linux
global options	C:\my.cnf, Windows\my.ini	/etc/my.cnf
user-specific options (no evaluation by mysqld)		~/.my.cnf
server-specifc options (for mysqld only)	DATADIR\my.cnf	DATADIR/my.cnf

The directory DATADIR is the default directory, which during compilation of MySQL is provided as data directory. Under Windows this is normally C:\mysql\data, while under Unix/Linux it is generally /usr/local/mysql/data or /usr/local/data. Please note that DATADIR need not be the directory in which MySQL actually stores the database files. This directory is usually set when the MySQL server is launched with the option --datadir. However, access to the configuration file takes place before this option is evaluated.

The syntax of the file is based on the following pattern:

```
# comment
[programname]
option1  # corresponds to --option1
option2=abc  # corresponds to --option2=abc
option3=var=efg  # corresponds to --option3 var=efg
```

These options are divided into groups for each program. Instead of *programname* you should specify the name of the program.

- Settings that are to be used by all programs other than mysqld are assigned to the group [client].

- Settings that relate only to the server are assigned to the group [mysqld]. (The group [server] is also used by mysqld.)

- Settings special to the program *xyz* are assigned to the group [*xyz*].

Here option is the option name in long form, but without hyphens. (So, for example, the option --host in the configuration file becomes simply host.) If options expect parameters, then these are specified with =. The third option line comes into play with options like --set-variable, by means of which variables of the client program can be specified.

Let us see, finally, a concrete example of a configuration file:

```
# options for all MySQL tools
[client]
user=username
password=xxx
host=uranus.sol
# options for mysqldump
[mysqldump]
force
# options for mysql (monitor)
[mysql]
set-variable=select_limit=30
```

TIP *Changes to configuration files are effective only after a restart of the program in question. This holds in particular for the MySQL server (thus for options in the group* [mysqld]*).*

CAUTION *Please be sure that the options specified in the* [client] *section are truly supported by all MySQL tools. If a MySQL tool finds an unknown option in the* [client] *section, then the command is terminated with an error message.*

CAUTION *If you wish under Unix/Linux to execute user-specific options settings in* ~/.my.cnf *and possibly specify passwords there, then ensure that no other users are able to read this file.*

```
user$ chmod 600 ~/.my.cnf
```

> **CAUTION** *If you specify Windows paths or directories in a configuration file, then you must use / or \\ instead of the backslash \. (In the Windows version of MySQL the backslash is used as escape character.)*
>
> *Furthermore, paths cannot be placed in quotation marks within a configuration file (even if the path contains space characters).*
>
> *Please note that these rules are different from those that obtain for a direct setting of options with --option = ...*

> **TIP** *Under Unix/Linux you can use the program* my_print_defaults *grp to determine the options set for [grp] in the configuration file. The program is particularly suited for use in custom scripts.*

Options in Environment Variables (aka System Variables)

An additional possibility for specifying options are environment variables at the level of the operating system. (Under Windows these variables are usually known as system variables.)

The following list names the most important of these variables. To set such variables under Windows you use the dialog for system control (see Figure 4-1). Under Linux you can define such variables in script files (e.g., in /etc/profile or ~/.profile) with export. Depending on which shell you use, you may use the command declare -x or setenv instead of export.

Import and Environment Variables for mysql, mysqladmin, mysqld, mysqldump, ...

MYSQL_TCP_PORT	specifies the port number for the TCP/IP connection to MySQL (generally 3306)
MYSQL_UNIX_PORT	specifies the socket file for local communication under Linux/Unix (e.g., /var/mysql.lock)
TMPDIR	specifies the directory to be used for temporary files; this directory is also used for temporary tables
USER	specifies the user name

Precedence

Option settings are read in the following order: environment variables, configuration files, options at program startup.

In the case of contradictory settings the last setting read takes precedence. For example, options at program startup supersede settings in environment variables.

mysqld (Server)

The following lists, organized by topic, summarize the most-used mysqld options.

> **POINTER** *An almost complete reference to the long list of* mysqld *options can be obtained in* mysqld --help. *A brief description of most options can be found in the chapter "Installing MySQL" in the MySQL documentation. The options for replication and binary logging are described separately, in the chapter "Replication."*

mysqld *Options: Directories and Files*

-b *p*	--basedir=path		uses the given directory as base directory (installation directory)
	--character-sets-dir=*path*		specifies the directory in which the character set files are located
-h *p*	--datadir=*path*		reads database files from the specified directory
	--defaults-extra-file=*fn*		specifies an additional configuration file that is read after all the others; this option must be passed as the first option to mysqld; this option cannot be given in a configuration file
	--pid-file= *filename*		specifies the file in which the process ID number should be stored (under Unix/Linux only); the file is evaluated by the init-V script to terminate mysqld
	--socket=*file*		specifies the file name mysql.sock (default: /tmp/mysql.sock)

mysqld *Options: Language Setting*

	--default-characterset=*name*	specifies the character set to be used (for sorting, comparison, etc.)
-L *n*	--language=*name*	specifies the language in which error messages, etc., are to be output

mysqld *Options: Security*

	--myisam-recover[=opt1, opt2 ...]	has the effect that at startup all damaged MyISAM tables are automatically restored; the possible options are *DEFAULT, BACKUP, FORCE, QUICK*; they correspond to the myisamchk options
	--safe-show-database	has the effect that *SHOW DATABASES* displays only those tables that the user is permitted to access
	--secure	ensures that the association between computer names and IP numbers is correct; this makes it difficult for an attacker to disguise himself with a false host name; the option is activated by default unless --skip-host-cache is used
	--skip-grant-tables	omits input of the *mysql* database with access information; caution: anyone can then change any database!
	--skip-host-cache	does not use a cache to store the association between computer names and IP numbers
	--skip-show-database	has the effect that *SHOW DATABASES* can be executed only by users with the *PROCESS* privilege
-u *n*	--user=*name*	specifies the Unix/Linux account under which mysqld is to be executed; for the switch to work after startup, mysqld must be started up from *root*

mysqld *Options: Logging*

-l	--log[=*file*]	logs every connection as well as all SQL commands; if no file name is specifies, then MySQL uses the file name *hostname.log* in the database directory
	--log-bin-index=*file*	specifies the file in which the file name for the binary logging files is stored
	--log-long-format	logs the time and user in the change log (valid for --log-update)
	--log-slow-queries[=*file*]	logs queries whose execution takes longer than the time specified in the variable *long_query_time*
	--log-update[=*file*]	logs all SQL commands that make a change in data (thus in particular, *INSERT, UPDATE, DELETE*); if a file name is specified, then MySQL stores the changes in the file *file.n*; if no file name, then the logging file is created in the database directory and it uses the file name *hostname.n*; in both cases *n* is a three-digit integer, so that the logging files are sequentially numbered
	--log-bin[=*file*]	logs as in --log-update all SQL commands that change data; however, here a binary format is used (more compact, required for replication)

mysqld *Options: BDB Tables*

--skip-bdb	indicates that BDB is not to be used
--bdb-home=*path*	specifies the directory with the database files (corresponds to --basedir)
--bdb-tmpdir=*path*	specifies the directory for temporary BDB files
--bdb-log-dir=*path*	specifies the directory for BDB logging files
--bdb-no-sync	has the effect that changes in the logging file are not saved there at each change; thus BDB tables are more efficient, but less secure
--bdb-no-recover	has the effect that at startup of the server no attempt is made to recreate BDB tables

mysqld `Options: InnoDB Tables`

`--skip-innodb`	specifies that the InnoDB table driver is not to be loaded; this makes sense if no InnoDB tables are used and memory is thereby to be saved
`--innodb_data_home_dir=`*p*	specifies InnoDB directory; additional directory or file specifications relative to the path *p*
`--innodb_data_file_path=`*ts*	specifies the tablespace for all InnoDB tables; this can involve one or more files; the size of each file must be specified in bytes, megabytes (M), or gigabytes (G); example: `inno1:600M;inno2:1G`
`--innodb_log_group_home_dir=`*lp*	specifies directory for InnoDB logging files

mysqld `Variables: InnoDB Tables`

The following variables can be set with `--set-variable` = varname=*value*. Tips for optimal settings can be found in the InnoDB documentation in the chapter "MySQL Table Types" of the MySQL documentation.

`innodb_log_files_in_group=`*n*	specifies how many logging files will be used; the InnoDB table driver fills these files in order; once all files have been filled, the first is overwritten with new data, etc.; default: 2
`innodb_log_file_size=`*n*	specifies how large each individual logging file should be; larger files are a help to speed, but increase the time needed to restore the database after a crash; the size is usually given in megabytes (e.g., 10M); default value: 5M
`innodb_log_buffer_size=`*n*	specifies how much RAM is to be used for writing logging files; default value: 1M
`innodb_buffer_pool_size=`*n*	specifies how much RAM is to be used for intermediate storage of table data and indexes; this parameter has a great influence on speed; the larger, the better (with respect to the amount of RAM available, of course); default value: 8M
`innodb_additional_mem_pool_size=`*n*	specifies how much RAM is to be allocated to various internal management structures; default value: 1M
`innodb_lock_wait_timeout=`*n*	specifies the maximum wait (in seconds) for the completion of a lock; after this period of time the transaction will be canceled with *ROLLBACK*; default value: infinite

mysqld `Options: Gemini Tables`

`--skip-gemini`	specifies that the Gemini table driver should not be loaded; this makes sense if no Gemini tables are to be used and therefore memory is to be saved
`--gemini-flush-log-at-commit`	has the effect that the logging file is updated immediately after the end of a transaction; this is very secure, but very slow
`--gemini-recovery=FULL|NONE`	specifies whether Gemini tables should be recreated automatically after a crash at the next launch of MySQL (default value: `FULL`)
`--transaction-isolation=`*isl*	sets the default isolation level for transactions; possible settings for `isl` are: `UNCOMMITTED` | `READ-COMMITTED` | `REPEATABLE-READ` | `SERIALIZABLE`; the default setting is `READ-COMMITTED`

mysqld `Variables: Gemini Tables`

The following variables can be set with `--set-variable = `*varname=value*. Some tips on the optimal setting can be found in the Gemini documentation in the chapter "MySQL Table Types" in the MySQL documentation.

`gemini_connection_limit=`*n*	specifies the maximum number of connections; the overhead is about one kilybyte per connection; default setting: 100
`gemini_lock_table_size=`*n*	determines the maximum number of simultaneous locks; default setting: 4096
`gemini_buffer_cache=`*n*	specifies the amount of RAM for table data and indexes; the size is in bytes, megabytes (M), or gigabytes (G); this parameter has a great influence on the speed; the Gemini documentation recommends that the cache be at least ten percent of the space used by the Gemini tables (assuming that there is enough available RAM); default setting: 1M
`gemini_lock_wait_timeout=`*n*	specifes how long (in seconds) a wait there should be for the resolution of locks; after this time period the transaction will be terminated with *ROLLBACK*; default setting: 10

mysqld `Options: Replication/Master`

`--log-bin`	activates binary logging
`--server-id=n`	assigns the server a unique ID number; the range of values for n is between 1 and 2^{31}
`--binlog-do-db=dbname`	has the effect that only changes to the specified database are logged in the logging file
`--binlog-ignore-db=dbname`	has the effect that changes to the specified database are not logged in the logging file

mysqld `Options: Replication/Client`

`--server-id=n`	assigns the server a unique ID number
`--master-host=hostname`	specifies the host name or the IP address of the replication master
`--master-user=username`	specifies the username for replication communication
`--master-password=pword`	specifies the associated password
`--master-connect-retry=n`	specifies after how many seconds an attempt should be made to restore a broken connection to the master

mysqld `Options: Other`

	`--bind-address=ipadr`	specifies the IP address that MySQL should use; this option is important if the computer is so configured that it uses several IP addresses
	`--default-table-type=type`	specifies the table type that new tables are to use if the type is not explicitly given
`-P n`	`--port=n`	specifies the IP port that the server should use (default 3306).

> **CAUTION** *If you specify an option in a configuration file that* mysqld *does not know about (for example, due to a silly typo), then the server cannot start up. So watch out!!*

Variables

Many additional settings can be carried out with MySQL variables. For this you specify --set-variable=var=value at server startup or add the line set-variable=var=value in the configuration file. Some variables can be changed while the server is running with the SQL command *SET*.

> **POINTER** *A reference to all variables is displayed by* mysql --help. *A brief description of most variables can be found in the MySQL documentation under the description of the SQL commands* SET *and* SHOW VARIABLES *(chapter "Language Reference"). Hints on configuring options and variables with a view to optimal performance can also be found in the MySQL documentation (the chapter "Getting Maximum Performance").*

mysql (SQL Command Interpreter)

The monitor mysql allows interactive execution of SQL commands. This program can also be run in batch mode for many administrative tasks, including the generation of HTML tables. The commands are input from a file with < *file*. All SQL commands can be used in this file. The commands must be followed by a semicolon. Comments are introduced with the character #. (All additional characters to the end of the line are then ignored.)

At the launch of mysql numerous options can be specified. Furthermore, an optional database name can be given, in which case this database becomes the default database (corresponds to the command *USE databasename*).

mysql: *Syntax*

---

mysql [options] [databasename] [< commands.sql]

---

mysql: *General Options*

-e *cmd*	--execute=*cmd*	executes the given command(s); commands must be separated by semicolons; mysql is then terminated; contrary to the information in the help text to mysql, the results are not formatted as with --batch, that is, this option must be specified as needed (and in fact, before --execute); the entire option should be put in quotation marks
-i	--ignore-space	recognizes functions even if there are spaces between function names and their parameters; with -i, for example, *SUM (price)* is allowed, while without the option it must be written *SUM(price)*
-L	--skip-line-numbers	displays error messages without line numbers; the line numbers otherwise displayed refer to the location at which the faulty SQL command is located in a batch file and is generally an aid in debugging
-U	--i-am-a-dummy or --safe-updates	permits *UPDATE* and *DELETE* commands only if the effective range is limited with *WHERE* or *LIMIT*; furthermore, there is a maximum number of query results from *SELECT* commands as well as a maximum number of *JOIN*s
-V	--version	displays the version of mysql; mysql is then terminated
	--tee=*filename*	copies all input and output into the specified logging file; this option is allowed only if mysql is used in interactive mode (not in batch mode)
	--no-tee	no logging (default condition)

---

mysql: *Formatting and Output Options*

-B	--batch	separates columns in tables by tab characters (instead of by spaces and lines); moreover, only results of queries are displayed, and no status information
-E	--vertical	lists the results of queries with columns displayed horizontally, one below the next (instead of with vertical columns, one next to the other); this option is particularly to be recommended if a query returns many columns but few rows (ideally only one); as with --batch only results of queries are shown, and no status information
-H	--html	formats the results of queries as HTML tables; as with --batch only results of queries are shown, and no status information
-N	--skip-column-names	leaves off column titles in the output of tables
-r	--raw	in query results outputs the characters ASCII-0, tab, newline, and \ unchanged; (normally, these characters are output as \0, \t, \n, and \\); this option is effective only in combination with --batch
-s	--silent	displays less status information than in normal mode; does not use costly table formatting
-t	--table	formats tables with lines and spaces (default setting)
-v	--verbose	displays extensive status information, more than in normal mode

mysql: *Commands for Interactive Mode*

\c	clear	interrupts input of a command; \c can be given at the end of a command and leads to the entire input being simply ignored
\e	edit	calls the external editor named in the environment variable *EDITOR* and there enables a change in the command; this works only under Unix/Linux; after the return to mysql the command given in the editor is not displayed in mysql, which makes this option somewhat confusing to use
\g	go	executes the command (corresponds to ; and Return)
\h	help	displays a list of commands
\p	print	displays the entire current command on the screen
\q	exit or quit	terminates mysql (under Unix/Linux this works also with Ctrl+D)
\r	connect	terminates the current connection to MySQL and creates a new connection; optionally, a database name and host name of the MySQL server can be given (in that order)
\s	status	displays status information about the MySQL server
\T [*f*]	tee [*filename*]	logs all input and output into the specified file; if no file name is given, then the file name used in the previous tee command is used; if the file already exists, then the input and output are appended to the end of the file
\t	notee	ends tee; logging can be resumed at any time with tee or \T
\u *db*	use *database*	makes the given database the default database
\#	rehash	creates an internal list of all mysql commands, the most important SQL key words, and all table and column names of the current database; in the sequel the input of the initial letters suffices; with Tab the abbreviation is extended to the full key word; works only under Unix/Linux
\. *fn*	source *filename*	executes the SQL commands contained in the file; the commands must be separated by semicolons

> **CAUTION** *If* mysql *is launched with MySQL 3.23.33 with the option* -p *or* --password *(the password must be input interactively), then the program ignores the setting of the option* character-sets-dir *in configuration files.*
>
> *You can get around this difficulty by specifying this option directly or by starting* mysql *with* --password=xy *(which, however, is insecure).*

mysqladmin (Administration)

Various administrative tasks can be accomplished with mysqladmin, such as creating new databases and changing passwords. There are several commands that can be passed to mysqladmin, which are then executed sequentially.

> **TIP** *The names of* mysqladmin *commands can be abbreviated to the point where the name remains unique (e.g.,* flush-l *instead of* flush-logs, *or* k *instead of* kill*).*
>
> *Most* mysqladmin *commands can also be executed as SQL commands, for example, by* CREATE DATABASE, DROP DATABASE, FLUSH, KILL, SHOW. *These commands are given in parentheses in the lists below. There is additional information in the SQL reference in Chapter 13.*

mysqladmin: *Syntax*

```
mysqladmin [options] command1 command2 ...
```

---

mysqladmin: *Options*

-f	--force	display no warnings (e.g., with drop database), execute further commands even after errors
-i *n*	--sleep=*n*	repeat command every *n* seconds (for example, for regular display of status or for ping); mysqladmin runs endlessly; under Unix/Linux it can be terminated with Ctrl+C, under Windows only by closing the DOS window
-r	--relative	displays, in combination with -i and the command extended-status, a change in the previous status
-E	--vertical	like --relative, but changes are displayed in a single, very long, line
-t *n*	--timeout=*n*	timeout time for establishing a connection to the server; if after *n* seconds no connection has been established, then mysqladmin is terminated
-w *n*	--wait=n	attempt a connection *n* times

mysqladmin: *Commands*

create *dbname*	generates a new database (corresponds to *CREATE DATABASE*)
drop *dbname*	deletes an existing database irrevocably (corresponds to *DROP DATABASE*)
extended-status	displays countless status variables of the server (*SHOW STATUS*)
flush-hosts	empties the host cache table (*FLUSH HOSTS*)
flush-logs	closes all logging files and then reopens them (*FLUSH LOGS*); with update logs a new file is created, where the number of the file ending is increased by 1 (e.g., *file.003 → file.004*).
flush-status	resets many status variables to 0 (*FLUSH STATUS*)
flush-tables	closes all open tables (*FLUSH TABLES*)
flush-threads	empties the thread cache

flush-privileges	reinputs the privileges database *mysql* (*FLUSH PRIVILEGES*)
kill *id1*, *id2*, ...	terminates the specified threads (*KILL*)
password *newpassw*	changes the password of the current user
ping	tests whether a connection to the server can be established
processlist	displays all threads (*SHOW THREADS*)
reload	reinputs the privileges database *mysql*
refresh	closes all tables and log files and then reopens them
shutdown	terminates the SQL server
status	displays some server status variables
variables	displays the system variables of the SQL server (*SHOW VARIABLES*)
version	determines the version of the MySQL server

mysqldump (Backup/Export)

With mysqldump you get a long list of all SQL commands that are necessary to recreate a database exactly as it was. There are three syntax variants of mysqldump, depending on whether a database, several enumerated databases, or all databases managed by MySQL are to be stored. Only with the first variant can the output be limited to particular tables.

mysqldump: *Syntax*

```
mysqldump [options] dbname [tables]

mysqldump [options] --databases [moreoptions] dbname1 [dbname2 ... ]

mysqldump [options] --all-databases [moreoptions]
```

mysqldump: *Options*

	--add-drop-table	inserts a *DROP TABLE* command before every *CREATE-TABLE*
	--add-locks	inserts *LOCK TABLE* before the first *IN-SERT* command and *UNLOCK* after the last *INSERT* command
	--all	specifies all MySQL-specific options in the *CREATE TABLE* command
-A	--all-databases	saves all databases managed by MySQL; *CRE-ATE DATABASE* and *USE* are placed in the backup file
-B	--databases	stores several databases
	--complete-inserts	generates for each data record a separate *INSERT* command; this is the default setting; use --extended-insert to minimize the size of the backup file
	--delayed-inserts	uses *INSERT* with the option *DELAYED*
-e	--extended-insert	generates only one *INSERT* command per table with which the data of all records are handled (more efficient)
-F	--flush-logs	updates the logging files before the backup is begun
-f	--force	continues even after errors
	--no-create-db	generate no *CREATE TABLE* commands (only *INSERT*s)
	--no-data	generate no INSERT commands (only *CREATE TABLE* commands to recreate the structure of the database)
-l	--lock-tables	executes a *LOCK TABLE READ* for all tables before the data are read; this ensures that no data can be changed while mysqldump is running; the obvious drawback is that all write processes are blocked until mysqldump is done, which can take a while with large databases
	--opt	shorthand for the following options: --add-drop-table, --add-locks --quick --all --extended-insert --lock-tables (in most cases this is an optimal setting)

-q	--quick	outputs results record by record without internal intermediate storage; without this option first the entire table is moved into RAM and then output; the advantage of --quick is the lower memory requirement, the disadvantage that the MySQL server is generally blocked for a longer period of time; --quick should definitely be used for very large tables (when the entire table cannot be held in RAM of the local computer)
-Q	--quote-names	encloses table and column names in single quotes (e.g., 'name')
-T *dir*	--tab=*dir*	writes the result directly into the specified directory, whereby for each table two files are created, one with the table structure (*.sql) and the second with the stored data in the format of the command *SELECT . . . INTO OUTFILE* (*.txt)
-w *cnd*	--where=*condition*	considers only data records that satisfy the *WHERE* condition *cnd* or *condition*; the entire option must be placed in quotation marks, e.g., " -wprice>5 " or " --where=ID=3 "

mysqldump: *Formatting Options (only in combination with --tab)*

--fields-terminated-by	see Chapter 13: *SELECT . . . INTO OUTFILE*
--fields-enclosed-by	
--fields-optionally-enclosed-by	
--fields-escaped-by	
--lines-terminated-by	

If you are using --tab, then the second file (tablename.txt) contains the contents of the table directly (that is, not in the form of *INSERT* commands). This has several advantages: The resulting file is somewhat more compact, and a later importation can be executed significantly more quickly. (However, the operation is more complex, and only a single table can be handled.)

The options --fields and --lines should each be set in quotation marks. The following example shows how you can pass the double quote itself as a character to the option:

```
> mysqldump -u root -p --tab /tmp "--fields-enclosed-by=\"" ...
```

To reinput the file thus generated (*.txt) with mysqldump you can use either the program mysqlimport, discussed in the following section, or the SQL command *LOAD DATA*.

mysqlimport (ASCII Import, Bulk Import)

With mysqlimport it is possible to import specially formatted ASCII files into MySQL tables. Here mysqlimport represents merely an interface to the command *LOAD DATA*, described in detail in Chapter 13.

mysqlimport: *Syntax*

```
mysqlimport [options] databasename filename
```

mysqlimport: *Options*

-d	--delete	deletes all existing records in the table before importation
-i	--ignore	ignores new records with an existing value for a *UNIQUE* or *PRIMARY KEY* column
-L	--local	reads the file from the local file system (not from that of the MySQL server)
-l	--lock-tables	blocks the tables for all other clients during importation
-r	--replace	overwrites existing records with the same value in a *UNIQUE* or *PRIMARY KEY* column
	--fields-terminated-by	affects special characters;
	--fields-enclosed-by	see *LOAD DATA* in Chapter 11
	--fields-optionally-enclosed-by	
	--fields-escaped-by	
	--lines-terminated-by	

mysqlshow (Displaying Information)

With `mysqlshow` you can quickly obtain an overview of the databases, tables, and columns managed by MySQL. Without parameters the command returns a list of all databases managed by MySQL. With parameters the command displays information on the specified database, table, or column.

mysqlshow: *Syntax*

```
mysqlshow [options] [databasename [tablename [columnname]]]
```

mysqlshow: *Options*

-i	--status	displays additional status for tables (table type, average record length, etc.)

mysqlbug (Sending Error Notification)

The script `mysqlbug` helps in composing error messages to `mysql@lists.mysql.com`. The script is available only under Unix/Linux. It collects the most important information about the MySQL version installed on the system (version number of the server, options used at compilation, version number of the libraries, version number of Perl, etc.) and then displays a text template using the editor specified by *$VISUAL*.

You can now report information on your problems or errors at the locations provided for. As soon as you leave the editor, you have the possibility of terminating the error report, sending it, or editing it.

> **TIP** *Under Windows you can create error reports with the dialog sheet* REPORT *of the program WinMySQLadmin, instead of with* `mysqlbug`.

myisamchk (Repairing MyISAM Files)

With myisamchk you can check the integrity of MyISAM database files (name.MYD and name.MYI). Damaged files and indexes can be repaired as required. Re-creation of the index is necessary as well if the sort order of the server was changed.

The parameters of myisamchk are tables names. Here the complete file name is given (either without ending or with the ending *.MYI). Depending on the options specified, however, both MyISAM files, that is, name.MYD and name.MYI, are analyzed or changed.

Please note that with myisamchk there are several options whose significance depends on whether the program is used simply for checking (without -r, -o, --recover, --saferecover) or for changing table files (with one of these options).

If you are still working with ISAM tables (usually with older versions of MySQL), you can repair their files with isamchk. However, the options here are somewhat different from those of myisamchk.

myisamchk: *Syntax*

```
myisamchk [options] tablename1 tablename2 ...
```

myisamchk: *Options (Analyze Table File without -r or -o)*

-c	--check	checks the integrity of the table files; -c is the default option if no options are specified
-e	--extend-check	checks most thoroughly (and slowly)
-F	--fast	check only tables whose files were not properly closed
-C	--check-only-changed	check only tables that were changed since the last check
-f	--force	restarts myisamchk with the option -r, if errors are discovered
-i	--information	displays statistical information about the tables
-m	--medium-check	checks more thoroughly (and slowly) than with -c
-U	--update-state	marks a file as damaged if errors are discovered
-T	--read-only	does not change the file

myisamchk: *Options (Repair and Change Table File with -r or -o)*

-B	--backup	creates the backup file name.bak for name.myi
-e	--extend-check	attempts to recreate every data record; however, this usually leads to many records with incorrect or deleted data; moreover, the repair takes a long time; this option should be used seldom
-f	--force	overwrites temporary files
-l	--no-symlinks	follows no symbolic links (that is, only those files are repaired that are found under the actual file name; available only under Unix/Linux)
-o	--safe-recover	like -r, but a different algorithm is used
-q	--quick	only an index file is repaired; the actual file is left untouched
-q -q		has almost the same effect as -q, but the data file is unchanged if key fields are not unique
-r	--recover	attempts to recreate defective files
-t *p*	--tmpdir=*path*	uses the specified directory for temporary files
-u	--unpack	decompresses table files that were compressed with myisampack
	--character-sets-dir=*dir*	reads character set data from the specified directory
	--set-character-set=*name*	uses the specified character set for recreating indexes

myisamchk: *Other Options*

-a	--analyze	analyzes and stores the distribution of key fields in the indexes; this can speed up table access somewhat
-A *n*	--set-auto-increment[=n]	uses as start value for *AUTO-INCREMENT* a number that is one greater than the highest value used so far, or else *n* (whichever is greater)
-d	--description	displays various information about the table (record format and length, character set, indexes, etc.)
-R	--sort-records=*idxnr*	sorts the records in the table file according to the specified index; the index is specified as a number (where this number can be determined first with -d); then nearby records in the index are located near each other in the table file as well; this can speed up access if records are frequently read in the order defined by the index
-S	--sort-index	sorts the blocks of the index file

myisamchk: *Variables for Memory Management*

-O key_buffer_size=*n*	specifies the size of the key buffer; the default is 512 kilobytes; *n* specifies the number of bytes (or *n*K for kilobytes, or *n*M for megabytes)
-O read_buffer_size=*n*	specifies the size of the read buffer; the default value is 256 kilobytes
-O sort_buffer_size=*n*	specifies the size of the sort buffer; the default value is 3 megabytes
-O write_buffer_size=*n*	specifies the size of the write buffer; the default value is 256 kilobytes

myisampack (Compressing MyISAM Files)

MyISAM database files (name.MYD) are compressed with myisampack. Thereby one can achieve drastic reductions in storage requirements for tables (often considerably more than one-half) and under some circumstances increased access speed to the data. However, the data can now no longer be changed.

myisampack: *Syntax*

```
myisampack [options] tablename1 tablename2 ...
```

myisampack: *Options*

-b	--backup	creates a backup name.old of the table file
-f	--force	executes the operation even if the resulting file is bigger than the original
-j	--join='*new_table_name*'	unites all tables specified into a single, large, file; the tables must all have exactly the same column definitions
-t	--test	executes myisampack provisionally without actually changing any data
-T *p*	--tmpdir=*path*	uses the specified directory for temporary files

#### CHAPTER 15

API Reference

THIS CHAPTER CONTAINS A REFERENCE to the APIs (application interfaces) between MySQL and PHP and between MySQL and Perl that were introduced in this book.

Chapter Overview

PHP API

This reference gives a compact overview of the PHP functions and their parameters for access to MySQL databases. First a few formal remarks:

- Square brackets in the left column indicate optional parameters.

- For all functions for which there is an enumeration over an index *n*, this index is in the range 0 to *nmax* − 1.

- Examples of the application of these functions can be found particularly in Chapters 3 and 8. Further references can be found in the Index.

Connection and Administration

$id =* **mysql_connect**(*$host, $user, $pw);	establishes a connection
$id=* **mysql_pconnect**(*$host, $user, $pw);	establishes a persistent connection (reused when a connection is renewed) and is thus more efficient
mysql_change_user(*$newuser, $passw*);	changes the user name for the connection
mysql_select_db(*$dbname*);	determines the default database
mysql_close(*[$id]*);	closes the connection

Generally, the specification *id* can be omitted as long as there is only one connection to MySQL and thus no possibility of confusion.

Administration, Error Evaluation

$result =* **mysql_list_dbs**(*[$id]);	determines a list of all known databases; the evaluation is like that of *SELECT* queries
$result =* **mysql_list_tables**(*$dbname [,$id]);	determines a list of all tables of the database; evaluation like that of *SELECT* queries
$result =* **mysql_list_fields**(*$dbn, $tbln [,$id]);	determines a list of all fields of the table; evaluation like that of *SELECT* queries
mysql_create_db(*$dbname [,$id]*);	creates a new database
$n =* **mysql_errno**(*[$id]);	determines the number of the most recent error
$txt =* **mysql_error**(*[$id]);	determines the error message

Executing SQL Commands

$result = **mysql_query**($sql [, $id])	execute SQL command for the default database
$result = **mysql_db_query**($db, $sql [, $id]);	as above, but for the database *db* (which becomes the default for all further queries)

Output of SELECT Query Results

mysql_data_seek($result, $rownr);	determines the active data record within the result
$row = **mysql_fetch_array**($result);	returns the next record of the result (or *false*); access to individual fields takes place with *row['fieldname']*, where case sensitivity is in force
$row = **mysql_fetch_row**($result);	returns the next record of the result (or *false*); access to individual fields is via *row[n]*
$row = **mysql_fetch_object**($result);	returns the next record of the result (or *false*); access to individual fields is via *row->fieldname*
$data = **mysql_result**($result, $rownr, $colnr);	returns the contents of the field in row *rownr* and column *colnr*; this function is slower than the other functions in this list and should therefore be used only in particular cases (such as to read a single value, e.g., SELECT COUNT(*))

Here *result* is a value that enables access to the list of data records from a *SELECT* query. In evaluation by the functions in the following list there is always one record in the list that is active. Usually, all records are output one after the other with *mysql_fetch_array*, *mysql_fetch_row*, or *mysql_fetch_object*. The next record then automatically becomes the active one. The active record can also be set with *mysql_data_seek*

The three functions *mysql_fetch_array*, *mysql_fetch_row*, and *mysql_fetch_object* differ only in the way in which individual fields of a record are accessed: *row['fieldname']*, *row[n]*, or *row->fieldname*. Of the three functions *mysql_fetch_row* is the most efficient, but the difference in speed is very small.

Metainformation on Query Results

$n = **mysql_num_rows**($result);	determines the number of result records (*SELECT*)
$n = **mysql_num_fields**($result);	determines the number of result columns (*SELECT*)
$n = **mysql_affected_rows**([$id]);	determines the number of records that were changed by the last SQL command (*INSERT, UPDATE, DELETE, CREATE, . . . , SELECT*)
$autoid = **mysql_insert_id**([$id]);	determines the *AUTO_INCREMENT* value generated by the last *INSERT* command
***mysql_free_result**($result);*	releases the query result immediately (otherwise, at the end of the script)

Metainformation on the Fields (Columns) of Query Results

$fname =* ***mysql_field_name**($result, $n);	returns the field name of column *n*
$tblname =* ***mysql_field_table**($result, $n);	returns the table name for coumn *n*
$typename =* ***mysql_field_type**($result, $n);	returns the data type of column *n* (e.g., *"TINYINT"*)
$length =* ***mysql_field_len**($result, $n);	returns the maximum length of the column
$lengths =* ***mysql_fetch_length**($result);	returns a field with length information for all fields of the last read data record; access with *lengths[n]*
$flags =* ***mysql_field_flags**($result, $n);	returns the attribute properties of a column as a character string (e.g., *"not_null primary_key"*); the properties are separated by spaces; evaluation is done most easily with *explode*
$info =* ***mysql_fetch_field**($result, $n);	returns information on column *n* as an object; evaluation proceeds with *info->name* (see the list below); note that *info* may contain, in part, properties other than *flags*

Attributes of `mysql_field_flags`

auto_increment	attribute *AUTO_INCREMENT*
binary	attribute *BINARY*
blob	data type *BLOB, TINYBLOB*, etc.
enum	data type *ENUM*
multiple_key	field is part of a nonunique index
not_null	attribute *NOT NULL*
primary_key	attribute *PRIMARY KEY*
timestamp	attribute *TIMESTAMP*
unique_key	attribute *UNIQUE*
unsigned	attribute *UNSIGNED*
zerofill	attribute *ZEROFILL*

Field Information for `mysql_fetch_field`

info->name	column name (field name)
info->table	name of the table from which the field comes
info->max_length	maximum length of the field
info->type	name of the data type of the field (e.g., *"TINYINT"*)
info->numeric	1 or 0, depending on whether the field contains numeric data
info->blob, not_null, multiple_key, primary_key, unique_key, unsigned, zerofill	1 or 0; see list above for interpretation

Perl DBI

> **REMARK** *Please note that this reference does not contain an exhaustive list of all DBI methods, functions, and attributes. We have included only those key words that are most relevant for everyday MySQL programming with Perl. A complete reference can be found in the* perldoc *documentation.*
>
> *In this book we generally place Perl methods in parentheses to improve readability. However, Perl syntax allows the execution of methods without parentheses, as in* $dbh->disconnect.

Common Variable Names

The Perl *DBI* module is object-oriented. Thus the key words introduced in this section relate in part to methods, which can be applied to specific objects (which in Perl are generally called *Handles*). In this reference the following variable names will be used for such objects:

Common Variable Names for DBI Handles

$dbh	(*database handle*)	represents the connection to the database
$sth	(*statement handle*)	enables evaluation of query results (with *SELECT* queries)
$h	(*handle*)	general handles, used in this section with methods that are available to *$dbh*, *$sth*, and *DBI*
$drh	(*driver handle*)	enables access to many administrative functions

Establishing the Connection

The Connection

use DBI();	activates the DBI module
$datasource = "DBI:mysql:dbname;" . *"host=hostname";*	specifies database names and computer names
$dbh = *DBI->**connect**($datasource, $username, $password [, %attributes]);*	creates the connection to the database

Within the *datasource* character string further parameters—separated by semicolons—may be given. (Information on setting up MySQL configuration files can be found in Chapter 14.)

Optional Parameters in the datasource Character String

host=hostname	name of the computer with the MySQL server (default: *localhost*)
port=n	IP port (default: 3306)
mysql_compression=0/1	compresses communication (default: 0)
mysql_read_default_file=filename	file name of a MySQL configuration file
mysql_read_default_group=mygroup	read group *[mygroup]* within the configuration (default: group *[client]*)

A list with attributes can be passed as an optional fourth parameter of *connect*. You can supply these attributes either directly or in the form of an array variable:

```
$dbh = DBI->connect($source, $user, $pw, Attr1=>val1, Attr2=>val2);
%attr = (Attr1=>val1, Attr2=>val2);
$dbh = DBI->connect($source, $user, $pw, \%attr);
```

To a great extent these attributes can be read and changed with *$dbh* after the connection has been established.

```
$dbh->'LongReadLen' = 1000000;
```

The following list describes the most important *connect* attributes.

Optional connect *Attributes* ($dbh *Attributes*)

RaiseError=>0/1	if the connection is not properly established, display error message and terminate program; default setting: 0
PrintError=>0/1	if the connection is not properly established, display error message but continue execution; default setting: 1
LongReadLen=>n	determines the maximum size of an individual data field in bytes (0: do not read long fields)
LongTruncOK=>0/1	specifies whether data fields that are too long should be truncated (1) or whether an error should be triggered (0)

Terminate Connection

*$dbh->**disconnect**();*	terminate connection to the database

Execute SQL Commands, Evaluate SELECT *Queries*

Execute Queries Without Return of Data Records

*$n = $dbh->**do**("INSERT ...");*	executes an SQL query without returning records; *$n* contains the number of records that were changed, or *0E0* if no records were changed, or *−1* if the number is unknown, or *undef* if an error has occurred
$n = $dbh->**do**($sql, \%attr, @values);	executes a parametrized query; *@values* contains values for the wild card expressed in the SQL command by *?*; these values are handled automatically with *quote()*; *%attr* can contain optional attributes (otherwise, specify *undef*)
*$id = $dbh->{'**mysql_insertid**'};*	returns the *AUTO_INCREMENT* value of the last record to be inserted; caution: the attribute *mysql_insertid* is MySQL-specific

Execute Queries with Return of Data Records

$sth = $dbh->**prepare**("SELECT . . . ");	prepares an SQL query (generally *SELECT* queries); all further operations proceed with the help of the *statement handle*
$sth->**execute**();	executes the query
$sth->**execute**(@values);	executes a parametrized query; *@values* contains values for the wild card expressed in the SQL command by *?*;
$sth->**fetchxxx**();	evaluate results (see below)
$sth->**finish**();	releases the resources of the *statement handle*

If a query was executed with *prepare* and *execute* and a list of records was returned as result, then this list can be evaluated with a number of *fetch* methods.

Evaluate List of Data Records

@row = $sth->**fetchrow_array**();	reads the next record into the array *@row*; if the end of the list is reached or if an error occurs, then *@row* contains an empty array; access to individual elements proceeds with *$row[n]* (where for the first column one has *n=0*)
@row = $sth->**fetch**();	corresponds to *fetchrow_array()*
$rowptr = $sth->**fetchrow_arrayref**();	like *fetchrow_array()*, but returns pointers to arrays (or *undef* if the end of the list of records is reached or an error occurs)
$row = $sth->**fetchrow_hashref**();	reads the next record into the associated array *$row*; if the end of the list of records is reached or if an error occurs, then *$row* contains the value *undef*; access to individual elements proceeds with *$row->{'columnname'}*, where case sensitivity is in force
$result = $sth->**fetchall_arrayref**();	reads all records and returns a pointer to an array of pointers to the individual records; access to individual elements proceeds with *$result->[$row][$col]*
$result = $sth->**fetchall_arrayref**();	as above, but the records are now associative arrays; access is via *$result->[$row]->'columnname'*

Bind Variables to Columns (for `fetchrow_array`)

$sth->**bind_col**($n, \$var);	binds the column *n* to the variable *$var* (where for the first column we have, exceptionally, *n=1*); the variable is automatically updated when the next record is read; *bind_col* must be executed after *execute*; the function returns *false* if an error occurs
*$sth->**bind_columns**(\$var1, \$var2, . . .);*	like *bind_col*, but variables are assigned to all columns of the query; make sure you have the correct number of variables

Metainformation on SQL Commands

*$n = $sth->{'**NUM_OF_FIELDS**' };*	returns the number of result columns (after *SELECT*)
*$n = $sth->{'**NUM_OF_PARAMS**' };*	returns the number of parameters in queries with wild cards
*$sql = $sth->{'**Statement**' };*	returns the underlying SQL command

Shorthand Notation

@row = $dbh->**selectrow_array**($sql);	corresponds to a combination of *prepare*, *execute*, and *fetchrow_array*; the result is an array of the first result data record; access to further records is not possible
$result = $dbh->**selectrow_array**($sql);	as above, but *$result* contains the value of the first column of the first result record
$result = $dbh->**selectall_arrayref**($sql);	corresponds to *prepare*, *execute*, and *fetchall_arrayref*; for evaluation of *$result* see *fetchall_arrayref*

Marking Special Characters in Character Strings and BLOBs with the Backslash

$dbh->**quote**($data);	prefixes the contents of *$data* between single quotes, prefixes \ and ' with \, and replaces 0-bytes by \0; if *$data* is empty (*undef*), then *quote()* returns the character string *NULL*

Determine Column Names, Data Types, etc., of SELECT Results

*$array_ref = $sth->{'**NAME**'};*	returns a pointer to an array with the names of all columns; evaluation with @*$array_ref[$n]*, where *n* ranges from 0 to *$sth->{'NUM_OF_FIELDS' -1*
*$array_ref = $sth->{'**NAME_lc**'};*	as above, but names in lowercase
*$array_ref = $sth->{'**NAME_uc**'};*	as above, but names in uppercase
*$array_ref = $sth->{'**NULLABLE**'};*	specifies for each column whether *NULL* may be stored there (1) or not (0); if this information cannot be determined, then the array contains the value 2 for this column
*$array_ref = $sth->{'**PRECISION**'};*	specifies the precision in the sense of ODBC; here is meant the maximum column width
*$array_ref = $sth->{'**SCALE**'};*	specifies the number of decimal places for floating-point numbers
*$array_ref = $sth->{'**TYPE**'};*	specifies the data type of all columns in the form of numerical values; the values relate to the ODBC standard; tests determined the following values: *CHAR: 12, INT: 4, TEXT/BLOB: −1, DATE: 9, TIME: 10, TIMESTAMP: 11, FLOAT: 7, DECIMAL: 3, ENUM/SET: 1*

Error Handling

Methods for Error Handling

*$h->**err**();*	error number of the last error (0: no error)
*$h->**errstr**();*	describes the last error (empty character string: no error)
$h->**trace**($n [, $filename]);	logs all internal MySQL data accesses and redirects output to *STDERR* or the given file; *n* specifies the degree of detail to be logged (0 deactivates logging, 9 logs everything)

Auxiliary Functions

DBI Functions

@bool = DBI::**looks_like_a_number**(@data);	tests for each element in the array @data whether it is a number and returns *true* or *undef* in the result array
$result = DBI::**neat**($data [, $maxlen]);	formats the character string contained in *$data* in a form suitable for output; character strings are placed in single quotes; non-ASCII characters are replaced by a period; if the character string is longer than *$maxlen* characters (default: 400), then it is truncated and terminated with . . .
$result = DBI::**neat_list**(\@listref, $maxlen, $sep);	as above, but for an entire array of data; the individual elements are connected by *$sep* (default: ",") into the resulting character string

$dbh Methods

$ok = $dbh->**ping**();	tests whether the connection to MySQL still exists and returns *true* or *false* accordingly

MySQL-Specific Extension of the DBD::mysql Driver

If you use the *DBI* module for access to MySQL databases, then there are some supplementary functions available via *DBI* methods and attributes, of which we shall now describe some of the most important. The use of these functions can simplify programming and can make Perl programs more efficient. However, the code will no longer be portable; that is, a later change to another database system will require additional work.

Administrative Functions Based on a Separated Connection

$drh = DBI->install_driver('mysql');	returns a *driver handle*
*$drh->func('**createdb**', $database,* *$host, $user, $password, 'admin');*	creates a new database; a new connection is used for this
*$drh->func('**dropdb**', $database,* *$host, $user, $password, 'admin');*	deletes a database
*$drh->func('**shutdown**', $host,* *$user, $password, 'admin');*	shuts down the MySQL server
*$drh->func('**reload**', $host, $user,* *$password, 'admin');*	reinputs all MySQL tables (including the *mysql* tables with privilege management)

Administrative Functions Within the Current Connection

$dbh->func('**createdb**',* *$database, 'admin');	creates a new database
$dbh->func('**dropdb**',* *$database, 'admin');	deletes a database
*$dbh->func('**shutdown**', 'admin');*	shuts down the MySQL server
*$dbh->func('**reload**', 'admin');*	reinputs all MySQL tables

$dbh Attributes

*$id = $dbh->'**mysql_insertid**';*	returns the *AUTO_INCREMENT* value of the most recently inserted data record
*$info = $dbh->'**info**';*	after certain special SQL commands is supposed to return a character string with information about the command (e.g., after an *UPDATE* command: *Rows matched: 13 Changed: 13 Warnings: 0*); however, several tests of this attribute were unsuccessful
*$threadid = $dhb->'**thread_id**';*	returns the thread ID number of the current connection to MySQL

$sth *Methods and Attributes*

*$sth->**rows**();*	returns after *SELECT* queries the number of data records found by *SELECT*; caution: does not work if *$sth->'mysql_use_result' =1* holds
*$sth->'**mysql_store_result**' =1;*	activates *mysql_store_result*, so that with *SELECT* queries all results are stored temporarily on the client computer (default setting)
*$sth->'**mysql_use_result**' =1;*	activates *mysql_use_result*, so that with *SELECT* queries only a single record is stored temporarily on the client

$sth *Attributes for Determining Metadata on* SELECT *Results*

*$ar_ref = $sth->'**MYSQL_IS_BLOB**';*	returns a pointer to an array whose values specify whether the column contains BLOBs; evaluation with *@$ar_ref[$n]*, where *n* ranges from 0 to *$sth->'NUM_OF_FIELDS' -1*
*$ar_ref = $sth->'**MYSQL_IS_KEY**';*	specifies whether the columns are indexed
*$ar_ref = $sth->'**MYSQL_IS_NOT_NULL**';*	specifies whether the attribute *NOT NULL* holds for the columns
*$ar_ref = $sth->'**MYSQL_IS_NUM**';*	specifies whether numerical data are stored in the columns
*$ar_ref = $sth->'**MYSQL_IS_PRI_KEY**';*	specifies which columns are part of the primary index
*$ar_ref = $sth->'**MYSQL_MAX_LENGTH**';*	specifies the maximum column width of the query results
*$ar_ref = $sth->'**MYSQL_TABLE**';*	specifies the underlying table names for all columns
*$ar_ref = $sth->'**MYSQL_TYPE_NAME**';*	specifies the names of the data types for all columns

Part VI

Appendices

MySQL Error Numbers

THIS APPENDIX CONTAINS A REFERENCE to the error numbers that you will frequently have to deal with in the development of MySQL programs.

POINTER *In the MySQL documentation you will find in the chapter "Problems and Common Errors" a description of the causes of some frequently occurring MySQL errors.*

Error Numbers for the MySQL Server

The error numbers for the MySQL server are defined in the source code in the file include/mysqld_error.h. The associated texts can be found, in the local language, in sql/share/*language*/errmsg.txt.

Unfortunately, it is relatively burdensome to bring the two files into alignment, since the text constants in errmsg.txt are given as an unnumbered list. The file Docs/mysqld_err.txt should be of help in associating the two files, but this file is no longer current, and it contains only some of the error messages. Therefore, the following list should be of some help. It contains all error messages of MySQL version 3.23.32.

1004	Can't create file *
1005	Can't create table *
1006	Can't create database *.
1007	Can't create database *. Database exists
1008	Can't drop database *. Database doesn't exist
1009	Error dropping database (can't delete *)
1010	Error dropping database (can't rmdir *)
1011	Error on delete of *
1012	Can't read record in system table
1013	Can't get status of *

1014	Can't get working directory
1015	Can't lock file
1016	Can't open file: *.
1017	Can't find file: *
1018	Can't read dir of *
1019	Can't change dir to *
1020	Record has changed since last read in table *
1021	Disk full (*). Waiting for someone to free some space . . . .
1022	Can't write, duplicate key in table *
1023	Error on close of *
1024	Error reading file *
1025	Error on rename of * to *
1026	Error writing file *
1027	* is locked against change
1028	Sort aborted
1029	View * doesn't exist for *
1030	Got error * from table handler
1031	Table handler for * doesn't have this option
1032	Can't find record in *
1033	Incorrect information in file: *
1034	Incorrect key file for table: *. Try to repair it
1035	Old key file for table *; Repair it!
1036	Table * is read only
1037	Out of memory. Restart daemon and try again (needed * bytes)
1038	Out of sort memory. Increase daemon sort buffer size
1039	Unexpected eof found when reading file *
1040	Too many connections
1041	Out of memory; Check if mysqld or some other process uses all available memory. If not you may have to use 'ulimit' to allow mysqld to use more memory or you can add more swap space
1042	Can't get hostname for your address
1043	Bad handshake
1044	Access denied for user: *@* to database *
1045	Access denied for user: *@* (Using password: *)
1046	No Database Selected
1047	Unknown command
1048	Column * cannot be null
1049	Unknown database *

1050	Table * already exists
1051	Unknown table *
1052	Column: * in * is ambiguous
1053	Server shutdown in progress
1054	Unknown column * in *
1055	* isn't in GROUP BY
1056	Can't group on *
1057	Statement has sum functions and columns in same statement
1058	Column count doesn't match value count
1059	Identifier name * is too long
1060	Duplicate column name *
1061	Duplicate key name *
1062	Duplicate entry * for key *
1063	Incorrect column specifier for column *
1064	* near * at line *
1065	Query was empty
1066	Not unique table/alias: *
1067	Invalid default value for *
1068	Multiple primary key defined
1069	Too many keys specified. Max * keys allowed
1070	Too many key parts specified. Max * parts allowed
1071	Specified key was too long. Max key length is *
1072	Key column * doesn't exist in table
1073	BLOB column * can't be used in key specification with the used table type
1074	Too big column length for column * (max = *). Use BLOB instead
1075	Incorrect table definition; There can only be one auto column and it must be defined as a key
1076	*: ready for connections
1077	*: Normal shutdown
1078	*: Got signal *. Aborting!
1079	*: Shutdown Complete
1080	*: Forcing close of thread * user: *
1081	Can't create IP socket
1082	Table * has no index like the one used in CREATE INDEX. Recreate the table
1083	Field separator argument is not what is expected. Check the manual.
1084	You can't use fixed rowlength with BLOBs. Please use 'fields terminated by '.

1085	The file * must be in the database directory or be readable by all
1086	File * already exists
1087	Records: * Deleted: * Skipped: * Warnings: *
1088	Records: * Duplicates: *
1089	Incorrect sub part key. The used key part isn't a string or the used length is longer than the key part
1090	You can't delete all columns with ALTER TABLE. Use DROP TABLE instead
1091	Can't DROP *. Check that column/key exists
1092	Records: * Duplicates: * Warnings: *
1093	INSERT TABLE * isn't allowed in FROM table list
1094	Unknown thread id:
1095	You are not owner of thread
1096	No tables used
1097	Too many strings for column * and SET
1098	Can't generate a unique log-filename *.(1-999)\n
1099	Table * was locked with a READ lock and can't be updated
1100	Table * was not locked with LOCK TABLES
1101	BLOB column * can't have a default value
1102	Incorrect database name *
1103	Incorrect table name *
1104	The SELECT would examine too many records and probably take a very long time. Check your WHERE and use SET OPTION SQL_BIG_SELECTS=1 if the SELECT is ok
1105	Unknown error
1106	Unknown procedure *
1107	Incorrect parameter count to procedure *
1108	Incorrect parameters to procedure *
1109	Unknown table * in *
1110	Column * specified twice
1111	Invalid use of group function
1112	Table * uses an extension that doesn't exist in this MySQL version
1113	A table must have at least 1 column
1114	The table * is full
1115	Unknown character set: *
1116	Too many tables. MySQL can only use * tables in a join
1117	Too many columns
1118	Too big row size. The maximum row size, not counting BLOBs, is *. You have to change some fields to BLOBs

1119	Thread stack overrun: Used: * of a * stack. Use 'mysqld -O thread_stack=#' to specify a bigger stack if needed
1120	Cross dependency found in OUTER JOIN. Examine your ON conditions
1121	Column * is used with UNIQUE or INDEX but is not defined as NOT NULL
1122	Can't load function *
1123	Can't initialize function *; *
1124	No paths allowed for shared library
1125	Function * already exist
1126	Can't open shared library * (errno: * *)
1127	Can't find function * in library
1128	Function * is not defined
1129	Host * is blocked because of many connection errors. Unblock with 'mysqladmin flush-hosts'
1130	Host * is not allowed to connect to this MySQL server
1131	You are using MySQL as an anonymous user and anonymous users are not allowed to change passwords
1132	You must have privileges to update tables in the mysql database to be able to change passwords for others
1133	Can't find any matching row in the user table
1134	Rows matched: * Changed: * Warnings: *
1135	Can't create a new thread (errno *). If you are not out of available memory, you can consult the manual for a possible OS-dependent bug
1136	Column count doesn't match value count at row *
1137	Can't reopen table: *
1138	Invalid use of NULL value
1139	Got error * from regexp
1140	Mixing of GROUP columns (MIN(),MAX(),COUNT() . . .) with no GROUP columns is illegal if there is no GROUP BY clause
1141	There is no such grant defined for user '*' on host *
1142	* command denied to user: '*@*' for table *
1143	* command denied to user: '*@*' for column * in table *
1144	Illegal GRANT/REVOKE command. Please consult the manual which privileges can be used.
1145	The host or user argument to GRANT is too long
1146	Table '*.*' doesn't exist
1147	There is no such grant defined for user '*' on host * on table *
1148	The used command is not allowed with this MySQL version

1149	You have an error in your SQL syntax
1150	Delayed insert thread couldn't get requested lock for table *
1151	Too many delayed threads in use
1152	Aborted connection * to db: * user: '*' (*)
1153	Got a packet bigger than 'max_allowed_packet'
1154	Got a read error from the connection pipe
1155	Got an error from fcntl()
1156	Got packets out of order
1157	Couldn't uncompress communication packet
1158	Got an error reading communication packets
1159	Got timeout reading communication packets
1160	Got an error writing communication packets
1161	Got timeout writing communication packets
1162	Result string is longer than max_allowed_packet
1163	The used table type doesn't support BLOB/TEXT columns
1164	The used table type doesn't support AUTO_INCREMENT columns
1165	INSERT DELAYED can't be used with table *, because it is locked with LOCK TABLES
1166	Incorrect column name *
1167	The used table handler can't index column *
1168	All tables in the MERGE table are not identically defined
1169	Can't write, because of unique constraint, to table *
1170	BLOB column * used in key specification without a key length
1171	All parts of a PRIMARY KEY must be NOT NULL; If you need NULL in a key, use UNIQUE instead
1172	Result consisted of more than one row
1173	This table type requires a primary key
1174	This version of MySQL is not compiled with RAID support
1175	You are using safe update mode and you tried to update a table without a WHERE that uses a KEY column
1176	Key * doesn't exist in table *
1177	Can't open table
1178	The handler for the table doesn't support check/repair
1179	You are not allowed to execute this command in a transaction
1180	Got error * during COMMIT
1181	Got error * during ROLLBACK
1182	Got error * during FLUSH_LOGS
1183	Got error * during CHECKPOINT

1184	Aborted connection * to db: * user: '*' host: '*' (*)
1185	The handler for the table does not support binary table dump
1186	Binlog closed while trying to FLUSH MASTER
1187	Failed rebuilding the index of dumped table *
1188	Error from master: *
1189	Net error reading from master
1190	Net error writing to master
1191	Can't find FULLTEXT index matching the column list
1192	Can't execute the given command because you have active locked tables or an active transaction
1193	Unknown system variable *
1194	Table * is marked as crashed and should be repaired
1195	Table * is marked as crashed and last (automatic?) repair failed
1196	Warning: Some non-transactional changed tables couldn't be rolled back
1197	Multi-statement transaction required more than 'max_binlog_cache_size' bytes of storage. Increase this mysqld variable and try again.

Client Error Numbers

Client programs (e.g., `mysql`, `mysqladmin`, but also all programs that use the MySQL library `libmysqlclient`) can return two kinds of errors: errors from the server (see above) and their own errors. In the latter case the error numbers are defined in `include/errmsg.h`. The associated texts are located, in various languages, in `libmysql/errmsg.c`.

2000	Unknown MySQL error
2001	Can't create UNIX socket (*)
2002	Can't connect to local MySQL server through socket * (*)
2003	Can't connect to MySQL server on * (*)
2004	Can't create TCP/IP socket (*)
2005	Unknown MySQL Server Host * (*)
2006	MySQL server has gone away
2007	Protocol mismatch. Server Version = * Client Version = *
2008	MySQL client run out of memory
2009	Wrong host info
2010	Localhost via UNIX socket
2011	* via TCP/IP
2012	Error in server handshake

2013	Lost connection to MySQL server during query
2014	Commands out of sync; You can't run this command now
2015	* via named pipe
2016	Can't wait for named pipe to host: * pipe: * (*)
2017	Can't open named pipe to host: * pipe: * (*)
2018	Can't set state of named pipe to host: * pipe: * (*)
2019	Can't initialize character set * (path: *)
2020	Got packet bigger than 'max_allowed_packet'

Operating System Errors and Errors of the MyISAM Table Driver

Many errors are triggered by problems at the operating-system level (for example, when the hard drive is full). A further group of errors can arise when the (My)ISAM table driver has problems in reading or changing table or index files. The most likely cause of this problem is defective table files (for example, after a crash). In such cases you can get help from myisamchk (see Chapter 1).

Common to both groups of errors are that the error numbers are smaller than 1000 and that the error text can be recovered with perror. Given an error number this command returns the operating system's error text (*Error code n:* . . .) and the (My)ISAM error text (*n =* . . .). In the following examples error 28 is an operating system error, while error 137 is a (My)ISAM error.

```
root# perror 28
Error code 28: No space left on device

root# perror 137
Error code 137: Unknown error 137
137 = No more records (read after end of file)
```

In most cases the error number is unique, as in the examples above. That is, it is either an operating system error or a (My)ISAM error. However, there are cases of duplication, as the following example shows:

```
root# perror 120
Error code 120: Is a named type file
120 = Didn't find key on read or update
```

Finally, please note that the operating system error numbers are dependent on the operating system. Error 120 above was returned by Linux. This error does not exist under Windows.

> **TIP** *A current list of all error numbers can be obtained under Unix/Linux*
> *with the following bash command:*
>
> ```
> i=1; while [ $i -le 200 ]; do perror $i; i=$[$i+1]; done > err.txt
> ```

MyISAM Error Numbers

The following list gives only the (My)ISAM errors. (We have omitted the operating system error numbers.)

120	Didn't find key on read or update
121	Duplicate key on write or update
123	Someone has changed the row since it was read; Update with is recoverable
124	Wrong index given to function
126	Index file is crashed / Wrong file format
127	Record-file is crashed
131	Command not supported by database
132	Old database file
133	No record read before update
134	Record was already deleted (or record file crashed)
135	No more room in record file
136	No more room in index file
137	No more records (read after end of file)
138	Unsupported extension used for table
139	Too big row (>= 16 M)
140	Wrong create options
141	Duplicate unique key or constraint on write or update
142	Unknown character set used
143	Conflicting table definition between MERGE and mapped table
144	Table is crashed and last repair failed
145	Table was marked as crashed and should be repaired

The Web Site
for This Book

AT THE WEB SITE WWW.KOFLER.CC/MYSQL you will find not only miscellaneous background information and extensive links to this book, but also, and above all, the examples presented in the previous chapters of this book (databases and code). A large portion of the examples (all PHP scripts and all Perl-CGI scripts) can be tried out directly at the web site.

Decompressing Example Files

All example files are available as compressed archives both in *.zip and *.tgz formats. Decompress with Winzip or tar -xzf.

Setting Up the Databases

The example databases *test_vote* (introduced in Chapter 3), *books*, *mylibrary*, *myforum*, and *exceptions* (all presented in Chapter 5) are available as *.sql files.

Before you can input the *.sql file in MySQL you must first create the database with mysqladmin (here, for example, the database *mylibrary*):

```
> mysqladmin -u root -p create mylibrary
Enter password: xxx
```

Then use mysql to move the database:

```
> mysql -u root -p mylibrary < mylibrary.sql
Enter password: xxx
```

To be allowed to execute these two commands you need, of course, to possess sufficient access privileges (see Chapter 7).

You can also create and input the databases with phpMyAdmin. To do this, click first on HOME and create the database (CREATE NEW DATABASE). Then input the SQL file with RUN SQL QUERIES. To do this, click on BROWSE, select the database file, and start the importation with OK. (An extensive description of phpMyAdmin including possible importation problems can be found in Chapter 4.)

All example programs function only if the databases described in this book are available (see above) and if you change the user names and passwords used in the code.

PHP Examples

All PHP files assume PHP4 and use the ending *.php.

The *mylibrary* and *myforum* scripts begin with an *include* instruction, with which the file read-connectfunctions.php is read from the local directory. The only task of read-connectfunctions.php consists in rereading the file myforumconnect.inc.php or mylibraryconnect.inc.php.

Among the example files, this second include file is also located in the local directory. It contains the code for creating the database connection (including the password in plain text). For security reasons this file should be moved to a directory that is externally inaccessible (i.e., via a web browser). Then you must change the path for the *include* command in read-connectfunctions.php. (This two-pronged process was chosen so that you do not have to change the *include* command in all *.php files, but only in connectfunctions.php.)

Further information on the example programs appears in Chapter 8. There you will find a description of why it makes sense with PHP not to place files with passwords in the same directory as other PHP files.

Perl Examples

Under Unix/Linux you must also execute chmod u+x so that the files will be recognized as executable programs. With some programs we are dealing with CGI scripts. Further information on the example programs can be found in Chapter 9.

Visual Basic Examples

To be able to use the programs off the shelf you must have Visual Basic 6. If you use VBA instead, you must open the *.frm files in a text editor and copy the relevant code segments from there into the VBA editor. Under certain circumstances some small changes will be necessary. Further information on these example programs appears in Chapter 10.

APPENDIX C
Bibliography

1. Sharon Bjeletich et al. *Microsoft SQL Server 7.0 Unleashed*. SAMS, 1999.

2. Rich Bowen et al. *Apache Server Unleashed*, SAMS, 2000.

3. Chris Date, Hugh Darwen. *A Guide to the SQL Standard*. Addison-Wesley Longman, 1998.

4. Paul DuBois. *MySQL*. New Riders, 2000.

5. W. J. Gilmore. *A Programmer's Introduction to PHP 4.0*. Apress, 2000.

6. Michael Kofler. *Definitive Guide to Excel VBA*. Apress, 2000.

7. Michael Kofler. *Linux: Installation, Configuration, and Use*, 2nd edition. Addison-Wesley, 1999.

8. Michael Kofler. *Visual Basic Database Programming*. Addison-Wesley, 2001.

9. Laura Lemay. *Teach Yourself Perl in 21 Days*. SAMS, 1999.

10. Robert Orfali, Dan Harkey, Jeri Edwards. *Client/Server Survival Guide*, 3rd edition. John Wiley & Sons, 1999.

11. Tobias Ratschiller, Till Gerken. *Web Application Development with PHP 4.0*. New Riders, 2000.

12. David Solomon et al. *Microsoft SQL Server 6.5 Unleashed*. SAMS, 1996.

13. Randy Yarger, George Reese, Tim King. *MySQL & mSQL*. O'Reilly, 1999.

Index